Critical Readings on Latinos and Education

This critical anthology showcases an interdisciplinary forum of scholars sharing a common interest in the analysis, discussion, critique, and dissemination of educational issues impacting Latinos. Drawing on the best of the past 20 years of the *Journal of Latinos and Education*, the collection highlights work that has been seminal in addressing complex educational issues affecting and influencing the growing Latina and Latino population. Chapters discuss the production and application of wisdom and knowledge to real-world problems while engaging and collaborating with the interests of key stakeholders in other sectors outside the "traditional" academy. Organized thematically around issues related to policy, research, practice, and creative and literary works, the collection is sure to extend and encourage novel ways of thinking about the ongoing and emerging questions around the unifying thread of Latinos and education.

Enrique G. Murillo, Jr. is Professor of Education at California State University, San Bernardino. He is the founding Editor-in-Chief of the *Journal of Latinos and Education* (*JLE*), and of the *Handbook of Latinos and Education* (*HLE*). Additionally, he is the founder of the National Latino Education Network (NLEN), and Latino Education & Advocacy Days (LEAD), the objective of which is to promote a broad-based awareness of the crisis in Latino education and to enhance the intellectual, cultural, and personal development of our community's educators, administrators, leaders, and students.

Critical Readings on Latinos and Education

Tasks, Themes, and Solutions

Edited by
Enrique G. Murillo, Jr.

NEW YORK AND LONDON

First published 2019
by Routledge
52 Vanderbilt Avenue, New York, NY 10017

and by Routledge
2 Park Square, Milton Park, Abingdon, Oxon, OX14 4RN

Routledge is an imprint of the Taylor & Francis Group, an informa business

© 2019 Taylor & Francis

The right of Enrique G. Murillo, Jr. to be identified as the author of the editorial material, and of the authors for their individual chapters, has been asserted in accordance with sections 77 and 78 of the Copyright, Designs and Patents Act 1988.

All rights reserved. No part of this book may be reprinted or reproduced or utilised in any form or by any electronic, mechanical, or other means, now known or hereafter invented, including photocopying and recording, or in any information storage or retrieval system, without permission in writing from the publishers.

Trademark notice: Product or corporate names may be trademarks or registered trademarks, and are used only for identification and explanation without intent to infringe.

Library of Congress Cataloging-in-Publication Data
A catalog record for this book has been requested

ISBN: 978-0-367-07526-2 (hbk)
ISBN: 978-0-367-07528-6 (pbk)
ISBN: 978-0-429-02120-6 (ebk)

Typeset in Bembo
by Apex CoVantage, LLC

This anthology is dedicated to the memory of my late father, Enrique A. Murillo, Sr. (1928–2017).

Enrique Murillo Araujo, who later simply became Enrique A. Murillo, was born in El Barrio, Sinaloa (an area near the city of Culiacán). His father was Arturo Murillo Retamoza, a bank associate and administrator and high-ranking officer in Pancho Villa's army, whose family came from Amaculí, Durango. His mother was Alejandrina Araujo Armienta, born in Las Tapias, Culiacán, but whose family had come from both Tameapa and Cosalá, Sinaloa.

My father was among the hardest-working people that I ever met. It is from him that I got my work ethic. He would wake early to go work, then come home to eat and nap, and then go to work again. He had come to the U.S. at the age of about 28, and he spent most of his working years as a general laborer, as an ironworker, and working with scaffolding and painting.

As his son, on the weekends he'd force me to wake up early, and I was his helper. There was always work to be done to the house, things to be fixed. He built things, was an avid carpenter, and repaired TVs and much more. He could never sit still.

As a child, school was the only way I could escape the work assignments. I was excused from helping him as long as it was a school-related reason, such as homework. Early on he had told me that if I didn't want to work so hard at physically demanding labor, then I'd better do well in school. He'd constantly point out how tired he was and for me to take note.

My father cared a great deal about people and loved his community. He came to make a better life for himself in Los Angeles, California in 1956, with his then–young wife, Maria Luisa. He later settled in the city of Huntington Park, and thanks to his aunts (rest in peace) Catalina Parrales and Elisa Araujo, who sponsored his immigration, he was able to settle and grow roots.

He lived a shared experience of having family on both sides of the border. He dreamt of buying a house and raising children, and of being able to help his family back in Mexico. His eyes lit up with optimism and the belief that if he worked hard enough, he would elevate his humble place in life and the lives of his children.

My father was a union man and labor organizer, advocate, activist, and community leader. To be of SERVICE to others is by far the greatest gift and legacy he left me. He was always there when family, friends, and even strangers needed him. He helped countless numbers of people. I miss my father more than words can say. I miss him dearly and will never forget him.

Contents

Biographical Sketch   xi
El Futuro es Nuestro: *From the Editor's Desk*   xiii
Credits   xxxiii

SECTION I
Tasks   1

1 "Mexican Americans Don't Value Education!": On
   the Basis of the Myth, Mythmaking, and Debunking   3
   RICHARD R. VALENCIA AND MARY S. BLACK

2 Funds of Knowledge: An Approach to Studying
   Latina(o) Students' Transition to College   26
   CECILIA RIOS-AGUILAR AND JUDY MARQUEZ KIYAMA

3 All for Our Children: Migrant Families and Parent
   Participation in an Alternative Education Program   44
   PABLO JASIS AND DOUGLAS MARRIOTT

4 Quantitative Intersectionality: A Critical Race
   Analysis of the Chicana/o Educational Pipeline   59
   ALEJANDRO COVARRUBIAS

5 Challenges Facing Hispanic-Serving Institutions in
   the First Decade of the 21st Century   78
   ALFREDO G. DE LOS SANTOS JR. AND KARINA MICHELLE CUAMEA

6 *Nuestro Camino*: A Review of Literature Surrounding
   the Latino Teacher Pipeline   95
   KELLY M. OCASIO

SECTION II
Themes 117

7 *Francisco Maestas et al. v. George H. Shone et al.*:
   Mexican American Resistance to School Segregation
   in the Hispano Homeland, 1912–1914 119
   RUBEN DONATO, GONZALO GUZMÁN, AND JARROD HANSON

8 Latino English Language Learners: Bridging
   Achievement and Cultural Gaps Between Schools
   and Families 141
   MARY ELLEN GOOD, SOPHIA MASEWICZ, AND LINDA VOGEL

9 Understanding Latina/o School Pushout: Experiences
   of Students Who Left School Before Graduating 159
   NORA LUNA AND ANITA TIJERINA REVILLA

10 *Compartiendo Nuestras Historias*: Five *Testimonios*
   of Schooling and Survival 178
   WANDA ALARCÓN, CINDY CRUZ, LINDA GUARDIA JACKSON,
   LINDA PRIETO, AND SANDRA RODRIGUEZ-ARROYO

11 The Value of Education and *Educación*: Nurturing
   Mexican American Children's Educational Aspirations
   to the Doctorate 190
   MICHELLE M. ESPINO

12 Mapping and Recontextualizing the Evolution of
   the Term *Latinx*: An Environmental Scanning in
   Higher Education 216
   CRISTOBAL SALINAS JR. AND ADELE LOZANO

SECTION III
Solutions 237

13 *Abuelita* Epistemologies: Counteracting Subtractive
   Schools in American Education 239
   SANDRA M. GONZALES

14 Sustaining a Dual Language Immersion Program:
   Features of Success 257
   ILIANA ALANÍS AND MARIELA A. RODRÍGUEZ

15 Beginning With *El Barrio*: Learning From Exemplary
   Teachers of Latino Students   271
   JASON G. IRIZARRY AND JOHN RAIBLE

16 The Relationship Between a College Preparation
   Program and At-Risk Students' College Readiness   288
   JENNIFER T. CATES AND SCOTT E. SCHAEFLE

17 Latina/o Parent Organizing for Educational Justice:
   An Ethnographic Account of Community Building
   and Radical Healing   302
   KYSA NYGREEN

18 Dream Big: Exploring Empowering Processes of
   DREAM Act Advocacy in a Focal State   321
   BRAD FORENZA AND CAROLINA MENDONCA

19 Multiple Ethnic, Racial, and Cultural Identities in
   Action: From Marginality to a New Cultural Capital
   in Modern Society   337
   HENRY T. TRUEBA

   Index   359

Biographical Sketch

Enrique G. Murillo, Jr., PhD is Professor of Education at California State University, San Bernardino. He is a first-generation Chicano, born and raised on the Eastside of Greater Los Angeles, and a native bilingual speaker in Spanish and English.

He completed his PhD in the Social Foundations of Education program at the University of North Carolina at Chapel Hill. His master's degree from California State University, Los Angeles is in the same area, with coursework toward the bilingual multiple-subject teaching credential; his bachelor's degree is in psychology, received from the University of California, Los Angeles. He offers both a generalist background in education and schooling, with cognate disciplines in sociology and anthropology. His specialty areas include foundations of education, research methods, critical ethnography, educational anthropology, and cultural studies.

He is the founding Editor-in-Chief of both the *Journal of Latinos and Education* (*JLE*), published quarterly by Taylor & Francis, and of the *Handbook of Latinos and Education* (*HLE*), Routledge. Additionally, he is the founder of the National Latino Education Network (NLEN).

Dr. Murillo is former California Student Aid Commissioner (CSAC) and served while implementing the California DREAM Act. CSAC is the principal state agency responsible for administering financial aid programs for students attending public and private universities, colleges, and vocational schools in California. He also served as the president and the chair of the EdFund Board.

He is Founder and Executive Director of the LEAD organization (Latino Education & Advocacy Days). The objective of LEAD is to promote a broad-based awareness of the crisis in Latino education and to enhance the intellectual, cultural, and personal development of our community's educators, administrators, leaders, and students. Under the LEAD banner, Dr. Murillo has initiated or facilitated numerous programs and projects, such as the IE Regional Collaborative, Cash for College FAFSA Workshops, the Student Parent Academic Resource Campaign, Feria Educativa College & Career Fair, the LEAD Virtual Classroom and Webinar Series, Portraits of Hope Novela Educativa Video Series, LEAD Social Media Ambassadors, the Binational Parent Leadership Institute, and finally, the LEAD Summit.

Most recently, Dr. Murillo has served as President of the Southern California Consortium of Hispanic-Serving Institutions (SCCHSI). The SCCHSI comprises all the regional community colleges and four-year universities that are federal Department of Education–designated Hispanic-Serving Institutions (HSIs) in Southern California, from Santa Barbara to the southern border. There are more than 70 HSIs in the region, the highest number and concentration in the United States.

He has authored/edited more than 120 publications, has presented at more than 135 professional conferences, and is the recipient of numerous awards, including NBC News Education Nation Thought Leader, the Outstanding Professor in Professional Growth Accomplishments, Outstanding Advisor, the Outstanding Young Alumnus Award by the University of North Carolina at Chapel Hill, Educator of the Year, the Outstanding Support of Hispanic Issues in Higher Education Award by the American Association of Hispanics in Higher Education, the California State University Forgivable Loan, the National Hispanic Scholarship Fund, the Southern Oral History Award, the prestigious Outstanding Dissertation Award from Phi Delta Kappa, and Top 5 Outstanding Dissertation Award from the American Educational Research Association.

Dr. Murillo has been recognized with more than 45 local, regional, state, national, and international governmental and congressional commendations. In 2016, he was awarded the Lifetime Achievement Volunteer Service Award by President Barack Obama, and has twice attended special functions at the White House; in 2014, he was bestowed the Mexican government's Ohtli Award [*Reconocimiento Ohtli*]. It is the highest honor presented to a civilian outside Mexico for "services rendered to the dissemination of Mexican culture abroad."

El Futuro es Nuestro
From the Editor's Desk

Several decades ago as I entered a new space as a "native" ethnographer, educational anthropologist/sociologist, scholar-activist, and public intellectual, I decreed (with others of my generation) a new pioneering motto of "Public or Perish." This was a word-play on "Publish or Perish," a phrase describing the pressure in academia to rapidly and continually publish academic work to sustain or further one's career. As a Chicano-Indígena,[1] the precept of "Public" was consistent, as a means to extend the tenants of the now-famous El Plan de Santa Bárbara,[2] that had guided Chicano scholars to not only serve and give back to the communities on whose giant shoulders we stood on but also to create sustainable educational models by which to bridge the campuses of higher education with the barrios, fields, and factories—from which we found ourselves in diaspora (1970).

In just a few decades, the U.S. Census Bureau, Census 2000 (albeit undercounted Latinos, as arguably has always been the case) had confirmed what the few of us at the time, across all the various fields and disciplines, had already foreshadowed.[3] While Latino children had already formed the largest demographic group in many of our public schools, and Latinos would then soon emerge as the largest minority in the United States, our educational attainment was unfortunately not keeping pace. With all the problems that we were facing at that historical cusp: the economy, the environment, the politics of immigration—our Latino communities had added yet another quandary to our list. As a community, we were in the middle of an educational crisis.[4]

With the need to create a paradigm shift to more aggressively address our low formal educational attainment vis-à-vis access to quality pre-K programs, our children attending schools with fewer resources, test scores, mismatch between home and school cultures, high mobility rates, racially segregated communities with high poverty rates, high school graduation rates, college admission requirements, community college transfer rates, and overall higher education completion rates,[5] I founded in 1999 a set of innovative and productive Latino education programs, publications, and events. What is known currently as LEAD (Latino Education & Advocacy Days) came to be housed on the campus of California State University, San Bernardino (CSUSB) and would attempt to address our educational crisis head-on.

In coetaneous sync, among the first courses I developed or reformulated for the Teaching Credential and Masters courses in Education at California State University, San Bernardino (CSUSB), were "Culture and Schooling," "Pedagogical Foundations for English Language Learners," "Social and Cultural Contexts for School Learning," "Educational Foundations," and "Educational Research"; and later on as a tenured full professor, "Advanced Qualitative Research Methods," and "Diversity and Equity in Education" for the Doctorate in Educational Leadership. All these course curricula and andragogy were very specifically articulated and aligned as forms of community resource mapping, public engagement, and service learning opportunities that marry the university campus with the communities we strive to serve.

Like many scholars of my generation, especially the Chicano/Latino, we found ourselves working and producing educational knowledge from the margins. The modern and postcolonial writings of scholars such as Paulo Freire (1970) had nudged many of us to theorize about oppression, consciousness, power, and action. The 1980s then found us reacting to the neoliberal renaissance of marketized and privatized education, with the distinctly negative social consequences that resulted from the emergence and promotion of a national-level discourse that positioned schools in the service of the economy.[6] Then in the 1990s we were also responding all the more to the Eurocentric, critical, and poststructuralist frameworks that had reinscribed Latinos under an abstract concept of difference and the false Black/White racial binary in the social imagination and discourse (Murillo, 1999).

The turns to postmodern abstractions had also affected our theoretical perspectives of cultural domains in radical ways. I have sometimes described my experiences in the academy as traveling those blurred boundaries when Other becomes researcher, narrated become narrator, translated becomes translator, native becomes anthropologist, and how one emergent and intermittent identity continuously informs the other. After decades of intense social struggle, albeit much has been accomplished in education, many challenges sadly remain. We still need to address the dearth in the literature and the limitations of previous research and to keep an emphasis on alternative scholarship.

The aforementioned were the very reasons I worked to become a "native" scholar, university professor, and teacher educator in the first place, as a more strategic means to improve education and schooling across the board and to speak to the social nature of our community lives, and our attempts to understand both what and how we learn from it and apply it to the classroom. The LEAD projects, then, became an extension of the regular classroom, with the need to go beyond the constraints of the four walls and tap into the community funds of knowledge[7] as to integrate students' culture and background into our instruction to be more effective.

The impact and success of LEAD had to be grounded in collaboration, participation, and outreach. Our work, by necessity, involves significant participation and partnerships in the region and nationally, and strong interactive connections with Latino networks in the United States, as well as Latin Americans and Indigenous Peoples throughout the Americas and the world.

The LEAD movement has primarily resided in higher education institutions, which are criticized—often for good reason—for our tendency to isolate ourselves from our surrounding contexts and for not being more engaged with the issues that affect the communities in which we are located. The various LEAD networks reach agreement that there are important issues that directly or indirectly affect institutions and the multiple communities we straddle that required us to "climb out of the ivory tower," to do the action work that is most relevant for the local context and in such a way that they can be used to inform and shape policy.

"NetRoots" is one way to describe our methods of awareness-raising, education, promotion, advocacy, activism, analysis, discussion, critique, and dissemination of educational issues that impact Latinos. The word is a combination of "internet and grassroots," reflecting the technological innovations, participatory democracy, and campaign-oriented activities that set our techniques apart from other forms of education and advocacy. Our work propels through local and regional efforts—with supra-local interlinks via national and global web-based connectiveness—that organize communication points that spread out but are not directed outward to, or from, any one singular point.

The curricular and extended activities of LEAD Week, with its annual signature Summit (with media reach of more than 300 million households), is the showcase. But behind the scenes, the protractive action, both democratic and collective, definitely takes place. Over the past decades, the LEAD projects have enacted the necessary groundwork and campaign for our extraordinary new future. Our netroots movement long decided that we no longer have to jump in front of trains or dodge bullets to convince others of our orientation to action. Put simply, the LEAD movement engages with and believes that the singular accomplishable solution to our educational dilemma lies in community activism and democratic participation.

In fact, most of the work of the LEAD organization has flown well below the conventional radar, at the level of the infra-political—despite the highly visible success of the annual summit. Twenty years ago, with the birth of the *Journal of Latinos and Education* (*JLE*), the primary motivation was to build an education movement that was neither primarily ideational nor ideological, but a praxis based on scientific approaches. At the time there were still too few major publications on Latinos and education. There were research reports published all over the place or in highly specialized books and journals. Furthermore, there was no one comprehensive published review of theory, research, and practice on the topic. Despite some seminal publications, Latino issues remained often seen as limited in focus (academic colonialism). Mainstream publications tended to consider Latino issues as peripheral to broader issues in the discipline. Mainstream publications also tended to focus on nationally known "Latino" authors and look only to the work of a few to publish.

As its Founding Editor-in-Chief, we changed that! Housed in the College of Education at CSUSB, *JLE* became a premier academic journal. *JLE* provides a cross-, multi-, and interdisciplinary forum for scholars and writers of diverse disciplines who share a common interest in the analysis, discussion, critique, and dissemination of educational issues that impact Latinos. It is published quarterly by Routledge, and with many thousands of subscriptions, downloads, and readers, our work informs a basis for current action to address the educational crisis, of which Latino students are emblematic.

JLE was first conceived when a group of scholars and activists from CSUSB presented a symposium on the effects of California's Proposition 227 at the American Educational Studies Association in 1999. During this conference, we conversed and proposed the collaborative creation of a new academic journal to specifically address issues surrounding the education, broadly defined, of Latinos in the United States.

Upon return, the group that included members of the Center for Equity in Education at CSUSB met regularly over the course of a full year to design and create the journal. In conducting a comprehensive document analysis and review of existing academic journals, it became evident that articles on Latinos and education were being published sporadically, appearing singly, apart, or in isolated instances in highly specialized journals, or were simply absent. This situation is created by a combination of factors including but not limited to a lack of interest in these issues, high competition for public space, and/or lack of opportunity to publish.

In April 2000 we met with Lawrence Erlbaum (of LEA Publishing Co.) and cemented our collaborative venture. The mission and editorial scope of *JLE* is a cross-, multi-, and interdisciplinary forum for scholars and writers who share a common interest in the analysis, discussion, critique, and dissemination of educational issues that impact Latinos. We identified these four broad arenas that encompass issues of relevance: (a) policy, (b) research, (c) practice, and (d) creative and literary works.

We recruited numerous scholars, practitioners, and community representatives at the forefront of their chosen fields and disciplines to serve on the inaugural *JLE* Editorial Advisory Board. We were confident that the scholarship, learnedness, and expertise the editorial advisory board brought to this collaborative venture had established its reputation as a high-quality, credible academic peer-reviewed journal.

As mentioned previously, a critical factor we considered as we took on the venture was the ongoing demographic increase in Latinos. As our numbers grew, there would be a concomitant increase in articles on research, policy, and status related to Latinos. The Black–White social order has faded with the old century, and we had inaugurated the new millennium as the largest minority group in the United States. In K–12 public schools, we, too, had surpassed the number of African American students. Nevertheless, despite our social, political, and historical presence and our memory and discussions about the impact of race and other social forces, the equitable education of

Latino students often remained as "Other," mired in this artificial Black–White binary of popular social imagination. The demographics augured for both an increase in publications on Latinos and education and for an increase in consumers of those publications.

In our vision we committed to cover education in the broad cultural sense, including formal and informal schooling. Although there were journals in the other disciplines that may have addressed these issues, too often they were treated peripherally and relevant scholarship on Latinos was not well represented, if at all. Latino issues are often seen as limited in focus due to academic colonialism and epistemological racism. Established mainstream journals, as mentioned, also were inclined to center on but a few "nationally known" Latino authors and looked only to the work of a small number of us to publish. We expected that *JLE* would serve as an impetus to raise the consciousness and integrity of other journals.

JLE gave authors and researchers from other disciplines and authorial locations a place to publish. *JLE* also created opportunities for new perspectives to be published. Topics that were usually not published (nor popular) in research journals, such as parent education and community outreach, would offer new visions to readers. *JLE* also looked at new dissertation research that focuses on Latino issues and created opportunities for new voices and ideas to be heard. We also invited voices of the community, such as activists, students, teachers, and parents, to express their thoughts and analyses. One of the goals of *JLE* was to actively mentor the next generation of scholars and researchers working with our populations.

Although those of us of Mexican origin were (and remain) the majority of Latinos in the United States, particular attention had to be given to geographical equity to assure representation of all regions and "Latino" groups in the United States. Policies and practices promoting equity and social justice for linguistically and culturally diverse groups were particularly encouraged and welcomed for consideration.

Also, we believed language barriers could also be crossed by the journal. We have served as a link to Latin America and addressed hemispheric issues of common interest, such as immigration, poverty, indigenous rights, globalization, and so forth. A common language, Spanish, the third-most spoken language in the world, also helped to create an international audience for *JLE*. Although English has been our principal print language, we had soon worked on publishing special issues and feature articles in bilingual form.

The momentum of *JLE* led me to found and enact the next LEAD project, the National Latino Education Network, whose electronic portal (serving as an electronic "barrio") allowed for exchange among thousands and predated the cusp of the social media revolution. The NetRoots movement expanded among the broad spectrum of researchers, teaching professionals and educators, academics, scholars, administrators, independent writers and artists, policy and program specialists, students, parents, families, civic leaders, activists, and advocates. Among the primary action items was to compile a resource guide/clearinghouse that allows members to search and browse for resources, opportunities and activities in the Latino educational community, which was nonexistent or incomplete at the time.

The next LEAD project was the *Handbook of Latinos and Education* (*HLE*) (Murillo, et al. 2010) and had the unique purpose and function of profiling the scope and terrain of this particular domain. As its Founding Editor-in-Chief, I admit my bias that it remains the most significant and influential groundbreaking publication or compilation in the field of Latino education, in terms of its contributions to research, to professional practice, and to the emergence of related interdisciplinary studies and theory. It symbolizes an important transition in Education and the continual consciousness of Latinos. At core exists the struggle for educational equity and rights, with the conceptualization of social justice embedded, and support structure helping the plight of schools that are underfunded and racially organized in the most stereotypic of ways.

Few know this, but the evolution of the annual LEAD Summit (Latino Education & Advocacy Days) sprang from the launching this Handbook, as it was a means to reach stakeholders beyond higher education campuses to showcase not our "problems" or "deficits" but to flip the script toward the already-developed, new, and imaginative solution-based approaches and action-oriented initiatives to solve our educational crisis.

Next came the *Feria Educativa* College and Career Fair, which in its inaugural year (2011) was the first-ever educational fair of its kind in CSUSB history, that both brought thousands of Latino students and families onto our campus and was broadcasted a live television show on Telemundo Spanish-language TV. The *Feria Educativa* College & Career Fair remains as one of my favorite LEAD projects as a community-engagement activity during which we inform and inspire, including enthuse a college-going and career-readiness culture for all students to be prepared for a full range of postsecondary options; engage parents and families, with special efforts to reach Latinos, as a critical component in believing that their children are "college material" and offer opportunities to understand their role in the college process, as well as other postsecondary career opportunities; distribute/exhibit/present educational and career information, postsecondary opportunities, and other materials pertinent to community well-being (e.g., health, immigration, and civic engagement) and be available to support families; and build collective commitment and a partnership model that includes active involvement from all sectors of the regional community.

From the need to plan and execute such large-scale educational fairs, LEAD comprised a broad array of community stakeholders and organizations intended to involve, engage, inspire, and inform families along their educational journey. We called this LEAD project the Inland Empire Regional Collaborative, and we were one of only three models praised by the Obama White House, as LEAD also had the honor of principally coordinating the only White House Initiatives Summit held in our region.

From here so many other initiatives came about through our various partnerships; the Binational Parent Leadership Institute, Cash for College, the Student Parent Academic Resource Campaign, and the High School Equivalency Program are among the most notable.

The principal purpose of all the LEAD events, programs, and projects are to support closing (dismantling) the achievement gap among low-income, historically underrepresented students and their peers. Over the past decades, Latinos have finally emerged as the largest minority in the nation, with majority populations in many states and regions and, in some cases, the majority demographic among school-aged children. Yet, Latinos continue to have some of the highest dropout/pushout rates, score among the lowest on achievement tests, and have low college enrollment and graduation rates. Both Latino students and teachers have a high mobility rate, are located in racially segregated communities with high poverty rates, and attend schools with fewer resources, staffing, and programs.

Many of our communities are losing the battle to keep our focus on educational equity and achievement, including attending college and beyond. The strengths of our communities will continue to depend, to a large extent, on the positive educational outcomes of Latino students. Thus, our objectives are to promote a broad-based awareness of the crisis in Latino education and to enhance the intellectual, cultural, and personal development of our community's educators, administrators, leaders, and students.

All the publications, curricula, programs, and events aim to support and accelerate student success through a broad range of topics on the educational issues that impact Latinos, particularly students and families. The components that encompass most issues of relevance are Community Engagement, Professional Development, Parental Involvement, and Youth Leadership; Schooling Conditions and Outcomes/Educational Pipeline; Culture, Identity, and Diversity; Immigration, Globalization, and Transnationalism; Language Policies and Politics; Early Childhood; Latino Perspectives on School Reform; Culturally Responsive Pedagogies and Effective Practices; High Stakes Testing and Accountability; Community Activism and Advocacy; and Higher Education Eligibility, Enrollment, and Attainment.

Community collaboration and change are evident in all the many networks I have formed or given shape to over these several decades, including the thousands of LEAD members and affiliates and the hundreds of events I have coordinated and hosted. California State has even declared the last week of March as a Week of Latino Education and Advocacy and has specifically mentioned LEAD through various Assembly Concurrent Resolutions.[8]

Over the years, LEAD has amassed more than 200 regional, state, and national partners and has formed more than 1,600 chapters across 40 countries. Together with our nearly 20 media partners, we are able to reach the aforementioned 300 million households. Yet with all our programs and events, we always make special efforts to bring community to our campus. In 2018 LEAD Week brought nearly 2,000 attendees and, with our Social Media

Ambassadors, amassed more than 20,300,000 Social Media Engagement & Impressions.[9] Our activities have helped boost the Binational Parent Leadership Institute, the Catholic Schools EXPO, the PUENTE Project Student Leadership Forum, the VIP Welcome Dinner, the LEAD Summit, the César E. Chávez Memorial Breakfast, and the Southern California Consortium of Hispanic Serving Institutions.[10]

HSIs are defined in federal law as accredited and degree-granting public or private nonprofit institutions of higher education with 25 percent or more total undergraduate Hispanic full-time equivalent student enrollment. The Southern California Consortium of Hispanic Serving Institutions is the largest of its kind, with more than 70 HSIs in our Southern California region. Our goals are to increase the access, retention, and success of Latino students in higher education; to partner and network to secure funding for member institutions; to advance the development of Latino leadership at member institutions; to serve as the venue for sharing information on funding, legislation, and other matters that advance the interests of member institutions; to collaborate with communities, businesses, government, and other organizations to leverage resources; to support and improve resource development and staff development, including sharing best practices and strategies; and to support and work collaboratively with state- and national-level organizations, agencies, and associations who share a common interest and mission to support HSIs and/or underserved populations in higher education.

Many of our consortium members are at a historical juncture. Our student bodies are diversifying faster than our faculty, and compared to their peers, Latino students are more likely to still be enrolled beyond 6 years on their path toward a degree. We must better and continue to prepare Latino students for tomorrow's challenges through collaboration and leveraging institutional strengths and resources. We must provide a cooperative vehicle to enhance our success in reaching our individual and collective goals, such as developing an intentional campus culture and redesigning curricula; to include more community engagement and/or community-based learning and research; to enhance faculty development, and equity agenda in faculty hiring, tenure, and promotion; and to nurture a mutual vision and alliance across disciplines, colleges, and/or institutions.

Education is the civil rights issue of our generation; it's a right, not a privilege. All LEAD activities, be it a program, publication, or event, are not only community-engaged and community-driven but actually are forms and extensions of scholarship. This current book is an anthology made up of select bodies of work that previously were published in the *JLE*, and as its founding editor-in-chief, I feel could best exemplify that spirit of community-engaged and community-driven Scholarship.

In line with the scope and aims of *JLE*, and LEAD projects overall, this anthology appeals to a cross-, multi-, and interdisciplinary forum of stakeholders who share a common interest in the analysis, discussion, critique, and dissemination of educational issues that have an impact on Latinos.

The four broad arenas that encompass most issues of relevance are the same: (1) Policy, (2) Research, (3) Practice, and (4) Creative & Literary works. It extends and encourages novel ways of thinking about the ongoing and emerging questions around the unifying thread of Latinos and education—for researchers, practitioners, authors, and other stakeholders who are working to advance understanding at all levels and aspects—be it theoretical, conceptual, empirical, clinical, historical, methodological, and/or other in scope.

The various manifestations of the diverse frameworks and topical areas typically range anywhere from—but aren't limited to—theoretical and empirical analyses, policy discussions, research reports, program recommendations, evaluation studies, finding and improving practical applications, carefully documenting the transition of theory into real-world practice, and linking theory and research, new dissertation research, literature reviews, reflective discussions, cultural studies, and literary works. *Education* will be defined in the broad cultural sense and not be limited to just formal schooling, and particular attention is given to geographical equity to assure representation of all regions and "Latino" groups in the United States.

Two sets of (overlapping) guidelines served as my criteria in the selection of what critical readings might best exemplify the scholarship on Latinos and education. As a first rung, I employed very broad criteria. As mentioned previously, after the *HLE* was published in 2010, I organized (along with a team of planners) the LEAD Summit to launch it. The summit has thus far lasted the test of time and still continues annually. It is a large conference with as many as 1,000 participants in-person, 1,600 viewing partners across 40 countries watching via the internet webcast and many thousands more listening and watching via our numerous media partners.

From the early years we enacted a "chat room" function via the internet, where our individual viewers and town hall viewing sites (LEAD chapters), as they were watching the live webcast, were able to simultaneously converse and chat about all the topics around Latinos and education.

In line with building on the inaugural LEAD summit's goals, many participants, starting at our second annual summit, via online social media and our global virtual classroom, have had ample opportunities to exchange and forge future action items. This process, which makes the LEAD Summit *not* only a conference *but* also an action-planning forum, is one which helps focus ideas and to decide what steps needed to take to achieve particular goals.

Of course, there was disagreement, but overall there was some general agreement on certain items. Some agreement was achieved not only among educators but among the larger forum that included businesses, parents, and community organizations. This anthology, then, serves to highlight or illuminate some, or all, of these recurring themes, thus making for a community-engaged and community-driven scholarship.

The following are the recurring tasks, themes, and solutions (not in order of importance or priority), amassed over the years at the annual Latino

Education & Advocacy Days, on the Latino Education Action Items with which we must collectively engage:

- Learn the traits, backgrounds, cultural histories, and diversity of—and among—Latino groups.
- Build teacher and counselor education programs that have an explicit student–home culture component so that educators are not only sympathetic but also appreciative and sensitive of students' backgrounds and are willing to structure the schooling experiences to be compatible with students.
- Create qualified teachers that have specialized knowledge and skills in language acquisition, biliteracy, and cross-cultural learning. Build "grow your own" teacher recruitment and education programs, with candidates who have organic linkages to the communities in which they intend to serve.
- Research the social reception received by Latino families and the impact of this on the learning of children.
- Combat the deficit views of Latinos; incorporate students' language, culture, and experiential knowledge into schools; acknowledge that an educator's responsibility for providing students with particular academic content knowledge and learning skills should not conflict.
- Create meaningful, trusting horizontal and reciprocal relationships with Latino parents and extended family.
- Short of a constitutional mandate for schooling at the federal level, acknowledge that fundamentally significant educational action is historically conducted at the level of states and our localities, thus where much of our attention should remain.
- Draw together many diverse constituencies of vested interest and facilitate the growth or cluster of collaboratives or action zones that work together to meet educational targets for improvement. These include engagement among parents, students, and other concerned citizens into a movement of transnational proportions that will enable our voices to be heard in the public policy arena. These, in turn, foster creative learning and collaborative leadership projects among and within the action zones.
- Maintain a basic ethos motivated by research, policy analysis and advocacy, education and community action. Foster the practice of research-based teaching and learning, and resist cooptation by political rhetoric, political parties, or unfunded governmental mandates.
- Acknowledge that partnership building is an action-based strategy and that no responsible change comes without the public pressure that requires it.
- Help empower Latino families with information and resources to succeed in the education system, thus fostering a strong culture in academic achievement and college aspiration.

After a narrative analysis of these action items that were offered by the LEAD Summit participants, a second rung was employed, thus narrowing the criteria and strengthening the foundation. These elements are what is offered to the reader:

- Reinforces the positive views of education held by Latinos, especially newcomer families.
- Validates Latino cultural identities, experiences, and ways of knowing that inform those views of education.
- Imparts Latino educational models of what knowledge, skills, and dispositions are worthy of respect and have utility.
- Elaborates the ways how parents and community members can help improve student performance and enrichment and provides a setting for educators, parents and community advocates to share their knowledge, concerns, program needs, and ideas and seek answers to questions that can promote better educational transformations.
- Expands those Latino views of education so as to enthuse a college-going and career-readiness culture for all students to be prepared for a full range of postsecondary options.
- Engages parents and families as to the general expectations of U.S. schooling and as to how they are a critical component in the success of their child's education.
- Expands Latino parents' beliefs that their children are "college material" and offer opportunities to understand their role in the college process, as well as other postsecondary career opportunities.
- Distributes/exhibits/presents educational and career information and postsecondary opportunities, and other materials pertinent to community well-being and be available to support families.
- Builds collective commitment and a partnership model that includes active involvement from all sectors of the regional community.
- Convenes the various sectors of the community together in a way that promotes collaboration, cooperation, and coordination among and between educational/school programs and community-based initiatives.

These critical readings on Latinos and education are organized thematically: tasks, themes, and solutions. I began by looking at the most-cited articles but then rounded it off with the "Editor's picks." Of interest to me were those articles that have been seminal in addressing complex issues, producing and applying wisdom and knowledge to real-world problems while engaging and collaborating with the interests of key stakeholders in other sectors outside the "traditional" academy.

SECTION I (Tasks) begins with Richard R. Valencia (2002), whose seminal piece probes and punctures the long-standing fiction that Mexican Americans, particularly parents of low socioeconomic status, do not value education.

He suggests that the underpinning for the myth lies in the pseudoscientific notion of "deficit thinking," shaped by the fusion of ideology and science, that blames the victim. His piece explores the succession of the mythmaking itself, examining "scholarly" and other sources, and then provides the reader with discourse on how the myth can be discredited with heavy evidence to the contrary. As he wrote, in the production of scholarship we often have to deconstruct mistaken and insubstantial writings before we can construct new ones. Without conceding this fact, it is taxing to continue the ongoing proactive scholarship on the Mexican American family with respect to the importance of the institution of education and schooling.

Next, Cecilia Rios-Aguilar and Judy Marquez Kiyama (2012) well articulate the significance of higher education to the Latina(o) population, as it simply cannot be overstated, as our growing youth populations are among those who have been the least well served by the educational system from K–12 to postsecondary school. As they write, notwithstanding efforts to upsurge college access, college enrollment, and completion rates, they remain stratified by socioeconomic status (Titus, 2006) and by race and ethnicity (Baum & Ma, 2007). Their contribution examines the much-cited conceptual framework of "Funds of Knowledge" and its implications for the college transition process for Latina/o students. Moreover, the authors discuss the strengths and limitations of this framework and make valuable recommendations for its continued use in Latina/o educational research to unlearn, disrupt, and reframe deficit thinking.

The third contribution, by Pablo Jasis and Douglas Marriott (2010), problematizes the all-too-common characterizations educators often hold of low-income migrant parents as "uncaring" or "not interested" in the schooling lives of their children. These authors describe and analyze school participation among a group of migrant parents enrolled in a community-based adult education program. This study clearly points to the notion that migrant parents are willing to assume active roles in the schooling of their children when schools are willing to establish and facilitate the cultural conditions that are necessary to help parents feel welcome, valued, and respected. Moreover, the establishment and facilitation of these cultural conditions are only possible when parents' ways of knowing are honored and woven into the very fabric of any educational program that purports to serve the needs of its students, families, and communities.

Next, Alejandro Covarrubias (2011) updates our view of the Chicano educational pipeline with a unique methodological approach that produces subtle quantitative patterns at the intersection of race, class, gender, and citizenship status. This critical race framework of intersectionality disaggregates data along the intersections, thus providing a filled portrait of the educational trajectory of Mexican-origin people living under distinct conditions. Covarrubias states that this portrait can allow us to capture the nuanced educational outcomes for this demographic as they are shaped by the intersecting systems of oppression and privilege.

Alfredo G. de los Santos Jr. and Karina Michelle Cuamea (2010) describe the severe challenges that face HSIs in the 21st century. Presidents and chancellors of HSIs were surveyed, and their comments revealed five challenges that they feel have the potential to seriously hinder the viability of these higher education institutions. As de los Santos Jr. and Cuamea note, these challenges are further compounded when one takes into consideration the need to educate the rapidly growing Hispanic population, which is now the largest racial/ethnic group in the United States. Hence, policymakers must seriously consider these challenges and devise ways to alleviate them so Hispanics will have the necessary opportunities to enroll in and graduate from colleges and universities.

The last contribution to this section is by Kelly M. Ocasio (2014), who traces what the author calls the discrete points or junctures within the teacher pipeline beginning with successful graduation from high school to persistence and completion of a college degree, teaching certification, or alternative pathway and, finally, to securing a job as a classroom teacher. She identifies significant barriers, including the alarming 50 percent graduation rates at the high school level, poor preparation, financial need, and a lack of college knowledge that have an impact on college admissions and retention. Teacher preparation has several routes, including the traditional university path, 2-year college and alternative paths, paraprofessionals becoming teachers, and career pathway programs—all important gateways. Finally, once in the classroom, Latina/o teachers are motivated by their strong commitment to combating their own negative experiences with schooling and to opening up new opportunities for Latina/o children. The teacher pipeline is a story of significant racialized barriers but also one of inspiring motivation and accomplishment.

SECTION II (Themes) begins with the leading-edge work of Ruben Donato, Gonzalo Guzmán, and Jarrod Hanson (2017). The authors brilliantly describe the case history of *Francisco Maestas et al. v. George H. Shone et al.*, which had been rendered invisible in the educational legislative research literature until now. Their rich description of this case serves as a reminder that parents and allies from the legal field have historically fought for their children's access to equitable schooling in spite of deficit notions that parents of color "do not care" about the life chances of their children.

Next, Mary Ellen Good, Sophia Masewicz, and Linda Vogel (2010) present a research study that explores the cultural-ecological barriers to academic achievement that Latino English Language Learners (ELLs) currently face. The researchers worked with parents and teachers from a rural school district in the Rocky Mountain region to investigate barriers to academic achievement. Findings included barriers related to communication gaps; culture clashes; poorly articulated ELL plans; a lack of teacher preparation in multiculturalism, language acquisition, and ELL instructional strategies; and a lack of support systems for families transitioning to a new environment and culture. Their contribution provides a series of important and concrete recommendations for teachers, school administrators, community/school liaisons, and others working with families in schools.

Next, Nora Luna and Anita Tijerina Revilla (2013) describe narratives of school experiences of Latina/o early school leavers and examined their reasons for leaving Clark County schools before graduating. They then analyzed the responses using the resistance model laid out previously by Solórzano and Delgado Bernal (2001). Then, next, those reasons are compared to the district exit surveys. In two focus groups and two in-depth interviews, a total of 17 participants (10 males and 7 females) disclose the major institutional and personal categories that led them to leave school early. The authors do well in using the term *pushout* as opposed to *dropout* to illuminate the data that students' decisions to leave school are not solely an individual choice but, rather, also result from institutional practices/policies and social forces.

Wanda Alarcón, Cindy Cruz, Linda Guardia Jackson, Linda Prieto, and Sandra Rodriguez-Arroyo (2011) provide a dynamic cacophony of narratives on schooling and survival. Originally published in the VOCES section of *JLE*, the authors offer a deeply personal series of five *testimonios*[11] that resonate with the many narratives of justice, ideology, language, discrimination, and epistemology. They present a critique of prevailing conditions that have conspired to treat them as "alien[s] in [their] own country." As Latina scholars in the academy, their willingness to engage and articulate their personal histories in the form of *testimonios* constitutes a form of both revolution and resistance. The authors use the tradition of "radical storytelling" to problematize the multiple instantiations of oppression and subordination that have been consistent companions throughout their formal education. In the final analysis, these are expressions of cultural and personal affirmation and resistance to individual subjugation and *comunidad*[12] misrepresentations.

Next, Michelle M. Espino (2016) focuses on the issue of Latino parental engagement. Espino explores the narratives of Mexican American doctoral students who describe their experiences and feelings about their parents' pedagogies and engagement with schooling. Espino is interested in how her participants interpreted their parents' and families' messages about education and schooling and the extent to which these messages and experiences served to shape their educational aspirations. Drawing on Tara Yosso and Solórzano's (2005) and Yosso's (2006) conceptualization of community cultural wealth, Espino identifies many instances of home *educación*[13] and support not readily perceptible in dominant conceptions of parental educational engagement. She also finds stories of parents' concern for economic survival and simultaneous inattention to their children's schooling and college-going aspirations. The challenge for the field of Latino education is to contextualize the complexities and contradictions of the different and very real parental messages as experienced and interpreted by adult children.

Ending this section, Cristobal Salinas Jr. and Adele Lozano (2017) explore and map the ways of which the recent linguistic turn toward "Latinx" is currently used within higher education contexts, especially student affairs, and provide an analysis of how it can unsettle the outmoded notions of inclusivity and contour the institutional understandings of intersectionality. As they write, the term *Latinx* emerged recently as a gender-neutral label for Latino/a and Latin@. Findings indicate a weighty trend or turn toward usage of *Latinx* in social media and its emergent usage within institutions of higher learning. Being that empirical studies centering on the creation and evolution of the Latinx terminology are nonexistent, the authors further our understanding, recontextualizing the usage of language that aims to advocate for people who are living in the fluid borderlands of gender and sexuality.

SECTION III (Solutions) begins with Sandra M. Gonzales (2015), who introduced the use of autoethnographic inquiry to study the role of the grandmother (*abuelita*) in preventing the abandonment of Mexican culture. Representing arguably a significant departure from prevailing research themes targeting Latinos, the study of *abuelita* epistemologies represents new terrain in understanding the rich and complex Latino/a community. Gonzales describes a sustained history of subjugation, subordination, and de-Indianization experienced by modern Mexicans, Mexican Americans, and Chicanas/os. She seeks to counter this circumstance from an unapologetically transgressive and disruptive narrative of "*abuela* as educator, tradition keeper, and cultural warrior." As if a contemporary migrant stepping over borders and boundaries, the author audaciously purports that grandmothers possess the capacity to disrupt subtractive or delimiting schooling practices and appreciably improve the academic success of Latino/a students. The study provides a vibrant and inspiring examination of a topic that many Latinos/as are inherently familiar with, namely, the profoundly intellectual and spiritual role of grandparents in the Latino/a community. It is appropriate that her work narrates a story of the epistemological informants of grandparents and elders and their profound impact on helping mitigate the subtractive consequences of suppressive schooling conditions experienced by Latino/a students.

Next, Iliana Alanís and Mariela A. Rodríguez (2008) take readers to the world of a successful dual-language immersion program offering Spanish and English. Often, dual-language immersion programs start off with the view of bilingualism as an asset; however, soon afterward they revert to a remedial orientation that then undermines the efficacy of dual-language instruction toward bilingualism/biliteracy and school achievement. Through qualitative data collection and analysis, Alanís and Rodríguez identified the factors that have contributed to the success of one dual-language program focused on native language as enrichment rather than remediation. These factors include pedagogical equity with rigorous content standards and equal status of both languages; qualified bilingual teachers who are provided institutional support for collaboration and professional development; active parent–home collaboration, including parent-planned programming; and knowledgeable leadership that fosters a proactive school climate for high academic goals.

Jason G. Irizarry and John Raible (2011) identify the values and practices of effective and "exemplary" teachers of Latino students. Drawing on a qualitative, phenomenological interview-based study of a diverse group of 10 teachers in an urban context, they analytically review the participants' biographies and document those factors most cited as the most relevant and prominent to informing their practice and engagement with Latino students. They appropriately position and situate the academic performance of Latino youth in the broader discourses that push beyond the more typical deficit perspectives that often decontextualize and oversimplify underachievement and failure (poverty, little parental involvement, etc.) by considering the additional sociocultural influences of significance (family, neighborhood, race, language, and personal interactions). They describe the teachers' immersion experiences in Latino communities, classroom and community curricular connections, and linguistic and other assets. Flipping the notions of "student as problem," their expansion of barrio-based epistemologies and ontologies describes how these teachers develop ways of being and knowing through close contact with the Latino community.

As habitually under-examined as are the notions of barrio-based epistemologies and ontologies, the persistent under-realization of Latinos in higher education appears equally intractable. Jennifer T. Cates and Scott E. Schaefle (2011) consider the relationship between a college preparation program and "at-risk" students' college readiness in their contribution. Programs to increase the higher education participation of students identified as "at risk" have historically included information on promoting academic preparedness, higher education pathway information, and information on internal motivation. Despite persistent efforts to mitigate the conspicuous underrepresentation of minorities in higher education, the so-called achievement gap continues to exist, and in some areas of educational performance, the gap is expanding. Although fundamental and critical program elements have been identified previously, little is still known about how these elements are related to college readiness. Thus, there is a lack of information about program outcomes and outcome research overall for college outreach programs. The authors suggest that one salient variable for higher education participation remains material wealth, or income, and further assert that Latinos' class location prevents them from acquiring a unique social-cultural cache.[14]

Next, Kysa Nygreen (2017) discusses findings from research with a grassroots, community-based organization working with Latina/o immigrant parents. Presented is an alternative understanding to the too-often pervasive deficit view of Latina/o parent involvement that frames parents as passive and unengaged. The study, instead, demonstrates partnerships that work to strengthen parents' critical consciousness and advocacy skills. In narrative form, the author highlights the Freirean popular education approach utilized by the organization in their workshops where women—like Zoraya—shared with pride stories of school advocacy and engagement. In line with a *mujerist* point of view that looks at the struggles, resiliency, and survival of Chicanas/Latinas, Nygreen also documents the insecurities and fears that Latina mothers contend with in an anti-Latino immigrant climate that speak to a humanizing and context-specific approach to parent engagement. That is, it is about meeting the needs of community members on their terms regardless of the initial objectives or intentions of the organization.

Brad Forenza and Carolina Mendonca (2017) examine the lessons and advocacy narrated by five college-aged undocumented DREAM Act supporters interviewed about their beliefs, role, participation, and leadership in advancing the DREAM Act in their state. In tandem with the four dimensions of intra-organizational empowerment, they found that these activists shared a desire to change the status quo in favor of one of the most disenfranchised groups in the United States (DREAMers), acknowledged the importance of solidarity and coalition building with other advocates to advance the cause, advocated a need to confront and challenge stigmas around the undocumented status, and came to understand the political process (via civic literacy).

Last, I chose to end as we had begun, with Henry T. Trueba's (2002) inaugural contribution to *JLE*'s very first issue, in which he posited that immigrants possess a unique skill and flexibility to acquire and manage different identities that coexist and function without conflicts in different contexts simultaneously. Latino immigrants, especially, used to be conceived of as "handicapped" because of their experience of oppression and their low economic status. They were seen as lacking the necessary cultural capital to succeed at the level of mainstream populations. However, as the demographics change, those individuals who can best function in a diverse society will have greater ability to function effectively. The mastery of different languages, the ability to cross racial and ethnic boundaries, and a general resiliency associated with the ability to endure hardships and overcome obstacles will clearly be recognized as a new cultural capital that will be crucial for success in a modern diversified society, not a handicap.

Continue to read ahead and enjoy the full value and complexity of the anthology presented by *Critical Readings on Latinos and Education: Tasks, Themes, and Solutions*. I extend my appreciation to the authors for their respective contributions and commend them for their contributions to the field of Latinos and education. I must also extend my gratitude to the editorial staff, associates, board, and reviewers of *JLE* for these last 2 decades for their initiative in supporting the continued research and practices that illuminate the myriad circumstances in which Latinas/os and their families continue to struggle for educational excellence and equity. Last, I must thank all the LEAD projects' staff, planners, sponsors, partners, and chapters for affirming the importance of scholarship and creative analysis that attempt to give voice to a community of learners that is silent no longer.

Thank You—*Muchísimas Gracias*—*Tlazokamate*.

Enrique G. Murillo, Jr., PhD
Professor, College of Education
Executive Director, Latino Education &
Advocacy Days (Lead) Organization
Editor in Chief, *Journal of Latinos and Education*
California State University, San Bernardino

Notes

1. Indigenous, Native, Original Inhabitant to the Americas or Western Hemisphere.
2. *El Plan de Santa Bárbara: A Chicano Plan for Higher Education* was written by the Chicano Coordinating Council on Higher Education as a manifesto recognizing the central role of knowledge and representation in power structures and in producing real social change.
3. Keep in mind that Chicano/Latino PhDs were only about 0.5 percent of all persons holding a doctorate at the time.
4. See Gándara and Contreras (2009).
5. See Valencia (2010), where he prolifically challenges leaders, educators, researchers, and advocates alike to grapple with the unequal social, political, and cultural systems of U.S. communities.
6. See Bartlett, Fredrick, Guldbrandsen, and Murillo (2002).
7. *Funds of Knowledge* is a term coined by Luis Moll and extended by many other scholars since, describing the prior knowledge students bring into the classroom because of their unique familial, cultural, and experiential backgrounds (L.C. Moll, C. Amanti, D. Neff and N. González, 1992; L. Moll and N. González, 1997).
8. Assembly Concurrent Resolution (ACR 137): http://leginfo.legislature.ca.gov/faces/billTextClient.xhtml?bill_id=200920100ACR137
9. For more information, please visit: http://lead.csusb.edu/ and http://leadsummit.csusb.edu/
10. The Southern California Consortium of Hispanic Serving Institutions started as a CSUSB initiative, and I currently serve as its president.
11. *Testimonio* is a form of testimonial narrative account, rich in its Latin American roots, especially in indigenous villages, and its power lies in their metaphor of "witnessing" through real-life experience and bringing immediate and emotive attention to an issue.
12. Community and community experience.
13. The concept of *educación* incorporates ways that families place value on personal development and respect for others as part of what it means to be "educated" as well as layer lessons taught in the home with lessons taught in the classroom. It includes ethical, social, and moral character; manner; and rectitude. See Valenzuela (1999), Auerbach (2002), and Villenas (2006).
14. See Bourdieu (1977) and Bourdieu and Passeron (1977) on "Cultural Capital", here referring to the prolonged and organic accumulation of sensibilities, disposition, and predilections that fundamentally inform the critical decisions of one's life, including the desire and commitment to pursue higher education.

References

Alanís, I. & Rodríguez, M. A. (2008). Sustaining a Dual Language Immersion Program: Features of Success. *Journal of Latinos and Education*, 7(4), 305–319.

Alarcón, W., Cruz, C., Guardia Jackson, L., Prieto, L., & Rodriguez-Arroyo, S. (2011). *Compartiendo Nuestras Historias*: Five *Testimonios* of Schooling and Survival. *Journal of Latinos and Education*, 10(4), 369–381.

Auerbach, S. (2002). Why Do They Give the Good Classes to Some and Not to Others? Latino Parent Narratives of Struggle in a College Access Program. *Teachers College Record*, 104(7), 1369–1392.

Bartlett, L., Fredrick, M., Guldbrandsen, T., & Murillo, E. G., Jr. (2002). The Marketization of Education: Public Schools for Private Ends. *Anthropology & Education Quarterly*, 33(1), 1–25.

Baum, S. & Ma, J. (2007). *Education Pays 2007*. Washington, DC: College Board.

Bourdieu, P. (1977). Cultural Reproduction and Social Reproduction. In J. Karabel & A. H. Halsey (eds), *Power and Ideology in Education* (pp. 487–511). New York: Oxford University Press.

Bourdieu, P. & Passeron, J. C. (1977). *Reproduction in Education, Society, and Culture*. Beverly Hills, CA: Sage.

Cates, J. T. & Schaefle, S. E. (2011). The Relationship Between a College Preparation Program and At-Risk Students' College Readiness. *Journal of Latinos and Education*, 10(4), 320–334.

Chicano Coordinating Council on Higher Education. (1970). *El Plan de Santa Bárbara: A Chicano Plan for Higher Education*. Oakland, CA: La Causa Publications.

Covarrubias, A. (2011). Quantitative Intersectionality: A Critical Race Analysis of the Chicana/o Educational Pipeline. *Journal of Latinos and Education*, 10(2), 86–105.

de los Santos, A. G., Jr. & Cuamea, K. M. (2010). Challenges Facing Hispanic-Serving Institutions in the First Decade of the 21st Century. *Journal of Latinos and Education*, 9(2), 90–107.

Donato, R., Guzmán, G., & Hanson, J. (2017). *Francisco Maestas et al. v. George H. Shone et al.*: Mexican American Resistance to School Segregation in the Hispano Homeland, 1912–1914. *Journal of Latinos and Education*, 16(1), 3–17.

Espino, M. M. (2016). The Value of Education and *Educación*: Nurturing Mexican American Children's Educational Aspirations to the Doctorate. *Journal of Latinos and Education*, 15(2), 73–90.

Forenza, B. & Mendonca, C. (2017). Dream Big: Exploring Empowering Processes of DREAM Act Advocacy in a Focal State. *Journal of Latinos and Education*, 16(4), 290–300.

Freire, P. (1970). *Pedagogy of the Oppressed*. New York: Seabury Press.

Gándara, P. & Contreras, F. (2009). *The Latino Education Crisis: The Consequences of Failed Social Policies*. Cambridge, MA: Harvard University Press.

Gonzales, S. M. (2015). *Abuelita* Epistemologies: Counteracting Subtractive Schools in American Education. *Journal of Latinos and Education*, 14(1), 40–54.

Good, M. E., Masewicz, S., & Vogel, L. (2010). Latino English Language Learners: Bridging Achievement and Cultural Gaps Between Schools and Families. *Journal of Latinos and Education*, 9(4), 321–339.

Irizarry, J. G. & Raible, J. (2011). Beginning with *El Barrio*: Learning From Exemplary Teachers of Latino Students. *Journal of Latinos and Education*, 10(3), 186–203.

Jasis, P. & Marriott, D. (2010). All for Our Children: Migrant Families and Parent Participation in an Alternative Education Program. *Journal of Latinos and Education*, 9(2), 126–140.

Luna, N. & Tijerina Revilla, A. (2013). Understanding Latina/o School Pushout: Experiences of Students Who Left School Before Graduating. *Journal of Latinos and Education*, 12(1), 22–37.

Moll, L. C., Amanti, C., Neff, D., & Gonzalez, N. (1992). Funds of Knowledge for Teaching: Using a Qualitative Approach to Connect Homes and Classrooms. *Theory into Practice*, 31(2), 132–141.

Moll, L. C. & González, N. (1997). Beginning Where the Children Are. In O. S. Ana (ed.), *Tongue-tied: The Lives of Multilingual Children in Public Education* (pp. 152–156). Lanham, MD: Rowman & Littlefield.

Murillo, E. G., Jr. (1999). Mojado Crossings Along Neoliberal Borderlands. *Educational Foundations*, 13(1), 7–30.

Murillo, E. G., Jr. et al. (2002). From the Editor's Desk. *Journal of Latinos and Education*, *1*(1), 1–5.

Murillo, E. G., Jr. et al. (eds). (2010). *Handbook of Latinos and Education: Theory, Research & Practice*. Philadelphia, PA: Routledge.

Nygreen, K. (2017). Latina/o Parent Organizing for Educational Justice: An Ethnographic Account of Community Building and Radical Healing. *Journal of Latinos and Education*, *16*(4), 301–313.

Ocasio, K. M. (2014). *Nuestro Camino*: A Review of Literature Surrounding the Latino Teacher Pipeline. *Journal of Latinos and Education*, *13*(4), 244–261.

Rios-Aguilar, C. & Marquez Kiyama, J. (2012). Funds of Knowledge: An Approach to Studying Latina(o) Students' Transition to College. *Journal of Latinos and Education*, *11*(1), 2–16.

Salinas, C., Jr. & Lozano, A. (2017). Mapping and Recontextualizing the Evolution of the Term *Latinx*: An Environmental Scanning in Higher Education. *Journal of Latinos and Education*. Published online 16 November 2017.

Solórzano, D. G. & Delgado Bernal, D. (2001). Critical Race Theory, Transformational Resistance, and Social Justice: Chicana and Chicano Students in an Urban Context. *Urban Education*, *36*, 308–342.

Titus, M. (2006). Understanding the Influence of the Financial Context of Institutions on Student Persistence at Four-Year Colleges and Universities. *Journal of Higher Education*, *77*, 353–375.

Trueba, H. T. (2002). Multiple Ethnic, Racial, and Cultural Identities in Action: From Marginality to a New Cultural Capital in Modern Society. *Journal of Latinos and Education*, *1*(1), 7–28.

U.S. Census Bureau, Census 2000 (2000). Summary File 1; 1990 Census of Population, General Population Characteristics (CP-1-1).

Valencia, R. R. (2002). "Mexican Americans Don't Value Education!"—On the Basis of the Myth, Mythmaking, and Debunking. *Journal of Latinos and Education*, *1*(2), 81–103.

Valencia, R. R. (2010). *Chicano School Failure and Success: Past, Present, and Future* (3rd edn). Abingdon: Routledge.

Valenzuela, A. (1999). *Subtractive Schooling: U.S.-Mexican Youth and the Politics of Caring*. Albany, NY: State University of New York Press.

Villenas, S. (2006). Pedagogical Moments in the Borderland: Latina Mothers Teaching and Learning. In D. Delgado Bernal, C. A. Elenes, F. E. Godínez, & S. Villenas (eds), *Chicana/Latina Education in Everyday Life: Feminista Perspectives on Pedagogy and Epistemology* (pp. 147–159). Albany, NY: State University of New York Press.

Yosso, T. J. (2006). *Critical Race Counterstories Along the Chicana/Chicano Educational Pipeline*. New York, NY: Routledge.

Yosso, T. J. & Solórzano, D. G. (2005). Conceptualizing a Critical Race Theory in Sociology. In M. Romero & E. Margolis (eds), *The Blackwell Companion to Social Inequalities* (pp. 117–146). Malden, MA: Blackwell.

Credits

Section I: Tasks

Chapter 1: Richard R. Valencia and Mary S. Black (2002) "Mexican Americans Don't Value Education!"—On the Basis of the Myth, Mythmaking, and Debunking, *Journal of Latinos and Education*, *1*(2), 81–103, DOI: 10.1207/S1532771XJLE0102_2

Chapter 2: Cecilia Rios-Aguilar and Judy Marquez Kiyama (2012) Funds of Knowledge: An Approach to Studying Latina(o) Students' Transition to College, *Journal of Latinos and Education*, *11*(1), 2–16, DOI: 10.1080/15348431.2012.631430

Chapter 3: Pablo Jasis and Douglas Marriott (2010) All for Our Children: Migrant Families and Parent Participation in an Alternative Education Program, *Journal of Latinos and Education*, *9*(2), 126–140, DOI: 10.1080/15348431003617814

Chapter 4: Alejandro Covarrubias (2011) Quantitative Intersectionality: A Critical Race Analysis of the Chicana/o Educational Pipeline, *Journal of Latinos and Education*, *10*(2), 86–105, DOI: 10.1080/15348431.2011.556519

Chapter 5: Alfredo G. de los Santos Jr. and Karina Michelle Cuamea (2010) Challenges Facing Hispanic-Serving Institutions in the First Decade of the 21st Century, *Journal of Latinos and Education*, *9*(2), 90–107, DOI: 10.1080/15348431003617798

Chapter 6: Kelly M. Ocasio (2014) *Nuestro Camino*: A Review of Literature Surrounding the Latino Teacher Pipeline, *Journal of Latinos and Education*, *13*(4), 244–261, DOI: 10.1080/15348431.2014.887467

Section II: Themes

Chapter 7: Ruben Donato, Gonzalo Guzmán, and Jarrod Hanson (2017) *Francisco Maestas et al. v. George H. Shone et al.*: Mexican American Resistance to School Segregation in the Hispano Homeland, 1912–1914, *Journal of Latinos and Education*, *16*(1), 3–17, DOI: 10.1080/15348431.2016.1179190

Chapter 8: Mary Ellen Good, Sophia Masewicz, and Linda Vogel (2010) Latino English Language Learners: Bridging Achievement and Cultural Gaps Between Schools and Families, *Journal of Latinos and Education*, *9*(4), 321–339, DOI: 10.1080/15348431.2010.491048

Chapter 9: Nora Luna and Anita Tijerina Revilla (2013) Understanding Latina/o School Pushout: Experiences of Students Who Left School Before Graduating, *Journal of Latinos and Education*, *12*(1), 22–37, DOI: 10.1080/15348431.2012.734247

Chapter 10: Wanda Alarcón, Cindy Cruz, Linda Guardia Jackson, Linda Prieto, and Sandra Rodriguez-Arroyo (2011) *Compartiendo Nuestras Historias*: Five *Testimonios* of Schooling and Survival, *Journal of Latinos and Education*, *10*(4), 369–381, DOI: 10.1080/15348431.2011.605690

Chapter 11: Michelle M. Espino (2016) The Value of Education and *Educación*: Nurturing Mexican American Children's Educational Aspirations to the Doctorate, *Journal of Latinos and Education*, *15*(2), 73–90, DOI: 10.1080/15348431.2015.1066250

Chapter 12: Cristobal Salinas Jr. and Adele Lozano (2017) Mapping and Recontextualizing the Evolution of the Term *Latinx*: An Environmental Scanning in Higher Education, *Journal of Latinos and Education*, 1–14, DOI: 10.1080/15348431.2017.1390464

Section III: Solutions

Chapter 13: Sandra M. Gonzales (2015) *Abuelita* Epistemologies: Counteracting Subtractive Schools in American Education, *Journal of Latinos and Education*, *14*(1), 40–54, DOI: 10.1080/15348431.2014.944703

Chapter 14: Iliana Alanís and Mariela A. Rodríguez (2008) Sustaining a Dual Language Immersion Program: Features of Success, *Journal of Latinos and Education*, 7(4), 305–319, DOI: 10.1080/15348430802143378

Chapter 15: Jason G. Irizarry and John Raible (2011) Beginning With *El Barrio*: Learning From Exemplary Teachers of Latino Students, *Journal of Latinos and Education*, *10*(3), 186–203, DOI: 10.1080/15348431.2011.581102

Chapter 16: Jennifer T. Cates and Scott E. Schaefle (2011) The Relationship Between a College Preparation Program and At-Risk Students' College Readiness, *Journal of Latinos and Education*, *10*(4), 320–334, DOI: 10.1080/15348431.2011.605683

Chapter 17: Kysa Nygreen (2017) Latina/o Parent Organizing for Educational Justice: An Ethnographic Account of Community Building and Radical Healing, *Journal of Latinos and Education*, *16*(4), 301–313, DOI: 10.1080/15348431.2016.1247706

Chapter 18: Brad Forenza and Carolina Mendonca (2017) Dream Big: Exploring Empowering Processes of DREAM Act Advocacy in a Focal State, *Journal of Latinos and Education*, *16*(4), 290–300, DOI: 10.1080/15348431.2016.1240077

Chapter 19: Henry T. Trueba (2002) Multiple Ethnic, Racial, and Cultural Identities in Action: From Marginality to a New Cultural Capital in Modern Society, *Journal of Latinos and Education*, *1*(1), 7–28, DOI: 10.1207/S1532771XJLE0101_2

Section I
Tasks

1 "Mexican Americans Don't Value Education!"

On the Basis of the Myth, Mythmaking, and Debunking

Richard R. Valencia and Mary S. Black

Economist Thomas Sowell wrote the following in his chapter on "The Mexicans" (*Ethnic America: A History*, 1981): "*The goals and values of Mexican Americans have never centered on education*" [italics added] (p. 266). Historically and contemporarily, there have been numerous assertions by individuals in the scholarly literature and in media outlets that Mexican American parents, particularly of low-socioeconomic status (SES) background, do not value education. Thus, they fail to inculcate this value in their children via academic socialization, and seldom participate in parental involvement activities in their home or the school.[1] As a consequence, the myth contends, Mexican American children tend to perform poorly in school (e.g., low academic achievement). These allegations cannot be taken lightly, as there is substantial evidence that, in general, "when parents are involved in their youths' schooling, children do better in school" (Marburger, 1990, p. 82).[2]

Our intent in this article is to

1. Shed some light on the fundamental basis of the myth that Mexican Americans do not value education.
2. Advance an understanding of the myth by identifying the sources of this false, unsupported assertion—the mythmakers themselves.
3. Debunk the myth by discussing literature that has demonstrated Mexican Americans do indeed value education.
4. Present a case study of Mexican American parental involvement in education (i.e., a transgenerational analysis of 6 families in Austin, Texas).

The Fundamental Basis of the Myth

We contend that the basis of the myth—Mexican Americans don't value education—lies in the pseudoscientific notion of "deficit thinking" (see Valencia, 1997a, for a comprehensive discussion of the evolution of deficit thinking in educational thought and practice from the American Colonial period to the contemporary period). Deficit thinking refers to the idea that students, particularly of low-SES background and of color, fail in school because they and their families have internal defects, or deficits, that thwart the learning process. The theory of deficit thinking has its roots in the racial climate of the American Colonial period (Menchaca, 1997), and has evolved as a protean model. Depending on the zeitgeist of the time period, the variants of deficit thinking have included genetic (Valencia, 1997b), cultural (Foley, 1997), familial (Pearl, 1997), and genetic–cultural–familial explanations (Valencia & Solórzano, 1997). Deficit thinking, an endogenous theory of school failure, "blames the victim" rather than examining how schools and the political economy are structured to prevent students from learning optimally. As such, the theory asserts that poor schooling performance of students of color is rooted in the students' (alleged) cognitive and motivational deficits, while institutional structures and inequitable schooling arrangements that exclude students from learning are held blameless (Valencia, 1997a). The basis for the myth that Mexican Americans do not value education stems from the general model of deficit thinking, and from the specific variant of familial deficits. The argument goes as follows: Given that Mexican Americans (allegedly) do not hold education high in their value hierarchy, this leads to inadequate familial socialization for academic competence, which in turn contributes to the school failure of Mexican American children and youths.

Furthermore, the myth of Mexican Americans' indifference to the value of education can be more fully understood when viewed as part of a historical tradition of deficit thinking. In this tradition, Mexican Americans are described under the "Mexican American cultural model (stereotype)" in which their value orientations are presented as the root cause of their social problems (Hernández, 1970), including school failure (for overviews and critiques of the model, see, e.g., Menchaca, 2000; Romano-V, 1968). In a broader sense, the Mexican American stereotype model is grounded in the long-standing myth that behavior is equated with values (Valencia & Solórzano, 1997). As Allen (1970) has noted,

> Behavior cannot be equated with values. In other words, simply because a person behaves in a certain way does not mean he desires to do so because of his beliefs or values. Another problem is that the concept is tautological: Values inferred from behavior are used to explain behavior. To be useful for explaining behavior, values should be measured independent of the behavior to be explained, or no advantage can be claimed for the gratuitous labeling of the behavior.
>
> (pp. 372–373)

Mythmaking

The assertion that Mexican Americans are indifferent toward and devalue education has been communicated in various ways. These expressions are particularly seen in (a) some very early master's theses (1920s, 1930s), (b) published scholarly literature, and (c) opinions voiced in media outlets. In this section, we discuss examples of this mythmaking from these three categories.

Early Master's Theses

Taylor (1927) sought to investigate the possible reasons for "pedagogical retardation" (being overage for grade level) among young school-age Mexican American children in Albuquerque, New Mexico. The author concluded that mental retardation, lack of knowledge in English, excessive school transfers, and poor nutrition were contributing factors to pedagogical retardation among a substantial percentage of the students. Taylor also honed in on the "indifference of [the] family toward [the] value of education" (p. 173). Specifically contextualizing such "indifference" in school attendance issues, Taylor commented,

> Every possible effort is made in Albuquerque toward the enforcement of regular attendance, insofar as the administrative officers are concerned. The difficulty lies in the home. A serious lack of the realization of the importance of regular attendance is the source of the trouble in these schools. The large percentage of illiterate parents, found especially among the Mexican population, *fails to understand the full value of the opportunity offered by the public schools* [italics added].
> (pp. 176–177)

Other examples of these mythmakers of the past are

1. Gould (1932, southern California area study): "*As a general rule, the [Mexican] parents lack any desire for education*" [italics added]
   (p. 2).

2. Lyon (1933, Los Angeles City School District study): "The greatest cause of [intercultural] conflict arises from the attitude toward education on the part of the parents and . . . Mexican girls. *The parents feel that the child is needed in the home and do not understand the necessity for education*" [italics added]
   (pp. 42–43).

The assertions by Taylor (1927), Gould (1932), and Lyon (1933) were not uncommon voices from the past regarding the establishment and perpetuation of the myth that Mexican Americans do not value education. Such contentions were based on deficit thinking and stereotypes. These newly credentialed individuals with their master's degrees failed to acknowledge the forces and conditions that likely created obstacles for Mexican American parents to fully express their appreciation for and value of education—for example, not being welcome at schools because of racial animus, language barriers, and the need for their children to contribute economically to the household due to exploitative arrangements the parents faced in the world of work. This non-deficit thinking perspective can be seen, however, in a small number of master's theses from this period. Pratt (1938) investigated schooling conditions, SES background, and academic achievement of Mexican American and White children in Delta, Colorado (an agricultural community in which most of the Mexican Americans worked in the local sugar beet industry, and supplemented their income by harvesting other crops). Pratt found that the reasons (provided by the parents) for the Mexican American children's attendance problems were "no shoes to wear, no clothes to wear, too sick, had to work [most frequent response], and girls kept at home so they would not run around with the boys" (p. 96). Rather than blaming the victim, Pratt interpreted the children's poor attendance—which could have been viewed under a deficit thinking framework as parental indifference to education—to be related to serious economic problems: "It would seem that many of the deplorable circumstances of these impoverished people would and could be alleviated if the wage scale of the Mexican were raised to a higher level" (p. 102).

Scholarly Literature

To be sure, master's theses are considered as scholarly literature. Here, however, the focus is on literature (e.g., books, book chapters in edited volumes, journal articles) that, we assume, has gone through the rigors of peer review. We examine examples of mythmaking from three categories of scholarly literature: (a) the "culturally deprived" child literature of the 1960s, (b) the "at risk" child and family literature of the 1980s and 1990s, and (c) an "other" category.

"Cultural Deprivation" Literature

In the 1960s, the "culturally deprived" child (also referred to as the "culturally disadvantaged," "intellectually deprived," and "socially disadvantaged" child) was socially constructed (see Pearl, 1997, for a sustained coverage of this era). Voluminous literature spoke to the culturally deprived child and his or her (allegedly) socially pathological family and impoverished home environment (e.g., Frost & Hawkes, 1966; Hellmuth, 1967). As we previously discussed (see Footnote 1), Mexican American children and their families (particularly of low SES background) were, among other racial and ethnic groups, a targeted population of the 1960s mythmakers (see Marans & Lourie, 1967). Havighurst (1966), in a chapter titled "Who are the Socially Disadvantaged?" (a discussion on the general socially disadvantaged population), presented a brief list of "family characteristics" the socially disadvantaged child lacks, compared to "modern urban" families (meaning middle class). The characteristic most germane to our discussion is that "the socially disadvantaged child lacks.... *Two parents who:* read a good deal; read to him; show him that *they believe in the value of education* [italics added]; reward him for good school achievement" (p. 18). Another example of mythmaking during the era of cultural deprivation is seen in Dougherty (1966), who—without the support of a single citation—commented, "*Parental indifference to the value of education is transmitted to the children* [italics added], where school careers are naturally characterized by poor attention, low achievement, and early leaving. Thus, the cycle of hopelessness and despair is repeated from generation to generation" (p. 389).

It is beyond the scope of this article to discuss critiques of the cultural deprivation literature. We refer the interested reader to the writings of Baratz and Baratz (1970), Labov (1970), Pearl (1997), and Valencia and Solórzano (1997). Critiques of the cultural deprivation literature model have centered, for example, on the framework's racist and classist nature, theoretical weaknesses, and methodological shortcomings of this body of research.

The "At Risk" Child Literature[3]

First popularized in the educational policy circles of the early 1980s, the label *at risk* is now entrenched in the educational literature as well as in the talk of educators and policymakers (Valencia & Solórzano, 1997). Writing in 1995, Swadener and Lubeck (1995a) reported that since 1989 over 2,500 articles and conference papers have dealt with the at risk construct. Given their overrepresentation among the poor and low-SES families, Mexican Americans and other Latinos are considered by scholars of the at risk literature to be part of this group. Sleeter (1995) has asserted that the new term *at risk* is a resurrected metaphor for the cultural deprivation and culturally disadvantaged terms used with great frequency in the 1960s (also, see Valencia & Solórzano, 1997).

Although some of the literature on at risk students and their families alludes to unfavorable schooling conditions (e.g., low expectations of students, curriculum differentiation) and societal conditions (e.g., racism, lack of opportunity) that likely place students at risk for school failure, the *primary focus* is on *familial* characteristics (e.g., race or ethnicity, poverty, single parenthood) and *personal* characteristics of students (e.g., poor self-concept, self-destructive behaviors, English as second language, juvenile delinquency; see, e.g., Manning & Baruth, 1995; Vaughn, Bos, & Schumm, 1997).

Regarding the role of the home and parents, "the 'at risk' label alleges that a child suffers some environmentally induced deficiency . . . [and] by implication or design, mothers are presumed to be the *source* of the problems children experience" (Lubeck, 1995, p. 54). Furthermore, "If a child does not fare well, emotionally, socially, or academically, it is the family—but the mother specifically—who is implicated" (Lubeck, p. 54). Lubeck (1995) pointed to a statewide (North Carolina) survey of principals and superintendents, in which the respondents associated at risk status with maternal employment, poverty, single parenting, and minority status. Administrators made reference to the roots of these problems mainly through innuendo:

> We have large numbers of children who come from homes with *no emphasis on education* [italics added]. . . . Large numbers of youngsters come into

school with absolutely no background, either academic or social. . . . Many of our five-year-olds come to kindergarten with minimal experiences and marginal skills partially due to poor parenting skills. Many parents are "drop-outs" and lack the know-how and ability to provide quality preschool experiences for their child [*sic*] . . . . Many of our homes do not offer children the support needed to develop emotionally, socially, and academically.

(Lubeck & Garrett, 1990, pp. 336–337)

In sum, a strong case can be made that the notion of at risk denotes a form of deficit thinking (Valencia & Solórzano, 1997; also, see Fine, 1995; Richardson, Casanova, Placier, & Guilfoyle, 1989). Part of the problem with the concept of at risk is that it tends to overlook any strengths and promise of the student so labeled, while drawing attention to the presumed shortcomings of the individual (Ronda & Valencia, 1994; Swadener & Lubeck, 1995b). Students continue to be defined as at risk based on "personal and familial characteristics" (Donmoyer & Kos, 1993, p. 9). As such, at risk has become a person-centered explanation of school failure. The construct of at risk is preoccupied with describing "deficiencies" in students, particularly alleged shortcomings rooted in familial and economic backgrounds of students. Finally, the concept of at risk qualifies to be under the rubric of deficit thinking in that the notion pays little, if any, attention to how schools are institutionally implicated in ways that exclude students from learning (see Valencia, in press). The idea of at risk blames the victim, as does the notion of deficit thinking. The deficit model turns students into burdens and trades potential for risk.

Other Literature

Another category of scholarly literature in which mythmaking can be seen regarding the alleged indifference Mexican Americans have toward education is what we refer to as "other" literature. This category contains literature that does not snugly fit into either the cultural deprivation or at risk camps, although such scholarship shares the common feature of being heavily shaped by deficit thinking. Here we briefly discuss two examples of this other literature: Sowell (1981) and Dunn (1987).

This article opened with a quote by Sowell (1981) that is worth repeating: "*The goals and values of Mexican Americans have never centered on education*" [italics added] (p. 266). How does Sowell, who has written a history of racial and ethnic groups in the United States, support this sweeping generalization? What specific evidence does he marshal to defend such a blatant assertion? He does so by noting comparative high school completion rates across race and ethnicity: "As of 1960, only 13% of Hispanics in the Southwest completed high school, compared to only 17 percent for blacks in the same region, 28% among non-Hispanic Whites, and 39 percent among Japanese Americans"

(p. 266). It appears that Sowell is making this argument: *Because Mexican Americans have the lowest high school completion rate of the groups he compares,*[4] *then this means that Mexican Americans do not value education.* Clearly, Sowell frames his interpretation of the racial and ethnic high school completion gap in a deficit thinking manner. Explicit in his argument is that Mexican Americans are the makers of their own educational shortcomings. Furthermore, he fails to discuss the far different interpretations of the achievement gap proffered by the authors who presented the original data Sowell describes above (Grebler, Moore, & Guzmán, 1970, p. 143, Table 7–1). Grebler et al. attribute the achievement gap, in part, to intragroup (i.e., Anglo and Mexican American) variations in "rural–urban background, to immigrant status, and to poverty and other aspects of the home environment" (p. 170). Grebler et al. also present a structural inequality hypothesis to explain the gap:

> *The extreme disparities in different locales suggests [sic] also an [sic] hypothesis concerning a strategic determinant in a larger society: the extent to which local social systems and, through these, the school systems have held the Mexican American population in a subordinate position.*
>
> (p. 170)[5]

Sowell's (1981) claim that Mexican Americans' goals and values have never focused on education is one of the most egregious and unfounded statements ever made about Mexican Americans and their schooling. His assertion is not only wrong (as we shall see later when we debunk the myth), but it is presented in a book on the history of racial and ethnic groups in the United States—a type of source that should be committed to the highest level of interpretive scholarship, not mythmaking.

A second example of mythmaking from the scholarly literature regarding the allegation that Mexican Americans do not value education is seen in Lloyd M. Dunn's (1987) research monograph, *Bilingual Hispanic Children on the U.S. Mainland: A Review of Research on Their Cognitive, Linguistic, and Scholastic Development.*[6] While acknowledging that the schools have, in part, been implicated in not serving Latino pupils (i.e., Mexican American and Puerto Rican), Dunn places the blame on parents who, he contends, do not care about education. This is a major factor, Dunn argues, that explains why Latinos, as a group, have academic problems in schools.[7] He opines, "it would be more correct to point out that these Hispanic pupils and their parents have also failed the schools and society, because *they have not been motivated and dedicated enough to make the system work for them*" [italics added] (p. 78). Furthermore, in the absence of any supportive data or sources, Dunn asserts, "*It* [valuing education] *is a tradition that Hispanics in general do not appear to have*" [italics added] (p. 80). Once again, we see a scholar evoke a long-standing deficit thinking tactic of shifting culpability away from structural problems in the schools (such as segregation, financial inequalities, and curriculum differentiation), to the backs and shoulders of Latino parents who are expected to carry the near exclusive burden of school success for their children. Moreover, Dunn is either unaware of or chooses to disregard the available literature that Latinos do value and do get involved in their children's education, an area we discuss shortly.

Media Expressions

A third way in which the myth of Mexican Americans' indifference to the importance of education has been expressed is through individuals making such pronouncements in some forum that subsequently capture the attention of the media (particularly newspapers and television). We discuss two cases in point: Lauro Cavazos and Lino Graglia.

Lauro Cavazos, former United States Secretary of Education (and the top-ranking Latino) in President George H. Bush's administration, made some comments in early April 1990 that set off a maelstrom of disputation. Cavazos made his comments at a press conference in San Antonio that was concerned with the first of a series of five regional hearings on Hispanic educational problems. He stated, "*Hispanics have always valued education . . . but somewhere along the line we've lost that. I really believe that, today, there is not that emphasis*" [italics added] (Snider, 1990, p. 1). There was immediate response from the media. The headlines of the *San Antonio Light* pronounced, "Cavazos Says Attitude Hurts Hispanics" (Snider, 1990, p. 1). The *New York Times'* headline of a front-page story proclaimed, "Education Secretary Criticizes the Values of Hispanic Parents" (Snider, 1990, p. 1).

Suffice it to say, Cavazos's pronouncements provoked considerable public clamor, particularly from Mexican American San Antonians. Dr. José A. Cárdenas, Executive Director of the Intercultural Development Research Association and lifelong educational activist commented, "It's [Cavazos's assertion] a simple case of the victim being blamed for the crime" (Snider, 1990, p. 1). James A. Vásquez, Superintendent for the San Antonio Edgewood Independent School, responded, "The terrible thing is . . . that he's denying what's happened to Mexican Americans in the history of this state, how we've been discriminated against in every way. It proves he continues to be very far removed from the community" (Snider, 1990, p. 2). Vásquez's contention of a history of widespread discrimination, including educational inequalities in Texas, can be amply documented by existing scholarship (see De León, 1983; Feagin & Booher Feagin, 1999; San Miguel, 1987; San Miguel & Valencia, 1998; Valencia, 2000).

Cavazos's unfounded and insulting statements about Hispanics' attitude toward education certainly provoked outcries. This resultant uproar paled, however, in comparison to the commotion generated by similar comments that constitutional law Professor Lino Graglia made at a news conference on September 10, 1997, at The University of Texas at Austin. At that time, Graglia was chosen as honorary co-chairman of the newly established group, Students for Equal Opportunity—a group who was "tired of hearing only from supporters of affirmative action" (Roser, 1997, p. B1). At the campus press conference, where the new student group made its debut, Graglia made the following remarks regarding affirmative action, race, and academic performance at The University of Texas School of Law:

> The central problem is that Blacks and Mexican Americans are not academically competitive [with Whites]. . . . Various studies seem to show that Blacks [and] Mexican Americans spend less time in school. *They have a culture that seems not to encourage achievement* [italics added] . . . failure is not looked upon with disgrace.[8]

In an NBC *Today* interview with reporter Matt Lauer on September 12, 1997, Graglia was asked if he had any statistical backing for his cultural statements about minority students and educational achievement:

Graglia: I'm not an expert on educational matters.
Lauer: But you do agree with the statement that came out of yours that says they [Blacks and Mexican Americans] have a culture that seems not to encourage achievement?
Graglia: Well, I meant to say that there are some cultures, like some of the Asian cultures that insist more highly on the students going to school and achieving in school . . .

Ramiro Canales (a member of the Chicano/Hispanic Law Students Association at UT) was also interviewed by Lauer, who asked Canales how he felt about the cultural issues Graglia raised.

Canales: Professor Graglia is not qualified to make cultural assessments. He is a law school professor and not a cultural anthropologist, and when he makes these generalizations they not only promote racial stereotypes but also distort reality as it is in Texas. I think both African American and Mexican American cultures promote success. I think that the parents of all the minority law students want their students [*sic*] to succeed.

The nefarious pronouncements from Graglia, who has a long history of speaking out against affirmative action and using busing for school desegregation (Roser & Tanamachi, 1997), drew national and international media coverage and swift denunciations.[9] Included among the public condemnors were UT School of Law Dean Michael Sharlot, UT Interim President Peter Flawn, UT System Chancellor William Cunningham, student organizations, professors, civil rights organizations, and racial and ethnic minority lawmakers (Martin, 1997; Roser & Tanamachi, 1997). Regarding the latter group, Hispanic state lawmakers called for Graglia's resignation. Senator Gregory Luna, head of the State Hispanic Caucus, stated, "It seems we're in an era where the Ku Klux Klan does not come in white robes but in the robes of academe" (Martin, 1997, p. 1). UT students of color were also very involved in the protest against Graglia. They staged a sit-in at the School of Law, and helped organize a political rally in which Reverend Jesse Jackson, in front of 5,000 people, lambasted Graglia (Roser & Tanamachi, 1997).

The Cavazos and Graglia incidents serve as reminders that statements made about racial or ethnic groups—in which the remarks are shaped by deficit thinking, ahistoricism, ignorance of scholarly literature, and bigotry—have no value in promoting further understanding of the achievement gap between White and minority student groups. These incidents also should remind us that we need to be vigilant in responding to unfounded comments about Mexican Americans and other people of color.

In conclusion, it is quite evident that the myth of Mexican Americans not valuing education has evolved into a stereotype of epic proportions. Apparently having its roots in the 1920s master's theses, it has flourished as it has been promulgated in the scholarly literature of the culture of poverty, culturally deprived, and at risk child, in texts on racial and ethnic history and cross-cultural cognitive and academic achievement assessments, and statements by individuals that are deemed newsworthy by the media. There is no doubt that many Mexican American school-age children and youths experience, on the average, school failure. Valencia (in press) discusses 15 different schooling conditions and outcomes that help to understand the nature of such school failure. To attribute the persistent and pervasive achievement gap between Mexican American students and their White peers to a value orientation of Mexican American indifference to the importance of education is baseless, irresponsible, and racist. Furthermore, and very importantly, this assertion of not valuing education is a *myth*. Next, we bring forth evidence to demonstrate how this myth can be exposed.

Debunking the Myth

The indiscriminate comments that we have reviewed by a number of individuals who contend that Mexican Americans have never had education as a goal, nor valued it, is far from the truth. For example, had Sowell (1981) carefully done his historical research he would have found that Mexican Americans have rallied around education for many decades (see, e.g., San Miguel & Valencia, 1998). In this section, we debunk the myth of Mexican American indifference to the importance of education by providing three evidentiary forms: (a) the historical and contemporary struggle for equal educational opportunity, (b) the scholarly literature documenting parental involvement, and (c) a case study of transgenerational parental involvement.

Historical and Contemporary Struggle for Equal Educational Opportunity

The history and contemporary endeavors of the Mexican American community's quest for equal educational opportunity has been so extensive and rich that the first author (R. R. Valencia) is able to teach an undergraduate course,

"Chicano Educational Struggles," at The University of Texas at Austin on this topic. The course is an analysis of how Mexican Americans have struggled for better education via five historical and contemporary processes. In brief, they are

1. Litigation. Since the 1930s, Mexican Americans have brought forth lawsuits of various types in their efforts to improve the educational lot of their children and youths. Such litigation has involved, for example, segregation (for a discussion of key cases see San Miguel & Valencia, 1998; Valencia, Menchaca, & Donato, in press), special education (Henderson & Valencia, 1985), school financing (Valencia, in press), school closures (Valencia, 1980, 1984a, 1984b), undocumented children (Cárdenas & Cortez, 1986), and high-stakes testing (Valencia & Bernal, 2000).[10] Notwithstanding the range of outcomes of this litigation as a whole (bittersweet ones, some losses, and some victories), taking their cases to court for over the last 70 years speaks to the reality that Mexican Americans highly value education.
2. Advocacy Organizations. In their pursuit of improved education for their community, Mexican American parents, scholars, lawyers, and youths have founded a number of advocacy organizations. Beginning with the establishment of the League of United Latin American Citizens in 1929 (LULAC; Márquez, 1993), many advocacy groups, in which better education is a rallying point for action, have been founded over the years. Examples of these highly visible organizations are the American GI Forum (Ramos, 1998), Mexican American Legal Defense and Educational Fund (MALDEF; O'Connor & Epstein, 1984), and Movimiento Estudiantil Chicano de Aztlán (MEChA; Muñoz, 1989). These advocacy organizations, and many others, have played critical roles in the identification of issues and in the advancement of improved educational conditions and outcomes for Mexican American students. For example, San Miguel and Valencia (1998) note, "Over the last three decades, MALDEF has evolved into a chief source of successful education litigation for the Mexican American community, winning many lawsuits and setting highly influential case law" (p. 388).
3. Individual Activists. Another indication that Mexican Americans value education stems from the work of scores of individuals who have championed the cause, that is, the Mexican American community's historical and contemporary resolve for the pursuit and attainment of educational equality. Historically, there have been, for example, the likes of grassroots organizer Eleuterio Escobar in San Antonio, Texas, in the 1930s, 1940s, and 1950s (García, 1979); Héctor García, founder of the American GI Forum in Texas in 1948 (Ramos, 1998); George I. Sánchez, scholar and civil rights activist from the 1930s to 1970s (Romo, 1986); Pete Tijerina, founder of MALDEF in San Antonio, Texas, in 1968 (O'Connor & Epstein, 1984); and Mari-Luci Jaramillo, pioneer of bilingual and bicultural education in New Mexico (Vásquez, 1994). To this illustrious list, we can add numerous other individual activists:

university professors, lawyers, students, parents, community organizers, schoolteachers, politicians, and so forth.

4. **Political Demonstrations.** For decades, Mexican Americans have expressed their collective interest and action in promoting better education for children and youths by engaging in public confrontations in a display of dissatisfaction with oppression, with the goal of gaining resources. One of the more common forms of political demonstrations has been the strategy of a "blowout" (school walkout). It appears that the first such blowout occurred in 1910 in San Angelo, Texas, lasting through 1915 (De León, 1974). At the heart of the blowout was the Tejano community's demand that its children be allowed to attend the superior White schools. Other well-known blowouts transpired in East Los Angeles in 1968 (Rosen, 1974), and in Crystal City, Texas, in 1969 (Navarro, 1995).

5. **Legislation.** A final form of struggle in which Mexican Americans have expressed their resolve in improving the educational lot for their children and youths is seen in legislative efforts. One example is the long struggle for bilingual education in Texas in which State Senator Joe Bernal and State Representative Carlos Truan persevered from 1969 to 1981 to institutionalize bilingual education (San Miguel, 1987; Vega, 1983). Another example is the "Top Ten Percent Plan," a law that went into effect in Texas in Fall 1998. The bill, written by State Representative Irma Rangel and State Senator Gonzalo Barrientos, allows high school students who graduate in the top 10% of their graduating classes to be automatically admitted to any public 4-year institution of higher education in Texas, including its premier institutions (see Chapa, 1997).

Parental Involvement Literature

Studies of Mexican American parental involvement in education over the past 10 years present a more nuanced and sympathetic view than in earlier decades. Recent ethnographic studies give powerful testimony to the cultural strengths and assets of Latino families (for a review of seven studies, see Villenas & Deyhle, 1999; also see Villenas & Foley, in press). For example, Romo and Falbo (1996) conducted a 4-year longitudinal study of 100 Latino students (overwhelmingly Mexican Americans) deemed at risk by their school districts. The commitment of the students' families to education surfaced time after time through *consejos* (advice-giving narratives). While many other factors also affect educational outcomes, it is wrong to say that Mexican American parents don't care. Similarly Suárez-Orozco and Suárez-Orozco (1995) found in their study of 189 Latino adolescents that immigrant parents had a fierce desire for their children to achieve academically.

Many studies have identified effective parental teaching strategies initiated by both Mexican American parents and schools (Hernández, 1995; Lesar, Espinosa, & Diaz, 1997; López, Scribner, & Mahitivanichcha, 2001; Moreno, 1997, 2000; Morrow & Young, 1997; Nistler & Maiers, 1999; Rodríguez-Brown,

Li, & Albom, 1999). Likewise, "funds of knowledge" about the work-a-day world within Mexican American families (topics of which may differ from other racial and ethnic groups) are also being recognized as important educational resources often overlooked in the past (González et al., 1995; Moll, Amanti, Neff, & González, 1992).

Furthermore, the myth of lack of concern about education is effectively disassembled by literature documenting the high expectations for children's education and positive beliefs held by Mexican American families. Numerous studies have identified high expectations for children's academic achievement and a multitude of supportive behaviors in Mexican American homes that counter the long-standing myth about Mexican American parents' disregard for education (see, e.g., Achor & Morales, 1990; Delgado-Gaitán, 1992; Delgado-Gaitán & Trueba, 1991; Gándara, 1982; Laosa, 1978; Moll et al., 1992; Moreno & López, 1999; Moreno & Valencia, in press).

In-depth interviews with Mexican American mothers by Lara-Alecio, Irby, and Ebener (1997) demonstrate three categories of Mexican American parental behaviors that support high achievement by low-income students. These include (a) high expectations, (b) belief in education, and (c) parents as links between home and school. Setting high expectations for the completion of school and expressing the desire for children to further their education, or become more educated than the parents, appear to be powerful and pervasive beliefs and attitudes among Mexican American families.

In an examination of data concerning 1,714 eighth-grade Mexican American students from the National Educational Longitudinal Study (NELS) of 1988, Keith and Lichtman (1994) confirmed the importance of parental involvement and found that parents who set high educational goals for their children appeared to improve their children's academic success. Moreno and López (1999) studied a sample of 158 Latina mothers and found that even though less acculturated women reported less knowledge about school activities and more barriers to involvement, they nonetheless reported high educational expectations for their children.

Morrow and Young (1997) found that children and parents enjoyed working with each other on literacy tasks, and that even though low-SES families often found it difficult to shoulder more responsibility, they were sincerely interested in their children's educational welfare. Quantitative research by Okagaki and Frensch (1998) shows that Latino parents hold approximately the same ideals of children's academic attainment as Whites. In addition, both groups had similar expectations concerning college enrollment for their children. In *Great Expectations* (Immerwahr & Foleno, 2000), one of the most comprehensive national surveys of the public's attitudes and opinions regarding higher education ever conducted, the authors' results laid to rest the myth that minority parents don't value higher education as highly as Whites:

> It is . . . sometimes suggested that members of these minority groups [Hispanic and African American] compared to other populations, do

not place as high a value on higher education. The findings from this study seem conclusively to eliminate this . . . reason. *Higher education is important for all Americans, but it is especially important to African American and Hispanic parents, who are significantly more likely to emphasize higher education than either White parents or the population as a whole.* [italics added]

(p. 4)

Several studies report that *all* the families in their interview samples held high aspirations for their children's academic success (Delgado-Gaitán, 1992; Moll et al., 1992). "The common thread with all parents was that they cared about their children's education," according to Delgado-Gaitán (p. 495). The study by Moll et al. included 25 Mexican American families in Arizona and approximately 100 observations in the homes. Moll and his colleagues said, "[They—the families] have a very strong philosophy of childrearing that is supportive of education . . . they have goals of a university education for their children . . . all the households we visited possess similar values" (p. 137).

Transgenerational Parental Involvement: A Case Study

Mexican American parents are interested and involved in their children's education as demonstrated through school activities as well as behaviors strictly within the home. The internal home behaviors by Mexican Americans concerning school have been little studied, but are of critical importance to understanding parental attitudes towards the value of education (see Henderson, 1966; Henderson & Merritt, 1968; Laosa, 1978, 1980). While some parents cannot become *externally* involved with education at the school itself, the families in the present case study were all deeply involved *internally*, that is, within the home.

Interviews with 10 adults (4 grandparents and 6 parents) from 6 Mexican American families in Austin, Texas, illustrate both internal and external involvement in education (Black, 1996). All adults were bilingual or English-speaking and had resided in Texas from 2 to 5 generations. The economic histories of all 6 families consistently told of great difficulties and sacrifices by grandparents and others, culminating in stable, if modest employment in the parents' generation.

Parental interactions with school, such as attendance at meetings and volunteering for school activities, are examples of *external*, or public, involvement in education. As López et al. (2001) have pointed out, these are the types of behaviors most often mentioned in the parental involvement literature (also see Epstein, 1990). Further, these authors distinguish between school involvement on the part of the parents and home involvement on the part of the school (such as training parents in child literacy strategies). The present case study illustrates a more subtle type of parental involvement that is often difficult to capture: the attitudes and practices concerning school that are initiated by the family and found exclusively in the home itself (Laosa & Henderson,

1991). Such actions as telling family stories about school experiences and making sure children arrive at school on time each day are examples of parents' involvement with school *internally*, that is, through private, family behaviors within the home (Delgado-Gaitán, 1994; Leichter, 1973).

1. External Involvement With School. Members of these families discussed their external involvement in education through service, teacher contacts, and school visits. Several members of these families played active roles in the Parent Teacher Association (PTA) of their child's school. For example, one grandmother was a life member of the PTA, and one parent—who had been forced to drop out of high school when she became pregnant as a teenager—later served as PTA president of her child's school. Some parents initiated contact with teachers in other ways. "I never hesitated to call the teacher when [my daughter] needed it," commented another mother; "I even called one of them [in the] last six weeks to check on things." When the daughter was in elementary school, this mother admitted she called the teacher every Friday to find out about homework due on Monday. One father visits the school periodically, surprising his son occasionally for lunch in the cafeteria or visiting his classroom.
2. Internal Involvement With School. Many of the grandparents and parents had work obligations and transportation issues that prevented them from participating outside the home in the school life of their children. Members of all 6 families reported behaviors within the home, however, that demonstrate the value they place on schooling. Besides seemingly straightforward concerns like homework and school attendance, family conversations within the home reveal attitudes toward education that go a long way to explode the myth of lack of concern (Delgado-Gaitán, 1994; Romo & Falbo, 1996).

"We help our kids with homework around the kitchen table every night," said one father. "One child is accelerated, but the other one needs more help," he continued. "I always sit down with them to do homework," claimed another mother. She remembered her older siblings always helped her with homework as well. "The older ones were smarter, and they helped the younger ones," she said. "I couldn't help them," one grandmother with only 2 years of schooling explained, "but my husband always did." Within these 6 families, at least, homework is seen as important and steps are taken to make sure it gets done.

Another grandmother spoke of getting her children to school. In the late 1950s and early 1960s, her husband used to walk their seven children the three blocks from their house to school every morning and walk them back every afternoon. "He was lucky," she said, "because his boss would let him do that."

Some of the stories by the grandmothers in these families of their own school experiences clearly illustrate the high value they placed on education.

One woman started school at age 10 in a segregated school for Mexican-origin children in Texas. Being older than most first graders, the teacher asked her to help the younger ones. So, in essence, she became the teacher's aide. She finished the sixth grade at age 16. In those days, no opportunity for further schooling was available to her in that town, so her formal education ended. She was, however, immediately hired as the school caretaker. She swept the school, built the fire in the stove on cold days, and cooked soup for the children during the Depression. In later life she worked in her own children's elementary school cafeteria for 20 years. She became a life member of the PTA and volunteered many hours at the school after she retired. She was "at school" almost every working day of her life since age 10 in one way or another.

"I cried and cried for days when I had to quit school," recalled another Mexican American grandmother who had to quit school during the Depression, "I didn't want to quit, but it was a matter of some of us not having enough to eat if I didn't." She took a job as a maid, washing clothes on a scrub board for $2.50 per week. "Reading was my favorite subject," she said, "I went to a spelling bee once on the radio . . . but I didn't win. I loved going to school." Here was clearly a child who valued school, but was forced by extreme circumstances to end her formal education in order to help support her family.

Besides family stories that are often retold within the family group, other family conversation also reflects high value for education. "We talk to our kids about their ambitions," a father said, "'Anyone can flip a burger. You're not gonna do that. You're gonna need more education,' we say. We want them to be successful. . . . If you really want to make a difference, you've got to stay in school and go as far as you can," he added. One mother described her communication with her daughter as "always frank and open. We always talk about the consequences of our actions. I tell her 'my job is to feed you and clothe you; your job is to go to school and learn,'" she continued.

One grandmother told of scolding her daughter, who did not want to go to school one day. "Do you want to be like me," she asked, "and know nothing? The only job I could get is in the laundry or the kitchen. No money. Do you want that?" (see Romo & Falbo, 1996, for examples of similar cautions to children). The parents and grandparents in this case study explicitly connect, through *consejos*, academic success with college and later adult economic security. "Children need to go to college today in order to get good jobs," commented one mother. "Kids need a whole lot of education," another parent said. "The teachers are preparing them for college, saying 'you can do it.' [When I was in school] I don't think I ever heard the word college. I would like to see my son go to college and be the best he can be," she continued. Another mother summed up the reality: "The job market requires college now," she said, "It's important to get further education to get a good job. That's the only way to break the cycle [of poverty] that our parents and grandparents went through."

Conclusion

In the final analysis, it is important for scholars to be steadfast in debunking the myth that Mexican Americans don't value education. Although such debunking may be deemed reactive, it is necessary. In the production of scholarship dealing with Mexican Americans, we often have to deconstruct inaccurate and unsound writings before we can construct new works. Without acknowledging this reality, it is difficult to continue the ongoing proactive scholarship on the Mexican American family and its rich, varied, and positive expressions regarding the importance of the institution of education.

Notes

1. This note is excerpted, with minor modifications, from Valencia and Solórzano (1997, p. 192). Mexican Americans have not been alone in being pegged as not valuing education. During the 1960s, when familial forms of deficit thinking were widespread in the literature, the target populations were the all too familiar "culturally disadvantaged," that is, ". . . Whites, Negroes, Puerto Ricans, Mexicans, and all others of the poverty group who basically share a common design for living" (Marans & Lourie, 1967, p. 20). The carriers of the deficit were frequently identified as inadequate mothers and fathers who ". . . seem to perpetuate their own conditions in their children through their childrearing patterns . . . [and who] . . . produce a disproportionate incidence of academic failures and of lower socioeconomic memberships among their full-grown offspring" (Marans & Lourie, 1967, p. 21). Implied in these assertions was that these parents did not value education (nor work, economic progress, and mobility).
2. Numerous studies have documented the positive association between parental involvement and children's academic performance (e.g., Chavin & Williams, 1988; Comer, 1986; Dornbusch & Ritter, 1988; Keith & Lichtman, 1994; Moreno & López, 1999). Regarding the long-standing importance of parental involvement in children's schooling performance, Rosado and Aaron (1991) comment,

    > Since the beginning of the American education system, parental involvement has played an important role in education (Cremin, 1977). This involvement has continued through the years, but in the last decade (1980s), it has gained momentum. Following the report of the National Commission on Excellence in Education in 1983, *A Nation at Risk*, parental involvement became a key issue in education.
    >
    > (p. 24)

3. Parts of this section are excerpted, with minor modifications, from Valencia and Solórzano (1997, pp. 196–197).
4. Actually, it was American Indians who had the lowest high school completion rate (11.4%), not Mexican Americans (see Grebler et al., 1970, p. 143, Table 7–1).
5. It appears that Carter's (1970) book, *Mexican Americans in Schools: A History of Educational Neglect*, was influential in shaping this structural inequality hypothesis offered by Grebler et al., who based their section "General School Practices Affecting Mexican Americans" (pp. 155–159) on Carter's book. This was not mentioned by Sowell (1981).
6. This section on Dunn is excerpted, with minor modifications, from Valencia & Solórzano (1997, pp. 190–191).
7. In his monograph, Dunn's (1987) comments on Latino parents' indifference to the importance of education were indeed controversial. The most disputatious section of

his monograph, however, was his position that there was a "probability that inherited genetic material is a contributing factor" (p. 63) to the low scores of Mexican American and Puerto Rican children on measures of intelligence. For discussion and critique of Dunn's genetic interpretation, see Valencia and Solórzano (1997) and Valencia and Suzuki (2001).
8. This quote by Graglia is taken from a newsclip (of the September 10, 1997 news conference at UT) shown on NBC *Today*, September 12, 1997 (Lauer, 1997).
9. It appears that Graglia's views on affirmative action have hurt him. According to Martin, reporter of the UT *Daily Texan*, "former President Ronald Reagan [in 1986] pulled away from appointing Graglia to the 5th U.S. Circuit Court of Appeals after complaints about his remarks regarding affirmative action" (1997, p. 2).
10. For citations of legal cases germane to most of these various categories of litigation noted here, see San Miguel and Valencia (1998).

References

Achor, S., & Morales, A. (1990). Chicanas holding doctoral degrees: Social reproduction and cultural ecological approaches. *Anthropology and Education Quarterly, 21,* 269–287.

Allen, V. L. (1970). The psychology of poverty: Problems and prospects. In V. L. Allen (Ed.), *Psychological factors in poverty* (pp. 367–383). Chicago: Markham Press.

Baratz, S. S., & Baratz, J. C. (1970). Early childhood intervention: The social science base of institutional racism. *Harvard Educational Review, 40,* 29–50.

Black, M. S. (1996). *Historical factors affecting Mexican American parental involvement and educational outcomes: The Texas environment from 1910–1996.* Unpublished doctoral dissertation, Harvard University, Cambridge, MA.

Cárdenas, J. A., & Cortez, A. (1986). The impact of *Plyer v. Doe* upon Texas public schools. *Journal of Law & Education, 15,* 1–17.

Carter, T. (1970). *Mexican Americans in schools: A history of educational neglect.* New York: College Entrance Examination Board.

Chapa, J. (1997, December). *The Hopwood decision in Texas as an attack on Latino access to selective higher education programs.* Paper presented at the Harvard University Civil Rights Project, Research Conference on the Latino Civil Rights Crisis, Los Angeles, CA, and Washington, DC.

Chavin, N. F., & Williams, D. L. (1988). Critical issues in teacher training for parental involvement. *Educational Horizons, 6,* 87–89.

Comer, J. P. (1986). Parent participation in the schools. *Phi Delta Kappan, 67,* 442–446.

De León, A. (1974). Blowout 1910 style: A Chicano school boycott in West Texas. *Texana, 12,* 125–140.

De León, A. (1983). *They called them greasers: Anglo attitudes towards Mexicans in Texas, 1821–1900.* Austin: University of Texas Press.

Delgado-Gaitán, C. (1992). School matters in the Mexican American home: Socializing children to education. *American Educational Research Journal, 29,* 495–513.

Delgado-Gaitán, C. (1994). Consejos: The power of cultural narrative. *Anthropology and Education Quarterly, 25,* 298–316.

Delgado-Gaitán, C., & Trueba, H. (1991). *Crossing cultural borders: Education for immigrant families in America.* London: Falmer.

Donmoyer, R., & Kos, R. (Eds.). (1993). *At-risk students: Portraits, policies, programs, and practices.* Albany: State University of New York Press.

Dornbusch, S. M., & Ritter, P. L. (1988). Parents of high school students: A neglected resource. *Educational Horizons, 6,* 75–77.

Dougherty, L. G. (1966). Working with disadvantaged parents. In J. F. Frost & G. R. Hawkes (Eds.), *The disadvantaged child: Issues and innovations* (pp. 389–394). New York: Houghton Mifflin.

Dunn, L. M. (1987). *Bilingual Hispanic children on the U.S. mainland: A review of research on their cognitive, linguistic, and scholastic development.* Circle Pines, MN: American Guidance Service.

Epstein, J. L. (1990). School and family connections: Theory, research and implications for integrating sociologies of education and family. *Marriage and Family Review, 15,* 99–127.

Feagin, J. R., & Booher Feagin, C. (1999). *Racial and ethnic relations* (6th ed.). Upper Saddle River, NJ: Merrill/Prentice Hall.

Fine, M. (1995). The politics of who is "at risk." In B. B. Swadener & S. Lubeck (Eds.), *Children and families "at promise": Deconstructing the discourse of risk* (pp. 76–94). Albany, NY: State University of New York Press.

Foley, D. E. (1997). Deficit thinking models based on culture: The anthropological protest. In R. R. Valencia (Ed.), *The evolution of deficit thinking: Educational thought and practice* (pp. 113–131). The Stanford Series on Education and Public Policy. London: Falmer.

Frost, J. F., & Hawkes, G. R. (1966). (Eds.). *The disadvantaged child: Issues and innovations.* New York: Houghton Mifflin.

Gándara, P. (1982). Passing through the eye of the needle: High-achieving Chicanas. *Hispanic Journal of Behavioral Sciences, 4,* 167–179.

García, M. T. (1979). *Mexican Americans: Leadership, ideology, and identity, 1930–1960.* New Haven, CT: Yale University Press.

González, N., Moll, L. C., Tenery, M. F., Rivera, A., Rendon, R., González, R., & Amanti, C. (1995). Funds of knowledge for teaching in Latino households. *Urban Education, 29,* 443–470.

Gould, B. (1932). *Methods of teaching Mexicans.* Unpublished master's thesis, University of Southern California, Los Angeles.

Grebler, L., Moore, J. W., & Guzmán, R. C. (1970). *The Mexican-American people: The nation's second largest minority.* New York: Free Press.

Havighurst, R. J. (1966). Who are the socially disadvantaged? In J. F. Frost & G. R. Hawkes (Eds.), *The disadvantaged child: Issues and innovations* (pp. 15–23). New York, NY: Houghton Mifflin.

Hellmuth, J. (Ed.). (1967). *Disadvantaged child* (Vol. 1). New York, NY: Brunner/Mazel.

Henderson, R. W. (1966). *Environmental stimulation and intellectual development of Mexican American children.* Unpublished doctoral dissertation, University of Arizona, Tucson.

Henderson, R. W., & Merritt, C. B. (1968). Environmental background of Mexican American children with different potentials for school success. *Journal of School Psychology, 75,* 101–106.

Henderson, R. W., & Valencia, R. R. (1985). Nondiscriminatory school psychological services: Beyond nonbiased assessment. In J. R. Bergan (Ed.), *School psychology in contemporary society* (pp. 340–377). Columbus, OH: Charles E. Merrill.

Hernández, A. E. (1995). Enhancing the academic success of Hispanic females. *Contemporary Education, 67,* 18–20.

Hernández, D. (1970). *Mexican American challenge to a sacred cow* (Monograph No. 1). Los Angeles: Mexican American Cultural Center, University of California.

Immerwahr, J., & Foleno, T. (2000). *Great expectations: How the public and parents—White, African American, and Hispanic—view higher education.* New York: Public Agenda.

Keith, P. B., & Lichtman, M. V. (1994). Does parental involvement influence the academic achievement of Mexican-American eighth graders? Results from the National Education Longitudinal Study. *School Psychology Quarterly, 9,* 256–272.

Labov, W. (1970). The logic of nonstandard English. In F. Williams (Ed.), *Language and poverty* (pp. 153–187). Chicago: Markham Press.

Laosa, L. M. (1978). Maternal teaching strategies in Chicano families of varied educational and socio-economic levels. *Child Development, 49,* 1129–1135.

Laosa, L. M. (1980). Maternal teaching strategies in Chicano and Anglo-American families: The influence of culture and education on maternal behavior. *Child Development, 51,* 759–765.

Laosa, L. M., & Henderson, R. W. (1991). Cognitive socialization and competence: The academic development of Chicanos. In R. R. Valencia (Ed.), *Chicano school failure and success: Research and policy agendas for the 1990s* (pp. 164–199). The Stanford Series on Education and Public Policy. London: Falmer.

Lara-Alecio, R., Irby, B., & Ebener, R. (1997). Developing academically supportive behaviors among Hispanic parents: What elementary teachers and administrators can do. *Preventing School Failure, 42,* 27–32.

Lauer, M. (1997, September 12). *Today.* New York, NY: National Broadcasting Corporation.

Leichter, H. J. (1973). The concept of educative style. *Teachers College Record, 75,* 239–250.

Lesar, S., Espinosa, L., & Diaz, R. (1997). Maternal teaching behaviors of preschool children in Hispanic families: Does a home intervention program make a difference? *Journal of Research in Childhood Education, 11,* 163–170.

López, G. R., Scribner, J. D., & Mahitivanichcha, K. (2001). Redefining parental involvement: Lessons from high-performing migrant-impacted schools. *American Educational Research Journal, 38,* 253–288.

Lubeck, S. (1995). Mothers at risk. In B. B. Swadener & S. Lubeck (Eds.), *Children and families "at promise": Deconstructing the discourse of risk* (pp. 50–75). Albany, NY: State University of New York Press.

Lubeck, S., & Garrett, P. (1990). The social construction of the "at-risk" child. *British Journal of Sociology of Education, 11,* 327–340.

Lyon, L. L. (1933). *Investigation of the program for the adjustment of Mexican girls to the high schools of the San Fernando Valley.* Unpublished master's thesis, University of Southern California, Los Angeles.

Manning, M. L., & Baruth, L. G. (1995). *Students at risk.* Boston, MA: Allyn & Bacon.

Marans, A. E., & Lourie, R. (1967). Hypotheses regarding the effects of child-rearing patterns on the disadvantaged child. In J. Hellmuth (Ed.), *Disadvantaged child* (Vol. 1, pp. 17–41). New York, NY: Brunner/Mazel.

Marburger, C. L. (1990). The school site level: Involving parents in reform. In S. B. Bacharach (Ed.), *Education reform: Making sense of it all* (pp. 82–91). Boston, MA: Allyn & Bacon.

Márquez, B. (1993). *LULAC: The evolution of a Mexican American political organization.* Austin, TX: University of Texas Press.

Martin, D. H. (1997, September 12). Remarks raise lawmakers' ire. *Daily Texan,* pp. 1–2.

Menchaca, M. (1997). Early racist discourses: Roots of deficit thinking. In R. R. Valencia (Ed.), *The evolution of deficit thinking: Educational thought and practice* (pp. 13–40). The Stanford Series on Education and Public Policy. London: Falmer.

Menchaca, M. (2000). History and anthropology: Conducting Chicano research. In R. Rochín & D. Valdés (Eds.), *Toward a new Chicano history* (pp. 167–181). East Lansing, MI: Michigan State University Press.

Moll, L. C., Amanti, C., Neff, D., & González, N. (1992). Funds of knowledge for teaching: Using a qualitative approach to connect homes and classrooms. *Theory into Practice, 31*, 132–141.

Moreno, R. P. (1997). Everyday instruction: A comparison of Mexican American and Anglo mothers and their preschool children. *Hispanic Journal of Behavioral Sciences, 19*, 527–539.

Moreno, R. P. (2000). Teaching practices of Mexican American mothers with everyday and school-related tasks. *Merrill-Palmer Quarterly, 46*, 613–631.

Moreno, R. P., & López, J. A. (1999). Latino parent involvement: The role of maternal acculturation and education. *School Community Quarterly, 9*, 83–101.

Moreno, R. P., & Valencia, R. R. (in press). Chicano families and schools: Myths, knowledge, and future directions for understanding. In R. R. Valencia (Ed.), *Chicano school failure and success: Past, present, and future* (2nd ed.). London: RoutledgeFalmer.

Morrow, L. M., & Young, J. (1997). A family literacy program connecting school and home: Effects on attitude, motivation, and literacy achievement. *Journal of Educational Psychology, 89*, 736–742.

Muñoz, C. (1989). *Youth, identity, power: The Chicano movement.* New York: Verso.

National Commission on Excellence in Education. (1983). *A nation at risk: The imperative for educational reform.* Washington, DC: U.S. Government Printing Office.

Navarro, A. (1995). *Mexican American Youth Organization: Avant-garde of the Chicano movement in Texas.* Austin: University of Texas Press.

Nistler, R. J., & Maiers, A. (1999). Exploring home-school connections: A family literacy perspective on improving urban schools. *Education and Urban Society, 32*, 3–17.

O'Connor, K., & Epstein, L. (1984). A legal voice for the Chicano community: The activities of the Mexican American Legal Defense and Educational Fund, 1968–1982. *Social Science Quarterly, 65*, 245–256.

Okagaki, L., & Frensch, P. A. (1998). Parenting and children's school achievement: A multiethnic perspective. *American Educational Research Journal, 35*, 123–144.

Pearl, A. (1997). Cultural and accumulated environmental deficit models. In R. R. Valencia (Ed.), *The evolution of deficit thinking: Educational thought and practice* (pp. 132–159). The Stanford Series on Education and Public Policy. London: Falmer.

Pratt, P. S. (1938). *A comparison of the school achievement and socio-economic background of Mexican and White children in a Delta Colorado elementary school.* Unpublished master's thesis, University of Southern California, Los Angeles.

Ramos, H. A. J. (1998). *The American GI Forum: In pursuit of the dream, 1948–1983.* Houston: Arte Público Press.

Richardson, V., Casanova, U., Placier, P., & Guilfoyle, K. (1989). *School children at risk: Schools as communities of support.* London: Falmer.

Rodríguez-Brown, F. V., Li, R. F., & Albom, J. B. (1999). Hispanic parents awareness and use of literacy-rich environments at home and in the community. *Education and Urban Society, 32*, 41–58.

Romano-V, O. I. (1968). The anthropology and sociology of the Mexican Americans: The distortion of Mexican-American history. *El Grito, 2*, 13–26.

Romo, H., & Falbo, T. (1996). *Latino high school graduation.* Austin: University of Texas Press. Romo, R. (1986). George I. Sánchez and the civil rights movement: 1940 to 1960. *La Raza Law Journal, 1*, 342–362.

Ronda, M. A., & Valencia, R. R. (1994). "At-risk" Chicano students: The institutional and communicative life of a category. *Hispanic Journal of Behavioral Sciences, 16*, 363–395.

Rosado, L. A., & Aaron, E. B. (1991). Parental involvement: Addressing the educational needs of Hispanic inner-city parents. *Journal of Educational Issues of Language Minority Students, 8,* 23–29.

Rosen, G. (1974). The development of the Chicano movement in Los Angeles from 1967 to 1969. *Aztlán, 4,* 155–183.

Roser, M. A. (1997, September 11). UT group praises Hopwood ruling. *Austin American-Statesman,* p. B1.

Roser, M. A., & Tanamachi, C. (1997, September 17). Jackson urges UT to fight racism. *Austin American-Statesman,* pp. A1, A10.

San Miguel, G., Jr. (1987). *"Let all of them take heed": Mexican Americans and the campaign for educational equality in Texas, 1910–1981.* Austin, TX: University of Texas Press.

San Miguel, G., Jr., & Valencia, R. R. (1998). From the Treaty of Guadalupe Hidalgo to *Hopwood*: The educational plight and struggle of Mexican Americans in the Southwest. *Harvard Educational Review, 68,* 353–412.

Sleeter, C. E. (1995). Foreword. In B. B. Swadener & S. Lubeck (Eds.), *Children and families "at promise": Deconstructing the discourse of risk* (pp. ix–xi). Albany, NY: State University of New York Press.

Snider, W. (1990, April 18). Outcry follows Cavazos comments on the values of Hispanic parents. *Education Week,* pp. 1–2.

Sowell, T. (1981). *Ethnic America: A history.* New York, NY: Basic Books.

Suárez-Orozco, C., & Suárez-Orozco, M. (1995). *Transformations: Migration, family life, and achievement motivation among Latino adolescents.* Stanford, CA: Stanford University Press.

Swadener, B. B., & Lubeck, S. (1995a). The social construction of children and families "at risk": An introduction. In B. B. Swadener & S. Lubeck (Eds.), *Children and families "at promise": Deconstructing the discourse of risk* (pp. 1–14). Albany, NY: State University of New York Press.

Swadener, B. B., & Lubeck, S. (Eds.). (1995b). *Children and families "at promise": Deconstructing the discourse of risk.* Albany: State University of New York Press.

Taylor, M. C. (1927). *Retardation of Mexican children in the Albuquerque schools.* Unpublished master's thesis, Leland Stanford Junior University, Stanford, CA.

Valencia, R. R. (in press). The plight of Chicano students: An overview of schooling conditions and outcomes. In R. R. Valencia (Ed.), *Chicano school failure and success: Past, present, and future* (2nd ed.). London: RoutledgeFalmer.

Valencia, R. R. (1980). The school closure issue and the Chicano community. *Urban Review, 12,* 5–21.

Valencia, R. R. (1984a). *School closures and policy issues* (Policy Paper No. 84-C3). Stanford University, CA: Institute for Research on Educational Finance and Governance.

Valencia, R. R. (1984b). The school closure issue and the Chicano community: A follow-up study of the *Angeles* case. *Urban Review, 16,* 145–163.

Valencia, R. R. (Ed.). (1997a). *The evolution of deficit thinking: Educational thought and practice.* The Stanford Series on Education and Public Policy. London: Falmer.

Valencia, R. R. (1997b). Genetic pathology model of deficit thinking. In R. R. Valencia (Ed.), *The evolution of deficit thinking: Educational thought and practice* (pp. 41–112). The Stanford Series on Education and Public Policy. London: Falmer.

Valencia, R. R. (2000). Inequalities and the schooling of minority students in Texas: Historical and contemporary conditions. *Hispanic Journal of Behavioral Sciences, 22,* 445–459.

Valencia, R. R., & Bernal, E. M. (Eds.). (2000). The Texas Assessment of Academic Skills (TAAS) case: Perspectives from plaintiffs' experts [Special issue]. *Hispanic Journal of Behavioral Sciences, 22*(4).

Valencia, R. R., Menchaca, M., & Donato, R. (in press). Segregation, desegregation, and integration: Old and new realities. In R. R. Valencia (Ed.), *Chicano school failure and success: Past, present, and future* (2nd ed.). London: RoutledgeFalmer.

Valencia, R. R., & Solórzano, D. G. (1997). Contemporary deficit thinking: In R. R. Valencia (Ed.), *The evolution of deficit thinking: Educational thought and practice* (pp. 160–210). The Stanford Series on Education and Public Policy. London: Falmer.

Valencia, R. R., & Suzuki, L. A. (2001). *Intelligence testing and minority students: Foundations, performance factors, and assessment issues.* Thousand Oaks, CA: Sage.

Vásquez, O. (1994). Mari-Luci Jaramillo. In M. S. Seller (Ed.), *Women educators in the United States, 1820–1993: A biographical sourcebook* (pp. 258–264). Westport, CT: Greenwood Press.

Vaughn, S., Bos, C. S., & Schumm, J. S. (1997). *Teaching mainstreamed, diverse, and at-risk students in the general education classroom.* Boston, MA: Allyn & Bacon.

Vega, J. E. (1983). *Education, politics, and bilingualism in Texas.* Washington, DC: University Press of America.

Villenas, S., & Deyhle, D. (1999). Critical race theory and ethnographies challenging the stereotypes: Latino families, schooling, resilience and resistance. *Curriculum Inquiry, 29,* 413–445.

Villenas, S., & Foley, D. E. (in press). Chicano/Latino critical ethnography of education: Cultural production from *La Frontera*. In R. R. Valencia (Ed.), *Chicano school failure and success: Past, present, and future* (2nd ed.). London: RoutledgeFalmer.

2 Funds of Knowledge
An Approach to Studying Latina(o) Students' Transition to College

Cecilia Rios-Aguilar and Judy Marquez Kiyama

The United States is more racially and ethnically diverse today than at any other time in its history, and the near future promises a continuation of this trend (Swail, Cabrera, & Lee, 2004). The fastest growing youth populations, including Latina(o)s, are those who have been the least well served by the educational system from K–12 to postsecondary school (García & Figueroa, 2002). They are the underrepresented minority and lower income youth who are less likely than their White, higher income peers to graduate from high school (Pew Hispanic Center, 2004), to go to college (Perna, 2000), and to complete college (Swail et al., 2004). Thus, the significance of higher education to the Latina(o) population cannot be overstated. Indeed, for poor and working class Latina(o)s, who constitute the majority of the Latina(o) population in the United States, a college degree is an important route to a professional career, a well-paying job, and a better life (Quintana, Vogel, & Ybarra, 1991).

Despite efforts to increase college access, college enrollment and completion rates remain stratified by socioeconomic status (Titus, 2006) and by race and ethnicity (Baum & Ma, 2007). For example, Latina(o)s represented almost 14% of high school graduates in the 2004–2005 academic year but received only 11% of associate's degrees, 7% of bachelor's degrees, 5% of master's degrees, 5% of first-professional degrees, and just 3% of doctoral degrees awarded in the 2005–2006 academic year (National Center for Education Statistics, 2007). Moreover, Marin et al. (2008) found that although more minorities are attending college, many do not graduate. Indeed, they found that the percentage of Hispanic high school graduates entering college increased from 47% in 1972 to 70% in 1992; at the same time, the percentage of Hispanics completing college declined from 40% in 1975 to 34% in 2004.

A distinguishing characteristic of most of the existing literature on minority students' transition to college is the preponderance of models—economic and sociological—that assume that the transition to college is a linear process (Perna, 2006). In other occasions, these models suggest that something is *wrong* with students (and their families) simply because they are perceived to not have the characteristics, the capital, and the resources needed to participate and to succeed in college. As argued by Bensimon (2007), the scholarship in higher education has "imagined" (Moll, 2000) what students need to have and to do to be successful based on what these dominant models have found to be important factors associated with access to college. Consequently, the existing "politics of representation" (Holquist, 1983) have *not* resulted in increased college attendance and completion rates among minority students, including Latina(o)s.

In this article we discuss how the theoretical framework of funds of knowledge—the existing resources, knowledge, and skills embedded in students and their families (Moll, Amanti, Neff, & González, 1992)—can guide researchers in higher education as they conduct research on Latina(o) students' transition to college. We concentrate our attention on examining specific components of the transition to college among Latina(o) students: (a) college preparation, (b) college access, and (c) the development of career aspirations. We are aware that there are other components of the transition to college—college persistence and success—that are not covered in this paper.

We first review the existing literature on college opportunity and the transition to college. Next we discuss and critique some of the most dominant conceptual frameworks used to study students' transition to college. Next we briefly examine the origins of the concept of funds of knowledge. Then we discuss how funds of knowledge can be used by researchers in higher education to study Latina(o) students' transition to college. In doing so we rely heavily on existing research on funds of knowledge as well as on our own work with different samples of Latina(o) students and families. Immediately following this we discuss the limitations of using a funds of knowledge approach in higher education. We conclude by offering a research agenda that promises to close existing knowledge gaps.

Latina(o) College Access and Opportunity

Studies spanning nearly 15 years have indicated that although Latina(o) students and families are likely to emphasize the importance of a college education, students often do not complete a 2- or 4-year degree (Immerwahr, 2003). This disconnect has resulted in a number of outcomes, including a nontransition from middle to high school at rates of 48%–55%, with half of the students who do continue to high school leaving prior to graduation (Oliva & Nora, 2004). It is estimated that of the Latina(o) students who graduate from high school, only 35% will continue on to college (Oliva & Nora, 2004). Two-year colleges are often the starting point for Latina(o) students, who enroll at disproportionate numbers compared with other groups (58% vs. 40% of all 18- to 24-year-olds in the year 2000; Gándara, 2005). Unfortunately, the fact remains that transfer rates from community colleges to 4-year institutions are low (between 20% and 25%), and dropout rates from the freshmen to sophomore year remain high (between 55% and 65%; Oliva & Nora, 2004).

Sadly, in many studies, one sees responsibility and blame placed on the Latina(o) student (and his or her family) with no acknowledgment of the institutional barriers associated with college opportunity for this population. In reality, institutional forces and systemic barriers also create many of the roadblocks to college attainment for minority students (Deil-Amen & López Turley, 2007). Such is the case with policies directly impacting the enrollment of Latina(o) students based on race/ethnicity (such as Proposition 209 in California) or based on state residency status (such as Proposition 300 in Arizona). Flores, Horn, and Crisp (2006) explained that both old and new policies restrict college-going opportunities for undocumented Latina(o) immigrants. K–12 schools present another set of barriers for Latina(o) students, as variations exist in the investment in and expectations of Latina(o) students by school personnel. Often these expectations are low and impact students' ability to navigate courses, college requirements, and school structures, ultimately channeling students into a less rigorous and non-college track curriculum (K. González, Stone, & Jovel, 2003; Martinez, 2003).

It is clear that Latina(o) students are not attending or graduating from college at the same rate as their peers. It is also evident that a number of factors affect students' transition to college. We focus the next section of this paper on discussing existing conceptual frameworks that have been used to study the transition to college among underrepresented students, including Latina(o)s.

Latina(o) Students' Transition to College: An Economic and Sociological Perspective

Most of the literature that examines students' transition to college focuses its attention on individual-level explanations for why certain students do not do as well as others. Such work focuses on factors, including students' socioeconomic status, academic preparation, motivation, or college-choice processes, that sometimes presume student or family deficiencies with respect to their ability to do what is necessary to achieve desired academic outcomes (Oliva, 2008). In what follows we present two approaches that have been extensively used to examine students' transition to college.

The Economic Approach

In an attempt to explain students' transition to college, considerable economic research has emerged (Perna, 2006). A number of researchers (e.g., Paulsen, 1990) have used economic models of human capital investment to examine students' college choices. In particular, human capital models examine how students make choices of whether or not to attend college based on certain information, including college prices and financial aid. Moreover, these models suggest that information is crucial because it is associated with numerous outcomes, such as college expectations, application, enrollment, and choice (Perna, 2000, 2006). Research along this line of inquiry has also shown that parents and students, particularly African Americans and Latina(o)s, are uninformed or poorly informed, even when they expect or plan to attend college (Perna & Titus, 2005). Although these models have provided insight into how students make decisions about going to college, they lack a clear understanding of how information and other nonmonetary factors, such as exchanges of ideas and access to certain social networks, influence students' decision to go to college.

Sociological Approaches

In addition to human capital models, the transition to college literature in sociology reflects the dominance of the status attainment model (Deil-Amen & López Turley, 2007). The status attainment model focuses on analyzing the effect of socioeconomic status on students' educational attainment. Findings from this line of inquiry suggest that socioeconomic status is the most important factor associated with students' outcomes, including academic achievement and postsecondary outcomes (Sewell, 1971). More recent sociological research has focused on the ways in which the sociological constructs of cultural and social capital influence students' transition to college (Cabrera et al., 2006; McDonough, 1997; Nora, 2004; Pérez & McDonough, 2008; Perna & Titus, 2005).

Cultural capital refers to the system of qualities, such as language skills and cultural knowledge, that is derived, in part, from one's family and that defines a person's class position (Bourdieu, 1986). According to this framework, students of lower socioeconomic status are disadvantaged in the competition for academic rewards because their sociocultural environment may not provide the types of cultural capital required for success in school, such as academic attention, certain linguistic patterns, behavioral traits, orientation toward schooling, high expectations, or encouragement of college aspirations (Cabrera et al., 2006; McDonough, 1997; Perna, 2006).

Social capital is composed of contacts and memberships in networks that can be used for personal gain (Bourdieu, 1986). Researchers (e.g., Cabrera et al., 2006; K. González et al., 2003; Perna, 2006; Perna & Titus, 2005) have found that students who lack access to specific forms of social capital may have decreased chances of attending college. In sum, empirical studies that use these sociological approaches provide evidence that family background and social and cultural capital have a significant impact on educational aspirations, persistence, and attainment from the earliest schooling experiences through high school to college (Walpole, 2003).

Critiques of the Economic and Sociological Approaches

A considerable amount of research on students' transition to college has emerged; nevertheless, we argue that existing capital frameworks are insufficient to understand the complexities embedded in this process, particularly for Latina(o) students. In what follows we offer a critique of both approaches.

Rational choice theory (Becker, 1976), on which human capital theory is based, argues that human behavior is governed by the principle of maximization of goals (e.g., college attendance) under given constraints (e.g., constraints related to time and financial resources). In other words, the theory suggests that youth act as "adolescent econometricians" (Beattie, 2002, p. 19) as they evaluate the benefits of further education in terms of the income increase that would result from their gains in human capital—knowledge and skills. The rational choice model is based on a set of assumptions that need to be questioned, particularly when referring to minority students, including Latina(o)s. First, the rational choice theorist often presumes that the individual decision-making unit in question, usually the student, is "typical" or "representative" of some larger group (e.g., Latina[o]s). There is great heterogeneity among Latina(o) students, so having one econometric model for all Latina(o)s is probably not helpful in understanding how they make decisions related to college enrollment. Researchers need be cautious in taking findings from one subgroup of Latina(o) students and translating them to another subgroup. Second, it is assumed that the individual student is the *only* one who decides how much to invest in his or her education. The existing literature on higher education has strongly advocated for such an individualistic approach despite a variety of studies (e.g., Knight, Norton, Bentley, & Dixon, 2004; Pérez & McDonough, 2008) that show how important other contexts, including the influence of many family members and peers, are in minority students' decisions to attend and to succeed in college.

Third, rational choice models assume that individuals choose their preferred option among a set of alternatives. But most Latina(o) students living in economically poor conditions rarely face the opportunity to choose among several options. Indeed, these students tend to attend schools characterized by high levels of poverty and low quality. Deil-Amen and López Turley (2007) clearly pointed out that schools, as educational institutions, interact with other contexts (e.g., family and neighborhoods) to potentially reinforce existing inequalities. What this means for students attending schools with the characteristics mentioned previously is that they do *not* have as many options as their peers to attend a wide variety of colleges and universities. Furthermore, there is empirical evidence to suggest that it is theoretically problematic to assume that all youth form expectations about future outcomes in the same way (Beattie, 2002). It is very likely that the rational choice model does not reflect the number of concrete opportunities that minority students have to attend college (and, presumably, to improve their quality of life).

In contrast, sociological approaches shed light on the ways in which students' (and families') social and cultural capital affect students' chances of attending college. For example, studies (e.g., Perna & Titus, 2005) have found that social capital (primarily understood as parent involvement) influences college attendance. Nevertheless, these findings need to be carefully reviewed because social capital is generally operationalized using just one indicator rather than a multidimensional construct (Perna & Titus, 2005). Exceptions do exist, and one such example is the work of Stanton-Salazar (2001), who used the concepts of social capital, social networks, and a help-seeking orientation to understand the educational experiences of low-income Mexican students. Findings showed how elements of a student's experience (community, school, families) are organized to reproduce social inequality, how networks can lead to resource sharing and exclusion, and how human bridges and advocacy are important in creating access to new educational opportunities and resources.

Similarly, researchers (e.g., Nora, 2004; Perna, 2000) have found that cultural capital—a composite of cultural activities, attitudes, and knowledge—influences students' decisions to attend college. The use of such proxies can result in promoting a specific representation of students (and their families) as "deficient, disinterested, with confused priorities, and responsible for their youth's failure to enter college" (Knight et al., 2004, p. 100). This deficit perspective states that lower class culture has distinct values and forms of social organization. Although their interpretations vary, most of the research studies that use such proxies suggest that lower class and working-class families do not value education as highly as middle-class families do (Valencia & Black, 2002).

Another critical assumption of existing sociological approaches is that educationally successful groups possess social and cultural capital by virtue of their success; those groups that are not as successful, meaning those not going to college, are assumed to lack these forms of capital to be able to do better if only they possessed and/or acquired more of it. This retrospective analysis of social and cultural capital often remains bound in the context of structural resources and interests rather than accounting for the ways in which students (and their families) navigate their interests in between and in spite of structural constraints (Cammarota, Moll, Cannella, & González, 2010).

Furthermore, it is unfortunate that educational research on social and cultural capital continues to pay considerable attention to adopting and operationalizing these terms rather than modifying the theory and applying it to various U.S. contexts—not only the upper class but a broad range of social classes and racial/ethnic groups. Finally, with some exceptions (e.g., K. González et al., 2003; Stanton-Salazar, 2001), studies that use sociological approaches to examine Latina(o) students' transition to college use *individuals* or *parents* as their primary unit of analysis. These approaches severely limit who should be involved in youths' college-going process, inaccurately perpetuating the worldviews that all students are solely raised and supported by their parents (Knight et al., 2004).

We argue here that in order for experts to fully understand Latina(o) students' transition to college, dominant models must be challenged, and students and their families need to be studied from integrated perspectives. It is important to state that we are not arguing that economic and sociological perspectives should not be utilized to examine Latina(o) students' transition to college. Instead, we argue for the need to use multiple perspectives to advance an understanding of a very complex process. In particular, we claim that incorporating a funds of knowledge approach to study the transition to college among Latina(o)s will improve our understanding of power and equity in educational opportunity.

Funds of Knowledge

Funds of Knowledge: Origins and the Study of Household Practices

The concept of funds of knowledge was first introduced by anthropologists Carlos Vélez-Ibañez and James Greenberg (1992) as part of their household analysis of working-class Mexican families in the southwestern United States. In particular, they studied how working-class and economically marginalized families used their social networks, and the social and economic exchange relations that such networks facilitate, to mediate the uncertainty of their socioeconomic disadvantage. Funds of knowledge, then, were described in this work as an array of knowledge and skills that are of strategic importance to working-class households living in the U.S.–Mexico border region (Vélez-Ibañez & Greenberg, 1992). For example, many Mexican households have accumulated a wide breadth of knowledge in areas such as mining and metallurgy, ranching and animal husbandry, and trans-border transactions related to their sector of the economy in their particular region of the country (Moll et al., 1992). Other types of such funds include information concerning access to institutional assistance, legal help, occupational opportunities, and the most inexpensive places to procure needed goods and services. The theoretical framework of funds of knowledge has primarily been used by researchers, mostly in the K–12 sector, to document the wealth of knowledge existing in low-income households, to help teachers link the school curriculum to students' lives (Rios-Aguilar, Kiyama, Gravitt, & Moll, in press), and to challenge the deficit model that has characterized much educational theorizing about low-income children and families (Olmedo, 1997).

Funds of Knowledge in the Scholarship of Higher Education

In her presidential address to the Association for the Study of Higher Education, Bensimon (2007) noted "a lack of scholarly and practical attention toward understanding how the practitioner—her knowledge, beliefs, experiences, education, sense of self-efficacy, etc.—affects how students experience their education" (p. 444). Bensimon highlighted the role that funds of knowledge play in helping faculty to see students and families in terms of possibilities. Thus, countering the negative representations of minority students, usually known for such characteristics as speaking language(s) other than English, living in households with either one or many adults, and working too many hours—highly correlated with "risk" in educational research is critical to help students (and their families and communities) to succeed in school and in life. Most important, Bensimon encouraged researchers in higher education to use a conceptual framework that could assist in understanding how funds of knowledge shape faculty practices. Bensimon's article is the first attempt to use a funds of knowledge perspective in the scholarship of higher education. However, we argue here that this is not the only way that researchers can use funds of knowledge to study issues in higher education. The following sections discuss an alternative approach.

Funds of Knowledge: A Proposed Approach to Studying Latina(o) Students' Transition to College

We have stated here that there is a need for research that examines how households' funds of knowledge affect students' transition to college, particularly among Latina(o)s. By no means are we suggesting that using a funds of knowledge approach is the panacea for all of the problems related to the transition to college. Indeed, there is a need to critically examine what funds of knowledge can (and cannot) do to improve researchers' understanding of students' transition to college.

The Influence of Funds of Knowledge on College Preparation Among Latina(o) Students

The literature on college preparation typically focuses on academic achievement, which is usually measured by grades and coursework (Deil-Amen & López Turley, 2007). Findings suggest that a number of individual attributes (e.g., socioeconomic status, gender, and race/ethnicity) are associated with Latina(o) students' academic achievement (Portes, 2000). Without any doubt, these studies have contributed to explaining some variation in Latina(o) students' academic achievement. However, several other resources that affect college preparation have not been taken into consideration, and thus a large proportion of the variation in the academic achievement of students remains unexplained. For this reason, in what follows we provide a discussion of how funds of knowledge can inform research on college preparation. Specifically, we focus our attention on two issues: (a) the choice of the unit of analysis and (b) the analysis of variation in funds of knowledge. To illustrate these points, we rely on empirical data (previously collected) that examine the relationship between households' funds of knowledge and Latina(o) students' academic and nonacademic outcomes (see Rios-Aguilar, 2010, for methodological details for the data presented here).

Unit of Analysis: The Role of Households in the College Preparation of Latina(o) Students

Most research in higher education (e.g., Tierney & Auerbach, 2004) has focused on the influence of attributes such as parental involvement on students' college preparation. Yet varying notions of involvement have different impacts on the academic outcomes of students from different ethnicities (López, Barrueco, Feinauer, & Miles, 2007). In addition, most studies on college preparation focus on parent characteristics (e.g., level of education) and activities (e.g., attending school activities and visiting college campuses) that may not reflect the many influences embedded in the contexts of Latina(o) students' lives. Thus, we propose to use a household approach such as the one used in existing research on funds of knowledge.

To support the claim that a household approach is needed, we rely on empirical research on funds of knowledge that was previously conducted. Table 2.1 is an illustration of the diverse household configurations in which Latina(o) students are embedded. One type of household is a more traditional configuration with two adults living in the household, and the other is a less traditional configuration with more than two adults living in the household (including older children and relatives).

Given these household configurations, we claim that researchers in higher education need to think more carefully about how to incorporate households

Table 2.1 Selected Demographic Characteristics of Puerto Rican Households

Characteristic	Profile 1[a]	Profile 2[b]
Relationship with respondent		
Spouse	67%	11%
Children	14%	58%
Relative	6%	23%
Friend	5%	4%
Other	7%	4%
Country of birth		
Born outside the United States	58%	60%
Level of education		
Elementary	8%	11%
Middle school	23%	19%
High school	44%	43%
Some college	16%	19%
Bachelor's degree	5%	4%
Graduate degree	4%	4%
English proficiency		
Speak English very well	51%	54%
Speak English well	21%	20%
Speak English little	17%	13%
Speak English very little	11%	13%

a Two adults living in the household.
b Two or more adults living in the household.

into their analyses as a primary unit of analysis. The first step that needs to be taken is to collect data (both qualitative and quantitative) about Latina(o) households. One way to accomplish this goal is to use more sophisticated methods to examine the influence of distinct household configurations on students' transition to college. If researchers choose a qualitative approach, then they could follow N. González, Moll, and Amanti's (2005) three-interview model to examine the data collected. However, if a statistical approach is selected, then researchers could analyze the household data using appropriate multilevel techniques, such as a cross-classified random effects model (see Raudenbush & Bryk, 2002, for details). An advantage of using a multilevel approach is that it can examine a student nested simultaneously in different contexts (e.g., households and schools). The data gathering and estimating procedures that we suggest here are very complex. Nevertheless, they represent feasible options that researchers in higher education must explore if they aspire to conduct research that can increase the college enrollment rates of Latina(o)s.

Examining the Variation in Households' Funds of Knowledge

Unlike existing research that focuses exclusively on certain forms of capital to examine college preparation, in this section we consider some preliminary analyses of the variation in the funds of knowledge existing in Latina(o) households using a random sample of Puerto Rican households (see Rios-Aguilar, 2010, for details on the characteristics of the sample). What we offer here is a descriptive analysis of the richness and diversity embedded in Latina(o) households and how the academic outcomes of students vary according to this diversity.

We focus our examination of variation on two key elements of funds of knowledge: social reciprocity (a measure of the networks of exchange among different Latina(o) households) and household activities (a measure of the type of activities families and students engage in together). The reason for choosing to study the social reciprocity and household routine practices of these families is because it helps to develop a composite and multidimensional index of the range of possible funds of knowledge available in these households (N. González et al., 2005).

Indexes of "intensity" were created for both measures: social reciprocity and household activities. The idea of creating intensity indexes came from an analysis conducted by Deil-Amen, Prabhu, Terenzini, and Cabrera (2005) to assess the effectiveness of intervention programs aimed at increasing college awareness among at-risk students. The intensity indexes can be interpreted as proxies for how *frequently* families received and/or provided help and support to other families and how *frequently* families engaged with students in certain household activities. Table 2.2 shows the descriptive analyses for the intensity in social reciprocity and household practices. Perhaps the most revealing findings are that (a) there is variation in households' funds of knowledge and

Table 2.2 Descriptive Analysis of Intensity in Social Reciprocity Among Latina(o) Households

Characteristic	Low-Intensity Social Reciprocity (N = 89)	High-Intensity Social Reciprocity (N = 109)	Low-Intensity Household Practices	High-Intensity Household Practices
Characteristics of parents, %				
Female	90	86	92	92
Not born in the United States	55	60	56	56
Occupation				
Office and administrative assistant	24	22	26	26
Manufacturing	13	13	13	13
Services	29	33	32	32
Professional and business	11	13	11	11
Highest level of education completed				
Elementary	7	4	7	7
Middle school	27	28	22	22
High school	39	24	38	38
Some college	18	27	20	20
College	7	15	9	9
English proficiency				
Speak English well or very well	45	45	47	47
Spanish proficiency				
Speak Spanish well or very well	63	60	60	
Characteristics of students, M (SD)				
Stanford achievement performance level (1–4)	2.05 (.46)	1.94 (.41)	2.04 (.53)	2.00 (.37)
English language arts performance level (1–4)	2.05 (.77)	2.48 (.58)	2.12 (.78)	2.32 (.68)
Grade point average (0–4.5)	2.21 (.98)	2.48 (.91)	2.52 (.25)	2.09 (.92)
English literacy outcomes (0–45)	22.14 (13.48)	27.41 (12.2)	19.81 (11.91)	27.79 (13.24)
Spanish literacy outcomes (0–45)	21.53 (14.83)	27.46 (12.8)	17.80 (13.10)	28.94 (13.96)

Note. See Rios-Aguilar (2010) for details on the data collected.

(b) there are differences in the academic achievement of Latina(o) students depending on the intensity of social reciprocity and household activities.

The data analyses shown here are limited in several ways. For instance, these analyses are just descriptive (no statistical tests for differences were conducted). They do *not* examine how the varying intensity levels are related to students' academic achievement. In addition, only proxies for students' college preparation were measured and analyzed here. Future research needs to broaden the range of outcomes studied. For example, researchers need to analyze the relationship between funds of knowledge and college attendance and persistence. In addition, researchers must start to examine other noncognitive outcomes (e.g., resiliency and community engagement) that may also be relevant when one is utilizing a funds of knowledge approach.

Funds of Knowledge, College Access, and the Development of Career Aspirations

When disaggregating the multiple layers influencing college access and specifically examining the role of families, one sees that Latina(o) families have consistently been represented as deficient. These deficiency beliefs discount parents' values and views about education (Lott, 2001). Oftentimes parents from Latina(o) populations are perceived by school administrators and teachers as resistant to school efforts and uncommitted to their children's learning process. The literature challenging this dominant perspective clearly demonstrates that Latina(o) parents value education (Valencia & Black, 2002). In conducting a study that focused on the funds of knowledge and educational ideologies of six Mexican American families in a university outreach program, Kiyama (2010) found additional evidence that families form college ideologies in a variety ways, and many times those ideologies serve as positive influences. Findings from the same study also suggest that familial funds of knowledge influence the development of future career aspirations. Thus, the subsequent sections here focus on a discussion of how funds of knowledge can inform two specific processes: (a) getting into college and (b) the development of career aspirations.

"Getting in" College: Latino Families and College Access

Although dominant frameworks fail to acknowledge the college knowledge present in Latina(o) families, Kiyama's (2010) work illustrated that families' knowledge comes from firsthand experiences as well as the experiences of extended family members. Here we share a brief conversation about college costs and financial aid, two factors that might typically be considered a barrier for low-income and Latina(o) families. Although the families in the study acknowledged the financial challenges of attending college, they were determined not to let finances deter their children from "getting in." In a conversation about potential barriers to college, this mother expressed that she was not concerned about paying for college because she had gone through this process with her husband, who was currently enrolled in classes through the local community college:

Danielle: I went through it [financial aid process] with my husband so I never was scared about that.
Interviewer: Do you feel comfortable looking for financial aid and scholarships?
Danielle: Yeah. Even if they wanted a loan and pay it back when you are done, it doesn't matter. It gets paid back. . . . It doesn't scare me.

Danielle was familiar with different types of financial aid and knew that loans were available and could be repaid after graduation. Danielle's experience reminds us that we as researchers cannot continue to assume that families are lacking information about college. Danielle represents just one example of families who have college knowledge, often stemming from direct experiences and extended familial networks. These networks are important in providing information about both K–12 and higher education. Clearly, she was informed about the financial process of "getting in." It seems reasonable then to claim that researchers in higher education must examine what kinds of knowledge already exist in households and expand on them or help parents activate such knowledge into concrete strategies or actions that will enhance students' chances of enrolling and succeeding in college.

Funds of Knowledge and the Development of Career Aspirations

Occupational titles both carry a social status of how one is identified and represent how society values the notion of professional success. Here we share an example of a mother who describes the potential future occupations of her daughter—what the child would like to be and what the mother considers a successful path for her child. Valerie wanted her daughter Aracely (age 7) to go on to college, but she had concrete ideas about what Aracely's future might look like.

> I told her you can go to college and be a cheerleader and go be a teacher. I think her main one was cheerleader/coach type thing—teacher. From what it sounds like it is always going to be teaching something. Teaching other people to do it, and I am kind of saying, no, you are going to be a doctor. You are going to be a lawyer.

Although Aracely enjoys teaching and often plays school at home, Valerie expects that her future will be in a profession that is perceivably more successful. She rationalized this by explaining that Aracely likes to argue; therefore being a lawyer would be a better fit for her. All of the families had ideas about their children pursuing a college education, but their perceptions of successful careers were often limited by how narrowly professional success is defined in U.S. society. This mirrors the narrow definitions that educational researchers continue to draw upon when linking academic success with academic achievement. In this case, we argue that utilizing a funds of knowledge framework can help people to understand aspirations beyond college and professional aspirations. The framework can also help people to understand how and what career-like characteristics students are developing and experimenting with in the home.

Future research on Latina(o) families must begin to identify how families construct "getting out" of college. Research should also expand upon the role that Latina(o) families play in the retention and graduation processes of their students. Finally, additional research should understand how families create ideologies about career and professional aspirations.

Limitations of the Funds of Knowledge Approach

The intent of this paper is not to present a new study but instead to continue the discussion on funds of knowledge and highlight how this framework might help people to better understand college readiness, choice, access, and success among Latina(o) students. However, the funds of knowledge framework is not without limitations.

As researchers we must understand the processes of the development and acquisition of funds of knowledge. We currently have well-documented accounts of some of these processes, but we must build upon how, when, and by whom funds of knowledge are negotiated, activated, and expanded upon. It is very likely that in order to help Latina(o) students succeed in college the funds of knowledge approach needs to move from recognizing students to expanding and enriching these sources of knowledge beyond K–12. This begins with developing research with the goal of understanding the social networks of households and how these affect students' outcomes, including college access and success.

It is difficult to expand upon the types of funds of knowledge found in different types of households without also broadening the concept of the term *household*. However, as researchers introduce funds of knowledge into the college access, transition, and persistence literature they must reconceptualize the notion of "household." Households may begin to represent significant relationships outside of the family setting and into the collegiate setting. These may extend into residence halls and living/learning communities, fraternity and sorority involvement, and summer transition and retention programs in which a significant sense of community is developed. Finally, the majority of funds of knowledge research has been focused on Latina(o) families. Therefore, researchers' understanding of funds of knowledge is based on and limited by a Latina(o) perspective. It is important for the development and understanding of funds of knowledge to also include other subgroups of Latina(o) students and other ethnic minority, immigrant, and low-income families.

Implications for Further Research

Although we have gained a new perspective on the meaning of various funds of knowledge, we are still restricted in our knowledge of how these funds of knowledge are applied to the transitions into and out of college. Therefore, we propose the following as implications for future research:

1. *Refining units of analysis when studying funds of knowledge.* Future research must begin to incorporate into analyses of funds of knowledge and college access the role that siblings, extended families members, and communities play in this process.
2. *Examining the variation in households' funds of knowledge.* Future research on funds of knowledge needs to continue using both qualitative and quantitative methodologies to study different dimensions and variations of funds of knowledge as they apply to academic preparation and college access among Latina(o) students. Further research should expand upon this quantitative approach.
3. *Understanding the role of funds of knowledge in college access and the development of career aspirations.* Future college access research should examine how families construct the processes of getting into *and* getting out of college as well as how families develop career aspirations for their children.

Finally, future research should examine how and if those funds of knowledge are being converted into concrete educational opportunities for children throughout the course of their K–12 experience, into their college-going process, and into their persistence in college.

Conclusion

Throughout this article we have argued that there is a need to challenge existing frameworks used to study Latina(o) students' transition to college. We urge researchers to focus on the process of unlearning, disrupting, and reframing deficit thinking when it comes to studying Latina(o)s in higher education (Milner, 2007). By doing so, they will create a process of holding themselves more accountable to the students, families, and communities with whom they conduct research, as it is sometimes researchers' own belief systems and preexisting knowledge that contribute to deficit discourses and thinking (Milner, 2007). We aim to build on the recommendations of Milner (2007) and Young (1999), who proposed new frameworks for studying students and families of color, frameworks that challenge researchers to understand, interpret, and represent diverse communities in ways that maintain their integrity and illustrate their strengths. In doing so, we urge researchers in higher education not only to recognize the existence of funds of knowledge but also to assist students and families in expanding their use of funds of knowledge, in accessing other forms of capital (social and cultural capital), and in activating all of these to increase their academic and professional success.

References

Baum, S., & Ma, J. (2007). *Education pays 2007.* Washington, DC: College Board.

Beattie, I. (2002). Are all "adolescent econometricians" created equal? Racial, class, and gender differences in college enrollment. *Sociology of Education, 75*(1), 19–43.

Becker, G. (1976). *The economic approach to human behavior.* Chicago: University of Chicago Press.

Bensimon, E. (2007). The underestimated significance of practitioner knowledge in the scholarship of student success. *The Review of Higher Education, 30,* 441–469.

Bourdieu, P. (1986). The forms of capital. In J. G. Richardson (Ed.), *Handbook of theory and research for the sociology of education* (pp. 241–258). Westport, CT: Greenwood Press.

Cabrera, A. F., Prabhu, R., Deil-Amen, R., Terenzini, P. T., Lee, C., & Franklin, R. F., Jr. (2006). Increasing the college preparedness of at-risk students. *Journal of Latinos & Education, 5*(2), 79–97.

Cammarota, J., Moll, L. C., Cannella, C., & González, M. (2010). Sociocultural perspectives on interpersonal relationships in school. In S. Nieto & M. Rivera (Eds.), *Charting a new course: Understanding the sociocultural, political, economic, and historical context of Latino/a education in the United States.* Synthesis volume funded by the Spencer Foundation. Austin, TX: National Latino Education Research Agenda Project [NLERAP].

Deil-Amen, R., Prabhu, R., Terenzini, P., & Cabrera, A. (2005, April). *Reawakening the dream deferred: Can comprehensive intervention programs increase college awareness among at-risk students?* Paper presented at the annual meeting of the American Educational Research Association, Montreal, Quebec, Canada.

Deil-Amen, R., & López Turley, R. (2007). A review of the transition to college literature in sociology. *Teachers College Record, 109,* 2324–2366.

Flores, S. M., Horn, C. L., & Crisp, G. (2006). Community colleges, public policy, and Latino student opportunity. *New Directions for Community Colleges, 133,* 71–80.

Gándara, P. (2005). Addressing educational inequities for Latino students: The politics of "forgetting." *Journal of Hispanic Higher Education, 4*(3), 295–313.

García, E., & Figueroa, J. (2002). Access and participation of Latina(o)s in the University of California: A current macro and micro perspective. *Social Justice, 29,* 47–59.

González, K., Stone, C., & Jovel, J. (2003). Understanding the role of social capital in access to college for Latinas: Toward a college opportunity framework. *Journal of Hispanic Higher Education, 2,* 146–170.

González, N., Moll, L., & Amanti, C. (2005). *Funds of knowledge: Theorizing practices in households, communities, and classrooms.* Mahwah, NJ: Erlbaum.

Holquist, M. (1983). The politics of representation. *The Quarterly Newsletter of the Laboratory of Comparative Human Cognition, 5,* 2–9.

Immerwahr, J. (2003). *With diploma in hand: Hispanic high school seniors talk about their future.* Washington, DC: National Center for Public Policy and Higher Education.

Kiyama, J. M. (2010). College aspirations and limitations: The role of educational ideologies and funds of knowledge in Mexican American families. *American Educational Research Journal, 47,* 330–356.

Knight, M., Norton, N., Bentley, C., & Dixon, I. (2004). The power of Black and Latina/o counterstories: Urban families and college-going processes. *Anthropology & Education Quarterly, 35*(1), 99–120.

López, M., Barrueco, S., Feinauer, E., & Miles, J. (2007). *Young Latino infants and families: Parental involvement implications from a recent national study.* Cambridge, MA: Harvard Family Research Project.

Lott, B. (2001, August). *Recognizing and welcoming the standpoint of low-income parents in the public schools*. Presentation at the 109th Annual Conference of the American Psychological Association, San Francisco, CA.

Marin, P., Yun, J. T., Lee, C., Heller, D. E., Kurlaender, M., Felts, E., et al. (2008, March). *The educational pipeline and its consequences for students: Realizing Bakke's legacy*. Presidential session presented at annual meeting of the American Educational Research Association, New York, NY.

Martinez, M. (2003). Missing in action: Reconstructing hope and possibility among Latino students placed at risk. *Journal of Latinos & Education, 2*(1), 13–21.

McDonough, P. (1997). *Choosing colleges: How social class and schools structure opportunity*. Albany, NY: State University of New York Press.

Milner, R. (2007). Race, culture, and researcher positionality: Working through dangers seen, unseen, and unforeseen. *Educational Researcher, 36*(7), 388–400.

Moll, L. (2000). Inspired by Vygotsky: Ethnographic experiments in education. In C. Lee & P. Smagorinsky (Eds.), *Vygostkyan perspectives on literacy research: Constructing meaning through collaborative inquiry* (pp. 256–268). New York, NY: Cambridge University Press.

Moll, L., Amanti, C., Neff, D., & González, N. (1992). Funds of knowledge for teaching: Using a qualitative approach to connect homes and classrooms. *Theory Into Practice, 31*, 132–141.

National Center for Education Statistics. (2007). *Digest of education statistics 2007*. Retrieved April 1, 2008, from http://nces.ed.gov/programs/digest/d07/

Nora, A. (2004). The role of habitus and cultural capital in choosing a college, transitioning from high school to higher education, and persisting in college among minority and nonminority students. *Journal of Hispanic Higher Education, 3*(2), 180–208.

Oliva, M. (2008). Latino access to college: Actualizing the promise and potential of K-16 partnerships. *Journal of Hispanic Higher Education, 7*, 119–130.

Oliva, M., & Nora, A. (2004). College access and the K-16 pipeline: Connecting policy and practice for Latino student success. *Journal of Hispanic Higher Education, 3*(2), 117–124.

Olmedo, P. (1997). Voices of our past: Using oral history to explore funds of knowledge within a Puerto Rican family. *Anthropology & Education Quarterly, 28*, 550–573.

Paulsen, M. (1990). *College choice: Understanding student enrollment behavior* (ASHE-ERIC Higher Education Report No. 6). Washington, DC: George Washington University, School of Education and Human Development.

Pérez, P., & McDonough, P. (2008). Understanding Latina and Latino college choice: A social capital and chain migration analysis. *Journal of Hispanic Higher Education, 7*, 249–265.

Perna, L. (2000). Differences in the decision to attend college among African Americans, Hispanics, and Whites. *Journal of Higher Education, 71*(2), 117–141.

Perna, L. (2006). Studying college access and choice: A proposed conceptual model. In J. Smart (Ed.), *Higher education: Handbook of theory and research* (Vol. 21, pp. 99–157). New York: Agathon Press.

Perna, L., & Titus, M. (2005). The relationship between parental involvement as social capital and college enrollment: An examination of racial/ethnic group differences. *Journal of Higher Education, 76*, 485–518.

Pew Hispanic Center. (2004). *National survey of Latina(o)s: Education, summary and chartpack*. Washington, DC: Author.

Portes, A. (2000). The two meanings of social capital. *Sociological Forum, 15*, 1–12.

Quintana, S., Vogel, M., & Ybarra, V. (1991). Meta-analysis of Latino students' adjustment in higher education. *Hispanic Journal of Behavioral Sciences, 13*(2), 155–168.

Raudenbush, S. W., & Bryk, A. S. (2002). *Hierarchical linear models: Applications and data analysis methods*. Thousand Oaks, CA: Sage.

Rios-Aguilar, C. (2010). Measuring funds of knowledge: Contributions to Latina/o students' academic and non-academic outcomes. *Teachers College Record, 112*, 2209–2257.

Rios-Aguilar, C., Kiyama, J., Gravitt, M., & Moll, L. (2011). Funds of knowledge for the poor and forms of capital for the rich? A capital approach to examining funds of knowledge. *Theory and Research in Education, 9*(2), 163–184.

Sewell, W. H. (1971). Inequality of opportunity for higher education. *American Sociological Review, 36*, 793–809.

Stanton-Salazar, R. D. (2001). *Manufacturing hope and despair: The school and kin networks of U.S. Mexican Youth*. New York: Teachers College Press.

Swail, W., Cabrera, A., & Lee, C. (2004). *Latino youth and the pathway to college*. Washington, DC: Pew Hispanic Center.

Tierney, W. G., & Auerbach, S. (2004). Toward developing an untapped resource: The role of families in college preparation. In W. G. Tierney, Z. Corwin, & J. E. Colyar (Eds.), *Preparing for college: Nine elements of effective outreach* (Chapter 2). Albany, NY: State University of New York Press.

Titus, M. (2006). Understanding the influence of the financial context of institutions on student persistence at four-year colleges and universities. *Journal of Higher Education, 77*, 353–375.

Valencia, R., & Black, M. (2002). Mexican Americans don't value education! On the basis of myth, mythmaking, and debunking. *Journal of Latinos & Education, 1*(2), 81–103.

Vélez-Ibañez, C., & Greenberg, J. (1992). Formation and transformation of funds of knowledge among U.S.-Mexican households. *Anthropology & Education Quarterly, 23*, 313–335.

Walpole, M. (2003). Socioeconomic status and college: How SES affects college experiences and outcomes. *The Review of Higher Education, 27*(1), 45–73.

Young, M. (1999). Multifocal educational policy research: Toward a method for enhancing traditional educational policy studies. *American Educational Research Journal, 36*, 677–714.

3 All for Our Children

Migrant Families and Parent Participation in an Alternative Education Program

Pablo Jasis and Douglas Marriott

In this study, we examined several cohorts of Latino parents who were participants in Project Avanzando (Spanish for "advancing" or "moving forward"), a community-based alternative adult education program, and describe participants' increased participation in their children's schooling. Project Avanzando provides general education diploma (GED) instruction, transition to college services, and support services to adult migrant and seasonal farm workers. The program's services are offered under the umbrella of the Migrant Education Program, a nationwide effort to provide educational opportunities to agricultural families whose children's schooling is often disrupted or negatively affected because of the seasonal and migratory nature of agricultural employment. All participants at Project Avanzando are parents of school-age children.

This study explores the process of educational awareness and school involvement among a group of parents who are migrant farm workers, exploring the notion that Latino parents who are organized in educational or community activities are likely to engage more actively in their children's education (Delgado-Gaitán, 1994; Osterling, 2001; Valdés, 1996). Their emerging involvement is reflected in their increasingly active role in formal avenues of parent participation (Parent–Teacher Association [PTA], school events, etc.), their more assertive interactions with school personnel, and their increased participation in school-related activities (homework, visits to schools, classroom observations, field trips, etc.). The study suggests that participation in a community-based education program such as Project Avanzando can lead to a validation of the critical role such participants can play as partners in the successful schooling of their children and of themselves as effective learners, often promoting an invigorated appreciation of the value of education in the lives of their families.

Migrant Agricultural Families: A Marginalized Community

Although the generally low school achievement of Latino students across the nation has been attributed to a number of factors, one factor commonly cited by school personnel is "lack of parental involvement" in the schooling of this student population (Jasis, 2000; Jasis & Ordoñez-Jasis, 2005). Migrant or seasonal farm worker families are a particularly marginalized segment of the Latino population, whose socioeconomic, school achievement, and parent participation indicators have historically been below those of the rest of the community (Levine, 2009; National Agricultural Worker Survey (NAWS), 2002). Typically, agricultural workers and their families must piece together a series of jobs throughout the year, alternating with periods of no available work. Exacerbating the situation is the surplus of farm labor in the form of new rural immigrants and the use of farm labor contractors or "middle men," which has led to a dramatic lowering of wages in recent years. NAWS data indicate a decrease in the hourly wage from $6.89 in 1989 to $6.18 in 2000. The socioeconomic situation of today's farm workers is at its most dire point in recent history, as wages, standard of living, health status, and future prospects continue to lose significant ground.

Viewed as a segment of the larger farm worker population, the participants of Project Avanzando and their families mirror the social and educational profile of agricultural communities in the Southwest. The lives of these workers and their families are harsh. Available data on agricultural workers in California's San Gabriel Valley (the Project Avanzando service area) indicate that more than 90% are foreign born, originating primarily from Mexico's highlands; 93% are limited English proficient, with an average sixth-grade education; and 50% of families live below the poverty level (California Agricultural Census, 2002). Together, these factors have a profound negative impact on the children of these agricultural workers. Available socioeconomic and school achievement data indicate the severity of the education problems of these children (see Table 3.1).

In sum, despite considerable gains throughout the past decades—mainly resulting from the efforts of the Migrant Education Program—poverty, residential dislocation due to migration or seasonal work, and low English language proficiency are still critical factors affecting the schooling of migrant children (Migrant Education Program, Los Angeles County Office

Table 3.1 Socio-Economic and Educational Profile of Migrant Children in Los Angeles School District

Characteristic	Value
Migrant students (*n*)	18,239
Free or reduced lunch (%)	89.3
Non-English home language (%)	95
English learners (%)	63
Scores far below basic up to basic (%)	89
Dropout rate (%)	50

Note. Data are from Migrant Education Program, Los Angeles County Office of Education (2004).

of Education, 2004). The search for educational alternatives for these families points to the need to continue strengthening school services as well as to improve rates of parental involvement and family education (Martinez, Cranston-Gingras, & Velazquez, 2001).

Migrant Families and Schools: A Theoretical Framework

Adding to their challenging socioeconomic situation, most migrant parents have little knowledge about their children's schooling or about their opportunities and the school's expectations for their participation. Personnel in local schools and districts often assume that migrant parents' lack of visible involvement, such as attendance at PTA meetings or school–family events, is probably due to a lack of interest in their children's success (Cranston-Gingras, 2003; Jasis, 2000). A common perception of school personnel regarding migrant families is that because of their lower socioeconomic status, as well as their demanding work schedules, they are "a well-meaning, but hard-to-reach, hard-to-involve community" (Unpublished school staff interviews, 2004). Such perceptions have been amply chronicled and analyzed throughout the literature (Osterling, 2001; Valdés, 1996). Often, lower school performance by Latino students from low-income families is accompanied by negative perceptions on the part of their teachers about the parents' role in their children's schooling (Laureau, 1994). Historically, responsibility for the educational "failure" of Latino children has been at times shifted from the family to the community and vice versa, often assigning to students' families an inherently neglectful attitude toward school (Jasis, 2000). Often, parents such as our Avanzando participants tend to be perceived by teachers and school administrators as being uninterested in their children's education and even a negative influence on their children's school performance (Laureau, 1994). However, after conducting and examining extensive interviews and observations with Latino immigrant families, Valdés (1996), Delgado-Gaitán (1994), and Scribner, Young, and Pedroza (1999) have consistently refuted what they consider to be a misconstrued notion of an inherent educational apathy among these parents and families. Rather, they have found among this population a rich source of family values of unity, solidarity, and support and particularly strong views of what constitutes success and failure in education. In addition, Valdés argued convincingly that many schools and the society at large tend to have little regard for the values of these families.

The concept of parental involvement in public schooling has gained national momentum since the 1990s (Riley and Shalala, 2000; Warshaw, 1995). However, these efforts have yet to fully benefit minority communities, such as Latino migrant parents. In fact, research has indicated that turnout tends to be low at parent workshops about support for schools aimed at minority families, and report cards and school newsletters are often not understood by parents (Epstein, 1994; Martinez et al., 2001). Recruited volunteers, PTA and Parents and Teacher Organizations (PTO) members, and school leaders are often not representative of the school's populations, and school staff are seldom trained to interact with diverse parents (Warshaw, 1995). The very meanings of the words *parental involvement, participation*, and the like usually signify different things to the various actors in a school community. Laureau (1994) argued that many teachers' notions about parental involvement are narrow and are usually confined to parents attending parent–teacher conferences, volunteering at classroom activities, raising funds for the school, and helping with homework; these notions are often affected by the assumption that many minority parents lack the necessary skills to help their children with schoolwork. A variety of other possible contributions by working-class or minority parents tend to go unnoticed or unrecognized (Laureau, 1994). As a result, certain parents and families end up in a much better position than others to perform according to teachers' expectations in terms of "parent involvement." In addition, recent studies have suggested that school–family interactions are more effective when the process is inclusive, with clearly delineated expectations by all participants, yet flexible enough to accommodate diverse parental styles, community agendas, and cultures (Cranston-Gingras, 2003; Jasis & Ordonez-Jasis, 2005).

Project Avanzando: An Alternative, Community-Based Educational Effort

Project Avanzando reaches out to the parents and caregivers of migrant children with evening instructional services, child care, counseling, and activities centered around transitioning to higher education or work training. The program is located at six community sites in the San Gabriel Valley of Eastern Los Angeles County. Project Avanzando staff describe the program as "learner-centered"; program literature defines the program as "respecting the prior knowledge of the learner and seeing him/her as a co-facilitator of their [*sic*] learning process," using a "constructivist approach to adult education," providing support to participants by establishing "clear communication of expectations, and creating a joint model of accountability between participants and instructors" (Jasis & Marriott, 2004).

Since its inception, the design and implementation of Project Avanzando has actively promoted the need to provide for a student voice at all levels of the program, from classroom management decisions to programmatic governance (Arriaza, 2002). The incorporation of the adult participants' voices into the planning and implementation of the project has proved critical in overcoming the traditional barriers faced by adult learners, such as challenging work schedules, lack of child care, negative peer pressure, lack of time and sleep, lack of confidence or motivation, and transportation (Literacy Network of Greater Los Angeles, 2004). This approach, in turn, has greatly improved the retention rate of the participants. A respect for learners as decision makers, according to Vella (2002), is a core principle for effective adult learning and is part of the vision of Project Avanzando at all levels of programming. The program has consistently provided critical support services requested by the participants, such as free child care and transportation, counseling, and transition-to-college activities. Of the program's students, 73% are young mothers who consider the offering of safe, onsite child care as the critical component that makes possible their attendance and participation. An average of 80 children between the ages of 3 and 12 years regularly attend the program's child care service, offered concurrently with the adult classes in an adjacent classroom.

In its 7 years of implementation, Project Avanzando has graduated close to 600 farm workers or their adult dependents, 35% of whom have transitioned into higher education at local community colleges. Independent yearly evaluations of the program attribute the effectiveness of Project Avanzando among the farm worker population to the staff's ability to understand the academic and life challenges of the agricultural participants, as well as to the culture of inclusiveness and *empowerment* created at all programmatic levels. This notion of empowerment, which is discussed later in this article, involves a distinctive approach to leading the program's adult education classrooms, staff activities and interactions, as well as active community support and inclusive decision making (Arriaza, 2002; Murillo, 2005). These same programmatic dispositions are reflected in the program's child care offering, which motivated the many discussions the participants had about their changing relationship with the schooling of their children.

Examining Project Avanzando: Our Methodology

This study's ethnographic analysis was conceived under the notion advanced by Osterling (2001) that local communities are the main sources of valuable assets to be tapped for their own revitalization and growth. This examination of Project Avanzando and its preliminary findings are part of a larger study that examined the program since its inception, and for the following 2 years of implementation. Findings were articulated through the voices of the adult participants by interweaving personal and group narratives of parents, teachers, adult learners, and program staff and administrators to identify the pedagogical patterns that defined the program's approach to parent participation and empowerment, among other areas of programmatic impact. The findings of this article reflect an analysis of the views of the participating parents, which will be compared and contrasted with the voices of teachers and school administrators and with school performance data at a later stage in the study.

The concept of narrative is used here as a "means of imparting meaning to the events of our own lives, as a system of sense-making" (Greene, 1994, p. 14). It is also informed by Brunner (1994), who viewed narratives as a "continuing interpretation and re-interpretation of our experience" (p. 28), in which "life as *led* is inseparable from life as *told*" (p. 36, italics added in the original). This approach also involves the notion of *testimonio* (Beverley, 2009), or first-person narration, in which participants recall reflectively and purposely to give meaning to their lives and connect their stories with larger sociohistorical themes from an often marginalized or subaltern social positioning. It is also approached as the examination of a reflective dialogue among participants, a process that requires one to "begin, maintain, and nurture" (Vella, 2002, p. 4) a dialogical relationship toward a meaningful pedagogy.

Informed by these qualitative notions, the data collection activities related to this study were consistent with such an ethnographic approach: We conducted 32 in-depth individual and group interviews, 20 hr of classroom observations, two program surveys, and three focus groups. Three yearly evaluations and student data conducted on Project Avanzando were also examined to assess participant recruitment, retention, and graduation rates and other significant program activities. Informal discussions with participants in out-of-school settings were recorded through notes and were also included in the analysis. All data were collected, coded, and analyzed for larger thematic connections.

From a Program of *Service* to a Program of *Empowerment*

Since the inception of Project Avanzando, there has been a clear understanding by all organizational stakeholders—the sponsoring nonprofit agency, migrant education representatives, and community-based organizations—that the population to be *served* should be fully integrated into the design and implementation of the program (Art, Research and Curriculum Associates (ARC) Proposal—U.S. Department of Education, 2000). That understanding was implemented in practice through a series of community meetings, focus groups, and grassroots conversations that created the foundation for the educational practices and support services that would later be provided by Project Avanzando. The same basic approach was used to recruit and retain adult participants and their families during the first months of the program: There was a joint disposition of program staff and community supporters toward learning about and from the participating migrant families and adjusting and improving the program's core goals, objectives, and practices to better *serve* the participants.

Many of the shared concepts that framed the initial developments and the work ethos of Project Avanzando among program staff and an emerging collective of volunteers and community collaborators helped guide the program's first year of implementation. The main assumption of both groups was that there was a needy, hard-to-reach, and undereducated rural population in the area that could be well *served* with traditional, top-down GED instruction to improve their employment prospects and, thus, the economic future of their families. However, as knowledge about and from the community of learners deepened and a stronger rapport between staff and participants developed, many of the original assumptions about the program's practices and its sense of effectiveness began to change. As a result, a series of discussions took place among staff and participants toward the second year of implementation. These discussions encompassed a whole new direction for Project Avanzando as well as a distinct approach to implementing the adult education program. This new vision had the common goal of transitioning it from a program of *service* to a program of *empowerment* (Cruikshank, 1999; Freire, 1994; Jasis, 2000, Jasis & Ordonez-Jasis, 2005). The concept of *empowerment* is used here as it was by Cruikshank, who saw it as challenging the basic power relationships in society. It begins when "people change their ideas about the causes of their powerlessness, when they recognize the systemic forces that oppress them and act to change the conditions of their lives" (p. 70). The more common concept of *service*, in contrast, was increasingly seen as an engagement associated with a "work or duty performed for others, an assistance or benefit" ("Webster's II New Riverside Dictionary," 2004, p. 621) and generally associated with a manner of duty among two main participants with distinctive decision-making authority and a clear difference of power. Thus, the notion of service was perceived in this context as a way of establishing an unequal power relationship between the *provider* and the object of the *provision*, an approach that was purposely challenged by both staff and participants alike throughout the process of transforming Project Avanzando.

In practice, this process of change resulted in a program that became more learner centered and *constructivist* in its teaching–learning practices or, in other words, that was consciously built by experiential learning and implemented through a system of joint accountability involving individual and group commitment at various levels. Consistent with these implementation and governance changes, the program soon generated its own peer-training units on adult education, produced many of its own assessment and instructional materials, and provided for student and community voice as well as decision making while creating an accelerated timeline more in tune with students' emerging capabilities and needs (Murillo, 2005). This new *empowerment* approach was also reflected in the program's support services, particularly its child care and student support offerings, which provided an opportunity for participants to articulate and practice a new, more active appreciation of their children's schooling and their own emerging role in it. It is this particular area of the program on which the present study is focused.

Project Avanzando Parents and Their Children's Schooling

As mentioned earlier, the schooling of migrant children has historically been affected by low student achievement, poor parental involvement, and frequent disruptions and dislocations in the school calendar (Office of Migrant Education, 2004). These characterizations resonated loudly in the words of a local school principal, who explained that the few migrant students in her school were "definitely behind academically, coming from families that are working hard but are difficult to reach because they don't come to the school. These children often have attendance problems, among many other problems" (Staff interviews, 2005).

Although they shared much of the general migrant profile, the majority of parents participating in Project Avanzando lived in a largely urban environment and lived a less migratory life than other farm worker families, because many of the agricultural jobs were located within the same geographic region. At the time of recruitment into the program, the parents often described their relationship with their children's school personnel as distant and at times conflictive, as illustrated in the following testimonies:

> *A veces creo que mi hija no recibe atención en la escuela, su maestra anterior de matemáticas nunca respondía a mis preguntas ni hacía ningún esfuerzo para ayudarla, ahora la nueva maestra es mejor pero todavía no me dice qué tengo que hacer como mamá· para ayudarla.* (Sometimes I think my daughter does not receive attention at school, her former math teacher never answered my questions or made any effort to help her. Her new teacher is better but still does not tell me how I can help her as a parent.)
> (Adult learner interviews, 2005)

> *Antes sentía como que los maestros me hablaban* a *mí en las conferencias de la escuela, pero que realmente no hablaban conmigo.* (I used to feel that the teachers would speak *at* me during the [parent] conferences, but that they really were not really talking *with* me.)
> (Adult learner interviews, 2005, emphasis added by speaker)

Preliminary data from participating parents, however, showed a change in these parents' disposition toward their children's schooling as they became more active and effective in pursuing their own educational goals. Out of 45 parents who had attended the Avanzando program for 5 months or longer and who were closer to graduation, 90% wrote that they had gained a "better appreciation" of education and schooling; 85% wrote that they felt "better prepared" and "more motivated" to participate in their children's school activities, such as by helping with homework; 60% wrote that they now communicated more with their children's teachers; 70% said they visited their children's school more often; and all said that they now read more often with their children. One parent described her participation in the program as directly affecting her attitude toward her children's schooling:

> *Ahora comprendo más la importancia de participar en la escuela, los puedo ayudar más y quiero un mejor futuro para mis hijos!* (Now I understand better the importance of participating in their school, I can help them more, and I want a better future for my children!")
> (Adult learner interviews, 2005)

Martha Iniguez, the program's Student Services Coordinator, commented on her daily conversations with Avanzando parents, which she described as follows:

> We always talk about the importance of visiting their children's schools, of talking with teachers and asking questions, and if they don't get a good answer then talk with the principal until they feel satisfied and well informed. When they feel insecure about their studies, right before their GED exams, I remind them how important this [is] not only for themselves, but for their kids, that they are like little sponges that absorb everything, good and bad, and that gets these parents motivated to forget their fears, *they tell me they would do anything for their children!*
> (Staff interviews, 2005, informant's own emphasis)

The newly found appreciation and assertiveness regarding schooling that was reflected in these testimonies was also reflected in participants' relationships with their older children, who became active supporters of their parents' efforts. One mother emotionally recounted a recent conversation with her 19-year-old daughter, who was applying for college:

> *Ella me vio estudiando para mi examen y me dijo: mamá yo siempre supe que tú eras muy inteligente pero nomás nadie te había dado la chance de superarte, ahora debiéramos de estudiar juntas tú y yo.* (She saw me studying for my exam and she said, "Mom, I always knew you were very intelligent, but no one gave you a chance to improve yourself, now we should start studying together, you and me.")
> (Adult learner interviews, 2005)

Building an Adult Educational Alternative, Affecting Children's Schooling

The preliminary findings of this exploration of the community-based Project Avanzando suggest an improved, more participatory disposition among these parents toward involvement in their children's schooling. Our examination also points to an increased sense of self-efficacy and assertiveness among parents when helping their children with homework, reading with them at home, and even visiting and interacting with school personnel. And although the study has not yet examined the direct impact of this increased parental participation on students' school achievement as measured by test scores, these families clearly expressed a more positive view of schoolwork and schooling in general. One program parent wrote the following:

> *El programa ha despertado en todos nosotros el hábito de estudiar y leer.* (The program has awaken in all of us [her family] the habit of studying and reading.)
> (Adult learner interviews, 2005)

In our exploration of Project Avanzando, we identified a set of programmatic *features*, meaning salient, identifiable approaches, dispositions, and practices that help explain these positive findings while also illustrating the depth and the context of the program's impact. Some of these features were initiated by participants, whereas some others originated from program staff or community supporters.

Building a Strong Community of Learners

Project Avanzando was conceived on the notion that effective adult learning takes place within a *community of learners* (De La Rosa, 1986; Freire, 1986). That is, participants learned from one another's experiences and coconstructed knowledge in the process, enriching the learning process for everyone and often blurring the barriers between teachers and students. Typically, the program's GED instruction "delivery" was structured in a more interactive fashion and in a relaxed, less formal environment, with the participants sitting at a set of roundtables, integrating live discussions with a series of generating *themes* (Freire, 1974) that were intertwined with the standard requirements of GED exam preparation. Also, the program's instructors actively promoted the strengthening of student cohorts through academic peer support, small study groups, and a joint pace of instruction that allowed for the whole group to make progress toward examination and graduation on a similar timeline. Almost half of the students at the program sites shared with the researchers that they often used the same learning configurations for study sessions at home and for homework time with their children.

The Family Enterprise Approach

As part of the programmatic transformation toward an *empowerment* effort, Project Avanzando staff made a concerted effort to actively involve as many members as possible from each participant's family. The assumption was that in order to be effective, the efforts of each adult student needed to be supported and sustained by all family members in a joint, structured, and agreed-upon fashion. The program's message was this: In order for a migrant mother of school-age children to regularly attend GED classes and to successfully complete her course of studies, her spouse may have to cook meals some evenings or help get the children ready for school, and supportive children will have to make time each day for their mother to study by doing their own homework or playing quietly in their room at a specific time. In sum, a change in family dynamics was necessary to support each participating parent in succeeding at Project Avanzando. It thus became clear for all participants that success in the program was not to be an individual effort but an actual *family enterprise*, in which each family member had an active role to play. Staff implemented this notion by meeting with participants' family members at the time of intake and by formalizing *family enterprise* goals and commitments into an actual written, signed contract to support each of the program's parents. During times of occasional family distress, this signed contract was clearly a very valuable tool for program retention and successful GED completion.

Reflection, Discussion, and Writing Sessions

The program has made it a priority activity to regularly spend quality classroom time discussing and reflecting as a group on topics of interest to its adult participants. The instructors often found creative ways to connect these inclusive, in-depth conversations to the thematic units of GED preparation, including topics such as the local economy and politics, schooling, nutrition, health care, education, and even recreation and sports. Meaningful words or sentences from these conversations were often analyzed and dissected, and new meanings were introduced and discussed with an eye toward articulating and expanding a common knowledge base. The writing sessions that concluded these exercises significantly advanced the parents' sense of improved self-expression, public voice, and group leadership; these sessions also motivated parents to enhance their writing skills, which was critical to passing their GED exam. Participating parents reported that these group discussions helped prepare them for their interactions with their children's school personnel. They also reported that they learned how to better organize their thoughts, set clearer goals for their school meetings, and strengthen their public voices, helping them fight their fears of inadequacy or shyness when dealing with persons in positions of authority, such as teachers or school administrators.

Supplemental Reading Material

Through in-service workshops, the program's leadership trained its instructors to introduce and use in class supplemental reading materials, such as newspapers, magazines, school report cards, written pieces of general interest, and instruction manuals. Emphasis was placed on reading and analyzing selected literary materials within the time constraints of GED preparation and testing. As a result, Latin American novels, poetry, plays, and short stories were regularly read and examined in class. Working with more formal literature familiarized the participants with higher quality writing and promoted family reading and cultural pride, which in turn benefited participants' children in school. Some parents have suggested to their children's teachers (with some success) the use of these higher quality materials to promote and discuss recognized Spanish-language authors in their classrooms.

Intergenerational Participation

Many agricultural families in the Southwest have worked on the land for generations. Project Avanzando participants were no exception. The success of the program motivated these parents to invite their grown, out-of-school children as well as their own aging parents to attend GED classes, and many have graduated together. This intergenerational participation has had great meaning for local families and communities, promoting a positive *educational climate* for the whole family and stimulating conversations about the importance of schooling and the reasons why some older generations of lower income Latinos had restricted access to education.

Empowering Classroom Practices: Archival Note Taking, Portfolios, Self-Publication, and Journals

Participating parents were asked to identify a set of classroom practices that were particularly useful for their own GED instructional process and that were also transferable to their educational activities with their children at home. Led by their instructors, participants created archives with their own written class notes and suggestions about various topics across the five GED subjects, and they produced comprehensive writing portfolios with their articles and opinion pieces. They created and updated personal and group journals chronicling their learning process. Currently, they are focusing on self-publication of these materials through their emerging use of the Internet. Many of these practices were enthusiastically replicated with children at home and were often suggested to their children's teachers. Parents reported that most teachers responded positively to their suggestions.

Role Modeling by Program Alumni

Staff invited many of the program's graduates to speak to current adult learners about their experiences and challenges while participating in Project Avanzando. These conversations were critical in terms of addressing participants' fears and anxieties, particularly before GED exams. Graduates chronicled the remarkable impact that their studies, their graduation, and often their postsecondary career had on their own children's schooling. They often emphasized their increased ability to support their children academically, as well as the more active role they have since taken as advocates for their children's schooling. The challenges and daily achievements described in graduates' first-hand recollections and experiences strongly resonated with current students.

Conclusion

The preliminary findings of this examination of the community-based Project Avanzando suggest a significant connection between the participating parents' emerging involvement—and often activism—in their children's schooling and their participation in an organized adult education program based on a coconstructed model of *student empowerment.* Because the program targets a particularly underserved population such as migrant and seasonal farm workers, the pedagogical links of this multilevel connection may have significant implications for educators and researchers: Findings point to the need to implement and articulate effective educational programs involving the whole family. The impact of the parents' ongoing education process and their emerging use of the most effective classroom practices to help their children seems to have increased parents' sense of self-efficacy when dealing with their children's schooling, as reflected in parents' testimonies and through the observations of the program staff.

However, this study's preliminary findings need to be complemented with a comprehensive examination of the children's school performance as well as with an exploration of the feedback obtained from teachers and school administrators. The attitudinal changes among the parents are also the result of the program's specific offerings, which were designed and implemented with the active participation of the community. Thus, programmatic features such as learner-centered instructional delivery, inclusive governance and decision making, free child care and transportation, retention counseling, and transition-to-college activities clearly respond to specific participant needs and have resulted in increased attendance and academic success for both parents and their children. Finally, and equally important, this examination of Project Avanzando points to a foundational notion: Traditionally underserved minority families and communities can participate effectively in the education of their children when the conditions for their involvement are facilitated and when their culture and particular ways of engagement are validated and encouraged. Community-based adult education efforts such as Project Avanzando should be replicated and tapped into to increase awareness of parent participation and thus improve minority schooling. An examination of the data obtained also suggests that community-based adult education programs can become spaces of participation in school and in society, engaging families in valuable exercises of grassroots democracy and the development of voice (Jasis, 2000).

References

Arriaza, G. (2002). *HEP mid-year evaluations*. Washington, DC: U.S. Department of Education.

Art, Research and Curriculum Associates. (2005). *HEP proposal to the U.S. Department of Education*. Whittier, CA: Author.

ARC HEP Proposal (2000). Art, Research and Curriculum Associates, HEP Proposal to the US Department of Education. US Department of Education, 2000.

Beverley, J. (2009). Testimonio, subalternity and narrative authority. In N. Denzin & Y. Lincoln (Eds.), *The Sage handbook of qualitative research* (pp. 547–547). Thousand Oaks, CA: Sage.

Brunner, J. (1994). Life as a narrative. *Social Research, 71*(3), 691–710.

California Agricultural Census (2002). Retrieved March, 2010, from www.census.gov/econ/census02/data/ca/CA000_42.HTM

Cranston-Gingras, A. (2003). Reconnecting youth from migrant farmworker families. *Reclaiming Children and Youth, 11*(4), 242–246.

Cruikshank, B. (1999). *The will to empower: Democratic citizens and other subjects.* Ithaca, NY: Cornell University Press.

De La Rosa, M. (1986). *Alfabetizar concientizando.* Tijuana, B. C., Mexico: Promoción Popular Urbana.

Delgado-Gaitán, C. (1994). Spanish-Speaking families' involvement in schools. In C. L. Fagnano & B. Z. Weber (Eds.), *School, family and community interaction. A view from the firing lines* (pp. 85–98). San Francisco: Westview Press.

Epstein, J. (1994). Theory to Practice: School and Family Partnerships Lead to School Improvement and Student Success. In C. Fagnano and B. Werber, *School, Family, and Community Interactions: A View from the Firing Lines.* Boulder, CO: Westview Press.

Freire, P. (1985). Dialogicidad y diálogo. In A. Molina (Ed.), *Diálogo e interacción en el proceso pedagógico.*

Freire, P. (1986). *La educación como práctica de la libertad.* [Education as a Practice of Freedom]. 1986. Mexico, DF Mexico: Siglo XXI Editores.

Freire, P. (1994). *Pedagogy of hope: Reliving pedagogy of the oppressed.* New York, NY: Continuum.

Greene, M. (1994). Multiculturalism, community and the arts. In A. Dyson & C. Genishi (Eds.), *The need for story: Cultural diversity in classroom and community* (pp. 133–149). Urbana, IL: National Council of Teachers of English.

Jasis, P. (2000). *Building La Familia: Organization and empowerment with Latino parents in a public school.* Unpublished doctoral dissertation, University of California, Berkeley.

Jasis, P., & Marriott, D. (2004, November). *Community education for empowerment.* Presentation at the annual meeting of the American Educational Studies Association, Kansas City, MO.

Jasis, P., & Ordoñez-Jasis, R. (2005). Convivencia to empowerment: Latino parent organizing at La Familia. *The High School Journal, 88*(2), 33–43.

Laureau, A. (1994). Parent involvement in schooling: A dissenting view. In C. Fagnano & B. Werber (Eds.), *School, family and community interactions* (pp. 180–183). Boulder, CO: Westview Press.

Literacy Network of Greater Los Angeles. (2004). *Literacy@Work: The L.A. Workforce Literacy Project Skills Today, Jobs Tomorrow.* literacynetwork.org/literacynetwork_la/pdf/2005_ann_rpt.pdf

Martinez, Y., Cranston-Gingras, A., & Velazquez, J. (2001). Youth from migrant farm worker families: Perspectives of school personnel. *Journal of At-Risk Issues, 7*(3), 4–11.

Migrant Education Program, Los Angeles County Office of Education. (2004). *Migrant education reports, Region 10.*

Murillo, E. (2005). *HEP-Project Avanzando Mid-Year Evaluation, US Department of Education.*

National Agricultural Workers Survey (NAWS) (2002). Retrieved February 21, 2010, from are.berkeley.edu/APMP/pubs/Cal-NAWS/Cal-NAWS.pdf

Office of Migrant Education (2004). MEP-LACOE, Los Angeles County Office of Education, *Migrant Education Reports*, Region 10, Los Angeles, CA.

Osterling, J. (2001). Waking the sleeping giant: Engaging and capitalizing on the strengths of the Latino community. *Bilingual Research Journal, 25*(2), retrieved May 12, 2009, from http://brj.asu.edu, 59–88.

Riley, R. & Shalala, D. (2000). A Call to Commitment: Fathers' Involvement in Children's Learning. Retrieved from www.parentinvolvementmatters.org/research.php.

Scribner, J., Young, M., & Pedroza, A. (1999). Building collaborative relations with parents. In P. Reyes, J. Scribner, & A. Paredes Scribner (Eds.), *Lessons from high performing*

Hispanic schools: Creating learning communities (pp. 167–189). New York: Teachers College Press.

Valdés, G. (1996). *Con respeto: Bridging the distances between culturally diverse families and schools.* New York: Teachers College Press.

Vella, J. (2002). *Learning to listen, learning to teach: The power of dialogue in educating adults.* San Francisco: Wiley.

Warshaw, R. (1995). Forging a strong alliance. *America's Agenda Magazine, 5*(1), 22.

Webster's II New Riverside dictionary. (2004). Boston, MA: Houghton Mifflin.

4 Quantitative Intersectionality

A Critical Race Analysis of the Chicana/o Educational Pipeline

Alejandro Covarrubias

As a child, I was intrigued by exploring the most despised words in the American language within dictionaries. A native Spanish speaker, I looked to the dictionary as a resource to teach me about America's standard language, the "language of power" (Delpit, 2006). In my home we were permitted to speak only Spanish by our father; he told us of the great assets we would become in a changing American society as bilingual adults. Yet in the public sphere, especially in school, the power of the English language was clear. My second-grade teacher would teach me this poignant lesson the day she decided to change my name to its anglicized version by declaring, "I will call you Alex." She would rob me of that part of my identity until I would have the courage to reclaim it as an undergraduate in college.

I guess I was always a critical race theorist, conducting my own content analysis of dictionaries, looking up the words *bitch*, *wetback*, *nigger*, *fag*, and many others that demarcated the ways in which power was used to construct our intersecting identities and carry out its violence upon us. In the fifth grade, my attempt to problematize one of these words got me into serious trouble with my White, 30something teacher. After encountering the word *bitch* in one of *her* dictionaries, I used it in its grammatically correct form referring to the family dog, which was female. I remember that my intentional construction of the essay revolved around my desire to use the word, so I built my story around it.

This pivotal decision was preceded by me approaching the teacher in astonishment at the fact that the word *bitch* was in an American dictionary. She immediately forbade me to use it without any discussion of its historical violence upon women. In reflection, I wonder whether she was attempting to intervene in my emerging matriculation into patriarchal norms or whether she was recentering her Whiteness in this power struggle between herself and an 11-year-old Mexican boy. Nonetheless, that moment would transform my educational experience and lead to many incidents of her targeting me as a "temperamental" child who "talked too much," labels that would follow me through my journey along the educational pipeline.

On a recent trip to the library at a small liberal arts college near my home, I encountered one of the biggest dictionaries I have ever seen: an aged

Webster's Dictionary that must have weighed about 40 pounds. I happened upon this formidable document perched upon its own ornate pedestal, making its importance known to the passerby. My curiosity immediately took me to the copyright page of this record to discover its 1976 publication date. I immediately jumped to the N's, encountering the most reviled word in America's heritage. Its meaning of record indicated what I read as an uncommitted attempt to critique the word's usage and history: "1a: NEGRO— usu. Taken to be offensive b: a member (as an East Indian, a Filipino, an Egyptian) of any very dark-skinned race—usu. Taken to be offensive . . ." (Grove, 1976). I then jumped to the W's and read what I interpreted as a matter-of-fact and contemptuous depiction of Mexicans with no critique of the word's practice: "a Mexican who enters the U.S. illegally (as by wading or swimming the Rio Grande) <~s . . . willing to work for nothing if a rancher would conceal them—Irving Shulman>—compare to Bracero" (Grove, 1976). As my daughter walked up behind me, I hurriedly changed the page, responding vaguely, "I was looking up something," when she asked, "What are you doing?"

There are many formal and concrete ways that we are taught to look at differences among people. Often, we learn to assign value to these differences that serve to elevate the status of some people while diminishing the worth of others. These differences and their value, in turn, become "natural" to us because they become so widespread and consistently used. Just as these variations are made concrete and assigned a value within this dictionary, they are also assigned value and formalized through our educational experiences in schools. There, we again are taught to place positive and negative values on differences that may exist among various types of students. These distinctions then lead educators, administrators, and students themselves to perceive various groups of students differently. Perceptions of students ultimately become so persistent and pervasive that they can impact educational outcomes for people who are labeled by these terms, in some cases diminishing their potential.

The microagressions (Solorzano, 1998) found in the dictionary and in the classroom are merely reflections of the highly organized, historical relationships that have utilized the social constructions of race, class, gender, sexuality, and immigration status to separate people and assign them disparate value. Although it is widely recognized that these identity markers are historically and socially constructed, this does not negate the fact that they create uniquely lived experiences for people labeled by them, including creating disadvantage for some while privileging others. The relationship systems that use these identifiers (i.e., racism, sexism, nativism, class-based discrimination, etc.) also intersect in people's daily lives so that they have the potential to simultaneously create privilege and oppressive conditions for the same individuals within different conditions. For example, a man of color can simultaneously be paid more for the same job that a woman of color may be paid for but much less than his White counterpart. Hence, there can be simultaneously oppressive and privileging conditions based on the intersection of these systems. Schools have traditionally been one of the institutions that have served to create and maintain such demarcations among people and to establish and sustain their corresponding systems of relationships. They are often the places where we learn to "act like boys," first express our sexuality, perform our class identities, identify the "aliens" among us, and claim a racial or ethnic identity.

Schools are often the site of the adoption of such constructs by individuals and the site where those in power simultaneously ascribe these labels and their accompanying characteristics to students; both processes often have significant consequences for our educational opportunities and trajectories, as they will frequently impact the expectations and aspirations we have for ourselves and those that others have of us. Such belief systems can, and regularly do, lead to a distinction of resource availability for different groups that can significantly shape educational outcomes at all levels.

In this article, I utilize the framework of intersectionality to explore the educational trajectory of those who identify themselves as being of Mexican ancestry.[1] Coined by Kimberly Crenshaw (1989), *intersectionality* refers to the ways in which interconnected systems of domination based on race, class, gender, sexuality, and other social constructions simultaneously impact the lives of all people as they engage in socially mediated relationships and in their interaction with society and its institutions (Crenshaw, 1989, 1991). It seeks to move beyond singularly defined sociological theories that reduce our experiences as influenced by narrow and essentialist definitions of the self (Valdes, 1995, 1997). Intersectionality similarly challenges the notion that we live in a postcolonialist society in which these socially constructed divisions no longer impact or are impacted by power. Furthermore, it posits that institutions remain impacted by political projects that are guided by maintaining existing power relations at the expense of vulnerable populations along multiple intersecting continuums of difference. These political projects both are guided by and predictably, yet variably, influence the complex social relationships in which people partake daily—thus, this intersectionality happens at the macro levels of society and its institutions and at the same time is played out in our micro and intimate relationships on a day-to-day basis.

The Chicana/o Pipeline

The Chicana/o educational pipeline, first introduced by Daniel G. Solorzano (Solorzano, Villalpando, & Oseguera, 2005), has been widely utilized to (a) capture a snapshot of current educational realities for people of Mexican descent, (b) depict a predictable pattern of educational outcomes, and (c) offer policy recommendations aimed at transforming the unjust experiences summarized by the pipeline. Despite its obvious utility for these efforts, to date the pipeline has conflated many variables that limit our ability to truly describe the nuanced experiences of those of Mexican descent. This conflation challenges our ability to provide specifically effective policy and practice recommendations that address the various dimensions of diversity within this population, including race, gender, immigration status, and class. The homogenization of this population has also led many to essentialize the Chicano experience and to make that of the Chicano citizen the norm.

Following the critical race tradition of "asking the race question," Daniel Solorzano would transform the framework of the "educational pipeline" by prioritizing race as an analytical lens. Impressed by the work of Alexander "Sandy" Astin, who originated the pipeline as a conceptual framework, Solorzano,[2] similar to critical race theorists who would put race and racism at the forefront of the study of jurisprudence, would capture a snapshot of the educational outcomes for the most numerous racial groups in America. The education pipeline model has been useful for presenting data, revealing trends, and presenting the sequential patterns of success or failure for groups along their academic journeys. It has similarly been useful for educators and policymakers to make meaningful decisions about where to concentrate efforts and resources for addressing leakage points, or the many points of exit for students from various educational institutions.

Intersectionality Along the Educational Pipeline

Those familiar with the educational pipeline were accustomed to seeing it as an excellent tool for visually displaying the educational path of various racial groups as they collectively made their way through their academic careers. Of course, the pipelines we were used to seeing often showed us that the academic careers of people of color were short lived and that most Chicanas and Chicanos never made it past high school. Nonetheless, the tool was useful and we were amazed at the simple elegance of this framework for helping us share our stories. We were especially impressed when the pipeline began with the simple yet telling intersection of race and gender, giving us the capacity to witness the points of divergence between male and female students and eventually the slow but inevitable higher academic outcomes for women of color compared to men of color. When I presented these data to my students, they questioned whether the data accounted for their various experiences—How about immigrants? How about working-class people? What about the middle-class U.S. citizen? All of these questions led me on a quest to "ask the other question" (Matsuda, 1991, p. 1189).

The goal of this quest was to do what many scholars had effectively done for the past few decades: that is, to capture the nuances of our lives as the intersecting systems of oppression simultaneously acted upon us while we resisted or reenacted them. Much of this work has effectively demonstrated that our lives and relationships to others, and institutions, are complicated. We experience these relationships through the simultaneity of our multiple political and social identities as mediated by external conditions and context. Hence, we live a life in which we are constantly recreating ourselves while the inertia of power continues to maintain itself and define us in ways that shape our opportunities.

Schools, at all levels, often serve to try to make us fit within these prescribed norms (Freire, 2008). Although many of us constantly attempt to deconstruct and resist existing prescriptive social constructs and expected roles for those constructs, they are accepted by most and often ratified in policies and practices. For example, we know that in schools, most Chicanas and Chicanos are not tracked toward college readiness but rather relegated to underresourced, overcrowded schools where they are taught by less experienced teachers and are often taught curricula that are the least valued (Oakes, 1985; Valencia, 2002; Yosso, 2006). Both Chicanas and Chicanos, although often relegated to vocational tracks, are tracked distinctly based on their gender. Chicanas are often tracked into courses like home economics, typing, sewing, and cooking, whereas Chicanos are steered into woodshop, auto mechanics, welding, and sports. These directives can often shape what we perceive as being within our capacity to do. They also ultimately can shape our career decisions and life opportunities.

The intersectional analysis of the Chicana/Chicano educational pipeline, therefore, becomes critical to understanding how practices and policies within educational institutions have impacted our eventual outcomes. Although it does not provide us a detailed narrative of what happened within the schooling experiences of the diverse members of this diverse group, it gives us the patterns that have resulted from varied experiences shaped by the prescriptions that have often been imposed on its members. Qualitative research has done a great deal to help us understand these narratives, and it provides rich counterstories that shed light on the lived experiences of diverse people of color (Delgado Bernal, 2001; Solorzano, 1998; Solórzano & Yosso, 2001, 2002a, 2002b; Yosso, 2006). But quantitative intersectionality helps tell a broader story and captures patterns that cut across space and time. The quantitative intersectionality in this study uses the most recent census data to capture the impact of the intersection of race/ethnicity, class, gender, and citizenship status.

Methodology

Data for this study were gathered through the publicly available Census software Data Ferret. This software makes several Census databases available to the public for research purposes. For this project, I used the March 2009 Supplement of the Current Population Survey, the most complete, recent data available with the variables of interest. These data are gathered and reported annually for a strategic and representative sample of the general population that is then statistically extrapolated to provide accurate projections of the rest of the population. The Current Population Survey is collected monthly for 50,000 American households and is used to report national labor statistics. It also contains detailed data on educational attainment for all respondents. I was specifically interested in gathering data on educational attainment for people of Mexican descent and disaggregating them by multiple factors. Thus, I was able to download these data along race/ethnicity and select for those Latinas/os who identified as "Mexican." I further disaggregated these data by gender, class, and citizenship status using the five categories of citizenship used by the Census: (a) born in the United States, (b) born in Puerto Rico or another outlying area of the United States, (c) born abroad of U.S.-citizen parents, (d) naturalized citizen, and (e) noncitizen. For the purpose of creating these intersectional pipelines, the focus was on categories (a), (d), and (e), as these represented the highest number of respondents among Mexican-origin people.

Attainment data for this study only utilized data for the population aged 25 and older. This approach has been used by several scholars to gather (Rumberger, 1991), disaggregate, and analyze data on attainment rates, as it usually is able to capture the most representational sample of the population to attain terminal degrees (meaning these people are not likely to return to earn a high school diploma beyond this age or to earn advanced degrees prior to it, either). Of course, this creates some limitations in that it may not capture those cases in which older adults return to school to complete a high school degree or other cases in which advanced degrees are earned at a very young age. Nonetheless, it is the most representative sample of the population available and is a method utilized consistently across comparison groups.

The U.S. Census does not have a measure of wealth that can be accurately used to account for class status. Hence, I used family income to come up with four equally distributed quartiles as a proxy for class. It is recognized that family income does not capture the importance of accumulated wealth for determining class, especially privilege. However, it does provide a consistently reported measure that was used to compare groups' economic circumstances.

Findings

An updated analysis of the Chicano educational pipeline demonstrates that people of Mexican origin continue to be failed by American educational institutions at all levels. Figure 4.1 demonstrates that 44% of students entering the educational pipeline are eventually pushed out before completing a high school diploma. Of the remaining 56% who graduate from high school, 27 will enroll in college, some going to community college and others enrolling in 4-year universities. We find that of the 27 who move on to college, 5 will terminate their educational journey having earned only an associate's degree, whereas 10 will earn a baccalaureate. Still, of those who enter college, 12 (44%) will be pushed out prematurely, having earned no degree. Of the 10 with a bachelor's degree, only 2 will earn a graduate or professional degree, and an insufficient 0.2 will earn a doctorate.

These findings, although showing some improvements from 2000 Census data for this group (Yosso & Solorzano, 2006), continue to illustrate that Chicanas/os are the poorest served students of all of America's sizeable racialized

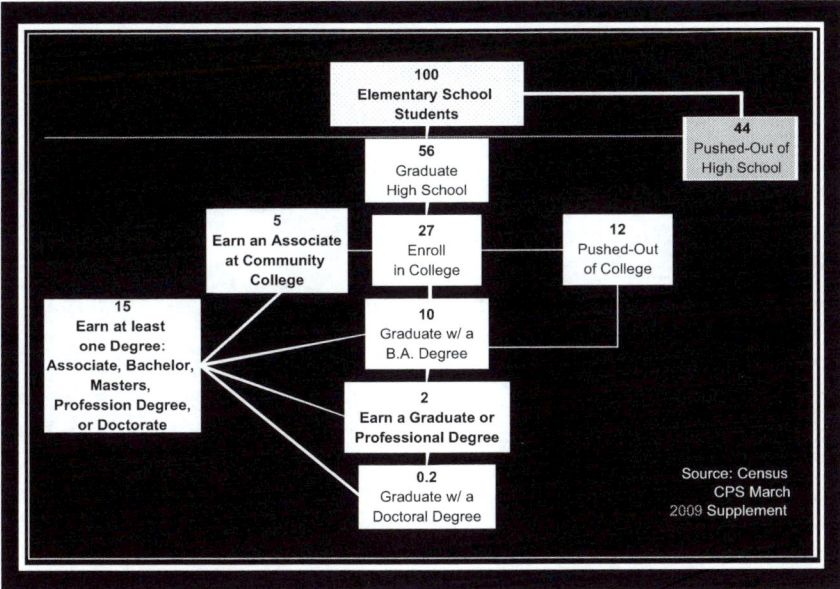

Figure 4.1 The Chicana/o (Mexican) Educational Pipeline.

B.A.=bachelor's degree; CPS=Current Population Survey. (Figure is provided in color online.)

groups. Nonetheless, race alone cannot account for the disparate outcomes captured in the pipeline.

As previously demonstrated by Yosso and Solorzano (2006), disaggregating educational outcomes for Mexican-origin people by gender provides a more complete portrait of the state of education for Chicanas and Chicanos. Figure 4.2 shows that when the data are disaggregated, Chicanas outperform their Chicano counterparts at all points along the educational pipeline. Chicanos are pushed out of high school at higher rates; earn fewer high school diplomas; and earn fewer associate's, bachelor's, master's, professional, and doctoral degrees. And although fewer Chicanos than Chicanas are pushed out of college, this is only the case because they enroll in college in fewer numbers—the college push-out rate for Chicanas is 46% compared to 45% for Chicanos. This pattern reveals a trend that has been in the making for more than two decades, as Chicanas were once outperformed by Chicanos at all levels of education. Even so, finding the distinct outcomes for Chicanos and Chicanas is only part of the quest to understand the varied educational outcomes and experiences of people of Mexican ancestry and to capture the impact of socially constructed variables that make up different aspects of our identity.

Although the intersections of race/ethnicity and gender yield a telling pipeline, there remains a conflation of citizenship that conceals vast educational outcomes for Mexican-origin people of distinct legal statuses. In order

66 *Alejandro Covarrubias*

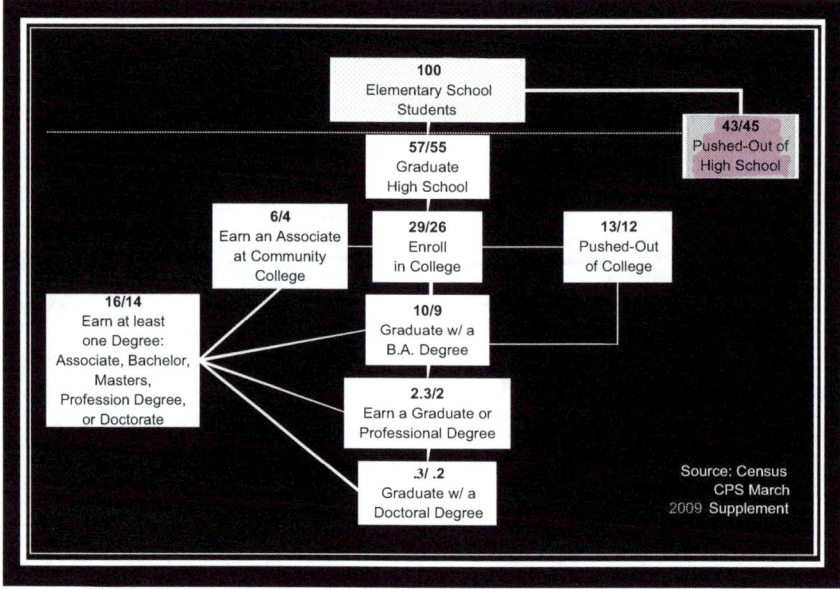

Figure 4.2 The Chicana/o (Mexican) Educational Pipeline Disaggregated by Gender.
B.A.=bachelor's degree; CPS=Current Population Survey. (Figure is provided in color online.)

to exhibit this varied range of achievement as impacted by legal status, I offer Figures 4.3–4.5 to illustrate the educational outcomes for Mexican-origin people who are noncitizens, U.S.-born citizens, and foreign-born naturalized citizens, respectively.

Figure 4.3 presents the dismal educational outcomes for noncitizen Mexicans. It shows that nearly two-thirds of noncitizen men and women are pushed out of school before being presented with a high school diploma, leaving slightly more than a third to continue their perilous trek through the educational pipeline. Of those who do get a high school diploma, only about a third will enroll in college, with only five earning a baccalaureate and one receiving a graduate or professional degree. Although we see the pattern of Chicanas outperforming Chicanos at different levels of education, we also see that compared to the pipeline in Figure 4.2, this one shows a couple locations where Chicanos outperform Chicanas. For example, men attain doctoral degrees at twice the rate of women, and Chicanas are pushed out of college at a slightly higher rate than Chicanos. Thus, the broader Chicana/o educational pipeline obscures differences in educational outcomes associated with the intersection of race, gender, and noncitizenship status.

Figure 4.4 illustrates the clear privilege of American citizenship. Those Mexican-origin people granted citizenship by virtue of their birthright are more than twice as likely as noncitizen Mexicans to earn a high school diploma and nearly 3 times less likely to be pushed out before receiving

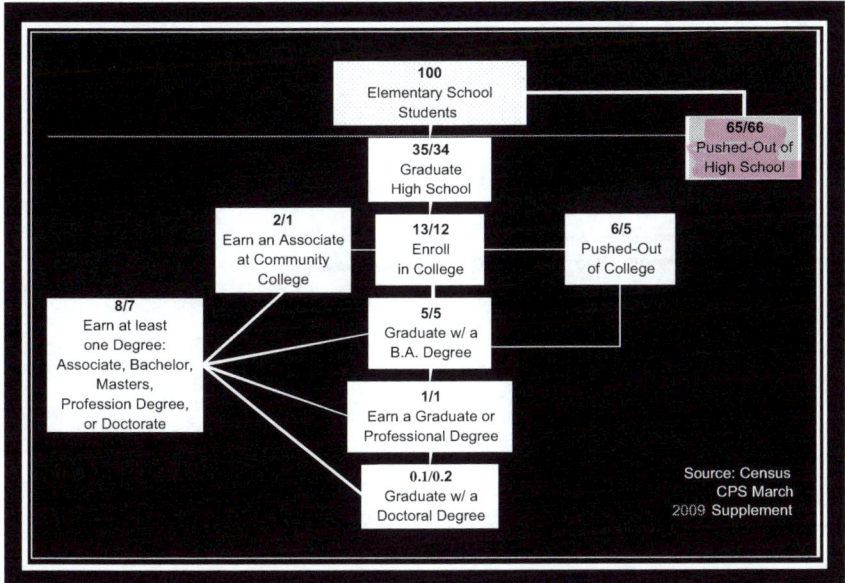

Figure 4.3 The Noncitizen Mexican Educational Pipeline Disaggregated by Gender.
B.A.=bachelor's degree; CPS=Current Population Survey. (Figure is provided in color online.)

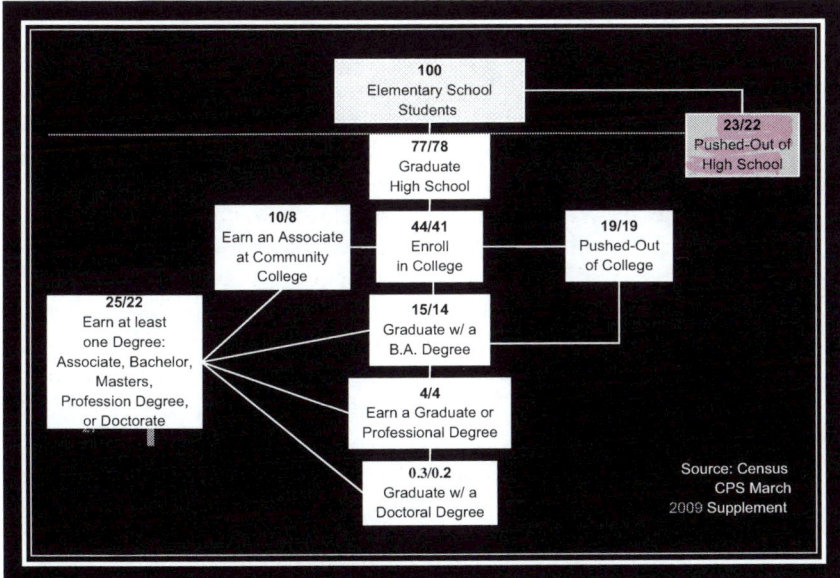

Figure 4.4 The U.S.-Born Mexican Educational Pipeline Disaggregated by Gender.
B.A.=bachelor's degree; CPS=Current Population Survey. (Figure is provided in color online.)

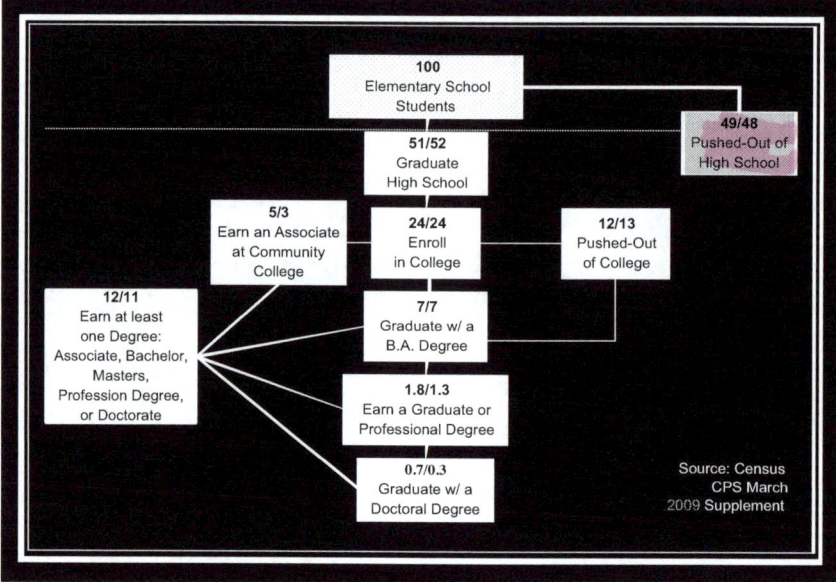

Figure 4.5 The Foreign-Born Naturalized Mexican Educational Pipeline Disaggregated by Gender.
B.A.=bachelor's degree; CPS=Current Population Survey. (Figure is provided in color online.)

their diploma. In addition, more than 4 in 10 of the original 100 U.S.-born Mexican-origin students who enter elementary school will enroll in college, with women having a higher likelihood of enrolling and earning some type of degree. These numbers are roughly 3 times the rate of their noncitizen Mexican counterparts. Moreover, 15 U.S.-born Mexican-origin women will earn a bachelor's degree compared to 14 U.S.-born Mexican-origin men, whereas 10 of the original 100 women will end their academic careers with an associate's degree and 8 men will do the same. The baccalaureate degree attainment rate for U.S.-born women is 3 times the rate for noncitizen Mexican women, and the bachelor's degree rate is nearly 3 times more for U.S.-born Mexican-origin men than for noncitizen Mexican men. Of those who make it beyond the bachelor's, four men and four women of Mexican origin who are U.S. born will earn a graduate or professional degree, with 50% more women (0.3 of the original 100 female students) earning doctorates than men (0.2 of the original 100 male students). Again, we see a fourfold graduate or professional degree attainment rate for U.S.-born Mexican-origin men and women in relation to noncitizen U.S.-born men and women. These consistently and significantly higher attainment rates for the U.S.-born Mexican-origin population than noncitizen Mexican-origin people point to the importance of citizenship and the rights and privileges associated with this sociopolitical designation. They also affirm the significance of nativist racist ideologies that drive down attainment rates for Mexican transnational migrants (Perez Huber, Benavidez Lopes, Malagon, Velez, & Solórzano, 2008).

Foreign-born Mexicans who eventually become citizens gain legal, social, and political status that can lead to educational privileges, resulting in generally higher educational attainment rates than for Mexican nationals in the United States who are noncitizens. Still, they attain lower rates than U.S.-born Chicanos. Figure 4.5 shows that 51 (51%) girls and 52 (52%) boys out of 100 elementary students who are naturalized citizens of Mexican descent successfully earn high school diplomas, with 24 of each group successfully enrolling in college. These college enrollment numbers for Mexican-born naturalized Americans are twice as high as those for noncitizens of Mexican origin and nearly half those for U.S.-born Chicanas/os, again showing an impact continuum for citizenship status. Naturalized Mexicans demonstrate an outlier in this consistent citizenship pattern given that 0.7% of female students will earn a doctoral degree, more than twice the rate for men in this group, 7 times the rate for female noncitizens, and 2.5 times the rate for U.S.-born women. This result challenges the additive perspective of understanding the combined and simultaneously nuanced manner that different systems of oppression take on when they intersect.

Figures 4.3, 4.4, and 4.5 provide evidence that the intersection of race, gender, and immigration status consistently leads to women outperforming men, woven in with an upswing in performance as legal rights and social status increase through citizenship. These patterns, however, do not explain all of the variability that exists in educational attainment among a heterogeneous Mexican-origin population. Another clear pattern that occurs when the data are disaggregated is the positively correlated relationship between class and educational attainment rate—that is, as class increases for Mexican-origin Americans, these people have greater educational success (see Figure 4.6). The high school push-out rate for the Mexican-origin population decreases as their income level rises, from a high of 60% for the lowest quartile to 16% for the highest quartile. Conversely, high school attainment rates increase for Chicanas/os as their income level rises, from as low as 40% for the lowest quartile to as high as 84% for the highest quartile. These skewed outcomes typically result in the Mexican-origin population having generally low attainment rates, because most Chicanas/os live in working-class conditions in which they face underresourced schools that spend a great deal of money on surveillance and enforcement, have the least experienced teachers, have densely populated schools, and are marked by other factors that hinder educational success. Case in point, as few as 3 of the original 100 Mexican-origin students from the lowest quartile will successfully navigate the pipeline to earn a baccalaureate, and only 0.6 will get a master's or professional degree. On the other end of the spectrum, nearly 7 in 10 (67%) Chicanas/os from the highest quartile will enroll in college, with 30 (30%) continuing on to a bachelor's, 9 (9%) getting a graduate or professional degree, and 0.73 earning their doctorate. This developing trend demonstrates the effects of class privilege.

70 *Alejandro Covarrubias*

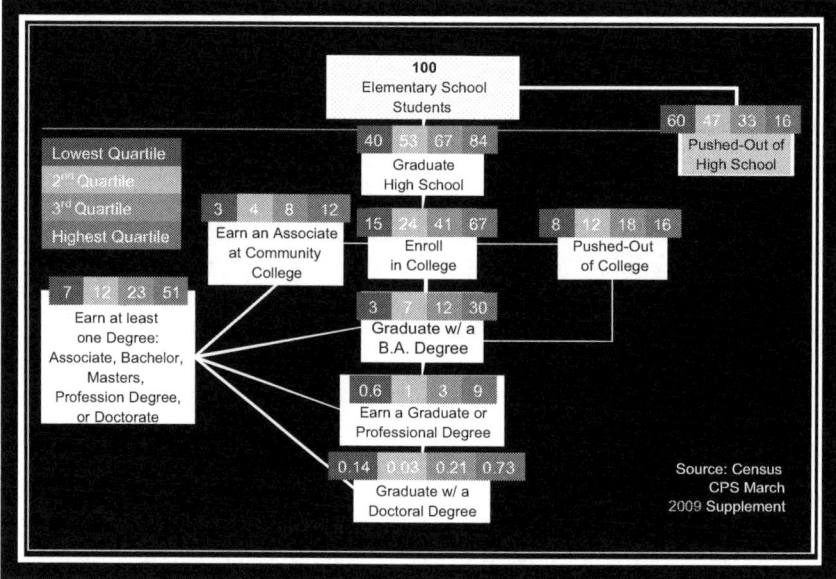

Figure 4.6 The Chicana/o (Mexican) Educational Pipeline by Class.
B.A.=bachelor's degree; CPS=Current Population Survey. (Figure is provided in color online.)

Clearly, the pattern of class being positively correlated with educational attainment continues throughout the educational pipeline with a couple exceptions. The highest college push-out numbers (18 and 16) are concentrated in the two highest quartiles; however, this is only a reflection of the very high college enrollment numbers. These numbers represent 44% (third quartile) and 24% (highest quartile) of college push-out rates within their class, well above the 53% (lowest quartile) and 50% (second quartile) for the lowest two income brackets. Among doctoral degree recipients we see that the lowest quartile of Mexican-origin people has more than 4 times the rate (0.14) of doctorates compared to the second quartile (0.03). The doctoral degree attainment for those earning a bachelor's degree is 5%, one tenth of 1%, 2%, and 2% for Quartiles 1, 2, 3, and 4, respectively. This marks a significant break in the pattern revealed throughout the pipeline that may signal a resilience attribute (Yosso, 2006) and perseverance among lower income Chicanas/os. This finding requires more research to learn what may impede doctoral degree attainment for second-quartile Chicanas/os.

Even when class was controlled across all of the major groups in the United States, we find that Latinas/os generally, and Chicanas/os specifically, continue to be pushed out at the highest levels among all major racialized groups in the United States, regardless of class status (see Figure 4.7). A baseline for all of the distinct racialized groups combined yields a 13% push-out rate for Whites, 16% for African Americans, 12% for Asian Americans, 26% for

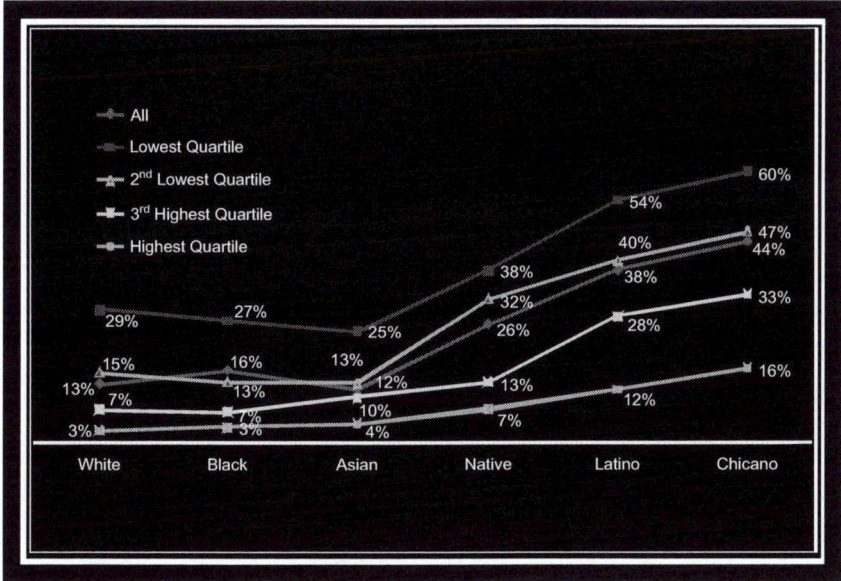

Figure 4.7 Push-Out Rates Controlled by Class.
Native = Native American. (Figure is provided in color online.)

Native Americans, 38% for Latinas/os, and 44% for Chicanas/os. Among those in the lowest quartile for each group, Whites have a 29% push-out rate, Blacks a 27% rate, Asians 25%, Native Americans 38%, Latinas/os 54%, and Chicanas/os a whopping 60%. This method of controlling for class reveals a surprisingly higher push-out rate for Whites than African Americans at the lowest quartile. Nonetheless, Native Americans, Latinas/os, and Chicanas/os are ejected from schools prematurely at significantly higher rates in this quartile. In the second quartile the pattern is repeated, although at a lower level: Whites (15%), Blacks (13%), Asians (13%), Native Americans (32%), Latinas/os (40%), and Chicanas/os (47%). Clearly, there remains a class impact across the board such that all push-out rates decrease as class increases, but Latinas/os and Chicanas/os continue to be disproportionately and negatively impacted. Asians and Blacks in this quartile are pushed out at the same rate, and Whites remain with a higher push-out rate compared to both. It is Native Americans, Latinas/os, and Chicanas/os who are pushed out at 2.5 times, 3 times, and 3.5 times the rates of others, respectively. In the fourth quartile, 7% of Whites and Blacks, 10% of Asians, 13% of Native Americans, 28% of Latinas/os, and 33% of Chicanas/os are pushed out before receiving their high school diploma. Most disturbing for this income bracket is that Chicanas/os within this third quartile are pushed out at a higher rate (33%) than Whites (29%), Blacks (27%), and Asians (25%) of the lowest quartile. These numbers should sound the alarm for policymakers and practitioners who suggest that with income comes access to schools with greater resources, which leads to better outcomes. For Latinas/os generally and for Chicanas/os specifically, access to quality education can clearly not be reduced to class alone. Nonetheless, there is also convincing evidence that for the most part, class is a predictable indicator of educational attainment for most groups and can at times reduce, but not eliminate, the impact of race. Finally, among the highest quartile individuals the marked distinctions from the previous series of data have been diminished but not erased: Whites (3%), Blacks (3%), Asians (4%), Native Americans (7%), Latinas/os (12%), and Chicanas/os (16%). In the last two quartiles class seems to have negated the attainment difference between Whites and Blacks, yet Asians remain undoubtedly more likely to complete their diploma. Still, Chicanos are as much as 5 times more likely to be pushed out, even in this class-privileged group. Evidently, a simple class-based analysis of the distinct educational outcomes for the different racial groups will not suffice. We need to utilize a more complex intersectional analysis that captures the various impacts of these multiple social constructions.

Figures 4.8 and 4.9 capture the intersection of race, class, gender, and citizenship status in relation to being pushed out before earning a high school diploma and attaining a bachelor's degree, respectively. These figures offer a multidimensional cross-tabulation, or a quantitative intersectional analysis that provides the most complete account of the simultaneous impact of race,

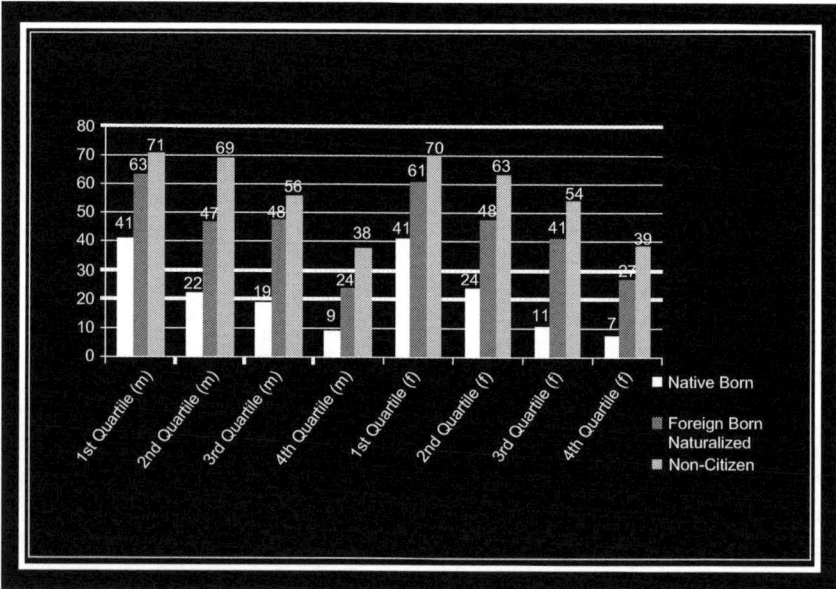

Figure 4.8 Chicano/a High School Push-Out by Class, Gender, and Citizenship Status. (Figure is provided in color online.)

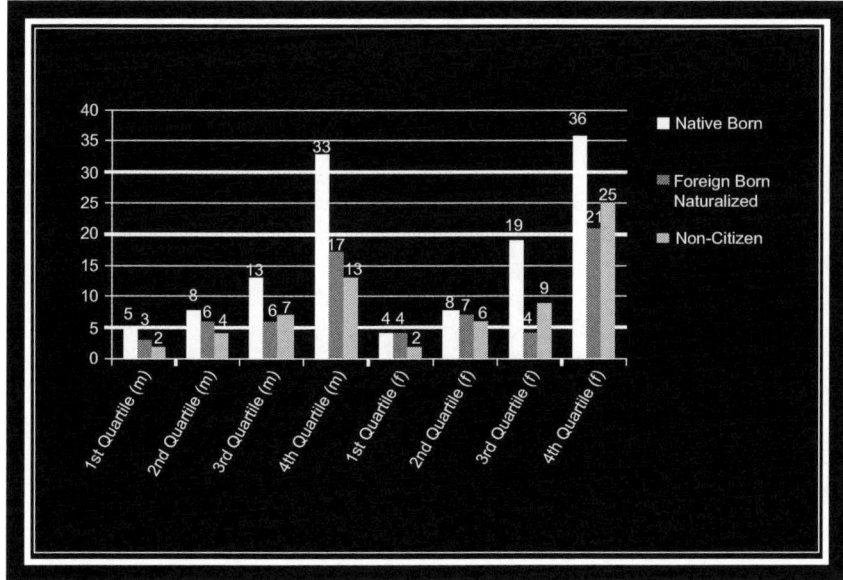

Figure 4.9 Chicano/a Baccalaureates by Class, Gender, and Citizenship Status.
(Figure is provided in color online.)

class, gender, and immigration status on Chicanas and Chicanos. With it, we can trace the clear patterns that each of these social constructs has on this population individually and collectively. We can also arrive at more sophisticated within-group comparisons. For example, in Figure 4.8 we can see that although native-born Chicanas/os tend to get pushed out in lesser numbers than their foreign-born Mexican brothers and sisters, native-born immigrant men from the lowest class quartile (41%) are pushed out more frequently than fourth-quartile noncitizen Mexican-origin women (39%). This type of analysis reveals the complexity of intersectionality, that it does not allow us to essentialize the Chicana/o experience but rather complicates our investigation to expose more multifaceted relationships.

In many of the previous pipelines we saw an overwhelming pattern of Chicanos being outperformed by their Chicana counterparts. However, this intersectional analysis brings to light that this pattern is often disrupted by the intersection of multiple constructs. For instance, if one looks at native-born Mexican-origin men from the first to the fourth quartiles, their push-out rates predictably decrease (first, 41%; second, 22%; third, 19%; and fourth, 9%). Similarly, native-born Mexican-origin women's push-out rates decrease as their family income levels rise (first, 41%; second, 24%; third, 11%; and fourth, 7%). Still, the once predictable pattern of women outperforming men is interrupted. In the lowest quartile, native-born Chicanas and Chicanos are pushed out at the same rates. In the second quartile, U.S.-born Chicanos are pushed out less (22%). Surprisingly, in the third quartile, U.S.-born Chicanos are pushed out at a 73% higher rate (19%) than native-born Chicanas in the same quartile (11%). Returning to the often seen pattern, we find that Chicanos who are U.S. born and who are from the fourth quartile are more likely to be pushed out (9%) than U.S.-born female fourth-quartilers of Mexican origin (7%).

Another clear benefit of quantitative intersectionality is the ability to uncover often concealed anomalies that may require further investigation, including qualitative intersectional analyses. Figure 4.8 unravels several noteworthy comparisons that raise more questions for investigation. Quartile 3 is the location of a couple of these: Both foreign-born naturalized (48%) and U.S.-born (19%) Mexican-origin men from the third quartile are pushed out at dramatically higher rates than their female counterparts (41% and 11%, respectively). These findings beg the question of why there is such a pronounced gender difference in push-out rates in this third quartile that seemingly disproportionately impacts Chicano citizen men. Another equally intriguing disparity is exposed within the second quartile, in which noncitizen Mexican-descent men (69%) are much more likely to be pushed out than noncitizen Mexican-descent women (63%) in the same quartile. These obvious patterns require that we hear from the people most impacted by these outcomes, those living with their implications. They require that we qualitatively investigate the stories of those at the "bottom of the well" (Bell, 1992) and provide the rich counternarratives (Yosso, 2006) that can help us make sense of these patterns. However, these patterns would have been nearly impossible to capture had a quantitative intersectional approach not been utilized. Figure 4.9 provides more evidence of the utility of this approach.

Figure 4.9 shows an intersectional analysis of how race, class, gender, and citizenship status impact baccalaureate degree attainment for Mexican-origin people residing in the United States. Evident are the expected patterns: The greater one's income, the greater the likelihood of attaining a bachelor's degree; citizenship is more strongly associated with baccalaureate attainment than noncitizenship; and Mexican-origin women generally outperform Mexican-origin men. Though these findings are important, an intersectional analysis puts this portrait more in focus, revealing many of the details lost in general investigations using singular analytical lenses (i.e., race, class, gender, or citizenship). A case in point is an analysis of the third quartile, in which we find that 13% of U.S.-born men of Mexican origin earn a bachelor's degree compared to 19% of U.S.-born women of Mexican origin. This intersection reveals a distinct effect that leads to a significant difference in baccalaureate attainment between men and women within such conditions. There is an even more fascinating discovery in the fourth quartile, in which noncitizen Chicanas earn bachelor's degrees at more than 100% the rate of noncitizen Chicanos. This finding demonstrates a never before captured pattern that challenges deficit-based perspectives of immigrant women. It also compels researchers to investigate further this important disparity, as this group of noncitizen women outperforms both men and women of all quartiles and all citizens with the exception of U.S. native-born Chicanas/os of the fourth quartile. It challenges us to explore the cultural assets that these women share that make them persevere despite adverse conditions.

Conclusions

Latinas/os, two thirds of whom are of Mexican origin, have been the largest minority group in the United States for more than a decade, yet they continue to be the most poorly served by American educational institutions. We have found here what others have found elsewhere, that at all levels of the educational pipeline Chicana/o educational outcome rates are alarming (Valencia, 2002; Yosso & Solorzano, 2006). Indeed, Chicanas/os are pushed out before completing their high school diploma at much higher rates, and they earn fewer baccalaureate, graduate, professional, and doctoral degrees than any other major racialized group in the United States (Covarrubias, Solorzano, & Velez, 2010). Still, these trends conceal within-group patterns that tell of the distinct impact of various forms of subordinations. Lost is often the impact of gender-based discrimination, patriarchy, class inequality, nativist racism, and their interconnected effects. This study has demonstrated that, undeniably, there exists an intersectional effect that leads to disparate within-group educational outcomes. Armed with this information, gathered only through a quantitative intersectional analysis, practitioners, researchers, policymakers, and families can begin to make intentional and concerted efforts to understand and address the impact of these power relations, especially where they intersect.

Clearly, this methodological approach warrants further exploration as it unmistakably produces elusive quantitative patterns at the intersection of race, class, gender, and citizenship status. Notwithstanding this fact, there remains the need to expand intersectional analyses to capture the impact of other forms of subordination, including those related to disability, sexuality, language and others, at their intersection with those explored here. We must also explore how these intersections impact other racialized groups historically so as to capture and understand the historically nuanced ways in which diverse Americans have experienced various intersections. Lastly, findings from any research are only as good as the data source. Without a doubt, Census data are the most widely available data, used regularly to record trends and predict patterns throughout the country. However, Census Current Population Survey data, which are gathered monthly, although more comprehensive, have a much lower completion rate than decennial Census data. Therefore, there remains a need to capture more educational data at smaller geographic levels in order to have greater control and more precise predictability.

Critical race theorists and others before them have long made the case for telling our own stories to counter the often prescriptively destructive grand narratives about our communities, especially for those most impacted by injustice (Delgado, 1999; Yosso, 2006). Many of us have done so, relying on qualitative research to richly detail the particulars of our experiences. These often vivid depictions are capable of peeling back the layers of injustice, capturing the distinct and interconnected nature of various forms of subordination. However, the method used in this study can provide us with an alternative way of telling our collective stories by uncovering the specific and intersectional effects of the multiple constructs that help shape our realities, especially as they relate to our educational experiences and outcomes across the Chicana and Chicano educational pipelines.

Notes

1. *People of Mexican descent, Mexican origin,* and *Mexican ancestry* are used interchangeably in this article to signify all people who are themselves of Mexican background or whose family lineage is of Mexican origin. *Chicana* and *Chicano* are also used to refer to this same group on several occasions. Chicana and Chicano is a sociopolitical identity adopted by many people of Mexican origin who are committed to the political project of transforming unjust relations of power.
2. Although Daniel Solorzano is well known for his work with educational pipelines, he credits Alexander "Sandy" Austin, his colleague, for introducing him to this method of capturing and presenting data (D. Solorzano, personal conversation, May 14, 2010).

References

Bell, D. (1992). *Faces at the bottom of the well: The permanence of racism.* New York, NY: Basic Books.

Covarrubias, A., Solorzano, D., & Velez, V. (2010). *The Chicana/o pipeline revisited: Ten years later.* Unpublished manuscript, UCLA Chicano Studies Research Center, Los Angeles, CA.

Crenshaw, K. (1989). Demarginalizing the intersection of race and sex: A black feminist critique of antidiscrimination doctrine, feminist theory and antiracist politics. *University of Chicago Legal Forum, 1989,* 139–166.

Crenshaw, K. (1991). Mapping the margins: Intersectionality, identity politics, and violence against women of color. *Stanford Law Review, 43,* 1241–1252.

Delgado, R. (1999). *When equality ends: Stories about race and resistance.* Boulder, CO: Westview.

Delgado Bernal, D. (2001). Learning and living pedagogies of the home: The Mestiza consciousness of Chicana students. *International Journal of Qualitative Studies in Education, 14,* 623–639.

Delpit, L. (2006). *Other people's Children: Cultural conflict in the classroom.* New York, NY: New Press.

Freire, P. (2008). *Education for critical consciousness.* London: Continuum.

Grove, P. B. (Ed.). (1976). *Webster's third new international dictionary of the English language unabridged.* Springfield, MA: G. & C. Merriam.

Matsuda, M. (1991). Beside my sister, facing the enemy: Legal theory out of coalition. *Stanford Law Review, 43,* 1183–1189.

Matsuda, M. (1996). *Where is your body? And other essays on race, gender and the law.* Boston, MA: Beacon.

Oakes, J. (1985). *Keeping track: How schools structure inequality*. New Haven, CT: Yale University Press.
Perez Huber, L., Benavidez Lopes, C., Malagon, M., Velez, V., & Solórzano, D. (2008). Getting beyond the "symptom," acknowledging the "disease": Theorizing racist nativism. *Contemporary Justice Review, 11*(1), 39–51.
Rumberger, R. (1991). Chicano drop-out: A review of research and policy issues. In R. Valencia (Ed.), *Chicano school failure and success: research and policy agendas for the 1990's* (pp. 64–89). London: Falmer.
Solorzano, D. G. (1998). Critical race theory, race and gender microaggressions, and the experience of Chicana and Chicano scholars. *Qualitative Studies in Education, 11*(1), 121–136.
Solorzano, D. G., Villalpando, O., & Oseguera, L. (2005). Educational inequities and Latina/o undergraduate students in the United States: A critical race analysis of their educational progress. *Journal of Hispanic Higher Education, 4*(3), 272–294.
Solórzano, D. G., & Yosso, T. (2001). Critical race and LatCrit theory and method: Counterstorytelling Chicana and Chicano graduate school experiences. *International Journal of Qualitative Studies in Education, 14*, 471–495.
Solórzano, D. G., & Yosso, T. (2002a). A critical race counterstory of affirmative action in higher education. *Equity and Excellence in Education, 35*, 155–168.
Solórzano, D. G., & Yosso, T. (2002b). Critical race methodology: Counterstorytelling as an analytical framework for education research. *Qualitative Inquiry, 8*, 23–44.
Valdes, F. (1995). Sex and race in queer legal culture: Ruminations on identities and interconnectivities. *Southern California Review of Law and Women Studies, 5*, 25–49.
Valdes, F. (1997). Under construction: LatCrit consciousness, community, and theory. *California Law Review, 85*(5), 1087–1142.
Valencia, R. (Ed.). (2002). *Chicano school failure and success: Past, present, and future* (2nd ed.). New York, NY: Routledge Falmer.
Yosso, T. (2006). *Critical race counterstories along the Chicana/o educational pipeline*. New York, NY: Routledge.
Yosso, T., & Solorzano, D. G. (2006, March). *Leaks in the Chicana and Chicano educational pipeline* (Latino Policy & Issues Brief No. 13). Los Angeles, CA: UCLA Chicano Studies Research Center.

5 Challenges Facing Hispanic-Serving Institutions in the First Decade of the 21st Century

Alfredo G. de los Santos Jr. and Karina Michelle Cuamea

Educational excellence for Hispanics is a manifest destiny for America's economic and democratic success.—Thomas M. Fallo,[1] President, El Camino College, Torrance, CA

At the end of the first decade of the 21st century, the United States is having difficulty competing in a global economy that depends on a well-prepared workforce. At the same time, the country has experienced significant demographic changes that will affect future generations. Hispanics are now the largest minority group, making up 14.8% of the U.S. population; in 2006, 1 in 7 persons in the United States was Hispanic.[2] Hispanics as a group have a lower socioeconomic background compared to the total population. Hispanics, one of the youngest of all the racial/ethnic groups in the United States, are also less prepared to compete in the global marketplace.

Hispanics have historically enrolled in a relatively small number of institutions of higher education, creating what are now called Hispanic-serving institutions (HSIs).[3] The Hispanic population in the United States, which is projected to represent 1 in 5 Americans by 2030, could potentially become the workforce that will drive the economy in years to come, if a quality education is provided. The challenges and issues faced by the institutions that enroll 60% of Hispanic college students are thus important to the economic well-being of all Americans.

Review of the Literature

In this section we first provide a brief overview of the new economy and the importance of a prepared workforce, which is followed by some recent demographic data on Hispanics. After that, we provide the most recent data on Hispanics and higher education as well as projections of Hispanic high school graduation and college enrollment rates. This is followed by information about HSIs and the reasons Hispanics decide to enroll in these institutions.

The New Economy and Hispanics

In this section we provide information from recent national reports about the new economy, the current status of the United States in the global marketplace, and the importance of an educated and prepared workforce. In 1999, the Morrison Institute for Public Policy at Arizona State University described the

> new economy in terms of eight broad characteristics: (1) Technology is a given, (2) Globalism is here to stay, (3) Knowledge builds wealth, (4) People are the most important raw material, (5) There's no such thing as a smooth ride, (6) Competition is relentless, (7) Alliances are the way to get things done, (8) Place still matters—but for different reasons.
>
> (p. 7)

Two recent reports, both of which used a storm as a metaphor, have raised questions about the ability of the United States to compete successfully. *America's Perfect Storm: Three Forces Changing Our Nation's Future* focused on divergent skill distribution, the economy, and demographic trends (Kirsch, Braum, Yamamoto, & Sum, 2007). The first force, skill distribution,

> is evident in the findings of large-scale national and international surveys conducted over the past decades, which show that large numbers of our nation's adults do not have sufficient command of the literacy and numeracy skills needed to function effectively in an increasingly competitive work environment.
>
> (p. 6)

Almost one half (49%) of Hispanic adults tested at the lowest level for literacy, and one third (33%) tested at the second lowest level. Only 3% tested at the highest level, and 13% tested at the second highest level (p. 12).

The "seismic changes in our economy that have resulted in new sources of wealth, novel patterns of international trade, and a shift in the balance between capital and labor" make up the second major force that will affect the United States. These changes "have been driven by both technological innovation and globalization, resulting in a profound restructuring in the U.S. workplace" (Kirsch et al., 2007, p. 6).

The third force, sweeping demographic changes, will have a major effect on the country.

> Our population will become increasingly older and more diverse, with immigration having a significant impact on the composition of the workforce . . . Fueled by high birth rates and by immigration, the Hispanic share of the population is expected to grow from 14 percent in 2005 to slightly more than 20 percent by 2030.
>
> (Kirsch et al., 2007, p. 6)

Kirsch et al. (2007) noted that the United States is

> in the midst of a perfect storm in which these three powerful forces are combining to generate waves that already have had considerable

impact. . . . The forces behind this storm continue to gain strength, and calm seas are nowhere in sight.

(p. 7)

Similarly, the other report using a storm as a metaphor, *Rising Above the Gathering Storm: Energizing and Employing America for a Brighter Economic Future*, stressed the urgent need to preserve U.S. economic security, with a focus on science, technology, engineering, and mathematics (Committee on Prosperity in the Global Economy of the 21st Century, 2006). The Committee noted that the

> nation must prepare with great urgency to preserve its strategic and economic security. Because other countries have, and probably will continue to have, the competitive advantage of a low-wage structure, the United States must compete by optimizing its knowledge based resources, particularly in science and technology.
>
> (p. 4)

Two of the Committee's four recommendations focused specifically on education: K–12 education and higher education. One recommendation focused on strengthening the skills of teachers, which would in turn strengthen the skills of the students who will become our future leaders. The other recommendation focused on increasing the number of U.S. citizens achieving degrees in the sciences while continuing to improve the Visa process for international students and scholars (Committee on Prosperity in the Global Economy of the 21st Century, 2006, p. 4).

To summarize, recent reports have noted that, in a global economy that depends on a prepared, educated workforce and in which wealth is created by knowledge, the people who are projected to make up more than one fifth of the U.S. population by 2030—Hispanics—are some of the least educated and least prepared.

Demographics: Hispanics in the United States

In this section we discuss the growth of the Hispanic population in the United States (including both native-born and foreign-born Hispanics) and the median age of both native-born and foreign-born Hispanics.

In 2006, the Hispanic population of 44,298,975 represented 14.8% of the total population in the United States. Whereas the total population in the country increased by 6.1% from 2000 to 2006 (from 281,421,906 to 299,398,485), the Hispanic population increased by 25.8%. Of the total Hispanic population in 2006, 26,608,451, were native born, whereas 17,690,524 were foreign born (Pew Hispanic Center, 2008). Thus, in 2006, 1 out of 7 persons in the United States was Hispanic. By 2006, Hispanics were the largest minority group in the country. Moreover, 6 out of 10 Hispanics were native born.

The median age of U.S. Hispanics in 2006 was 27 years compared to 36 years for the total population. The median age of native-born female Hispanics was 18, and that of foreign-born female Hispanics was 37. The median age of male Hispanics born in the United States was only 17 compared to 35 among foreign-born male Hispanics (Pew Hispanic Center, 2008).

In 2006, the highest percentage of native-born U.S. Hispanics—8.7% female and 8.4% male, for a total of 17.1%—were 4 years of age or younger, compared to only 0.8% of foreign-born Hispanics. More than 4.59 million native-born Hispanics were 4 years old or younger! More than one fourth (26.6%) of native-born female Hispanics—a total of 7,095,884 million—were 19 years or younger in 2006 compared to 5.4% of female Hispanics who were foreign born. Almost 3 out of 10 (27.7%) male Hispanics born in the United States—a total of 7,295,884 million—were 19 years of age or younger in 2006, whereas 6.1% of foreign-born male Hispanics were in this age group (Pew Hispanic Center, 2008).

To summarize, in 2006, both female and male Hispanics born in the United States were younger than Hispanics who were foreign born. Thus, of the 26.6 million native-born Hispanics, more than one half, or 14.4 million, were 19 years of age or younger and potential college students. The dramatic differences in the age distribution of foreign and native-born Hispanics can be seen in the population pyramid in Figure 5.1.

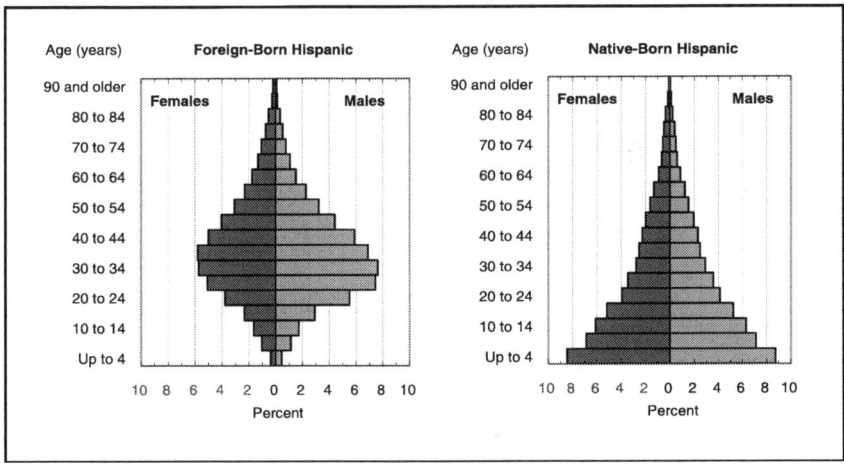

Figure 5.1 Age and Gender Distributions for Foreign- and Native-Born Hispanics, 2006. This figure was adapted from Table 9a in the *Statistical Portrait of Hispanics in the United States, 2006* (Pew Hispanic Center, 2008). © 2009 Pew Hispanic Center, a Pew Research Center project, *Statistical Portrait of Hispanics in the United States, 2007.* http://pewhispanic.org/files/factsheets/hispanics2007/Table-9a.pdf. Reprinted with permission.

Hispanics and Higher Education

This section includes data about Hispanics and higher education in the United States, including high school completion rates, college participation rates, college and university enrollment rates, and degrees earned. In addition, projections of Hispanic high school graduation rates are included.

In 2005, 65.9% of 18-to 24-year-old Hispanics were high school graduates, compared to 82.9% of 18-to 24-year-olds of all races. Whereas 38.9% of *all* 18- to 24-year-old high school graduates were enrolled in college, only 24.8% of 18- to 24-year-old Hispanics were enrolled in college (Cook & Cordova, 2007).

In 2005, the rate of college enrollment among all high school graduates was 38.9%. However, only 24.8% of Hispanic high school graduates enrolled in college (Cook & Cordova, 2007). Almost 4 of 10 of *all* high school graduates in 2005 were enrolled in college compared to only 1 of 4 Hispanic high school graduates.

In the Fall 2004 semester, the total enrollment at all institutions of higher education in the United States was 17,282.044, which represented a 21.3% increase from the Fall 1994 enrollment of 14,245,602. In the Fall 2004 semester, a total of 1,679,924 Hispanics were enrolled, a 67% increase from the 1,005,965 enrolled in 1994. Of all Hispanics enrolled that fall, 913,145 were enrolled in 2-year institutions, and 766,779 were enrolled in 4-year institutions (Cook & Cordova, 2007).

Of the 697,649 associate's degrees earned in 2004–2005, Hispanics earned 74,339 (10.7%). In 2004–2005, a total of 1,516,229 bachelor's degrees were awarded, and Hispanics earned 99,924 (6.6%) of these degrees (Cook & Cordova, 2007).

Hispanics earned 28,574 (4.9%) of the 578,812 master's degrees awarded in 2004–2005. Of the 87,289 professional degrees awarded in 2004–2005, Hispanics earned only 4,196 (4.8%). Hispanics earned 1,693 doctoral degrees in 2004–2005, or only 3.2% of the total 52,705 doctoral degrees awarded (Cook & Cordova, 2007).

In summary, even though Hispanics represented 14.8% of the total U.S. population in 2006, they earned only 10.7% of associate's degrees, 6.6% of bachelor's degrees, 4.9% of master's degrees, 4.8% of professional degrees, and 3.2% of doctoral degrees awarded in 2004–2005.

Hispanic High School Graduation and College Enrollment Projections

Between 2004–2005 and 2021–2022, the number of Hispanic students who will graduate from public high schools in the United States is projected to more than double, from 380,736 to 780,268. During this same period, the number of non-Hispanic White high school graduates is projected to decrease from 1,851,095 to 1,588,455 (Western Interstate Commission for

Higher Education, 2008). In 2021–2022, Hispanic high school graduates will represent 20.4% of the total number of high school graduates; thus, 1 out of every 5 high school graduates will be Hispanic.

In some states, increases in the number of Hispanic high school graduates will also be significant. In Texas, the number of Hispanic high school graduates is projected to almost double, from 84,566 in 2004–2005 to 164,269 in 2021–2022. In California, the projected number of Hispanic high school graduates in 2021–2022 will be more than double the number of non-Hispanic Whites projected to graduate: 184,108 Hispanics versus 90,258 non-Hispanic Whites (Western Interstate Commission for Higher Education, 2008).

In 1999, Carnevale and Fry projected that the number of Hispanics who will enroll in college will increase to 2.46 million in 2015 from 1.43 million in 1995 (p. 86). This represents an increase of 72% in the number of Hispanics projected to enroll in college.

Hispanics and HSIs

This section provides information on the enrollment patterns of Hispanics in institutions of higher education in the United States and the reasons Hispanic students select HSIs. In 1979, Olivas, the first scholar to document the fact that minority students actually enroll in a small number of institutions, wrote that "83 urban two year institutions represent more than 40% of minority two year enrollments: 21% American Indian, 43% black, 43% Hispanic, and 43% Asian" (p. 28).

Although Olivas focused on 2-year colleges, this same pattern holds true in all types of institutions 30 years later. In a publication on the characteristics of minority-serving institutions, the National Center for Education Statistics reported that in 2004, "Hispanic-serving institutions as one subgroup of [minority-serving institutions] alone enrolled 50 percent of all Hispanic undergraduates" (Li, 2007, p. 16). Of the 1,666,859 Hispanic undergraduates in 2004, a total of 836,677 (50.2%) were enrolled in HSIs. A total of 611,419 Hispanics (36.7%) were enrolled in non-minority-serving institutions. The rest were enrolled in Black-serving institutions, non-historically Black colleges and universities, Asian-serving institutions, and other institutions (Li, 2007, p. 16).

The Hispanic Association of Colleges and Universities (HACU; 2008) noted, "Although our member institutions in the U.S. represent less than 10% of all higher education institutions nationwide, together they are home to more than two-thirds of all Hispanic college students." It is clear that the majority of Hispanic students enrolled in institutions of higher education in the United States are enrolled in a relatively small number of institutions. In effect, this is what creates HSIs.

In a study of HSIs, Santiago (2007) reported that the

> classification of a campus as an HSI shows no evidence of influencing student college choices. However, most HSIs have institutional

characteristics that align with Latino student priorities and needs and explain why so many students choose HSIs. For example many Latino students at HSIs identified low college costs, proximity to where they lived and an approachable campus as their priorities for choosing a college. In tandem with student priorities, HSIs are generally less expensive than other institutions, are located in large Latino communities, and tend to be more accessible compared to other institutions.

(p. 3)

Purpose of the Study

The purpose of the present study was to identify the challenges and issues facing HSIs as defined by the presidents and chancellors of these institutions as they look toward the end of the first decade of the 21st century. In effect, this study emanates from one of the recommendations made in a 2003 article by de los Santos and de los Santos that also focused on the issues, challenges, and problems faced by HSIs.

Methodology

In October 2007, we sent a survey to presidents, chancellors, and chief executive officers of 209 HSIs in the United States and Puerto Rico that were members of the HACU.[4] They were asked to respond to two questions:

1. As you look to the end of this, the first decade of the 21st century, what are the three most important challenges/issues/problems facing your institution?
2. Are any of these challenges/issues/problems related directly to the fact that your institution is an HSI? Why? How?

The respondents were asked to list challenges in order of priority and to provide a short explanation. Finally, the survey asked for additional comments or "quotable quotes."

The responses were reviewed by both of us and transcribed. We developed categories and prepared a coding system. Finally, the responses were classified into the categories.

Limitations of the Study

This study has a number of limitations. One is that the sample included only the presidents or chancellors of the 209 HSIs that were members of the HACU in 2007. Another limitation is the response rate: Only 86 useful completed surveys were returned, a response rate of 41%.

Another limitation, and one that is inherent in studies such as this one, is that the responses represent each individual respondent's perspective on the matter. Finally, another limitation was posed by our reviewing and analyzing the data and classifying them into six major themes and several subthemes. It is possible that other researchers would have divided the responses into different categories or subthemes.

Findings: Challenges Facing HSIs

This section is divided into two major subsections corresponding to the two questions asked in the survey. In the first section we outline and describe the challenges identified by the presidents. The question of whether these challenges are related to the institutions being HSIs is addressed in the second section.

Challenges Facing HSIs

In this section we present the responses to the first research question, in order of priority: funding, student preparedness, student retention/success, faculty, and affordability. For each issue, problem, or challenge, we describe subthemes that emerged in the responses.

Funding

The challenge cited most often by the presidents was funding. As shown in Table 5.1, 78.8% of presidents indicated that financial issues were placing constraints on the institutions they led. Of the 85 presidents who responded to the survey, 67 said that funding was an issue. More than one third (34.1%)

Table 5.1 Issues Facing Hispanic-Serving Institutions as Defined by Presidents/ Chief Executive Officers, 2007–2008

Issue	Priority 1	Priority 2	Priority 3	Total	% of Total
Funding	29	21	17	67	78.8%
	34.1%	24.7%	20.0%		
Student preparedness	16	11	6	33	38.8%
	18.8%	12.9%	7.1%		
Student retention/success	12	10	5	27	31.8%
	14.1%	11.8%	5.9%		
Faculty	7	9	8	24	28.3%
	8.3%	10.6%	9.4%		
Affordability	2	6	5	13	15.4%
	2.4%	7.1%	5.9%		

Note. The number in the *total* columns represents those respondents who listed funding as their first, second, or third priority. For example, 67 of the 85 respondents, or 78.8%, listed funding as an issue.

of presidents listed funding as the most important issue. Almost one fourth ($n = 17$, or 24.7%) indicated that funding was the second most important issue; and 17 (20%) listed funding as the third most important issue.

The presidents used different terms and words to express the issue: "decrease in financial resources," "erosion of funding," "inadequate resources," "continued declined in 'real' funding," "tighter and tighter funding," and "resource challenged."

A number of presidents focused on the lack of state funding, an important subtheme. The chancellor of a large community college in Arizona wrote that the financial problems at his institution were as a result of "disinvestment in community colleges by the legislature." The president of a small rural Texas community college wrote that in the 1980s, 80% of the budget at his institution had come from the state; now, state funds make up only 25% of the budget. The president of one of the campuses in the California State University system wrote that the "amount of state resources available to support the university continues to dwindle. It will be necessary to generate alternative sources of revenues."

Another subtheme that emerged from the responses focused on the uncertainty and inadequacy of funding. The president of a large community college in California wrote that his institution lacked "appropriate funding to hire faculty and provide services." The president of a public university in Colorado indicated that the state "funds its institutions of higher education at a very low level, relative to other states. As an HSI serving a low income area of the state, this institution faces significant challenges in attracting and retaining qualified faculty and staff." The president of a New Jersey community college called for "a reasonable and reliable annual state appropriation."

Another subtheme was the rising costs of education at both the community college and university levels and the consequences of this. The president of a multicampus university in Puerto Rico wrote that part of the problem was the increasing costs of operating the university. The president of a university in California noted that although costs were increasing, the state appropriations for higher education as a percentage of the budget were decreasing. The president of a small, private 2-year college in Illinois wrote, "Operational costs, including payroll and benefits for faculty/staff, energy, maintenance, security, etc. have increased at much faster rate than tuition. This is affecting colleges serving minorities because we keep tuition low."

The president of a public university in Florida wrote that state funding

> has been declining at the same time that the number of residents seeking higher education has been increasing. This places the university in the untenable position of denying access or reducing the quality or doing a little bit of both. . . . Recently we have decided that we will have to deny access because we cannot reduce quality.

Student preparedness

The second challenge most often cited was student preparedness. According to Table 5.1, nearly 40% of respondents stated that a large number of students entering their colleges and universities were significantly underprepared to do college-level work. Almost 20% of respondents listed student preparedness as the most pressing issue in their institutions, approximately 13% stated that it was the second most pressing issue, and just more than 7% stated that it was the third most pressing issue. The terms and words used to depict the issue included "lack academic readiness/preparedness," "need remedial work in math/English," "students arrive with developmental needs," and "need precollegiate basic skills."

The high percentage of students needing remedial and developmental courses was a subtheme that surfaced among the nearly 40% of presidents who stated that student preparedness was a major issue. The president of a small California community college stated that "80% of entering freshmen need at least one developmental education course, which inevitably diverts resources to remediate students in math, writing and reading before they are 'college ready.'" Likewise, the president of multicampus community college in Arizona stated that "80% of new students need remedial work in math." Lastly, the president of a university in Puerto Rico expressed that "students need a solid academic education in reading, writing and math in order to succeed in today's society."

The president of a community college in New Jersey expressed that currently 75% of students at his campus have a remediation issue, and 25% of his students are entering through the portal of English as a Second Language (ESL) and bilingual education. This leads to the topic of English language learners, which arose as a subtheme among the survey responses. The president of a California university explained that English language learners at his university present challenges to the faculty and to the students themselves. This in turn creates a problem because students taking remedial courses carry no course credit and do not earn resources for the university. The president of a junior college in Texas expressed that "the close proximity of the college to Mexico and the influx of students whose command of English is weak; [*sic*] create the large number of developmental classes."

Another subtheme was the lack of alignment between high school and college curricula. The president of a Florida university expressed that "the current PK–12 educational system is not efficiently preparing students for a college level education." A California community college president expressed that his campus needs "more coordination with feeder high schools in order to insure [*sic*] a smoother transition for students from high school to college."

Student retention/success

The third most mentioned challenge was student retention/success. As shown in Table 5.1, almost 32% of respondents felt that this was an important issue that needs to be improved. They expressed that low retention rates result in low graduation rates. Just more than 14% of respondents listed student retention/success as the most important issue at their institution, almost 12% listed it as the second most important issue, and nearly 6% listed it as the third most important issue. The terms and words used to explain the issue included "low retention due to preparation issues," "student success is the most pressing and critical challenge," and "our key focus is ensuring students are retained and graduate."

Many presidents identified student underpreparedness as a subtheme related to the issue of student retention/success. The president of a community college in New York said that "weaknesses in writing, quantitative analysis and critical thinking skills cause students to struggle which leads them to under perform [sic] and fail." The president of a community college in California stated that "student success is affected by unprepared students out of K–12."

A president/superintendent of a community college in California stated that 70% of students enter his institution under prepared for college level courses which affects student success. The president of a university in California stated that the recruitment, retention, and graduation of underrepresented students in science, technology, engineering, and mathematics disciplines and fields was a major challenge at his institution.

Another subtheme related to student retention/success was the low socio-economic status (SES) of some students. The president of a community college in New York stated that a large majority of her students live in the poorest district, below the poverty level. According to this president, these students are "ill-prepared for college [which] combined with their staggering personal life problems impedes their graduation." A chancellor from Texas explained that "it is important to increase the number of underserved and lower SES students from high school and adults going to college." The president of a community college in Colorado stated that students at his institution are "unable to complete a degree in four years due to societal and economic challenges."

Faculty

The fourth most cited issue had to do with faculty. Table 5.1 shows that more than 28% of presidents were concerned with different aspects affecting faculty on their campuses. The following were key phrases used to express the issue: "building an appropriately diverse faculty and staff," "hiring adequate prepared faculty," and "no comparable pool of new faculty or administrative leadership."

From the responses, the following subthemes emerged: replacing retired faculty with adequate faculty, and the need for diverse faculty who understand and are willing to address the needs of underserved students. The president of a community college in California expressed that the lack of adequate faculty and administrator pools was the most important issue at his institution. The president of a university in California stated that "the cost of living makes it difficult to recruit new faculty to replace an aging workforce." Meanwhile, the president of a university in Texas expressed concern that in the years to come large numbers of "the most experienced faculty and administrators will be joining the ranks of retirees leaving no comparable pool of new faculty or administrative leadership to represent a diverse population prepared to take their place at higher education institutions."

Another subtheme addressed the need for diverse faculty. The president of a small university in California expressed that building an appropriate diverse faculty and staff to serve the diverse student body at his institution was an issue. He stated that "it is challenging for smaller regional institutions to attract candidates of color." The president of a community college in Chicago was concerned with hiring diverse and qualified faculty that reflected the student body. She expressed that "there is a limited pool of graduates in today's universities being trained to become teaching faculty or higher education administrators."

Affordability

The final challenge mentioned by respondents was affordability. Table 5.1 shows that more than 15% of presidents designated affordability as a concern within their institutions. The following were key terms and words used to express the issue: "high quality of education is expensive," "struggle to pay for college while raising families," and "educational cost increase." Two subthemes emerged: an increase in the costs of higher education, and low-SES students.

The president of a university in Texas stated that "costs of higher education are increasing at a time when the state appropriations are decreasing and pushing the cost to the students and their parents." The president of a university in Puerto Rico stated that the increasing cost of education "has a direct impact on access, so that increases in cost are understandably of great concern to students, parents and education policy makers."

The other subtheme, low-SES students, was noted as a concern by the president of a community college in California, who expressed, "Our low-income adults struggle to pay for college while raising families." The president of another university in California stated that "non-resident students struggle with financial assistance, yet poor socio-economic conditions only exacerbate the problem."

Relation of Challenges and HSI Status

This section outlines the presidents' responses to the question about whether the challenges and issues identified were directly related to the institutions being designated as HSIs. Respondents noted a relationship for only two issues: funding and student retention/success.

A very small number of respondents indicated that the issue of funding was directly related to the fact that their institution was an HSI. Only 11 of the

67 respondents who identified funding as an issue found such a relationship. Those who responded positively to this yes/no question used the students the institutions serve as part of their rationale.

The president of a community college in Texas wrote, "Funding is related to our HSI status only in that we work with students who are first generation college students, students who are often unprepared for the rigors of a college education and are economically challenged." The president of a large public university in Florida echoed this thought: "The reduction of state funding will be partially compensated [for] by an increase in tuition. This will reduce access to our students, many of whom are first generation in [sic] college students who come from families with fewer financial resources."

The chancellor of a community college district in California noted that the relationship "is based on the fact that 43% of our students are Hispanic and 29% are first generation college students. A high percentage of these student groups are in the [sic] need of programs and services for which we lack funding."

Finally, the president of a public university in Texas based the relationship on geography:

> HSIs are more likely to be located in parts of the country that are also experiencing growth in the population. The infrastructures of these communities are tightly stretched. Competition for scarce resources will continue to be a serious problem, especially characteristics of fast growth regions.

The presidents who listed student retention/success as an issue generally did not relate it to the institution being an HSI. The president of a university in Texas reflected the point of view of many other presidents when he noted that this "challenge is more related to our demography. We are applying 20th century public policy to 21st century students."

One reason that student retention/success is a challenge, as stated by the president of a college in New York, is that "urban IHEs [institutions of higher education] have more difficulty because their mission is to serve populations that come from public schools where many do not receive proper preparation for higher education." The president of a private university in Puerto Rico noted that the low retention rate "is due to the low academic profile of the students and their need to earn an income."

Family income is an important reason students do not succeed, according to the president of a community college in California who wrote that poverty is a factor, adding, "So many are season [sic] workers with low pay and intermittent work." Other presidents mentioned additional factors. The president of a community college in New Mexico wrote that "Hispanic, immigrant and other minority students face even greater pressures/stresses: finances, childcare, academic preparation, transportation."

The president of a California university noted that because of "poor preparation, less inclination to borrow, likelihood to work too many hours and to frontloaded [sic] time spent on remediation, Latino students have been less likely to graduate in a timely way."

Summary of Findings

This study identified five key challenges faced by HSIs, listed here in the order mentioned by respondents: funding, student preparedness, student retention/success, faculty, and affordability. Respondents in a study by de los Santos and de los Santos (2003) identified five other challenges as the most pressing: funding; technology; faculty; growth and diversity; and student preparedness, retention, and graduation. Thus, four out of five issues in this study were recurring issues; however, the level of importance was not the same in all cases.

Funding was once again the highest ranked issue among respondents. In 2007, a total of 78.8% of presidents and chancellors identified funding as the main issue on their campuses, compared to 81.3% in 2003. In the present study, 38.8% of respondents recognized student preparedness as the second most pressing issue at their institutions, and 31.8% identified student retention/success as the third most important issue. This is comparable to the 31.7% of respondents who in 2003 identified student preparedness, retention, and graduation as the fifth most important issue facing their institutions (de los Santos & de los Santos, 2003).

In 2003, 38.5% of respondents identified faculty as the third most significant issue, whereas in 2007, 28.2% of respondents stated that faculty was the fourth most significant at their institutions. Affordability (15.3%) was the fifth most cited issue in the present study. This challenge was not identified in de los Santos and de los Santos's 2003 study.

Recommendations for Future Research

This study raises a number of questions and issues that warrant further research. Consider the quote by Thomas M. Fallo at the beginning of this article: "Educational excellence for Hispanics is a manifest destiny for America's economic and democratic success." What could be the impact on the economic success of the United States if not enough Hispanics are provided with a quality education? What does Fallo mean by "democratic success"?

Another possibility for future research would be to conduct a similar survey to the one described here among presidents of a matched set of institutions that are not HSIs. Are there differences between these institutions and HSIs? A similar survey should be conducted among a sample of trustees of HSIs to determine what challenges they consider most important. Future studies might also focus on best practices used by HSIs to successfully serve Hispanic students even with limited fiscal resources. In addition, have any HSIs been successful in recruiting and retaining faculty and administrators who mirror the racial/ethnic make-up of their students? How have they done this?

Other studies could project the resources—both capital funds for constructing and equipping facilities and resources for operations—that would be needed 5–10 years from now in states such as Texas and California that will experience significant increases in the enrollment of Hispanic students. What options are feasible for providing these resources, other than continuing to increase tuition and fees?

Finally, this study should be replicated again in another 4–5 years.

View of the Future

The presidents' views of the capacity of HSIs to continue to prepare Hispanics to be a significant part of the future workforce for the United States are directly related to the challenges they outlined. Although the survey did not include a question about the future, some of the respondents gave their views of the future in the explanation section of the survey. Because of their richness, we include some responses here.

Focusing on the future impact of the lack of funding in the recent past, the president of a college if New York City wrote that the

> accumulation over many years of deficits due to inadequate budgets has resulted in gaps in staffing (faculty and other professionals as well as in general maintenance) and deferred maintenance of facilities. Monies obtained from external sources via indirect costs recovery (grants for training, research and other purposes) are used to fill in some of the gaps, but they are woefully insufficient, given the needs of the institution.

Focusing on institutional capacity versus projected need, the president of one of the campuses in the University of Texas system stated that an increasing number of Hispanic students will face challenges in the future.

> Texas is expected to experience an unprecedented amount of growth over the next 30 years. The growth is expected to occur predominantly in the Hispanic population. California is in a very similar situation. Yet, neither state is significantly growing capacity in the institutions of higher education. That means that over a million new seats will be needed in California and 600,000 more in Texas, with very little actual growth in capacity funded.

The chancellor of a community college in California wrote that higher education

> needs new types of faculty and administrators who want to attack the problems of serving those who are not being served. . . . There is need for new resources, not just new money, but a mixing of existing resources

and the sharing of faculty, teachers, facilities so that new types of clienteles can be served.

It is interesting to note that many of the views of the future focus on the challenges HSIs will face because of the projected increase in the number of Hispanic students who will enroll and the inability of the institutions to adequately serve them. As noted by many of the respondents, many of these students have need for both academic and student support services because of their academic preparedness. The principal reason for this dilemma is the lack of adequate and reliable funding.

This is happening at a time when the U.S. economy is having difficulty and some states—one of the important sources of funding for institutions of higher education—are facing deficits. The Center for Budget and Policy Priorities reported in August 2008 that 29 states and the District of Columbia were facing deficits for fiscal year 2009, which began in July 2008 (McNichol & Lav, 2008).

Some of the states facing deficits are those with large concentrations of Hispanics, including Arizona, California, Florida, Illinois, New Jersey, and New York. For example, Arizona faced a budget deficit for fiscal year 2009 of $1.9 billion, which represented 17.8% of the fiscal year 2008 budget. California's 2009 deficit of $22.2 billion represented 21.3% of the budget for fiscal year 2008 (McNichol & Lay, 2008).

In the face of all this, HSIs, in all probability, will continue to face similar challenges and issues to the ones identified in this study. But the responsibility for educating the increasing number of Hispanics students will still remain.

Perhaps the best way to end the article is to quote Thomas M. Fallo: "Educational excellence for Hispanics is a manifest destiny for America's economic and democratic success."

Notes

1. The only respondent whose name is used in this article is Thomas M. Fallo, President of El Camino College. He generously allowed the use of his quote and his name. We thank him not only for the quote but also for permission to use his name.
2. The terms *Hispanic* and *Latino* are used interchangeably to identify people from the Caribbean, Central American, Mexico, Puerto Rico, South America, Spain, and other countries where Spanish is the primary language.
3. Although a number of definitions of the term *Hispanic-serving institution* are available, the definition used in this article is the definition used by the Hispanic Association of Colleges and Universities (2008): "Colleges, universities or systems/districts where total Hispanic enrollment constitutes a minimum of 25% of the total enrollment, including full-time and part-time students whether at the undergraduate or graduate level (including professional schools), or both (headcount, for-credit students)."
4. We want to extend our thanks to Dr. Antonio Flores, President of the HACU, for his generosity in allowing us to use the mailing list of presidents and chancellors of HACU member institutions. We also want to thank Imelda Bósquez, Executive Assistant to the President, for her quick and positive response to our requests. To both we say, ¡Muchas gracias!

References

Carnevale, A. P., & Fry, R. A. (1999). *Crossing the great divide: Can we achieve equity when generation Y goes to college?* Princeton, NJ: Educational Testing Service.

Committee on Prosperity in the Global Economy of the 21st Century. (2006). *Rising above the gathering storm: Energizing and employing America for a brighter economic future.* Washington, DC: National Academies Press.

Cook, B. J., & Cordova, D. I. (2007). *Minorities in higher education: Twenty-second annual status report 2007 supplement.* Washington, DC: American Council on Education.

de los Santos, A. G., Jr., & de los Santos, G. E. (2003). Hispanic-serving institutions in the 21st century: Overview, challenges and opportunities. *Journal of Hispanic Higher Education, 4,* 337–391.

Hispanic Association of Colleges and Universities. (2008, April 10). *2007 membership dues information.* Retrieved April 10, 2008, from www.hacu.net/hacu/Dues_EN.asp?SnID=945587643

Kirsch, I., Braum, H., Yamamoto, K., & Sum, A. (2007). *America's perfect storm: Three forces changing our nation's future.* Princeton, NJ: Educational Testing Service.

Li, X. (2007). *Characteristics of minority-serving institutions and minority undergraduates enrolled in these institutions* (Report No. 2008–256). Washington, DC: National Center for Education Statistics.

McNichol, E. C., & Lav, I. J. (August 2008). *29 states face total budget shortfall of at least $48 million, in fiscal 2009.* Washington, DC: Center on Budget and Policy Priorities. Retrieved February 19, 2010, from http://www.cbpp.org/files/1-15-08sfp.pdf/files/

Olivas, M. A. (1979). *The dilemma of access: Minorities in two-year colleges.* Washington, DC: Howard University Press and the Institute of Educational Policy.

Pew Hispanic Center. (2008, January). *Statistical portrait of Hispanics in the United States, 2006.* Retrieved May 5, 2008, from http://pewhispanic.org/factsheets/factsheet.php?FactsheetID=35

Santiago, D. A. (2007). *Choosing Hispanic-serving institutions: A closer look at Latino students' college choice.* Washington, DC: Excelencia in Education.

Western Interstate Commission for Higher Education. (2008). *Knocking at the college door: Projections of high school graduates by state and race/ethnicity 1992–2022.* Boulder, CO: Author.

6   *Nuestro Camino*
A Review of Literature Surrounding the Latino Teacher Pipeline

Kelly M. Ocasio

Latinos face an educational crisis as they lag behind their peers throughout the educational pipeline, particularly in high school graduation and college enrollment rates. For every 100 Latino students, 21 will go to college, 8 will earn a graduate degree and less than 0.2% will earn a doctoral degree (Huber, Huidor, Malagon, Sanchez, & Solorzano, 2006; Sólorzano, Villalpando, & Oseguera, 2005). The disheartening academic outcomes for many Latinos can be connected, at least in part, to the lack of Latino teachers who may be uniquely equipped to meet the needs of this group (Irizarry & Donaldson, 2012; Monzo & Rueda, 2001; Ochoa, 2007). In order to create spaces where Latino students are growing up to pursue their dreams of higher education, classrooms must be equipped with teachers who can relate to these students and serve as role models on their journeys to success.

One of the most compelling arguments in favor of an increase in teachers of color is that these teachers act as role models for students, often playing a huge role in student achievement (Bustos Flores, Riojas Clark, Claeys, & Villareal, 2007; Frankenberg, 2009; Ochoa, 2007; Salinas & Castro, 2010). These teachers may provide a rich learning environment for their students, as they tend to hold higher expectations for students of color and have an ability to relate to them both culturally and linguistically (Frankenberg, 2009; Irizarry & Donaldson, 2012; Monzo & Rueda, 2001; Ochoa, 2007; Quiocho & Rios, 2000). Teachers of color may also help strengthen ties between home and school for students of color, as they are more likely to value the cultural funds of knowledge that students bring to school (Frankenberg, 2009; Irizarry & Donaldson, 2012; Moll, Amanti, Neff, & Gonzalez, 1992; Monzo & Rueda, 2001).

Bustos Flores et al. (2007) also asserted that teachers of color bring a unique critical perspective to schooling because of their personal experiences. These teachers typically enter the profession with a heightened awareness of the sociopolitical contexts in which students of color are educated (Irizarry & Donaldson, 2012; Quiocho & Rios, 2000). Once teachers of color get to the classroom, they are also more likely to work in high-minority, hard-to-staff schools and have greater retention rates in those settings (Ingersoll & May, 2011; Irizarry & Donaldson, 2012; Villegas, 2009). The benefits of staffing classrooms with teachers of colors accrue as one looks at the academic success of students of color as well as awareness and equity for all. There is certainly a desperate need for the United States to employ a diverse teaching staff that includes teachers who are culturally representative of the diverse student body they serve (Frankenberg, 2009; Gomez & Rodriguez, 2011; Sakash & Chou, 2007).

The diversification of the teacher workforce not only benefits students of color. Non-White educators play an important role in the desegregation of schools by equalizing power among teachers from all backgrounds (Frankenberg, 2009). Teachers of color "bring knowledge, insights, and perspectives to schools that otherwise would not be there, including raising issues of structural inequality present in schools and society" (Frankenberg, 2009, p. 4). They raise awareness among White teachers and expose White students to new ideas and perspectives to better prepare students for a racially diverse society (Orfield & Lee, 2007). White students who work with teachers of color are more likely to challenge their own racial stereotypes, possibly leading to reduced prejudice for all students (Frankenberg, 2009).

In spite of these benefits, there remains a lack of ethnic minority teachers in schools and classrooms today (Frankenberg, 2009; National Center for Education Statistics [NCES], 2008; Pew Hispanic Center, 2011). NCES (2008) data confirm that teachers of color are a much smaller percentage of the teaching force than students of color are in comparison to the entire student population. This fact rings especially true for the Latino population. According to the 2007–2008 NCES Schools and Staffing Survey (NCES, 2008), only 6% of public school teachers nationwide are Latino. In comparison with the 19% of students who identify as Latino who are in classrooms, there is clearly a disproportionate number of Latino teachers to the students they serve. Latino students often enter their K–12 classrooms to face educators who do not share their cultural background. Although some non-Latino educators may be effective teachers for Latino students, there are a myriad of social, academic, and psychological benefits to students of color who are taught by teachers of color (Dee, 2004; Dillard, 1994; Gay, Dingus, & Jackson, 2003; Irizarry & Donaldson, 2012; Villegas & Lucas, 2004).

It becomes apparent that the lack of minority teachers, specifically Latino teachers, has a negative impact on Latino student achievement and persistence in education (Frankenberg, 2009; Irizarry & Donaldson, 2012). This issue is likely to grow even more acute as the Latino population continues to grow steadily across the nation (Bustos Flores & Claeys, 2011; Pew Hispanic Center, 2011; U.S. Census Bureau, 2009). In fact, U.S. Census Bureau (2009) data predict that by 2050, the Hispanic population in the U.S. will double in size.

In order to provide rich learning environments for these students and improve graduation and success rates for the Latino student population, teaching staff at the K – 12 level need to diversify and include more Latino teachers. The first step in recruiting, preparing, and retaining high-quality and culturally responsive Latino teachers is to understand the Latino teacher pipeline. This article explores the Latino teacher pipeline experience, identifying points within the pipeline that present problems for Latinos as well as identifying points of success or possibilities for strengthening this pipeline.

Terminology

Throughout the educational leadership literature, pipeline terminology is widely used to discuss the fluidity of the educational experience from pre-kindergarten through college graduation (Huber et al., 2006). It is sometimes referred to as the *P – 20 pipeline* or the *K – 16 pipeline*, but most often simply the *educational pipeline*. It is also true that pipeline terminology has historically been used in discussions about marginalized groups of people. It is often used to describe the seemingly constant flow of particular students into various systems, such as the judicial system, as in the *school-to-prison pipeline*. Regardless of the various ways in which the term is used, a pipeline is reminiscent of a fluid process—a "direct channel" or pathway (Merriam-Webster, 2014)—an accurate description of the pathway followed by many individuals in their pursuit of a career.

I have chosen this term to discuss a very particular process—the process of a person becoming a teacher, or the *teacher pipeline*. Although not widely used in this way across empirical research, some literature discusses the teacher pipeline as the career pathway that a teacher follows once he or she successfully secures a classroom teaching role and following retention strategies in these settings. However, this article emphasizes the fluidity of the teacher pipeline from a broader perspective and begins much earlier in the educational pipeline. Although I have chosen this terminology, my intent is not to imply that this process is seamless and smooth for those who travel through it. In fact, the teacher pipeline is one that is complex and multifaceted, particularly for marginalized educators such as Latinos.

This article includes discussion of discrete points (or junctures) within the teacher pipeline: successful graduation from high school; enrollment and persistence throughout college; earning teaching certification; and lastly, securing a position as a classroom teacher. The broader teacher pipeline discussion, of course, continues well beyond the recruitment of teachers, as the issue of teacher retention is critical to the success of K – 12 classrooms. Experts must not only get teachers into the classroom but also address how to keep them there. Although the concept of the teacher pipeline does not end as a teacher gets his or her first job, this article focuses explicitly on this earlier portion of the pipeline, specifically for Latinos.

Discussion

Educational leaders and policymakers have long struggled with ways to increase diversity in the teaching workforce (Gonzalez, 1997; Ochoa, 2007; Sakash & Chou, 2007). Some innovative programs aimed at increasing interest and persistence in the field of teaching have targeted Latino students throughout the K – 16 pipeline, although the majority of efforts have included an emphasis on improving schools of education and/or teacher education programs (Bustos Flores & Claeys, 2011; Gomez, Rodriguez, & Agosto, 2008; Weisman & Hansen, 2008). Whether these programs have focused on better recruitment efforts and college access for Latino students or have strengthened diversity initiatives within schools of education and teacher preparation programs, there continues to exist a shortage of Latino teachers in the field.

The majority of research surrounding teacher recruitment and retention focuses on the majority population that is currently in the classroom: White, middle-class, female teachers (Bragg, 2007; Guarino, Santibanez, & Daley, 2006; Irizarry & Donaldson, 2012). The teaching profession as a whole is composed mainly of "good girls" (Galman, 2006, p. 48) who have been drawn into teaching by intrinsic motivators—wanting to work with children, making a difference in the lives of their students, enjoying their schooling experience and wanting to continue their experience with it (Berry, 1986; Goodlad, 1984; Irizarry & Donaldson, 2012; Lortie, 1975).

Financial incentives are not a primary motivator in the master narrative of wanting to teach. Rather, the many aforementioned intrinsic motivators are the main reasons that teachers choose to enter the classroom (Guarino et al., 2006; Irizarry & Donaldson, 2012). Although intrinsic motivators have been proven to be the guiding factor in teacher recruitment, teacher salary does play a role in teacher retention. In their analysis of the teacher workforce, Guarino et al. (2006) noted that teachers who are paid a higher salary have a lower attrition rate, suggesting that at some point in the teacher pipeline financial incentives may play more of a role than at earlier points in the pipeline.

Although there is certainly diversity among the pipeline experiences of White female teachers who currently make up the teacher labor market, the dominant teacher pipeline includes a traditional pathway to teaching: graduating successfully from high school, enrolling and persisting through a 4-year college degree while earning a teaching certification along the way, then attaining a classroom teaching position (Darling-Hammond, Chung, & Frelow, 2002). Recently, with the high demand for teachers, particularly in urban classrooms, alternative pathways to the classroom have become a part of the dominant discourse around the teacher pipeline literature. Alternative pathways include those that are an alternative to the traditional 4-year undergraduate program. Most states have alternative programs available for candidates who hold a bachelor's degree and wish to become teachers (Feistritzer, 1998). These alternative pathways vary from summer-long intensive programs to lengthier programs entailing enrollment in a college.

Although alternative routes to the classroom have become somewhat more common within the dominant narrative on teacher pipelines, the traditional university-based teacher education route remains the most commonly traveled pathway to the classroom among the general teacher labor market

(Darling-Hammond et al., 2002). Consequently, as I show here, the Latino pipeline into teaching includes a heavy reliance on these alternative paths to the classroom.

Juncture 1: Latino High School Completion

The teacher pipeline is one that requires a certain level of education as well as aspirations to continue going to school, earn a specialized degree, and attain a teaching position. Latino students lag behind their peers in academic achievement, graduation, and persistence throughout the educational pipeline (Huber et al., 2006). Moreover, critical junctures within the Latino K – 16 educational pipeline that present a significant barrier for Latinos include persisting through high school, getting into college, and persisting through college. In their study, Huber et al. (2006) demonstrated that Latinos lag behind their other racial/ethnic counterparts in graduating students at all points of the educational pipeline, beginning in elementary school.

Embedded within the discourse on low high school graduation rates is a discussion of student success early on within K–12 education. Studies have found substantial differences in children's test scores by race and ethnicity as early as kindergarten (Burkam & Lee, 2002; Green, 2008; Rumberger & Angulano, 2004). Latino students are said to be at a disadvantage compared to their non-Latino peers even before they enter kindergarten (Rumberger & Angulano, 2004). In fact, Latino students may be up to 2 years behind their White peers in reading and math by third grade (Green, 2008). The average elementary math achievement scores are 19% lower for Latinos than they are for White students (Burkam & Lee, 2002). Clearly, there exists an achievement gap between Latino students and their non-Latino peers early on in their educational career, culminating with low high school graduation rates.

With only roughly 50% of Latinos graduating from high school, a main challenge in ensuring Latino educational success is obviously beginning with student persistence throughout K–12. It is impossible to address teacher pipeline shortages when students struggle with mere high school completion rates and student achievement scores in early elementary school. But why do Latino students struggle so significantly during their K–12 schooling experience? The lack of Latino teachers to serve as role models for these students accounts, at least in part, for the students' lack of academic achievement. Although there is not one main struggle that Latinos face, the challenges that they face result in their lack of academic achievement, often pushing them off of the educational trajectory.

The National Education Longitudinal Study (NELS), a study begun in 1988 with eighth-grade students, followed students along their individual career pipelines with follow-up surveys all the way up until 2000. Swail, Cabrera, and Lee (2014) used these data to analyze Latino pathways, specifically looking at preparation and aspirations. In terms of their high school years specifically, Latino students are more likely to be held back in school, take lower forms of mathematics (lower math achievement is a predictor of a reduced likelihood of completing high school, limited admission to many postsecondary institutions, and limited access to higher paying jobs), change high schools more than twice, earn a C or less, leave high school before graduation, and earn a general equivalency diploma (Swail et al., 2014). These many alarming realities that Latino students face compound, creating a significant barrier for them as they continue on their educational path.

Not only are Latino students not adequately prepared to traverse the educational pipeline, but their aspirations were the lowest of any group of students (Swail et al., 2014). The NELS data suggested that only 55% of Latinos aspired to a bachelor's degree (a full 20% lower than the national average). This is problematic, as students who do not aspire to postsecondary education "self-select out of the educational pipeline" (Swail et al., 2014, p. 25). Consequently, one quarter of the NELS Latino students (those without aspirations to attend postsecondary education of any kind) were on a noncollege trajectory by the eighth grade.

These findings provide strong evidence that Latinos are not only failing to persist through the educational pipeline at the same rate as their peers but are much less prepared and hold lower aspirations than their counterparts. Latino students are clearly at a disadvantage in their preparation for postsecondary education. This critical juncture of the teacher pipeline offers significant barriers to students that must be considered in finding ways to strengthen the pipeline for Latino teachers.

Juncture 2: Latino College Access

The next critical juncture in this pipeline includes college student access—both enrollment in college and persistence through postsecondary education. The Latino pipeline into higher education has been more well documented throughout the literature than the Latino teacher pipeline (Behnke, Piercy, & Diversi, 2004; Cooper, 2002; Gandara, 2002; Huber et al., 2006). There are many barriers that Latino students face in pursuing a postsecondary education. One of the main challenges faced by Latinos is the increased cost of college attendance and the lack of financial assistance for college when Latino families generally earn well below their White counterparts (Downs, Martin, Fossum, Martinez, Solorio, & Martinez, 2008; Swail et al., 2014). With the rising costs of attending college, Latino students face a substantial barrier in accessing a higher level of education.

Another barrier to higher education relates back to students' experiences in the K–12 system and their lack of preparation for college (Downs et al., 2008; Swail et al., 2014). Latino students are often not encouraged to take college preparation courses, lack support and guidance from counselors, and are tracked throughout their schooling into lower level courses (Thomas, 1998; Vela-Gude et al., 2009). This leads to them graduating from high school without being prepared to enter college. The lack of academic achievement among Latinos is a major concern, often forcing the Latino students who do enroll in college to take remedial courses to better prepare for the rigor of college-level courses (Cohen & Brawer, 2003).

The lack of college knowledge among students and families is one of the primary and most significant barriers that Latino students face in attending college (Auerbach, 2002, 2011; Downs et al., 2008; Gandara, 2002). As many Latino students are first-generation college students, they simply lack knowledge of the college application process (Auerbach, 2004; Vela-Gude et al., 2009). As their parents do not know how to navigate the pathway to college, these students must rely on outside assistance to pave the way. In addition, many students and Latino families face a language barrier from accessing resources needed to achieve higher education; face limited access to technology and resources; and experience a general lack of outreach efforts on the part of schools, counselors, and admissions personnel and administrators to assist students (Auerbach, 2004; Downs et al., 2008; Gandara, 2002; Tornatzky, Cutler, & Lee, 2002; Vela-Gude et al., 2009). This knowledge is often taken for granted by individuals with a college trajectory in mind. However, for many Latino students, their lack of information presents a significant barrier to their educational success.

In efforts to increase the college enrollment and success rates of Latino students, many college access programs have sprung up across the country, taking many shapes and forms. College access programs aim to increase the college enrollment rates of students who lack the resources and tools necessary to successfully enroll in college (Cooper, 2002; Gandara, 2002). These programs offer support for students while they are still in high school and prepare them for a postsecondary education. Gandara (2002), in her study of a college access program geared toward Latino students, found that Latino students consistently exhibit lower academic aspirations and preparation for college. Although college access programs targeting Latino and other minority students have been implemented across the country, a system-wide change in the way in which students are educated in every classroom is needed (Gandara, 2002). College access programs are successful in taking students and maximizing their potential, given the situation they are in, as a result of a poor education system that has not served their needs for decades (Cooper, 2002).

Cooper (2002), in her longitudinal case study, suggested five bridges that are at work in college access programs geared toward Latino students: families' involvement, teachers' intensive instruction, guidance counseling, mentoring, and support of college-bound peers. She asserted that "these component bridges play complementary roles in supporting [students'] pathways to college" (p. 609). In understanding Latino students' pipeline to college, one must look at these different bridges that play a significant role in their access to education. Only in looking at how these bridges function can one begin to find ways to strengthen students' access and persistence to higher levels of education. In hoping to understand more about the Latino teacher pipeline, it becomes important to consider how these bridges may or may not play a role in these students' access as well.

Behnke et al. (2004), in their study, offered research about how academic and occupational aspirations are fostered in Latino families. This is important information that is needed to understand the impact of families, expectations, and *consejos* on Latinos' aspirations for becoming teachers. Both Behnke et al. and Gomez (2010) discussed the impact that families (particularly mothers) have on Latino students' aspirations and experiences in education. In looking at the Latino pipeline into teaching, it becomes apparent that Latino parents are an important bridge to students' success in education and beyond.

The conversation around Latino college access must be held alongside a discussion of the Latino teacher pipeline. As teaching requires a 4-year postsecondary degree, getting Latino students to persist through college is critical if people want more Latino teachers in the classroom. Incidentally, as students of color pursue a college education, the majority of minority college students pursue degrees in business, engineering, and social science (Haberman, 1988). There are even higher numbers of students who are undeclared than there are students pursuing an education degree (Haberman, 1988). This fact underscores the need to better understand the reasons behind minority college students not choosing a path into teaching.

Latino students who persist and do attend college often feel the pressure that is placed on them to utilize their education as a means of social advancement (Valadez, 2008). As many Latino students struggle to persist through higher education, as a result of the variety of challenges outlined, the goal of achieving a college degree may be synonymous with changing the discourse of poverty that has been ever present in many of these students' lives. For this reason, teaching becomes a risky choice for Latinos who do make it through the system and hope to find good-paying jobs upon graduation. In society, teaching is often viewed as a low-status, low-respect, and low-paying position that is often occupied by privileged individuals who do not earn a degree as a means to advance socially (Bragg, 2007; Goodlad, 1984). Often teachers go into debt pursuing this low-paying career (Darling-Hammond, 2011). As was explored, the dominant narrative surrounding teaching includes middle-class individuals who pursue this path for intrinsic motivational reasons, not because of financial benefits (Guarino et al., 2006; Irizarry & Donaldson, 2012). Because so many Latinos and other students of color use education as a means of social and financial advancement, teaching may not always be the most popular choice of a career.

Considering the already small sample size of Latino college graduates available, it is no surprise that so few Latino teachers are available to teach youth. Clearly, Latino students face various barriers to becoming future educators—lack of college preparation, lack of support early in their educational careers, being tracked into lower level academic courses, and being pushed to pursue other professions that will promote social advancement. In looking at policies and innovative programs that will target Latino populations to pursue teaching paths, college access will inevitably be a primary factor in these conversations. The discourse around college recruitment, access, and persistence must include an emphasis not only on getting Latinos into college but also on finding ways to make the teaching profession more appealing and accessible to this population that already faces significant barriers.

Juncture 3: Obtaining a Teaching Degree

The next critical juncture in the teaching pipeline that I explore is obtaining an actual teaching license or certification. Although the traditional teacher pipeline reflects a pathway that often includes teacher certification as a part of traditional teacher education programs in postsecondary institutions, the Latino pursuit of teaching credentials is often much less traditional. Latino teachers make it to the classroom through various pathways. For some teachers, this process is a part of the college access conversation. A need to strengthen college access for Latinos is definitely the first critical step in securing a more diverse teacher workforce. However, there other pathways that Latinos follow in obtaining teacher certification that do not include the traditional 4-year college route.

Some of the pathways that Latino teachers have followed in their personal teacher pipelines include the traditional teacher education route, the 2-year college route, paraprofessionals becoming teachers, alternative teaching certification (such as Teach for America [TFA]), and career pathway programs (schools targeting K–12 students interested in careers in teaching). The traditional teacher pipeline will undoubtedly be explored from the perspective of Latinos, as this remains an important pathway. In addition, these alternative paths to teaching, which are not as frequently presented in research, serve an important role in understanding the Latino teacher pipeline and the diversity of experiences of Latino educators.

Latinos in Teacher Education

The route to teaching through a traditional teacher education preparation program remains an important route into teaching. Sadly, the number of undergraduate bachelor's degrees conferred each year in the nation to Latino students has declined by 11% since 1992 (American Council on Education, 1995). In fact, the number of students of color in teacher education programs remains disproportionately low (Darling-Hammond et al., 2002; Ingle & Castro, 1993; Irizarry & Raible, 2011). Less than 2% of teacher education students identify as Latino (Ingle & Castro, 1993). As these programs are not representative of a diverse student population, this leaves students of color feeling uncomfortable and out of place within these programs (Galindo, 1996; Gomez et al., 2008; Gonzalez, 1997; Salinas & Castro, 2010).

Consequently, teacher education programs have long been struggling to find ways to recruit, prepare, and retain a more diverse teaching staff in schools

(Bustos Flores et al., 2007; Gomez et al., 2008; Gonzalez, 1997). The goal of employing a diverse and culturally responsive teaching staff has been at the heart of these efforts (Salinas & Castro, 2010; Weisman & Hansen, 2008). It is simply not enough to have teachers of color; rather, schools must employ teachers who are constructive and culturally responsive and who challenge the curriculum and official knowledge of schools.

When looking at the teacher pipeline, a primary point of consideration in wanting to strengthen it includes a thorough investigation of how schools of education can better recruit and prepare future educators. In fact, much of the literature surrounding the Latino teacher pipeline focuses on experiences of students within teacher education programs—an ironic fact considering the low representation of Latinos within these programs. There is no doubt that the experiences of Latino students within traditional teacher education programs are important narratives in understanding how to recruit and retain more qualified teachers in the Latino teacher pipeline more broadly. In fact, Irizarry and Raible (2011) asserted that "teacher education can play a significant role in transforming the teaching force in ways that become more responsive to the needs of Latino communities and students" (p. 189). The opportunity that schools of education offer in strengthening the Latino pipeline abound, making this juncture one of interest in the desire to strengthen this pipeline.

The Academy for Teacher Excellence (ATE) at the University of Texas at San Antonio is a federally funded program that aims to increase the recruitment, preparation, and retention of "culturally efficacious" Latino students into specific teaching shortage areas in the state of Texas (Bustos Flores et al., 2007, p. 56). Recruitment strategies that were found to work at ATE included early identification of students and purposive outreach efforts. Most important in this program was working with Latino students on retention strategies (Bustos Flores et al., 2007). Providing connections for these Latino preservice teachers proved to be critical in retaining and preparing them for the classrooms—efforts such as providing mentoring, counseling, advising, and summer bridge activities. These professional, academic, and personal strands were found to be powerful in recruiting, preparing, and retaining Latino teachers through ATE (Bustos Flores et al., 2007). As experts look to continue strengthening Latino college access, attracting more Latinos into teacher education must be done hand in hand with these efforts.

Two-Year College Route

Two-year institutions are important bridges to education for many students in the landscape of American institutions of higher education. Often more affordable, serving their communities' needs and offering a unique curriculum, 2-year colleges provide a niche in higher education that is often sought after by Latino students (Bragg, 2007; Cohen & Brawer, 2003; Wilson, 2001). Consequently, Latinos are much more likely to enroll in 2-year institutions than any other ethnic group of students (Swail et al., 2014).

As community colleges provide liberal arts and transfer education, a developmental and remedial curriculum, and continuing education, often students needing this programming will seek the 2-year college route (Bragg, 2007; Cohen & Brawer, 2003). These institutions allow students who may not want to attend a 4-year college or who need remediation or language support to attend college in a setting that is geared toward their needs. For Latinos specifically, community colleges and other 2-year institutions are an important gateway to America's educational opportunities (De los Santos & De los Santos, 2006). There is little doubt that these institutions are critical for many Latino students' college experiences, as approximately 60% of all Latino students enrolled in postsecondary education in 2000–2001 were enrolled in 2-year institutions (Harvey, 2003; Swail et al., 2014). Cohen and Brawer (2003) also asserted that community colleges have been a primary point of entry into higher education for Latinos. With more than half of the Latino college population attending these institutions, this route becomes one that needs to be further explored in understanding Latino teacher pipelines (Wilson, 2001).

As teaching certification often requires more than a 2-year degree (although requirements vary by state), students who begin at community colleges with hopes of becoming teachers must transfer to a 4-year campus to finish their career. However, the transfer rate of Latino students into 4-year campuses is drastically low (Dilworth, 1990). For this reason, it is important to strengthen the partnerships between 2-year and 4-year institutions in bridging students' pathways into teaching. In navigating the path to teaching via community colleges, Latino students may face challenges along the way—some of which could be lessened through increased collaboration and partnerships between institutions (Villegas & Clewell, 1998; Wilson, 2001). Students often do not know how to ensure that the courses they are taking at the community college will transfer directly to 4-year campuses, and students may not meet criteria for transfer admission at these institutions (Villegas & Clewell, 1998). Increased collaboration between institutions could help Latino students navigate the transfer process more fluidly, guaranteeing that they meet admission criteria and take appropriate coursework at the 2-year college to put them on the transfer track.

The community-based mission of community colleges often serves the needs of the Latino population in many unique ways. In responding to shortages in local teacher labor markets, some community colleges have begun partnerships with 4-year colleges and universities, strengthening their articulation agreements and transfer programs for students to begin their teacher education coursework at the 2-year level and finish at a 4-year institution (Bragg, 2007; Floyd & Walker, 2003; Townsend & Ignash, 2003). Equally as important in strengthening the Latino teacher workforce is the fact that community colleges have played a critical role in the creation and administration of career ladder programs that provide part-time programs to students who work and would like to advance into a specific career, such as teaching

(Villegas & Clewell, 1998). Villegas and Clewell (1998) described a career ladder program that targets paraprofessionals wanting to pursue a teaching career path. It is specialized to ensure that these teachers persist through their programs and earn a degree. The program that these authors discussed has had great success in taking paraprofessionals and creating an academic program that addresses their needs and helps them achieve their goal of obtaining a teaching certificate. Lastly, community colleges also provide programming and community resources earlier in students' pipelines, often while they are still within K – 12 schools. Finding ways to tap into students' early interest in teaching and support those interests are ways in which community colleges fill niches within the teacher pipeline.

Two-year institutions are important gateways to teaching that can strengthen the Latino pipeline to teaching (Bragg, 2007; Haberman, 1988). The importance of 2-year institutions for the Latino educational pipeline suggests that more data need to be explored about how these institutions partner with the community to address the lack of Latino educators in classrooms. Researchers have suggested for years that if the nation hopes to recruit, prepare, and retain more teachers of color, there must be more collaboration between 2-year institutions and 4-year campuses (Haberman, 1988), in regard to both 2-year institutions being a bridge to 4-year institutions as well as possibly providing preparation, training, and specialization for students throughout their lives.

Paraprofessionals Becoming Teachers

Searches of electronic databases for literature surrounding the Latino teacher pipeline yielded a number of articles related to a paraprofessional-to-teacher pipeline (Bonner, Pacino, & Hardcastle Standford, 2011; Monzo & Rueda, 2001; Villegas & Clewell, 1998). The route to a teaching career via a paraprofessional career is actually an important route to teaching, especially for Latino teachers. Although it is not known how many teachers nationwide pursue a path through the paraprofessional route, research has indicated its importance for Latino educators. This pathway to teaching provides Latino educators in classrooms who are often closely tied to the school communities in which they teach, as paraprofessional educators are generally employed close to their home communities and often reflect the culture and community of the students in their classrooms (Monzo & Rueda, 2001). The cultural connection that paraprofessionals can provide to the students they teach is unique to this group of educators. Not only do paraprofessionals become educators with a deep cultural, emotional, and linguistic connection to their students (Bonner et al., 2011; Monzo & Rueda, 2001), but these educators serve as role models for themselves and other Latinos in their communities, with the ability to shift the trajectory for their own children, families, and other individuals in their communities (Bonner et al., 2011).

As some Latinos who wish to become teachers may not have the education necessary or financial means to pursue a degree, becoming a paraprofessional at a local school is often a path that is chosen. This work allows these individuals to work within a classroom context without needing the credentials of a regular classroom teacher. Paraprofessionals who work in bilingual schools may also be able to use their native Spanish should English be a barrier to their employment at other jobs. Paraprofessional positions allow Latinos a step on the path to becoming a teacher. As many individuals will choose to move on and pursue a teaching career as a result of this experience, this route offers an opportunity for growth and support in the Latino teacher pipeline.

Latinos who begin as paraprofessionals may encounter barriers to actually becoming teachers, including the financial burden of returning to school, language barriers, and lack of schooling (Bonner et al., 2011; Monzo & Rueda, 2001). Paraprofessionals are more likely to be older, have children, and bear full financial responsibility in their households (Villegas & Clewell, 1998). They are also more likely to have academic gaps, particularly in communication and mathematics (Villegas & Clewell, 1998). As most have not gone through the college pipeline themselves, they tend to feel insecure in a college setting (Villegas & Clewell, 1998). For these many reasons, a network is often needed for these individuals to traverse this pathway successfully.

Alternatively, Villegas and Clewell (1998) identified five strategies that contribute to Latino paraprofessionals successfully pursuing a teaching degree: establishing partnerships with school districts, using multiple sources of information, providing academic and social support services, modifying the teacher education program, and securing tuition assistance. These strategies help support the unique needs of paraprofessionals on their paths to a teaching degree. The paraprofessional-to-teacher pipeline is one that is less traditional but important for many Latinos who pursue a teaching degree (Bonner et al., 2011; Valenciana, Morin, & Morales, 2005; Villegas & Clewell, 1998).

Career Pathway Programs

Career pathway programs that begin at the K–12 level have been in existence for some time. These programs begin preparing students for occupations well before they finish their K–12 schooling. This early preparation for specific skills strengthens individual pipelines into specific career fields for students. Early recruitment and preparation are the key components to the success of these programs. Many believe that "teacher career pathways are increasing access and representation within the teaching profession by strategically targeting historically underrepresented student populations for teacher workforce development" (Embry Jenlink, 2012, p. 1). These programs strengthen relationships between academic studies, educational aspirations, and career goals, thus strengthening the fluidity of the pipeline for these students (Bragg, 2007; Embry Jenlink, 2012). Although these programs are noted as contributing to the teacher pipeline dialogue, it can be seen as problematic to track students in this way—into a feminized position such as teaching. This pathway may be one answer in alternative pathways to the classroom, but it may not necessarily be the *best* answer in getting there.

Teacher training magnet schools (a form of a career pathway program) are a unique pathway to teaching for some communities, particularly Latino communities. These schools are created with the intention of recruiting, preparing, and training teachers early in their schooling experience (within the K–12 setting). Students eventually go on to a 4-year program through a partnership school to complete their teacher education. Oliva and Staudt (2003) reported on one such program at the University of Texas at El Paso through a partnership with Riverside High School's Socratic Institute that specifically targeted Latino students. Findings suggested that this magnet school program was successful because it fostered the notion that teaching is a calling rather than just a profession (Oliva & Staudt, 2003). For this reason, a magnet school that taps into students' passions and interests early on connects to good teaching later on (Oliva & Staudt, 2003).

This type of program supports Latino students in persevering through a more traditional teacher pipeline framework—starting with high school graduation and navigating the college pipeline. All of the students in this program indicated that they intended to attend a postsecondary institution, applying for college and most enrolling in a local community college (Oliva & Staudt, 2003). Although data were not reported on the students' persistence through later parts of the teacher pipeline, students' exposure to this program helped them decide early on whether a teaching career was something they really wanted. Rather than pushing these Latino students into the classroom with hopes of their changing an institution that did not serve them, this program hopes to pull them into teaching for intrinsic reasons, much like traditional teacher education students. This program continues to recruit students and serve as a model for other academies.

Another career pathway program, the Grow Your Own (GYO) initiative, aims to provide access for underrepresented students into college and eventually into the classroom (Hallett, 2012). GYO students often begin their postsecondary careers at a 2-year institution but transfer to a 4-year program, where they attend a standard teacher education program. This community-based approach to preparing teachers of color is gaining interest and strengthening relationships between communities, K–12 schools, community colleges, and 4-year institutions (Hallett, 2012). As GYO programs are still relatively new, it is difficult to determine the long-term effectiveness of such programs at this time, although at this point the GYO Illinois program reports a high retention rate of students, demonstrations of content knowledge, classroom management, and engaging students and parents (Hallett, 2012). This pathway is one that certainly has the potential to play an important role in the landscape of the Latino teacher pipeline.

Alternative Certification Paths

Latino teachers are in short supply across the nation but especially in urban areas, where Latino and minority populations tend to be largest. As is true within the general teacher pipeline, alternative certification programs have begun to become popular across the nation in an effort to fill the need for certified teachers in these high-need areas (Darling-Hammond et al., 2002). Alternative certification programs have gained in popularity in the landscape of the teacher pipeline. In fact, it is believed that nearly 18.3% of all teachers enter the profession through an alternative certification program (U.S. Department of Education, 2008). Most states have alternative pathways to the classroom for college graduates wishing to pursue a teaching career and get alternatively certified as a classroom teacher (Irizarry & Donaldson, 2012). These pathways may include emergency licensure that fills teacher shortages in high-need areas.

TFA is one example of an alternative path to teaching that has become an important alternative route to teaching across the nation (Darling-Hammond, 2011; Donaldson & Johnson, 2010). TFA recruits recent college graduates to teach in high-need urban areas of the United States with a shortage of qualified teachers (Donaldson & Johnson, 2010). TFA is a key component of Latino student success because of the increased presence of TFA partner schools in areas with a high Latino population (Irizarry & Donaldson, 2012). The need to fill these schools with Latino teachers as role models is important to consider. Some evidence supports the fact that programs such as TFA are good minority teacher recruitment tools (Nadler & Peterson, 2009) that place these teachers back in urban contexts. In fact, in many states, the majority of teachers who are certified through alternative routes are minority teachers (Nadler & Peterson, 2009). TFA specifically is important for the Latino teacher pipeline not only as an entry point for Latinos pursuing teaching but also for retention (Irizarry & Donaldson, 2012). Latinos are much more likely than Whites to be retained in the high-need-area schools in which TFA places them (Irizarry & Donaldson, 2012).

Although TFA has been praised by some researchers as being an important gateway for teachers of color, TFA can also be viewed as a problematic solution to the teacher shortages facing high-need schools. This program does not equip future educators with the pedagogical content knowledge that teacher preparations programs include. Teacher quality and effectiveness may be compromised when using a stop-gap method of filling classrooms with uncertified teachers. In a study by Darling-Hammond, Holtzman, Gatlin, and Vasquez Heilig (2005), TFA teachers were proven to be less effective in terms of student achievement gains than certified teachers. Certified teachers consistently produce higher academic gains among students, thus reaffirming the need not just for warm bodies in the classroom but for highly qualified staff in schools. Regardless of the critiques of TFA, this is a pathway to teaching that is important within the discourse on the Latino teacher pipeline, as it has been successful in getting Latinos into the classroom.

In the Chicago public schools, a program called Project 29 was implemented to increase the pool of Latino teachers in the district (Sakash & Chou, 2007). Project 29, a federally funded initiative, enrolled candidates from diverse backgrounds—many from diverse professions such as law, business, engineering, and others (Sakash & Chou, 2007). The majority had provisional teaching certifications but needed a teaching degree to continue working in the classroom. This program has proven to be extremely successful in increasing the number of effective and highly qualified Latino teachers who become leaders in Chicago public schools (Sakash & Chou, 2007). The Project 29 teachers were more likely to teach in Chicago public schools, schools with predominantly Latino enrollment and slightly lower achieving schools than their peers (Sakash & Chou, 2007). As is true with TFA, these teachers also had greater retention rates than their peers (Sakash & Chou, 2007). These impressive statistics show the value of alternative certification programs as they relate to the Latino teacher pipeline. Attention should be given to finding ways to continue supporting students of color, specifically Latinos, through these alternative programs.

Juncture 4: Landscape of Latino Teachers in the Field

Although the voices of Latino teachers are not as readily available in the empirical literature, a small handful of researchers have begun to pull together voices of Latino educators. Although the dominant narrative of teaching includes individuals who have had a positive experience with schooling, and being inspired by teachers they had as students (Irizarry & Donaldson, 2012; Lortie, 1975), Latino teachers have primarily been motivated by a desire to combat negative experiences they had as students, hoping to create a better future for the students they teach (Irizarry & Donaldson, 2012). In their study of both preservice Latino teachers and TFA Latino teachers, Irizarry and Donaldson (2012) found that the participants in their studies "consistently described teaching as a platform from which to challenge the injustices they experienced in schools [and want to] transform the institutions they viewed as critical to shaping the opportunities available to Latina/o youth" (p. 168). This push into the classroom differs greatly from the mainstream teacher pipeline.

Latino teachers who make it to the classroom must sometimes defy the expectations set upon them by family and those around them. Some teachers must challenge the traditional cultural pathway that is expected of them in order to leave home, get a higher education, and become an educator (Galindo, 1996; Ochoa, 2007). Ochoa (2007) shared narratives of Latino teachers, including reflections on these teachers' progress through the educational pipeline. The barriers articulated throughout this article are present within these stories. However, one also hears about ways that these teachers overcame these struggles. Many of the Latino teachers reflected on the support systems that surrounded them and helped them achieve their goal of becoming a teacher (Ochoa, 2007). Whether these networks were individual teachers, counselors, role models, mentors, or even organizations and community programs, these support systems were critical in ensuring academic excellence for the teachers in Ochoa's study.

Like Ochoa, Galindo (1996) shared the Latino teacher experience in his work. He highlighted three Chicano teachers as he explored their teacher role identity while arguing for the need to share more narratives of Latino teachers within various contexts, including teacher education, to create supportive environments that value the backgrounds and experiences of these educators. It is clear that these Latino teachers' family values became important in their teacher identity roles as well, something that may be unique to Latino teachers (Galindo, 1996).

The benefits that accrue as schools are able to recruit more Latinos into the classroom are evident through a study conducted by Weisman and Hansen (2008). They found that Latino teachers note a stronger connection to their Latino students and families as well as an affinity to teach in urban, low-income districts with high Latino populations (Weisman & Hansen, 2008). Latino teachers want to provide a cultural and linguistic role model to their Latino students (Weisman & Hansen, 2008). Latino teachers' ability to relate to the experiences of their students makes them well equipped to tackle the challenge of increasing student achievement for their Latino students.

Conclusion

Through this literature review, it has become clear that the critical junctures of the Latino teacher pipeline that were explored present challenges to Latinos pursuing a teaching career. Educators and policymakers wanting to strengthen the Latino teacher pipeline must begin by addressing the alarming facts about the lack of Latinos who are making it through the educational system. Attention must be paid to finding ways to address the gaps in the educational achievement of Latino youth, who will one day become future educators. An important step in this process includes getting more Latino teachers as role models in the classroom. However, that step cannot be achieved if experts do not address the achievement gap of Latinos, as Latinos will not make it past the first step of the teacher pipeline. This becomes a cyclical problem that must be addressed immediately.

The Latino teacher pipeline is often nontraditional and does not mirror the dominant narrative of teacher pipelines. The traditional teacher education program continues to lack diversity and is not necessarily the most common pathway followed by Latinos into the classroom. Alternative certification programs, 2-year college enrollment followed by a 4-year degree, the paraprofessional-to-teacher pipeline, and career pathway programs are all important in the Latino teacher pipeline. Although it is definitely important to continue to find ways to strengthen the traditional teacher pipeline for Latino educators, it must also be acknowledged and accepted that the Latino teacher pipeline is often a nontraditional pathway to the classroom. For this reason, alternative pathways must be explored and strengthened for Latino teachers as well.

Overall, this comprehensive review points to the fact that more empirical data are needed about the Latino teacher pipeline in general. Data across each of the critical junctures of the pipeline are necessary, but more information is definitely needed from the perspective of Latino teachers who have successfully navigated the teacher pipeline. It is evident that many of the challenges that Latinos face are highlighted in the literature. However, the areas of opportunity that may strengthen the pipeline are not as readily available. The most important source of support is to begin with Latino teachers themselves. However, this marginalized group of teachers does not yet have a strong voice in the landscape of the teacher pipeline literature. Their experiences will help illustrate barriers and support networks that Latino teachers face in their pursuit of a teaching degree. These data are important for educators and policymakers to use in finding ways to strengthen this pipeline. This should serve as a call for action—more empirical data from Latino teachers are needed in order to strengthen the teacher pipeline.

References

American Council on Education. (1995). *Minorities in higher education: Thirteenth annual status report*. Washington, DC: Office of Minority Concerns.

Auerbach, S. (2002). "Why do they give the good classes to some and not to others?" Latino parent narratives of struggle in a college access program. *Teachers College Record*, 104, 1369–1392.

Auerbach, S. (2004). Engaging Latino parents in supporting college pathways: Lessons from a college access program. *Journal of Hispanic Higher Education*, 3(2), 125–145.

Auerbach, S. (2011). Learning from Latino families. *Educational Leadership*, 68(8), 16–21.

Behnke, A. O., Piercy, K. W., & Diversi, M. (2004). Educational and occupational aspirations of Latino youth and their parents. *Hispanic Journal of Behavioral Sciences*, 26(1), 16–35.

Berry, B. (1986). Why bright college students won't teach. *Urban Review*, 18(4), 269–280.

Bonner, P. J., Pacino, M. A., & Hardcastle Standford, B. (2011). Transition from paraprofessionals to bilingual teachers: Latino voices and experiences in education. *Journal of Hispanic Higher Education*, 10(3), 212–225.

Bragg, D. (2007). Teacher pipelines: Career pathways extending from high school to community college to university. *Community College Review*, 35(1), 10–29.

Burkam, D. T., & Lee, V. E. (2002). *Inequality at the starting gate: Social background differences in achievement as children begin school*. Retrieved from the Economic Policy Institute website: http://www.epi.org/publication/ books_starting_gate/

Bustos Flores, B., & Claeys, L. (2011). Academy for Teacher Excellence: Maximizing synergy among partners for promoting college access for Latino teacher candidates. *Urban Review*, 43, 321–338.

Bustos Flores, B., Riojas Clark, E., Claeys, L., & Villareal, A. (2007). Academy for Teacher Excellence: Recruiting, preparing and retaining Latino teachers through learning communities. *Teacher Education Quarterly*, 34(4), 53–69.

Cohen, A. M., & Brawer, F. B. (2003). *The American community college* (4th ed.). San Francisco, CA: Jossey-Bass.

Cooper, C. R. (2002). Five bridges along students' pathways to college: A developmental blueprint of families, teachers, counselors, mentors and peers in the Puente project. *Educational Policy, 16,* 607–622.

Darling-Hammond, L. (2011). Teacher preparation: Build on what works. *Education Week, 30*(24), 36–26.

Darling-Hammond, L., Chung, R., & Frelow, F. (2002). Variation in teacher preparation: How well do different pathways prepare teachers to teach? *Journal of Teacher Education, 53*(4), 286–302.

Darling-Hammond, L., Holtzman, D., Gatlin, S. J., & Vasquez Heilig, J. (2005). Does teacher preparation matter? Evidence about teacher certification, Teach for America, and teacher effectiveness. *Education Policy Analysis Archives, 13*(42). Retrieved from https://epaa.asu.edu/epaa/v13n42/

De los Santos, A. G., & De los Santos, G. E. (2006). Latina/os and community colleges: A pathway to graduate studies? In J. Castellanos, A. M. Gloria, & M. Kaminura (Eds.), *The Latino/a pathway to the Ph.D.: Abriendo caminos* (pp. 37–54). Sterling, VA: Stylus.

Dee, T. (2004). Teachers, race, and student achievement in a randomized experiment. *Review of Economics and Statistics, 86,* 195–210.

Dillard, C. (1994). Beyond supply and demand: Critical pedagogy, ethnicity and empowerment in recruiting teachers of color. *Journal of Teacher Education, 45*(1), 9–17.

Dilworth, M. E. (1990). *Reading between the lines: Teachers and their racial/ethnic cultures* (Teacher Education Monograph No. 11). Washington, DC: ERIC Clearinghouse on Teacher Education and American Association of Colleges for Teacher Education.

Donaldson, M. L., & Johnson, S. M. (2010). The price of misassignment: The role of teaching assignments in Teach for American teachers' exit from low-income schools and the teaching profession. *Educational Evaluation and Policy Analysis, 32*(2), 299–323.

Downs, A., Martin, J., Fossum, M., Martinez, S., Solorio, M., & Martinez, H. (2008). Parents teaching parents: A career and college knowledge program for Latino families. *Journal of Latinos and Education, 7*(3), 227–240.

Embry Jenlink, K. (2012). *Teacher preparation in career pathways: The future of America's teacher pipeline.* Lanham, MD: Rowman & Littlefield Education.

Feistritzer, C. E. (1998). *Alternative teacher certification—An overview.* Washington, DC: National Center for Education Information.

Floyd, D., & Walker, D. (2003). Community college teacher education: A typology, challenging issues, and state views. *Community College Journal of Research and Practice, 27,* 643–663.

Frankenberg, E. (2009). The segregation of American teachers. *Education Policy Analysis Archives, 17*(1). Retrieved from http://epaa.asu.edu/epaa/v17n1/

Galindo, R. (1996). Reframing the past in the present: Chicana teacher role identity as a bridging identity. *Education and Urban Society, 29*(1), 85–102.

Galman, S. (2006). Rich White girls: Developing critical identities in teacher education and novice teaching settings. *International Journal of Learning, 13*(3), 47–55.

Gandara, P. (2002). A study of high school puente: What we have learned about preparing Latino youth for postsecondary education. *Educational Policy, 16,* 474–495.

Gay, G., Dingus, J., & Jackson, C. (2003). *The presence and performance of teachers of color in the profession* [Monograph]. Washington, DC: Community Teachers Institute.

Gomez, M. L. (2010). Talking about ourselves, talking about our mothers: Latina prospective teachers narrate their life experiences. *Urban Review, 42,* 81–101.

Gomez, M. L., & Rodriguez, T. L. (2011). Imagining the knowledge, strength and skills of a Latina prospective teacher. *Teacher Education Quarterly*, *38*(1), 127–146.

Gomez, M. L., Rodriguez, T. L., & Agosto, V. (2008). Who are Latino prospective teachers and what do they bring to U.S. schools? *Race and Ethnicity Education*, *11*(3), 267–283.

Gonzalez, J. M. (1997). Recruiting and training minority teachers: Student views of the pre-service program. *Equity and Excellence in Education*, *30*(1), 56–64.

Goodlad, J. (1984). *A place called school*. New York, NY: McGraw-Hill.

Green, T. M. (2008). The racial academic achievement gap. Retrieved from http://files.eric.ed.gov/fulltext/ED500218.pdf

Guarino, C., Santibanez, L., & Daley, G. (2006). Teacher recruitment and retention: A review of the recent empirical literature. *Review of Educational Research*, *76*(2), 173–208.

Haberman, M. (1988). Proposals for recruiting minority teachers: Promising practices and attractive detours. *Journal of Teacher Education*, *39*(4), 38–44.

Hallett, A. C. (2012). Grow Your Own Illinois: Taking action in Chicago neighborhood schools. In K. Embry Jenlink (Ed.), *Teacher preparation in career pathways: The future of America's teacher pipeline* (pp. 65–77). Lanham, MD: Rowman & Littlefield Education.

Harvey, W. B. (2003). *Minorities in higher education, 2001–02: Twentieth anniversary annual status report*. Washington, DC: American Council on Education.

Huber, L. P., Huidor, O., Malagon, M., Sanchez, G., & Solorzano, D. (2006). *Falling through the cracks: Critical transitions in the Latino/a educational pipeline*. Los Angeles: University of California, Los Angeles, Chicano Studies Research Center.

Ingersoll, R., & May, H. (2011). The minority teacher shortage: Fact or fable? *Phi Delta Kappan*, *93*(1), 62–65.

Ingle, Y., & Castro, R. (1993). *Resolving a crisis in education: Latino teachers for tomorrow's classrooms*. Claremont, CA: Tomas Rivera Center.

Irizarry, J., & Donaldson, M. (2012). Teach for America: The Latinization of U.S. schools and the critical shortage of Latino/a teachers. *American Educational Research Journal*, *49*(1), 155–194.

Irizarry, J., & Raible, J. (2011). Beginning with El Barrio: Learning from exemplary teachers of Latino students. *Journal of Latinos & Education*, *10*(3), 186–203.

Lortie, D. (1975). *Schoolteacher: A sociological study*. Chicago, IL: University of Chicago Press.

Merriam-Webster (2014). *Pipeline [Def. 2]*. Retrieved from http://www.merriam-webster.com/dictionary/pipeline

Moll, L., Amanti, C., Neff, D., & Gonzalez, N. (1992). Funds of knowledge for teaching: Using a qualitative approach to connect homes and classrooms. *Theory Into Practice*, *31*(2), 132–141.

Monzo, L. D., & Rueda, R. S. (2001). Professional roles, caring and scaffolds: Latino teachers' and paraeducators' interaction with Latino students. *American Journal of Education*, *109*, 438–472.

Nadler, D., & Peterson, P. E. (2009). What happens when states have genuine alternative certification? We get more minority teachers and test scores rise. *Education Digest: Essential Readings Condensed for Quick Review*, *75*(1), 57–60.

National Center for Education Statistics. (2008). *Schools and Staffing Survey (SASS), percentage distribution of school teachers, by race/ethnicity, school type, and selected school characteristics, 2007–2008*. Retrieved from http://nces.ed.gov/pubs2009/2009324/tables.asp

Ochoa, G. L. (2007). *Learning from Latino teachers*. San Francisco, CA: Jossey-Bass Education Series.

Oliva, M., & Staudt, K. (2003). Pathways to teaching: Latino student choice and professional identity development in a teacher training magnet program. *Equity and Excellence in Education, 36*(1), 270–279.

Orfield, G., & Lee, C. (2007). *Historic reversals, accelerating resegregation, and the need for new integration strategies.* Cambridge, MA: Civil Rights Project at Harvard University.

Pew Hispanic Center. (2011). *Statistical portrait of Hispanics in the United States, 2010.* Retrieved from http://www.pewhispanic.org/2012/02/21/statistical-portrait-of-hispanics-in-the-united-states-2010/#1

Quiocho, A., & Rios, F. (2000). The power of their presence: Minority group teachers and schooling. *Review of Educational Research, 70,* 485–528.

Rumberger, R. W., & Angulano, B. A. (2004). *Understanding and addressing the California Latino achievement gap in early elementary school.* Retrieved from the University of California Linguistic Minority Research Institute website: http://escholarship.org/uc/item/65d6v84n

Sakash, K., & Chou, V. (2007). Increasing the supply of Latino bilingual teachers for the Chicago public schools. *Teacher Education Quarterly, 34*(4), 41–52.

Salinas, C., & Castro, A. J. (2010). Disrupting the official curriculum: Cultural biography and the curriculum decision making of Latino preservice teachers. *Theory and Research in Social Education, 38,* 428–463.

Sólorzano, D. G., Villalpando, O., & Oseguera, L. (2005). Educational inequities and Latina/o undergraduate students in the United States: A critical race analysis of their educational progress. *Journal of Hispanic Higher Education, 4*(3), 272–294.

Swail, W. S., Cabrera, A. F., & Lee, C. (2004). *Latino youth and pathway to college.* Washington, DC: Pew Hispanic Center Study.

Thomas, R. S. (1998, April). Black and Latino college enrollment: Effects of background, high school preparation, family and peer influence, and financial aid. *American Educational Research Association.* Retrieved from http://files.eric.ed.gov/fulltext/ED420253.pdf

Tornatzky, L. G., Cutler, R., & Lee, J. (2002). *College knowledge: What Latino parents need to know and why they don't know it.* Chicago, IL: Tomás Rivera Policy Institute.

Townsend, B., & Ignash, J. (Eds.). (2003). The role of the community college in teacher education. *New Directions for Community Colleges, 121,* pp. 37–46.

U.S. Census Bureau (2009). *United States Population Projections 2000 to 2050.* Retrieved from http://www.census.gov/population/projections/files/analytical-document09.pdf.

U.S. Department of Education (2008). National Center for Education Statistics, Schools and Staffing Survey (SASS), "Public School Teacher Questionnaire," 2007–08. Retrieved from http://nces.ed.gov/surveys/ctes/tables/h120.asp

Valadez, J. R. (2008). Shaping the educational decisions of Mexican immigrant high school students. *American Educational Research Journal, 45,* 834–860.

Valenciana, C., Morin, J. A., & Morales, R. S. (2005). Meeting the challenge: Building university school district partnerships for a successful career ladder program for teachers of English learners. *Action in Teacher Education, 33*(1), 20–32.

Vela-Gude, L., Cavazos, J., Johnson, M., Fielding, C., Campos, L., & Rodriguez, I. (2009). "My counselors were never there": Perceptions from Latino college students. *Professional School Counseling, 12*(4), 272–279.

Villegas, A. (2009, February). *Hispanic research agenda: Teacher preparation.* Paper presented at the National Latino/a Education Research Agenda Project, New York, NY.

Villegas, A. M., & Clewell, B. C. (1998). Increasing teacher diversity by tapping the paraprofessional pool. *Theory Into Practice, 37*(2), 121–130.

Villegas, A., & Lucas, T. (2004). Diversifying the teacher workforce: A retrospective and prospective analysis. In M. A. Smylie & D. Miretzky (Eds.), *Developing the teacher workforce: 103rd yearbook of the National Society for the Study of Education* (pp. 70–104). Chicago, IL: University of Chicago Press.

Weisman, E. M., & Hansen, L. E. (2008). Student teaching in urban and suburban schools: Perspectives of Latino preservice teachers. *Urban Education, 43*, 653–670.

Wilson, E. V. (2001). Pathways to teacher education: Factors critical to the retention and graduation of community college transfer students in teacher education programs. *Inquiry, 6*(2), 17–27.

Section II
Themes

7 *Francisco Maestas et al. v. George H. Shone et al.*

Mexican American Resistance to School Segregation in the Hispano Homeland, 1912–1914

Ruben Donato, Gonzalo Guzmán, and Jarrod Hanson

This article chronicles a school desegregation lawsuit, *Francisco Maestas et al. v. George H. Shone et al.* (1914), filed by Mexican Americans in Alamosa, Colorado, against the Alamosa School District Superintendent and Board of Education in 1913.[1] The *Maestas* lawsuit provides a portrait of a community organizing to advocate for the education of their children. This case is important because it precedes other challenges to the segregation of Mexican children in public schools. The *Maestas* case was tried 16 years before *Del Rio ISD v. Salvatierra* (Texas, 1930) and 17 years before *Alvarez v. Lemon Grove* (California, 1931). Both of those cases became highly visible in the history of education literature, and *Alvarez* became known as the first successful Mexican American school desegregation case in the United States.[2] The *Maestas* case, however, is different from *Salvatierra* and *Alvarez* in three fundamental ways that are important to highlight prior to describing the case.

First, unlike *Salvatierra* in Del Rio and *Alvarez* in Lemon Grove—communities that were located along, or close to, the U.S.–Mexico border—the *Maestas* lawsuit was filed in Alamosa. Located in Colorado's San Luis Valley, this is part of the country that historian Richard Nostrand called the "Hispano homeland." Nostrand maintained that southern Colorado (and northern New Mexico) was a location where people of Mexican descent were isolated and culturally removed from Mexico. It was a place where unique "Mexican" identities (i.e., Spanish American or Hispanos Americano) evolved over time.[3]

Second, how race was used to challenge school segregation in the *Maestas* lawsuit differed from how it was used in *Salvatierra* and *Alvarez*. In *Salvatierra* the Mexican plaintiffs argued that Mexicans were part of the "other white race" and were exempt from legal segregation under the laws of Texas.[4] Similarly, plaintiffs in *Alvarez* argued that California did not have a law that allowed for the segregation of Mexican children, whereas there were laws that explicitly permitted the segregation of other named races.[5] In *Maestas*, Mexican American plaintiffs asserted that race was a driving force behind the school officials' actions to segregate their children. Defendants responded that Mexican American students were White and therefore race could not have motivated their decisions.

Third, Mexican American plaintiffs in Alamosa did not receive legal assistance from the Mexican government. They were historically removed from Mexico and had deep roots in northern New Mexico and southern Colorado.[6] Because of the longstanding roots of many Mexicans in the San Luis Valley and the plaintiffs' status as American citizens, the Mexican Consulate was not used as a resource either politically or legally in the community's fight against segregation.

In this article we argue that the *Maestas* lawsuit is one of the earliest Mexican-American-led school desegregation lawsuits in the United States. In fact, the *Denver Catholic Register* noted in 1914 that the lawsuit "was the first time in the history of America that a court fight was made over an attempt to segregate Mexicans in school."[7] We further argue that this lawsuit is unique not only because of its geographical location and because Mexican Americans did not have support from the Mexican government but—most important— because a novel strategy was used at the time to challenge the segregation of their children. Mexican Americans rejected their legal White status, claimed that they were racially distinct, and used the Colorado State Constitution to challenge segregation because it was illegal for schools to distinguish and classify children in public schools according to color or race.[8]

The Emergence of a Lawsuit

The *Maestas* lawsuit was triggered when the school board and superintendent established a policy to send *all* Mexican children into the district's newly constructed Mexican School in 1912.[9] The school was built in 1909, when the Alamosa School Board of Education purchased a piece of property on the "Mexican side" of town with the intent to build a school to serve non-English-speaking Mexican American children.[10] When the school was constructed, it was a modest building with four classrooms, was staffed by three teachers, and served approximately 140 Mexican American children.[11] Once completed, the school attracted much local interest, with one newspaper editor from Creede, Colorado, reporting, "Back east and south they build separate schools for negro children. At Alamosa they have just built one exclusively for Spanish children."[12]

In 1912, not long after the school opened, a local newspaper reported that a group of Mexican Americans filed a complaint "to see if the school board has any authority to compel Mexican children to attend any particular school building when another one is more convenient."[13] Mexican American parents viewed the policy change as a matter of racial discrimination. A visiting Jesuit priest during the same year reflected on the social environment, stating that "the Americans in that community had built a school where the Mexicans alone came together so that the American boys would not have to mingle with the Mexicans." The social conditions were so disconcerting that "Americans treated those poor Mexicans as the black sons of Africa."[14] Another year and a half passed before the *Rocky Mountain News* in Denver reported that Mexican Americans in Alamosa had complained to the Colorado state superintendent of instruction, Mary C. C. Bradford, to see whether school officials in Alamosa had the authority to segregate their children in one school. The story described how Mexican children in the district were forced to attend one school in the community. State Superintendent Bradford told the press that she was going to ask the Colorado attorney general for an opinion about the complaint.[15]

The *Denver Catholic Register* further added that racial tension in Alamosa was escalating because Mexican American families believed school officials were segregating their children unjustly.[16] Two days later, the *Denver Times* reported that the "State Board Cannot Stop Segregation of Mexicans" and that Mexican children in Alamosa "must continue to attend a school in which they are segregated from whites and blacks." The story was clear that after an investigation into its powers, the "state board of education can do nothing in the matter."[17] Similarly, the *Alamosa Independent Journal* reported the same outcome and added that "Mexican children of Alamosa must continue to attend a special school in which they are segregated from whites and blacks [or] appeal to the county school board or take the case into the courts."[18]

Seeing that the Alamosa School Board of Education, the school district superintendent, the Colorado State Board of Education, and the Colorado State Attorney General were unable or unwilling to address their complaint, Mexican Americans organized, pulled their children out of the Mexican School, staged a boycott, and filed a lawsuit in the District Court.[19] As these actions unfolded, the *Denver Catholic Register* explained that Mexican American parents challenged school officials' assertion that their children were being segregated because they lacked English language skills. Mexican American parents believed that language was being used as an excuse to segregate their children when race was the real issue behind school board and superintendent actions.[20] As a result, Mexican American parents staged a walkout in the fall of 1913 and refused to send their children to the Mexican School. The *Denver Post* reported that a "school strike, engineered by the Mexicans of Alamosa against the public school of the city, reached such a serious state yesterday that a court fight became the only solution."[21] The *Denver Catholic Register* also noted that "rather than retract from its stand," school officials "let the children go without education."[22]

Grassroots Activism

The lawsuit was a significant undertaking for the Mexican American community. Unlike in later lawsuits challenging the segregation of Mexican children, the Mexican American community in Alamosa did not have the assistance of the Mexican Consulate, as the plaintiffs were U.S. citizens. In this section, we investigate the organizing that led to the lawsuit, who the leaders were, how they acquired legal counsel, and how the lawsuit was funded. In 1962, Luther Bean, Nancy Denious, and Elinor Kingery interviewed a former teacher and activist who was involved with the case. J. R. C. Ruybal was not only an activist in the community but one of the first teachers to teach at the Mexican School.[23] Ruybal, born in 1879, was 83 years old at the time of the interview and was 33 years old in 1913, the time when the lawsuit was being filed. By 1962, the time of the interview, 48 years had passed since the *Maestas* decision was handed down. In the interview, Ruybal explained that many Spanish Americans had moved to Alamosa from New Mexico to work on the railroads. As the Spanish American population in Alamosa began to grow, their children started to attend school. Teachers, he said, had problems in mixed classes. Ruybal explained that the Alamosa School Board and Superintendent Kendall decided to construct a Mexican School to serve non-English-speaking Mexican American children. At the time, Ruybal explained, he supported the Mexican School, which, he said, was a place where Mexican American children were taught in English but concepts were explained in Spanish.[24]

The problem started, according to Ruybal, when the school board and new school district superintendent, George Thompson, established a policy to segregate all Spanish Americans in the school district. "On February 5, 1912," said Ruybal, "the school board made all Mexican children go to the Mexican school." This was a problem, said Ruybal, because half of the Spanish American children in the district were able to speak English. After school officials began to force all Mexican American children into the Mexican School, Mexican Americans started to inquire about the policy. A group was subsequently formed—the Spanish American Union. The group met, discussed the issue, drafted a resolution, and met with the Alamosa School Board of Education. "We presented those resolutions to the board," said Ruybal, "protesting the segregation. They did not pay attention to us."[25] Ruybal and the Spanish American Union were disappointed that their concerns about the segregation of their children fell on deaf ears.

Because the school board and superintendent would not listen to their concerns, the Spanish American Union tried something else. They went to the *Alamosa Journal* with the intent to publish their resolution, but the editor of the newspaper, said Ruybal, refused to publish the document. At this time, Ruybal was still employed at the Mexican School, but his tenure at the school did not last long. Ruybal explained that the school board would not communicate with him. However, the board asked Mr. French, another teacher at the Mexican School, to speak to him. Mr. French asked Ruybal, "How long are you going to stay with these people?" Ruybal responded that he was going to "stay with them to the last." Ruybal said that "[Mr. French told me that I would] 'not last very long.' It was true. They refused me a position." Based on the interview, Ruybal suggested that he was fired because he was part of a group that was challenging the segregation of all Mexican children in the Mexican School.

After Ruybal was dismissed from the Mexican School, he purchased an interest in a Spanish American newspaper in Antonito, a small town south of Alamosa. Ruybal used the newspaper as a means of challenging the Alamosa schools. When Ruybal joined the newspaper, he began to write about various issues in the area. At first, he said, he was not writing about the Alamosa schools. But that quickly changed. He started to write about the Alamosa schools because a Mr. Gallegos tried to enroll his children at a White school in Alamosa that was closer to his home. His children were denied admission to the school. Mr. Gallegos wanted to challenge the school board and even thought about filing a lawsuit, but after Gallegos spoke with an attorney, he was discouraged from going forward. He was told it was expensive and that he had "no chance to win. So he stopped."[26]

Soon after, a Mr. Quintana contacted Ruybal and encouraged him to write about the segregation of Mexican American children in the Alamosa schools. But Quintana asked Ruybal to do more. He encouraged him to appeal to "Spanish Americans to raise money to fight the matter in court." Ruybal began to reach out to the Spanish American communities in the San Luis Valley, pleaded for their support, and asked them to contribute to a fund to begin a lawsuit. "Raising money to go to court," said Ruybal, "started to come in from the Spanish settlements." Many Spanish Americans were supportive of the lawsuit, and they contributed what they could.[27] Once money was raised, a committee was formed. It had 10 members, and Ruybal was part of the group. Among the members, said Ruybal, was "Father Montell, a Catholic priest." As the committee members started to strategize about how they were going to challenge the Alamosa School District, they knew it would be difficult to acquire legal counsel and that it would be expensive. But in one meeting, said Ruybal, "Father Montell said 'I know a young man. He is a very bright man. I believe I can get him for a reasonable price.' We told him to go ahead." Father Montel went to Denver and spoke with an attorney named Raymond Sullivan, and an agreement was made. Sullivan agreed to represent Mexican Americans in Alamosa and charged the group $200 plus expenses, Francisco Maestas was named plaintiff, and the lawsuit began.[28]

A Lawsuit Is Filed

In his petition to the District Court, Raymond Sullivan described the Alamosa context and the school board's actions from the Mexican American parents' perspective. At the time, there were approximately 800 Mexicans in the city, and 150 of them were between 6 and 21 years old. The district had three schools: the North Side or High School (it also included a primary or grammar school) in Ward 1 at Bell Avenue and Main Street; the South Side School, situated in Ward 4 at Eleventh Street and Hunt Avenue; and a third, "known as the Mexican school, in Ward Three at Ninth Street and Ross."[29] Sullivan averred that

> all the Mexican children or children of Mexican descent are and have been for more than two years last past, obligated by order of said Board of Education to attend said Mexican School up to the fifth grade thereof, where other children were and are permitted to attend the schools most convenient to their residence.

Sullivan pointed out that some schools were "convenient to the residence of the Mexican children and from which they are excluded on account of their race."[30]

Sullivan explained that the "plaintiff who is himself of the Mexican race" went to see School District Superintendent George O. Thompson to enroll his 11-year-old son, Miguel, in a school that was more convenient to his home, but on September 2, 1913, Superintendent Thompson "refused to admit said child as a pupil and directed him to attend the Mexican School."[31] Sullivan added that on August 25, 1913, a group of Mexican American parents contacted the Alamosa School Board of Education for permission to enroll their children at the North Side School because it was more convenient to their homes. School board officials informed Mexican American parents that "their children and all children of Mexican descent would be confined to the Mexican school up to the fifth grade."[32] Sullivan explained that Francisco Maestas's son was "forced to cross and re-cross said tracks in his travel to and from the said Mexican School to his great danger and to plaintiff's distress of mind."[33]

Sullivan maintained that by denying the Maestas children access to the closest school and thereby forcing them to attend the Mexican School, school officials were making a "distinction and classification of pupils in the public schools on account of race or color contrary to the Constitution of the laws of the State of Colorado." Article IX, Section 8 of the Colorado Constitution stated that "no sectarian tenets or doctrines shall ever be taught in the public schools, nor shall any distinction and classification of pupils be made on account of race or color."[34]

Sullivan asked for an alternative writ of mandamus to be issued by the court directing the school board and superintendent to

> admit the said child of plaintiff to the North Side School or the most convenient of the public schools of said city to which he has the right of admission without any distinction or classification on account of his race or color, and pay the costs of this action, or to show cause why they should not do so.[35]

As the news media covered the case, the *Alamosa Independent Journal* reported that the decision to segregate Mexican American children was "adopted several years ago by the directors, and it has been proven that it was the best system ever inaugurated in any school district" and that the "percentage of those Spanish American children who advance beyond the fourth grade has steadily increased." The paper also reported that "last year's advancement of scholars increased over 400 per cent over the number of those advanced before the system was inaugurated five years ago, with practically the same attendance."[36] The *Alamosa Independent Journal* clearly supported the school board of education and school district superintendent. The paper claimed that school officials were "giving the children of the Spanish American families of this city advantages they have never enjoyed elsewhere" and also cautioned that "if the board is wrong they will simply have to go back to the old and far inferior system of educating the children of these citizens."[37]

In response to the Mexican Americans' complaint, District Court Judge Charles Holbrook determined that the *Maestas* petition had made a sufficient case for admittance of the students that he issued an order to the school board and superintendent to either admit the children to the most convenient public school or file an answer arguing why they should not.[38]

The Answer

John T. Adams responded to Raymond Sullivan's petition on behalf of the school board. In his answer, Adams specified what the Alamosa School Board of Education and the school district superintendent admitted and what they denied. Among other things, they admitted that Francisco Maestas was a U.S. citizen and a tax-paying resident of Alamosa. The answer also admitted that Francisco Maestas tried to enroll his son Miguel (i.e., Mike) at North Side High School on September 2, 1913, and that Superintendent Thompson refused to admit Miguel into the North Side School and ordered him to attend the preparatory school.[39]

Adams, however, challenged Sullivan on several counts. Adams denied that school officials ordered all Mexican children to attend the preparatory school, denied that the school board and school district superintendent had distinguished or classified Mexican children based on color or race, and denied that Mexican children were excluded from any school that was convenient to their residence because of their race.[40]

Adams argued that Miguel Maestas and other Mexican American children were not segregated on account of race because the Mexican American children were in fact "Caucasian." He argued that "all of the children of said school district are of the same race and color, to-wit, white children of the Caucasian race, with the exception of a few negroes."[41] Adams was trying to make the case that school officials were not segregating Mexican children based on race because Mexican children were Caucasian.[42]

Instead he argued that Miguel Maestas was denied admission to the North Side School because he lacked English skills and was academically unprepared. He pointed out that Miguel had failed an English exam and that he was "behind in all of his classes and studies, and . . . unable to carry on the work thereof." Miguel was also behind academically, said Adams, because his parents had "permitted" him to stay out of school for 3 months (because of the walkout).[43] Adams then maintained that Miguel was required to attend the preparatory school "where special facilities were and are provided for the use of all children who are deficient in a working knowledge of the English language."[44]

Building on the argument that language was the key issue, Adams argued that the school had employed teachers with special skills at the school and that it offered the "best and most efficient system of teaching pupils unfamiliar with English language and where a new language must be taught and learned." Adams also argued that Mexican children received "more individual attention from the teachers in the use of English language; and the course of general (manual training) is the same for the children attending the school."[45]

Perhaps in a nod to *Plessy v. Ferguson*, Adams also made a case for the quality (and equality) of the facilities at the Mexican School. Adams argued that the school building was one of the best in the city, that it was sanitary, and that the "equipment is equal to, if not superior to any other school building." Children at the school, Adams claimed, "receive equal educational advantages with all the children in the city."

Adams also challenged the idea that distance and safety were serious issues. He averred that the preparatory school was not far from the Maestas home and argued that it was not a perilous walk to the preparatory school and that, given the seven-block distance, it was "within reasonable walking distance from plaintiff's place of residence." He also claimed that Miguel's walk to the school was not dangerous because of passing trains, as railroad companies were required to protect pedestrians by using warning signs and signals and that walking across the tracks was no more dangerous than crossing any street in the city.[46]

Finally, Adams argued that segregation was important for the education of all students in Alamosa. He claimed that it was "impossible to efficiently teach the non-English-speaking children in said school district, in English grammar, or any other subject, without seriously retarding and impairing the educational advancement and development of the school children of said city."[47] Adams cautioned the court about allowing non-English-speaking Mexican American children to attend one of the other schools in the district where teachers did not understand Spanish and warned the court that

> the graded system of schools in said city would be seriously injured and impaired if not altogether destroyed, and the advancement of educational development of the pupils of the said city would be thereby retarded, including not only those speaking the Spanish language but also those speaking only the English language.

Adams asserted that it was impossible "to provide for adequate teaching facilities for said pupils in more than one of the buildings in said city." To "change the present system of instruction in said school district," he concluded, "would result in great and irreparable injury and loss to said school district and tax payers thereof."[48]

Adams ended by putting forth the board's perspective about who was behind the suit. He said that the defendants believed that the lawsuit was instigated by individuals who did not have children in the school district, individuals who did not pay taxes in the district, individuals who were of Mexican birth, and individuals who wanted to destroy and discredit the school and school officials for personal reasons. He said, in short, that it was individuals who wanted to embarrass and handicap the "principal and instructors in said schools, and the defendant directors of said School District."[49]

In the Court

There is no transcript from the trial, but there are some court records and newspaper accounts. In the trial, race became an issue because it was key to the plaintiffs' argument that Mexican Americans be understood as racially distinct. The *Alamosa Independent Journal*, however, reported how plaintiffs wanted to raise questions of race but that the "issue fell flat." It did so, the story noted, because the "general impression among our citizens seems to be that the Spanish Americans . . . are having their children take advantage of a system that is for the best interest of all concerned." It also pointed out that "these Spanish American parents, of which there are several hundred families represented in this city, appear to sincerely believe that they are not being treated justly."[50]

For its part, the school district subpoenaed a professor from the Greeley Normal School to testify on its behalf. Professor W. B. Mooney praised the school board and superintendent for the "good work done in the Alamosa schools through the segregation of the Spanish American scholars and the competent teachers for their instruction, who understood the custom and language of these children." Mooney declared that school officials were segregating Mexican children because it was pedagogically sound and praised them for hiring teachers with special skills at the school. The press described Professor Mooney as someone who was rational and stated that he was "very convincing to an unprejudiced mind."[51]

But the coverage by the *Alamosa Independent Journal* was limited. The *Denver Catholic Register* had more to report. It provided brief accounts of testimony from school board members, the superintendent, a principal, two teachers, several parents, a number of schoolchildren, and other community members. School District Superintendent George O. Thompson testified that Mexican American children were "put in a school by themselves because of their deficiency in the English language." He also told the court that no "American" children attended the school. When board member J. H. Darling took the stand, Sullivan asked him whether he thought there was racial prejudice toward Mexicans in Alamosa and whether he believed that "public sentiment had not been in favor of segregating their children in the public schools." Darling told Sullivan that he "would rather not answer the question."[52] Darling, however, not only admitted that he "would never permit his children to attend school with the Mexicans" but affirmed that "he was still of that mind." In addition, he also told the court that "the school set aside for the Mexican children was at all times designated the Mexican School in the official records of the board."[53]

George Shone, president of the school board, told the court that they acted in the best interest of all children. In his testimony, C. L. Lahrmann, treasurer of the school board and a baker by trade, suggested that he was responsible for conceptualizing the establishment of the Mexican School. But when he was asked whether "certain American persons had not called upon him and asserted that if the Mexican children were allowed to attend the American schools they would withdraw their children," Lahrmann told the court that he "could not remember—that he was not positive."[54]

Francisco Maestas and his son Miguel were also put on the stand. The *Register*, however, focused on Miguel. It reported how he "was timid and abashed by reason of the crowded court room." However, Miguel "understood and answered the questions put him by counsel in English." When defendants asked Miguel questions through an interpreter, "he responded in English before the interpreter could finish the questions." Miguel told the court that he was "often made late for school by reason of waiting for trains to pass." Other children were "put on the stand and answered readily in English the questions put to them by counsel."[55]

Other Mexican American parents and their children were put on the stand. Parent after parent testified that "their children knew English." One parent, Victor Gallegos, told the court that two of his children of school age "had been refused admission to the American school and that he had, rather than send them to the Mexican school, placed them in a convent in Denver." He said that he and his wife had spoken English to them since they were born and were well acquainted with the English language. Another Mexican American parent, Efren Quintana, claimed the "majority of the children in the Mexican school spoke English as well as his children and that he could see no reason except that of race prejudice as to why they were segregated." He maintained that the "great majority of the Mexican people wished to have their children attend the schools nearest to them without discrimination." Quintana also told the court that he had "never been in favor of a separate school" and that he had been a "member of a committee of Mexicans who appeared before the school board with a petition signed by 180 Mexican heads of families asking for their 'constitutional rights' in the schools." Quintana unabashedly told the court that the committee of Mexicans was "informed by Director Lahrmann that they had no rights."[56]

The principal of the South Side School in the district, Miss Carrie Body, testified, telling the court that she was ordered "to send all Mexican children to the Mexican School." Teachers from the Mexican School also testified. Miss Mary Lister asserted that "most of the children in her grades had a sufficient knowledge of the English to carry on the work in those grades." The other teacher at the Mexican School, Miss Loretta McGraw, stated that they spoke with "the children mostly in English and found that [was] the best way to teach them." But she told the court that they were "required by the board to use Spanish in teaching them." Miss McGraw concluded that "she was acquainted with all of the children in the school and that most of them spoke English."[57] Overwhelming evidence seemed to suggest that Mexican American children at the Mexican School were able to speak and understand English.

The Ruling

District Court Judge Charles Holbrook ruled in favor of Francisco Maestas and other Mexican American children in the Alamosa School District in March 1914. Judge Holbrook was convinced that school officials had used the English language deficiency and the academic unpreparedness of some Mexican American children as a rationale to send all Mexican American children to the Mexican School up to the fifth grade.[58] He explained that English-speaking Mexican American children had the right to attend public schools near their homes, or schools of their choice, in the Alamosa School District. In his decision, Holbrook ordered the school district to "admit Miguel Maestas, plaintiff's son, and the children of other Mexican people to attend the school or school nearest them respectively."[59]

In his decision, Judge Holbrook showed that he understood the school board's arguments about the educational purposes of the school. He noted that the "school was built for their [the Mexican students'] benefit, and supplied with teachers especially selected, because of their ability to speak both English and Spanish." Judge Holbrook believed that the Mexican School served a valuable service because "children sitting in a room wherein the instruction given is in a language which they do not understand, however, bright the child may be, cannot make progress, and must necessarily fall behind their classes."

However, he ultimately rejected those arguments and decided in favor of Maestas. He noted that some of the Mexican American children "in the lower grades may be able, and doubtless are able, to speak English."[60] He also understood why "Spanish speaking people believe that their children are excluded from the two English-speaking schools, upon account of race." Rejecting the school board's argument, he believed that this "feeling must be eradicated before the school can reach its greatest efficiency." He did not think it was just to send English-speaking Mexican children to the Mexican School because he saw "evidence [that showed there were] children in different grades in the Mexican Primary School, who know enough English to understand instruction in the same grades in the other schools." Thus, Holbrook stated that "in the opinion of the court . . . the only way to destroy this feeling of discontent and bitterness which has recently grown up, is to allow all children so prepared, to attend the school nearest them."[61]

Holbrook explained that

> Miguel Maestas, convinced the court that he is entitled to the privilege of attending the school nearest his home: and, the court is of the opinion that others in the primary school should be allowed to attend the schools nearest their respective places of residence.

Holbrook, however, stipulated that if there were any errors about the English language proficiency of children, the children themselves would know and would "soon ask to be returned to the primary school." In other words, Holbrook's ruling also meant that school officials were able to keep the non-English-speaking students at the Mexican School.[62]

The Media Reports the Decision

When Judge Holbrook delivered his decision in March 1914, a number of newspapers in Colorado and from neighboring states reported the outcome of the case. *The Rocky Mountain News* described how school officials in Alamosa had to admit "Mexican children as pupils and must give them the same instruction as is given the American children of the city." The press reported that school board members had "arbitrarily fixed a rule that Spanish-speaking pupils could not enter any of the other schools until after having completed the fourth grade in the Mexican school."[63]

On the following day, the *Denver Post* reported how "Mexican children have the same rights in the public schools in the state and cannot be lawfully segregated." The story explained that Judge Holbrook understood that the school in Alamosa was built for the benefit of children who could not speak English. But it was clear to Holbrook that Mexican American parents believed that their children were "excluded from the two English-Speaking schools on account of race." The press also explained that Holbrook understood that "the only way to destroy this feeling of discontent and bitterness that has grown up is to allow all the children so prepared to attend the schools nearest them."[64]

The *Denver Catholic Register* reported not only that the school segregation of Mexican American children had to stop in Alamosa but that the lawsuit was historic—that it "was the first time in the history of America that a court fight was made over an attempt to segregate Mexicans in school."[65] The front page of the *Alamosa Courier* read that Mexican Americans had won the court decision. The paper published Holbrook's entire decision and explained that the segregation was not because the Mexican children could not speak English "but because of race prejudice the school board and the city superintendent held against his people."[66]

In Akron, Colorado, a small community located in the northeastern part of the state, the newspaper reported that school officials in Alamosa had to admit Mexican children into their schools and "give them the same instruction as is given the American children of the city." The story in Akron reported that the school was built to serve non-English-speaking Mexican American children but that the "board arbitrarily fixed a rule that Spanish-Speaking pupils could not enter any of the other schools until after having completed the fourth grade in the Mexican school."[67]

Because the lawsuit was tried in the Hispano homeland, a Spanish-language newspaper, *La Revista de Taos* from Taos, New Mexico—a community located about 90 miles south of Alamosa—reported that Hispanos in Alamosa were victorious, that school officials in Alamosa had to admit Mexican American children into White schools, and that school officials had to provide them with the same instruction as American youth. In Spanish, the editor of La Revista told its readers, "*Congratulamos a los hispanos americanos residentes de Alamosa, estado de Colorado, por su valor y firmeza en defender sus garantias civicas como ciudadanos Americanos . . .*" Translated into English, the words congratulate the Hispanos Americanos of Alamosa for their courage and for defending their rights as American citizens.[68]

Legal Loose Ends

Although Holbrook's decision was public and many newspapers had reported his ruling, the lawsuit was not entirely over. John Adams filed a motion to vacate judgment and to dismiss action.[69] Judge Holbrook denied the motion to vacate on April 17, 1914. Adams filed a notice that the school board planned to appeal to the state supreme court; however, we could not find evidence of an appeal having been filed at or heard by the Colorado Supreme Court.[70]

Shortly after the trial, there was a handwritten order from Judge Holbrook regarding whether two additional students in the preparatory school could select another school in the district. It appears that Judge Holbrook examined the students' English abilities and determined that Juan Ortega was "qualified to receive instruction in English without retarding the class," and Judge Holbrook ordered that he be allowed to attend the school nearest his residence. However, he also determined that "Juan Maestas should acquire a little better knowledge of the English language, both for his own good and for the progress of the class to which he would be assigned" and ordered that he not be transferred until he was "able to pass a better examination in English."[71] This highlights the challenges the Mexican American community faced after the decision. Judge Holbrook made the determination about the language abilities of these two additional students, but the prospect of appealing the school district's determination about the language abilities of each Mexican student was impractical.

Discussion

The *Maestas v. Shone* case needs to be understood as one of the earliest Mexican American challenges to school segregation in the United States. The decision meant that the Alamosa School District was required to admit

English-speaking Mexican American children to White schools near their homes, but those who did not have a command of English were kept at the Mexican School. It is instructive to read how different newspapers interpreted the outcome of the case. The editor of the *Alamosa Leader*, for example, was partially correct. He reported that "the decision, in effect, is that the Mexican children can go to any school in Alamosa, nearest their homes, provided they are proficient to do so by having a knowledge of the English language." He also believed that "the decision was very fair." However, unlike other newspaper accounts, the editor distorted the recent past and discounted why Mexican Americans filed the lawsuit in the first place. He claimed the "Alamosa school board never contended that the Mexican children in this district should be barred from the north side school." The *Leader* was incorrect. Other newspapers were accurate about how the lawsuit came about. As the *Hooper-Mosca Tribune* noted, it was not about Miguel Maestas's inability to understand English but "because of race prejudice the school board and city super-intendent held against his people."[72]

What also became clear in this case was how Judge Holbrook showed confidence in his decision when he discussed the language deficiency of Mexican children. As we saw, he argued in his ruling that it made pedagogical sense to provide non-English-speaking children with teachers who understood their language. He believed that bright Mexican American children were unable to learn in an environment in which they did not understand the language. At the same time, Judge Holbrook appeared ambiguous, hesitant, and uncomfortable when race was concerned. Given Holbrook's hesitation on race, his ruling needs to be understood within that space and time. Racial politics in America were intense. It had only been 18 years since the 1896 landmark U.S. Supreme Court decision *Plessy v. Ferguson* upheld the constitutionality of state laws allowing racial segregation in public facilities under the "separate but equal" doctrine.[73] Moreover, the Colorado State Constitution prohibited schools from classifying and distinguishing children based on color or race.[74]

Judge Holbrook was astute. He most likely developed certain sensibilities about race because he was raised in the South. He was born in Virginia in 1848, was a former schoolteacher in Kentucky, was admitted to the Kentucky Bar in 1876, came to Colorado in 1877, and was elected a district attorney in District 12 in Colorado in 1881. Holbrook was so well regarded as a magistrate in Alamosa that he was put on the primary ballot to run for the Colorado State Supreme Court before he died in August 1914. As a judge, he was described as ruling on decisions "always as near fair as he could possibly render them, and he made it a rule to give no attorney the best or the worst of it."[75] Given Holbrook's ruling, school officials did not pursue an appeal, and it did not go to the Colorado Supreme Court.[76]

To the extent that Judge Holbrook was from the South, it is not certain how much he knew about the legal construction of race as it applied to Mexican Americans. The racial category of Mexican Americans had a complicated history. It was complicated because the federal government made the decision to grant American citizenship to Mexicans living in the territory newly ceded after the U.S.–Mexican War in 1848, an area that included Alamosa. The "Treaty of Guadalupe Hidalgo," said K. L. Bowman, "stipulated that former Mexican citizens were to be given 'all the rights of citizens of the United States.'"[77] Because people of color were ineligible for U.S. citizenship during the mid-19th century, the federal government categorized Mexicans as White.[78] Classifying Mexicans as White became a political act because most were racially mixed. Most were *mestizos*, a combination of Spanish and Indian.[79] But because the federal government was forced to make a decision about how to incorporate Mexicans into the newly ceded territory, the treaty, said George Martinez, turned Mexicans "into whites."[80]

Classifying Mexicans as White during the mid-19th century was not a simple narrative in which Mexicans became White U.S. citizens who were accepted in American society. Laura Gomez argued that for "many Americans, it was the fact of Mexicans' 'mongrel' status that most strongly signaled their racial inferiority." And because naturalization was restricted to White persons, Gomez maintained that the "Mexicans' collective naturalization in 1848 prompted a *legal* definition of Mexicans as 'White.'"[81] Legal scholar Ariela Gross argued that "while a small elite of Mexican-American landholders who could prove that they were 'Spanish' maintained white status, the majority of 'Mexicans' were viewed and treated by Anglos as a separate race."[82]

It is not surprising, then, that Judge Holbrook did not know how to respond to Raymond Sullivan's claim that Mexican children were racially distinct or John Adams's position that Mexican Americans were Caucasian and no different than other White children in the school district. Judge Holbrook did not respond to these issues in his decision. Given that Mexican Americans were legally White in the United States, Holbrook could have, in principle, agreed with Adams and ruled that Mexican American children were White and thus were not being segregated in the Mexican School.[83] But he did not. Holbrook did not seem to be convinced that Mexican American children were White, but he was also careful not to state that they were racially distinct.[84]

In his ruling, Holbrook suggested that school board members and the previous superintendent were well intentioned and that they had constructed the school to serve non-English-speaking children. But he also believed that the school board and superintendent had strayed from the original goal and implemented a policy that forced all Mexican American children into the Mexican School. Without officially stating that school board members had established a policy that was based on race, Holbrook forced school officials to admit English-speaking Mexican children to White schools near their homes.

After the decision was delivered, Raymond Sullivan was interviewed by the *Denver Catholic Register* and was asked to respond to the ruling. Sullivan told the *Denver Catholic Register* that the peremptory writ of mandamus granted by Judge Holbrook forced school board members to permit all children who understood English to attend schools near their homes. Sullivan was lukewarm about the decision but was satisfied because, he said, "the decree applies to practically all the Mexican children in Alamosa, as nearly all have the knowledge indicated." In other words, Sullivan seemed content with the ruling because very few Mexican American children were going to be relegated to the Mexican School. Nevertheless, he was bothered with the idea of segregated schooling based on language. In fact, he told the *Denver Catholic Register* that "it is still our contention that even though totally deficient in a knowledge of the English language, children cannot be placed in a separate race school in Colorado on that ground."[85] Sullivan understood the importance of local control and that school districts were given power to operate and govern their schools. But he told the *Denver Catholic Register* that "nowhere in the statute of Colorado are school boards authorized to segregate school children on account of language." He argued that when one segregates based on language, "you are getting perilously close to separation on account of race." Sullivan hypothesized that under "this theory you have to have separate schools for Germans, French, Italians, Greeks, Bulgarians and so on until every race is isolated and reared in a separate school." This separation, said Sullivan, was counterproductive to the spirit of the Colorado Constitution and went against the America ideal of being a nation "composed of many races and many peoples." Sullivan believed that racial diversity made America a "strong and united commonwealth." Separate schooling, he believed, "would tend toward race consciousness, dissolution and disintegration."[86]

We are not suggesting that with this victory, race relations in Alamosa were ameliorated. They were not. The Mexican American struggle for racial justice was far from over. Two years after the *Maestas* ruling, Raymond Sullivan returned to Alamosa. This time he came to assist the district attorney on a lawsuit brought on by a Mexican American against the owners of a bowling alley. The suit was filed under the Civil Rights Act of Colorado, which prohibited "the exclusion of any person from a public place of amusement on account of race or color." The owners of the bowling alley posted signs that read "Mexican trade not wanted." In this case, the jury found overwhelming evidence that Mexican Americans were being barred from that establishment. One of the owners was found guilty and the other was acquitted.[87] Our point here is that even though Mexican Americans were allowed to attend schools of their choice with White children after 1914, and although the district attorney forced some business owners to take Jim Crow signs down in 1916, racial discrimination continued for decades.[88] Like other Mexican American communities in the United States, *Hispanos Americanos* in Alamosa understood that they lived on the margins of American life, but they slowly started to move from the margins to the center of the struggle for racial equality.

Notes

1. Francisco Maestas, suing in his own behalf and in behalf of all others similarly situated, Plaintiff, v. Geo. H. Shone, C. L. Lahrmann, Joseph H. Darling as the Board of Education of School District No. 3 Conejos County; and Geo. O. Thompson,

as superintendent of School District No. 3, Conejos County. Defendants. Petition by Raymond Sullivan, Attorney for Plaintiffs. Alamosa County. Combined Court. Alamosa, CO 81101. District Civil Roll #1.
2. Independent School District v. Salvatierra, 33 S.W. 2d 790 (Tex.Civ.App. – San Antonio 1930); Alvarez v. Lemon Grove, Civil Action No. 66625 (Superior Court San Diego County, Cal. 1931). The *Maestas* case also preceded the *Romo v. Laird* case. See Laura K. Munoz, "Romo v. Laird: Mexican American Segregation and the Politics of Belonging in Arizona," *Western Legal History* 26, nos. 1 & 2 (2013):97–131.
3. Richard Nostrand, *The Hispano Homeland* (Norman: University of Oklahoma Press, 1992). In this article, various sources refer to Mexican Americans in Alamosa as "Mexican," "Spanish," and "Spanish Americans." We use the term *Mexican American* with the understanding that Nostrand was correct, that the Mexican American population is different from that of other states in the Southwest.
4. *Independent School District v. Salvatierra*, p. 795.
5. Robert R. Alvarez, Jr., "The Lemon Grove Incident: The Nation's First Successful Desegregation Court Case," *Journal of San Diego History* 32, no. 3 (1986): 10–11, http://www.sandiegohistory.org/journal/86spring/lemongrove.htm.
6. Mexican Americans in Alamosa did not have Mexican Consul support because they were U.S. citizens. Hispanos, or Spanish Americans, had deep roots in the region. Thirteenth Census of the United States: 1910-Population. Department of Commerce and Labor – Bureau of the Census. Colorado, Conejos County. Alamosa. Precinct 12. The 1910 census noted that Francisco (Frank) had roots to New Mexico, not Mexico. Maestas was also categorized as White in the census.
7. "Alamosa Mexicans Win School Court Fight," *Denver Catholic Register*, 26 March 1914. The *Register* noted that it "was the first time in the history of America that a court fight was made over an attempt to segregate Mexicans in school." The editor of the *Denver Catholic Register* understood that the *Maestas* lawsuit was unique. In another story, the *Register* noted that "never before has a question of school segregation arisen here. In some sections of the country court fights have been waged over colored, Chinese and Japanese children but never before have the Mexicans been mixed up in such a contest." "Alamosa School Fight Unique in Court Annuals of this State," *Denver Catholic Register*, 4 December 1913.
8. According to historian Danielle Olden, "It was not until the late 1960s that Mexican American civil rights attorneys began to abandon the 'other white' argument. After years of winning school desegregation cases on the basis of their other whiteness . . . Mexican American civil rights attorneys turned to a new argument that emphasized their racial distinctiveness," Danielle R. Olden, "Shifting the Lens: Using Critical Race Theory and Latino Critical Theory to Re-Examine the History of School Desegregation," *Qualitative Inquiry* 21, no. 3 (2015): 235. Also see Richard Valencia, *Chicano Students and Courts: The Mexican American Legal Struggle for Educational Equality* (New York: New York University Press, 2008), 67.
9. J. R. C. Ruybal, interview by Luther Bean, Nancy Denious, and Elinor Kingery, sound recording, Colorado Historical Society, Denver, Co., 20 November 1962, item ID: 33317710, call number OH 83. Also see *Alamosa Independent Journal*, 9 February 1912.
10. Alamosa Clerk and County Recorder, Records Conejos Co., Warranty Deed Record, Book 72, p. 278. The Alamosa School District purchased the property from Samuel. B. Scholz on August 7, 1909. The property was used to build the Mexican School.
11. "Mexican Kiddies Prove They Are Able to Speak English," *Denver Catholic Register*, 15 January 1914. School enrollments at the Mexican School were provided by School District Superintendent George Thompson at the trial. He also noted that the school had the capacity to serve 200 students. It is important to note that the name of the school evolved, but most official and unofficial records made clear that the school was intended to serve Mexican American children. For example, a photograph of

136   *Ruben Donato et al.*

the school in the *Alamosa Manual and Course of Study* in 1911 was captioned as the "Spanish School." The "Spanish School" was featured in the manual and was photographed. It read that "teachers in this school must be persons who can use the Spanish language," *Manual and Course of Study for the Public Schools of Alamosa. Used by Order of, and Approved by, The Board of Education*, 1 May 1911, p. 59. In 1912, a map company illustrating the town of Alamosa listed the school as the "Mexican Public School" in its index. Sandborn Map Company (11 Broadway, New York), October, 1912. It read that Alamosa had a population of 4,000 and was situated in Conejos County. Moreover, the Colorado Educational Directory in 1913–1914 listed the school as "Mexican Preparatory." Finally, some members of the community referred to it as the "Willis School," and others simply called it the "Mexican School."

12. "Southern Colorado: Items of Interest Gathered From Exchanges," Creede (Co.) Candle, 11 December 1909.
13. *Alamosa Independent Journal*, 9 February 1912.
14. Gerald McKevitt, *Brokers of Culture: Italian Jesuits in the American West, 1848–1919* (Stanford: Stanford University Press, 2007), 257.
15. "Mexicans in Alamosa Say the School Board Discriminates," *Rocky Mountain News*, 10 September 1913.
16. "More Discrimination by School Board," *Denver Catholic Register*, 11 September 1913.
17. "State Board Cannot Stop Segregation of Mexicans," *Denver Times*, 13 September 1913, p. 3. It was puzzling that the story in the *Rocky Mountain News* (September 10) noted that Colorado State Superintendent of Instruction Mary C. C. Bradford was going to seek advice (or an opinion) from Colorado Attorney General Fred Farrar in order to respond to the Mexican Americans' complaint about the school segregation of their children in Alamosa. Apparently Attorney General Farrar must have informed State Superintendent Bradford that the State Board of Education could not intervene. We searched for correspondence between State Superintendent of Instruction Mary C. C. Bradford and Colorado Attorney General Fred Farrar and found no record of such correspondence. However, in the Biennial Report of the Attorney General in 1913–1914, Attorney General Farrar responded to a query about the segregation of Mexican American children in the Durango School District, specifically citing the Mexican American segregation controversy in Alamosa in his response. The Durango School District Superintendent, Florence Salabar, wanted to know "whether or not it is legal to separate the Mexican children in the public schools, particularly in the first, second and third grades, for the other children." The Attorney General responded that school districts in the state had much discretion to operate their schools. However, he noted that as "a matter of law, if the children are excluded by reason of their race, there is no question that such exclusion is illegal." However, he claimed that "if the test is one of language, then it is perfectly proper for it is an exercise of the right of school officials to prescribe the course of study for the best interest of the school." Opinion, see *Biennial Report of the Attorney General of the State of Colorado, 1913–1914* (Denver, The Smith-Brooks Printing Co, State Printers, 1914), 124–125.
18. "State Board Cannot Stop Segregation of Mexicans," *Alamosa Independent Journal*, 19 September 1913. In addition to the *Alamosa Independent Journal* story, a newspaper from Pine Bluffs, Wyoming, wrote a short blurb about the incident in its Colorado events section. In brief, it reported that Mexican American parents in Alamosa had complained to the "state superintendent of public instruction that the school board of Alamosa has shown class distinction in building a separate school house for the Mexican children." "Colorado News: Gathered From All Parts of the State," *Pine Bluffs (Wy.) Post*, 14 February 1907.
19. "Trinidad Faces Race War Over Mexican Pupils: School Strike Against Foreigners Lands in Court," *Denver Post*, 21 November 1913.
20. "School Battle in Alamosa to Enter Courts," *Denver Catholic Register*, 20 November 1913.

21. "Trinidad Faces Race War Over Mexican Pupils: School Strike Against Foreigners Lands in Court," *Denver Post*, 21 November 1913. We interpreted the "strike" as parents refusing to send their children to the Mexican School. Other newspapers in the area did not seem to cover this story.
22. "School Battle in Alamosa to Enter Courts," *Denver Catholic Register*, 20 November 1913.
23. J. R. C. Ruybal, interview by Luther Bean, Nancy Denious, and Elinor Kingery, sound recording, Colorado Historical Society, Denver, Co., 20 November 1962, item ID: 33317710, call number OH 83. Luther Bean was one of the first faculty members at Adams State College, Alamosa, Co. www.museumtrail.org/luther-bean-museum.html.
24. J. R. C. Ruybal interview. Ruybal's interview coincided with what was described in the *1911 Manual and Course of Study for the Public Schools of Alamosa*. The Manual read that "teachers in this school must be persons who can use the Spanish language," p. 59. It should be noted that a Juan R. Borrego was hired by the Alamosa school board to teach all Spanish speaking children in the Alamosa schools in 1907, "Local Happenings Told in Short Paragraphs," *Saguache(Co.) Crescent*, 17 February 1907.
25. J. R. C. Ruybal interview. The press confirmed Ruybal's point that the Spanish American Union met with the board. It was noted that "the Spanish Americans of this city petitioned the school board for the admittance of their children to the nearest school to their homes. The petition cites that the laws of the U.S. or state of Colorado, do not justify a segregation of the scholars attending the public schools, and the practice in vogue in the city is therefore arbitrary. The school board will undoubtedly act upon the petition before the school opens next month." *Alamosa Independent Journal*, 8 August 1913. A week later the press noted that "a large delegation of Mexican residents in this city will meet with the school directors on Monday night, when the proposition of the segregation of the American and Spanish American scholars will be considered, and an endeavor made to have the former school board ruling annulled." *Alamosa Independent Journal*, 15 August 1913.
26. J. R. C. Ruybal interview. Most likely the "Spanish American Union" was associated with or was a Alamosa local chapter of La Sociedad de Protección Mutua de Trabajadores Unidos, a Mexican American mutual aid society based in Antonito, Colorado. See Jose A. Rivera, La Sociedad: Guardians of Hispanic Culture Along the Rio Grande (Albuquerque: University of New Mexico Press, 2010); "A Joke," *The Alamosa(Co.) Leader*, 27 December 1913.
27. "Alamosa Mexicans Plan to Battle for Rights," *Denver Catholic Register*, 23 October 1914. This article confirmed Ruybal's point that he was raising money to fund the lawsuit in the area.
28. J. R. C. Ruybal interview. In addition to Ruybal's interview, it made sense that Francisco Maestas would be named plaintiff because of where his family lived. There were 18 homes on Ross Avenue, and the Maestas family was the only Mexican American family. Maestas's home was seven blocks from the Mexican School. See F. A. McKinney's San Luis Directory, 1913–1914, p. 97.
29. *Maestas et al. v. Shone et al.*, Petition by Raymond Sullivan, Attorney for Plaintiffs, 1–2.
30. Ibid., 2.
31. Ibid., 2.
32. Ibid., 3.
33. Ibid., 3.
34. Ibid., 3–4. See also *The School Laws, Annotated, of the State of Colorado, as Amended to Date, 1 January 1912* (Denver: The Smith-Brooks Company, State Printers), 17.
35. *Maestas et al. v. Shone et al.*, Petition by Raymond Sullivan, Attorney for Plaintiffs, 2, 4.
36. "Directors Think They Are Right," *Alamosa Independent Journal*, 28 November 1913. This story suggested that the number of Mexican American children who were in school beyond the fourth grade increased more than 400%. This issue was not clear.

What was clear was that Mexican Americans were, for the most part, not making it to the local high school. Based on the *Sierra Blanca Journal* (high school yearbook), one Mexican American (Carlos Sanchez) graduated in 1913. Other than Carlos Sanchez, there were no Mexican Americans enrolled at Alamosa High School in 1913. In 1917, there were no Mexican Americans enrolled at Alamosa High School. See the Annual Echo, 1917. High school yearbooks can be retrieved from the Alamosa High School library.

37. "Directors Think They Are Right," *Alamosa Independent Journal*, 28 November 1913. A story in the *Denver Catholic Register* noted that "some of the Alamosa papers are bitterly fighting the Mexicans." See "Alamosa School Fight Unique in Court Annals of this State," *Denver Catholic Register*, 4 December 1913.
38. *Maestas et al. v. Shone et al.*, Order, Chas. C. Holbrook, Judge.
39. *Maestas et al. v. Shone et al.*, Defendants, Answer, John T. Adams, 3.
40. *Maestas et al. v. Shone et al.*, Defendants, Answer, John T. Adams, 3.
41. Ibid.
42. The *Denver Post* reported that Adams was trying to make the case that "Mexicans are not a distinct race, but are Caucasians, and therefore cannot be discriminated against as members of a distinct race by Americans." The story was short. It did not challenge Adams's argument about the racial background of Mexican American children, but it did ask its readers whether they thought Mexicans were "Caucasians." The way the headline of the story was framed seemed to question the idea that Americans would believe that Mexicans were Caucasians and think that they were indistinguishable from White children. See "Mexican Children Demand Schooling With Americans. Conejos Parents Suit Brought by Parents Against Education Board. Are They Caucasians? Authorities Say Discrimination Is Made Because They Speak no English," Denver Post, 14 January 1914.
43. Miguel Maestas was allowed to stay out of school by his father because it was part of the Mexican American parent protest in Alamosa to boycott the segregated Mexican School.
44. *Maestas et al. v. Shone et al.*, Answer, John T. Adams, 4.
45. Ibid., 7.
46. Ibid., 5.
47. Ibid., 6.
48. Ibid., 8–9.
49. Ibid., 10.
50. "School Board Trial," *Alamosa Independent Journal*, 9 January 1914.
51. "Happenings Epitomized," *Alamosa Independent Journal*, 9 January 1914.
52. "Mexican Kiddies Prove They Are Able to Speak English," *Denver Catholic Register*, 15 January 1914.
53. Ibid.
54. Ibid.
55. Ibid.
56. Ibid.
57. Ibid.
58. We acknowledge that sources in the Maestas case conflicted, as some claimed that Mexican American children were segregated up to the fourth grade. Others said it was the fifth grade.
59. *Maestas et al. v. Shone et al.*, Holbrook ruling. This story also has the entire ruling in "Mexican Patrons of Public Schools Win Court Decision," *Hooper-Mosca (Co.) Tribune*, 21 March 1914.
60. Ibid.
61. Ibid.
62. See Holbrook's ruling in "Mexican Patrons of Public Schools Win Court Decision," *Hooper-Mosca (Co.) Tribune*, 21 March 1914.

63. "Alamosa Must Give Mexicans Free Schooling: Court Grants Mandamus Prohibiting Segregation of Spanish Speaking Children," *Rocky Mountain News*, 22 March 1914, p. 6.
64. "Alamosa Schools Ordered to Admit Mexican Children: Bar Lifted by Court Order of Judge Holbrook, in Suit for Boy. 'Pupils Should Be Taken Out of Spanish Classes When They Speak English,'" *Denver Post*, 23 March 1914.
65. "Alamosa Mexicans Win School Court Fight: Segregation of Spanish Must Cease," *Denver Catholic Register*, 26 March 1914.
66. "Mexican Patrons of Public Schools Win Court Decision," *Alamosa Courier*, 21 March 1914.
67. "'Must Admit Mexicans,' to Have Free Schooling Same as American Children. Judge of District Court Grants Mandamus Prohibiting Segregation of the Spanish Speaking-Children," *Akron (Co.) Weekly Pioneer Press*, 27 March 1914.
68. "Los Ninos Mexicanos Victoriosos: La Corte Concede un 'Mandamus' Prohibiendo la Segregacion de los Niños de Habla Español," *La Revista de Taos*, 17 April 1914.
69. *Maestas et al. v. Shone et al.*, Defendants, Motion to Vacate Judgment and Decree and to Dismiss Action, Order, Chas. C. Holbrook. 17 April 1914, Judge. In the motion, Adams argued that Sullivan's amended petition was not sufficient enough to constitute a cause of action, that the court assumed it had jurisdiction over the lawsuit, and that the order had no support to issue a peremptory mandamus. Adams also argued that the judgment and decree failed to specify which Spanish-speaking children in the district – other than Miguel Maestas – possessed an understanding of English sufficient for admission to other schools.
70. *Maestas et al. v. Shone et al.*, Defendants, Motion to Vacate Judgment and Decree and to Dismiss Action, Order, Chas. C. Holbrook, 17 April 1914. Judge. J. R. C. Ruybal did not mention in his oral interview that the case was appealed to the Colorado State Supreme Court.
71. Order dated 24 April 1914, in the case of *Maestas v. Shone*.
72. "Mexican Patrons of Public Schools Win Court Decision: Judge Holbrook Finds Against Discrimination in Education," *Hooper-Mosca (Co.) Tribune*, 21 March 1914.
73. *Plessy v. Ferguson*, 163 U.S. 537 (1896).
74. Colorado Constitution, Section 427, Article 9.
75. "Judge Holbrook Dies," *The Alamosa Leader*, 29 August 1914.
76. The authors conducted the search of the Colorado State Archives. We also asked the librarian at the Colorado State Supreme Court Library to aid in finding record of the case. We found no record of the *Maestas et al. v. Shone et al.* (1914) case.
77. K. L. Bowman, "The New Face of School Desegregation," *Duke Law Journal* 50 (2001): 1751–1808. Brown v. Board of Educ., 374 U.S. 483 (1954), p. 1763. See also Ariela J. Gross, "'The Caucasian Cloak': Mexican Americans and the Politics of Whiteness in the 20th-Century Southwest," *Georgetown Law Journal* 95 (2006): 338–392. USC Law Legal Studies Paper No. 06–20. Available at SSRN: http://ssrn.com/abstract = 934574. http://heinonline.org/HOL/Page?handle = hein.journals/glj95&div = 17&g_sent = 1–404.
78. Gross, "The Caucasian Cloak," p. 347. See also G. A Martinez, "The Legal Construction of Race: Mexican Americans and Whiteness," *Harvard Latino Law Review* 2 (1997), 321–348. Clare Sheridan, "Another White Race: Mexican Americans and the Paradox of Whiteness in Jury Selection," *Law and History Review* 21, no. 1 (Spring, 2003): 1. www.jstor.org/stable/3595070.
79. S. H. Wilson, "Brown Over 'Other White': Mexican Americans' Legal Arguments and Litigation Strategy in School Desegregation Lawsuits," *Law and History Review* 21, no. 1 (2003): 145–194. Neil Foley, *The White Scourge: Blacks, Mexicans, and Poor Whites in Texas Cotton Culture* (Berkeley: University of California Press, 1997), 61. On this point, Foley noted that in 1920, the population in Mexico was about 14 million. Of that number, 10% were White, 30% Indian, and 60% mixed (*mestizo*).

80. Martinez, "The Legal Construction of Race," 327.
81. Laura E. Gomez, *Manifest Destinies: The Making of the Mexican American Race* (New York: New York University Press, 2007), 83.
82. Gross, "The Caucasian Cloak," 341.
83. Thirteenth Census of the United States: 1910-Population. Department of Commerce and Labor – Bureau of the Census, Colorado, Conejos County, Precinct 12, Alamosa, Sheet No. 22 B. The racial classification of Francisco Maestas and his family in 1910 Census was "W" for White.
84. *Maestas et al. v. Shone et al.,* Petition by Raymond Sullivan, Attorney for Plaintiffs, p. 2.
85. "Alamosa Mexicans Win School Court Fight," *Denver Catholic Register*, 26 March 1914.
86. Ibid.
87. "Suit That Alleges Discrimination Won by Alamosa Mexican," *Denver Catholic Register*, 23 March 1916. Also see *The People of the State of Colorado v. Henry H. Hamilton and James H. Williams*, Reference #32, Alamosa District Court, Alamosa, Colorado, Term: March 3–15, 1916.
88. As was noted in *United States v. Alamosa County*, Colo., 306 F. Supp. 2d 1016 (D. Colo. 2004), "Discriminatory practices existed in Alamosa County, particularly during the first half of the twentieth century. These practices created or exacerbated socioeconomic disparities between Hispanic and Anglo residents. Official action and social activism, particularly during the last fifty years, however, have reduced the discriminatory climate in the county. This has improved educational and socioeconomic conditions for Hispanic residents and contributed to increasing diversity within the Hispanic population."

8 Latino English Language Learners

Bridging Achievement and Cultural Gaps Between Schools and Families

Mary Ellen Good, Sophia Masewicz, and Linda Vogel

Closing the achievement gap between advantaged and disadvantaged students is at the core of national educational efforts. The federal No Child Left Behind Act of 2001 ignited a reform movement by establishing high expectations for *all* students and by creating strong accountability for public schools to demonstrate high student achievement. Accountability is a cornerstone of this law, which requires schools to disaggregate student performance on state-standardized assessments by subgroups: racial/ethnic, economically disadvantaged, students with disabilities, and students with limited English proficiency (No Child Left Behind Act, 2002).

Although the No Child Left Behind Act mandates grade-level proficiency for 100% of all student subgroups by the year 2014, some argue that this is not attainable without resources, capacity, and will (Linn, 2003; Public Education Network, 2007). This goal is especially challenging for Hispanic students who are also English language learners (ELLs). Nationwide, their academic performance consistently falls far below that of other students (Abedi & Dietel, 2004; *Impact of No Child Left Behind*, 2007; Kindler, 2002; Kohler & Lazarin, 2007; Lee, 2002; Viadero, 2001).

The underachievement of Hispanic ELL students is a problem that has caught the attention of educational leaders, policymakers, teachers, parents, and taxpayers alike. Data on student assessments demonstrate a growing problem, yet there is a lack of consensus about what causes the achievement gap and what solutions might close it. The purpose of this qualitative study was to gain a deeper understanding of some of the barriers that impede the academic achievement of Hispanic ELL students by exploring the perceptions and experiences of their parents and teachers.

Hispanics are now the largest and fastest growing minority group in the United States, a country that no longer has a majority ethnic group (Kohler & Lazarin, 2007; Perea, 2004). Traditional cultural values and beliefs of Hispanic families focus on relationships and not on competitive factors such as academic achievement. These values can contrast sharply with those of the mainstream U.S. educational system, in which individualism, self-reliance, and academic achievement are held in high regard (Perea, 2004).

Much of the existing research on academic achievement has addressed variables that schools can control, such as curriculum, best practices, professional development, class size, and funding (Marzano, 2003; Reeves, 2005; Schmoker, 1999). Studies of the academic success of Hispanics and ELLs have focused primarily on pedagogical approaches, teacher perceptions and expectations, and cultural and linguistic differences (Y. S. Freeman & Freeman, 2002; *Impact of No Child Left Behind*, 2007; Salinas, 2000). Much less research has been conducted on the social and cultural capital of Hispanic parents, their strengths, and their desire to connect with schools in ways that are meaningful to them (Brooks, 2005; Delgado-Gaitan, 2004; Perea, 2004). As critical researchers, we suspect that the power and influence Hispanic parents can have on their children's education has been ignored by many and underestimated by most.

Because the number of schools failing to meet ELL achievement goals continues to grow, many question whether it is even possible for schools to close the achievement gap (Public Education Network, 2007). Rothstein (2004) reviewed social class characteristics that influence the achievement gap and suggested that school reform efforts alone will not raise student achievement. He called for public policy to address the social and economic conditions of families that influence learning; schools will continue to fail if they work in isolation from parents, communities, and other critical entities (Rothstein, 2004).

For many decades, a deficit model has resonated in the literature, suggesting the cause of low achievement for Hispanic and other minority students is the students themselves (Valencia, 1986, 1993). Unequal treatment of Hispanic students has persisted over the past century (Flores, 1982, 1993). Hispanic students have been given hurtful and negative labels, such as *mentally retarded, linguistically handicapped, culturally and linguistically deprived,* and *at risk* (Flores, 1982, 1993). This attitude based on perceived deficits has permeated in schools, reinforcing preferences and the unequal treatment of Hispanic students and thus sustaining racial and discriminatory practices in society (Valencia, 1993).

Great debates continue over the causes of the achievement gap and strategies for closing it, yet few would argue that parental involvement is important for student success. When parents are involved in education, students and schools improve (Epstein, 1986, 1995; Gonzalez-DeHass, Willems, & Holbein, 2005). Collaboration between parents, teachers, and communities can lead to mutual understanding and partnerships that benefit all students (Delgado-Gaitan, 2004; Epstein et al., 2002). However, in spite of well-intended teachers and parents, the achievement gap between Hispanic ELL students and their peers continues to widen. This complicated problem cannot be solved if teachers and parents work in isolation.

What are the barriers to the academic success of Hispanic ELL students? To address this question, we conducted an exploratory qualitative study to gain a deeper understanding of what impedes the success of Hispanic ELL students in school. Because we were most interested in learning from their teachers and parents, we raised the following research question: What are the barriers to improving the academic achievement of Hispanic ELL students as perceived by their parents and teachers?

Methodology

Qualitative Tradition

Because the nature of our research question related to gaining understanding and explaining meaning, we used a qualitative methodology. *Qualitative research* has been defined as "an inquiry process of understanding based on distinct methodological traditions of inquiry that explore a social or human problem" (Creswell, 1998, p. 15). To maximize data collection we conducted focus group interviews of teachers and parents (Creswell, 1998; Patton, 1990).

Theoretical Framework

Inasmuch as constructivism provided the epistemological view for this study, our conceptual framework was grounded in two theoretical perspectives: critical inquiry (Freire, 1972) and the cultural-ecological adaptations of minority communities (Ogbu & Simons, 1998). Crotty (1998) described critical inquiry as an ongoing project that includes reflection and action to create a more just and freer society. Central to this theory are relationships between power, culture, privilege, and oppression (Crotty, 1998). Freire's critical theory, liberation philosophy, and emphasis on giving voice to marginalized people guided the design of this study.

A theoretical perspective promulgated by Ogbu and Simons (1998) also informed our research. This cultural-ecological theory takes into account societal and school effects as well as the dynamics within minority communities. The collective adaptation of immigrant minority groups is partly shaped by the group's history, why members immigrated to the United States, and the sociocultural adaptations of these minorities (Ogbu & Simons, 1998).

Ogbu's theory explains differences in school performance for minority students based on whether these students were voluntary or involuntary immigrants. Immigrant groups who voluntarily come to the United States tend to have higher achievement compared to involuntary immigrants (Ogbu & Simons, 1998). Voluntary immigrant minorities measure their economic condition by the standards of their homeland and are motivated to endure forms of injustices due to language or culture (Ogbu & Simons, 1998). Involuntary immigrant minorities include Native Americans, African Americans, Alaska Natives, early Mexican Americans, and Puerto Ricans, who were each conquered, enslaved, or colonized (Ogbu & Simons, 1998). These minority groups have developed a "folk theory" that educational credentials do not guarantee economic success in the mainstream society (Ogbu & Simons, 1998). Unlike voluntary immigrants, involuntary immigrants seek to be different from the mainstream culture to maintain an identity (Ogbu & Simons, 1998). The historical treatment of minorities in the United States and the politics of inequity shape minority groups' perceptions of school as a vehicle for social and economic advancement (Ogbu & Simons, 1998).

Researcher Personal Stance

We believe public education is a primary means of promoting democracy and a more just society. Immigrant families, like other minority families who live in poverty, struggle against oppression related to class, race, ethnicity, language, and national origin. Young (1990) described marginalization as a form of oppression. Our interpretation of marginalization and oppression is constructed from the many stories and experiences minority and immigrant families have shared with us for more than 20 years. The meaning we construct from their struggles resonates in our beliefs about social justice. In this study, our perspective on social justice centers on equity in public education (Marshall & Gerstl-Pepin, 2005). As criticalists, we believe that the oppression minority families confront in their day-to-day lives must be recognized and named (Young, 1995).

Participants and Setting

This study was conducted in a semirural community located in the Rocky Mountain region of the United States in a school district with a population of approximately 2,500 students. At the time of the study, 65% of the district's students were identified as Hispanic, and 36% were identified as ELLs (F. Wilson, personal communication, April 24, 2006).

Participants included teachers and parents of Hispanic ELL students who had attended school in the district for at least 1 year. We collected data from two different focus group interviews of parents and teachers. Parent participants were selected from a district-sponsored adult English (ESL) class. Selected were Hispanic parents who had ELL children enrolled in the district's elementary, middle, and high schools. The eight parent participants were all Spanish-speaking Hispanic mothers of Mexican origin who ranged in age from 28 to 43 years. They had all received their education in Mexico and had immigrated to the United States within the past 5 years.

Teacher participants were selected to include teachers from the district's elementary, middle, and high schools who had at least 3 years of experience teaching ELL students. They included four women (three Hispanics and one Caucasian) and one man (Hispanic) who ranged in age from 30 to 45 years. All of the teachers were fluent in both English and Spanish.

Design and Procedures

We used purposeful sampling to identify and select participants because we wanted to discover, to understand, and to gain insight from parents and teachers. Purposeful sampling involves selecting cases that are information rich, from which a great deal can be learned (Patton, 1990). We selected a sample most likely to provide the information and understanding we were seeking (Merriam, 1998; Patton, 1990). The district coordinator of federal programs and the district adult ESL instructor assisted in the identification of potential teacher and parent participants for the focus group interviews.

Focus groups use group interaction to produce data and insights that would be less accessible without group interaction (Morgan, 1997). The ideal size of a focus group depends on the research question, but as a rule of thumb Morgan suggests 6–10 participants. We invited eight participants to each focus group, hoping to have at least six in each group interview. All eight parents agreed to participate, and they all showed up for the interview. Likewise, all eight invited teachers agreed to participate; however, only five showed up for the focus group interview. The three teachers who did not show up each said that last-minute circumstances prevented their attendance.

Three weeks prior to the focus group interviews prospective participants were sent an invitation letter explaining the purpose of the study and the date, time, and location of the interview. They were told they would be offered a $25 gift certificate for a local grocery store in appreciation for their time and effort. Participants accepted the invitation by replying on a form we had sent them along with a self-addressed, stamped envelope. One week prior to the meeting, we met with the eight selected teachers to confirm their intent to participate and provided them with a copy of the interview questions. The adult ESL instructor did the same with the eight invited parent participants.

Both focus groups were convened on the same day for a 90-min, semi-structured, audiotaped interview. The teacher group met immediately after school, and the parent group was convened in the evening to allow working parents the opportunity to participate. Child care was provided at no cost to the parent participants, and light snacks were offered to both groups. All communication (written and oral) with parents was in Spanish, their native language.

Participants were informed that their participation was completely voluntary and that confidentiality would be maintained; they were told they could withdraw at any time. We explained the purpose of the study and why they had been selected to participate. Both groups were encouraged to ask questions before they signed the consent forms. The consent form was read aloud in Spanish by an eager parent volunteer to ensure parents' full understanding regardless of their literacy level. Eight open-ended questions guided the interviews which were both audiotaped.

Data Collection and Analysis

The main source of data in our study was transcripts from the two focus group interviews. We read and reread the transcripts many times to make sense of and to interpret meaning. Using a critical framework, we listened for the voice behind each participant's response as we moved back and forth in the process of consolidating, reducing, and interpreting the data (Merriam, 1998).

Categorical aggregation is a useful form of data analysis (Creswell, 1998). Using this approach, we looked for a collection of instances from the data, hoping for meaning to emerge (Creswell, 1998). In this way, participant responses were analyzed inductively to identify emergent themes and relevant meanings. Creswell described direct interpretation of data as a process of "pulling data apart and then putting them back together in more meaningful ways" (p. 154). We used open coding to individually analyze the transcripts and then shared our interpretations to identify core concepts. Peer examination allowed us to more fully explore the data (Merriam, 1998).

Meaning and insights were holistically elicited from the text. When we reflected on our critical framework, certain words jumped off the pages: "racism," "sacrifice," "chaos," and "discrimination." As we continued to break down the data, subthemes emerged and we were able to conceptualize connections. Our codes evolved into themes, which further developed into subthemes.

Having an understanding of critical theory (Freire, 1972), we framed our inquiry through a critical lens. In seeking to hear the parents' voices, we felt an obligation not only to listen but also to consider what changes, or actions, needed to be taken in the cause of social justice. Analysis in critical inquiry can never be seen as final; it is an ongoing project of reflection and action (Crotty, 1998).

Trustworthiness

Merriam (1998) listed strategies for enhancing trustworthiness in research, such as triangulation, checking interpretations with the individuals interviewed, asking peers to comment on emerging findings, and clarifying biases and assumptions. We enhanced trustworthiness by explaining our assumptions and how our theoretical frameworks guided the study, by triangulating data, by using peer examination, by thoroughly detailing the study, and by explaining how the findings were derived from the data (Merriam, 1998). We believe these approaches have resulted in data that are not only rich and profound but also trustworthy.

Findings

Five themes emerged from the collective responses of the parent and teacher participants: communication gaps; culture clashes; lack of a systemic, articulated district ELL plan; lack of teacher preparation in multiculturalism, language acquisition, and ELL instructional strategies; and a lack of support

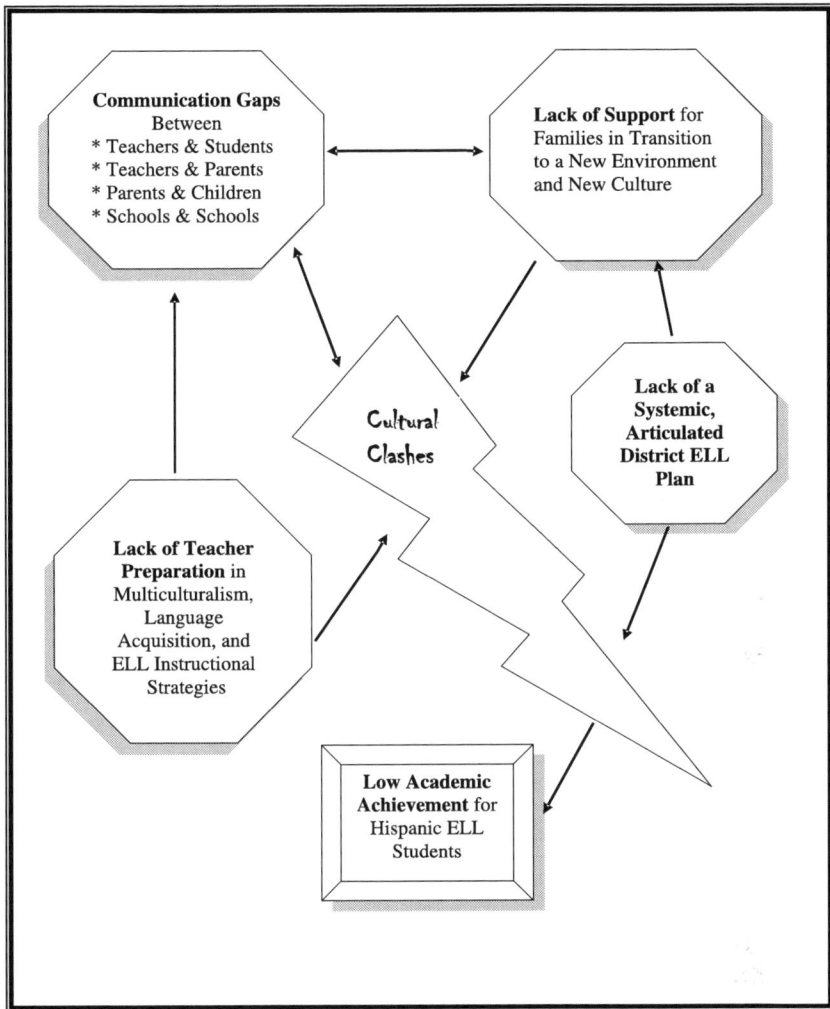

Figure 8.1 Barriers to Improving the Academic Achievement of Hispanic ELL Students. ELL = English Language Learner.

systems for families transitioning to a new environment and new culture. These findings are illustrated in Figure 8.1.

Communication Gaps

Both teacher and parent groups consistently identified communication gaps as the major barrier that impeded student achievement. The gaps they discussed pertained to relationships between four key groups: teachers and students, teachers and parents, parents and their children, and schools within the district.

Communication Gaps Between Teachers and Students

Participants expressed sadness related to language barriers that hindered communication between teachers and students. Teachers were frustrated that the majority of teachers in the district were not bilingual; those who were bilingual were not appreciated or valued. Parents shared their belief that if teachers do not speak the child's language or understand his or her culture, learning cannot be optimized. Both groups described feelings of frustration, anger, discomfort, and hurt when discussing communication between teachers and students. They felt that communication gaps negatively impacted student achievement.

Communication Gaps Between Teachers and Parents

Parents acknowledged that they lacked the English language skills needed to effectively communicate with teachers and school personnel. They desperately wanted to learn English and sincerely appreciated the district's efforts to provide ESL classes for parents. Beyond language barriers, parents felt the school environment was not welcoming and that some teachers were defensive. Parents could not have meaningful conversations with teachers because there just were not enough bilingual teachers or liaisons in the schools to serve as interpreters and translators to help bridge language gaps. Parents wanted to work with teachers to help their children with homework and studies, but two factors got in their way: parents' limited English skills and a lack of academic preparation in academic content areas.

Parents expressed a great desire to advocate for their children but felt that schools did not, or would not, listen to them. They wanted to have a voice in their children's education but felt that their voice had been silenced (Freire, 1972). They also wanted to be involved in the hiring of new teachers because they believed they were good judges of quality in choosing the best teachers for their children. Most educators enter low-income and diversely populated schools without an understanding of family backgrounds, concepts of caring, and the framework of partnerships (Epstein, 1995). As found in this study, a lack of mutual understanding creates barriers and conflicts between schools and families that negatively impact student achievement (Epstein, 1995).

Communication Gaps Between Schools Within the District

Teachers expressed a need to expand conversations across the district to help bridge gaps as students moved to higher grade levels. They did not know what was being taught in other school buildings and felt that student achievement would improve if teachers talked more with one another, especially across school buildings. Susana, a teacher, commented as follows:

> There are completely different philosophies of ESL happening in our different schools. There needs to be strategies where people are talking about

what is working and why they are doing things a certain way. What has been successful? What strategies haven't worked? We can learn from old lessons and create a scaffolding approach. We do that with our children, and it would be useful for us to do that as educators across the district.

Culture Clashes

There were obvious differences in the ways in which parents and teachers viewed the role of teachers. Both groups described misunderstandings and conflicts related to clashes between the U.S. school culture and the culture of families who had emigrated from Mexico (Perea, 2004). Luisa, a parent, shared her view of how Mexican parents perceive the teacher's role:

> In Mexico, teachers consider students as an extension of their own family and refer to them as *my* children. They not only see themselves as educators, but also as parents, counselors, grandparents, and even mothers, especially when they act as caretakers for sick students. As parents, we trust their judgment; we believe what they tell us. So when the teacher requires our cooperation, we cooperate. This seldom happens here.

One of the biggest concerns expressed by parents was that they did not feel that school personnel listened to them or respected their input. Parents had lost their sense of trust for the school. They felt that school personnel were condescending, were disrespectful, and discriminated against them based on stereotypes (Delgado-Gaitan, 2004; Valdes, 1996). Parents thought that school administrators viewed them and their families as *the* problem (Valencia, 1986). They used the word *racism* often, especially when asked what gets in the way of student success. Parents described a lack of respect and equality that would allow them to more fully participate in their child's development as a student and as a human being (Freire, 1972; Valdes, 1996).

When asked about cultural barriers, parents expressed a loss of cultural identity and cultural foundation when they emigrated from Mexico to the United States. They did not feel connected to the new culture in the United States, in the school, or in the community and described a loss of control. Teachers described their experiences working with youth who felt that they had lost control. They said immigrant students who feel out of control can overreact or behave in negative ways. Both parents and teachers shared experiences of immigrant students who had demonstrated behavioral problems in attempting to fit into a new school culture.

Parents expressed a sense of cultural deprivation as their children moved further away from their traditional cultural values and closer to mainstream U.S. culture (Delgado-Gaitan, 2004; Perea, 2004). They lamented a loss of ability due to language and cultural barriers to parent their children in the traditional ways they valued. Parents described family chaos resulting from the cultural conflicts their children faced as they traded one culture for another.

Lack of a Systemic, Articulated ELL Plan

Teachers did not feel that the district had a strategic, coordinated, or comprehensive plan for ELL students to acquire both English language proficiency and content knowledge within a realistic time frame. They expressed a need for greater native language support at the early grade levels, when many immigrant students first enter the English-speaking world. They were concerned about newly arrived students being placed in an environment that did not emotionally or psychologically support learning and felt that immigrant students needed a safe environment to deal with the multitude of changes that bombarded them on a daily basis. Rosario, a teacher, summed it up saying the following:

> We need to strategically place resources where they are needed—ESL teachers in specific places. We need a way to exit students out of the program and to transition them. It would be nice to have that whole system in a plan that is laid out. I feel like this hand doesn't know what the other hand is doing. I can be totally doing something that counteracts what the other side is doing. I think that we, as a whole school system, need to all be at the same table and talk about what is happening. It should be consistent at all grade levels. It is not.

These findings are reflected in ongoing debates about the effectiveness of English language acquisition models, programs, and strategies (Krashen, 1997). Bilingual education, English immersion, and sheltered English are examples of programs currently used to teach English language acquisition. When children receive a quality education in their first language they acquire knowledge and literacy in that primary language that can then be transferred to a second language (Krashen, 1997). Students in well-designed bilingual programs acquire academic English at least as well as, and often better than, children in English-only programs (Krashen, 1997). Piercynski, Matranga, and Peltier (1997) found that having bilingual teachers is especially helpful for ELL students as they transcend language barriers.

Contrary to these findings, the district in this study supported an English-only approach for ELL students to acquire English language skills. At the national level, the English Only movement has become the opposition to bilingual education (D. Freeman & Freeman, 2001). Many claim that English Only proponents have created negative attitudes not only toward bilingual education but toward bilingual people as well (D. Freeman & Freeman, 2001). Such debates continue to dominate the political landscape of the public education system.

Lack of Teacher Preparation in Multiculturalism, Language Acquisition, and ELL Instructional Strategies

Teachers and parents agreed that teachers lack preparation in three critical areas: multiculturalism, language acquisition, and ELL instructional strategies. They identified a need for more training and preparation for all district teachers on sheltered ESL strategies that are based on scientific research, engaging, and focused on best practices. In addition, they felt that all district teachers, not just those who taught English to ELL students, needed to better understand the impact of culture on teaching and learning.

Teachers overwhelmingly agreed that the district's current English-only approach to language acquisition did not allow enough processing time for students to grasp new concepts. Carmen, a teacher, shared the following:

> Teachers without training or experience in working with ELL students need to slow down to allow enough time for students to process and integrate knowledge. ELL students get frustrated when they can't understand the teacher, and school is not relevant if they are not engaged in learning.

Genesse and Richards (1994) found greater success when educators accepted and encouraged students to retain their culture and language while at the same time helping them learn about a new culture and language. Case studies have demonstrated the loss of heritage language as students transition to a new culture and a disruption in the acculturation process for Hispanics and other minority groups (Krashen, Tse, & McQuillan, 1998).

Parents and teachers were concerned because the best bilingual teachers left the school district for higher paying jobs in other districts where their bilingual skills were valued. They believed bilingual teaching is a specialty and that bilingual teachers should be fairly compensated for their extra training and skills. Parents suggested that schools compensate bilingual teachers more, because higher salaries would make the teachers feel valued and they would stay in the district. Teachers agreed that bilingual skills and ESL credentials are assets that merit higher compensation. The value parents and teachers placed on being bilingual did not align with the district's English-only philosophy.

Teachers and parents believed that administrators and board members might not fully understand the complexity of issues related to second language acquisition, culture, and the educational background of immigrant students. They wanted their educational leaders to fully understand the needs of ELL students when making policy decisions and when allocating resources to support effective programs and best practices.

Lack of Support Systems for Families in Transition to a New Environment and New Culture

Teachers and parents described the overwhelming challenges families face as they transition to a new country, a new language, and a new school system. High stress, emotional upheaval, anxiety, and difficulty coping were listed as common reactions to acculturation. Parents expressed a feeling of being trapped in the economic reality of having to work long hours for very low wages. Many immigrant parents in the district worked in seasonal agriculture and received low, unpredictable wages. They lived in a world dominated by poverty and uncertainty.

Parents verbalized feelings of alienation, isolation, and guilt. They did not have their traditional family support systems to rely upon and voiced a need for bicultural counselors, psychologists, and health professionals to assist them as their families adjusted to a new culture. For families living in poverty, these types of services are unaffordable luxuries, as Celia, a parent shared:

> There are situations when children need therapy in order to maintain their academic achievement. Loss of a loved one, divorce, and other problems at home affect their performance at school. We need to look for professional help outside of school, which places an additional financial burden on parents.

All parents in this study said that they were immigrants who had come to this country for reasons related to economics; their primary motivation was to find a better life for their family. Parents described the sacrifices they made to give their children a better life, one that could only be achieved through hard work. Carlos, a teacher and an immigrant himself, said the following:

> The main priority for immigrant parents is to find work; it is not education. This is not to suggest they don't place a high value on education, but when it comes to survival, education might have to wait. Education is not urgent; eating is.

Parents said they felt guilty about not being able to support their children's emotional needs as they struggled with enormous change and stress. Ofelia, a parent, expressed this feeling of guilt as follows:

> Our lives are consumed by work. When we first got here, my children used to cry. They would ask, "Mommy, why did you bring me here to be subjected to this?" I felt a knot in my throat and prone to tears.

Students too are deeply affected by the stress of cultural adaptation. Teachers said newly arrived students who do not feel like they fit into the school culture feel singled out and insecure. They experience a sense of not belonging in either world. Magda, a parent, described her son as being *"enclochado,"* meaning the clutch was stuck for him. He couldn't go forward or backward; he was unable to function in either the English- or Spanish-speaking worlds. He was simply stuck.

Teachers felt that all of the newness that immigrant students experience is sometimes just too much for them to handle, especially when they feel harassed and intimidated. They believed it is the teacher's role to create a safe environment in which students love to learn. Gloria, a teacher, shared the following:

> They need to learn everything, not just English. They need to learn to become educated. Students are losing the value of a quality education

if we focus on an English immersion model. If students are pushed too quickly into English without support, they lose their native language and don't develop academic skills in either language; they have no foundation in either language.

Teachers felt that when students are frustrated, they can become bored and discipline problems can occur. They said that some students rebel, especially older youth who resent their parents for taking them away from their lives, their family, and their friends in Mexico. Teachers thought that students might reject English as an act of rebellion. Parents and teachers shared a belief that discipline problems can be a result of anger experienced by immigrant children who leave behind a life they know and love in Mexico, oftentimes against their will. These beliefs are reflected in Ogbu's theory (Ogbu & Simons, 1998) related to voluntary and involuntary immigrants. Although the parents in this study voluntarily chose to immigrate to the United States, in many cases their children were involuntary immigrants with their own unique set of struggles. Teachers and parents described students whose behavior reflected a need, or perhaps a desire, to be different from the mainstream culture in order to maintain their own identity (Ogbu & Simons, 1998).

Conclusions and Recommendations

Based on our analysis of findings and our review of other studies in the literature, we have generated nine recommendations, which are presented in Table 8.1. Our recommendations are similar to those found in other research studies; what will make a difference is how they are implemented. Providing teacher training in multiculturalism and best practices related to language acquisition and ELL instructional strategies can be executed without great difficulty. However, changing a school culture and creating trust within and outside of the school system is a more complex challenge. Trust and a supportive school culture are key elements to improved student academic achievement. Without a cultural shift toward high expectations for *all* students, a shared vision and mission, a clearly articulated curriculum, meaningful parental involvement, and student engagement in school, the achievement gap for Hispanic ELL students will continue to widen.

The findings of this study shed further light on barriers for Hispanic ELLs and are supported by Perea's (2004) description of the norms in Hispanic and American culture. In the extreme, these norms are oppositional. Hispanic culture is highly relational, whereas American culture, as exemplified in schools, is individualistic and competitive (Perea, 2004).

For the Hispanic parents in this study, the communication gap reflected more than a lack of English or Spanish language skills; there was no relationship or connectedness for them, which is critical to an enmeshed culture. Communication barriers for parents were more deeply rooted in relationships than in language differences. Teachers, as representatives of the American school culture, also experienced communication gaps that impeded

Table 8.1 Recommendations for Improving the Achievement of Hispanic ELL Students

Recommendation	Rationale
1. Implement a district-wide systemic plan that addresses the language acquisition, content knowledge, and cultural needs of Hispanic ELL students.	Research supports bilingual or transitional models as best practices in helping ELL students acquire academic language and content knowledge.
2. Recruit and retain quality bilingual teachers, paraprofessionals, and liaisons to bridge language and cultural gaps.	Bilingual staff can enhance trust between schools and homes by opening access to school personnel, influencing decision making, and improving communication.
3. Conduct ongoing professional development for *all* teachers on multiculturalism and effective ELL instructional strategies.	Opportunities to learn and grow professionally help teachers effectively meet the learning needs of culturally and linguistically diverse students.
4. Provide ELL program articulation within schools and across the district.	Values, philosophy, and beliefs articulated in a comprehensive district-wide ELL program will systematize the program approach.
5. Recognize and respect the heritage of all families by honoring multiculturalism.	Recognition and respect for the importance of all cultures will strengthen bonds between schools and families and will support the aspirations, dreams, and values of both school and home cultures.
6. Provide academic and emotional support for students and their parents.	Welcome centers, community liaison positions, peer-to-peer mentors, teacher advisory programs, tutors, counselors, parent support groups, and referrals to community agencies such as health and social services support student success.
7. Create opportunities for parents to engage in authentic conversations about their children to increase their empowerment and sense of equality.	Research supports meaningful parental involvement as an important component of improving student achievement for all students.
8. Seek outside facilitation to create a district and school culture that engages Hispanic ELL students to succeed.	A culturally responsive approach is essential for creating and sustaining meaningful change.
9. Expand the present study to include students and principals.	Further studies are needed for a deeper understanding of Hispanic ELL student achievement. The perceptions of students and principals will add to the body of knowledge and enhance understanding of this complex issue.

Note. ELL = English Language Learner.

their relationships with Hispanic parents and students. For both parents and teachers, it was a lack of relationships that inhibited communication, mutual understanding, trust, and, subsequently, parental involvement. Communication gaps generated a great deal of fear for parents and teachers, who lamented the loss of heritage language and culture for immigrant children (Krashen, 1997). Parents believed this loss led to a crisis in a child's identity and slowed academic progress.

When parents were asked what they thought ELL students needed to succeed in school, they resoundingly said that schools must embrace and respect the culture of the families they serve. Culture clashes appeared to undermine the expectations and hopes teachers and parents had for students. There were distinct differences in how teachers and parents viewed their roles in the development of students. Parents entrusted their children to the school but did not feel that they could trust the school. Teachers were concerned that their general education teacher peers had limited understanding of the cultural, emotional, and academic support Hispanic ELL students need to succeed. Recruiting and retaining quality Hispanic bilingual teachers could help eliminate this barrier. Minority teachers are effective in meeting the learning needs of minority students because of shared deep cultural experiences (Salinas, 2000).

A primary concern of both parent and teacher participants was the lack of teacher preparation in multiculturalism. This barrier results in low expectations for Hispanic ELL students, devalues their native culture and language, reinforces the deficit model perception of Hispanic ELL students as *the* problem, and can alienate students from the school (Valencia, 1986). Without preparation in multiculturalism, teachers lack knowledge and skills to understand the community they serve. Teachers and parents believed a lack of trained, quality teachers across the system had led to low student achievement, a high dropout rate, and a disenfranchised Hispanic population.

Other concerns revolved around issues of class, race, and national origin. Parents felt that these issues were caused by a lack of cultural awareness and understanding by teachers; they called it racism. They felt that their concerns were not taken seriously and that they were not viewed as equal partners in the education of their children. Parents felt ignored when they tried to communicate with the school or express their views; they did not feel empowered to influence decisions affecting their children. These sentiments reflect the critical inquiry theoretical perspective of this study. Parents described oppressive experiences that created a state of marginalization and silenced their voices (Freire, 1972; Young, 1995). When presented with a gift certificate at the conclusion of the parent focus group, Lupe, a parent, smiled and sighed:

> It's not necessary for you to give me this. The real gift you gave me today was a voice. The fact that you invited me here and tape-recorded my words makes me believe that you are listening and what I have to say matters. *That* is a true gift!

Parents found a lack of support systems in their volatile transition to a new environment and new culture. Their children encountered the social stress of not fitting into the mainstream culture. Parents felt a loss of control in guiding the development of their children and faced enormous obstacles as they struggled to support their families financially. They grieved the loss of their traditional support system of their extended family when it came to raising children in a new and different culture. Their sacrifices appeared significant considering the loss of cultural continuity, the loss of connection to their homeland and heritage, and the loss of language and cultural identity for their children.

Immigrant families pay a high price as they transition to a new land hoping for economic opportunity. Instead of a welcome mat, many find chaos and conflict and are left to wonder whether the benefits are really worth the pain and hardships their families endure. Like everyone else, Hispanic immigrant parents also want to close the achievement gap, especially for their children. We believe the hopes and dreams of all families can be realized in a democratic society whose values are rooted in social justice and equity in public education.

References

Abedi, J., & Dietel, R. (2004). Challenges in the No Child Left Behind Act for English language learners. *Phi Delta Kappan, 85,* 782–785.

Brooks, S. M. (2005, November). *Increasing minority parent involvement by changing the parameters from teacher-centered to parent-centered models.* Paper presented at the annual meeting of the University Council for Educational Administration, Nashville, TN.

Creswell, J. W. (1998). *Qualitative inquiry and research design: Choosing among five traditions.* Thousand Oaks, CA: Sage.

Crotty, M. (1998). *The foundations of social research: Meaning and perspective in the research process.* London: Sage.

Delgado-Gaitan, C. (2004). *Raising student achievement through home-school partnerships.* Thousand Oaks, CA: Corwin Press.

Epstein, J. L. (1986). Parent involvement: Implications for limited English proficient parents. In C. Smith-Dudgeon (Ed.), *Issues of parent involvement and literacy* (pp. 6–16). Washington, DC: Trinity College.

Epstein, J. L. (1995). School family/community partnerships: Caring for the children we share. *Phi Delta Kappan, 76,* 701–712.

Epstein, J. L., Sanders, M. G., Simon, B. S., Salinas, K. C., Jansorn, N. R., & Van Vaoorhis, F. L. (2002). *School, family, and community partnerships: Your handbook for action* (2nd ed.). Thousand Oaks, CA: Corwin Press.

Flores, B. M. (1982). *Language interference or influence: Toward a theory for Hispanic bilingualism.* Unpublished doctoral dissertation, University of Arizona, Tucson.

Flores, B. M. (1993, April). *Interrogating the genesis of the deficit view of Latino children in the educational literature during the 20th century.* Paper presented at the annual meeting of the American Educational Research Association, Atlanta, GA.

Freeman, D., & Freeman, Y. (2001). *Between worlds: Access to second language acquisition.* Portsmouth, NH: Heinemann.

Freeman, Y. S., & Freeman, D. E. (2002). *Closing the achievement gap: How to reach limited-formal-schooling and long-term English learners.* Portsmouth, NH: Heinemann.

Freire, P. (1972). *Pedagogy of the oppressed.* Harmondsworth, England: Penguin.

Genesse, F., & Richards, J. C. (1994). *Educating second language children: The whole child, the whole curriculum, the whole community.* Cambridge: Cambridge University Press.

Gonzalez-DeHass, A. R., Willems, P., & Holbein, M. D. (2005). Examining the relationships between parental involvement and student motivation. *Educational Psychology Review, 17*(2), 99–123.

Impact of No Child Left Behind on English language learners: Hearing before the Subcommittee on Early Childhood, Elementary and Secondary Education of the Committee on Education Labor, House of Representatives, 110th Cong., 1 (2007).

Kindler, A. L. (2002). *Survey of the states' limited English proficient students and available educational programs and services: 2000–2001 summary report.* Washington, DC: National Clearinghouse for English Language Acquisition.

Kohler, A. D., & Lazarin, M. (2007). *Hispanic education in the United States* (Statistical Brief No. 8). Washington, DC: National Council of La Raza.

Krashen, S. D. (1997). *Why bilingual education?* Charleston, WV: ERIC/Clearinghouse on Rural Education and Small Schools. (ERIC Document Reproduction Service No. ED403101)

Krashen, S. D., Tse, L., & McQuillan, J. (Eds.). (1998). *Heritage language development.* Culver City, CA: Language Education.

Lee, J. (2002). Racial and ethnic achievement gap trends: Reversing the progress toward equity? *Educational Researcher, 31*(1), 3–12.

Linn, R. (2003, April). *Accountability: Responsibility and reasonable expectations.* Presidential address presented at the annual meeting of American Educational Research Association, Chicago, IL.

Marshall, C., & Gerstl-Pepin, C. (2005). *Re-framing educational politics for social justice.* Boston: Pearson.

Marzano, R. J. (2003). *What works in schools: Translating research into action.* Alexandria, VA: Association for Supervision and Curriculum Development.

Merriam, S. B. (1998). *Qualitative research and case study applications in education.* San Francisco: Jossey-Bass.

Morgan, D. L. (1997). *Focus groups as qualitative research* (2nd ed.). Thousand Oaks, CA: Sage. No Child Left Behind Act of 2001, Pub. L. No. 107–110, § 115, Stat. 1425 (2002).

Ogbu, J. U., & Simons, H. D. (1998). Voluntary and involuntary minorities: A cultural-ecological theory of school performance with some implications for education. *Anthropology & Education Quarterly, 29*(2), 155–188.

Patton, M. Q. (1990). *Qualitative evaluation and research methods* (2nd ed.). Thousand Oaks, CA: Sage.

Perea, S. (2004). *The New America: The America of the moo shoo burrito.* Denver, CO: HIS Ministries.

Piercynski, M., Matranga, M., & Peltier, G. (1997). Legislative appropriation for minority teacher recruitment: Did it really matter? *The Clearing House, 70,* 205–206.

Public Education Network. (2007). *Open to the public: How communities, parents and students assess the impact of the No Child Left Behind Act: The realities left behind.* Washington, DC: Author.

Reeves, D. B. (2005). *Accountability in action.* Englewood, CO: Advanced Learning Press.

Rothstein, R. (2004). *Class and schools: Using social, economic, and educational reform to close the black-white achievement gap.* Washington, DC: Economic Policy Institute.

Salinas, J. (2000, February). *The effectiveness of minority teachers on minority student success.* Paper presented at the National Association of African American Studies & National

Association of Hispanic and Latino Studies: 2000 Literature Monograph Series, Houston, TX. (ERIC Document Reproduction Service No. ED455235)

Schmoker, M. (1999). *Results: The key to continuous school improvement* (2nd ed.). Alexandria, VA: Association for Supervision and Curriculum Development.

Valdes, G. (1996). *Con respeto: Bridging the distances between culturally diverse families and schools: An ethnographic portrait.* New York: Teachers College Press.

Valencia, R. R. (1986, November). *Minority academic underachievement: Conceptual and theoretical considerations for understanding the achievement problems of Chicano students.* Paper presented to the Chicano Faculty Seminar, Stanford University, Stanford, CA.

Valencia, R. R. (Ed.). (1993). *Chicano school failure and success: Research and policy agendas for the 1990s.* Bristol, PA: Falmer Press. (ERIC Document Reproduction Service No. ED387279)

Viadero, D. (2001). Learning gap linked to LEP instruction. *Education Week, 20*(32), 8.

Young, M. I. (1990). *Justice and the politics of difference.* Princeton, NJ: Princeton University Press. Young, M. D., & Scribner, J. D. (1994). *Parental involvement in minority communities: A review of the research literature.* Austin, TX: The Effective Border Research and Development Initiative, The University of Texas.

9 Understanding Latina/o School Pushout

Experiences of Students Who Left School Before Graduating

Nora Luna and Anita Tijerina Revilla

Currently, the state of educational attainment for most Latina/o students is in crisis. (The term *Latina/o* is used here to respect both genders and more accurately reflect the political, geographical, and historical links among Latin American countries.) Compared with other groups, Latina/o students are more likely to be enrolled below grade level, are less likely to participate in preschool and after-school programs, drop out earlier and at higher rates, and have lower literacy rates (Gandara & Contreras, 2009). Latina/o students are less likely than their non-Latina/o peers to complete high school, and recent Latina/o immigrants are even more likely to drop out (Kohler & Lazarín, 2007). The Latina/o population aged 25 and older is less likely than non-Latina/o Whites to have at least graduated from high school (57.0% and 88.4%, respectively). In addition, more than one quarter of Latinas/os have less than a ninth-grade education (27.3%) compared with only 4.2% of non-Latina/o Whites. The proportion of those with a bachelor's degree or more is much lower for Latinas/os than for non-Latina/o Whites. Less than one quarter of Latina/o students aged 18 through 24 are enrolled in postsecondary degree-granting institutions. In addition, Latinas/os represent only 5% of graduate students in the nation (U.S. Census Bureau, 2005).

Using Census data and information from the National Center for Education Statistics, Yosso (2006) summarized it in the following manner:

> We begin with 100 Chicana and Chicano students at the elementary school level, noting that 56 drop out of high school and 44 continue on to graduate. (The term Chicana/Chicano is used to mean students of Mexican ancestry.) In Nevada, 72% of the Latina/o population is of Mexican descent. In addition, educational attainment and other statistics vary by nationality group. Of the 44 who graduate from high school, about 26 continue on toward some form of postsecondary education. Of those 26, approximately 17 enroll in community college and nine enroll in a 4-year institution. Of those 17 in community colleges, only one will transfer to a 4-year institution. Of the nine Chicanas/os attending a 4-year college and the one community college transfer student, seven will graduate with a baccalaureate degree. Finally, two Chicana/o students

will continue on to earn a graduate or professional school degree and less than one will receive a doctorate.

(p. 4)

Understanding Latina/o students' school experiences is one way to develop and implement strategies to support increased educational achievement. There is not one simple solution. This study provides a view into a window of possible solutions for the educational crisis faced by Latinas/os.

Purpose of the Study

The purpose of this study was to describe narratives of school experiences of Latina/o early school leavers, examine their reasons for leaving school before graduating, and analyze their responses using the resistance model laid out by Solórzano and Delgado Bernal (2001). In addition, the authors compare the participants' reasons for leaving school with data from the Clark County School District's (CCSD) 2007 Dropout Survey Report. The following research questions served as a guide for the study: Why do Latina/o students leave high school before graduating? What are the school experiences of Latina/o early school leavers? What are the perceptions of Latina/o early school leavers regarding the differences between them and students of other ethnic groups? How do participants' behaviors fit into the categories of resistance or oppositional behavior? Finally, how do the participants' reasons for leaving school early compare to the results of the school district's dropout survey report?

The term *pushout* is used as opposed to *dropout* because the data reveal that students' decisions to leave school are not solely an individual choice but rather a result of various factors, including institutional practices/policies and social forces that push students out. For example, some school staff may counsel students out in order to help meet academic goals. Other students are counseled out because they present discipline problems with which the school does not want to deal. In other instances, teacher and school personnel attitudes push students out by creating an unwelcoming and hostile environment.

Background: An Overview of the CCSD Dropout Survey Report

In an effort to examine the reasons why students leave school, personnel in the CCSD in Las Vegas, Nevada, contacted non-return students every year via the telephone. In November 2007, they collected some self-report data regarding the reasons students did not return to school (CCSD, n.d.). Counselors reached 1,020 of the 3,791 ninth through twelfth-grade students listed on the non-return report. The remainder (2,771 students) were unreachable because of disconnected phone lines and/or invalid emergency contact information.

According to survey results, the top reasons students who were reached gave for having left school were as follows: did not like school, found a job, or were credit deficient. Of the non-return students, 37.5% were White, 15.4% were Black, 6.2% were Asian, 1.1% were American Indian, and 39.8% were Hispanic. However, responses were not reported by race/ethnicity; therefore, it is not possible to know whether reasons for not returning to school varied by ethnic group.

Literature Review

Many researchers have examined the possible contributing causes to the Latina/o education crisis; some issues cited in the research as contributing factors include unequal funding for schools located in low-income areas (Kozol, 1991); the absence of qualified and caring teachers (Valenzuela, 1999); the dismantling of bilingual education programs (Crawford, 2004); and the imposition of disciplinary actions that reproduce conditions of dominance, subordination and institutional racism (e.g., low expectations; Espinoza-Herold, 2003). Other factors identified in the literature include the absence of meaningful participation by teachers in school reform efforts (Orfield, 2004); the tracking of students of color into vocational and special education classes; racial segregation; overcrowded schools; poorly maintained schools; untrained or uncredentialed teachers; a shortage of school supplies and textbooks; minimal access to college preparatory, Advanced Placement, and honors courses; an overreliance on biased standardized tests; and the dismissive treatment of Latina/o cultural strengths (Yosso, 2006).

Although little empirical evidence supports cultural deficit models (Solórzano & Solórzano, 1995; Valencia & Solórzano, 1997), these models are most often used to explain school failure among Latinas/os. Cultural deficit models blame Latina/o students, parents, and communities for lacking specific attributes, which in turn leads to academic failure. This model finds dysfunction in Latina/o cultural values and proposes that these values are to blame for low educational and occupational attainment (Ogbu, 1990). Some of the alleged deficient cultural values include immediate gratification, an emphasis on cooperation rather than competition, a present versus future time orientation, and a tendency to minimize the importance of education and upward mobility (Valencia, 1997). Furthermore, supporters of this model assert that Latina/o families (mainly Mexican or Chicana/o families) exhibit dysfunctional social structures: large, disorganized, female-headed, Spanish- or non-standard-English-speaking, and patriarchal or matriarchal family hierarchies that cause and perpetuate a culture of poverty (Sowell, 1981). In addition, the model argues that Latina/o parents fail to assimilate and embrace the educational values of the dominant group and socialize their children with values that do not support educational achievement (Banfield, 1974).

Deficit thinking permeates society today. Both schools and those who work in schools reflect this belief. Professional meetings, school personnel meetings, teacher training, and most places where people discuss the issue of Latina/o education or dropout include words such as *underclass, at risk*, and *disadvantaged* (Valencia & Solórzano, 1997). According to García and Guerra (2004), this reality calls for a critical review of the factors that perpetuate deficit thinking and in fact reproduce "educational inequalities for students from nondominant sociocultural and linguistic backgrounds" (p. 155).

Recently, researchers examining Mexican identity, such as Valenzuela (1999), have steadily shown that mainstream institutions continue to strip away the identities of Mexican children through educational systems that show a lack of caring for them and through subtractive assimilation practices. According to Valenzuela, this loss of Mexican identity, plus a continuous loss of social capital available to later generation Mexicans, negatively impacts the academic achievement and school success rates of many Mexican students.

Valenzuela (1999) asserted that schools subtract resources from U.S. Mexican youth. She argued that students do not fail school; schools fail students. Schools dismiss the definition of *educación* in the Mexican culture that assumes that an individual student's "progress" is lodged in the caring relationship developed between teacher and student.

> Although *educación* has implications for pedagogy, it is first a foundational cultural construct that provides instructions on how one should live in the world. With its emphasis on respect, responsibility, and sociality, it provides a benchmark against by which all humans are to be judged, formally educated or not.
> (Valenzuela, 1999, p. 21)

Valenzuela also argued that "subtractive schooling encompasses subtractive assimilation policies and practices that are designed to divest Mexican students of their culture and language" (p. 20). Schools are organized to perpetuate inequality through academic tracking, a cultural bias against Mexican culture and the Spanish language, and a legacy of ambiguous relations between themselves and the communities they serve.

Subtractive schooling is based on a 3-year ethnographic study at a predominantly Mexican and Mexican-American school in Houston, Texas. Schooling deprives the students at the high school of important social and cultural resources, leaving them more and more vulnerable to academic failure. For example, first-and often second-generation Mexican and Central American students outperform their third-and later generation counterparts (Suarez-Orozco, 1991; Vigil & Long, 1981). Mexican immigrant youth consistently fare better than U.S.-born Mexican students when grades, test scores, and dropout rates are examined (Valenzuela, 1999). Immigrant youth are more likely to be perceived by teachers as respectful, obedient, and deferential (Suarez-Orozco, 1991). Students who display these behaviors are rewarded by their teachers. Furthermore, this behavior is consistent with mainstream teachers' expectations of "Mexican" behavior. For immigrant youth, criticizing the school is seen as inappropriate and impolite. In contrast, the attitudes of U.S.-born youth are seen as "deficient," lacking in drive and motivation. These youth are viewed by school personnel as lacking the linguistic, cultural, moral, and intellectual traits the assimilationist curriculum requires (DeVillar, 1994). Valenzuela (1999) found that youth born in the United States are merely opposed to the "schooling process that disrespects them; they oppose not education, but *schooling*—the content of the education and the way it is offered" (p. 5, emphasis in original). School officials may see disengaged, rebellious, and defiant youth, but Valenzuela found youth who seek unconditional acceptance and caring relationships as the basis for teacher-learning experience. Teachers see students as not *caring*, and students see teachers as not *caring*. As one student said, "If the school doesn't care about my learning why should I care? Answer me that. Just answer me that!" (p. 3).

Furthermore, Valenzuela (1999) has proposed that schools are organized in such a way that fractures students' cultural and ethnic identities that create divisions among students and between students and staff. Teachers fail to make meaningful relationships with students; students are alienated from their teachers, and often first-generation and U.S.-born students are hostile toward one another. In general, the feeling that "no one cares" is pervasive.

In this framework, an authentically caring pedagogy would reverse the effects of subtractive schooling. "Additive" schooling would be about equalizing opportunities and about assimilating Mexicans into larger society. Students can be both Mexican and American. Addictive schooling is about the maintenance of community, including the home–school relationship.

Using critical race theory, Yosso (2006) shifted the view from a deficit perspective of communities of color and focused on community cultural wealth. Community cultural wealth includes an array of cultural knowledge, skills, abilities, and contacts of socially marginalized groups that usually go unrecognized, unacknowledged, or uncelebrated. Her approach to understanding student success and barriers brought to the forefront structural barriers and sociopolitical histories and contexts. The framework is based on the concept of social capital that originally appeared in the literature in the early 1900s (Hanifan, 1916). Yosso asserted that various forms of capital fostered through cultural wealth, including aspirational, linguistic, navigational, social, familial, and resistance capital, are used by communities of color to survive and resist oppression. These areas of capital are used by Latinos in order to survive the institutional neglect of the U.S. public school system that has consistently failed them. These categories are not static or mutually exclusive; they are dynamic processes that build on one another as part of community cultural wealth.

Theoretical Framework

At the forefront of critical education research are theories that contest schooling practices that maintain the subordination of "oppressed" people, including but not limited to poor, working-class, female, ethnic-/linguistic-minority, undocumented, disabled, and queer students and many other marginalized and discriminated populations. (The use of the word *queer* is related to the community activist practice of using the term *queer* as a reclaimed and redefined label that acts as an umbrella for many non-heteronormative identifications, including lesbian, gay, bisexual, transgender, intersex, questioning, allied, and fluid. It is a term that holds political significance and is heavily associated with the gay/queer rights movement.) Freire's (1994) work is the foundation for many of the efforts in this area, as he outlined a theoretical model for working with oppressed students many years ago. He focused primarily on those oppressed by their condition as exploited workers, but his theories have been expanded to include many more discriminated and exploited groups. Freire argued that dehumanization is the "result of an unjust order that engenders violence in the oppressors, which in turn dehumanizes the oppressed" (p. 26). He also asserted that "sooner or later being less human leads the oppressed to struggle against those who made them so" (p. 26). Hence, the oppressed will not be able to tolerate their continued oppression/dehumanization and will eventually have no other recourse but to resist and seek out their own liberation. According to Freire, the oppressed can and should be transformers of their world, and they can do this through a liberatory praxis that includes a critical consciousness/education, or *concientización*, and action.

Critical pedagogue Giroux (1983) also wrote that a radical pedagogy will be achieved only when there is a greater understanding of the relationships between power, resistance, and human agency. That is, power dynamics at play within schools are systematically disenfranchising particular students based on certain aspects of their identities and background. However, there are also many ways in which these students and their educators are strategically resisting oppression and pushout factors. Marginalized students and their allies have human agency, and they are surviving and thriving using their education and critical consciousness to navigate an unjust system. The majoritarian perspective that posits that all students have an equal opportunity and access to education is heavily contested by the work of critical scholars. The authors recognize the injustices but also realize that there are ways to change the expected outcomes.

Chicana and Chicano critical race education scholars Solórzano and Delgado Bernal (2001) expanded on Giroux's discussion of resistance as they examined the oppositional behavior of students from a critical race perspective. They analyzed the experiences of the students involved in the 1968 East Los Angeles School walkouts and 1993 University of California at Los Angeles Chicana and Chicano studies protests to explore student resistance. According to Solórzano and Delgado Bernal, students exhibit four distinct categories of resistance or oppositional behavior in response to social oppression. Reactionary or defiant behavior is not resistance because the students lack both a critique of their oppressive conditions and a motivation toward liberation or social justice. Self-defeating resistance is displayed by students who may have some type of critique of their oppressive social conditions but are not motivated by an interest in liberation or social justice. These students engage in behavior that is not transformational and in fact may help to recreate the oppressive conditions from which it originated. Conformist resistance refers to the oppositional behavior of students who are motivated by a need for liberation and social justice yet hold no critique of the systems of domination. These students are motivated by a desire to create social justice yet engage in activities and behavior within a more liberal tradition. They want things to get better for themselves and others, but they are likely to blame themselves, their families, or their culture for the negative conditions they find themselves in. Transformational resistance is a form of student behavior that is accompanied by a critique of domination and a desire for self-or social liberation. In other words, students must hold an awareness and critique of the oppressive conditions and structures of domination and must be motivated by a sense of social justice. With a deeper level of understanding and a social justice orientation, transformational resistance offers the greatest possibility for social change.

Methods

In an effort to understand the school experiences of Latina/o students and the reasons they drop out in Clark County, the researchers used a qualitative approach. This approach was suitable because it allowed the researchers to gain in-depth information about the participants and their entire school experience. Two focus groups and two in-depth interviews with a total of 17 participants were convened between October 2008 and March 2009. Ten males and 7 females participated. Eight participants were born in Mexico, two were born in El Salvador, and seven were born in the United States (five were of Mexican ancestry and two were of Central American ancestry). Fifteen participants were enrolled at an adult high school at the time of the focus groups and interviews; two participants were neither enrolled in school nor working. The focus groups and interviews lasted between 60 and 120 min each. All of the young adults had dropped out of a CCSD high school. Both focus groups were of mixed gender; one focus group included only immigrants to the United States. All of the participants were Latinas/os between the ages of 18 and 25 who had left high school before graduating.

Students were invited to participate in a focus group or interview through flyers posted around the adult high school, announcements made via the adult high school intercom system, and referrals made by staff at the adult high school. One focus group was funded by a grant that Nevada Kids Count received from the Annie E. Casey Foundation (students were given $60 in cash for participating). The other focus group and two interviews were funded by the University of Nevada Cooperative Extension general operating budget (students were given $15 gift cards for participating). The group facilitators were experienced bilingual Latina professors. The focus group started with general open-ended questions designed to establish rapport and encourage candid conversation. The facilitators guided the discussion around a series of questions. These questions were chosen for their direct relationship to the topic. One focus group was conducted in English, and the focus group with the immigrants was conducted in Spanish and English, as preferred by the participants. The focus groups were recorded and then transcribed. The transcriptions were translated into English where necessary. Institutional review board approval was sought and obtained for the study. All of the names used in this article have been changed to protect the identity and confidentiality of the participants.

Data Analysis

A coding system was developed and tracked on a tally sheet. The categories and codes were based on the domain or sphere of influence that a particular factor was in. For example, participants mentioned teachers and coursework; therefore, a "school" category was created, then subcategories were created for "teachers" and "coursework." Items that were related to personal choices, decisions, or circumstances were placed in a "personal" category. Comments were never assigned to more than one category. For example, participants mentioned peer pressure to ditch or use drugs; this reason was only placed in the "ditching" category and not in a "peer pressure" category.

The responses fit in two general categories: (a) school issues—discrimination or racial microaggressions, apathetic and bad teachers, bad school or negative school climate, irrelevant and boring coursework, and falling behind in grades and coursework; (b) personal issues—ditching, hanging around with the wrong crowd, cultural issues, not understanding English, using drugs, fighting, working, laziness and bad attitude.

Results and Discussion

Participants discussed several themes related to school issues, including discrimination and racial microaggressions, apathetic and bad teachers, a bad school or negative school environment, irrelevant and boring coursework, and falling behind in school. These themes were assigned to the "school" category. The themes assigned to the "personal" category included ditching, wrong crowd, drugs, fighting, and laziness; cultural issues; ESL; pregnancy; work; and mental health issues. Participant quotes are provided for each theme, and an analysis follows each category.

School Issues

Discrimination and Racial Microaggressions

Generally the most prominent theme discussed by participants had to do with issues at school, specifically discrimination and racial microaggressions by teachers and administrators. *Microaggressions* "are subtle, stunning, often automatic, and non-verbal exchanges which are 'put downs' of blacks by offenders. The offensive mechanisms used against blacks often are innocuous. The cumulative weight of their never-ending burden is the major ingredient in black-white interactions" (Pierce, Carew, Pierce-Gonzalez, & Wills, 1978, p. 66). Also, Davis (1989) defined *microaggressions* as "stunning, automatic acts of disregard that stem from unconscious attitudes of white superiority and constitute a verification of black inferiority" (p. 1576). Finally, Delgado and Stefancic (1992) further described examples of subtle racism as ones in which victims become sensitized to the subtle nuances and codewords of racism—the body language; averted gazes; exasperated looks; terms such as "you people," "innocent whites," "highly qualified black," "articulate," and so on—that, whether intended or not, convey racially charged meanings (p. 1283). These subtle forms of racism can have a dramatic effect on people of color.

Participants generally believed that teachers, administrators, and school personnel gave preferential treatment to Whites and Blacks and that they were treated negatively based on their ethnicity. One participant said that he got expelled for "just smoking, whereas White kids could do all kinds of things and nothing would happen." Another male participant said that he was blamed for stealing a box of suckers because he was the only Latino in the class. All participants provided personal experiences of feeling discriminated. One young man stated the following, very emotionally:

> With Latinos everything is gang related. If three Latinos are hanging out, it's a gang. They'll [school police] stop you and pull up your shirt to check out your tattoos then take pictures. I walked into one of my English classes and I just had a sweater and I just sat down and put my head down and the teacher actually, she called the school police thinking that I was going to shoot up the school only because I had my hoodie up and I put my hands down. . . . I saw an officer in front of me and he's asking me can I unzip my jacket. I was like okay. So I took off my sweater and then they searched me and they're like, "Oh no, we're just being precautious." I'm like being precautious by searching me because I got a hoodie on?

Participants definitely did not believe that their culture was valued and thought that it was seen as a negative. One student was told by his White Spanish teacher, "You speak slang Spanish not correct Spanish." He felt bad about this and said, "They just put you down." Students thought there was an ungenuine effort to appear to value their culture: "We only have 5 de Mayo even though it's Hispanic Month! We are feeling left out, they say it is Hispanic Month but don't do anything, don't teach us anything about our history." Another participant said that a teacher told the class, composed of mostly Mexican students, that "if they didn't study they would end up like the other Mexicans standing outside of Home Depot."

In summary, the theme of discrimination and racial microaggressions was the most salient. Racial microaggressions can have a tremendous impact on students' motivation and ability to persist in school. Students were very aware of teachers' attitudes and beliefs and how they were communicated, whether in subtle or not-so-subtle ways. For several participants, leaving school was done in resistance to the discrimination they experienced on a daily basis in school. This kind of resistance can be classified as self-defeating resistance, as noted previously (Solórzano & Delgado Bernal, 2001). However, if students have no articulated or conscious critique of discrimination, it can be viewed as reactionary behavior (unmotivated for social justice/liberation and lacking a critique of social oppression).

Apathetic and Bad Teachers

Another theme discussed by focus group participants had to do with teacher experiences. Participants were very critical of teachers, although they acknowledged that there were some good teachers. Participants perceived most teachers as apathetic and as not enjoying teaching. The following statements reflect their perceptions: "Even if students fail, teachers still get their check." "We are treated like little kids; they are constantly insulting our intelligence." "Some teachers hate their job and take it out on the student. Most teachers are not willing to help." "Teachers only focus on students who are doing well. They don't try to help kids who are struggling, they try to get you out." "Most just give you a worksheet and tell you to fill it out." "There are teachers that actually let students fight in the classroom . . . yeah, the [physical education] coach would be betting on it . . . they'd be like I'll bet $20 this one wins right here."

Linda, an immigrant from El Salvador, said,

> I had teachers who were Hispanic, but my teacher who was also from El Salvador . . . she told me that she didn't speak Spanish. But once I heard her speaking Spanish, and told her so, and she said yes, but not to you, but, I told her that I didn't know how to do my homework. She said I must do it anyway.

The teacher never helped Linda or explained the instructions in Spanish; therefore, she was not able to do her assignments. Several participants did remark that the adult high school they were attending had better teachers. One student said, "Teachers care," referring to the adult high school teachers.

Valenzuela's (1999) work on "caring" affirms many of the narratives heard from participants regarding this theme. Her research demonstrates that educational institutions continue to strip away the identities of Mexican children through a system that shows a lack of caring and through subtractive assimilation practices. Participants also confirmed what Valenzuela found, that teachers fail to make meaningful relationships with students; and, just as in Valenzuela's work, students generally believed that "no one cares."

Bad School or Negative School Climate

Participants were very aware of the disparities between schools. "It seems like people just go there [schools in "rich" neighborhoods] to do their work and just go. But these schools are so out of control," said one person. Another student agreed, "For some reason, the schools in the west side are the most messed up, the west and the east side, like the good schools are like down in the south." Alan said that people do not really hear about all of the problems at the school. He said that there was a big riot at his school and that people actually lit trashcans on fire, hit the dean with a bottle of Clorox, and had food fights. He said, "It's like hard to go to school and focus on school with all this stuff around you, there's so many problems you've got to worry about." He added, "It's getting hard out there, just hope you guys can make it better for those that are coming. They underestimate us and are quick to judge."

Students were fully aware of the fact that their schools were sorely under-resourced, and this had a direct impact on their perception of the value of their education and self-perception. Although they critiqued the educational system, many believed they have very little recourse and ability to create change around this reality. One participant said,

> They had to actually put in just single chairs without desks because they were running out of room ... sometimes you'd be like, "Well you got to go outside in the hall, here's your book ... if you have questions come inside." You just try to do the work, but if I don't get it, I'm going home.

Irrelevant and Boring Coursework

Another major reason cited for dropping out was irrelevant and boring coursework. Armando was placed in an "easy" English class. "They did work for kindergartners," he said. He still failed the class. "The work was too easy and boring," according to Armando. Adam kept being tested for ESL classes and he always passed; he said, "They underestimate people." Participants said that they sometimes got classes they did not need, and if they wanted to change the class, it would take months to do so. In third grade, Armando attended school in Mexico. He said classes were a lot more challenging there; he did work there that he later did in high school in the United States. Alan said that his English class was so easy "it makes you think 'Are you serious?' You think I'm that dumb?" The lack of culturally relevant pedagogy, coupled with low expectations of working-class and poor students, immigrant students, and students of color, is a strong indicator of a pushout factor in schools. However, although most student retention research focuses on student "failure," very little is being done to hold institutions of education accountable for changing the culture of the school from a focus on remedial work to high achievement and student-centered curriculum. Students' critiques speak to this area of need.

Falling Behind in Grades and Coursework

Several students discussed being credit deficient and not likely to graduate even if they stayed in school. A few students said that once they knew they were failing, they just "gave up." Other participants had no credits at all when they dropped out. One participant said that the only time he ever talked to his counselor in 4 years of school was the time she told him that he was credit deficient. Another male said that he was pretty much an "average kid, not bad or good," but that he was one credit short and ended up deciding to leave school before graduating.

Personal Issues

Ditching, Hanging Around With the Wrong Crowd, Drugs, Fighting, and Laziness

Despite all of the negative experiences and hardships in school, participants primarily blamed themselves for leaving school without graduating. They all regretted it and believed it was ultimately their mistakes that led them to leaving school early. Many participants said they ditched, hung out with the wrong crowd, did drugs, fought, and were lazy. Participants felt pressure from their peers to ditch and use drugs. They also acknowledged being "lazy" and having a "don't care attitude." They acknowledged being unmotivated and having procrastinated in school. The young adults did not believe that it was the school's role or responsibility to make school more interesting. "It's school, it's not supposed to be fun," said one young woman.

The need for intervention programs and early detection of student dropout and pushout is of the essence. Students take accountability and responsibility for their actions, but without proper guidance and navigation through the educational pipeline, falling behind in school and personal issues continue to be huge sources of concern.

Cultural Issues

Participants who came to the United States related stories about missing their county, having to learn a whole new system of life, and feeling frustration as a result of not understanding the language. Linda said the following:

> Well I used to live in Michoacan, it wasn't a city, it wasn't like here. Plus back there we would have to do all kinds of different stuff to obtain food . . . here you just go shopping and get everything, it was harder over there and it was easier here but either way you miss back home, you miss your family members back over there and just coming here and getting used to something that you basically have no idea what it is and everything, it was hard.

Efren said, "I just missed my country." Rocio said the biggest obstacle she encountered was "just getting used to a whole new country when you come from a whole different place where you basically don't know anything or anyone . . . but just getting used to here and having to learn everything." In response to the question "What are some of the differences in school experiences between Latinos and non-Latinos?" Carolina said the following:

> Our parents don't speak any, well my parents don't speak any English, I think that's pretty much why I think it's harder, just speaking everything and learning all the stuff. You know people that are from here usually know what you're getting yourself into and they teach their kids before they go to school and all of that. But us, I think that's pretty much the difference between us and them, but there's really no difference.
> *Question: What do you think they teach the kids?*
> Like if they start off as little kindergartners, probably just the ABCs and numbers, the few words that they have to know and us we go in there not knowing anything. Like I went in there not knowing nothing and it was, I think that was the only thing. I don't see any difference though between us and the other races or the people that were born here. I think we're pretty much all the same except we have to learn the language and they probably already know it, not all of them, but most of them do.

ESL

The focus group of Latina/o immigrants discussed the problems they encountered in school as a result of not understanding English. "For me it was hard, a little bit hard because I didn't understand the language, but then I got used to it. I started, you know, understanding and little by little it got better," said one female. Julio stated, "Well me, the teachers are always getting mad because I only spoke Spanish and well she would like say, 'Oh you're, well you guys are here in the U.S. now and you guys got to learn how to talk English.'" Julio was in third grade when he came to the United States. Carol came to the United States in fourth grade:

> My year was pretty hard because I was a fourth grader and my teacher didn't speak any Spanish and I didn't speak English, there were two of us that didn't speak any English at all. So the struggles were pretty much learning how to talk it, how to write it and to be in a whole class where everybody knew how to speak.

Another male participant said he struggled to do the work and understand the teacher. Linda said her teachers would tell her to get help from other students.
  Several of the examples of the two themes above were discussed in the work done by Yosso (2006) as she identified areas of community cultural wealth such as linguistic capital, familial, and social capital that many educators do

not view as assets. Instead, a student's bilingualism and multiculturalism are viewed as deficits. The student's experiences and culture are not valued, recognized, or acknowledged.

Pregnancy

Several participants mentioned knowing someone who had dropped out because of a pregnancy, but only two participants revealed that they had left school because they had gotten pregnant. Fabiola finished tenth grade, got married, had her baby, and moved in with her husband across town. Fabiola's husband, mother, and mother-in law all encouraged her to continue with school and were available to babysit. She had been highly encouraged by her teachers at Rancho High School to continue with school after her baby was born, and she was planning to do so. However, she started 11th grade at a new school and quit after a few weeks. Fabiola was failing her classes and could not get any help. She did not think that the teachers were helpful or friendly; she also did not make any friends at the new school, so she felt alone. "At Rancho they used to help me a lot. All the teachers I had for the two years they helped me really good and that's how I passed and any problems I had I used to go with them," said Fabiola. She did not think that she had the same support at the new school. Another female participant said that she ditched school and was not a good student when she became pregnant. She said her mother was very disappointed because she had brought her to the United States so she could be successful. However, she has returned to school to be a good role model for her baby daughter.

Talavera-Bustillos (1998) revealed that motherhood can also be a source of inspiration for continuing with education. According to Talavera-Bustillos, motherhood can foster resilience and be the reason that many young women return to school and continue on the path of education. This is pertinent for student retention research and needs to be explored further.

Work

Several participants worked full time or almost full time. These young people said that having a job made it easier for them to drop out. They agreed that they liked the money; one male said he was getting $14.86 an hour working in housekeeping at a hotel casino. Another male participant said he worked at a movie theater to have money for car insurance. Arnie worked on the weekends at a local dairy farm. He said he helped his family. According to the participants who worked, they did not quit school to work out of necessity but because they enjoyed having money. One female said the following:

> I wanted to work, I wanted to have my own things . . . I told my mom, "I want to work," and she didn't agree with it. She said I had to study and she got mad at me . . . I told her I could still go to school and work

at the same time. She said, "Do you promise?" I said, "Yeah." But then you know you start getting money ... then I gave up on school because of my work.

Economic survival is a key component of the decision to leave school early. Many students are financially responsible for themselves and their entire family very early in life. This is an incredible obstacle to school completion.

Mental Health Issues

Daisy dropped out of school for the first time when she was 12 years old. She tried to go back several times but kept getting into trouble. She said the primary problem she had in school had to do with mental health issues:

> When I started going [to school] I would always get nervous like because there was too many people. ... I guess you'd call it social anxiety, yeah I have problems with being with a lot of people, so. But then I had a depression problem so I didn't want to be in school ... that's just really what kept me from going to school. I would always get nervous or just always felt like someone was, I don't know, but the teachers weren't even helpful either. I would throw up before going to school. I would have one teacher that I could talk to which was good and was my history teacher, but she would kind of understand what was going on, so we need more teachers like that.

Latina/o youth are more likely to suffer from mental health issues such as depression. Frequently these issues are more likely to go untreated, leading to social and academic problems (Gandara & Contreras, 2009).

Discussion

For the most part, participants had a critique of their oppressive conditions but were not motivated by an interest in social justice; therefore, many of the behaviors described in this article fit into the *self-defeating resistance* category. Students described various forms of discrimination or racial microaggressions they experienced at school by teachers and administrators. There is powerful evidence that racism in subtle and not-so-subtle forms can have a tremendous impact on the lives of students of color (Espinoza, 1990). In this case, students resisted the discrimination and racial microaggressions by ultimately dropping out of school.

Participants in the study reacted to forms of oppression and racial microaggressions by teachers and school practices by engaging in behavior that was not transformational and that in fact led to the conditions that maintained their oppressive structures, such as purposefully not doing their work and ultimately leaving school before graduating. Some students said that once they knew they were failing they just "gave up," demonstrating reactionary or defiant behavior.

The narratives about teachers provided by the participants demonstrate the subtractive schooling practices documented in Valenzuela's (1999) research. Participants described teachers as not caring; they subsequently engaged in reactionary or defiant behavior or in self-defeating resistance. Students enrolled in the adult high school were all motivated and committed to completing their high school degree. They also frequently discussed the fact that teachers at the adult high school "care." Again, this confirms Valenzuela's research that students are seeking caring relationships as the basis for the learning experience.

Beginning in elementary school, Latina/o children begin to get tracked and placed in lower reading-ability groups. They are clustered into a lower level curriculum, setting them on a pathway that becomes more unequal in middle school. Students in these lower level groups will come to see themselves as slower and not as smart as other students, setting themselves on a path of low-level achievement.

Despite the critique of the teachers and the system, participants engaged in self-defeating resistance. These critiques can lead to transformational resistance, and in fact, as most of these students were enrolled in an adult high school, they had moved to conformist resistance. They blamed themselves, their families, and their culture for the negative conditions they found themselves in. In conformist resistance, students hold no critique of the system and want things to get better for themselves, but they engage in activities and behaviors within a more liberal tradition, such as returning to school but doing nothing about the system that led them to leave school in the first place.

By blaming themselves for leaving school without graduating, participants internalized the majoritarian narrative that blames students for "failure" instead of using a counterstory. Counterstory telling is a method of telling the experiences of racially marginalized people. Majoritarian narratives tell the story of those with racial and social privilege. Participants said that they did drugs and engaged in other self-defeating behavior such as ditching and having a "lazy" and "don't care" attitude. Although the issue of drug use is beyond the scope of this article, there is an abundance of research demonstrating the risk factors for substance use, which include the availability of drugs, the laws and norms of the community regarding drugs, and other issues that impact whether youth use substances—such as leaving school early. Drug use is not exclusively an individual decision but rather is influenced by social, biological, psychological, and environmental factors. Participants did not question what led to their "don't care attitude" and believed it was not the school's job to make school interesting, again internalizing the majoritarian narrative instead of reflecting on what led them to have the "I don't care attitude."

Students frequently mentioned missing their country and feeling alienated because of not understanding the language. As described earlier, Latina/o students' culture is often viewed not as a strength but rather as a deficit. If teachers engaged in culturally relevant and authentically caring pedagogy or understood the community cultural wealth (Yosso, 2006) that students brought with them to school, the students' experiences would be valued and legitimized and could be included as part of the curriculum. Also, teachers, with support from the system, could strive to make genuine connections with students.

Students who worked during high school did so to "help their families" and be able to "buy their own things." Perhaps students were able to obtain some respect and independence through working that they could not obtain in school. For the reasons mentioned previously, work was more rewarding and seemed to provide a feeling of autonomy. The question then becomes, Why does school not provide the rewarding feelings of being independent and autonomous?

Conclusion

In conclusion, there is not one primary reason participants gave for dropping out. Participants revealed various reasons for leaving school early, as well as many school experiences that resulted in overall negative experiences in school that may have led to a pushout factor. The focus group discussion revealed many points of possible intervention and prevention strategies. At the closing of the focus group, one participant said, "I hope you make it better for the ones that are coming. Being Hispanic you are considered low. They underestimate us."

Given these data, the authors believe that the *majoritarian* narrative that depicts students simply as dropouts is extremely narrow and unhelpful for student retention purposes. When the work of Solórzano and Delgado Bernal (2001) is considered, perhaps there is a possibility for critical education and thinking that will lead students toward transformational resistance, resilience, and persistence in school; that is, there is potential to foster and create a space for a heightened critique of social oppression that creates the incentive for students to pursue personal change as well as social change.

Comparison With the CCSD Dropout Survey Report

The dropout survey and the focus groups and interviews are very different methods and tools for gathering information; therefore, they cannot truly be compared. Nonetheless, this general comparison demonstrates some differences and similarities in Latina/o school experiences and reasons for leaving school early than for the early school leavers who were surveyed, as a group. The focus groups and interviews demonstrated school issues to be the primary cause of school dropout among Latina/o students; however, more personal issues were mentioned, as demonstrated by the list of factors. In other words, it seems that school structural and institutional issues generated more discussion and that there were more memories related to experiences such as discrimination, bad teachers, bad school climate, irrelevant coursework, and being credit deficient; however, participants mentioned as many personal issues, such as ditching and drug use, that affected school, but they did not spend as much time discussing those issues. The CCSD telephone survey demonstrated school issues and personal issues to be equally salient, as demonstrated by the percentage who responded to each reason; however, the report did not include any qualitative data or explanation, and therefore it is difficult to understand the context.

With thousands of students leaving school early every year, it is understandable that school district personnel want a fast method, such as a fill-in survey, to assess and assign reasons for this phenomenon. However, as the discussion with these 17 participants revealed, there is not one simple fill-in-the-blank reason. If a solution is to be developed, then it will be necessary to spend time understanding complex issues from students' and families' perspectives.

References

Banfield, E. C. (1974). Schooling versus education. In *The unhealthy city: The nature and future of our urban crisis* (pp. 132–157). Boston, MA: Little, Brown and Company.

Clark County School District. (n.d.). *Dropout rates fast facts*. Las Vegas, NV: author.

Crawford, J. (2004). *Educating English language learners: Language diversity in the classrooms* (5th ed.). Los Angeles, CA: Bilingual Educational Services.

Davis, P. (1989). Law as microaggression. *Yale Law Journal, 98*, 1559–1577.

Delgado, R., & Stefancic, J. (1992). Images of the outsider in American law and culture: Can free expression remedy systemic social ills? *Cornell Law Review, 77*, 1258–1297.

DeVillar, R. A. (1994). The rhetoric and practice of cultural diversity in U.S. schools: Socialization, resocialization, and quality schooling. In R. A. DeVillar, C. J. Faltis, & J. P. Cummins (Eds.), *Cultural diversity in schools: From rhetoric to practice* (pp. 25–56). Albany, NY: State University of New York Press.

Espinoza, L. G. (1990). Masks and other disguises: Exposing legal academia. *Harvard Law Review, 103*, 1878–1886.

Espinoza-Herold, M. (2003). *Issues in Latino education: Race, school culture and the politics of academic success*. Boston, MA: Allyn & Bacon.

Freire, P. (1994). *Pedagogy of hope*. New York, NY: Continuum.

Gandara, P., & Contreras, F. (2009). *The Latino education crisis: The consequences of failed social policies*. Cambridge, MA: Harvard University Press.

García, S. B., & Guerra, P. (2004). Deconstructing deficit thinking: Working with educators to create more equitable learning environments. *Education and Urban Society, 36*(2), 150–168.

Giroux, H. A. (1983). Theories of reproduction and resistance in the new sociology of education: A critical analysis. *Harvard Educational Review, 55*, 257–293.

Hanifan, L. J. (1916). The rural school community center. *Annals of the American Academy of Political and Social Science, 67*, 130–138.

Kohler, A. D., & Lazarín, M. (2007). *Hispanic education in the United States* (Statistical Brief No. 8). Washington, DC: National Council of La Raza.

Kozol, J. (1991). *Savage inequalities: Children in America's schools* (1st ed.). New York, NY: Crown.

Ogbu, J. (1990). Minority education in comparative perspective. *Journal of Negro Education*, *59*, 45–57.
Orfield, G. (2004). Losing our future: Minority youth left out. In G. Orfield (Ed.), *America: Confronting the graduation crisis* (pp. 1–11). Cambridge, MA: Harvard Education Press.
Pierce, C., Carew, J., Pierce-Gonzalez, D., & Wills, D. (1978). An experiment in racism: TV commercials. In C. Pierce (Ed.), *Television and education* (pp. 62–88). Beverly Hills, CA: Sage.
Solórzano, D. G., & Delgado Bernal, D. (2001). Critical race theory, transformational resistance, and social justice: Chicana and Chicano students in an urban context. *Urban Education*, *36*, 308–342.
Solórzano, D. G., & Solórzano, R. (1995). The Chicano educational experience: A proposed framework for effective schools in Chicano communities. *Educational Policy*, *9*, 293–314.
Sowell, T. (1981). *Ethnic America: A history*. New York, NY: Basic Books.
Suarez-Orozco, M. (1991). Migration, minority status, and education: European dilemmas and responses in the 1990s. *Anthropology and Education Quarterly*, *22*(2), 99–199.
Talavera-Bustillos, V. (1998). *Chicana college choice and resistance: An exploratory study of first generation college students*. Unpublished doctoral dissertation, University of California, Los Angeles.
U.S. Census Bureau. (2005). *School enrollment-social and economic characteristics of students: October 2003*. Washington, DC: U.S. Department of Commerce. Retrieved from http://www.census.gov/prod/2005pubs/p20-554.pdf
Valencia, R. R. (Ed.). (1997). *The evolution of deficit thinking: Educational thought and practice*. Washington, DC: Falmer.
Valencia, R. R., & Solórzano, D. G. (1997). Contemporary deficit thinking. In R. Valencia (Ed.), *The evolution of deficit thinking: Educational thought and practice* (pp. 160–210). Washington, DC: Falmer.
Valenzuela, A. (1999). *Subtractive schooling: U.S.–Mexican youth and the politics of caring*. Albany: State University of New York Press.
Vigil, J. D., & Long, J. M. (1981). Unidirectional or nativist acculturation: Chicano paths to school achievement. *Human Organization*, *40*, 273–277.
Yosso, T. J. (2006). *Critical race counterstories along the Chicana/Chicano educational pipeline*. New York, NY: Taylor & Francis.

10 *Compartiendo Nuestras Historias*
Five *Testimonios* of Schooling and Survival

Wanda Alarcón, Cindy Cruz, Linda Guardia Jackson, Linda Prieto, and Sandra Rodriguez-Arroyo

When Margaret Randall (1984) stated that "it is no accident, because recognition of, knowledge of, and understanding of one's personal and collective identity is essential to people's revolution" (p. 10), the telling of our personal histories and *testimonios* as Chicanas and Latinas in the academy becomes nothing less than transformational. Our use of the *testimonio* narrative reflects a praxis grounded in the community work and activist scholarship that we engage with as we negotiate the academy as working-class women of color. To read and to listen to these stories is to commit to another kind of understanding—one of solidarity—of the challenges of language and assimilation, of gender and race and the violence of patriarchy, of the experiences of being treated as an "alien" in one's own country. *Testimonio* requires a deep learning, necessitating an openness to give oneself to the other. It requires what Emmanuel Levinas (1994) described as "receiving the lesson so deeply [that] the lesson of truth is not held in one consciousness. It explodes toward the other" (p. 80).

This compilation of testimonial narratives comes from the hundreds of hours that we have collectively shared and analyzed our experiences as we move forward in our educational trajectories. Our stories are not part of the national discourse of "pulling ourselves up by our bootstraps"—the individualistic, nation-building narratives of the hegemony. These stories stand in for the hundreds and thousands of women of color who are also struggling to achieve the credentials necessary to survive, to begin this larger project of racial, gendered, and economic transformation in our communities. *Testimonio* is one tool we own, this radical storytelling that we learned as cultural workers and community activists, and we carry it into the academy along with the political and social capital we bring to our scholarly lives.

John Beverley (1993) stated that stories "centered on the 'I' and personal experience, serving those subjects—the child, the 'native,' the woman, the insane, the criminal, the worker" (p. 71) "[evoke] an absent polyphony of other voices, other possible lives and experiences" (p. 75). Our stories, polyphonic and urgent, are an offering to those who would stand in solidarity with us, a theory in the flesh, and a process of healing. We progress with every truth-telling; every story we begin strips away at these inscriptions of race, poverty, violence, and homophobia; with every spoken word we heal. The personal is indeed political as we acknowledge our collective memories, our shared histories. Through *testimonio* we acknowledge our own resiliency and the histories of our resistance.

The educational *testimonios* we present here were first organized and shared at the 2009 American Association of Hispanics in Higher Education annual conference in San Antonio, Texas. In this space where we told our own stories, our audience responded powerfully and testified about their own experiences in schools, and our panel was no longer a staid academic space but one in which we heard one another's voices, transforming the place into one of mutual support and solidarity.

Wanda Alarcón

I didn't always know it, but English is not my first language. I came to understand this through a memory that feels to me like a scene from an old home movie, frozen in time. *Cut to: Inside of a fifth-grade classroom in the pueblo Reyes Acozac, Mexico. La maestra* says to the class, "*Atención niños, hoy tenemos una estudiante nueva.*" She turns to me and asks me to say my name to the class. I do as I'm told, and I say, "*Me llamo Wanda Ah-lahr-cone.*" With a smile, my teacher gently corrects my watery Americanized pronunciation and says, "*Tu nombre es Wanda Alarcón.*"

I was born in East Los Angeles to Guadalupe and Amando, Mexicano immigrants. Born and raised in Reyes Acozac, a little pueblo just outside of Mexico City, they married in their 20s and came to the United States to work and raise a family. Before I ever heard the A-E-I-O-U & sometimes Y song I remember how my father taught me the vowels with a funny song he would sing to me like this: "A"—*chaka chaka chaka chaka chaka chaka cha . . .* "E"—*cheke cheke cheke cheke checke cheke che . . .* and so on. My parents were wholly in charge of my education for the first 5 years of my life. Of course, Spanish was my first language. Other than what I might have absorbed from *Sesame Street*, I did not speak English when I started kindergarten. But I quickly learned it, and so did my brothers, with so much proficiency that in four more years English became our primary language. My parents regularly objected to our casual Americanisms, like "You guys." "*¡¿Como que you guys? Nosotros no somos* "you guys," *somos sus papás!*" And my father soon made a decision to intervene on our behalf because it was clear to him that our language and identity were at stake. It seemed to me that one minute he declared "*¡Mis hijos no van a crecer pochos!*" and the next we were living in Reyes with my grandparents.

That first day of fifth grade in Mexico, I don't remember feeling shame over not knowing how to pronounce my own name. I wasn't alarmed over my assimilation like my father was, and in fact I didn't even notice that I was growing up "American." Life in Mexico changed all of that. At a time when the Chicano movement was redefining first-, second-, third-generation Mexicanos in the United States, my parents drilled into us that we were not Mexican Americans, *pochos, cholos*, and whatever a Chicano was. They insisted that we would always be, above all, Mexicanos and that the United States was, therefore, a foreign land. To lose our language was akin to losing our identity, our history, and even our sense of family.

We spent a year in Mexico; my mother, brothers, and I all went to school, fifth grade for me. My sister was born in Mexico while my father stayed in the United States to work and save money for a house. My grandmother taught me my first piano lessons and solfeggio on my grandfather's upright piano: *do re mi fa sol fami re do*. By the end of that year we were the perfectly bilingual *familia* Alarcón. But I didn't so much experience that move as an intentional plan for a radical education transformation, not the way my father had in mind, but rather thought that we moved from the United States to Mexico, English to Spanish, because that's how our family looked and worked. My father's parents had migrated to the United States to work, but all of my mother's family, my *abuelitos* and *tíos*, lived in Mexico. We drove from Los Angeles to Mexico and back so many times for long summer vacations—I think it was in part my parents' sense of adventure to come to the United States in the first place. My father loved to drive and my mother loved new places. The memories of driving into calm beach cities at dawn, Mazatlán, Hermosillo, and having breakfast in a bustling *plazita*, the heady aroma of toasted corn and ripe fruit all around, crossing from the United States into Mexico and noticing the signs for Coca-Cola on both sides of the border gave me an education about life across the *frontera* from both perspectives. That was a long time ago.

Now I claim the name Chicana for myself for all it contains intellectually, politically, creatively. But in many ways the Mexican and the American experiences I've traveled and crossed all of my life have yet to meet. For my own survival, I retrace the palimpsest of my history through these early memories of songs and rhymes, desert landscapes, school in the pueblo and the city, our first home in the Los Angeles eastside, multiple crossings at the Tijuana border—my parents and siblings having to declare our various citizenships. Sometimes these experiences I've carried for a long time come to me as fleeting impressions and I am not sure I can fully grasp their meaning. But in that space of intangibility there is also perception. I remember a history that began with the sound of my parents' voices, and with that, I can be certain of what I know. No, English was not my first language.

Cindy Cruz

When I was in the fifth grade, a girl from my school said she liked me as she thought I was a boy. We all laughed, my friends and I, when we heard that. She even tried to talk with me during recess, but I was too busy playing soccer to listen to this girl who was so dumb she couldn't tell if I was a boy or a girl. But the misrecognition bothered me (it always did), and I often wondered why people put so much investment in my appearance, what rule was I breaking? At home I looked at myself in the mirror—this body that enjoyed running and soccer and was as good as any boy, kung fu mock-fighting with them. Maybe it was my hair cut short by my *Tia* who just graduated from beauty school that confused this girl? Was it the boots I wore every day? Or the silver cowboy belt buckle my father bought for me at the rodeo last year?

As I got older, my gender did matter to people when I looked or played or walked like a boy. People felt free to police my gender—my clothes, or the way that I talked, or my hair. Sometimes it was teachers or nurses who questioned my gender and other parents asking me even while I was standing in the grocery line with my mother! My mother would tell them to mind their own business and a few other things. They knew I was different, but they didn't know why. Some of them thought they knew what to do with my difference.

I walked home from school every day with my neighbors, but on this day I was late, as music kept me later than I usual. Noticing the time, I grabbed my instrument case and made my way home. The streets were so quiet. I thought it was strange because usually there were kids playing and riding their bikes in the streets until nightfall. I remembered a book I read that talked about how birds and other animals instinctively hide away before a storm or a tornado. My boots echoed through the empty streets and I heard whisperings on my left near a row of vacated houses: "Wetback, go home." I bit my lip nervously, as I was a little scared of older boys. They seemed to be the ones most outraged at my transgressions. I walked a little faster and noticed who lived nearby, just in case I had to make a run for it. I heard those words again, "Wetback, go home," but this time it was a little louder. I walked to the middle of the street and shouted back to them, "Don't call me a wetback, you assholes!" Three White teenagers came out of the house on my left, blocking my way home. I froze. "Calling us assholes, you little spic?" said the tallest boy, SWP (supreme White power) tattooed on his left arm. "Are you a boy or a girl?" the second one sneered. "Maybe we should find out," said the third and started toward me. I tried to shout for help, but my vocal cords wouldn't work. As the third boy grabbed me and started to drag me into the empty row of houses, the adrenaline rushed through me and I slammed my instrument case into his groin. He fell to his knees in pain and I ran as fast as I could from the other two boys who now had to get their Aryan Youth companion out of the street.

When I got home, I thought that this must be how people are going to react to me and my boots and short hair and cowboy belt buckles. I felt sick and insecure about my "looks"—I allowed my hair to grow out and wore more clothing made for girls. I hated how men and boys would stare at me. By junior high, other students made obscure comments about my sexuality, or lack thereof. Other classmates were more blatant, tagging "jota" or "dyke" on my locker in *placas* (graffiti) that I recognized. But the words did not stick to me, and I was fortunate to be placed in a pre-college track at my school. It kept the overt heterosexuality at bay. But the storm of drugs, sex, and alcohol swirled around me and I buried myself in my books. If outside the classroom was about the brutality of adolescent boys, then inside the classroom, where literature took me far away from my dusty hometown, I excelled. When the steel mill closed and my father and everyone around us lost their jobs, I didn't ask for money for books, so I shoplifted what I wanted and searched the thrift stores for literature. I could get Michael Herr's *Dispatches* for 25 cents, James Baldwin's *The Fire Next Time*, or five books for a dollar at the local secondhand store. I had teachers in high school, some of whom were lesbian or gay, who loaned me books or allowed me to search through the department libraries for literature and poetry. I read everything I could get my hands on.

During my first year of college, someone gave me a copy of *This Bridge Called My Back: Writings by Radical Women of Color* (Moraga & Anzaldúa, 1983). It made such a profound impact to read these testimonials from working-class writers of color, that *Bridge* was a space where women of color, particularly lesbians of color, were at the center of a radical politic. Their critique of U.S. imperialism, of racism and homophobia, of the image in the foreword of a world on fire reverberated through my own histories and those of my family. *Bridge* gave me a language to begin to make sense of my world, and I understood that these writers made the political decision to be the connections between communities. But most important, it was reading the stories of Gloria Anzaldúa, Nellie Wong, Cherríe Moraga, and Audre Lorde and my intensely personal connection to their brutal honesty about themselves, their families, and how the shit comes down on women of color in this country. I recognized my histories in their words, my history of false rewards for my family's assimilation into the language of this country, and my own queerness. I recognized my own resiliency. And despite all they've experienced, I recognized that these writers still choose to use their own bodies for political work—the human *Bridge*, the back that gets walked on over and over.

I believe that my experience growing up queer didn't necessarily mean "homosexual." In Fontana it was a queer thing to want to go to college. I want to believe that my socialization as an assertive and righteous girl cut me out of the crowd. Maybe it was the fact that I didn't speak with an accent, or maybe it was my refusal to play by the rules ascribed to my race and gender. It made sense to call myself a *lesbian* early on, as it was a term that described what I was experiencing, but maybe the term *dyke* would be a better fit for me—one that announces my hard-scrabble working-class history. When I hear other people tell stories about growing up and going to school, so normal and unassuming, I hesitate to tell my own stories. School was a safe space for me. I didn't have to "come out" of any closet, but my standpoint begins where race and capitalism and gender are hopelessly entangled. My life moves away from those I went to school with every time I claim my queer body. I am convinced that had I not been a lesbian, I would not have survived this. I would not have survived.

Linda Guardia Jackson

"You're just a dirty Meskin," my playmate from next door yelled at me after I had won, again, at the game of jacks. The words plunged into my being as hot and searing as that Texas summer afternoon. My 9-year-old mind didn't intellectually understand the epithet, but emotionally the words felt like a sharp knife cutting into my stomach. It was the first and only time anyone has made such a blatantly racist remark directly to me, but indirectly south Texas racism against Mexican Americans was always all around me. The words from that long-ago summer remain a hard kernel inside of me that I take out periodically to examine.

We were the only Mexican American family in an Anglo[1] neighborhood, and I attended predominantly Anglo schools. I spoke English at home and school, but the sounds of Spanish swirled around me in conversations among my mother, father, *abuelos*, *tias*, and *tios* were never directed toward my sisters, cousins, or me. I later asked myself how I had not absorbed this "secret" language that the adults spoke with one another. Now I realize how the hegemony of English and the oppression of all things Mexican deeply affected my family and my life. At an early age, I noticed that my elders spoke Spanish to one another only at home and not in public. My mother must have felt deeply stigmatized in order to deny me her mother tongue.

I do know from her stories that my mother had been educated in a public school system in San Antonio that punished students for speaking Spanish and that she had not been allowed to speak English at home. I believe my mother's historical moment and geographical space led her to feel shame about her language that she wanted to spare her children.

As a result, I am, as Dr. Kathy Escamilla once stated, a recovering monolingual. In my early years, I was neither allowed to speak Spanish at school nor encouraged to speak it at home. Later in life, I made a conscious effort to learn the language that my *abuelos* and my parents spoke. Because I had been unable to have a lengthy conversation with my monolingual Spanish-speaking grandmother while I was growing up, I never got to hear her *cuentos* directly from her, even though she lived with us. This saddens me to this day.

I do, however, have physical and sensorial memories that connect me to my maternal grandmother. I remember her washing my below-the-waist hair with rainwater she collected just for that purpose. I remember sitting close to her side as I learned to crochet and embroider in the backyard on some of those beautiful days we can sometimes have in San Antonio. Another powerful memory is of our shared task of plucking out the little rocks that hid in the pile of dried pinto beans, which she would transform into her delicious *frijoles enteros*. Our communication had been nonverbal; she had not learned English, and at that time I spoke little Spanish.

Someone once asked why my parents had not spoken Spanish to me during my childhood. I did not have an immediate response and paused to think about the interplay between language and identity that I have found so difficult to understand and that, through the years, has elicited many different emotions in me. I have felt shame about my lack of fluency in Spanish and guilt about my success in school. My experiences moved me to learn Spanish as a second language and work in bilingual education.

I end with two stories that were told to me by Dr. Angela Valenzuela—one is an event and the other is the myth of Coyolxauhqui, Aztec goddess of the moon. The event happened in 1978: Electrical workers installing underground cables in Mexico City found a sculpture relief made of volcanic stone weighing 8 tons. It showed the goddess decapitated with arms and legs dismembered. The myth involves Coyolxauhqui, goddess of the moon, and her brother, Huitzilopochtil. The brother springs full grown out of their mother's womb and kills his sister because Coyolxauhqui was going to kill their mother. Her brother cuts off Coyolxauhqui's limbs and head and casts her down from the top of a hill.

I relate the event and the myth to the identity-making of Latinas who pursue a higher education degree. The covering and the (un)covering of the relief itself and the dismembering and the (re)membering connect to how I view the possibility of healing the wounds inflicted by our daily lived experiences through telling story, sharing story, and listening to story. The (re)discovery of the sculpture is sad because of the many lost years without it. The myth is violent. But schooling that is subtractive of language and culture is also violent and sad. However, Coyolxauhqui symbolizes the possibility of (un)covering, (re)discovering, and (re)membering through telling.

Linda Prieto

My *testimonio* speaks to my experiences as the daughter of Mexican immigrants growing up during the 1980s and early 1990s in the Central San Joaquin Valley of California, which is my backdrop. My family taught me difficult and valuable lessons through their words, actions, and expressions, lessons that I carry to this day. On long cold nights my mom made us *avena o una tacita de chocolate caliente* (oatmeal or a small cup of hot chocolate) to nourish us as we finished our homework, and in the mornings we awoke to the *tlac, tlac* of the rolling pin shaping perfectly round *tortillas de harina* (flour tortillas) on the kitchen counter, the smell wafting down the trailer corridor accompanied by that of *frijoles* (beans). These expressions of love provided physical, emotional, and mental nourishment that contributed to my academic success in the classroom. My mom also struggled to send us to school looking our best every day. Our clothes might have been secondhand but our attitudes were first class. We were clean, neatly dressed children. My sister and

I wore ponytails or *trenzas* (braids) in our hair adorned with ribbons. Even though I had classmates who refused to play with me because my clothing didn't match, our appearance characterized quiet, hardworking students and was well received by our principal and teachers.

However, community and family relations would present their own conflicts. I had to learn to critique and question these systems as well. I am still learning. At a friend's house, my mom sat quietly as a *tía política* (aunt by marriage) commented, "*Las mujeres que se van de la casa y no visten de blanco son unas perdidas*" (Women who leave their homes before marriage are fallen from grace). My mom knew the intent of her comment because my sister would soon leave home of her own accord to attend Stanford and not to get married as was culturally expected. Three days after I arrived at Stanford as a new student, I asked my sister and four of her Chicana friends to accompany me to the hair salon. Growing up, my dad did not allow us to cut our hair. His reasoning was that because we belonged to him, *con más ganas* so did our hair. He decided when it needed a trim and cut it himself. So on that sunny afternoon, we drove to a salon on a mission. I was assigned to the only Chicano hairdresser and shared with him that I wanted to have my waist-length hair cut. Later that day I took my *trenza*, placed it in an envelope, and mailed it to my father. No further explanation was needed. I stared in the mirror and reimagined a new self.

While at Stanford, my mom, sister, and I sat around the kitchen table in our apartment as the mom of one of our friends advised us on having children: "*Miren muchachas, si pa' los 36 no se han casado, que le hace; nomas encuentrensen un cabron que valga la pena y abran le las piernas*" (Look, girls, if by the time you're 36 you haven't married, it doesn't matter; just find a halfway decent jerk and open your legs to him). Growing up I never heard my mom use such expressions, unlike my father, for whom every other word was a curse word. We looked around the table at one another open mouthed as we processed her advice. Years later I was visiting a cousin when she made the following comment, "*Una mujer que no se casa y tiene hijos no es una mujer*" (A woman who doesn't marry and bear children is not a real woman). Being the only 30-something in the room who was unmarried and without children I pretended not to hear. Perhaps in their cultural world, one in which I didn't completely belong, it seemed unfathomable that I would want to be something other than a housewife and mother.

Resisting the patriarchal structure experienced at home also served to strengthen me. Although my father's character as a strong and committed worker gave me strength to endure hostilities outside of the home, I was also challenged by the role his male authority had over everyone and everything pertaining to the family. Day-to-day activities in the home (e.g., cooking, cleaning, washing) were the responsibilities of women. However, outside of the home my mother's duties were also numerous. Growing up, we raised farm animals and later consumed them and their offspring as a way to subsidize our income. I remember how my hands trembled as I helped my mother kill chickens and rabbits she later prepared as *caldos* (stews) or *moles*. Even when my father slaughtered the larger animals (e.g., pigs, goats, calves) it was my mother who prepped the tools and hot water beforehand and cured, stored, and prepared the meat afterward. One of the duties I most despised was cleaning the small intestines of the pigs, even when they later resulted in deliciously fried *tripitas* (small intestines). I was exposed to skill sets designed to benefit my survival in a poor rural context while I simultaneously learned to negotiate the means by which they were employed. As a result I was better able to navigate lived tensions outside of the home as well.

Through our daily routines we learned the strategies of organization, structure, doing for others, love, survival, and accountability. These tools became scripted in our bodies. I grew up in California during a time, much like the present, when immigration raids were common. For me and other children of immigration, the raids presented fears and frustrations that did not enter the classroom discourse. Growing up my mom refused to learn English. She forbid my siblings and I from speaking it at home, and now she surprises me with how much of it she really understands. I carry my family's sacrifices on my back, like a tortoise carries her shell, a constant reminder of what we have been through and what we have had to endure. But in my lifetime I have also struggled with the cultural traditions and values that weigh us down; like an unbreakable iron clasp these traditions at times squeeze my very spirit. Like a *Nahual* I am learning to transform. Sometimes I am the like the breeze that carries my *abuelita's* (grandma's) untold stories across the lands and whispers them in my ear. Other times I am caught off guard by the slap of patriarchy passed down from my father's family to him, an inheritance I refuse. Still I am the *fuego ardiente* (burning fire) of which Anzaldúa (1987/1999) wrote:

> The spirit of the fire spurs [me] to fight for [my] own skin and a piece of ground to stand on, a ground from which to view the world—a perspective, a homeground where [I] can plumb the rich ancestral roots into [my] own ample mestiza heart.
>
> (p. 45)

Sandra Rodriguez-Arroyo

Jorge Duany (2000) described Puerto Ricans/*Boricuas* as a *nación en vaivén* (a nation on the move), always in this constant back-and-forth move from Puerto Rico to the United States. My *testimonio* is based on five personal narratives to show this notion and how even with all these *vaivenes* (traveling back and forth from one country to another) I have always returned to my roots.

The Red Nightgown

The day before I was born my father decided to go to a baptism party. It was Christmas day, and he did not want to stay home. My mother was furious!

So my father devised a plan to solve his "problem." If my mother felt that it was time for her to give birth, she had to put on a red nightgown, go outside of our little yellow house, climb the little hill beside it, and stand on top of the hill. If he kept an eye on our house from the other hill where the party was taking place, he could see my mother's red nightgown *moviéndose con el viento* (moving with the wind), and he would return as soon as possible. Thank God I was not born that day! Ever since, when my mother told me this story, I always envisioned my mother with her red nightgown standing on top of the hill and my father running back home as fast as he could in a drunken state. I love that story! It is part of the beginning of my life back in Puerto Rico, and the little yellow house near the little hill was my first home.

Boston

When my parents decided to move to Boston looking for a better future, I was only 2 years old. We spent 5 years in a place that fascinated and terrified me at the same time. I was fascinated with my bilingual school and by Boston Commons, but I was terrified with the gang fights and gun shootings around the public housing project where we lived. To survive in the projects either you did not talk to your neighbors or you became the neighbor everybody was afraid to talk to. My sister and I had to learn how to remain quiet and not look around us when we walked around those dark brown buildings. Through those 5 years my father worked hard in all sorts of jobs (e.g., hotel housekeeping, salad man, handyman, school lunchroom assistant) to save money to buy a new house in Puerto Rico. My kindergarten teacher once mentioned that she never met my dad. The only time I actually remember that my dad went to my school was one night for a school presentation. I treasure in my memory the feeling of walking through the school halls with his hand holding mine and feeling so proud to finally show him off.

Llegamos a *Puerto Rico*

After 5 years of living in Boston, my parents decided that it was time to move back to Puerto Rico. The first thing that my mom did to prepare my sister and me for school on the island was to take us to get very short haircuts to avoid getting *piojos* (lice) at our new school; the strategy didn't quite work because we still got them. At our Puerto Rican school, we had to wear these dark green uniforms, and my classmates started calling me "Nuyorican." It took me years to understand the demeaning use of that word among Puerto Ricans from the island. But at that young age I associated the word with New York, so I would yell back to them, "I lived in Boston, not New York!" Our new house made all kind of noises when we walked in it, and hurricanes scared me to death. My dad started working in construction, and my mom got a job as a lunch lady in the school my sister and I attended. They left the house before 6 a.m., so my sister and I had to wake up, prepare breakfast, and get ready for school on our own. When we got to school every day we *had* to stop by the lunchroom and report to my mom with a simple *llegamos* (we are here) and with a sense of relief she would always respond *¡Qué bueno!* (I am glad!). My sister and I grew up knowing that they were working hard to provide us with opportunities, so unless we *really* needed something, they were not going to buy it for us. There were other priorities, like fixing the house to make it a safer place and paying the bills. They instilled in us the importance of studying and working hard to have a better future. This is the main reason I decided to pursue graduate school.

Puerto Ricans Are Not International Students

On my way to graduate school at Penn State on a very cold, cold January morning, I took a bus ride from Pittsburgh to State College. I was scared to death as I watched through the big windows all the accumulated snow and ice on both sides of the roads. For the first time in my life I prayed the rosary on my own four times. I finally arrived to Penn State after 7 hours of bus travel and somebody told me to report to the International Students' Office. I did as I was told and I got in line with international students waiting to be helped with their paperwork. When it was my turn to receive help the lady who was to help me couldn't find my paperwork. After an hour of visiting offices to find out the reason for this incident someone finally told me, "Oh, I am sorry to tell you that as a Puerto Rican you are not considered an international student. Therefore, our office cannot help you." I had no other option than to return to the cold weather, and with some difficulties I finally found out how to register and get my student identification card. At the end of that long day I was starving and tired, but I survived. Ever since that first day at Penn State I have seen my years in grad school as a time of survival, but I have also worked hard on finding ways to help new Puerto Rican graduate students when they arrive on campus. Puerto Ricans, the same as many other students coming from other countries and states, also need help to navigate our new surroundings.

Can I Come Back Home?

Now I feel the urge to finish my doctorate and I recognize that on my quest to help others survive graduate school, I forgot about myself. And like the prodigal son, I had a hard time accepting the fact that I needed help to finish my doctoral degree. Last spring I called my *mami* (mommy) and asked her if I could return home to Puerto Rico to write my dissertation, and she said, "*Sí*" (yes). As when I was a little girl, the moment I arrived at my parents' home, I said, "*Llegué*" (I am here). My *mami* said, "*¡Qué bueno!*" and gave me a big hug. I am now closer to my goal of finishing my dissertation, and I recognize that without my family I could have not come this far.

I recognize that my personal experiences are very similar to the ones lived by many Puerto Ricans. As *Boricuas* we are aware that our constant *vaivenes* from Puerto Rico to the United States could make us feel extremely confused, with the constant question of what makes Puerto Rico not an international country but a U.S. territory. However, we know something for sure—our Puerto Rican roots, our families, are what hold us together no matter where we are.

Acknowledgments

We gratefully thank our friend and mentor Dr. Sofia Villenas for her support of our work and our stories.

Note

1. In south Texas, *Anglo* is a term used to refer to White Euro-Americans.

References

Anzaldúa, G. (1999). *Borderlands/La frontera: The new mestiza*. San Francisco: Aunt Lute Books. (Original work published 1987)

Beverley, J. (1993). *Against literature*. Minneapolis: University of Minnesota Press.

Duany, J. (2000). Nation on the move: The construction of cultural identities in Puerto Rico and the diaspora. *American Ethnologist, 27*(1), 5–30.

Levinas, E. (1994). *Outside the subject/Emmanuel Levinas* (M. B. Smith, Trans.). Palo Alto, CA: Stanford University Press.

Moraga, C. and Anzaldúa, G. (1983). *This bridge called my back: Writings by radical women of color*. Boston: Kitchen Press.

Randall, M. (1984). *Testimonios: A guide to oral history*. Toronto, Ontario, Canada: Participatory Research Group.

11 The Value of Education and *Educación*

Nurturing Mexican American Children's Educational Aspirations to the Doctorate

Michelle M. Espino

After the Latina/o population became the largest minority group in the United States (U.S. Census Bureau, 2004), projections of garnering greater influence in society and within institutions, such as education, were widespread in the media (El Nasser, 2003; Schmidt, 2003a, 2003b). These projections are not yet realized in the area of educational attainment, particularly for Mexican Americans, the largest ethnic group within the Latina/o population.[1] As of 2010, 57.4% of Mexican Americans older than the age of 25 had graduated from high school compared to 62.9% of the entire Hispanic population (U.S. Census Bureau, 2012). In terms of attaining postsecondary education, only 10.6% of Mexican Americans older than the age of 25 have earned a bachelor's degree or higher compared to 13.9% of the total Hispanic population and 29.9% of the entire U.S. population.

The purported causes of these disparities can be traced over decades of educational research and practice. As early as 1916, for example, discriminatory educational policies across the country used linguistic differences and phenotype to segregate Mexican American children from White classrooms and placed Spanish-speaking children and children with Spanish surnames in segregated schools (Fernández & Guskin, 1981). Americanization programs coordinated at local schools dispossessed Mexican Americans of their culture and language by enforcing American values that Mexican Americans supposedly lacked, such as proper hygiene (Delgado Bernal, 2000; Fernández & Guskin, 1981). In addition, culturally determinist theoretical models were used to perpetuate negative cultural stereotypes and criticize values such as "present versus future time orientation, immediate instead of deferred gratification . . . cooperation rather than competition" (Solórzano & Solórzano, 1995, p. 297). Presently, Mexican American families are blamed or held accountable for low rates of educational attainment despite countless efforts to dispel these stereotypes (Ceja, 2004; Solórzano & Yosso, 2001; Valencia & Black, 2002). Decades of research have critiqued the ethnocentric nearsightedness of educational research pertaining to Mexican American communities, yet the deficit discourse continues to affect how educators and researchers perceive and work with Mexican American students and families at various educational levels (Ceballo, 2004). Little consideration is given to the moral development (i.e., *educación*) that families provide in the home that complements the formal education received at school (Valdes, 1996; Valenzuela, 1999). The master narrative that Mexican American communities[2] do not value education is pervasive in thought and practice despite substantial evidence to the contrary; this narrative has become a convenient excuse to deny support to these communities.

This article describes the interpretations and (re)tellings of parental/familial messages about education that affected the formation of educational aspirations of seven Mexican American PhDs. These participants were selected from a larger study focused on the life narratives of 33 Mexican American PhDs (Espino, 2008) because they identified as low income or working class in their childhoods, they were the first in their families to attend college, and their "parents' highest level of education [was] a high school diploma or less" (Ceja, 2006, p. 91). Because much of the parental involvement literature focuses on families from low-income backgrounds and those with lower levels of educational attainment, I focused on participants who reflected similar backgrounds in an effort to illuminate and reject deficit-centered findings in the literature about this population. The primary research questions were as follows: (a) In what ways did Mexican American PhDs interpret their parents' and families' messages about education and *educación*? and (b) To what extent did parents' and families' messages about education and *educación* shape the educational aspirations of these Mexican American PhDs? This study contributes to literature that substantiates parental messages about education and parental support that can lead to positive outcomes in educational attainment. In addition, this study adds complexity to the scholarship on educational attainment, considering the multiple facets that lead to the development of educational aspirations and the convergence of parental/familial support and structural educational opportunities. The (re)tellings of parental/ familial messages as shared from the perspectives of adult children contribute to the discourse regarding the extent to which children internalize and interpret parental/familial messages about education and how the messages shared through word and example can be forms of parental/familial involvement.

Literature Review

In an effort to contextualize the role of Mexican American parents and families in the formation of educational aspirations and the extent to which their messages about education and *educación* are internalized, I provide an overview of how educational research positions parental involvement and how parental/familial messages can be interpreted as a form of parental involvement.

Parental/Familial Involvement

The roles that researchers and practitioners claim that parents and families should have in students' education have fluctuated over time (Tierney & Auerbach, 2004). These claims fall along a spectrum that categorizes forms of involvement, or the purported lack thereof, across race and social class (Freeman, 2010). Quantifiable behavior such as rates of parental participation in schools, the frequency of discussing educational issues with children, and rates of contact with teachers pertaining to academic issues are often the only forms of parental involvement supported in the literature (Altschul, 2011; Perna & Titus, 2005).

The myopic view of parental involvement within research is also translated to practice. For example, teachers who have lower expectations for ethnic minority students or students from lower socioeconomic backgrounds transfer their expectations into classroom environments and students' classroom behavior. Such teachers are less likely to praise and reward students, "wait less time for a response to a question . . . [are] more likely to criticize a wrong answer, interpret [student] behavior in more negative ways, and teach less material . . . than teachers with high expectations" (Solórzano & Solórzano, 1995, p. 304). Administrators and teachers, even those with the best of intentions, can show a lack of care or personal concern for students of color, marginalizing them in the process. Through their interactions in classroom environments and school structures, students of color (sub)consciously recognize that they are Othered as individuals and members of communities whose cultures, language(s), religious beliefs, and traditions are marginalized in education and society (Valenzuela, 1999). School administrators expect particular actions taken on the part of parents and families, centering all school activities around school schedules and on school grounds rather than extending the school into the community and arranging events and activities around family time. For parents who actively engage in school activities or attend parent–teacher conferences, activation of accepted forms of capital can result in greater access to and support from teachers (Lareau & Horvat, 1999; Monkman, Ronald, & Theramene, 2005). Conversely, approaching teachers and school administrators with forms of capital that are not valued can lead to barriers between teachers and parents (Lareau & Horvat, 1999). Families from lower socioeconomic backgrounds or with children who are first-generation college students do not necessarily have access to these resources and are held accountable for not performing normative forms of parental involvement (López, 2001).

In such environments, Mexican Americans are forced to live among incongruent worlds, with the pressure of assimilating to the dominant culture while struggling to maintain connections with family through languages, cultures, and values. Mexican American and Latino families may not demonstrate parental involvement in normative ways, but there is ample evidence that these families place education and *educación* at the forefront of their values (Auerbach, 2006; Quiñones & Marquez Kiyama, 2014; Valdes, 1996; Valenzuela, 1999). The concept of *educación* refers to the ways in which Mexican American families incorporate the values of personal development and respect for others as part of what it means to be educated as well as layer lessons taught in the home with lessons taught in the classroom (Auerbach,

2002; Valenzuela, 1999; Yosso, 2006). According to Auerbach (2006), "The cultural schema of *educación* has a powerful impact on how Latino immigrant parents participate in their children's education," which often entails offering "moral support on the sidelines" rather than performing normative forms of parental involvement (p. 278). As a result, parents and families emphasize the moral development of their children in the home while encouraging good behavior at school.

Assessing the level of involvement for low-income Mexican American families is difficult, especially when the "not so visible ways" of parental action are neglected in the research (Auerbach, 2002, p. 1385). Parental involvement should be "reframed as a multidimensional concept inclusive of family-school engagement practices and educational expectations and aspirations, anchored in Latino-centered views of education" (Quiñones & Marquez Kiyama, 2014, p. 150). In this instance, the educational aspirations shared and (re)interpreted throughout a child's formative and young adult life should be analyzed more critically as an imaginative aspect of agency that is "shaped by parents' social location, cultural models, and family dynamics" (Auerbach, 2006, p. 276). Parents' educational aspirations—verbal, embodied, and performed—demonstrate the various ways in which parents and families "address, respond to, and struggle with dominant beliefs and ideologies" as well as provide venues for "creative meaning-making and improvisations—a different kind of power" found within marginalized communities (Villenas, 2006, p. 150). The "pain, joy, and contradictions" (Villenas, 2006, p. 149) expressed in these messages may ultimately affect access and retention in college and graduate school as Mexican American students negotiate the possible tensions between conflicting messages of what it means to be educated and *bién educados* (i.e., welleducated, well-mannered; Auerbach, 2006; Gándara, 1995).

Parental and Familial Aspirations

Parents' aspirations are based on their own educational experiences, insider knowledge about educational systems, as well as their perceptions of school climate and perceptions of their children's academic abilities (Ceja, 2004; Spera, Wentzel, & Matto, 2009). In addition, parents tend to have higher expectations of children finishing college, even if this is something that they were unable to accomplish themselves (Bank, Slavings, & Biddle, 1990). Latina/o parents are cited as having more influence over their children's educational aspirations than other ethnic groups (Clayton, 1993; Qian & Blair, 1999). Latina/o parents who express their interest in advancing their own education have children with higher educational aspirations and believe that such aspirations are achievable (Behnke, Piercy, & Diversi, 2004). However, barriers as cited in the research exist, such as lack of time to dedicate to furthering parents' education because of work obligations, lack of understanding of how children's aspirations could actually become reality, and limited

English language proficiency that constrains the type of assistance that parents can provide with homework (Behnke et al., 2004).

For Latina/o families, aspirations are often manifested in parental/familial *consejos* (advice) shared within the home that motivate children (Auerbach, 2002, 2006) and lead to advocacy for children in schools (Delgado-Gaitan, 1994). Stories play a powerful role in Latina/o families because they establish a sense of worth and build resistance against the challenges faced outside of the home (Gándara, 1995). These stories become embedded in how the child perceives himself or herself as well because they "reinforce the sense of mutual obligation among family members" (Auerbach, 2006, p. 278). At times, the stories are manifested in behavior and life experience, as noted by Ceja (2004), who found that the parents of Chicana college students did not have to talk directly about college to instill in their daughters the importance of higher education. Children can observe the challenges that parents experience as a result of not having an education (Auerbach, 2006; Ceja, 2004; López, 2001). These observations can uplift and motivate children, as well as serve as an added weight as children contend with the pressures of advancing their families and communities through education (Fisher & Padmawidjaja, 1999). Parental/familial agency and shared *consejos* cannot solely resolve the challenges that Mexican American communities face in advancing through various educational systems, but the stories gathered from this study offer greater depth to understanding the wealth of support that parents provide that is often overlooked in the educational literature.

Conceptual Framework

In order to address the deficit discourse about Mexican American students, families, and communities that is found in the parental involvement literature, I use Yosso's (2005, 2006) concept of community cultural wealth. Community cultural wealth challenges the specific focus on cultural capital, a concept that reminds scholars as well as students of color that communities of color lack the knowledge that is most valued in schools. This section focuses on the origins of the community cultural wealth framework and the extent to which this framework can uncover the imaginative aspects of agency found within the recollections of parental/familial *consejos* and narratives.

Critical Race Theory (CRT) as the Foundation of Community Cultural Wealth

CRT places race and racism at the center of political, social, and educational discourses. The larger umbrella of CRT focuses on counter-storytelling, which is "a method of telling a story that casts doubts on the validity of accepted . . . myths, especially ones held by the majority" and the permanence of racism (Delgado & Stefancic, 2001, p. 144). Four tenets guide CRT scholarship: (a) Racism is ordinary and not aberrational, (b) U.S. society is based on a "White-over-color ascendancy" that advances White supremacy and provides a scapegoat (i.e., communities of color) for working-class communities, (c) race and racism are social constructions, and (d) storytelling "urges Black and Brown writers to recount their experiences with racism . . . and to apply their own unique perspectives to assess . . . master narratives" (Delgado & Stefancic, 2001, pp. 7–9).

In the mid-1990s, researchers defined CRT in education as "a set of . . . perspectives, methods, and pedagogy that seeks to identify, analyze, and transform those structural, cultural, and interpersonal aspects of education that maintain the subordination of [students] of color" (Solórzano, 1998, p. 123). Education is viewed as an institution that "operate[s] in contradictory ways, with the potential to oppress and marginalize co-existing with the potential to emancipate and empower" (Solórzano & Yosso, 2001, p. 479). The critical race scholar in education can counter the deficit model by focusing on Mexican American students' and families' assets and lived experiences and, through careful analysis of the data, inspire action through the counterstories constructed.

Community Cultural Wealth

Asset-based models such as funds of knowledge (Moll & González, 2004; Vélez-Ibañez & Greenberg, 1992) and community cultural wealth (Yosso, 2005, 2006; Yosso & Solórzano, 2005) have not only challenged deficit-centered discourses but helped scholars to reconceptualize how Latinas/os navigate educational pathways. Yosso's community cultural wealth framework was first introduced in 2005 as an organization of literature based on decades of research on Latina/o educational experiences. She drew from a branch of CRT called *Latina/o critical race theory* that not only centered race and racism as an inherent part of the struggles faced by Latinas/os in U.S. society but also recognized that the intersections of language, immigrant status, accent, phenotype, and surname contributed to the subjugation of Latina/o communities (Solórzano & Yosso, 2001).

Because wealth is not merely an accumulation of income but an accumulation of "assets and resources, [such as] stocks, savings, owning a home or business" (p. 40), Yosso (2006) theorized that assets and resources found in communities of color had the potential to support students along their educational pathways. She aggregated studies about these assets and resources into categories of capital that would "account for how students of color may simultaneously promote the practice of both dominant and transformative forms of cultural and social capital to achieve academic success" (Maldonado, Rhoads, & Buenavista, 2005, p. 633).

The categories of capital within a community cultural wealth framework are aspirational, linguistic, navigational, social, familial, and resistant. *Aspirational capital* is parental transmission and maintenance of dreams and goals "beyond present circumstances" throughout the children's educational journeys despite "real or perceived barriers and, often, without the resources or other objective means to attain these goals" (Yosso & Solórzano, 2005, p. 130). Mexican American children who know multiple languages and communication methods can serve as language brokers for their families and build "connections between racialized cultural history and language" (p. 132). These real-world literacy skills engender *linguistic capital*, or the "intellectual and social tools attained through communication experiences in more than one language and/or style" (p. 132). By traversing through social institutions and dominant structures, Mexican American children gain *navigational capital*, which is a "set of social-psychological skills that assist[s] individuals and groups to maneuver through structures of inequality . . . [and] acknowledges individual agency within institutional constraints" (p. 131). Kinship networks and loose ties to other social networks and resources, or *social capital*, help children and families gather resources and information to navigate social structures and give back to social networks. *Familial capital* is nurtured through kinship networks and includes cultural identity(ies) as well as community history and well-being. "From these kinship ties, [Mexican American children] learn the importance of emotional, moral, educational, and occupational consciousness" (p. 130). Finally, *resistant capital* is developed through awareness of and agency against forms of oppression as well as "the willingness to challenge [and transform] inequalities" and prove others wrong (p. 155).

The accumulation of various forms of capital can provide the springboard for Mexican Americans to navigate through educational systems. From the standpoint of educational research, focusing on different forms of capital (in addition to cultural capital) can help affirm the values inherent within Mexican American communities and develop better strategies for accessing and completing postsecondary education.

Methodological Approach

This article is part of a larger study that analyzed the life narratives of 33 Mexican American PhDs along their journeys to the doctorate (Espino, 2008). I used narrative analysis, which "takes as its object of investigation the story itself" and analyzes how the story is ordered (Riessman, 1993, p. 1). Context is especially important because it involves the "historical moment of the telling; the race, class, and gender systems the [participants] manipulate to survive and within which their talk has to be interpreted" (Riessman, 1993, p. 21). This approach dispels dominant cultural assumptions and encourages reflexive relationships between the researcher and participants (Auerbach, 2002).

Participants

The participant sample extracted for this article consisted of two females and five males of Mexican descent who successfully completed their doctorates at five different U.S. universities between 2004 and 2006. Recruitment e-mails encouraged participants from any discipline and were distributed widely through social networks and organizational listservs, such as the National Latina/o Psychological Association and the Society for the Advancement of Chicanas/os and Native Americans in the Sciences. Interested participants completed a demographic form that included open-ended questions about racial/ethnic identity(ies), gender, academic discipline, current occupation, pseudonym, and contact information. I ascertained participants' social class backgrounds during the interviews as well as additional background information regarding their immigrant status and parental educational attainment. The participants incorporated into this article were the first in their families to attend college, had parents who did not enroll in college, and identified themselves as working class or poor. The participants were raised in Arizona, California, and Texas; two participants had been born in Mexico and then raised in the United States. I categorized participants' doctoral disciplines based on the National Research Council's (2006) taxonomy of doctoral fields: arts and humanities (two participants), education (three participants), and social and behavioral sciences (two participants). Five of the participants were faculty members, one was a university researcher/analyst, and one was a therapist. The participants spoke English and Spanish throughout the interviews and often alternated between the two languages. I made every effort to respect how the participants chose to identify themselves; therefore, their chosen racial/ethnic identities are included in their quotes.

I conducted all of the semistructured interviews via telephone with the exception of two participants whom I interviewed in person while attending two separate education conferences. The interview protocol focused on participants' family histories, their educational experiences, and the structures or mechanisms they used to successfully complete the doctorate. Each audio-recorded interview lasted at least 1.5 hours, and participants were interviewed at least twice to ensure that the interview protocol questions were answered. To mitigate concerns regarding data collection, I focused on being an empathetic interviewer (Fontana & Fey, 2005), developing rapport and trust with the participants by listening carefully to their stories and providing opportunities for reciprocal conversations that would help "create the space for [us] to reflect on the meaning-making process together" (Jones, Torres, & Arminio, 2006, p. 166). Centering personal truths and experiential knowledge in this study meant that I made space for the lived experiences of individuals from working-class backgrounds who identified as first-generation college students.

Data Analysis

I approached the data through a narrative analysis perspective, which meant that my role was to (re) present participants' stories and (re)interpretations, considering five levels of representation. Participants first think about their experiences (attending to experience) and then decide how they will share those experiences with others (telling about experience). The audience will largely determine how those experiences are explicated, as the telling of experiences demonstrates how participants want to be known to the audience. The experiences are recorded and then (re)presented in text, which is a "fixation of language . . . into written speech" (transcribing experience; Riessman, 1993, p. 11). The researcher-interpreter then critically evaluates the transcribed experiences and, based on his or her theoretical framework and positionality, formulates similarities and differences in experiences across the sample and then discusses "what the interview narratives signify; editing, and reshaping what was told" (p. 13). The final level in representation is reading experience, whereby participants or external readers encounter the written work and provide feedback on how the narratives are (re)presented.

The data from the larger study were analyzed as "verbal action . . . explaining, informing, defending, complaining, and confirming or challenging the status quo" (Chase, 2005, p. 657). I maintained a journal of my interpretations in an effort to (re)consider the themes that were emerging and the multiple interpretations that could explain the participants' life narratives. For the purposes of this article, I further analyzed how the seven participants interpreted the parental/ familial messages they recalled from memories and forms of capital that were acquired through those parental/familial messages, if any. The narratives shared and analyzed were (re)presentations of the realities experienced and remembered by the participants at particular moments in time.

Trustworthiness

A critical tool in narrative analysis is the use of member checks or external readers who can provide feedback on the (re)presentations and (re)interpretations of participants' realities (Jones et al., 2006). When asked to provide feedback on the transcription drafts, participants added new narratives and requested edits to their responses in order to protect themselves when referencing racist interactions with colleagues and faculty; one returned the actual transcriptions with corrections. I utilized the finalized transcripts when interpreting the data.

I felt an obligation to (re)present the participants' narratives in a responsible manner. Many of these participants are the only Mexican Americans or faculty of color in their departments and may be easily recognizable depending on their disciplines and social identities. In an effort to protect their anonymity, I do not include the names of any institutions attended, graduation dates, or ages and only describe doctoral discipline and general geographic location, if necessary, within the context of the narratives.

Positionality

Disclosing one's "understandings, beliefs, biases . . . and theories" is helpful in addressing how the researcher (re)presents the findings (van Manen, 1990, p. 47). My decision to analyze the life narratives of Mexican American PhDs was based on uncovering and addressing my own journey as a Mexican American/Chicana, middle-class, first-generation college student who is not proficient in Spanish and who was the first in my extended families to obtain a doctorate. Some of my most treasured memories of being with my family involve storytelling around the kitchen table. The stories shared helped me learn about the history of my family, the values we espouse, and the role that I play in paving the trail for future generations. I have observed how the same story that has been recited many times through the years shifts and changes, inflected with new lessons or given a different emphasis based on what I am supposed to learn that day. My parents and extended kin have wisdom that goes beyond formal schooling, and I believe that the cultural assets that they brought to that kitchen table and imparted on me have been and continue to be vital to my educational success and to my personal development. I am driven to write about parental/familial *consejos* in an effort to combat the master narrative that Mexican American parents and families do not value education and to honor the imaginative aspect of agency embedded within the stories shared while also attending to the contradictions found within the *consejos* that may reflect dominant paradigms. The concept of community cultural wealth challenges me to consider how asset-based models facilitate better understandings of the complex experiences of Mexican American communities that should not fit the deficit-centered discourse on Latina/o educational attainment.

Limitations

This study illuminates the experiences of a small group of Mexican American PhDs who successfully navigated through educational systems and cannot necessarily be generalized to the entire population of current Mexican American PhDs or to those who aspire to earn the doctorate. In addition, the memories shared cannot be verified, as these are interpretations made by adult children about events that occurred in childhood. However, the (re)interpretations of those memories are still salient because the extent to which the participants internalized these messages led to real outcomes as evidenced in the findings. Despite these limitations, I understood the power I had as an interviewer to guide the interviews and my role as a narrator, weaving together participants' recollections into a larger story about Mexican American educational attainment and taking the responsibility for (re)presenting these narratives with care and respect.

Findings

> We are the manifestations of all of our parents' hopes and dreams. It's always because of our parents. That's the way I see it. I belong to them and whatever I become was just because of them.
> (Christine, Mexican American/Chicana, social behavioral sciences)

The participants' recollections of parental/familial messages about education illustrate forms of capital as described in Yosso's (2005, 2006) community cultural wealth framework. With particular attention to the imaginative aspects of agency activated through word and example, the findings demonstrate the formation and maintenance of familial, aspirational, and resistance capital, which were at the forefront of the narratives shared. In an effort to dispel the assumption that Mexican American communities are monolithic on issues related to education, I also present the contradicting messages found within some of the participants' attempts to interpret parental/familial *consejos* about education (Auerbach, 2007). On the surface, the stories shared could be misconstrued by the reader as perpetuating the master narrative that Mexican American parents/families do not value education. It is important to move beyond a deficit-centered approach and recognize that these are adult children's interpretations of their parents' motivations and that systemic and structural barriers can affect parental/familial perspectives on social mobility through education and the subsequent *consejos* that are shared with younger generations (see Villenas, 2006).

Tearing Down the Drywall

Jesús Pierda's (Chicano, social behavioral sciences) father worked in construction and would often take him to work. Jesús recounted his father presenting a set of choices regarding education that inadvertently led to building resistant capital (Yosso, 2005, 2006):

> When I was in high school, he starts shooting acoustic and texture on the walls, but it's really hard work . . . and my dad would tell me, "You can do this, or you can go to school. What do you want?" When I was a kid. . . . I was not a very good student. In fact, I was a poor student. But, nevertheless, I knew that my way out of this life . . . was in education.

Watching his father work in construction motivated Jesús to succeed in school. His narrative extended to discussions about resistance, explaining moments when he witnessed his father fight against unfair practices at work:

> He would work for [White men], but they wouldn't pay him. He'd go and call them, go to their houses . . . and I saw that, you know? "*Lo dieron el nopal en la frente*" (They tried to take advantage of me), as he would say. So they wouldn't pay my dad . . . and we'd go knock the drywall down. I always thought that was a lot of fun and it was good to get back at the man, you know? I mean, of course, I didn't think about it in these terms at that time, but I knew it was because we were Mexican and because we were disregarded. And there was honor [in taking down the drywall].

Jesús discussed the ways in which his academic training gave him a new language that he could incorporate into reflections about his family's involvement in developing his educational aspirations. As a child, Jesús could not articulate the racism and mistreatment his father experienced, but he understood the forces that were situating his father in a lower social position because of his race/ethnicity and his limited English language proficiency:

> I remember when I'd go to work with my dad . . . at these people's homes and they'd speak to me in [English] because I spoke to my dad in Spanish and I remember the condescending attitude that people had and . . . to this day I was disturbed by that. So these little experiences really helped to shape an understanding of myself.

Working next to his father in construction, Jesús developed a strong work ethic as well as a sense of workmanship. Witnessing his father confront contractors who mistreated him and would not pay him for his labor led to the development of resistant capital (Yosso, 2005, 2006), and Jesús learned that he could fight against "the man" by refusing to let those in positions of power take his labor (i.e., knowledge production) for granted.

There Are No Borders for You

Monique's (Chicana, education) family had lived in the same town on the West Coast "since before desegregation." Stories passed down through generations detailed the extended family's experiences with racism and segregation. Older family members drew from that history to offer advice and talk about educational possibilities with younger generations:

> At family parties, my uncles would say, "You were born [in California] and your family's from Mexico. There are no borders for you here. You should be able to go wherever you want. You should be able to cross wherever you want". . . and so [my university] was cited as another place where there were no borders.

Monique's generation of cousins was raised with messages transmitted in the form of resistant capital (Yosso, 2005, 2006) that encouraged that generation to cross physical and metaphorical boundaries in their journeys to college. These messages were further solidified in seventh grade when Monique's father expressed his expectations: "[My dad] sat me down formally and said, 'I expect you to go to college and we expect you to help all your cousins go.'" As the oldest cousin, Monique took her role very seriously, recalling her family's stories of resistance when the pressures of attending a private research-intensive university were overwhelming. The power of familial capital (Yosso, 2005, 2006) was vital to her educational survival and coaxed her younger sibling and cousins to consider college.

Carlos and the Sewing Machine

Throughout his childhood, Carlos's (Mexican, education) family maintained a small factory that made clothes. He remembered his home filled with garments and *máquinas de cocer* (sewing machines). He and his siblings were responsible for trimming the thread from the garments, "so you walk in and it was like a maze of clothing and machines and everything and our responsibility, as kids . . . was sort of routine, every day, 'Come home, do your homework and then, start trimming some of these things.'" Carlos did not always enjoy being part of the family business:

> I remember sometimes walking in from school and I knew when there was going to be a lot of work that day when I saw that big bag of stuff, "Oh my goodness! That's mine! That's my bag right there!" And so, there was this expectation that we would help out with the family business either at the house or during the weekends . . .

From a deficit perspective, putting children to work in the family business could deter them from their studies. However, as Carlos mentioned, completing homework was always the first priority. In addition, he understood the invaluable role he played in contributing to the family:

> What I understood was that I was trying to sell stuff that my parents made, but, as you grow older, you start looking at some of these things and you realize, "You know, they really counted on that five bucks," . . . or maybe, on a Sunday I sold $25 worth of things, that probably bought the milk and bread and some of the necessities, right? I think me and my older brother . . . were at the age where . . . we could start appreciating some of that stuff because we saw how hard my parents were working.

Through their example, Carlos understood the value of working hard as well as the importance of education:

> It was clear . . . that education was always important, despite the circumstances, despite the fact that there was always a lot of work to be done, education came first, so at no point during my elementary or junior high or even at my high school years, were we told . . . or pushed towards becoming more involved in the family business . . . at the expense of our . . . schooling.

Because Carlos's parents had limited English language proficiency and limited educational attainment, they seldom reviewed his homework, but they fostered a sense of responsibility in Carlos to do his homework and study. He remembered receiving stern messages from his father when he did not want to complete his homework:

> [My dad] would say, "Look, if you don't wanna do your homework, if you don't wanna do good in school, that's fine. Let me know and I'll buy another *máquina de cocer*. . . . You could help your mom sew. . . . I can take you out of school now and you could start working." I think the effect he was after was for us to say, "Oh, hell no," because, [I thought,] "I hate trimming [threads], I don't wanna be sewing." And so, from a young age . . . school was important.

Carlos's recollection illustrates the way that *consejos* were connected to parental labor. As an integral part of the family business, Carlos knew that the only way to move out of manufacturing clothes was to obtain an education. In this sense, the shame of sewing clothes as a career kept Carlos focused on completing his homework and aspiring for a different life. His parents used their work as a tool to leverage their children's educational aspirations. From an early age, he gathered aspirational capital (Yosso, 2005, 2006) that led him to succeed in school and eventually enroll in higher education.

Participants' parents were often subjected to labor-intensive and, as a few noted, humiliating jobs that yielded little pay and limited respect from the White middle-class communities that hired them. As children, the participants understood the importance of education because their parents articulated the sacrifices that they made by ensuring their children attended school and placed homework above work. Although their parents often told the participants that education was important, it was rarely forced. Parents challenged their children to make their own decisions about obtaining an education, which supports earlier research on Latina/o parental facilitation of autonomy (Ceballo, 2004). Participants were given a choice: Do this labor-intensive work or get an education. Obtaining an education was perceived as a way to move out of the current class stratum. Although their parents did not necessarily know how to navigate through educational processes, they believed that education was the key to success and to "indoor work." The children learned that hard work was important, but if hard work did not lead to something substantial, they would never advance. Working smarter instead of harder and fighting for fair payment for their labor were aspects of these participants' belief systems.

Also present in these narratives were tensions among different family members regarding what advanced education would mean. The following narratives are intended to illustrate the challenges that some participants had in interpreting memories of parents and family members who, faced with social realities, projected low or conflicting educational expectations on their children that affected their educational aspirations.

A Loss of Respect

Dr. O (Mexican American, social behavioral sciences) was raised by a father who had completed high school and a mother who had earned a general equivalency diploma when Dr. O was a child. Throughout his interview, Dr. O talked about the role of his mother and the aspirational capital (Yosso, 2005, 2006) that she instilled in him through her example and her resistance against family members who worried about the consequences of formal education:

> [My uncle asked], "Why is Dr. O even going to school?" So my mom said, "He's going because he wants to better himself." And my *tio's* [uncle's] response . . . was, "Why do you want him smarter than you? Once he thinks that he's smarter than you, he's going to treat you differently. In fact, he's going to have less respect for you." And my mom says, "I beg to differ. He's going to respect us more . . ."

Because of his mother's support and resistance, Dr. O persevered in college and inspired his cousins to pursue higher education. His interactions with extended kin illustrate the role of familial capital (Yosso, 2005, 2006) in forming and maintaining educational aspirations across a generation, as illustrated in Dr. O's conversation with his cousin:

> I had *primos* [cousins] that were roughly my age . . . who thought that Dr. O walked on water. As a matter of fact, one of my *primos* . . . went for his master's because he said I inspired him to go on. That was just amazing to hear. And after he heard that I was pursuing a PhD program, he's even talking about that now. He says, "Dr. O, when I saw that you did it and we grew up together. . . . I thought, 'Man . . . if Dr. O can do it, I can do it.'"

Juxtaposed against the conversation between Dr. O's uncle and mother at the beginning of the vignette, this quote demonstrates the philosophical transitions that occurred in Dr. O's family. Although older generations feared how educational attainment could influence their children (i.e., lack of respect, limited enactment of *educación*), by paving the way for his cousins, Dr. O demonstrated that educational attainment was possible and could keep him connected to his family. His narrative illustrates the complexity within individuals and family structures to simultaneously support and constrain educational aspirations.

You're on Your Own

Cuahtemoc (Chicano, education) was born in Mexico and moved with his parents and siblings to California. As the sole financial supporter, his father worked constantly, and his mother was responsible for the children's upbringing and education. Cuahtemoc concluded that their decision to change the manner in which they raised their children was a reflection of pressures from working multiple jobs and managing the children's daily activities:

> At some point [my parents] realized the whole concept of biculturalism and that they were in a new environment . . . and you have . . . a lot less control over your kids, especially if you have six of them . . . so . . . I grew up in the *barrio* where there was absolutely no parental supervision . . . telling you when to eat dinner, when to come home, when to go to sleep, none of that . . . So [I] learned, "Holy shit . . . I need to study 'cause no one's gonna tell me to study. If I don't do it, I fail . . . Nobody cares what I do." Well, it's not that my parents didn't care, but, in a way, they didn't really care . . .

Cuahtemoc believed that transitioning to a new country and a new culture, along with the strains of trying to support the family, led his parents to set aside their cultural traditions and espouse what they perceived as American cultural values, which were individualist in nature. He perceived that his parents' newly adopted sense of individualism led to a laissez-faire approach to his upbringing and, as he concluded, a lack of investment in his educational pursuits:

> [In] American culture, individualism is very valued, and [in] my parents' culture, from México, community is valued and so when you're a bicultural individual, you're living in both of these worlds. How [do] you manage that? Well, you look at that concept of individualism, that's what [my family] really focused on. They focused on themselves, advancing themselves economically . . .

Cuahtemoc believed that he was on his own to construct his educational success and keep track of his homework and school responsibilities without parental assistance. Despite his efforts to downplay the critique of his parents, Cuahtemoc blamed biculturalism for leading to his parents' limited, normative forms of involvement in his education. Although he did not connect his mother's constant presence at the schools, "help[ing] the teachers with whatever they needed," with five of the six siblings attending college, Cuahtemoc believed that articulating one's survival within U.S. society meant losing the family's culture, traditions, and sense of connection. His sense of loss was made even more evident when he recalled a time when he shared his goal of attending college:

> I was like, "I think I wanna go to college," and [my parents said], "Oh, well, good luck, Do whatever you gotta do." I once asked for financial support [for college] and [they said], "Well, we said, 'Good luck,' so you have to do it on your own," and I did. I had to get a job. I had to pay for everything. Complete individualism from the ground up and that's

been the way in our family, right? And there's some criticism in that, you know. . . . Where's family? Where's community? Where's what we had when we came from *México?*

Cuahtemoc's parents may not have been able to help him navigate college admissions processes or provide funding for college, but they encouraged him to seek educational opportunities and maneuver through the financial aid process on his own. From Cuahtemoc's perspective, the freedom they gave him to make his own decisions was stripping him and his family of a Latina/o collective identity and made Cuahtemoc feel isolated and unsupported in his educational journey.

Nieves, You're Gonna Sink Us

Nieves (Chicano, arts and humanities) was 9 years old when his parents divorced. He and his two brothers lived with his mother, and the family qualified for food stamps until Nieves's youngest brother was 18 years old. Nieves shared stories of growing up as a middle child and described the ways in which he was ignored by his brothers and felt unappreciated by his mother. When asked about his parents' involvement in education, Nieves struggled to describe whether he believed that they supported him:

> In terms of everyday stuff, [my parents] never really . . . told us to do our homework . . . 'cause they really didn't know the answers. . . . I feel bad for saying this, but it just wasn't that high of priority, you know . . . as long as you went and came back, every day. . . . They just put all the trust in the school.

Nieves and his brothers attended private Catholic schools until high school, when they could each decide to continue in private school. When Nieves was in eighth grade he received a scholarship for a private Catholic high school along with a group of

> . . . strong students. It was kind of an unprecedented thing; they didn't do it every year. [The school] knew that . . . all of us were gonna go off to public school. . . . We didn't have the money or whatever. We're all working class kids . . .

In return for receiving the scholarships, which included "my books and everything," Nieves and his friends spent the summer before high school working at the local church. As the summer ended, Nieves recounted the pressure he faced from his family to withdraw from the private high school and the ways that he perceived his mother distancing herself from his educational pursuits:

> My mom was always like, "Catholic school, they may pay for your tuition, but they're still gonna nickel and dime us for money. We need

to sell these tickets, you need to buy this, and everything," and she hated that. She was not a [parent—teacher association] mom; she never wanted to go to the school at all. . . . If they said there was a parent—teacher conference, she would just tell us not to bring the letter home . . .

After 1 week in Catholic school, Nieves dropped out:

> I had a full scholarship and everything . . . but . . . they were like, "Eh, it's a pain to get you out there." I think, one time, I walked . . . it was like 5 miles and I couldn't get a ride. No one really helped me.

Nieves felt guilty about the financial constraints that private schooling required and attempted to dismiss this pressure by rationalizing his mother's actions:

> My mom made it seem like . . . I was gonna sink her financially going to the school. So, maybe it would have. I don't think she was just trying to take something away from me . . . they weren't trying to punish me . . . everyone was just trying to make it . . .

Nieves often credited himself for his academic accomplishments in high school and his college aspirations, noting that he seldom felt any support from his family. He remarked that his mother was "more concerned that [he] mowed the lawn" than concerned with his educational pursuits. It is possible that Nieves's mother was concerned about the hidden costs of the scholarship, especially considering that the family qualified for welfare and food stamps. In addition, as a single parent of three boys, Nieves's mother may have been concerned with juggling the additional demands of a private school education while contending with limited resources. As his mother stated, a scholarship did not preclude the school from requesting additional funds through fundraising and school involvement. Instead of disappointing her son later in the year as more financial demands were requested from the school, perhaps Nieves's mother thought that she would stem potential embarrassment by dissuading him from attending the private high school.

We're Service People, Araceli

Although a college degree can be viewed as an avenue to social mobility, Araceli's (Mexican American, arts and humanities) story illustrates that the pull of maintaining class status through social reproduction can override the dream of higher education. Growing up in a Texas town with few Mexican families, Araceli relied on her family for support. While her father cleaned tables at a local restaurant, Araceli's mother, who spent most of her childhood working in agricultural fields, found work for the children cleaning cotton fields on a local farm. Araceli and her siblings worked in the fields for "4 years up until high school." When Araceli was a sophomore, her father was promoted through the ranks to restaurant manager in a nearby city and gave her a job as a waitress. Working in a larger city gave her an opportunity to escape the racism she experienced in high school. She witnessed teachers favoring the White ranchers' children, who were encouraged to apply for scholarships and meet with college admissions counselors while the Mexican children were ignored. In her senior year, Araceli earned a scholarship based on a beauty contest and began discussing the possibility of attending college:

> I think [my parents] were hesitant about [college]. Even though I had, by my senior year, gathered $12,000 to go somewhere. . . . I remember my dad saying, "What are you gonna do with a college degree? What are you gonna study?" because they were working-class people. It's like, "Well, what are you gonna do, practically?" because . . . my dad had a fifth-grade education; my mom had a sixth-grade education . . .

Moving outside the confines of service work was beyond her parents' hopes and seemed impractical. Obtaining an education was only a means for "employment in the service industry." Anything beyond that was deemed only appropriate for the affluent: "I think [my dad] highlighted the fact that, 'We're the working class of America and education is for the *ricos* [rich people] and . . . we're not rich.'" Araceli's narrative illustrates the difficult negotiations that some Mexican American children face within family units as they apply for college. Similar to other participants who shared stories about labor-intensive work, Araceli felt a sense of shame and guilt for admitting that she did not want to remain a restaurant worker:

> When I laid it out for them, I said, "Well, I graduated from high school. What am I gonna do?" And I didn't want to degrade what my dad was doing. I didn't want to say, "What? Work at the cafeteria the rest of my life?" I just told them, "Am I gonna be a waitress for the rest of my life? I wanna go to college and get an education."

According to Araceli, her parents, particularly her father, indicated that college was not the place for working-class people and that earning a college degree was a futile exercise if it did not provide skills that helped her serve others. The pull of social reproduction is evident in her depiction of her father's hesitancy and skepticism of social mobility through education. It is possible that her parents not only worried about funding higher education but feared that Araceli would lose her connection to her family and the values inherent in *educación*. Despite her parents' ambivalence, Araceli was able to leverage her educational goals by obtaining a scholarship, enrolling at a nearby junior college, and subsequently transferring to a 4-year institution a few hours away from home.

Three of the participants in the sample portrayed their parents as less engaged in their children's education based on normative forms of parental involvement, and one participant shared the fears that extended family members had about the consequences of higher education. The portrayals of their parents' and relatives' ambivalence toward higher education often reflected "misinformed upward mobility and generational thinking [that] perpetuate[d] low expectations" as well as social and structural barriers that limited children's educational aspirations (Quiñones & Marquez Kiyama, 2014, p. 163). For some families, providing alternatives to higher education might have been better than the physical, emotional, and perhaps intellectual distances (i.e., the loss of *educación*) that they feared could result from a college or graduate degree. It is also possible that previous experiences with schools, a lack of trust in teachers and administrators, and institutional racism could also have affected parents' trust in higher education (Quiñones & Marquez Kiyama, 2014). The power of educational systems to press on children a negative, deficit perspective about their own communities is also evident in the ways in which participants depicted their parents, who had never attended college yet were faulted for not providing tangible tools for navigating educational structures (i.e., normative forms of parental involvement). Each of the participants was given the freedom to make decisions about his or her education, which is consistent with literature on the extent to which parents see themselves as motivators rather than facilitators of college knowledge (Auerbach, 2006). Participants' portrayals, in many respects, failed to consider the potential struggles to maintain households with limited incomes and the potential community cultural wealth inherent in Mexican American families and communities. Their depictions illustrate, yet again, the tensions expressed by participants between being grateful for (in)tangible resources and support they received from their families and, as formally educated PhDs, knowing that these resources and familial support structures are not necessarily valued in educational contexts. The participants' stories suggest a multifaceted set of parental/familial perspectives on the value of education and *educación* within their families. Based on the literature and participants' recollections, it seems that some families embraced formal education and encouraged their children's educational aspirations in ways that challenged normative forms of parental involvement.

Discussion

In an effort to interrogate the deficit discourse and contribute to asset-based educational research, this article focused on the interpretations and (re)tellings of parental/familial messages about education that affected the formation of the educational aspirations of seven Mexican American PhDs. This study is a critique of dominant culture normativity and ethnocentric nearsightedness that envelops the discourse on parental involvement and the extent to which educational researchers exclude (under the guise of cultural norms) other viable pathways to and processes involving educational attainment. To this end, I used the framework of community cultural wealth (Yosso, 2005, 2006) to uncover various forms of capital embedded in word and example that are often overlooked in the mainstream literature as well as the tensions expressed by participants as they navigated between education and *educación* while resisting hegemonic forces that support school rather than community expectations of parental involvement. Along their journeys, most of the participants gathered and activated familial, aspirational, and resistant capital (Yosso, 2005, 2006), even when the dominant culture found little value in their stories, culture, language, and traditions. This study was a (re)presentation of Mexican American PhDs' memories and perceptions of invisible forms of parental involvement that were essential to cultivating and, at times, lessening the participants' educational aspirations along their journeys to the doctorate.

The participants' educational accomplishments, despite institutional and societal barriers, serve as inspiration for the next generation, but at what cost? All of the participants' recollections involved great concern for the outcomes of formal education. The majority of the participants acknowledged how formal education could create physical, intellectual, and emotional distances between them and their families. Unfortunately, their school environments did little to bring together the values of home and school. Because educational systems are composed of sorting mechanisms along the lines of knowledge and labor production (Bowles & Gintis, 1976), few mechanisms are available to help students become interdependent and socialized to value traditions, customs, and languages found in the home, community, *and* school. In addition, because these participants had to successfully navigate through multiple hostile schooling environments (secondary, college, and graduate school), it is not surprising how they articulated their survival in academe, perhaps resisting traditional forms of *educación* (e.g., respecting authority) in order to be the first in their families to graduate from college.

In three instances, families with differing perspectives and experiences appeared to question the benefits of continuing education. Participants who received conflicting messages about education had difficulty expressing their understanding and interpretations of what their families were able to do for them as well as, from their perspectives and rooted in normative forms of parental involvement, were not able to do to nurture a culture of possibility. Developing a more nuanced understanding of why some families did not seem to activate forms of cultural wealth (Yosso, 2005, 2006) within the family and community structure as a form of resistance against normative forms of parental involvement is beyond the scope of this study; however, possible explanations may be rooted in familial experiences with formal education, racism, the demands of managing the household, and limited contact with others who have accessed higher education.

This study focused on the ways in which the accumulation of various forms of capital and retention of cultural integrity can provide the springboard for Mexican Americans to successfully navigate through educational systems, regardless of whether parents/families use normative forms of parental involvement. As a result, what is perceived externally as valuing education may be consistent with the stories of what higher education means for Mexican American families. Because these imaginative aspects of agency are not validated by the dominant culture, Mexican American families are misconstrued as not valuing education, and students are forced to experience tensions between what it means to be educated and what it means to be *bién educados* (i.e., well-educated, well-mannered; Auerbach, 2006). Stories are an important imaginative form of agency that not only build self-efficacy but remind the children about their role within the family and the costs that could be incurred if the children left their families for individual educational pursuits. Stories tell people about themselves and what is possible and appropriate within familial and cultural contexts. Further research should explore the extent to which Mexican American children make meaning of these tensions, especially while they are in the process of forging through various educational systems.

Future research should also focus on the perspectives of Mexican American parents and extended kin to gain greater understanding of the rationale behind decisions that are made with regard to their children's educational aspirations and pathways to college and graduate school. In addition, the majority of the participants had siblings and cousins who also attended college. Further research should analyze the influence of parental, sibling, and extended kin involvement on the entire family's educational aspirations, which may contribute to perspectives divergent from the current college choice literature (see Ceja, 2006, for a discussion of the role of Chicana/o siblings in college choice processes).

Outreach to families is essential, particularly in communities with under-resourced schools. As illustrated in the narratives presented here, participants' feelings of shame in childhood were often associated with parents' occupations and perceived lack of involvement at school functions and interaction with teachers and administrators. Empowering children through classroom discussions about the skills and knowledge gained from parents, siblings, and extended kin; the various forms of capital (aspirational, linguistic, navigational, social, familial, and resistant; Yosso, 2005, 2006) that they have accumulated in their home environments; and the historical significance of their families and culture(s) can provide the foundation for higher levels of self-efficacy, cultural integrity, and educational aspirations. Projects that involve partnerships between communities and schools; research opportunities among various stakeholders, including local colleges; and environments that inspire an ethic of care that integrates practices in the home with practices in the schools can help children articulate their familial and community assets and integrate them into their classroom learning.

Along their journeys to the doctorate, Mexican Americans gather knowledge, skills, and abilities from families and communities and activate their community cultural wealth, even when the dominant culture and educational researchers find little value in Mexican American culture, language, and traditions. Mexican Americans find strength in the margins. Their ability to access and complete college and graduate school, in spite of the tensions between education and *educación*, is a reflection of parental and familial aspirations—forms of capital that will help to inspire the next generation.

Acknowledgments

I wish to thank Judy Marquez Kiyama and Rebeca Burciaga for helpful feedback in the preparation of this article.

Funding

This article is based on data used in my doctoral dissertation at the University of Arizona, which was supported in part by a dissertation fellowship from the Ford Foundation.

Notes

1. The term *Mexican American* is defined as individuals of Mexican descent living in the United States. When drawing from participants' narratives, I use personal racial/ethnic identifiers ascribed by the participants as well as terms used by studies cited to describe Mexican American communities (e.g., *Hispanic, Chicana/o,* or *Latina/o*).
2. *Mexican American communities* is a phrase used to critique deficit models that present a static, uniform, and uncomplicated community of color as well as recognize the diversity in social class, sexual orientation, phenotype, geographic location, educational attainment, and language acquisition, among other areas, within this population.

References

Altschul, I. (2011). Parental involvement and the academic achievement of Mexican American youths: What kinds of involvement in youths' education matter most? *Social Work Research, 35*(3), 159–170. doi:10.1093/swr/35.3.159

Auerbach, S. (2002). Why do they give the good classes to some and not to others? Latino parent narratives of struggle in a college access program. *Teachers College Record, 104*(7), 1369–1392. doi:10.1111/tcre.2002.104.issue-7

Auerbach, S. (2006). "If the student is good, let him fly": Moral support for college among Latino immigrant parents. *Journal of Latinos and Education, 5*(4), 275–292. doi:10.1207/s1532771xjle0504_4

Auerbach, S. (2007). From moral supporters to struggling advocates: Reconceptualizing parent roles in education through the experience of working-class families of color. *Urban Education, 42*(3), 250–283. doi:10.1177/0042085907300433

Bank, B. J., Slavings, R. L., & Biddle, B. J. (1990). Effects of peer, faculty, and parental influences on students' persistence. *Sociology of Education, 63*(3), 208–225. doi:10.2307/2112838

Behnke, A. O., Piercy, K. W., & Diversi, M. (2004). Educational and occupational aspirations of Latino youth and their parents. *Hispanic Journal of Behavioral Sciences, 26*(1), 16–35. doi:10.1177/0739986303262329

Bowles, S., & Gintis, H. (1976). *Schooling in capitalist America: Educational reform and the contradictions of economic life*. New York, NY: Basic Books.

Ceballo, R. (2004). From barrios to Yale: The role of parenting strategies in Latino families. *Hispanic Journal of Behavioral Sciences, 26*(2), 171–186. doi:10.1177/0739986304264572

Ceja, M. (2004). Chicana college aspirations and the role of parents: Developing educational resiliency. *Journal of Hispanic Higher Education, 3*(4), 338–362. doi:10.1177/1538192704268428

Ceja, M. (2006). Understanding the role of parents and siblings as information sources in the college choice process of Chicana students. *Journal of College Student Development, 47*(1), 87–104. doi:10.1353/csd.2006.0003

Chase, S. E. (2005). Narrative inquiry: Multiple lenses, approaches, voices. In N. K. Denzin & Y. S. Lincoln (Eds.), The Sage handbook of qualitative research (3rd ed., pp. 651–679). Thousand Oaks, CA: Sage.

Clayton, K. K. (1993, December). *Family influence over the occupational and educational choices of Mexican American students*. Paper presented at the annual meeting of the American Vocational Association, Nashville, Tennessee. Delgado, R., & Stefancic, J. (2001). *Critical race theory: An introduction*. New York, NY: New York University Press.

Delgado Bernal, D. (2000). Historical struggles for educational equity: Setting the context for Chicana/o schools today. In C. Tejeda, C. Martinez, & Z. Leonardo (Eds.), *Charting new terrains of Chicana(o)/Latina(o) education* (pp. 67–90). Cresskill, NJ: Hampton Press.

Delgado-Gaitan, C. (1994). "Consejos": The power of cultural narratives. *Anthropology & Education Quarterly, 25*(3), 298–316. doi:10.1525/aeq.1994.25.3.04x0146p

El Nasser, H. (2003, June 19). *39 million make Hispanics largest U.S. minority group*. Retrieved from www.usatoday.com/news/nation/census/2003-06-18-Census_x.htm

Espino, M. M. (2008). *Master narratives and counter-narratives: An analysis of Mexican American life stories of oppression and resistance along the journeys to the doctorate* (Unpublished doctoral dissertation). The University of Arizona, Tucson, AZ.

Fernández, R. R., & Guskin, J. T. (1981). Hispanic students and school desegregation. In W. D. Hawley (Ed.), *Effective school desegregation: Equity, quality, and feasibility* (pp. 107–140). Beverly Hills, CA: Sage.

Fisher, T. A., & Padmawidjaja, I. (1999). Parental influences on career development perceived by African American and Mexican American college students. *Journal of Multicultural Counseling & Development, 27*(3), 136–152. doi:10.1002/jmcd.1999.27.issue-3

Fontana, A., & Fey, J. (2005). The interview: From neutral stance to political involvement. In N. Denzin & Y. S. Lincoln (Eds.), *The Sage handbook of qualitative research* (3rd ed., pp. 695–727). Thousand Oaks, CA: Sage.

Freeman, M. (2010). "Knowledge is acting": Working-class parents' intentional acts of positioning within the discursive practice of involvement. *International Journal of Qualitative Studies in Education, 23*(2), 181–198. doi:10.1080/09518390903081629

Gándara, P. C. (1995). *Over the ivy walls: The educational mobility of low-income Chicanos*. Albany, NY: State University of New York Press.

Jones, S. R., Torres, V., & Arminio, J. (2006). *Negotiating the complexities of qualitative research in higher education: Fundamental elements and issues*. New York, NY: Routledge.

Lareau, A., & Horvat, E. M. (1999). Moments of social inclusion and exclusion: Race, class, and cultural capital in family-school relationships. *Sociology of Education, 72*, 37–53. doi:10.2307/2673185

López, G. R. (2001). The value of hard work: Lessons on parent involvement from an (im)migrant household. *Harvard Educational Review, 71*(3), 416–437. doi:10.17763/haer.71.3.43x7k542x023767u

Maldonado, D. E. Z., Rhoads, R., & Buenavista, T. L. (2005). The student-initiated retention program: Theoretical contributions and the role of self-empowerment. *American Educational Research Association Journal, 42*(4), 605–638. doi:10.3102/00028312042004605

Moll, L. C., & González, N. (2004). Engaging life: A funds of knowledge approach to multicultural education. In J. Banks & C. McGee Banks (Eds.), *Handbook of research on multicultural education* (2nd ed., pp. 699–715). New York, NY: Jossey-Bass.

Monkman, K., Ronald, M., & Theramene, F. D. (2005). Social and cultural capital in an urban Latino school community. *Urban Education, 40*(1), 4–33. doi:10.1177/0042085904270416

National Research Council. (2006). *Taxonomy of fields.* Retrieved from http://www7.nationalacademies.org/resdoc/Taxonomy_list.html

Perna, L. W., & Titus, M. A. (2005). The relationship between parental involvement as social capital and college enrollment: An examination of racial/ethnic group differences. *Journal of Higher Education, 76*(5), 485–518. doi:10.1353/jhe.2005.0036

Qian, Z., & Blair, S. L. (1999). Racial/ethnic differences in educational aspirations of high school seniors. *Sociological Perspectives, 42*, 605–625. doi:10.2307/1389576

Quiñones, S., & Marquez Kiyama, J. (2014). Contra la corriente (Against the current): The role of Latino fathers in family-school engagement. *School Community Journal, 24*(1), 149–176.

Riessman, C. K. (1993). *Narrative analysis.* Thousand Oaks, CA: Sage.

Schmidt, P. (2003a, 28 November). Academe's Hispanic future. *The Chronicle of Higher Education, 50*(14), A6–A12.

Schmidt, P. (2003b, 28 November). Educating the largest minority group. *The Chronicle of Higher Education, 50*(14), B6–B9.

Solórzano, D. G. (1998). Critical race theory, race and gender microaggressions, and the experiences of Chicana and Chicano scholars. *Qualitative Studies in Education, 11*(1), 121–136. doi:10.1080/095183998236926

Solórzano, D. G., & Solórzano, R. W. (1995). The Chicano educational experience: A framework for effective schools in Chicano communities. *Educational Policy, 9*(3), 293–314. doi:10.1177/0895904895009003005

Solórzano, D. G., & Yosso, T. J. (2001). Critical race and LatCrit theory and method: Counter-storytelling. *Qualitative Studies in Education, 14*(4), 471–495. doi:10.1080/09518390110063365

Spera, C., Wentzel, K. R., & Matto, H. C. (2009). Parental aspirations for their children's educational attainment: Relations to ethnicity, parental education, children's academic performance, and parental perceptions of school climate. *Journal of Youth and Adolescence, 38*(8), 1140–1152. doi:10.1007/s10964-008-9314-7

Tierney, W. G., & Auerbach, S. (2004). Toward developing an untapped resource: The role of families in college preparation. In W. J. Tierney, Z. B. Corwin, & J. E. Colyar (Eds.), *Preparing for college: Nine elements of effective outreach* (pp. 29–48). Albany, NY: State University of New York Press.

U.S. Census Bureau. (2004). *Race and Hispanic origin.* Retrieved from http://www.census.gov/pubinfo/www/multi media/LULAC.html

U.S. Census Bureau. (2012). *Educational attainment by race and Hispanic origin: 1970–2010.* Retrieved from http://www.census.gov/compendia/statab/2012/tables/12s0229.pdf

Valdes, G. (1996). *Con respeto: Bridging the distances between culturally diverse families and schools.* New York, NY: Teachers College Press.

Valencia, R. R., & Black, M. S. (2002). "Mexican Americans don't value education!" On the basis of the myth, mythmaking, and debunking. *Journal of Latinos and Education, 1*(2), 81–103. doi:10.1207/S1532771XJLE0102_2

Valenzuela, A. (1999). *Subtractive schooling: U.S.-Mexican youth and the politics of caring.* Albany, NY: State University of New York Press.

van Manen, M. (1990). *Researching lived experience: Human science for an action sensitive pedagogy.* Albany, NY: State University of New York.

Vélez-Ibañez, C. G., & Greenberg, J. (1992). Formation and transformation of funds of knowledge among U.S. Mexican households. *Anthropology & Education Quarterly, 23*(4), 313–335. doi:10.1525/aeq.1992.23.4.05x1582v

Villenas, S. (2006). Pedagogical moments in the borderland: Latina mothers teaching and learning. In D. Delgado Bernal, C. A. Elenes, F. E. Godínez, & S. Villenas (Eds.), *Chicana/Latina education in everyday life: Feminista perspectives on pedagogy and epistemology* (pp. 147–159). Albany, NY: State University of New York Press.

Yosso, T. J. (2005). Whose culture has capital? A CRT discussion of community cultural wealth. *Race Ethnicity and Education, 8*(1), 69–91. doi:10.1080/1361332052000341006

Yosso, T. J. (2006). *Critical race counterstories along the Chicana/Chicano educational pipeline.* New York, NY: Routledge.

Yosso, T. J., & Solórzano, D. G. (2005). Conceptualizing a critical race theory in sociology. In M. Romero & E. Margolis (Eds.), *The Blackwell companion to social inequalities* (pp. 117–146). Malden, MA: Blackwell.

12 Mapping and Recontextualizing the Evolution of the Term *Latinx*

An Environmental Scanning in Higher Education

Cristobal Salinas Jr. and Adele Lozano

Populations in the United States that identify as having Latin American ancestry have used various labels to self-identify, including Latino, Hispanic, Mexican American, Chicano, Puerto Rican, Cuban American, etc. In 2014, a new term—*Latinx*—began appearing on Internet and social media sites, causing confusion for those who did not know what it meant or how to pronounce it. Since then, the online presence of this term has continued to grow. According to Google Trends (2016), an analytics tool that tracks how often a particular search term is entered on the Google search engine, the number of times *Latinx* was used as a search term spiked in the U.S. in 2016. What is this nascent term and how is it being perceived and used in higher education? What significance does it hold for researchers who study this population? Is it simply a passing fad? These questions offer a starting point to examine the significance of an emerging label—one that focuses on the fastest-growing ethnic group in the United States. (U.S. Census, 2015).

Empirical studies focusing on the creation and evolution of the term *Latinx* are nonexistent, although a search of the literature reveals that some scholars in the field of education have begun using the term in their research. For instance, using two database tools, ERIC and Education Research Complete, the authors conducted a search for peer-reviewed articles that contain the term *Latinx*, which yielded only nine results (all published before the summer of 2016, which is when the search was conducted). None of these articles focused specifically on the meaning and use of the term *Latinx*, but rather used the term as a label or descriptor of a population. Of the small number of scholars who used the term in peer-reviewed articles, only two offered a footnote to explain the term to their readers (see Johnston-Guerrero, 2016; Monzo, 2016). The dearth of literature regarding the significance of this emerging label for a large segment of the U.S. population has created a knowledge gap within higher education.

The purpose of this article is to examine ways in which *Latinx* is used within the context of higher education and student affairs, and to provide an analysis of how the term can disrupt traditional notions of inclusivity and shape institutional understandings of intersectionality. The research questions that guide this study are: (1) How do higher education and student affairs stakeholders use the term *Latinx*? And (2) How does the term *Latinx* disrupt traditional notions of inclusivity for communities of people in higher education settings? While recognizing the lack of research on the use of the term *Latinx* in a broader context, the authors focus specifically on how stakeholders (e.g., faculty, staff, administrators, students) in the field of higher education and student affairs use the term *Latinx*. This article is one of the first to explore, map, and recontextualize the usage of the term *Latinx* within the fields of higher education and student affairs. The authors acknowledge the need for more research that examines the use of the term in K–12 educational settings and across disciplines. The authors further recognize that the term *Latinx* challenges the ideologies of language, culture, and gender, and is a way to recognize the importance of the intersectionality of social identities.

In this article, the authors provide a brief overview of pan-ethnic labels used for people of Latin American descent, as well as a definition of the term *Latinx* based on its current use in the literature, academic conferences, and in social media. Using environmental scanning as method, the authors analyze the use of the term within institutions of higher education and provide final conclusions regarding the future of this term and its impact within higher education environments. Throughout this article, the authors use the term "people of Latin American descent" to refer to the indigenous populations, citizens, and communities of people from Latin American countries and dependencies; the authors use *Latino, Latino/a, Latin@, Latinx,* or *Hispanic* when referencing studies or reports that used those categories.

Latino vs Hispanic

As researchers who study the experience of students of Latin American descent in higher education, the authors are continually navigating the nomenclature used for this population. *Latino* and *Hispanic* are two traditional, yet often misunderstood, labels used in higher education research and practice. The term *Latino*, which traditionally encompassed both male and female genders according to the rules of the Spanish language, has evolved within the literature and in daily conversations as *Latin, Latino/a, Latin@,* and *Latinx*. The term *Hispanic* was first adopted by the U.S. government during the Nixon administration and was implemented in the U.S. Census in 1980 (Delgado-Romero, Manlove, Manlove, & Hernandez, 2006). *Hispanic* derives from the Latin word *Hispania*, which later became *España* (Spain). *Hispanic* refers to people who are from countries where the primary language is Spanish (e.g., Spain, Columbia, Argentina, Mexico, Peru, Dominican Republic, among others) (Salinas, 2015). By contrast, the term *Latino* was adapted by the U.S. government to label individuals who identify as *mestizo or mulato* (mixed White, with Black and Native) people of Central or South America (Delgado-Romero et al., 2006). The term *Latino* refers to people from the Caribbean, as well as Mexico, and the countries that comprise Central and South America, even those countries that are not Spanish-speaking (Belize,

Brazil, French Guiana, Guyana, and Suriname) (De Luca & Escoto, 2012). It is important to understand the historical similarities and differences between *Hispanic* and *Latino*, which have resulted in different meanings for these two terms. A key similarity between these pan-ethnic terms is that they both refer to a cultural and ethnic group, not a race. Indeed, people of Latin American descent comprise various races, depending on ancestry and context, as the social construction of race continues to change through time. Furthermore, a 2012 report by the Pew Research Center found that when it comes to self-identification, "most Hispanics prefer their family's country of origin over pan-ethnic terms" (Taylor, Lopez, Martínez, & Velasco, 2012, p. 2).

The Emergence of Latinx

A comprehensive search of academic literature in the field of education, using common scholarly database tools (ERIC and EBSCOhost), indicates that historical research regarding the origins of the term *Latinx* does not yet exist. Various non-scholarly articles and opinion pieces provide some insight regarding how and why the term emerged. Padilla (2016) states that *Latinx* first emerged in 2004 among "left-leaning and queer communities as a way to promote inclusivity in language" (para. 6). With the rise of social media, the term then "gained a foothold by mid-2015, and its use began spreading beyond LGBTQIA communities" (para. 6). Sharrön-Del Río and Aja (2015) argue that the term *Latinx* was "born out of a collective aim to move beyond the masculine-centric 'Latino' and the gender inclusive but binary embedded 'Latin@'" (para. 1). While it may not be possible to pinpoint the exact time and place the term emerged, it appears to have been born out of the LGBTQIA community in the U.S. as a way to resist the gender binary.

Methods

The authors conducted an environmental scan to gather data for this research study. Originally developed as an analytical tool for use in business organizations, environmental scanning is now commonly used in higher education as part of the strategic planning process (Lapin, 2004; Morrison, 1992; Ritchie, Patrick, Corbould, Harper, & Oddson, 2016). Environmental scanning is the systematic collection of information (events, trends, relationships) to improve an organization's ability to adapt to its external environment (Choo, 2001). Lapin (2004) posits that environmental scanning's purpose is to enable an organization to develop or change a strategic plan based on the trends noted. Ritchie et al. (2016) maintain that environmental scanning data collection incorporates the following: an appropriate combination of literature reviews, systematic reviews, scoping reviews, web searches, questionnaires, focus groups, and interviews with key informants to uncover the range of perspectives related to a research question, topic, or key term. Additionally, the analysis of data collected through environmental scanning allows researchers to: (1) detect changes in the external environment; (2) define the potential threats or opportunities and potential changes for the organization caused by these changes; (3) promote a future orientation in leadership in the organization; and (4) alert leadership to trends and emerging issues and their future direction (Lapin, 2004). Insights gained through environmental scanning, particularly uncovering trends and emerging issues related to those trends, made this method of data collection appropriate for this study.

The data collection process incorporated four forms of environmental scanning on the use of the term *Latinx*: (1) search of the literature; (2) examination of higher education websites; (3) examination of higher education conferences; and (4) review of social media sites (Facebook, Instagram, and Twitter). Although the authors did not conduct focus groups or interviews to analyze perspectives of people on the use of the term *Latinx*, they were able to analyze a range of perspectives of the term *Latinx* through myriad opinion pieces on various social media sites. The approach to environmental scanning is informed by Lapin's (2004) method of *trend spotting* to detect "a behavior or change in the external environment and its likely future direction" (p. 106). In this case, the authors examined how behavior with the use of the term *Latinx* might impact the ways in which higher education environments acknowledge intersecting identities. Environmental scanning enables researchers to identify and analyze events, trends, and emerging understandings of the usage of Latinx. This method allowed the authors to document and recontextualize the evolution of the term *Latinx*.

Review of the Findings

Academic Journals

The search of the literature for this study, focusing on research articles that examined the use of the term "*Latinx*," yielded no results. This search was completed by using library search engines from two different universities (Florida Atlantic University and University of Wisconsin–La Crosse). Conducting two academic engine searches allowed the authors to gain a broader range of literature as part of the environmental scan. Although the literature did not include any scholarship examining the term *Latinx*, a number of peer-reviewed articles included the term *Latinx* as part of the title or within the article as a demographic descriptor or label. Out of nine articles, only two included a definition of *Latinx* as a way of informing the reader about the meaning of this label and how the author was using it. Johnston-Guerrero (2016) explains the term as: "Latinx (an inclusive, gender non-specific term replacing Latino/a)" (p. 44). Similar to Johnston-Guerrero, Monzo (2016) provides the following explanation for the use of the term:

> I use the term Latinx (as well as Chicanx) in order to be gender inclusive when referring to peoples of Latin American descent. However,

> traditional gender assignments (whether self-imposed or assigned) have an important impact on almost every aspect of people's lives and thus I use the gendered forms, Latina and Latino, when referring to specific individual.
>
> (p. 164)

The remaining seven articles do not provide a definition or context for use of the term *Latinx*. This implies that the authors expected the reader to be familiar with the term.

By contrast, a search of the ProQuest Theses & Dissertations Global database using the search term *Latinx* for anything published between 2010 and the summer of 2016 yielded 52 results: 45 published in 2016, six published in 2015, one in 2014, and nothing between 2010 and 2013. Although none of the authors of the 52 research studies examined the emergence and use of the term *Latinx* as the central focus of their research, four of them used the term in their title as well as throughout their article. The majority of the authors did not include *Latinx* as part of their article's title, but incorporated the term within their article as a demographic label. The authors of this study limited the search of dissertations and theses to the ProQuest database because it offers the most comprehensive collection of full-text dissertations and theses. They acknowledge that some relevant dissertations and theses may not be included in this database.

Similar to the results of the search of peer-reviewed articles, many of the 52 theses and dissertations included an explanation of the term *Latinx*. Some authors offered a brief definition for the reader either as a footnote or within the "definitions" or "methods" section of their paper: "Latinx (pronounced la-teen-ex) is a gender-neutral word for Latino/a, which is the commonly used word to distinguish genders" (Leek, 2016, p. 51). Others offered a more detailed and nuanced explanation of the term:

> The term Latinx provides a social identifier that aims to neutralize the sex-gender binary inherent in the Spanish language and thus, the ethnic category formally known as Latino. It offers an alternative to a) the general and masculine-centric ethnic term "Latino," b) the inherently gendered terms Latina/o, as well as c) the more recent gender inclusive but binary embedded term, Latin@. Its use elucidates the diversity of genders and sexualities of people who identify with Latinidad as an ethnic identity and is meant to connote inclusivity rather than exclusivity (not meant to be used exclusively as an identifier for gender-nonconforming or trans people of Latin American descent).
>
> (Haddock-Lazala, 2016, p. 1)

Still others provided their own positionality on the term *Latinx* in addition to a definition:

> I purposefully use the term "Latin@/x" to encompass Latin@ identities beyond a gender binary. . . . Using Latin@ assumes that all students were

cisgender, therefore I use Latin@/x instead. I also note, however, that my using Latinx as a White person could be contentious. Therefore, I cautiously proceed using Latin@/x, but recognize that terminology may evolve as the term Latinx is relatively new.

(Kilgo, 2016, p. 64)

The newness of the term *Latinx* created a temporal dilemma for some scholars who completed their dissertations in 2015, just as the term was gaining credence. As Arce (2015) explained:

Latinx is a relatively new way of referring to Latina/o population in a way that does not conform to a gender binary. This term gained popularity during the final stages of me completing this project, so the rest of the dissertation refers to Latina/os. Nevertheless, it is a new alternative that more adequately captures transgender, gender queer populations.

(p. v)

Gonzalez (2015) offers insight into a scholar's struggle to balance inclusive, albeit emerging, terminology with the expediency of maintaining traditionally accepted terminology:

Variations on the theme have come to appear in scholarly literature and popular culture alike, including the more inclusive but grammatically clunky "Latina/o" and "Latin@" which add a second gender dimension but err in their encouraging a gender binary. Much more recently the LGBTQ-friendly but largely unknown, "Latinx" (pronounced "Latinex") has entered the Latino lexicon, a term that is inclusive of the continuum of gender identities as a whole, but whose existence raises the question of whether the gender-neutral English version, "Latin," does not suffice, as it has greater currency and a deep history on the East Coast. Far from a question of simple semantics, the discussion of terminology adds a dimension of clarity, as it is my intention to discuss not only the lives of Latin-American men, but of Latin American people of all genders and ages. However, the census term "Latino" is preferred here, despite its decidedly patriarchal connotation, for its currency and widespread usage. This is carried out with hesitation and in hopes that readers can forgive the uninclusive language with the knowledge that better nomenclature is on the way.

(p. 14)

Based on the analysis of the use of the term *Latinx* in theses and dissertations, three patterns emerged. First, although the term initially appeared in 2014, it has only been within the past year that scholars have begun to use it more consistently as a gender-inclusive alternative to "Latino," "Latina/o," and "Latin@." Second, several scholars were compelled to offer a definition and/or positionality statement to the reader regarding the use of the term

Latinx in their thesis or dissertation. Third, the majority of scholars did not feel the need to define the term or explain their use of it. These findings are indicative of how and why current scholars are using the term *Latinx* and lead the authors to conclude that its use in higher education literature will continue to grow. Given the number of emerging scholars who used the term in their thesis or dissertation, it is reasonable to assume that these individuals will continue to incorporate the term *Latinx* into their research as they enter academia as faculty members or administrators. Thus, the term is more likely to become accepted and institutionalized within higher education.

Online Media: News Articles and Blogs

The Google search engine was used to collect online media documents, including news articles and blogs. As stated previously, and in accordance to the methods for this study, news articles and blogs were gathered to gain a deeper understanding of the events and trends regarding the use of the term *Latinx*. News articles and blogs have been a major source for the use of the term *Latinx* by scholars and activists. Through opinion pieces in news articles, scholars and activist have shared their standpoints on and definitions of the term *Latinx*. Many of these scholars and activists agree that the term *Latinx* has evolved and is being adopted as a genderless variant in efforts to be more inclusive of all gender identities (Armus, 2015; Logue, 2015; Princeton, n.d.; Ramirez & Blay, 2016; Sabate, 2015; van Horne, 2016). van Horne (2016) argues that the term "*Latinx* is practically the only explicitly ungendered term that has gained traction outside of academic circles" (para. 5). Other scholars, in efforts to expand on the understanding of the term *Latinx*, call attention to issues of intersectionality of language, culture, and gender (Padilla, 2016, Scharrón-Del Rio & Aja, 2015; Sosa, 2016). However, the term is not universally accepted or enthusiastically embraced by all scholars, activists, and people of Latin American descent. For example, Guerrera and Orbea (2015) argue against the use of the term *Latinx*. They claim that the term *Latinx* is becoming a buzzword, that the term is a blatant form of linguistic imperialism, that it is being used in the United States only, and that its use cannot be considered as "speaking Spanish." In pointing to another issue, Scharrón-Del Río and Aja (2015) argue that much of the perspective taking on the term *Latinx* demonstrates a "reactionary response that fails to substantively consider intersecting areas of privilege and oppression" (para. 3). These arguments emphasize the importance of recognizing that the term *Latinx* has multiple, and often complex, implications for individuals, scholarship, advocacy, and policy that scholars and educators need to deconstruct.

The examination of online newspaper articles and blogs provided insight regarding the emergence and evolution of *Latinx*. The authors found evidence that college students began using the term to challenge the ideologies of language, culture, and gender, and as a way to recognize the importance of the intersectionality of social identities. For example, Armus (2015) notes that, in December 2014, a Mexican American student group at Columbia University changed their group name from Chicano Caucus to *Chicanx* Caucus to be a gender-neutral student organization. Since the name of the *Chicanx* Caucus changed, the names of other programs and student organizations on campuses started to change (i.e., *Latinx* Heritage Month) (Armus, 2015; Logue, 2015). This appears to be the beginning of a national trend across colleges and universities in the United States. While the alteration of student organization names from *Latino* or *Latina* to *Latinx* has been a recent phenomenon, Logue (2015) notes the use of the word "x" first appeared in Puerto Rican psychological periodicals to challenge the gender binaries encoded in the Spanish language. For example, to challenge the masculine-centric nature of the Spanish language, authors use "*lxs estudiantes*" (the students), changing the word *los* (the) to *lxs*.

Spanish is a gendered language, which means that all nouns have a gender. In general, most nouns in Spanish that end in "o" tend to be masculine, and those that end in "a" tend to be feminine. Thus, the Spanish language "reinforces patriarchal and heterosexist norms" (Padilla, 2016, para. 3). To challenge the norms of a male-centric language, the term *Latino* evolved into *Latino/a* or *Latin@*—two terms that reinforce the gender binary of male/female. Adding the "X" to the end of *Latinx* and other words makes them gender neutral, and more inclusive for people of Latin American descent "whose gender identities fluctuate along different pints of the spectrum, from agender or nonbinary to gender non-conforming, genderqueer and genderfluid" (Reichard, 2015, para. 3). Thus, "*Latinx* is an attempt in Spanish to include non-binary people, those who are neither male nor female" (van Horne, 2016, para. 4).

While the "X" is viewed as part of a broader Latino movement that is concerned with issues of gender (van Horne, 2016), it is still misunderstood. Most scholars and activists used the "X" at the end of personal nouns to be gender neutral and more inclusive (i.e., Latinx and Chicanx) (see Logue, 2015; Padilla, 2016; van Horne, 2016; Vega, 2015). Others have used the "X" at the beginning of the word Chicano/a, replacing the "Ch" to embrace their indigenous roots (i.e., Xicana/o) (Becerril, 2015; Noriega, Romo, & Rivas, 2012; Sosa, 2016). Becerril (2015) maintains that the usage of "X" "rejects separatist nationalism and instead situates itself in the context of an international and global struggle for liberation, proudly declaring itself in solidarity with indigenous, *mestizx*, colonized and dispossessed people everywhere" (para. 2).

When documenting the use of the term *Latinx*, the authors found that the intersection of language and gender plays a significant role in how scholars and activists understand and reproduce the discourse, ideology, and gender identity of people of Latin American descent. The authors argue that the term *Latinx* has evolved as new form of liberation for people of Latin American descent who hold nonconforming gender identities; that it is inclusive in that it recognizes the intersectionality of sexuality, language, ethnicity, culture, geography, and phenotype; and it is often misused and underexamined for the intersecting areas of privilege and oppression.

Professional Conferences

As stated earlier, the term *Latinx* first began to appear on Internet and social media sites in 2014. Through environmental scanning, the authors found that, within higher education, the term *Latinx* started to emerge when college students began changing the names of their organizations (Armus, 2015; Logue, 2015). However, it was in 2016 that scholars and practitioners of higher education started to use the term *Latinx* in conference and association presentations. It is important to note that the authors did not attend every conference presentation that included the term *Latinx*. However, they were able to determine, based on their review of presentation titles and abstracts, that while the term *Latinx* was used in presentation descriptions, the term itself (meaning, use, evolution, etc.) was not the main focus or purpose of the presentations.

To ensure a more comprehensive environmental scan with a high level of timeliness, accuracy, credibility, and evidence of quality control, the authors examined conference presentations hosted by five major higher education and student affairs associations for the years 2015 and 2016. These annual conferences include: Association for the Study of Hispanics in Higher Education (AAHHE), ACPA—College Student Educators International (ACPA), Association for the Study of Higher Education (ASHE), NASPA—Student Affairs Professionals in Higher Education (NASPA), and National Conference on Race and Ethnicity (NCORE). The authors found that, in 2015, there were no presentations in which *Latinx* was used in the title and/or in the abstract. In 2016, a total of 10 presentations used the term *Latinx* in the title and/or abstract: one at NASPA, four at NCORE, and five at ASHE.

The authors limited their analyses to five annual conferences that draw a large number of higher education professionals from the United States as well as internationally. It is important to acknowledge the likelihood that other conferences sponsored presentations with the term *Latinx* in the title. Similar to the authors' conclusion regarding the use of *Latinx* in academic publications, it is reasonable to assume that scholars, activists, and practitioners within higher education and student affairs will continue to incorporate the term *Latinx* into their conference presentations.

Social Media Sites

The authors of this study included social media sites in their environmental scan of the term *Latinx* because "social media has become an important source of news that influences the examination of society and culture, and its interaction of race, law, power and privilege" (Beatty & Salinas, 2016, p. 6). Within higher education, social media has become an important tool for students, faculty, staff, and administrators to understand what works and does not work with regards to student engagement, student identity development, and identification of learning outcomes for students (Junco, 2014). Social media can be used to think through and develop promising practices within the field of higher education and student affairs, and to share new research discoveries.

Using Talkwalker (2016), a social media tracking tool, the authors were able to apply social media analytics to the environmental scan to measure the performance of tags (hashtags; #) in three social media platforms: Facebook, Instagram, and Twitter. Talkwalker tracked the mentions, engagements, potential reach to other social media users, sentiments (positive and negative), and gender usage of the term *Latinx*. It also tracked the top countries in which the term *Latinx* is being used in these platforms. In order to assure accuracy of the usage of the term *Latinx* in the three platforms, the authors focused the examination of the analytics on a six-month period, from June to November 2016. Data for that period remained fairly constant from week to week. For purposes of this study, the authors only report data from a seven-day period—November 15 to November 21, 2016—because it provided the most recent data on usage of the term *Latinx* and because the data from this seven-day period were consistent with the other weeks within the six months.

The authors found that, in the seven-day period, the term *Latinx* was mentioned over 9,000 times, 39% of which were positive sentiments and 28% of which were negative sentiments towards the term *Latinx*. From those 9,000 mentions of the term *Latinx*, those posted on social media reached over 11.9 million social media users, with 42,800 engaged in the post. Females (58.5%) outnumber males (41.5%) on the usage of the term *Latinx* in social media platforms. Although the term *Latinx* is mostly used in the United States, the authors were able to track the top countries that used the term: United States (87.5%), Canada (0.9%), United Kingdom (0.8%), Argentina (0.5%), Colombia (0.5%), Spain (0.4%), France (0.4%), Germany (0.4%), Philippines (0.4%), and other (8.3%).

As part of this analysis, the authors also documented the various forms of usage of tags (hashtags; #) for the term *Latinx* on social media. While the use of the term *Latinx* with a hashtag (#Latinx) was most common, the authors also found 49 additional ways in which social media users on Facebook, Instagram, and Twitter tagged the term (see Appendix). These various tags with the term *Latinx* provide insight into how social media users are utilizing the term to express and demonstrate their attitudes, lifestyles, hobbies, and actions, as well as how they celebrate accomplishments, challenge power and privilege, and build community and support for other communities of color. Based on the analysis of these three social media platforms, it is clear that the term *Latinx* is being used in a wide variety of ways to influence how social media users understand and make meaning of sexualities and gender and their interaction with society, culture, power, and privilege.

Higher Education Institutional Websites

The authors conducted an environmental scan of the websites of 34 U.S. colleges and universities to track the appearance of the term *Latinx* within the institutions' web pages to determine who was using it. The authors were particularly interested in determining how often the term was being used and whether it was becoming institutionalized as a label. Their sample included two types of institutions: research universities and Hispanic Serving Institutions (HSIs). The authors narrowed the list of 115 institutions classified as "doctorate institutions—highest research activity" (R1) on the Carnegie Classification of Institutions of Higher Education (n.d.) to 14 institutions that participate in the Big 10 Conference. This list provided a sample of large, flagship institutions located mostly in the Midwest. The authors also examined the websites of a sample of 20 HSIs located in Florida, Texas, and California.

The findings yielded several insights about the use of the term *Latinx* in higher education. First, none of the institutions in this sample appeared to have replaced the more traditional terms *Latino*, *Latina/o*, or *Latin@* with the term *Latinx* as a matter of practice throughout their websites. Yet, in this sample, all but one of the research institutions' websites and half of the HISs' websites included at least one reference to the term *Latinx*. This leads to a second finding regarding who is using the term and how they are using it. The term appears most frequently on student-organization-sponsored events such as cultural activities, speakers, and film series. In a few cases, the term appeared as part of a promotion of an event focused on a discussion of the meaning of the term *Latinx*, as in an event advertised on the Ohio State University Ohio Union Activities Board (2016) webpage, titled: "It's Not a Typo: Using the Term Latinx." California State University (SCU), Chico, an HSI, offered a similar event sponsored by various diversity offices, titled "Hispanic, Latinx, Xicana. . . . What's in a Name?" (CSU, Chico, 2016). It is clear that the purpose of these events is to educate the campus community about an emerging term—one that may be unfamiliar or confusing to the majority of the campus population.

Of the myriad Latino-based student organizations located on the campuses in the sample, only a handful used the term *Latinx*. Examples include the "LatinX Social Work Coalition" at the University of Michigan—Ann Arbor, "Political Latinxs United for Movement and Action in Society" (PLUMAS) at the University of Maryland—College Park, and "Latinx Badgers" (LxB) at the University of Wisconsin—Madison. While most student organizations continue to use the more traditional Latina/o in their titles, it is clear, based on the titles of the numerous events and activities sponsored by Latino-based student organizations, that the term is gaining more widespread use.

In some cases, university departments sponsored events and activities that used the term *Latinx* in their title. For example, the University of Iowa Center for Diversity and Enrichment and the School of Social Work co-sponsored an annual conference: "The 18th Iowa Latinx Conference" (University of

Iowa, 2016). This conference was previously titled "The Iowa Latino Conference"—the switch to the term *Latinx* in the conference title was made in 2016 (University of Iowa, 2015). Other department-sponsored events using the term *Latinx* in the sample institutions included graduation celebrations, heritage month activities, and cultural events.

While it was evident that some institutional departments, particularly diversity offices, sponsored or co-sponsored events with the term *Latinx* in the title, only three institutions in the sample used the term as part of the title of an official departmental unit or subunit. The Housing Department at Indiana University—Bloomington (2016) offers a learning community titled "Luis Davila Latinx Thematic Learning Community." The Division of Student Affairs at the University of Maryland—College Park (2016) has a webpage titled "Latinx Student Involvement," which includes links to pages, all using the term *Latinx*. Similarly, the Office of Student Life at Ohio State University (2016) devotes a bilingual webpage titled "Latinx" to providing information about counseling services. The ways in which these three institutions have embraced the term Latinx—going beyond simply sponsoring or co-sponsoring activities that use the term to incorporating it into titles of official departmental programs and webpages—may indicate the beginning of a trend towards institutionalization of the term.

Finally, the environmental scan of institutional websites revealed a phenomenon regarding the use of the term *Latinx* that cannot be ignored. There appeared to be a disconnect between faculty use of the term *Latinx* and institutional recognition of the term. Several of the universities in the sample had a Latino cultural center and/or a Latino studies program. The authors were particularly interested in whether these entities had changed their names to incorporate the term *Latinx*. None of them had made the change. Various titles were used for Latino studies programs, including Latina & Latino Studies, Latin American and Latino Studies, Latina/Latino Studies, Latina/o Studies, Chicano & Latino Studies, and Chican@ and Latin@ Studies. However, several faculty members working *within* those programs referred to their field as "Latinx studies" in their bios. Several faculty members had also used the term *Latinx* in the titles of their publications. This phenomenon might be viewed as a form of resistance by faculty members to the institutional use of traditional binary labels (Latina/o). At the very least, it is an indication of incongruence between how faculty members prefer to self-identify and how their institutional departments label them. The rise in the use of the term *Latinx* by both students and faculty members may push more departments and units to officially incorporate the term as part of their nomenclature.

Recontextualizing Latinx: Discussion and Implications

The terms *Hispanic* and *Latino* have evolved in the United States and are now part of the traditional lexicon used to identify people of Latin American descent. Yet, it is also evident that the term *Latinx* has gained popularity within the past few years. As a recent phenomenon, *Latinx* is used mostly by students in college and universities. The term *Latinx* has not evolved within the general population; rather, it has gradually gained increased use in higher education scholarship with no standard or official definition. The authors define *Latinx* as an inclusive term that recognizes the intersectionality of sexuality, language, immigration, ethnicity, culture, and phenotype. While there are various arguments for the use of *Latinx*, it has evolved as new form of liberation for those individuals who do not identify within the gender binary of masculinity or femininity, and it is used to represent the various intersections of gender as it is understood in different ways within different communities of people. The authors' approach to examining and documenting the term *Latinx* is consistent with researchers who use Latino Critical Race Theory as a form of liberation for *Latinx* communities. Similar to Solorzano and Delgado's (2001) work, the authors center the term *Latinx* with a liberatory lens which "offers a liberatory or transformative response to racial, gender, and class oppression" (p. 315).

The authors recognize that people may avoid using the term *Latinx* due to transphobic and homophobic inner feelings towards individuals who do not identify within the male or female gender binary. Others might challenge the term based on a history of major terms/words being developed and used mainly by Western modernism culture to describe marginalized populations. For example, Scheurich and Young (1997) maintain that we are socialized and educated in Western modernism's epistemologies (studies the theory of knowledge) that have delegitimized the ways of knowing for communities of people of color:

> Consider who the major, influential philosophers, writers, politicians, corporate leaders, social scientists, educational leaders have been over the course of western modernism. . . . They have virtually all been White. And it is they who have constructed the world we live in—named it, discussed it, explain it. It is they who have developed the ontological and axiological categories or competes like individuality, truth, education, free enterprise, good conduct, social welfare, etc. that we use to think (that thinks us?) and that we use to socialize and educate children.
> (Scheurich & Young, 1997, p. 8)

Therefore, people from majoritized and minoritized racial backgrounds, including people of Latin America descent, might not understand the term *Latinx*, due to a lack of knowledge of, or resistance to, the concept of intersectionality of sexuality, language, immigration, race, ethnicity, culture, and phenotype.

When people of Latin American descent experience oppression based on the layers of race/ ethnicity, gender, sexuality, language, immigration, culture, and phenotype, they come to consciously recognize that they do not socially or institutionally fit in (Solorzano & Delgado, 2001). As a form of resistance, people from Latin America descent have developed new terminology to create awareness, resistance, and liberation. As the authors analyze the term *Latinx*, they understand that *Latinx* communities of people—oppressed people—have the "essential tool[s] to their own survival and liberation" (Delgado, 1989, p. 2436). The authors strongly believe that the term *Latinx* evolved as a form of liberation by communities of people as they have created "action and reflection . . . upon their world in order to transform it" (Freire, 2010, p. 79). These communities of people who create liberation through action and reflection theorize their lived experiences and are "linked to processes of self-recovery" (hooks, 1991, p. 2).

Throughout this article, the authors make the case that the term *Latinx* has evolved as new form of liberation for those individuals who do not identify with the gender binary of masculinity or femininity, and that it is used to represent the various intersections of gender. In addition, the term *Latinx* is influenced by indigenous people's sexuality and gender roots, as in the case of Juchitán de Zarragoza, Oaxaca, Mexico, a Zapotec community where a community of people use a third gender role for biologically sexed men (Stephen, 2002). This third gender of individuals are not men or women; rather, they have a gender identity known as *Muxes* (Cobelo, 2016; Stephen, 2002). Cobelo (2016) explains that *Muxes* are "born biologically male and dress as women—but they consider themselves neither cross-dressers nor transgender. Instead, they are treated as 'the third gender,' and they identify neither as men nor as women" (para. 2). Furthermore, *Muxes* are "persons who appear to be predominantly male but display certain female characteristics" and fill a "third gender role between men and women, taking some characteristics of each" (Chiña, as cited in Stephen, 2002, p. 43). Similar to *Muxes*, *Latinx* can be rooted in the "indigenous gender systems that allow for more flexible models not attached to specific sexual identities" (Stephen, 2002, p. 44).

While most of society and many scholars have adopted the two-gender system (male and female), Stephen (2002) concludes from an ethnography study that indigenous people from the Americas had different gender system constructs:

> The persistence of a third gender role among contemporary Zapotecs for bodies that are sexed as male suggests that state societies such as the Zapotec and the Mexica may have had overlapping gender systems that included not only elite gender complementarity but also other systems that allowed for three or more genders. Since it is often acknowledged that state societies such as the Mexica and the Zapotec incorporated other deities and religious ideas into local and regional cosmologies, it is not inconceivable that more than one system of structuring gender could have coexisted at the local level in Zapotec communities—one directed at elites and another more closely associated with commoners.
>
> (pp. 48–49)

It is evident, through the historical roots of sexuality and gender, that gender continues to a be a category of social organization and the most significant classification and understanding of sexual behavior (Stephan, 2002). Higher education scholars, practitioners, and activists must continue to create and promote an inclusive space for all genders and the intersections with sexuality, language, immigration, race, ethnicity, culture, and phenotype.

Finally, it is important to remember that using the term *Latinx* does not necessarily create inclusivity to all communities of people, as many people still have not seen or heard, agree with, or understand the term *Latinx*. Google Trends (2016) documents that the most related queries by users searching the term *Latinx* include: *Latinx* meaning; what is *Latinx; Latinx* definition, *Latinx* define; *Latinx* vs. Hispanic; *Latinx* pronunciation; *Latinx* origin; and *Latinx* diversity. It appears that the majority of the population in the United States and the world are not familiar with or do not understand the term *Latinx*. It is clear, from this environmental scan, that additional research is needed to contextualize the history, meaning, and usage of the term *Latinx*. The authors expect an increase in the usage of the term *Latinx* in scholarship and higher education settings. It is also expected that, by the time this article is published, the number of scholarly articles using the term *Latinx* will have increased exponentially.

As scholars and activists continue to engage in future research and practice within Latina/o/x communities, the authors encourage them to ask research participants how they self-identify, and include *Latinx* along with other choices (e.g., Latina, Latino, Hispanic). It is critical to ask individuals how they self-identify to avoid making assumptions regarding their gender identity. It is also important that scholars and activists avoid making assumptions about the participants' self-identification from the data. For example, if a study reports that six participants of a study self-identify as Latina and five as Latino, the term *Latinx* should not be used unless some of the participants self-identify as Latinx. To promote gender inclusivity, the term *Latina/o/x* should be used when the gender of the population is not known. Addressing the complexities and misunderstandings regarding the term *Latinx* is essential to creating an inclusive space for all in higher education. The goal of this study is to further the understandings of the use of the term *Latinx*, and to advocate for people who are living in the borderlands of gender.

Conclusion

In an attempt to understand the ways that scholars and activist in higher education use, promote, engage, and deliver the term *Latinx*, the authors provide an overview of the evolution, history, and perspectives that communities of people have created about the term *Latinx*. Through a document analysis, the authors examined ways in which *Latinx* is used within the higher education context, and provided an analysis of how the use of *Latinx* can disrupt traditional notions of inclusivity and shape institutional understandings of intersectionality. While this article provides an understanding of how the term *Latinx* is used in the United States, mainly in higher education, there is the need for future research that continues to explore the sentiments regarding the term *Latinx* within all communities of people.

Through environmental scanning, the authors document the usage of the term *Latinx* in academic journals, online news articles and blogs, social media, and higher education institutions and conferences. From the data collected and analyzed, the authors conclude that the term *Latinx* challenges the ideologies of language, culture, and gender, and is a way to recognize the importance of the intersectionality of social identities. The authors believe that the term *Latinx* is a movement that will continue to gain popularity among higher education scholars, practitioners, activist, students, faculty, and staff, while promoting awareness and understanding of how concepts of sexualities and gender interact with society, culture, power, and privilege.

For educators, researchers, administrators, and students who are engaged in the process of examining and recontextualizing an emerging identity label, it is important to share your own positionalities and reflectivity on the term *Latinx*. Guillemin and Gillam (2004) explain positionality and reflectivity as:

> a way of ensuring rigor . . . involves how critical reflection of how the researcher constructs knowledge from the research process—what sorts of factors influence the research's construction of knowledge and how these influences are revealed in the planning, conduct, and writing up the research.
>
> (p. 275)

Positionality is a form of sharing personal narratives as they relate to one's own social identities, personal biases, beliefs, and values. A deeper understanding and awareness of the complexities of the term *Latinx* require a willingness to consider one's positionality and engage in reflectivity.

In addition, reading and engaging in critical conversations with colleagues and friends can help one to understand the importance and significance of the term *Latinx*. Through these conversations, one can be challenged, confront fears, and refute the stereotypes of social identities other than your own. The term *Latinx* is a meaningful and transformative word that promotes gender inclusivity, and thus a respect for basic human dignity. As institutions of higher education continue to seek excellence in diversity, multiculturalism and social justice, they must understand the significance of gender-inclusive language and its impact on the campus community.

References

Arce, W. M. (2015). *Reel negotiations: Exploring the relationship between film, religion, and sexuality in the Latino community*. (Doctoral dissertation). Retrieved from ProQuest (10115574).

Armus, T. (2015, October 7). *Student groups shift toward use of Latinx to include all gender identities*. Columbia Daily Spectator. Retrieved from http://columbiaspectator.com/news/2015/10/07/student-groups-shift-toward-use-latinx-include-all-gender-identities

Beatty, C., & Salinas, C. (2016). Providing spaces on college campuses and through social media for men of color to offer counterstories. *Developments*, 13(4), 6–12.

Becerril, C. S. (2015, June 24). *What's with the "X" in "Xicanisma?"* Latino Rebels. Retrieved from http://www.latinorebels.com/2015/06/24/whats-with-the-x-in-xicanisma/The Carnegie Classification of Institutions of Higher Education.

California State University, Chico. (2016). *Student announcements webpage*. Retrieved from http://www.csuchico.edu/ announcements-student/announcements/archives/2016–9–8/diversity-conversations.shtml

Choo, C. W. (2001). Environmental scanning as information seeking and organization learning. *Information Research*, 7(1), 1–37.

Cobelo, L. (2016, May 30). *Cooking with Muxes, Mexico's third gender*. Munchies. Retrieved from https://munchies.vice. com/en/articles/cooking-with-muxes-mexicos-third-gender

De Luca, S. M., & Escoto, E. R. (2012). The recruitment and support of Latino faculty for tenure and promotion. *Journal of Hispanic Higher Education*, 11(1), 29–40.

Delgado, R. (1989). Story for oppositionist and others: A plea for narrative. *Michigan Law Review.*, 87, 2411–2441.

Delgado-Romero, E. A., Manlove, A. N., Manlove, J. D., & Hernandez, C. A. (2006). Controversial issues in the recruitment and retention of Latino/a faculty. *Journal of Hispanic Higher Education*, 6, 34–51.

Freire, P. (2010). *Pedagogy of the oppressed*. New York, NY: The Continuum International Publishing Group.

Gonzalez, A. D. (2015). *Turley's Mills and archaeology of Latinos in the United States*. (Doctoral dissertation). Retrieved from Proquest (3725262).

Guerrera, G., & Orbea, G. (2015, November 19). *The argument against the use of the term "Latinx."* The Phoenix. Retrieved from http://swarthmorephoenix.com/2015/11/19/the-argument-against-the-use-of-the-term-latinx/

Guillemin, M., & Gillam, L. (2004). Ethics, reflexivity and "ethically important moments" in research. *Qualitative Inquiry*, 10(2), 261–280.

Haddock-Lazala, C. M. (2016). *Life and breasts at the borderlands: The breast reconstruction decision-making experiences of Dominican and Puerto Rican Latinxs*. (Doctoral dissertation). Retrieved from ProQuest (10163151).

hooks, B. (1991). Theory as liberatory practice. *Yale Journal of Law & Feminism*, 4(1), 1–12.

Indiana University-Bloomington. (2016). *La casa*. Retrieved from http://www.indiana.edu/~lacasa/housing/Luis%20Davila%20Latinx%20Thematic%20Learning%20Community%20.shtml

Johnston-Gerrerro, M. P. (2016). Embracing the messiness: Critical and diverse perspectives on racial and ethnic identity development. *New Directions for Student Services*, 154, 43–55.

Junco, R. (2014). *Engaging students through social media: Evidence-based practices for use in student affairs*. San Francisco, CA: Jossey-Bass.

Kilgo, C. A. (2016). *An epistemological revolution: Using quantitative data to critically interrogate high-impact educational practices*. (Doctoral dissertation). Retrieved from ProQuest (10181823)

Lapin, J. D. (2004). Using external environmental scanning and forecasting to improve strategic planning. *Journal of Applied Research in the Community College*, 11(2), 105–113.

Leek, D. W. (2016). *Community cultural wealth and higher education success: An analysis of the cisgender Latina student experience at a predominantly White institution*. Retrieved from ProQuest (10183681).

Logue, J. (2015, December 8). *Latina/o/x*. Inside Higher Ed. Retrieved from https://www.insidehighered.com/news/2015/12/08/students-adopt-gender-nonspecific-term-latinx-be-more-inclusive

Monzo, L. D. (2016). "They don't know anything!" Latinx immigrant student appropriating the oppressor's voice. *Anthropolgy & Education Quarterly, 47*(2), 148–166.

Morrison, J. L. (1992). Environmental scanning. In M. A. Whitely, J. D. Porter, & R. H. Fenske (Eds.), *A primer for new institutional researchers* (pp. 86–99). Tallahassee, FL: The Association for Institutional Research.

Noriega, C. A., Romo, T., & Rivas, P. T. (2012). *L.A. Xicano*. Seattle, WA: University of Washington Press.

The Ohio State University. (2016). *Office of Student Life: Counseling and consultation service*. Retrieved from https://ccs.osu.edu/the-spice-of-life-celebrating-diversity/latinx/

Ohio Union Activities Board. (2016). *Events webpage*. Retrieved from http://ouab.osu.edu/events.aspx/2016/10/20/55318/it-is-not-a-typo-using-the-term-latinx-?d=8

Padilla, Y. (2016, April 18). *What does "Latinx" mean? A look at the term that's challenging gender norms*. Complex. Retrieved from www.complex.com/life/2016/04/latinx

Princeton, L. (n.d.) *What is Latinx*. Retrieved from http://princetonlatinos.weebly.com/latinx.html

Ramirez, T. L., & Blay, Z. (2016, July 6). *Why people are using the term "Latinx"?: Do you identify as "Latinx"?* The Huffington Post. Retrieved from http://www.huffingtonpost.com/entry/why-people-are-using-the-term-latinx_us_57753328e4b0cc0fa136a159

Reichard, R. (2015, August 29). *Why we say Latinx: Trans & gender non-conforming people explain*. Latina. Retrieved from www.latina.com/lifestyle/our-issues/why-we-say-latinx-trans-gender-non-conforming-people-explain#1

Ritchie, S. D., Patrick, K., Corbould, G. M., Harper, N. J., & Oddson, B. E. (2016). An environmental scan of adventure therapy in Canada. *Journal of Experiential Education, 39*(3), 303–320.

Sabate, I. (2015, May 6). *Academic diaspora: Why Harvard doesn't have Latinx studies*. Harvard Politics. Retrieved from http://harvardpolitics.com/online/academic-diaspora-harvard-doesnt-latinx-studies/

Salinas, C. (2015). Understanding and meeting the needs of Latina/o students in higher education. In P. Sasso & J. Devitis (Eds.), *Today's college students* (pp. 21–37). New York, NY: Peter Lang.

Scharrón-Del Rio, M. R., & Aja, A. A. (2015, December 5). *The case for "Latinx": Why intersectionality is not a choice*. Latino Rebels. Retrieved from http://www.latinorebels.com/2015/12/05/the-case-for-latinx-why-intersectionality-is-not-a-choice/

Scheurich, J. J., & Young, M. D. (1997). Coloring epistemologies: Are our research epistemologies racially biased? *Educational Research, 26*(4), 4–16.

Solorzano, D., & Delgado Bernal, D. (2001). Examining transformational resistance through a critical race and LatCrit theory framework. *Urban Education, 36*(3), 308–342.

Sosa, G. (2016, June 30). *Shifting identities: Hispanic vs. Latino vs. Latinx*. Dieste. Retrieved from http://dieste.com/provoke-weekly/2016/06/30/identity-latinx

Stephen, L. (2002). Sexual and gender in Zapotec Oaxaca. *Latin American Perspectives, 29*(2), 41–49.

Talkwalker. (2016). *Social media analytics*. Retrieved from https://www.talkwalker.com/

Taylor, P., Lopez, M. H., Martínez, & Velasco, G. (2012). *When labels don't fit: Hispanics and their views of identity*. Pew Research Center. Retrieved from http://www.pewhispanic.org/2012/04/04/when-labels-dont-fit-hispanics-and-their-views-of-identity/

Trends, G. (2016). *Google trends explore: Latinx*. Retrieved from https://www.google.com/trends/explore?date=all&q=Latinx&hl=en-US

U.S. Census Bureau. (2015, September 15). *Facts for features: Hispanic heritage month 2015*. U.S. Department of Commerce. Retrieved from http://www.census.gov/newsroom/facts-for-features/2015/cb15-ff18.html

University of Iowa. (2015). *The 17th Annual Iowa Latino Conference*. Retrieved from https://diversity.uiowa.edu/sites/diversity.uiowa.edu/files/wysiwyg_uploads/2015lys_schedule-_final.pdf

University of Iowa. (2016). *18th Iowa Latinx Conference*. Retrieved from https://uiowa.edu/iowalatinoconference/

University of Maryland—College Park. (2016). *The STAMP: Latinx student involvement*. Retrieved from http://thes tamp.umd.edu/multicultural_involvement_community_advocacy/student_involvement_areas/latinx_student_involvement

van Horne, P. (2016, June 21). *Writer Jack Qu'emi explains the meaning of "Latinx."* Public Radio Information. Retrieved from http://www.pri.org/stories/2016-06-21/writer-jack-quemi-explains-meaning-latinx

Vega, B. E. (2015, October). *The audacity of the Latinx voice and the purpose of the Latinx intellectual tradition*. Latino Rebels. Retrieved from http://www.latinorebels.com/2015/10/14/the-audacity-of-the-latinx-voice-and-the-purpose-of-the-latinx-intellectual-tradition/

Appendix Latinx Hashtags Categorized by General Topic

Education	Political Activism	Art/Literature	Children	Other
latinxgradcaps	latinxpride	latinxart	latinxdeafbabyweares	latinx
latinxgrad	latinxlivesmatter	latinxgirlbrujeria	latinxkidlit	latinxs
latinxgrads	latinxrebels	latinxplotdancestudios	latinxbarbie	latinxplot
Latinxatcolumbialaw	latinxpower	latinxpress		latinxmas
latinxgradcap	latinxvote	latinxheritagemonth		latinxwhoyoga
Latinxsatcolumbialaw	latinxforblacklives	latinxartist		latinxperience
	latinxempowerment	latinxartists		latinxco
		latinxplotdancestudio		latinxexcellence
		latinxpression		latinxtacy
		latinxwriters		latinxownedbusiness
				latinxspiritweek
				latinxbinary
				latinx16
				latinxplotfitnesstudio
				latinxo
				latinxxx
				latinxdeboarbershop
				latinxindc
				latinxlove
				latinxmagic
				latinxpinup
				latinxplosionar
				latinxplosion

Section III
Solutions

13 *Abuelita* Epistemologies
Counteracting Subtractive Schools in American Education

Sandra M. Gonzales

Introduction: Subtracting the "Sacred Hoop"

"In the beginning was thought, and her name was Woman," wrote Paula Gunn Allen (1992, p. 11) in *The Sacred Hoop*. She continued,

> The Mother, the Grandmother, recognized from the earliest times into the present among those peoples of the Americas who kept to the eldest traditions, is celebrated in social structures, architecture, law, custom, and the oral tradition. To her we owe our lives, and from her comes our ability to endure, regardless of the concerted assaults on our, on Her, being, for the past five hundred years of colonization.
>
> (p. 11)

As a Chicana scholar crossing borders, crossing time periods, and crossing disciplines, I seek to reveal aspects of indigeneity that live on in contemporary Mexican culture. I use the word *Mexican* to include Mexican Americans, Mexican nationals, Mexican Indians, and Chicanas/os while linking these identities to U.S. Native American and indigenous discourse.

In an ethnographic study of the Mexquitic Indians of what is now called Mexico, Frye (1996) described how the Mexquitic peoples were denied their indigeneity because of a system that forced them to identify themselves according to racial ideologies imposed by their captors. This is true for Chicanas/os, who have been forced to deidentify themselves by not just one but two different racial ideologies, imposed first by the Spanish conquerors and then later by the English. Deena J. González (2001) brought this issue to the forefront of Chicana/o identity. When examining indigeneity in the Americas, the term *Chicana/o* cannot be used to describe our forefathers and mothers in previous centuries because of the de-indianization referred to by Frye, and very few academicians are trained in Chicana/o history, leaving contemporary Chicana/o scholars like me to train ourselves (D. González, 2001).

Such challenges reveal how stories can heal the ruptures created by conquest. Richardson (1997) said that the use of personal narrative, or the autoethnography, in research has the power to link "separate individuals into a shared consciousness" (p. 33). This consciousness can be used by colonized groups as a form of resistance, according to Pratt (1992). Noted Chicana scholar Gloria Anzaldúa used self-narrative, or what she called "autohistoriateoría," to resist de-indianization and to contest subjugated spaces such as the U.S.–Mexican border (Aldama, 2001). For me, stories expose a common history and heritage that is often undermined by geopolitical constructs such as the U.S.–Mexican border, which prompts the entombment of precontact identities under nationalistic discourses meant to supplant them (Frye, 1996).

In this particular piece, I cross borders through personal narrative in order to examine the role of *las abuelitas*, or grandmothers, as educators in Mexican, Mexican American, and Chicana/o culture. Like Gunn Allen (1992), I too am conscious of the strong women educators in my family, especially my grandmother. And I too recognize that grandmothers are undervalued as educators in Western society. Despite the centrality and significance of the *abuela*[1] in Mexican families, this topic has been underresearched. Thus, I explore how Mexican grandmothers have been dislodged from their traditional role as educators by the process of colonization and subsequent subtractive educational policies and practices, arguing that grandmothers have the potential to counteract the subtractive schooling process and thus positively impact student adjustment and success.

In *Decolonizing Methodologies: Research and Indigenous Peoples*, Linda Tuhiwai Smith (2001) posited that for indigenous scholars, writing and theorizing about our personal histories helps us to recover the significance of our own stories as well as "our language and epistemological foundations" (p. 39). The methodology used to produce this article is an example of this kind of work. Through the use of autoethnography and previously established texts, I reveal how the role of *abuela* as educator, tradition keeper, and cultural warrior lives on in my family despite more than 500 years of conquest and de-indianization. I also demonstrate how my *abuelita*[2] pulled me back into what Gunn Allen (1992) called "the sacred hoop," or the traditional wisdom of my ancestors, despite my own experience of subtractive education in U.S. public schools.

Data: A Memory of My *Abuelita*

I remember when my *abuelita* would listen to *ranchera*[3] music while she sewed. Sometimes she would get up and sway her hips back and forth to the rhythm of the accordion as she glided past me to reach for something out of the drawer. She would turn to me with a raised eyebrow and a heavenly smile as her favorite song came on. I could always sense her connection to the music, to the culture. It filled her, inspired her. It brought her a sense of joy and nostalgia. Every once in a while, she would try to teach my clumsy feet a step or two, but I would shy away, embarrassed by my awkward movements.

"Your grandmother used to be a dancer," my *tía*[4] would say. "You should learn." But I didn't want to learn Mexican dances, and I didn't want to learn

Spanish either. "I'm American," I would say emphatically, "not Mexican!" But my protests were drowned out by the sound of the accordion. They couldn't hear me because the music was too loud, the *grito*[5] too strong. "I HATE Mexican music, *abuelita!* Nobody listens to that stuff anymore!" I would yell angrily. She would smile coyly and say, "I remember this song from when I was a little girl." I would turn my back to her and pretend not to listen. But I did listen. And I do remember.

Like me, Gloria Anzaldúa (1999) described growing up with feelings of ambivalence and shame with regard to Mexican music. She wrote, "People who were to amount to something didn't go to Mexican movies, or *bailes*[6] or tune their radios to *bolero*,[7] *rancherita*,[8] and *corrido*[9] music" (p. 82). Like Anzaldúa, I too had internalized the message that music meant something about you. Music indicated a sort of status, and Mexican music was low on the totem pole of acceptable music genres for young people who wanted to fit in . . . especially at school. Nonetheless, my *abuelita* was unfazed by the popular demands of contemporary school culture. She held tight to her traditions and immersed me in a world full of Mexican music, language, and culture. Stubbornly resistant—and yet equally mesmerized—I was drawn to her every movement and word.

My eyes would tear up and a lump would grow in my throat as she told me stories of her migrant farmworker days and how she had struggled under unfair labor practices to feed her children.

Wide eyed, I would lay in bed sleepless, petrified of the *fantasma*[10] she described that suddenly appeared at a *baile* with the head of a beautiful woman and the foot of a chicken.

With my mouth watering, I would watch her roll out a perfectly thin tortilla and cook it gently on the *comal*[11] before topping it with a chunk of sweet butter and a dash of salt "*¡Ay, qué rico!*"[12]

Regardless of whether I desired to participate in Mexican culture, my *abuelita* stood strong on sustaining valued traditions and was an overt and covert daily reminder of our linguistic and cultural heritage. She probably didn't recognize it as such, but her manner of teaching, the values she instilled, and the leadership she demonstrated were passed down from generation to generation and are part of a tradition that Ojibwa scholar Rosemary Christensen calls "elder epistemology" (Rodriguez, 2008). It is "knowledge that is embedded in peoples' daily lives, embedded in languages, daily diet, stories and narratives, not necessarily in books or monuments" (p. 81).

Although elder epistemology includes the teachings of grandmothers, it more accurately refers to the various ways in which knowledge is passed down by all elders in a community. These elders may or may not be internal to one's family. They are referred to as such because of considerations determined to be important or significant by their group. Because in this article I am specifically referring to grandmothers as educators, I refer to this knowledge set as *grandmother* or abuelita *epistemologies*.

Although there is a large body of literature about families and communities as educators, such works more broadly explore the significance of nuclear families and local communities to school and student success. Missing to a large extent is a critical examination of the centralized role grandmothers have in cultural and linguistic maintenance and survival; the techniques used to teach grandchildren about their heritage; and how these lessons can translate into (a) positive self-efficacy, (b) expanded social, emotional, and cognitive capabilities, and (c) a healthier lived context for Mexican American children and families.

Analysis: Grandmothers as Educators in Indigenous Communities

> Grandmother Turtle, Grandmother Spider, or just Grandma. She brought the people to earth and gave them the rules and knowledge they needed to live. Indian People have many grandmothers, real and mythic. Some are biological relatives, some adopted ones. Grandmothers raise children; they tell stories in the winter and teach children the skills they need for survival. Grandmothers are the central characters in the daily and symbolic lives of Native women—indeed, of Native people.
>
> (Green, as cited in Schweitzer, 1999, p. 1)

This quote underlines the sacred web of knowledge that grandmothers weave in indigenous America. And it also reminds us of a grandmother's power and strength as she carries the world and its people on her back. The status of grandmother in Native cosmology is evidenced by the number of oral and written creation stories, Native American literature on the topic, as well as the number of stories found in children's books. Many scholars (Gunn Allen, 1992; Kincheloe & Kincheloe, 1983; Leichter, 1974; Schweitzer, 1999) have noted how Native grandmothers in the Americas have pioneered new ways of thinking and new ways of being. According to these scholars, grandmothers help their families adapt to new contexts and new cultures while preserving sacred traditions and ways of knowing. And they perpetuate the culture and values that have helped to sustain their people for millennia.

Although the role that grandmothers have in Native communities is varied and complex, in the traditional kinship system the role of raising and educating the young often belonged to the grandparents because the parents were busy taking care of the family and ensuring the survival of the group (Jaimes*Guerrero, 2003). Although not all grandmothers took on the role of educating, those who did helped to nurture and cultivate the young and inform their understandings of life, of self, and of identity. Some grandmothers were venerated for being "Mujeres muy luchonas," or what Gonzales (2003, p. 146) described as women warriors for justice, noting that "when the abuelitas arrive it's as if The Heart had entered the room" (p. 146). Indeed, in many Native communities, it was the grandmothers who fought against the effects of not just acculturation but also imperialistic policies. Leichter (1974) posited that "among American Indian tribes, those tribes in which the grandparents had the greatest part in the education of children were the most resistant to change" (p. 70).

Many scholars in the field of Native American studies concur and point overwhelmingly to the role of grandmothers as tradition keepers, warriors, and cultural consultants. *American Indian Grandmothers* (Schweitzer, 1999) chronicles the historical and contemporary issues facing Native American grandmothers of various tribal affiliations, such as Hopi, Lakota, Shawnee, Puget Sound Salish, Navajo, and Otoe-Missouria. Schweitzer (1999) noted that although grandmotherhood was explored from different perspectives, two principal reoccurring themes with regard to grandmothers could be realized within the various texts. These reoccurring themes were: "(1) traditions, the persistence of cultural patterns and (2) transitions, adaptations related to cultural and historical changes" (p. 4). It was argued that grandmothers were able to honor their traditional ways while also teaching their grandchildren how to adapt and blend their cultural traditions according to changing needs and changing environments. Although this research is not exhaustive, it does point to the pivotal role grandmothers have in many families and communities.

In my own family, it was my grandmother who provided a sense of cultural permanency that was reflected in the rhythm, sights, sounds, and smells of our life. Though the project of acculturation was blasting forward at school, the project of Mexican culturalization was reinforced by Grandma at home. Outside of school, my grandmother was the educator, instructing me in the ways of our culture and teaching me to value myself and my roots. She was the tradition keeper.

The term *tradition keeper* for the non-native reader may denote a passive act of simply maintaining or holding onto traditional knowledge. However, for me the term is one of insightful action and a deliberate use of agency. Grandmothers do not just hold onto knowledge; they actively educate in a manner unique to their contextual histories as well as their ancestral knowledge base. In other words, grandmothers don't just keep traditions; grandmothers teach traditions, with intentionality. Those traditions are like a form of curriculum.

By telling me stories about her days as a migrant farmworker, my grandmother was teaching me about my identity; about my family's migration story to Detroit; and about the history of our people, how hard they worked, how they suffered, how they persevered, and, more important, how they continued to love and triumph in the face of adversity.

The music she chose further grounded me in the struggle against the exploitive nature of American politics. Two of her favorite Mexican music genres, *ranchera* and *corrido*, are stories recited through song, inspired by the oral tradition and transferred across generations. The lyrics exposed me to important counternarratives about the Alamo and the Mexican Revolution, familiarizing me with the history of Emiliano Zapata, Pancho Villa, La Valentina, and other heroes and heroines who were completely excluded from my school curricula. Much of the content shared in songs is not part of the central discourse or incorporated into mainstream media, nor is the content covered in accessible formats that speak to Mexican working-class experiences.

When writing about the *ranchera* musical tradition, Broyles-González (2002) described how social empowerment was formed and informed through the spread of songs about unfair power dynamics and unfair labor practices. Some of the more popular *rancheras* and *corridos* were those that contested the exploitation of Mexican people, like my *abuelita*, who was exploited as a migrant farm laborer.

Similarly, *corridos* were traditionally sung by a *cantadista*, or singer, who traveled with a guitar from town to town, talking with common folks about important events and other happenings that impacted their lives (Simmons, 1953). The *cantadista* then skillfully shaped these events into songs that are synonymous with a newspaper story, complete with dates and locations and the names of people who were then made into legends.

González (2011) concluded that *corridos* provided a desperately needed venue for people, especially those who didn't read or write, to keep apprised of historical information and news about people in other communities. Indeed, Simmons (1953) argued that "corridos when properly interpreted are important social and historical documents" (p. 34). Paredes and Herrera-Sobek (2012) concurred, noting that "the Mexican corrido is at one and the same time a literary text, a piece of music, a specific performance, and a historical and social-cultural phenomenon" (p. 26).

My *abuelita* understood the critical forms of literacy used by her people. Like school teachers use textbooks and lesson plans, my grandmother used *corrido* and *ranchera* music to teach a form of critical consciousness. This critical consciousness has evolved into a critical pedagogy that has become the foundation for my own work as a scholar.

Like the rhythms and lyrics of traditional Mexican music, the making of tortillas also perpetuated a form of critical consciousness. Tortilla making originated with Mexico's indigenous population and is filled with symbolism and meaning. Rolling the tortilla into a perfect circle and cooking it gently on the *comal* was an act that had been repeated throughout our ancestral heritage. This act went beyond the mere cooking of a favorite family recipe or highly notorious food source. Bonfil Batalla (2004) noted how the Mesoamerican home was organized around the hearth and around the *metate*, a grinding stone, where tortillas were created from ground corn and cooked on a *comal*, a kind of cookware designed for tortillas.

Roberto Rodriguez (2008) also described tortillas and tortilla making and the symbolism associated with them. He described how memory can survive through food items such as tortillas, which allows the past to communicate with the present. Despite attempts to de-indianize Mexicans, tortillas live on to communicate our indigeneity; our connection to this land; and our connection to one another in the north and in the south, despite the imposition of contemporary geopolitical borders. Rodriguez wrote, "Many Indigenous and Indigenous-based peoples from Mexico and Central America identify as 'Gente de maiz' or people of corn" (p. 160). Rodriguez went on to state that "maize literally signifies a rootedness to this continent. If anything, it is the quintessential symbol of Indigenous America, of Turtle Island or America" (p. 161). Inspired by the work of Mayan scholar Domingo Martínez Paredez, Rodriguez emphasized, "Maize is not simply sustenance. It is beyond the notion of: 'We are what we eat.' It is: 'This is who we are—This is what we are made of' and 'This is where we come from'" (pp. 161–162).

Even my *abuelita*'s story of the *fantasma* with the head of a beautiful woman and the foot of a chicken was meant to stretch my understanding of life beyond the visible and understood. Storytelling of this nature is very common in Mexican communities. In her groundbreaking work *Borderlands/La Frontera*, Gloria Anzaldúa (1999) wrote, "Nudge a Mexican and she or he will break out with a story" (p. 87). She then went on to recount a story that her own father told her about a giant phantom dog that would run along the side of her father's pickup truck. Though this story might not seem credible or significant in an empirical manner, Anzaldúa demonstrated how story in the Chicano community imparts a different kind of truth, a folk knowledge that speaks to life's deeper meaning.

Sometimes my grandmother's stories were about *brujería*,[13] *curanderas*[14] or supernatural phe-nomena, such as ghosts and apparitions, much like the phantom dog in Anzaldúa's (1999) story. Acclaimed indigenous scholar Vine Deloria (1997), in his book *Red Earth, White Lies*, wrote, "The oral tradition, people felt, was serious; it was knowledge, and even the most unlikely aspects might be understood as true" (p. 37).

Although it may be hard for the non-Mexican reader to understand, each story has a purpose: to teach survival, reverence, and respect for all things seen and unseen, understood and not understood, crazy and not so crazy. As a result of these epistemologies, I grew up understanding the nuances of language used in various kinds of narratives and I recognized the purpose of each story above and beyond the examination of facts. My *abuelita* prepared me to recognize that there are many different kinds of realities and many alternative ways of understanding the world.

Patricia Gonzales (2006) argued that the Spanish conquerors attempted to destroy all Mesoamerican knowledge constructs, such as the ones I am describing. She described how families were forced to hide their indigenous ways of knowing so deep that many of us do not recognize them anymore. However, they still live in people like my *abuelita* who carry forward this knowledge by passing it down to their children and grandchildren.

Grandmother epistemologies may be celebrated by other groups as well. Mahera Ruby (2012) noted in her study "The Role of a Grandmother in Maintaining Bangla With Her Granddaughter in East London" how the grandmother was relied on in one Bangla family to teach Bangla language and culture. And with regard to European families, Leichter (1974) explained how the arrival to the Americas changed the extended family model. Because many Europeans left their extended families to come to the "New World," they were forced to move to a nuclear family model. This changed the family-as-educator dynamic, as there were often no grandparents in the house through which to pass important traditions. Although there has been some breakdown, many Mexicans still honor the role of elders as tradition keepers, and *abuelitas* like mine still play an important role in educating their families. Largely missing from academic discourse is a better understanding of how schools are structured to subtract or erase *abuelita* epistemologies, which is discussed in the next sections.

Subtractive Schooling and Subtracting *Abuelita* Legacies

> Unassessed in current scholarship are the academic consequences to many Mexican youth who "learn" perhaps no stronger lesson in school than to devalue the Spanish language, Mexico, Mexican culture, and things Mexican.
> (Valenzuela, 1999, p. 19)

As a result of her 3-year ethnographic study of academic achievement among Mexican American students at a Houston, Texas, high school, Angela Valenzuela (1999) argued in her book *Subtractive Schooling: U.S.-Mexican Youth and the Politics of Caring* that Mexican youth are stripped of their linguistic and cultural resources, which leaves them vulnerable to academic failure. Schools fail to establish the kind of caring relationships that Mexican youth value. When teachers and administrators fail to connect with their students' style of dress, manner of behavior, or use of Spanglish instead of proper English, rather than bridging the cultural divide, Valenzuela found that schools are being programmed to view Mexican American youth as oppositional to academic success.

Rather than reinforce or scaffold the linguistic and cultural capital that students bring to school, both teachers and administrators in Valenzuela's (1999) study tended to view their manner of speaking and dressing as signs that they didn't care about education. Mexican American cultural aesthetics were thus perceived as deficits that needed to be subtracted in order for academic and personal achievement to occur. Though Mexican immigrant youth tended to perform better and were perceived more favorably because of their quiet comportment, the belief that Mexican culture overall, and especially the home culture, was somehow at odds with American educational values remained (Valenzuela, 1999).

What is interesting is that both the Mexican American and the Mexican immigrant youth in Valenzuela's (1999) study felt that they were being superficially misjudged, but for different reasons. The Mexican American students contended that they were not against receiving an education, but rather their behavior was meant to symbolize their resistance to the noncaring environment perpetuated within their school's culture (Valenzuela, 1999). In the same study, Mexican immigrant students, in contrast, noted that their "quiet comportment" was not due to acquiescence but rather due to their feelings of powerlessness. Unlike the Mexican American students, the Mexican immigrant students did not feel that they could "openly defy school authority" because of their vulnerable status as immigrants (p. 14).

Thus, Mexican immigrant and Mexican American students were both seeking an education that more authentically reflected the form of caring embodied in the Mexican concept of being *bien educado*, a relationship-based model of learning frequently taught by grandmothers. Valenzuela (1999) aligned the concept of *bien educado* with the work of Nel Noddings (1984, 1992), which advanced the importance of teaching as an emotionally connected endeavor that centers itself on student development and needs. The idea is that when teachers demonstrate authentic caring, they are more tuned in to the needs of their students, and thus more deep learning occurs.

Although Nel Noddings undoubtedly advanced a caring praxis grounded in a values-based education model, I believe influences for the Mexican theoretical framework called *bien educado*, or to have good values, are of indigenous origin, evidenced by the kinship system and concepts such as "In Lak Ech." All three concepts—*bien educado*, the kinship model, and In Lak Ech—are deeply rooted in interdependent concepts of unity such as helping one another, taking care of one another, thinking of others' needs before your own, respecting elders, respecting Mother Earth, and treating all things as sacred. "The ethos or philosophy of In Lak Ech means—there is no I (and there is no you or the 'other'). Instead, there is 'tu eres mi otro yo'—you are my other self" (Paredez, as cited by Rodriguez, 2008, p. 162). Similarly, with regard to the kinship system, the "recurring themes that denote indigenous kinship are communalism; egalitarianism; reciprocity with others and with nature; and a complementary relationship between women and men, with special respect granted to children and elders" (Jaimes★Guerrero, 2003, p. 65). These philosophies are akin to a moral code of conduct and are the bedrock for the values embodied by *abuelita* or grandmother epistemologies.

Valenzuela (1999) argued that most Westernized teachers are trained in what she called an "aesthetic" form of caring that she described as rooted in methods and ideas rather than caring relationships. These concepts and ideas prepare young people to enter the market economy; they educate young people to be what my grandmother would call *bien preparado*, or well prepared to get a job. My grandmother would always say that being *bien preparado* was not the same as being *bien educado*. Though one might have received the training and skills to go on to college and have a professional career, this did not mean that one had learned good moral or ethical values; it did not mean that one had been taught to be a kind and caring person. It is this kind of values-based education model that the Mexican and Mexican American students in Valenzuela's study sought; it is this kind of education that is at the heart of *abuelita* epistemologies.

In Valenzuela's (1999) study, she described how both teachers and administrators devalued this form of caring education; they failed to recognize how tracking policies negatively stigmatized the youth and their families. They weren't able to fully understand how the curriculum was culturally and linguistically biased, nor did they recognize the effect of this bias on their students. And they were unaware of how their own actions and reactions contributed to the development of a subtractive schooling environment. In addition, they likewise failed to realize how subtractive schooling was linked to a larger historical legacy of cultural and linguistic erasure in Mexican and Mexican American communities (Valenzuela, 1999).

Subtracting *Abuelita* Epistemologies

The literature on subtractive schooling is significant to my own struggles navigating the divergent spaces of home and school while growing up. I now recognize how the subtractive schooling process eroded my own confidence in my cultural and linguistic identity as well as my familial relationships.

As I reflect back on the story about my grandmother, I realize my protest wasn't just about Mexican music. The music was merely a trigger for a larger issue: In my school, there was a negative stigma associated with being a Mexican, and that stigma intensified if you were a Mexican who also spoke Spanish. Rosa Sheets (2005) corroborated, noting, "Some children refuse to speak their heritage language because they view their ethnic group in a low social status" (pp. 119–120). Although this was true in my case, it was more complex than that. I quickly noticed that there was a cultural and linguistic hierarchy in which the worst stigma of all befell those Mexicans who spoke Spanish and surrounded themselves with all "things Mexican" (Valenzuela, 1999, p. 19) instead of all things American. As a result, I was ashamed to be a Mexican who spoke Spanish and listened to Mexican music.

Petrified of the social condemnation this stigma might bring, I rebelled against my cultural identity and against any familial display of what I perceived to be Mexican-ness. Unlike other groups, being Mexican was associated with being an immigrant; it meant that I was less than American; it meant that I was foreign; and worst of all, it meant that I didn't belong. For me, Spanish felt like a condemnation rather than an asset, with Spanish fluency denoting my relative degree of Mexican-ness.

The project of acculturation created tensions between my family and me, between my home culture and my school culture, and between my Spanish and English language abilities. According to Jin Sook Lee and Eva Oxelson (2006),

> for linguistic minority children, losing proficiency in their heritage language is more than just a loss of a linguistic system; it is a separation from their roots, a denial of their ethnic identity, and a dismissal of their potential as a bilingual and bicultural member of society.

(p. 455)

Not only did I internalize the subtractive schooling hierarchies, I attempted to bring these hierarchies home and impose them on my own family. This was evidenced by comments such as, "I HATE Mexican music, Grandma! Nobody listens to that stuff anymore!"

In this statement, *nobody* meant that nobody of status listened to Mexican music. Therefore, my frustration was derived from my perception—developed through my formal education—that my grandmother would voluntarily choose music that would relegate both of us to a lower status position according to the subtractive schooling hierarchy. Laura Padilla (2001) called this "internalized oppression" (p. 67), when one internalizes the stereotypical and pejorative beliefs of the dominant culture and responds as if those beliefs were accurate. Sofia Villenas (1996) called this the colonizer/colonized phenomenon. It is exemplified when colonized groups are indoctrinated to play the role of the colonizer by an educational system that teaches them to reinforce the values, perspectives, and beliefs of the dominant culture.

Sadly, by disparaging my grandmother's choice in music as well as her linguistic heritage, I was propagating the injustices that had been inflicted on my group as a whole through a subtractive schooling process designed to subtract *abuela* epistemologies by utilizing young people like myself as the very instruments of colonization and "conversion" to the belief system of the dominant culture that was put into place during hundreds of years of colonization. Thankfully, my grandmother was there to undermine these attempts by instructing me in the power of a curriculum that taught one to be *bien educado* in addition to being merely *bien preparado*.

The trauma of deculturalization through subtractive schooling practices is also a generational one; in other words, the struggle against cultural erasure is passed down from generation to generation. My family had this struggle with me, and now I have this same struggle with my own children: the struggle to preserve a linguistic and cultural identity, the struggle to preserve indigenous knowledge. James (2000) highlighted the resistance parents encounter when they seek to pass on their heritage language and culture. Parents experience resistance from the school because of the assimilatory agenda espoused and resistance from their own children, who internalize the school's perspective of their culture.

This is a struggle made even more difficult given the recent cuts to bilingual education and Mexican American Studies as well as the rise in anti-immigrant legislation and an increasingly assimilationist social-political rhetoric. With an increasing breakdown in the extended family or kinship system, how can we help children to navigate these complexities and rise above the hate with their cultural identities intact?

Furthermore, many educational institutions in this country continue not only to discount *abuela* epistemologies but also to intentionally move students away from their elders, constructing oppositional relationships between home and school values while using students as instruments of conversion. This means that children are being used to help Westernize the family and suppress their own cultural heritage as a way to accelerate the process of acculturation and assimilation. Indeed, this is not without historical precedent, as the utilization of children in schools to help nationalize other members of indigenous societies was the colonial model of education that began with the missions, evolved into the boarding school model, and is still carried over today into our contemporary educational institutions. The following section expounds on the changes contributing to the destabilization of the role of grandmothers as educators.

Colonial Legacies: The Subtraction of *La Abuelita* as Educator

> Unlike the social purpose of skills development and cultural transfer for children in settlers' schools, systems of education in the Spanish missions were purposefully designed to replace a child's Native American language, religion, dress and other cultural attributes with the Spanish language, Roman Catholic faith, and European mores, values and customs. Although some priests learned native languages, the missions' role in the deculturalization of Native Americans was extensive.
>
> (MacDonald, 2004, p. 9)

The colonial system of knowledge production built in the 16th century was highly successful at legitimizing "dominant definitions of reality" (Grande, 2004, p. 71). So successful was this system that it continues to reign over our communities after more than 500 years. Education systems today continue to treat native people as inferior beings by dismissing the networks they created to protect sacred knowledge structures and even calling them myth based, superstitious, and primitive, the same adjectives used during the era of colonization (Deloria, 1997).

The failure of contemporary school systems to meet the needs of the Mexican and Mexican American community can be traced back to the colonization of the Americas. The core curriculum of our first institutionalized educational system consisted of de-indigenizing the natives by nationalizing them according to new geopolitical territories and assimilating them to the language and culture of the colonial power, which was Spain/Spanish. Nonetheless, Bonfil Batalla (2004) contended that the Mexican cultural reality is still rooted in Mesoamerican civilization despite the linguistic conversion to Spanish and the imposition of Western values. He called this "Mexico profundo" because despite conquest, the deeper and more profound parts of an indigenous Mexico survive in the daily lives of its people despite the Spanish colonial veneer.

However, when U.S. schools establish educational policies that suppress Mexican cultural and linguistic capital, it forces students and families to redefine their identities within the dictates of yet another colonial racial ideology (Frye, 1996) developed by the English. This is equivalent to a form of double colonization.

Historically speaking, the missionary schools were central to the indoctrination process, as religious conversion was perceived as necessary for cultural conversion. Ricard (1974) described how the natives were rounded up into "villages of evangelization" (p. 139) where "idols were destroyed, and pagan ceremonies put to an end such that the barbarous Indians could be initiated into civilized life" (p. 137). The missionary schools did this by breaking down the existing family and community-based education, or kinship, system in which grandmothers played a significant role in teaching linguistic and cultural traditions. The section that follows focuses on the changes that contributed to the destabilization of the role of grandmothers as educators.

In many indigenous American traditions, God, or the creator, is both man and woman (Gunn Allen, 1992), represented as Father Sky and Mother Earth, the unity of a grandfather spirit and a grandmother spirit. In this belief system, guidance and leadership within a community is a shared responsibility among elders regardless of gender. There are both medicine men and medicine women, priests and priestesses. Gonzales (2003) noted that the "Mayan medicine man Apolinario says our hearts have a female valve and a male valve. As males and females, and human being to human being, we must learn to treat each other differently" (p. 151). Gonzales (2003) went on to argue that "if humankind does not come into balance, the earth will not survive" (p. 151).

As a result of colonization in the Americas, a spiritual paradigm shift occurred that promoted a religious system founded on the belief that there was one Spirit God who was male and that he passed on his divinity to his son, whose own divine authority was perpetuated through a line of allmale priests (Gunn Allen, 1992). This male-dominated religious system reinforced a patriarchal world order, which had a devastating effect on indigenous women in general. Of course, the ramifications of this new patriarchal world order were particularly negative for grandmothers, who found themselves displaced from their traditional leadership roles in society as elders, educators, tradition keepers, and venerated members of the community who previously held power and status (Gunn Allen, 1992; Jaimes & Halsey, 1992). They were replaced by an all-male priesthood and other males who now occupied these and other high-level offices. According to Jaimes and Halsey (1992), "In none of the several thousand non-treaty agreements reached between the United States and these same nations, were federal representatives prepared to discuss anything at all with women" (p. 322).

Gunn Allen (1992), Gonzales (2003), and Jaimes and Halsey (1992) argued that the erasure of the feminine in Native cosmology has long been one of the priorities of the colonial world order. To terminate the transmission of culture meant that it was necessary to sever the power of women and grandmothers. It required physically, psychologically, and strategically coercing both Native men and women under the domain of a patriarchal world order.

> The colonizers saw (and rightly) that as long as women held unquestionable power of such magnitude, attempts at total conquest of the

continents were bound to fail. In the centuries since the first attempts at colonization in the early 1500s, the invaders have exerted every effort to remove Indian women from every position of authority, to obliterate all records pertaining to gynocratic social systems, and to ensure that no American and few American Indians would remember that gynocracy was the primary social order of Indian America prior to 1800.

(Gunn Allen, 1992, p. 3)

Patriarchy is a contested area in feminist thought. Many indigenous scholars, such as Gunn Allen (1992) and Jaimes and Halsey (1992), argue that patriarchy was brought by the conquerors and imposed on both Native men and women through the process of colonization. In addition to the disenfranchisement that occurred, they point out, there have also been attempts by White feminists to shift the narrative toward a belief that all cultures, even Native American, were patriarchal. Unfortunately, many White feminists try to convince Native women that they are especially vulnerable to abuse by savage black, brown, and red men. This is a stereotype reproduced by colonial ideologies that both White men and women continue to perpetuate with negative consequences for colonized communities of color. Maria Cotera (2010), quoting Jaimes and Halsey, contended,

"Many Indian women are uncomfortable [with feminist analysis] because they perceive it (correctly) as white-dominated." Noting that white middle-class women have been the beneficiaries of the colonial exploitation of Indigenous peoples, Jaimes and Halsey point out that white feminists have too often criticized Indian gender relations without exploring the ways in which colonialism has transformed these relations.

(p. 233)

This same critique can be applied to educational scholars and policymakers who are quick to blame the Latino achievement gap on the demise of the Latino family unit; or the lack of parental support; or the fact that parents lack resources, lack academic understanding, or aren't educated themselves. However, rarely is there an examination of "the ways in which colonialism has transformed these relations" Cotera (2010, p. 233), meaning our own preconquest relations and our indigenous understandings of education. As a result, contemporary education scholars, researchers, and policymakers may be in danger of falling into the trap of unintentionally perpetuating damaging ethnic stereotypes.

Many Native scholars (Gunn Allen, 1992; Jaimes & Halsey, 1992; Jaimes*Guerrero, 2003; McClintock, Mufti, & Shohat, 1997) differ from their White feminist sisters because, for them, the displacement of women of color is due to colonization, not patriarchy. Patriarchy, they maintain, reinforces the White worldview. The patriarchy imposed through colonization acted as a catalyst, breaking down an indigenous system of gender equity. With colonization, the balance between men and women was disrupted, and a significant facet of that disruption was the displacement of the sacred and venerable role that grandmothers played within the family unit.

Nevertheless, despite more than 500 years of colonization, many Mexican grandmothers, like mine, continue to act as educators and continue to resist systematic attempts at their displacement and erasure. Their pedagogical strategies and practices continue to live on. Only now, because this role is not valued by the dominant society, their work as educators must take place hidden in the home—in opposition to much of what is being taught in schools.

Conclusion: Returning to the Sacred Hoop

Grandmothers, a historical asset to education in the Mexican and Mexican American community, have been rendered invisible to schools. And this research seeks to rectify this subtractive tendency, establishing the grandmother (both figuratively in terms of a female elder and literally as one's kin) and *abuelita* epistemologies as a potential growth area for research in the field of bilingual-bicultural, family/community and critical studies in education, particularly with regard to democratizing schools, decolonizing knowledge, and rethinking the Latino achievement gap.

And although the focus of this essay was on the grandmother in particular, grandfathers are also significant to our understanding of elders as educators in the community. The deep respect that both are given as educators, and the tremendous loss that our schools and communities suffer when the epistemological legacies that they represent are subtracted from the classroom, is immeasurable.

Instead of being calling on to help ease the tensions between home and school, to bridge cultural conflicts, and to pioneer a new praxis, grandmothers have instead been put in a peripheral position that is subordinate to formal educational institutions and that negates the value of their roles as women and as educators. Indeed, they have been placed in an oppositional position by a discourse that favors the contemporary over the traditional, men over women, school values over home values, and Western positivism over indigenous ways of knowing. In this way, grandmothers have been forced to protect their grandchildren from the deculturalizing effects of Westernized schools (Kincheloe & Kincheloe, 1983).

With their traditional ways of knowing and ways of teaching pushed to the margins of formal institutions of learning, Mexican grandmothers, or *abuelitas*, rather than being invited to participate collaboratively in a child's education often use their agency to counteract the forces of subtractive education and resist the effects of colonization experienced by children in schools. Mexican grandmothers also resist their own erasure by the dominant culture, and not only do they teach their grandchildren how to protect themselves against the subtraction of these epistemological legacies, but through *abuelita* epistemologies they teach them how to avoid being used as instruments of indoctrination.

Furthermore, *abuelita* epistemologies ground the young in a linguistically rich and culturally dynamic praxis of justice while also teaching youth how to adapt to a changing world context. Such epistemologies have the potential to help bridge the disconnect between school culture and family culture, between the Indigenous and the Western. Sandy Grande (2004) called this skill set "self-conscious traditionalism" (p. 169), which is when individuals consciously weave the traditional into contemporary situations. Likewise, this skill set could help educators weave traditional knowledge and values into contemporary school practice, thereby producing a more caring and transformative environment for all.

Abuelita epistemologies push us to re-envision new curricular itineraries. They push us to go beyond our current content areas or educational activities; to go beyond the discourse of what can be assessed, graded, quantified, or commodified. *Abuelita* epistemologies cannot be confined to a school building or defined by a cookie-cutter curriculum or taught in a 1-hr lesson plan. Such knowledge goes beyond compartmentalized lessons divided into prepackaged periods of time. Grandmother epistemologies are grounded in relationships with all aspects of life, and thus call for students to unite with their elders and the natural cycles of life. A praxis that creates opportunities to learn from time, indeed with time, as opposed to learning from a worksheet or a single expert is needed (Maurial, 1999). *Abuelita* epistemologies call on us to cross borders and to cross disciplines, to examine the relationship between culture, school, and imperialism "and what is defined as successful learning" (Semali, 1999, p. 99). To do so requires a critical redefinition of knowledge, as well as how it is produced, validated, disseminated, and consumed.

An important part of the redefining process is naming and renaming our own knowledge. Smith (2001) argued that they who name the world, give voice to their reality. By naming our knowledge, our realities, we begin the process of decolonization. By remembering our stories and sharing them, we give a face to conquest. By revealing our journeys, we give testimony to ancestral pathways. Like grandmother spider, we start from our center and weave, allowing our stories to intersect and crisscross. We transform our fate by building and rebuilding our web of knowledge, our web of traditions and faith, calling and waiting for the structure to emerge into a web of influence and equilibrium in schools between the genders and among people of all races.

Notes

1. Grandmother.
2. A diminutive form of "grandmother," akin to "grandma."
3. A form of Mexican folk music.
4. Aunt.

5. A shout, sometimes used as a musical accompaniment or enhancement.
6. Dances.
7. Ballads.
8. A diminutive form of *ranchera*.
9. Another form of Mexican folk music.
10. Ghost.
11. A flat pan used to warm tortillas.
12. "Mmm . . . how yummy!"
13. Witchcraft.
14. Healers.

References

Aldama, A. (2001). *Disrupting savagism: Intersecting Chicana/o, Mexican immigrant, and Native American struggles for self-representation*. Durham, NC: Duke University Press.
Anzaldúa, G. (1999). *Borderlands/la frontera: The new mestiza*. San Francisco, CA: Aunt Lute Books.
Batalla, G. B. (2004). *México profundo: Reclaiming a civilization*. Austin: University of Texas Press.
Broyles-González, Y. (2002). Ranchera music(s) and the legendary Lydia Mendoza: Performing social location and relations. In N. E. Cantú & O. Nájera-Ramírez (Eds.), *Chicana traditions: Continuity and change* (pp. 117–132). Champaign, IL: University of Illinois Press.
Cotera, M. E. (2010). *Native speakers: Ella Deloria, Zora Neale Hurston, Jovita Gonzalez and the poetics of culture*. Austin: University of Texas Press.
Deloria, V., Jr. (1997). *Red earth, white lies: Native Americans and the myth of scientific fact*. Golden, CO: Fulcrum.
Frye, D. (1996). *Indians into Mexicans: History and identity in a Mexican town*. Austin: University of Texas Press.
Gonzales, P. (2003). *The mud people: Chronicles, testimonies and remembrances*. San Jose, CA: Chusma House.
Gonzales, P. (2006, May). *In the spirit of the ancestors: Reconciling post tribal stress disorder*. Retrieved from http:// www.sjsu.edu/people/marcos.pizarro/maestros/Gonzales.pdf
González, D. (2001). Chicana identity matters. In C. A. Noriega, E. R. Avila, K. M. Davalos, C. Sandoval, & R. Pérez-Torres (Eds.), *The Chicano studies reader: An anthology of Aztlán 1970–2000* (pp. 411–426). Los Angeles: University of California at Los Angeles Chicano Studies Research Center Publications.
González, J. (2011). *Harvest of empire: A history of Latinos in America*. New York, NY: Penguin Books.
Grande, S. (2004). *Red pedagogy: Native American social and political thought*. Lanham, MD: Rowman & Littlefield.
Gunn Allen, P. (1992). *The sacred hoop: Recovering the feminine in American Indian traditions*. Boston, MA: Beacon Press.
Jaimes, M. A., & Halsey, T. (1992). American Indian women: At the center of indigenous resistance in North America. In M. A. Jaimes (Ed.), *The state of Native America: Genocide, colonization, and resistance* (pp. 311–344). Boston, MA: South End Press.
Jaimes* Guerrero, M. A. (2003). "Patriarchal colonialism" and indigenism: Implications for Native feminist spirituality and Native womanism. *Hypatia*, *18*(2), 58–69.
James, M. (2000). Culture in ESL instruction: An analytic framework. *TESL Canada Journal/Revue TESL Du Canada*, *49*, 36–49.

Kincheloe, J. L., & Kincheloe, T. S. (1983). The cultural link: Sioux grandmothers as educators. *The Clearing House, 57*(3), 135–137.

Lee, J. S., & Oxelson, E. (2006). It's not my job: K–12 teacher attitudes toward students' heritage language maintenance. *Bilingual Research Journal, 30*(2), 453–477.

Leichter, H. J. (1974). *The family as educator.* New York, NY: Teachers College Press.

MacDonald, V. (2004). *Latino education in the United States: A narrated history from 1513–2000.* New York, NY: Palgrave Macmillan.

Maurial, M. (1999). Indigenous knowledge and schooling: A continuum between conflict and dialogue. In L. M. Semali & J. L. Kincheloe (Eds.), *What is indigenous knowledge? Voices from the academy* (pp. 59–77). New York, NY: Falmer Press.

McClintock, A., Mufti, A., & Shohat, E. (1997). *Dangerous liaisons: Gender, nation and postcolonial perspectives.* Minneapolis: University of Minnesota Press.

Noddings, N. (1984). *Caring: A feminine approach to ethics and moral education.* Berkeley: University of California Press.

Noddings, N. (1992). *The challenge to care in schools: An alternative approach to education. Advances in contemporary educational thought* (Vol. 8). New York, NY: Teachers College Press.

Padilla, L. (2001). But you're not a dirty Mexican: Internalized oppression, Latinos and law. *Texas Hispanic Journal of Law and Policy, 7*(1), 59–114.

Paredes, A., & Herrera-Sobek, M. (2012). The corrido: An invited lecture at the "Music in Culture" public lecture series. *Journal of the American Folklore Society, 125*(495), 23–44. doi:10.1353/jaf.21012.0009

Pratt, M. L. (1992). *Imperial eyes: Travel writing and transculturation.* London, England: Routledge.

Ricard, R. (1974). *The spiritual conquest of Mexico.* Berkeley: University of California Press.

Richardson, L. (1997). *Fields of play: Constructing an academic life.* Piscataway, NJ: Rutgers University Press.

Rodriguez, R. G. (2008). *Centeotzintli: Sacred maize a 7,000 year ceremonial discourse* (Doctoral dissertation). Retrieved from ProQuest. (OCLC: ocn351812119)

Ruby, M. (2012). The role of a grandmother in maintaining Bangla with her granddaughter in East London. *Journal of Multilingual and Multicultural Development, 33*(1), 67–83.

Schweitzer, M. M. (Ed.). (1999). *American Indian grandmothers: Traditions and transitions.* Albuquerque: University of New Mexico Press.

Semali, L. M. (1999). Community as classroom: (Re)valuing indigenous literacy. In L. M. Semali & J. L. Kincheloe (Eds.), *What is indigenous knowledge? Voices from the academy* (pp. 95–118). New York, NY: Falmer Press.

Sheets, R. H. (2005). *Diversity pedagogy: Examining the role of culture in the teaching-learning process.* Boston, MA: Pearson Education.

Simmons, M. E. (1953). Attitudes toward the United States revealed in Mexican corridos. *Hispania, 36*(1), 34–42.

Smith, L. T. (2001). *Decolonizing methodologies: Research and indigenous peoples.* New York, NY: Zed Books.

Valenzuela, A. (1999). *Subtractive schooling: U.S.-Mexican youth and the politics of caring.* New York: State University of New York Press.

Villenas, S. (1996). The colonizer/colonized Chicana ethnographer: Identity, marginalization, and co-optation in the field. *Harvard Educational Review, 66,* 711–732.

14 Sustaining a Dual Language Immersion Program

Features of Success

Iliana Alanís and Mariela A. Rodríguez

The continued growth in the number of speakers of languages other than English is reflected in the rapidly increasing number of students in U.S. schools for whom English is a second language. Data from the National Center for Education Statistics (2005) show that the number of school-age children who spoke a language other than English reached almost 10 million in 2004. Such a dramatic increase continually challenges educators to provide effective language programs with quality instruction for students who are culturally and linguistically diverse. Some educators choose to view these challenges as opportunities by offering a two-way bilingual program as an educational option for meeting the needs of both monolingual Spanish speakers and monolingual English speakers.

Review of the Literature

In dual language education, two languages are used in the classroom for instruction and learning. Biliteracy is as much an aim as full bilingualism, with literacy being acquired in both languages either simultaneously or with an initial emphasis on native language literacy (Baker, 1996). Only a small number of bilingual programs in the country have the continued maintenance of the first language as an explicit goal (Center for Applied Linguistics, 2005). Hence, many English learners (ELs) receive instructional programs that are too short term in focus and are not cognitively or academically challenging (Thomas & Collier, 1997a).

With respect to the ultimate goal for ELs, the policy of transitional bilingual education, or ESL programs whose aims are English language proficiency and assimilation, is explicitly non-bilingual. Because the focus is on learning English without a strong effort to retain the native language, these programs incorporate a minimalist form of bilingualism for the period of time that students are in them (Hakuta & Gould, 1987; Snow & Hakuta, 1992). Dual language bilingual programs are an attempt to eliminate this minimalist form of bilingualism and to promote academic achievement for ELs as well as foreign language immersion for English-dominant students (Alanís, 2000; Lindholm-Leary, 2001). The opportunity for students to become bilingual is increased by the dual language bilingual approach. ELs benefit from retention and development of their native language while acquiring English, and English speakers enjoy exposure to real speakers of the foreign language. The program provides an atmosphere that allows students to acquire a second language and learn about another culture without sacrificing their individual identities. In so doing, the dual language program is responsive to the needs of children, the school, and the community.

For many ELs, improved access to quality bilingual education programs (Lindholm-Leary, 2001; J. D. Ramirez, Yuen, & Ramey, 1991) can facilitate success in school. ELs who have failed in various types of ESL and transitional bilingual education programs have made phenomenal gains in dual language programs (Thomas & Collier, 2002). In addition, native English speakers in these programs, despite learning through two languages, excel in their native English, scoring higher than peers studying only in English (Thomas & Collier, 2003).

The dual language bilingual program represents a pluralistic view of language (Christian, 1996). Administrators and teachers assume that bilingualism is cognitively, socially, and affectively beneficial both for students learning English and for those who are English dominant. Several reviews have been conducted of research and evaluation studies concerning bilingual and immersion education that identify certain pedagogical and social factors that contribute to successful language education programs (Carter & Chatfield, 1986; Skutnabb-Kangas & Cummins, 1988; Thomas & Collier, 1997b; Willig, 1985). These factors form the core criteria of successful language education, particularly dual language education programs, and serve as a framework for effective implementation and successful outcomes (Lindholm-Leary, 2001). These criteria include (a) administrative and home support, (b) school environment, (c) high-quality instructional personnel, (d) professional development, and (e) instructional design and features. Because variations in program design and delivery occur within a particular sociopolitical context, it is necessary to look at individual programs to identify factors that may contribute to the effectiveness of this model (Freeman, 1998). In particular, it is imperative to examine the factors that contribute to program sustainability in an era of increasing hostility toward bilingual programs.

Modes of Inquiry

Purpose

The purpose of this research was to explore the factors that may have contributed to the success and sustainability of one dual language program in an inner city, urban-diverse campus. The aforementioned critical features of successful dual language education programs were used as a foundation from which to begin the research.

Research Questions

1. To what extent has participation in the program contributed to students' academic outcomes?
2. What factors contributed to the sustainability of the dual language program at City Elementary?

Procedures

To address the central questions set forth in this paper, we used three sources of data: (a) site visits and non-participant observations; (b) taped and transcribed key personnel interviews; and (c) data from the fifth-grade English Texas Assessment of Knowledge and Skills (TAKS) in reading, mathematics, and science.

We utilized purposeful sampling within a case study methodology to identify key personnel for focus group and individual interviews. Informants included 10 dual language teachers and 1 campus principal involved in dual language program implementation at the K–5 grade levels. The campus principal and 2 of the 10 teachers had participated in the original discussions and decisions regarding implementation of the dual language program more than a decade ago. All were female native Spanish speakers of Mexican American descent with various years of teaching experience ranging from 1 to 19 years in bilingual education.

Data Analysis

Teacher focus groups and individual interviews were audiotaped and transcribed for analysis. Transcripts of informant interviews, field notes, and documents were manually coded to generate meaning for analysis. As delineated by Miles and Huberman (1984), the data analysis proceeded from noting patterns and themes to arriving at comparisons and contrasts to determining conceptual explanations. Triangulations of multiple data sources (e.g., district-and state-level documents) were built into data collection and analysis for the purpose of achieving trustworthiness.

To determine if students enrolled in the dual language bilingual program were meeting minimum state expectation standards, we examined standard scores on the English TAKS reading and mathematics for the fifth grade. According to state accountability guidelines, minimum expectations were equivalent to approximately 70% of the items being correct on each subject area test. Qualitative data were analyzed along descriptive methods.

Background of the Study

City Elementary School, a K–5 school with 321 students, is located in the heart of an urban city in south central Texas. In all, 85% of the student body is classified as economically disadvantaged by state and federal guidelines; 87.8% of the student population is Mexican American, and 29.4% speak Spanish as a home language. Located in a historic area of the inner city, City Elementary is in the middle of a thriving retail community and many single family homes, including a large community-based homeless shelter. The dual language program has been educating children in English and Spanish since 1995 and serves as the bilingual program for the campus. English-speaking parents have the option of placing their students in the two-way program or in an all-English classroom. Based on state accountability ratings, City Elementary has achieved a rating of Exemplary or Recognized for the past 5 years.

Findings

City Elementary School implements the 90/10 model. The program begins in pre-kindergarten and kindergarten, although some children enter the program in first grade. During the first few years, the goal is to present 90% of the content instruction in Spanish and 10% in English. The percentage of instruction provided in English and Spanish per grade level is as follows: kindergarten and first (90% Spanish and 10% English), second (80% Spanish and 20% English), third (70% Spanish and 30% English), and fourth and fifth (50% Spanish and 50% English). The 90/10 model requires an initial emphasis on the minority language because this language is less supported by the broader society and, thus, academic uses of this language are less easily acquired outside of school (Collier & Thomas, 2004). Research studies on this model have indicated high academic achievement for both groups of students (Genesee, 1987; Lindholm-Leary, 2004).

According to the campus brochure, the dual language program at City has three main goals:

1. To promote high levels of oral language proficiency and literacy in both Spanish and English.
2. To achieve proficiency in all academic subjects, meeting or exceeding district and state standards.
3. To cultivate an understanding and appreciation of other cultures and to develop positive attitudes toward fellow students, their families, and the community.

Like all dual language programs, teachers attempt to achieve balanced numbers of language-majority students and ELs in the classroom so that each group can serve as a linguistic resource and peer model for the other. Exposure to the second language is important because learners can hear the language being used in different contexts and have extensive opportunities to use the target language (de Jong, 2002; Mora, Wink, & Wink, 2001). Heterogeneous classes address the concern that some transitional bilingual programs isolate

ELs from other students. Native English speakers may enter the program at the pre-K, kindergarten, or first-grade levels. Spanish speakers, however, may be admitted at any grade level. Although the most desirable student ratio in the classroom is 50% English speakers and 50% Spanish speakers, the program can operate successfully as long as neither language group falls below 30% of the classroom population.

Student Outcomes: Academic Data

The length of time spent in a dual language bilingual program is positively correlated with student academic achievement. Thomas, Collier, and Abbott (1993) found the most powerful predictor for EL achievement to be the amount of formal schooling in the native language (L1). Significant differences in program effects become cumulatively larger as students continue past the third grade when the curriculum becomes cognitively more complex. Therefore, only scores for the fifth grade were examined. Analyses began with the 1999–2000 school year (the year the first cohort of kindergarten students entered fifth grade). The three figures reflect scores for City Elementary in the areas of English reading, mathematics, and science.

Scores for the fifth-grade TAKS test in English reading indicated that students at City Elementary consistently outscored students across the district and, with the exception of 2001, around the state (see Figure 14.1). Students exhibited high scores in the 80–100 range. This finding is impressive given that students were tested in English even though students in the dual language program did not receive formal English reading until the third grade. Consequently, Spanish did not hinder the development of English for either the English-dominant or Spanish-dominant group.

TAKS scores for English mathematics indicated that students consistently outscored their peers across the district and across the state, with an impressive

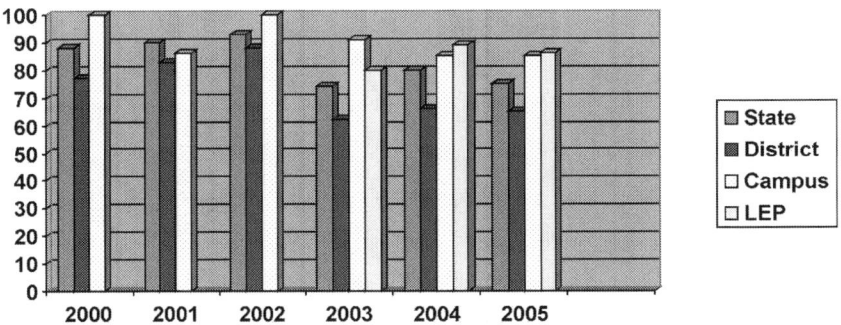

Figure 14.1 Grade 5 Texas Assessment of Knowledge and Skills: English reading. 2003 indicates a change in exam. LEP = limited English proficient.

Source: Texas Education Agency.

100% passing rate for the 2000–2002 academic years (see Figure 14.2). Similarly, the use of Spanish for instruction did not hinder the development of English for either the English-dominant or Spanish-dominant group in the dual language program.

Science scores for students at City Elementary paralleled those of mathematics and reading, reflecting a high degree of achievement (see Figure 14.3). This is significant given the context of science achievement in the state of Texas. During this 3-year period, the pattern of achievement levels across the state reflected little progress in science, as students' scores reflected 50% passing rates.

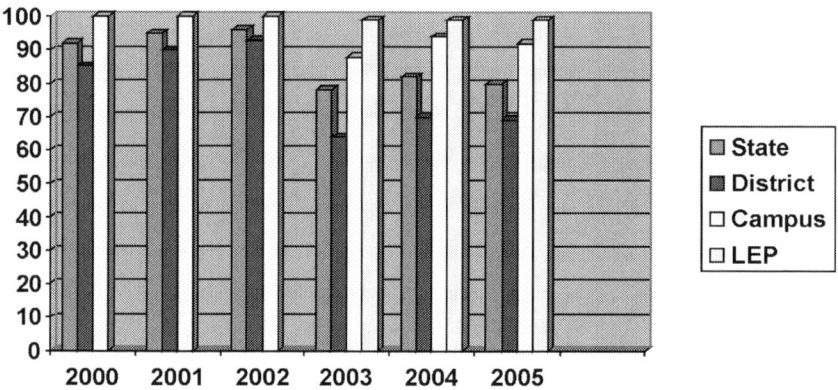

Figure 14.2 Grade 5 Texas Assessment of Knowledge and Skills: English mathematics. 2003 indicates a change in exam. LEP = limited English proficient.

Source: Texas Education Agency.

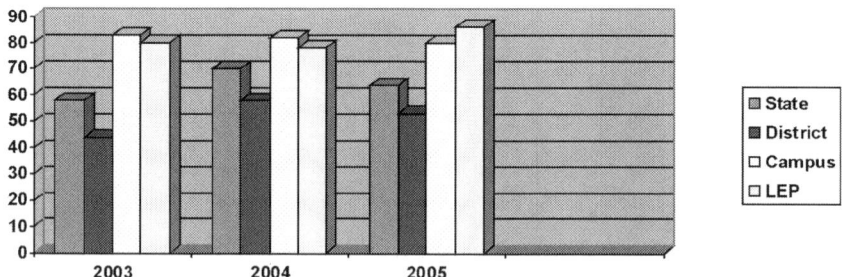

Figure 14.3 Grade 5 Texas Assessment of Knowledge and Skills: English science. 2003 indicates the first year science was assessed in Texas. LEP = limited English proficient.

Source: Texas Education Agency.

Discussion

TAKS results for reading, mathematics, and science indicate that students at City Elementary progressed in academic areas better than other students in the district and across the state based on state accountability standards. It appears that the dual language program's use of Spanish did not retard or impede children's acquisition of English or their English academic achievement. Given the gains in student achievement, our question was, what factors contributed to the success and sustainability of the dual language program at City Elementary?

Critical Features of the City Elementary Dual Language Program

Based on the dual language literature, we identified four factors that may have contributed to the success and sustainability of the dual language program at City Elementary. These are (a) pedagogical equity, (b) effective bilingual teachers, (c) active parent participation, (d) knowledgeable leadership and continuity.

Pedagogical Equity

The academic and linguistic success of Spanish-dominant children in dual language programs can be attributed to the use of the curricular mainstream taught in the child's native language as well as rigorous content standards regardless of the language of instruction. In contrast to remedial bilingual programs that offer "watered down" instruction, dual language enrichment models offer the curricular mainstream taught through two languages with rigorous content standards and high expectations. Such an environment is empowering, addressing issues of equity as well as test scores (Baker, 1996).

The dual language program at City Elementary remained true to research in second language acquisition, ensuring that students gained cognitive academic language proficiency and learning strategies in the native language before transfer to the second language was expected of them (Cummins, 1996). For example, all students were expected to read grade-level Spanish text as early as kindergarten, and math instruction, often cooperative in nature, required students to engage with one another as they worked through the learning process. In their desire to facilitate language acquisition and content area understanding, teachers made use of heterogeneously structured language pairing and peer-mediated instruction. Small student pairings allowed for the requirement of academic conversations that were important for cognitive as well as linguistic development. Thus, the potential for the cognitive benefits associated with full bilingualism were considerable.

In addition to rigorous content standards, the staff at City Elementary supported the notion of equal status of languages, as they were careful not to promote one language over the other, as suggested by one first-grade teacher:

"It is hard to elevate the Spanish language given the English influence, but we try everything we can to make students feel excited about knowing two languages." Teachers at City incorporated all forms of Spanish literature into their curriculum and lesson designs in their efforts not only to promote Spanish but also to increase the level of Spanish literacy.

The use of the first language promoted a stronger learning environment for native Spanish speakers and allowed for students to engage in the curriculum through active learning. Equally, native English speakers appreciated the value of acquiring a second language as they engaged in interactions with their Spanish-speaking classmates. According to another first-grade teacher, "English-speaking students feel proud about knowing and speaking Spanish." The positive attitude toward bilingualism was evident in teachers' classrooms as well as in the print along the hallways. Much of this print included representations of collaborative student work related to a variety of content areas and in both languages.

Effective Bilingual Teachers

According to Cloud, Genesee, and Hamayan (2000) complete understanding of the goals and philosophy of the bilingual program is crucial for teachers. Through this understanding, teachers at City Elementary believed in the value of the dual language program and displayed confidence in their instruction, as evidenced by the level of Spanish vocabulary introduced in every content area. Faculty at City Elementary believed that students must be actively engaged to learn and must take responsibility for their own learning. Consequently, teachers gathered regularly to discuss vertical alignment and were given the "green light" by their administrator to adjust the curriculum to meet the needs of their students. Teachers were constantly seeking to improve their teaching and worked together to promote a positive social and academic environment for all children, as evidenced by the following comment: "We make sure our curriculum is aligned to each grade level. If we don't have vertical alignment, that makes it much harder for us as teachers and for our students." In addition, the goal was balanced development in all three areas; the dual language teachers did not emphasize language development over academic and social development.

The dual language program followed the curriculum expectations as outlined for each grade level for the independent school district, yet teachers enhanced the curriculum via integrated instruction and project-based learning. Instructional approaches observed throughout the school to facilitate this process included hands-on mathematics and science, literature-based reading, and cooperative learning. Teachers made extensive use of heterogeneously structured groups to increase opportunities for language acquisition and understanding of content. Teachers asked children to work together on assignments that required active negotiation of meaning. Additionally, the use of manipulatives and experiential learning not only encouraged active engagement and higher order thinking skills but also provided a supportive context for integrating students of different levels of English/Spanish proficiency for content instruction.

To facilitate the academic process, teachers employed effective second language acquisition strategies to ensure comprehensible input for second language learners. Language was taught both formally and informally, and instruction was student centered. Partnering and the use of cooperative learning strategies both served as important stimuli to meet this cognitive and linguistic challenge. Teachers at City Elementary viewed all of these strategies as opportunities for meaningful language use and avenues for providing comprehensible content.

Based on our observations, the teachers at City Elementary were similar to those studied by García (1991), who identified attributes of effective teachers serving ELs. García characterized the following practices as exemplary: (a) a focus on instruction that is meaningful to the children with the use of themes as vehicles for language and literacy development, (b) opportunities for active learning through hands-on learning in collaborative groups, and (c) collaborative and cooperative interactions among the students that are heterogeneously organized. García also found that successful teachers held high expectations for their students and were receptive to suggestions and committed to culturally relevant pedagogy. All of these features were found to varying degrees at City. A quote by one second-grade teacher summed it up: "At this school, if you are not ready to work beyond your classroom, don't even come and apply." The teachers at City were committed to their students and to building partnerships with their students' parents.

Active Parent Participation

Although some parents have a limited awareness of the scope of their children's bilingual education program (Lee, 1999; Sheffer, 2003), parents whose children are enrolled in an immersion program tend to have high levels of involvement (Cloud et al., 2000). Parents at City Elementary played a critical role in program planning and sustainability. Based on parent meeting attendance, parents of students in the dual language program were committed to the bilingual and bicultural benefits afforded to their children. Parents were encouraged to volunteer in classrooms and to extend the learning process from school to home. Teachers' comments indicated that parents understood that program participation was not limited to their children but included their own involvement in all aspects of the dual language education program (Craig, 1996; Peña, 1998). Consequently, parents participated in semiannual parent meetings with the teaching staff to discuss issues and strategies for improving literacy and numeracy and agreed to meet with parents new to the program to offer support.

A final component of City Elementary's parent program was continuing education. Teachers at City Elementary offered parents classes for English and Spanish development. This allowed parents the "experience" of second language acquisition along with their children. Parents frequently approached the campus principal to discuss programmatic issues and anxiety over language development. One of the areas of concern for many parents was the decision regarding program placement. To offset this anxiety, the principal invited parents and children to observe classrooms as they made their decision regarding classroom placement. From our attendance at parent education meetings, it was clear that all key stakeholders were committed to the success of the program.

Knowledgeable Leadership and Continuity

Recent research has determined that the principal's level of commitment to a program is essential to implementing and maintaining enriched education programs such as dual language education. Principals who were well informed about the program (Aguirre-Baeza, 2001; Calderón & Carreón, 2001) fostered a proactive school climate that maintained high academic goals for all students (Lessow-Hurley, 2005; Montecel & Cortez, 2002). At City Elementary, the principal's level of knowledge about dual language programs and instructional practices for supporting ELs was evident through her discussions with parents and faculty. She remained current on dual language research, state law, and parent rights so that she could work with parents as she advocated for the program. She attended conferences with her teachers and read research articles during her own personal time. One teacher commented, ". . . She knows everything, and it's amazing to me how I might pick up a book and read it today, well, she already knows it. She already read it . . . she is very informed." As a savvy instructional leader, she maintained close ties with central office personnel to support her teachers and students. Through continued resource allocation she supported program implementation and professional development as indicated in the following statement: "Sometimes you have to be creative. You only have so much money to use for professional development. You need to figure out how to structure that." In addition, the principal worked hard to hire a qualified bilingual faculty as she developed staffing plans.

A unique but critical aspect at City Elementary School was the continuity of leadership. This principal had been instrumental in program implementation more than a decade ago. She attended numerous trainings and visited other dual language programs across the state. She also enlisted the help of local university faculty for questions and staff development. Teachers and parents had a strong voice in the option of implementation. This was not a top-down decision but a democratic process in which all involved had a say in the matter. This allowed teachers and parents to have ownership of the program, a crucial factor in establishing democratic leadership.

The consensus among teachers was that the principal's support and knowledge regarding dual language instruction had been crucial in program sustainability, as evidenced by the following comment: "It is because of her that our program has lasted for so long and been so strong." Another teacher commented, "I think that the strength of the program lies in that she's been able to provide that leadership. She has taken it from the beginning and helped nurture it, and soften rough spots that we've had." As a result, teacher turnover was low, a factor that has also facilitated the longevity of the program. A kindergarten dual language teacher referred to City's principal as a motivating force: "She expects a lot from us, and then I think that sort of turns around on us, and then we expect a lot from our parents and our kids, too."

A crucial factor in the success of this campus was the principal's desire to build leadership capacity among her teachers by allowing them to implement creative strategies in the classroom and encouraging them to take on leadership roles. She shared a democratic view of leadership as she consistently engaged teachers in the decision-making process: "Well, I can't make the decision for them. They have to decide for themselves." Each of these aspects demonstrated a sincere belief in the program and its level of effectiveness for all students and contributed strongly to the sustainability of the dual language program.

Educational Implications

The power of a dual language program is not just in its additive nature but in the pedagogical equity that exists for both language groups. It is not enough to merely adjust the language of instruction; teachers must adjust their philosophy, their teaching strategies, and their view of ELs. As teachers shift their belief about second language acquisition to one of enrichment versus one of remediation, the entire focus of the curriculum begins to shift as well. Teachers begin to evaluate how the curriculum best serves the needs of their students as they create the conditions under which children and parents can empower themselves. This cannot happen, however, without an administrator who understands the nature of bilingualism and the importance of advocacy for teachers, students, and biliteracy.

One common phrase among all interviewed was the continuing need to "fight" for the program with central office staff and some parents, as voiced by one teacher: "Although they do not inherently support the program, they do not block its implementation either." Administrators must be aware of the pitfalls and the need to support teachers at every step of the way. Otherwise, the influence of standardized testing and the desire for a quick transition to English overpowers teachers' best intentions and ultimately sabotages the program.

Conclusion

Dual language bilingual programs address several serious issues facing education in the United States. ELs are no longer segregated for any portion of the school day but are receiving the same core academic curriculum as their English-dominant peers. It is the kind of access ELs have to high-status knowledge and the quality of instructional interactions in dual language programs that defines educational quality and promotes greater equity. This is possible because effective dual language classrooms promote a high degree of student involvement (A. G. Ramirez & Stromquist, 1978; Strong, 1983), contextualize classroom discourse (Wong Fillmore & Valadez, 1986), and value students' cultural and linguistic backgrounds (García, 2005). This situation empowers native Spanish and native English speakers by promoting native Spanish and English language development as well as academic progress, and it nurtures a strong sense of self-identity (Christian, 1999; Thomas & Collier, 1999).

Changes in policies, programs, and practices that positively address the changing demographics by bringing disparate groups together are not only necessary but inevitable. The most significant reform in educational opportunities for ELs occurs when teachers and administrators at individual school sites work together at the campus level. These changes are not possible, however, without committed administrators, parents, and teachers who understand the process of bilingualism and the nature of schooling for language-minority children.

References

Aguirre-Baeza, L. (2001). Creating dual language dual language schools through effective leadership. *Educational Horizons*, 79(4), 167–170.

Alanís, I. (2000). An analysis of a Texas dual language bilingual program and its effects on linguistic and academic achievement. *Bilingual Research Journal*, 24, 225–248.

Baker, C. (1996). *Foundations of bilingual education and bilingualism* (2nd ed.). Philadelphia: Multilingual Matters.

Calderón, M., & Carreón, A. (2001). A dual language bilingual program: Promise, practice, and precautions. In R. E. Slavin & M. Calderón (Eds.), *Effective programs for Latino students* (pp. 125–170). Mahwah, NJ: Erlbaum.

Carter, T., & Chatfield, M. (1986). Effective bilingual schools: Implications for policy and practice. *American Journal of Education*, 95, 200–232.

Center for Applied Linguistics. (2007). *Directory of Two-Way Bilingual Immersion Programs in the U.S.* Retrieved July 23, 2007, from www.cal.org/twi/directory/

Christian, D. (1996). Two-way immersion education: Students learning through two languages. *The Modern Language Journal*, 80(1), 66–76.

Christian, D. (1999). Dual language bilingual education: Students learning through two languages. Educational Practice Report: 12. In *National Center for Research on Cultural Diversity and Second Language Learning*. Retrieved November 2, 2007, from http://repositories.cdlib.org/crede/ ncrcdslleducational/EPR12/

Cloud, N., Genesee, F., & Hamayan, E. (2000). *Dual language instruction: A handbook for enrichment education*. Boston: Heinle & Heinle.

Collier, V. P., & Thomas, W. P. (2004). The astounding effectiveness of dual language education for all. *NABE Journal of Research and Practice*, 2(1), 1–20.

Craig, B. A. (1996). Parental attitudes toward bilingualism in a local dual language immersion program. *Bilingual Research Journal*, 20, 383–410.

Cummins, J. (1996). *Negotiating identities: Education for empowerment in a diverse society*. Ontario: California Association for Bilingual Education.

de Jong, E. (2002). Effective bilingual education: From theory to academic achievement in a dual language bilingual program. *Bilingual Research Journal, 26*, 1–20.

Freeman, R. D. (1998). *Bilingual education and social change*. Philadelphia: Multilingual Matters.

García, E. E. (1991). Effective instruction for language minority students: The teacher. *Journal of Education, 173*, 130–141.

García, E. E. (2005). *Teaching and learning in two languages: Bilingualism and schooling in the United States*. New York: Teachers College Press.

Genesee, F. (1987). *Learning through two languages: Studies of immersion and bilingual education*. Cambridge, MA: Newbury House.

Hakuta, K., & Gould, L. (1987). Synthesis of research on bilingual education. *Educational Leadership, 44*(6), 39–45.

Hamayan, E., & Freeman, R. (Eds.). (2006). *English language learners at school: A guide for administrators*. Philadelphia: Caslon.

Lee, S. K. (1999). The linguistic minority parent's perceptions of bilingual education. *Bilingual Research Journal, 23*, 199–210.

Lessow-Hurley, J. (2005). *The foundations of dual language instruction* (4th ed.). New York: Addison Wesley Longman.

Lindholm-Leary, K. J. (2001). *Dual language education*. Clevedon, England: Multilingual Matters.

Lindholm-Leary, K. J. (2004/2005). The rich promise of two-way immersion. *Educational Leadership, 62*(4), 56–59.

Miles, M. B., & Huberman, A. M. (1984). Drawing valid meaning from qualitative data: Toward a shared craft. *Educational Researcher, 13*(5), 20–30.

Montecel, M. R., & Cortez, J. D. (2002). Successful bilingual education programs: Development and the dissemination of criteria to identify promising and exemplary practices in bilingual education at the national level. *Bilingual Research Journal, 26*, 1–21.

Mora, J., Wink, J., & Wink, D. (2001). Dueling models of dual language instruction: A critical review of the literature and program implementation guide. *Bilingual Research Journal, 25*, 417–442.

National Center for Education Statistics. (2005). *The condition of education 2005* (NCES Publication No. 2005–094). Washington, DC: U.S. Government Printing Office.

Peña, R. A. (1998). A case study of parental involvement in a conversion from transitional to dual language instruction. *Bilingual Research Journal, 22*, 237–259.

Ramirez, A. G., & Stromquist, N. P. (1978). *ESL methodology and student language learning in bilingual elementary schools*. Washington, DC: National Institute of Education. (ERIC Document Reproduction Service No. ED150879)

Ramirez, J. D., Yuen, S. D., & Ramey, D. R. (1991). *Final report: Longitudinal study of structured immersion strategy, early-exit and late-exit transitional bilingual education programs for language-minority children*. San Mateo, CA: Aguirre International.

Sheffer, C. S. (2003). Parents' lack of understanding of their children's bilingual education program. *Bilingual Research Journal, 27*, 333–341.

Skutnabb-Kangas, T., & Cummins, J. (1988). *Minority education: From shame to struggle*. Clevedon, England: Multilingual Matters.

Snow, C. E., & Hakuta, K. (1992). The costs of monolingualism. In J. Crawford (Ed.), *Language loyalties: A source book on the official English controversy* (pp. 384–394). Chicago: University of Chicago Press.

Strong, M. (1983). Social styles and the second language acquisition of Spanish-speaking kindergartners. *TESOL Quarterly, 17*(2), 241–258.

Thomas, W. P., & Collier, V. (1997a). *School effectiveness for language minority students.* Washington, DC: George Washington University, National Clearinghouse for Bilingual Education (NCBE)-Resource Collection Series.

Thomas, W. P., & Collier, V. P. (1997b). Two languages are better than one. *Educational Leadership, 55*(4), 23–26.

Thomas, W. P., & Collier, V. P. (1999). Accelerated schooling for English language learners. *Educational Leadership, 56*(7), 46–49.

Thomas, W. P., & Collier, V. P. (2002). *A national study of school effectiveness for language minority students' long-term academic achievement.* Santa Cruz, CA, and Washington, DC: Center for Research on Education, Diversity & Excellence. Retrieved September 26, 2007, from www.crede.ucsc. edu/research/llaa/l.l_final.html

Thomas, W. P., & Collier, V. P. (2003). The multiple benefits of dual language. *Educational Leadership, 61*(2), 61–64.

Thomas, W. P., Collier, V. P., & Abbott, M. (1993). Academic achievement through Japanese, Spanish, or French: The first two years of partial immersion. *Modern Languages Journal, 77*(ii), 170–179.

Willig, A. C. (1985). A meta-analysis of selected studies on the effectiveness of bilingual education. *Review of Educational Research, 55*(3), 269–317.

Wong Fillmore, L., & Valadez, C. (1986). Teaching bilingual learners. In M. C. Wittrock (Ed.), *Handbook of research on teaching* (3rd ed., pp. 648–685). New York: Macmillan.

15 Beginning With *El Barrio*
Learning From Exemplary Teachers of Latino Students

Jason G. Irizarry and John Raible

As educators and others search for remedies to address the problem of Latino student underachievement, they are often constrained by short-sighted interventions such as scripted curricula, rigid interpretations of the curriculum standards, and testing regimens to measure student performance over time (Giroux & Schmidt, 2004; Lipman, 2004; Valli & Buese, 2007). Such school-focused (rather than community-centered) interventions miss the mark when it comes to meaningfully improving the academic achievement of Latino students. The funds of knowledge (Moll et al., 1992) present in students' *barrios*, or neighborhoods, to use the Spanish phraseology for ethnic enclaves with large concentrations of Latinos, have the potential to positively inform teachers' work yet often remain untapped by schools. Consequently, the educational status of Latinos remains dire, as measured by traditional indicators of achievement such as high school completion, grade point average, and college attendance, suggesting that schools have grossly underserved this group of students.

This article documents the findings of an empirical study that examined the biographies of teachers who were identified by Latino students, parents, and community members as exemplary teachers. Our goal is to document and share the ways that the teachers developed the knowledge base that informs their practice with Latino students, thus making it more culturally responsive. In addition, we explore the implications that teachers' experiences present for the way in which institutions of higher education prepare teachers. The study was guided by two broad, overarching questions: (a) What are the experiences that exemplary teachers cite as central to their preparation to work with Latino students? and (b) How can the experiences of exemplary teachers inform teacher education efforts aimed at preparing teachers to work more effectively with Latino students?

Beginning in *El Barrio*

This study situates the academic performance of Latino students in broader discourses that go far beyond more typical deficit perspectives that tend to focus on decontextualized and oversimplified explanations of Latino underachievement, such as poverty or a lack of parental involvement, by considering additional sociocultural influences, such as the significance of family, neighborhood, race, language, and personal interactions. Moreover, rather than constructing students as the problem, we investigated the factors that contributed to the professional development of their *teachers*, and specifically those practices that allowed Latino community members to recognize certain teachers as particularly effective with their children.

Despite decades of school reform efforts aimed at improving academic outcomes for Latino youth, Latinos as a group still have alarmingly high dropout rates, and their college attendance and completion rates lag behind those of White and African American students. A number of reasons have been offered to explain the underachievement of Latinos in schools, including poverty, language barriers, cultural discontinuities between home and school, racism, and classism, among others. Based on our research with exemplary teachers, we suggest that school reform efforts will have only a minimal impact if the majority of teachers and administrators attempting to implement these programs remain culturally disconnected from the communities they serve.

The disconnect between a largely Anglo (i.e., White, U.S.-born, and monolingual English-speaking) teaching force and increasingly diverse and multilingual students can result in an interruption in the flow of accurate information from students' families and communities to their teachers. As a result, many teachers do not understand the sociocultural realities of their students' lives or the ways that schooling can help or hinder the realization of students' aspirations. In spite of this lack of information, this study points to ways in which some teachers were able to connect effectively with their Latino students despite huge obstacles.

Omnipresent structural inequalities that plague *barrio* schools that serve large percentages of students of color, including many English learners and students from lower socioeconomic strata, result often in the subsequent alienation and exclusion of students in droves. Nevertheless, some Latino students do experience academic success (Antróp-González, Vélez, & Garrett, 2005; Conchas, 2006; Gándara, 1995; Irizarry & Antróp-González, 2007). Research with Latino students suggests that academic achievement is predicated on the development of caring relationships between students and their teachers, counselors, administrators, and other school agents, which allows for more positive experiences in schools (De Jesús & Antróp-González, 2006; Flores-González, 2002; Irvine, 2003; Noddings, 1992; Rolón, 2000; Rolón-Dow, 2005). Unfortunately, Latino students are all too often confined to classrooms in which teachers cannot or will not cross cultural and linguistic boundaries to affirm their identities, implement modified teaching strategies that promote academic and personal success, or ally with diverse students and families. Although a body of literature regarding the characteristics of academically successful Latino students is emerging, there is relatively little empirical research regarding *teachers* who are especially effective with this group.

Our goal is not to overlook or ignore the powerful impact of structural factors that contribute to the suppressed performance of many Latino students and others traditionally underserved by schools. Rather, this study highlights the work of 10 exemplary teachers in the hope that their experiences may demonstrate to other educators ways in which pedagogy may become enhanced by more meaningful and sustained engagement with Latino communities. The implications of the teacher perspectives presented here suggest that it is through culturally responsive and critical pedagogical approaches that Latino students can become empowered to successfully navigate school and dismantle barriers to their success that exist in school and beyond. We call these approaches *barrio-based* because they intentionally draw on the funds of knowledge that become available when teachers immerse themselves in the social and cultural networks of their Latino students and their students' families.

We begin by offering a brief overview of the need for culturally responsive pedagogy with Latino students by presenting data regarding the demographics and characteristics of the current teaching force and the burgeoning student population, particularly in U.S. city schools. Next we provide a synopsis of the present study of exemplary teachers, including a description of the participants, the school and community settings, and the methods used in the study. Grounded in the analysis of the data, we forward and unpack the concept of *barrio-based epistemologies and ontologies*, which we define as ways of being and knowing that are informed by extended immersion in and connection to Latino cultural and linguistic communities, particularly as they are developed explicitly and leveraged to improve the education of Latino students. Finally, we discuss the implications of the findings for multicultural teacher education.

Who Will Teach Latino Children?

More than 11 million Latino children are currently enrolled in K–12 schools, representing approximately 20% of all public school students in the United States (Pew Hispanic Center, 2008). This population is expected to continue to grow at an unprecedented rate. The U.S. Census Bureau projects that by 2050 the population of school-age Latinos will soar to 28 million and surpass the number of non-Latino White students (Fry & Gonzales, 2008). It is significant that the demographics of the U.S. teaching force are not keeping pace with the "Latinization" of the school-age population. For example, 83% of all teachers are White EuroAmericans, and Latino teachers account for less than 7% of the teachers in the United States (National Center for Education Statistics, 2006). Judging by the characteristics of preservice teacher education programs, which typically attract primarily White, monocultural, English-speaking women, the demographics of the U.S. teaching force will not change significantly in the near future. Although recruiting greater numbers of Latinos into teacher education programs (and into the teaching profession more generally) is imperative, we also argue for the necessity and even desirability of *non*-Latino teachers embracing greater responsibility for the education of Latino students. In our view, teacher education can play a significant role in transforming the teaching force in ways that become more responsive to the needs of Latino communities and students. The challenges for multicultural teacher education are daunting but not insurmountable.

Preservice teacher candidates often enter teacher education programs with little experience with or knowledge of cultural differences. Research with preservice students indicates that many enter the profession believing negative stereotypes about urban children and their schools and having scant knowledge of structural barriers to student achievement such as racism and classism (Sleeter, 2001). In response, teacher education provides multicultural education courses and field experiences in diverse settings that begin to help preservice teachers to acquire the skills they will need to be successful in working with culturally diverse students. However, studies have shown that when not accompanied by an infusion of social justice perspectives throughout the teacher preparation curriculum, such diversity experiences can undermine the goals of multicultural education by reinforcing stereotypes, specifically among White preservice teachers (McDiarmid, 1990; Vavrus, 2002). Many teacher preparation programs still prepare teachers "from a monocultural perspective that eschews the pervasive impact of race, class, linguistic background, culture, gender, and ability and emphasizes instead a universal knowledge base for teaching" (Cochran-Smith, Davis, & Fries, 2004, p. 933). This knowledge base often excludes the cultural histories, "repertoires of practice" (Gutiérrez & Rogoff, 2003), and frames of reference of Latinos and other diverse communities.

Teacher preparation programs as well as district-based professional development efforts have been slow to respond to the needs of the burgeoning Latino population. Teacher educators in universities have not effectively made the case that comprehensive, culturally relevant pedagogy is an essential component of quality teacher education programs. Instead, many departments require that students enroll in only one course in multicultural education, or perhaps a single course in teaching English learners, effectively relegating multicultural education to the margins of teacher preparation programs (Nieto, 2000; Sleeter, 2001). Nearly 90% of teachers working with culturally and linguistically diverse students have not taken 8 or more hours of professional development aimed at preparing them to work effectively with this population (National Center for Education Statistics, 2002), and approximately one third of all English learner high school students nationwide had teachers who had not earned a major, minor, or certification in bilingual education or Teaching English to Speakers of Other Languages (TESOL) (Seastrom, Gruber, Henke, McGrath, & Cohen, 2002).

This under-preparation of teachers presents a significant challenge for Latino students, the largest group of English learners in P–12 schools. The question remains: If teacher education and professional development efforts are not able to adequately prepare teachers, and if so few teachers share or value the cultural heritages of Latino students, how then do teachers learn to become effective and culturally responsive to students from the largest and fastest growing yet most undereducated minority group in the United States?

Community and District Context of the Study

The urban community in which the study was conducted we refer to pseudonymously as Hoop City. The city has approximately 155,000 residents, making it the third largest city in its state (U.S. Census Bureau, 2006). According to the U.S. Census Bureau, approximately 50% of the residents identify as White, 28% as Latino (including 24% as Puerto Rican), and 20% as Black or African American. Like many other postindustrial cities, Hoop City faces a tough economic situation. The unemployment rate in this community is significantly higher than state and national averages, and those residents who do have jobs make on average $11,000 less than the national median household income. A local comparison of per capita income levels among Hoop City residents revealed racialized disparities that adversely impact Latino students and families. Latinos in Hoop City earn on average approximately $10,000 less than Whites and $5,000 less than African American residents.

Hoop City School District

The Hoop City Public Schools serve approximately 26,000 students. Latinos account for half of all of the students enrolled in the city's public schools. African Americans and Whites compose 28% and 20% of the school population, respectively. During the time of the study, the $6,692 average per-pupil expenditure for students in Hoop City fell far below the state average of $8,273. Approximately 1 in every 5 students spoke a language other than English as their primary language, and almost 3 out of every 4 students were eligible for free or reduced-fee lunch.

The high school dropout rate for the district is reported as 8%, a figure that is approximately 5% higher than the state average, and Latinos account for the largest percentage of dropouts. Although the reported district rate is alarmingly high, that figure only begins to tell a fraction of the story. The disparities between the reported dropout rate and the raw data regarding student enrollment paint contrasting pictures. An analysis of 5 years of enrollment data in Hoop City high schools suggested that more than 75% of Latino students enrolling in the ninth grade fail to progress to graduation in 4 years. It can be assumed that without any appreciable decline in the Latino population in Hoop City over this time, this alarming statistic represents casualties of the system who became dropouts or, in our view, push-outs.

Methods and Participants

This article draws on data collected as part of a larger study of exceptional teachers of Latino students (Irizarry, 2009; Irizarry & Antróp-González, 2007). The 10 participants in the study were identified as "exemplary" by members of the Hoop City Latino community using the community nomination method (Foster, 1991), an approach to sampling that entails "relying upon community members and community-sanctioned vehicles (for example, community newspapers and organizations) in order to judge people, places, and things within their own settings" (Foster, 1991, p. 147). The principal investigator (Jason G. Irizarry) approached students, parents, community-based organizations, and Latino employees of the local school district in order to solicit nominations for individuals they believed were exceptional teachers of Latino students. Teachers identified by more than one nominator were invited to participate.

This sampling method yielded a population of 10 potential participants, all of whom agreed to participate in the study. Five participants identified themselves as White, three as Latino, and two as African American. Participants ranged in age from 23 to 56, and the sample was split evenly between men and women. At the time of the study, the participants had completed anywhere from 2 to 36 years in the teaching profession. Three of the participants were elementary educators, whereas four taught in middle schools. One was an early childhood educator, and two participants had recently transitioned into positions as administrators. It is interesting that 8 of the 10 exemplary teachers lived in Hoop City in spite of the widespread poverty and related big city problems, a topic we return to later.

Data Collection and Analysis

The participants' experiences were documented using in-depth interviewing methods (Seidman, 1998). After transcribing the interviews, we analyzed the interview data by drawing on grounded theory (Glaser & Strauss, 1967; Strauss & Corbin, 1990). A thematic analysis was conducted by coding the interview data. Transcripts were analyzed for recurring themes, and theoretical implications were noted as they emerged. Data analysis was supported by additional archival research about community demographics, student achievement as reported by education reports, and other sources. In addition, in order to enhance the reliability and validity of the data, we systematically reviewed the findings for accuracy through member checking (Lincoln & Guba, 1985) with the study participants.

The Nominated Exemplary Teachers

Half of the teachers in the study could be described as "home grown," in that they were teaching in the same community in which they had been born and/or raised. The other five were "transplants," having originally come from communities other than Hoop City. In this section, we present brief profiles of the home-grown participants followed by the transplants.

Home-Grown Teachers

1. Jessica Helmsley is a White, 22-year-old middle school teacher. She grew up in Hoop City and attended public junior high and high schools in the city. Jessica worked as a substitute teacher while in college and

has been teaching full time for 2 years. She is fluent in Spanish and English and teaches in the English Language Learner Program.
2. Edward Black is a 25-year-old African American who was born and raised in Hoop City. He is a graduate of the Hoop City Public Schools and a local college in the city. Edward is currently an English teacher at a middle school in the district.
3. William Soto is a 31-year-old Puerto Rican social studies teacher in a local middle school. A product of the Hoop City Public Schools, he has been teaching for 10 years and was the department head of the bilingual program before recently accepting a position as a vice principal in his school.
4. James Talbert is 35 years old and identifies as African American. He was a teacher at a local high school for 6 years and has recently assumed an administrative position in the district. James attended Hoop City Public Schools and received his bachelor's and master's degrees from colleges in Hoop City.
5. Geraldo Peña, age 34, is a middle school teacher who identifies as Puerto Rican. He was born in the Midwest but was raised in Hoop City. He attended Hoop City Public Schools, receiving his undergraduate and graduate degrees from public institutions of higher education in the state.

Transplanted Teachers

6. Mario Cummings, age 39, is a White man who moved to Hoop City with his family in 2000. Born, raised, and educated in the Midwest, Mario taught in Colorado and Kansas before working in Hoop City Public Schools. He is a teacher at an elementary school in the Latino Northeast neighborhood.
7. Adelaide Morales was born in Puerto Rico and has been living in the contiguous United States for 15 years. She left Puerto Rico to teach in Hoop City and has been teaching in the city for 10 out of her 36 years in the profession. She is 56 years old. Adelaide is an early childhood educator in a 1-year sheltered immersion program for English learners.
8. Crystal Castro is a 30-year-old middle school teacher in the district. She identifies as Irish American. Crystal was born and raised in eastern Massachusetts and attended a state college. She is fluent in Spanish and English and has been teaching in Hoop City Public Schools for 6 years. She is married to a Puerto Rican man, hence her Spanish surname.
9. Sara Silver identifies as a White Eastern European Jew. She is 53 years old. She has been teaching for 26 years and currently works as a Collaborative Professional Development Teacher of Language Arts in an elementary school in the city.
10. June Hamilton is a 51-year-old woman who identifies as a White American. She has been teaching for 30 years and currently works with English learners in an elementary school in Hoop City. She is fluent in English and Spanish.

Findings

When we asked the teachers to identify the experiences that were most influential in preparing them to teach in urban schools, a pattern emerged to account for each teacher's effectiveness in working with Latino youth. It is significant that not one of the participants cited teacher education coursework. In fact, most teachers pointed out the shortcomings of teacher education relative to working with Latino youth. Throughout the interviews, a few teachers did acknowledge the importance of the foundation that teacher education established, equipping them, for example, with a general set of methods and important content knowledge. However, they also criticized their programs' lack of attention to working in specific contexts, such as in urban schools, or with students of culturally and linguistically diverse backgrounds. William Soto commented, "My teacher education program had one or two good courses, but most of that was generic, you know." James Talbert offered a similar critique, noting, "[In my program] we never talked about having a clue about the kids you work with. We just never talked about it."

Given the reported lack of attention to diversity in their teacher education programs, how did these teachers learn to become effective with Latino students? The consistent thread that emerged from the grounded theory analysis of the data was a pattern of sustained involvement with Latino communities both in the United States and abroad. This pattern signifies the important role played by *el barrio* in their personal and professional development. Three main findings have been organized into interrelated categories: (a) immersion experiences, (b) *barrio*–classroom connections, and (c) language and other assets. Each finding is discussed below, supported by examples from the interview data.

Finding 1: Immersion Experiences

The participants as a group centered the community in their teaching practice and cited their experiences pertaining to living with and learning from Latino families as some of the most influential factors in their development as teachers. For home-grown teachers, the process of learning about Latino culture was aided considerably by living in close proximity to Latinos in Hoop City. James Talbert, a life-long resident of Hoop City, put it succinctly: "The experience that helped the most for my work in the public schools was living in Hoop City. Working with young people, not in the classroom, but in general, doing different things to relate to the kids."

Growing up in Hoop City and attending its schools provided the home-grown teachers with a lifetime of experiences from which to draw. Despite the fact that Jessica Helmsley grew up in what she described as a "mostly White" neighborhood in Hoop City, she has learned more about the students she now serves and has refined her skills for crossing lines of cultural and linguistic difference, mainly through her participation in a religious community in which the congregation is largely Latino and the services are conducted in Spanish. Similarly, Ed Black credited growing up in a racially/ethnically mixed community with a large concentration of Latinos for shaping his perspectives about the education of Latino students and his work in Hoop City School District:

> One of the things that really helped prepare me for my work here was being a student in the Hoop City Public Schools. If I hadn't spent so much time here or in another urban city, I'd be lost. I was prepared by my life experience. I was prepared by all of the personal relationships that I had already formed prior to becoming a teacher. I grew up in housing projects across the city. My neighbors were mostly Latino and Black. We shared space and we shared culture.

James Talbert further underscored the importance of relationships with Latinos as a formidable influence on teacher preparation:

> My best friend growing up was Chico, who is Puerto Rican. I used to be at his house all the time, talking with his family, eating there, going to family functions and what have you. That was the best teacher, quite frankly. I was immersed in it; that was life for me. Since then, I have also read a lot about Latinos and specifically Puerto Ricans. I have a better understanding of their history and experiences in the United States. My teacher certification program didn't teach me any of that.

The community relationships they developed shaped the teachers as individuals. Like Ed and Jessica, William Soto continues to live in a Hoop City *barrio*. He cited the relationships he has developed over his years of living in that community as key to his work as a teacher:

> I teach and I live in the [Northeast Section]. It is a predominantly Puerto Rican community. I make enough money to live somewhere else, but I like living here. I run into my kids all the time. I am a stone's throw from the school. I live right next to the school. I see all of my kids. I know a lot of my kids' parents; we grew up together. We are friends. It's almost like I am an extension of their families when they come here.

Although not all home-grown teachers identified as Latino, some, such as Geraldo Peña, felt that their cultural identity added an important dimension:

> I'm Puerto Rican, and grew up and attended school in the city, so their culture is my culture. I live here and attend a predominantly Hispanic church. I am still very much connected to my culture and to the community.

Home-grown teachers, through their extended immersion in the community, all expressed feeling more familiar with the sociocultural and sociopolitical realities of *el barrio*. Even so, most teachers working with Latino students in urban communities like Hoop City do not live in the same communities as their students. Nevertheless, the transplanted teachers in this study have learned to be effective with Latino students. These participants explained the deliberate steps they took to seek experiences that enhanced their personal and professional development in relation to Latino students.

Some of the transplanted teachers in the study immersed themselves in the local Latino community, as did the home-grown teachers. Others found immersion experiences abroad. Transplanted teacher Mario Cummings spoke to the importance of teachers immersing themselves in their students' community, especially when the teachers themselves are not from that community:

> It's important to try to tap into the students and figure out who they were and talk to their parents and visit them in positive ways, not "your son or daughter is in trouble." Then you get kind of invited to social events, *quniceñeras* and things in the community . . . A large part is just listening to them and asking questions and talking with them, going into the neighborhood and visiting, and talking with people at [a local community-based organization].

All of the non-Latino teachers in the study made a conscious decision to cross lines of racial/ethnic and linguistic differences, and they cited these experiences as indispensable to their work with Latino students. Adelaide Morales, the only transplanted Latina teacher in the study, described the necessary work she undertook to familiarize herself with the particular sociocultural contexts of her new community and how these shaped her approaches to teaching and learning:

> I was born, raised, and educated in a rural part of Puerto Rico. Now I live in [Hoop City] right near the school. Even though most of my students are Puerto Rican, I was not prepared to work in an urban school district when I came here, but I made connections with the parents and the community, and that helped me a lot.

All of the transplanted teachers, whether they identified as Latino or not, referenced personal experiences in Latino communities as pivotal in their preparation to work with Latino youth and families. That is, they saw learning with and from the community as integral to their work in the classroom. Their dialectical relationships with students and families and their ongoing experiences in the community contributed to a knowledge base that informed their practice.

Finding 2: **Barrio–Classroom Connections**

Teachers' own immersion in the community of their students had a powerful influence on their professional preparation, as noted previously. However, perhaps even more significant is when teachers then brought that knowledge base into the classroom to make their practice more culturally responsive to the academic and personal needs of their students. The teachers all referenced examples of how they brought *el barrio* into their classrooms. For Ed Black, this involved drawing on his own personal biography to connect emotionally with his students, thus ensuring that community culture was reflected in his classroom:

> So many of my kids are so angry with their situation, with their lives in general. What I try to do is I constantly tell them about things that I had to fight through in my life. I tell them about being in a single family house, my mother not really being there the way I wanted her to be there, being on welfare, wearing the same clothes all the time. I try to show them that you can live that lifestyle and still come out relatively on top.

William Soto and Geraldo Peña described other approaches to using knowledge of the community in their classrooms. William Soto noted,

> Because of the nature of it, the classroom culture is representative of a lot of the kids. We constantly make analogies with our environments in class, and I think that connects pretty well with the culture of the students . . . Even within the city, we actually have a day where we raise the Puerto Rican flag at city hall. We talk about that and that becomes a part of the curriculum.

Reflecting on how, as a student, he had not seen his own experience mirrored in the curriculum, Geraldo Peña described the modifications he made to his teaching: "I teach history from the disenfranchised side, which includes the histories and perspectives of Latinos." Other teachers built on the human resources available in Hoop City, for example, by bringing in parents and other community members, not just to tell them about the performance of their children but to make vital contributions to the learning experiences of students. As Sara Silver noted, "Where we might be failing is in really finding ways to bring parents in." Instead of placing the blame for limited parental involvement completely on families, however, she implicated schools for their shortcomings in attracting parents and other stakeholders. Again, without exception, the teachers provided concrete examples of instances when they brought *el barrio* into the classroom. Crystal Castro explained,

> We had a high-ranking city official who is Puerto Rican come in and talk about his experience. . . . My kids need to hear about successful people.

It is rare that Puerto Rican students have Puerto Ricans as teachers. It is important to address that, but until we get more, I have to make sure my students see successful people of color.

Similarly, Adelaide Morales described her strategic use of parental involvement:

> This morning I had parents from Guatemala that came here and shared. This only happens because I have this initiative. If it depends on the principal, they never would have families in the classroom. That is not promoted. Love your students and try to get acquainted with the families, and tap into the richness that they are bringing to our school everyday.

Adelaide was willing to maintain this caring stance, even though the administration might not understand or approve.

Finding 3: Language and Other Assets

A number of originally monolingual English speakers described as highly significant their efforts to learn the language spoken by their students. June Hamilton noted,

> Studying abroad in Madrid helped me with my language acquisition. What really helped me with the Latino kids is just coming to the community and being there full time and forcing myself to speak Spanish, no matter what I sounded like. I didn't sound Puerto Rican with my college Spanish, so their lending an ear really helped me along. I have to attribute a lot to the parents and the kids; they helped me a lot.

Similarly, Sara Silver, who also spoke English as her first language, stressed the importance of learning Spanish for the impact it had on her practice:

> I thought that having a second language would be very beneficial. I used to save enough money, and every year I would take two to three weeks in a Latin American country. I still study it now to this day. I still try and get myself a little bit better . . . because I want to be able to talk with the kids. . . . It was something that I knew would make me a better teacher and a better communicator with the parents, which was very valuable. I *love* the Spanish language.

Crystal Castro and Jessica Helmsley both described how they refined their Spanish language skills and expanded their knowledge of Latino cultures through work and volunteer experiences in Latin America. Crystal Castro had worked in an orphanage in the Dominican Republic for three consecutive summers, whereas Jessica Helmsley used her vacation time to participate in church-led mission trips to various countries in South America.

Implications and Limitations

The experiences of exemplary teachers presented here, although certainly limited in terms of generalizability in part because of the study's small sample size, nevertheless stand as an important reminder of the extent to which teacher knowledge may be enriched through personal involvement in and relationships with students' families and communities. Because of the rigors of the methodology used, we remain reasonably confident that the study has adequately captured the factors that enabled this particular group of teachers to become effective with Latino students.

One limitation of the study may be the community nomination process itself. We chose not to problematize the definition of *exemplary*, making the strategic decision to trust the community's definitions instead. Although it could be argued that community members might favor bilingual teachers over monolingual English speakers (whom others could still deem "effective" based on supposedly objective measures such as student test scores or evaluations by their principals), this study intentionally privileged the assessment of Latino community members and, in effect, literally began in *el barrio*. Future research might address the community nomination process and tease out variables that could skew results in particular ways.

A related limitation is the study's sole use of qualitative methods. A mixed methods approach, which future research again could incorporate, might provide "harder" quantitative data on the students of these exemplary teachers, tracing, for instance, their attendance rates, tracing their academic progress toward graduation and college, and documenting how many may have left school when they moved on from these exemplary teachers' classrooms. Still another limitation is the study's reliance on self-disclosure, whereby it documented teachers' subjective reporting of what they believed made them effective teachers.

Having noted several research limitations, we maintain that there is much to be learned from the collective experiences that were empirically documented here. Here we present the major implications for effective pedagogy with Latino students. We highlight the emergence of what we refer to as barrio-*based epistemologies and ontologies* as particularly salient for culturally relevant pedagogy.

Eight of the 10 exemplary teachers in the study identified themselves as bilingual English–Spanish speakers. This statistic strikes us as remarkable, given that half of the cohort spoke English as their first language. These participants understood teaching as a linguistic act and therefore believed that their ability to communicate with students and families would be significantly enhanced by learning another language.

Beyond learning language in a college classroom, Sara, June, and Crystal, as well as several other participants, immersed themselves in Spanish-speaking communities, welcoming the opportunity to be taught by members of the community.

Their experiences with learning and using their second language facilitated the development of new understandings about their students and families, contributing to their knowledge base and their practice in the classroom. In addition, teachers placed value on the information networks and resources in the *barrios* from which their students came.

Both the transplanted and home-grown teachers suggested that their ability to create relationships, demonstrate care, and engage students in the teaching and learning process was strongly influenced by what they learned through their significant interactions with Latino students and families. Crystal Castro summed up this perspective, noting, "The kids taught me a lot. Parents and kids here can be great teachers."

The grounded analysis of the pattern of the ways in which *el barrio* came to be centered in exemplary teachers' professional development and classroom practice has led us to theorize a notion of barrio-*based epistemologies and ontologies*. In contrast to the external depiction of urban *barrios* as pathological, crime-ridden spaces that are devoid of educative resources, effective teachers of Latino students honor the knowledge and resources that do exist there and credit the community with significantly influencing their personal and professional development as teachers. As teachers, teacher educators, and district personnel search for ways to improve the academic achievement of Latino students, it is imperative that they include Latino communities as part of the process.

In our view, it is highly significant that the teachers nominated by community members as exceptional all described processes of becoming better teachers through close contact with the Latino community. Although the teachers in the study each had distinct experiences and unique pathways into the teaching profession, their collective experience reflects new ways of knowing and being that were shaped, in large part, by their sustained immersion in and connections to Latino communities. We refer to these as barrio-*based epistemologies and ontologies*.

Barrio-based epistemologies and ontologies are defined by several noteworthy characteristics. First, they are fundamentally *rooted in respect for students' cultures and identities*. Although the cultures and climates of many schools serving Latino students may be assimilationist, requiring that students shed aspects of their identities and adopt identities that are viewed more positively by those in power (see Valenzuela, 1999) for a chance at school success, effective teachers of Latinos in this study honored the cultures of their students and encouraged students to develop a positive sense of self, including a proud cultural self. They viewed students' cultures as worthy of inclusion in the classroom, not only as a bridge to master the mandated curriculum but also meriting their own space within the classroom. Moreover, teachers valued their students' home languages and rejected deficit perspectives and did *not* place the blame for Latino students' underachievement primarily on students and families. Effective teachers' respect for their students' cultures was further evidenced by the teachers' desire to remain connected to the Latino communities in which their students lived.

Second, *barrio*-based epistemologies are *based on the historical and contemporary sociopolitical context of the Latino community*. Latino students come from communities with distinct histories and experiences that have a direct impact on their relationships with social institutions such as schools. Teachers recognized the use of schooling as a vehicle to assimilate and subjugate Latinos (see Solís-Jordán, 1994; Spring, 2004). Effective teachers did not eschew the historical legacies of these communities and the struggles they have endured to gain access to equitable public education. Moreover, exemplary teachers did not see those struggles as part of an antiquated movement but rather as an unfinished struggle for social justice and educational equity that affected their students' lives in the present. Teachers understood their own work as part of this ongoing struggle.

Third, and related to the second characteristic, *barrio*-based epistemologies and ontologies *acknowledge the pervasiveness of race and racialization on teachers' lives and the lives of their Latino students*. Effective teachers of Latino students did not make futile attempts to become "color blind" or "culture blind" and instead acknowledged the impact of race and ethnicity on the lives of their students. Moreover, they strove to understand how their own racial/ethnic identities might impact their work with Latino students and families. Schools, like the communities in which they are located, are racialized spaces. Latinos, who can be of any race or multiple races, deal with racism as well as other forms of discrimination that impact their access to quality educational opportunities. Schools were viewed as a logical place to engage in conversations and develop the skills necessary to navigate, disrupt, and dismantle oppressive institutions that serve as gatekeepers for educational and other opportunities.

Fourth, *barrio*-based epistemologies and ontologies reflect teachers' *sustained commitment to and engagement with Latino communities*. The knowledge and skills necessary to be effective teachers of Latino students cannot be learned in one course or during a semester or two of "field placements" or practicum experiences. Rather, the experiences of teachers in the study suggest that a sustained commitment to and involvement with the community is required. This process should be about more than just schooling. Done correctly, it also has the potential to inform a process of "transracialization," through which dominant identities may be reinscribed, drawing on the knowledge base that is informed by immersion in subaltern social networks (Raible, 2005). Long-term immersion with racialized others has the potential to facilitate the emergence of new teacher identities, even though teacher may not come from the communities or racial backgrounds of their students (Raible & Irizarry, 2007).

Finally, *barrio*-based epistemologies and ontologies *inform both the pedagogy and language practices of effective teachers*. Learning multiple languages in order to connect to Latino students, families, and communities was important to the effectiveness of participants' teaching practices. Moreover, these teachers actively drew on their knowledge by translating it into liberating pedagogical practices. That is, they symbolically and virtually began their teaching in *el barrio* by centering classroom activities in the sociocultural realities of their Latino students' lives. Adelaide Morales perhaps summed it up best with her example of moving literally toward the children entrusted to her care: "Love your students and try to get acquainted with the families, and tap into the richness that they are bringing to our school everyday."

References

Antróp-González, R., Vélez, W., & Garrett, T. (2005). ¿Donde están los estudiantes puertorriqueños/os exitosos? [Where are the academically successful Puerto Rican students?]: Success factors of high-achieving Puerto Rican high school students. *Journal of Latinos & Education, 4*(2), 77–94.

Cochran-Smith, M., Davis, D., & Fries, K. (2004). Multicultural teacher education: Research, practice, and policy. In J. Banks (Ed.), *Handbook of research on multicultural education* (3rd ed.) (pp. 931–975). San Francisco: Jossey-Bass.

Conchas, G. Q. (2006). *The color of school success: Race and high-achieving urban youth.* New York: Teachers College Press.

De Jesús, A., & Antróp-González, R. (2006). Instrumental relationships and high expectations: Exploring critical care in two Latino/a community-based schools. *Intercultural Education, 17*(3), 281–299.

Flores-González, N. (2002). *School kids/street kids: Identity development in Latino students.* New York: Teachers College Press.

Foster, M. (1991). "Just got to find a way": Case studies of the lives and practice of exemplary black teachers. In M. Foster (Ed.), *Qualitative investigations into schooling* (pp. 273–309). New York: AMS Press.

Fry, R., & Gonzales, F. (2008). *One-in-five and growing fast: A profile of Hispanic public school students.* Washington, DC: Pew Hispanic Center.

Gándara, P. (1995). *Over the ivy walls: The educational mobility of low-income Chicanos.* Albany: State University of New York Press.

Giroux, H., & Schmidt, M. (2004). Closing the achievement gap: A metaphor for children left behind. *Journal of Educational Change, 5*, 213–228.

Glaser, B., & Strauss, A. (1967). *The discovery of grounded theory: Strategies for qualitative research.* Chicago: Aldine.

Gutiérrez, K. D., & Rogoff, B. (2003). Cultural ways of learning: Individual traits or repertoires of practice. *Educational Researcher, 32*(5), 19–25.

Irizarry, J. G. (2009). Representin': Drawing from urban youth culture to inform teacher preparation. *Education and Urban Society, 41*, 489–515.

Irizarry, J. G., & Antróp-González, R. (2007). RicanStructing the discourse and promoting school success: Extending a theory of CRP to DiaspoRicans. *Centro Journal of the Center for Puerto Rican Studies, 20*(2), 36–59.

Irvine, J. J. (2003). *Educating teachers for diversity: Seeing with a cultural eye.* New York: Teachers College Press.

Lincoln, Y. S., & Guba, E. (1985). *Naturalistic inquiry.* Newbury Park, CA: Sage.

Lipman, P. (2004). *High stakes education: Inequity, globalization, and urban school reform.* New York: Routledge.

McDiarmid, G. W. (1990). *What to do about difference? A study of multicultural education for teacher trainees in the Los Angeles Unified School District* (Research Report No. 90–11). East Lansing: National Center for Research on Teacher Education, Michigan State University.

Moll, L., Amanti, C., Neff, D., & Gonzalez, N. (1992). Funds of knowledge for teaching: Using a qualitative approach to connect homes and classrooms. *Theory Into Practice, 31*(2), 132–141.

National Center for Education Statistics (2002). *School and Staffing Survey 1999–2000: Overview of the data for public, private, public charter and Bureau of Indian Affairs elementary and secondary schools.* Washington, DC: U.S. Department of Education.

National Center for Education Statistics. (2006). Schools and Staffing Survey (SASS) 2003–2004, Public Teacher File. Washington, DC: U.S. Department of Education. Retrieved November 4, 2009, from http://nces.ed.gov/pubs2006/2006313.pdf

Nieto, S. (2000). Placing equity front and center: Some thoughts on transforming teaching education for a new century. *Journal of Teacher Education, 51*(3), 180–187.

Noddings, N. (1992). *The challenge to care in schools: An alternative approach to education.* New York: Teachers College Press.

Pew Hispanic Center. (2008). *U.S. population projections: 2005–2050.* Washington, DC: Author.

Raible, J. (2005). *Sharing the spotlight: The non-adopted siblings of transracial adoptees.* Unpublished doctoral dissertation, University of Massachusetts Amherst.

Raible, J., & Irizarry, J. G. (2007). Transracialized selves and the emergence of post-white teacher identities. *Race, Ethnicity, and Education, 10*(2), 177–198.

Rolón, C. (2000). Puerto Rican female narratives about self, school and success. In S. Nieto (Ed.), *Puerto Rican students in U.S. schools* (pp. 141–165). Mahwah, NJ: Erlbaum.

Rolón-Dow, R. (2005). Critical care: A color(full) analysis of care narratives in the schooling experiences of Puerto Rican girls. *American Educational Research Journal, 42*(1), 77–111.

Seastrom, M. M., Gruber, K. J., Henke, R., McGrath, D. J., & Cohen, B. A. (2002). *Qualifications of the public school teacher workforce: Prevalence of out-of-field teaching 1987–1988 to 1999–2000* (National Center for Education Statistics Publication No. 2002–603). Washington, DC: National Center for Education Statistics.

Seidman, I. (1998). *Interviewing as qualitative research: A guide for researchers in education and the social sciences.* New York: Teachers College Press.

Sleeter, C. E. (2001). Preparing teachers for culturally diverse schools: Research and the overwhelming presence of whiteness. *Journal of Teacher Education, 52*(2), 94–106.

Solís-Jordán, J. (1994). *Public school reform in Puerto Rico.* Westport, CT: Greenwood Press.

Spring, J. (2004). *Deculturalization and the struggle for equality: A brief history of the education of dominated cultures in the United States.* New York: McGraw-Hill.

Strauss, A., & Corbin, J. (1990). *Basics of qualitative research.* Newbury Park, CA: Sage.

U.S. Census Bureau. (2006). *Current Population Survey* (C2KBR-26). Washington, DC: Author.

Valenzuela, A. (1999). *Subtractive schooling: US–Mexican youth and the politics of caring.* Albany: State University of New York Press.

Valli, L., & Buese, D. (2007). The changing roles of teachers in an era of high-stakes accountability. *American Educational Research Journal, 44*, 519–558.

Vavrus, M. J. (2002). *Transforming the multicultural education of teachers.* New York: Teachers College Press.

16 The Relationship Between a College Preparation Program and At-Risk Students' College Readiness

Jennifer T. Cates and Scott E. Schaefle

There continues to be a persistent gap between groups of students who are more or less likely to attend college. Multiple factors have been identified that predict college enrollment or its absence, and these factors relate to different elements of the multistage process of enrolling in college. Among those groups of students who are least likely to attend college are Latina/o students from low-income backgrounds (Gándara & Bial, 2001; National Association for College Admissions Counseling [NACAC], 2004). In order to address this gap and distribute the benefits of higher education more broadly through society, many programs at the federal, state, and local levels have been established to support traditionally underrepresented groups of students in the pursuit of a college degree (Gándara & Bial, 2001; NACAC, 2004; Perna & Swail, 2001). Programs are often aimed at promoting academic preparedness, providing information about the path to college, and encouraging students to decide to attend college.

Gap in College Enrollment

Despite the overall rise in college enrollment rates, there are discrepancies between enrollment rates for low-and high-income students and students of different ethnic backgrounds. Latina/o students are less likely to attend college than White or African American students. In spite of increased overall Latina/o college enrollment rates over the past three decades, in 2006, 23.6% of Latinas/os aged 18–24 were enrolled in college compared with 41.0% of Whites and 32.6% of African Americans (National Center for Education Statistics [NCES], 2008). Swail, Cabrera, and Lee (2004) noted that Latinas/os enroll in 2-year or 4-year institutions at a rate of 65%, about 10% lower than for White students, and that Latina/o students enroll in 4-year colleges at about half the rate of White students. Even among high-achieving Latina/o students multiple factors often conspire to both block college enrollment and lead students to lower their educational expectations in terms of program selection (Gándara, 2005).

Low-income students are also less likely to enroll in college than higher income students (Cabrera, Burkum, & La Nasa, 2003). Even among high-ability students, low socioeconomic status (SES) students attend college at lower rates than their more well off counterparts (McDonough, 1997; Swail et al., 2004). Cabrera and La Nasa (2001) found that college-qualified students from low-SES backgrounds applied to 4-year colleges at a rate 17% lower than the national average for similarly qualified students. Latina/o students are far more likely to come from lower income families. More than half the Latina/o families studied by Swail et al. (2004) had incomes less than $25,000 compared with 23% of White students' families. Though students' low-income and ethnic minority statuses often overlap (Yampolskaya, Massey, & Greenbaum, 2006), it is clear that Latina/o students from low-income families are likely to experience low rates of college enrollment.

College-Track Course Enrollment

The problem of low enrollment is also affected by lower rates of college readiness among low-SES students (Cabrera & La Nasa, 2001). Adelman (1999) identified enrolling in advanced courses as one of the important steps in becoming qualified to attend college. Berkner and Chavez's (1997) index for college qualification includes an adjustment for rigorous coursework. According to the National Assessment of Educational Progress 2005 High School Transcript Study, Latinas/os are more likely than any other group to be enrolled in a "less than standard" curriculum. In addition to attending college at lower rates than more well-off students, lower SES students are also less likely to be enrolled in advanced math and science courses in high school (NCES, 2008). Low college enrollment rates are influenced by two factors: Latina/o and low-income students are less likely to attend college when they are qualified to do so, and they are less likely to be academically prepared to go to college.

Latina/o and low-income students are also less likely to have access to the social and cultural capital that can be crucial for college attendance. Social and cultural capital are concepts from the work of Bourdieu (1977; Bourdieu & Passeron, 1977). *Social capital* can be understood as specific knowledge or strategies that can be applied to the process that leads to college enrollment, and *cultural capital* can be understood as information about norms and expectations (Coleman, 1988; Perna, 2000b; Stanton-Salazar, 1997). The types of social and cultural capital that are most valuable for getting into college generally accrue more to upper income White students than to lower income or Latina/o students (Stanton-Salazar, 1997). For Latina/o and African American high school students, social and cultural capital may be as important as academic ability in the decision to attend a 4-year college (Perna, 2000b).

Latina/o students from low-income backgrounds often lack access to this type of capital in their families. Perna (2000a) suggested that parents' educational attainment can usefully serve as an indicator of cultural and social capital. In 2006, 32.4% of Latina/o students reported that their parents had less than a high school diploma compared with 4.0% of the White population

(NCES, 2008). Students whose parents have lower levels of educational attainment are less likely to take an advanced curriculum. In fact, 43% of the students who had a parent with less than a high school education were enrolled in a "less than standard" curriculum. In addition, students who were classified as "poor" were more likely to have parents with lower educational attainment, and 26.5% of Latina/o students were classified as poor (NCES, 2008). Latina/o students from low-income families are less likely to have parents with postsecondary education and are therefore less likely to have parents who can provide essential information and resources about the path to college.

Standardized Testing Preparation

The lack of social and cultural capital impacts another critical piece of the college admissions puzzle, standardized testing (Walpole et al., 2005). One of the first standardized tests related to college readiness that many students take is the Preliminary SAT (PSAT), which is generally taken early during the junior year and often during the freshman or sophomore year (College Board, n.d.). Taking the PSAT can serve several functions, including helping prepare students for the SAT I and II (Gándara, 2005), which are required for admission to many colleges. Berkner and Chavez (1997) reported that even college-qualified low-income Latina/o students are less likely to take college entrance exams. As with other academic areas, Latina/o students' SAT performance is often below that of White students and the student population as a whole. Gándara (2005) reported that even for the highest achieving Latina/o students, SAT scores are still lower than those of their White peers. These lower scores reflect, at least in part, a lack of access to social and cultural capital (Contreras, 2005). Walpole et al. (2005) suggested that knowledge about standardized admissions testing represents cultural capital. Therefore, student participation in the PSAT reflects some knowledge about the college admissions process. Participation reflects that students are thinking about college in their sophomore or junior year and are displaying a predisposition for college attendance. Taking the test can also be a step toward becoming prepared for the SAT I and qualifying for college admissions by succeeding on standardized tests.

College Plans and Expectations

A critical step on the path to college is that students develop expectations to go to college and plan to go to college (Cabrera & La Nasa, 2001). One of the widely cited models for understanding the college enrollment process is that proposed by Hossler and Gallagher (1987), which is composed of three stages: predisposition, search, and choice. The predisposition phase involves students making the decision to pursue a college education. In order to select college-track classes and take other steps toward qualification, students must first decide they want to go (Cabrera & La Nasa, 2000a, 2000b, 2001). Though having the predisposition to go to college is not sufficient to get a student enrolled, it is a critical first step (Perna, 2000a). Hossler, Schmit, and Vesper (1999) found that most high school students follow through with their educational plans. College plans and expectations are a crucial piece of the process of becoming qualified for college and of college outreach programs (Cabrera & La Nasa, 2001; Perna, 2002).

Elements of College Preparation Programs

Many programs exist to try to address the educational needs of less advantaged students. One of these is the GEAR UP program (Cabrera et al., 2006; NACAC, 2004; Perna, 2002; Swail, 2000). In 1998, Congress created the Gaining Early Awareness and Readiness for Undergraduate Programs (GEAR UP) program. GEAR UP differs from many other programs in that it targets entire cohorts or schools rather than individual students or specified at-risk groups. GEAR UP programs vary by site, but all are designed to be long term and address multiple areas of students' development. This approach is supported by the recognition that programs that are short term, discontinuous, and narrowly focused are not as effective as more long-term, integrated, broadly focused ones (Cabrera et al., 2006; Perna, 2002; Perna & Swail, 2001). GEAR UP programs do vary by site. The program described in the current study included 5 critical elements suggested by Perna (2002) and 11 elements identified as most important. The five elements identified as critical are goal of college attendance; college tours, visits, fairs; promoting rigorous course taking; parental involvement; and beginning by eighth grade. The 11 elements identified as most important include the five listed above and the following: college awareness or exposure, goal of promoting academic skills, parent college awareness, parent assistance with financial aid forms and involvement in student activities, SAT/ACT training, and tuition reimbursement.

The broad approach of the GEAR UP program in the current study addresses encouraging students to plan to attend college, increasing academic preparedness, and providing social and cultural capital to students and their families in order to help minimize the barriers to college attendance (Gándara & Bial, 2001; McDonough, 1997). GEAR UP attempts to provide students with access to the same kinds of social and cultural capital that are more commonly available to wealthier students (Cabrera et al., 2006).

Purpose of This Study

Although critical and important program elements have been identified, little is known about how different program elements are related to college readiness. Outcome research for college outreach programs is lacking in crucial areas. First, there is a lack of information about program outcomes. Gándara and Bial (2001) found that the lack of research about programs makes it difficult to know how effective they are, and Cabrera et al. (2006) found that there is a shortage of longitudinal research. Gándara and Bial also concluded that few programs engage in thorough evaluation and outcome studies. Similarly, Perna and Swail (2001) concluded that program evaluations are often just records of student participation. A second area for further research is the relationship between different program elements and outcomes. Most evaluations do not provide information on which program components are associated with various outcomes (Perna & Swail, 2001). Perna (2002) called for further research to better understand the effects of discrete program elements and combinations of elements. Gándara and Bial stated that one of the critical components for future research is determining which program elements are responsible for helping prepare students for postsecondary education.

After studying the relationship between GEAR UP program elements and various outcome variables, Yampolskaya et al. (2006) found that there is value in examining the amount of time spent in different program activities. They also found that students classified as "high participation" showed significant improvements in grade point average, whereas those classified as "low participation" did not. They concluded "that in order to improve academic outcomes students have to spend ample time in GEAR UP" (p. 473), and they stressed the need for additional studies to determine how program elements and amount of participation influence the students who are participating in GEAR UP programs.

The present study examines a group of students who participated in a GEAR UP program over a 6-year period, beginning in the sixth grade. We evaluate the relationship between the amount of participation in various GEAR UP program elements and components of college readiness. For the purposes of this study, we have included participation in college-track courses, PSAT participation in the sophomore or junior year, and plans and expectations to attend college as indicators of college readiness. More specifically, we investigated four questions:

1. What is the relationship between college-track course completion and hours of participation in the following program elements: tutoring, mentoring, advising, college visits, summer programs, educational field trips, and total hours?
2. What is the relationship between PSAT participation in 10th or 11th grade and hours of participation in the same program elements?
3. What program elements did students rank the highest for helping them decide to go to college?
4. What program elements correlated with students' self-reported expectations of going to college?

Method

Participants

The participants included in this study attended school in one of four school districts in a rural, western region that received GEAR UP services for a 6-year period. All four of the districts that received GEAR UP funding in this study had high percentages of students who received free and reduced-priced meals, between 70.4% and 77.8% of the students received this assistance. All participants included in this study were enrolled in one of these GEAR UP—funded schools for six of the years that the program was being administered. Only students for whom we had 6 years of participation and survey data were included.

There were a total of 187 participants. Of the participants, 131 were identified as Latina/o (70.1%), 54 were identified as White (28.9%), 1 was identified as "other" (0.5%), and there was no ethnicity information available for 1 of the participants (0.5%). Participants were 51.9% female ($n = 97$) and 47.6% male ($n = 89$), and gender information was missing for 0.5% ($n = 1$). The exact ages of the participants was not recorded, but all of the participants were in the 5th or 6th grade when data collection began, and they completed their 10th-or 11th-grade year during the final data collection period.

Data Collection

Hours of participation in program elements (tutoring, mentoring, advising, college visits, summer programs, and educational field trips and total hours) were recorded for all students over a 5-year period by the GEAR UP site directors in each of the schools. These data were then sent annually to the GEAR UP database manager for compilation and evaluation. In addition, site directors recorded the college-track classes that each student completed each year and sent this information to the database manager. The college-track courses included honors or advanced placement classes and math and science classes that are considered important for college preparation. Finally, site directors recorded whether students participated in the PSAT during their sophomore or junior year and also sent this information to the database manager.

An annual survey was administered by the database manager each spring toward the completion of the academic year. The surveys were administered by the database manager at each of the schools in the four districts. The survey included 40 items and was composed of closed questions with Likert-type response scales as well as some open questions. The questions generally inquired about students' preparation for and knowledge about college and financial aid, as well as their attitudes about GEAR UP activities and post-secondary education.

Two specific survey questions from the sixth-year survey are relevant to this study. The first survey item used in this study was the statement "I expect to go to college" followed by a response scale (1 = not at all, 2 = probably not, 3 = maybe, 4 = probably, 5 = definitely). The second survey item used in this study was the statement "The following activities helped me decide that I want to go to college." This statement was followed by 14 activities, each with a response scale below it (5 = a great deal, 4 = a lot, 3 = some, 2 = a little, 1 = none, or not applicable). The activities were visiting college campuses; participating in summer programs; tutoring; activities with mentors; talking with mentors; listening to GEAR UP guest speakers; 6th-grade trip to a 4-year university; 7th-grade trip, such as a film festival or Day of the Dead; 8th-grade career showcase at the community college; 9th-grade college planning at a 4-year college; 10th-grade speakers about college; college information booklets for each grade level; after-school GEAR UP activities, such as video production club or quilting club; and after-school homework help. All procedures for data collection and management were reviewed and approved by the university Human Subjects Review Committee.

Results

To address the first research question we conducted a standard multiple regression to determine the accuracy of the independent variables (hours of participation in tutoring, mentoring, advising, college visits, summer programs, and educational field trips and total hours) in predicting the number of college-track classes completed between Grades 7 and 11. Data screening for outliers using Mahalanobis Distance values led to the elimination of five cases. Evaluation of normality and linearity led to square root transformations of numbers of college classes, tutoring hours, college visit hours, and total participation hours; reflect and square root transformations of mentoring hours and advising hours; and natural log transformation of summer program hours. Regression results indicated that the overall model significantly predicted the number of completed college-track courses, $R^2 = .181$, R^2 adj $= .147$, $F(7, 172) = 5.42$, $p < .001$. This model accounted for 18.1% of the variance in the number of completed college-track classes. A summary of regression coefficients is presented in Table 16.1 and indicates that two of the seven variables contributed significantly to the model: advising hours and tutoring hours. Participation in advising was positively correlated with college-track

Table 16.1 Summary of Regression Coefficients for Program Elements Predicting College-Track Course Completion ($N = 180$)

Program Element	B	β	t	Bivariate r	Partial r
1. Tutoring	−.066	−.350	−2.116**	.053	−.159
2. Mentoring[a]	.037	.221	0.913	−.080	.069
3. Advising[a]	−.291	−.509	−3.810***	−.366	−.279
4. College visits	−.017	−.048	−0.422	.140	−.032
5. Summer programs	−.085	−.123	−0.949	.009	−.072
6. Educational field trips	.006	.099	0.086	−.080	.061
7. Total participation	.040	.375	0.852	.124	.065

[a] Interpretation of results should be reversed because of the use of reflection in the data transformation (Tabachnick & Fidell, 1996).

**$p < .05$.
***$p < .001$.

course completion, whereas participation in tutoring was negatively correlated with college-track course completion.

To address the second research question we conducted a discriminant analysis to determine whether six variables (hours of participation in tutoring, mentoring, advising, college visits, summer programs, and educational field trips) could predict whether students took or did not take the PSAT. Prior to analysis five outliers were identified and eliminated. Because of non-normality, square root transformations were used for tutoring, mentoring, and advising and a natural log transformation was used for summer program hours. The function that was generated was significant, $A = .840$, $\chi 2\,(6, n = 180) = 30.488, p < .001$, indicating that the function of predictors significantly differentiated between students who took the PSAT and those who did not. PSAT participation was found to account for 16.0% of the function variance. Standardized function coefficients and correlation coefficients (see Table 16.2) revealed that the variables of advising hours, summer program hours, educational field trip hours, and college campus visit hours were most associated with the function. Based upon these results, the function was labeled *Advising and College Campus Visitation*. Original classification results revealed that 92.9% of the students who did not take the PSAT were correctly classified and 29.6% of the students who took the PSAT were correctly classified. For the overall sample, 73.9% of the students were correctly classified. Cross-validation derived 72.2% accuracy for the total sample. The means of the discriminant functions were consistent with these results. Students who did not take the PSAT had a function mean of .284, and students who did take the PSAT had a function mean of -.663. These results suggest that students with less advising hours and less college visit hours (including summer program and educational field trips hours) are less likely to have taken the PSAT.

To address the third research question regarding which of 14 program elements students ranked the highest for helping them decide to go to college, we ranked the means for each item on a self-report survey in order from highest to

Table 16.2 Summary of Correlation Coefficients for Program Elements Predicting Preliminary SAT Participation ($N = 180$)

Program Element	Correlation Coefficient With Discriminant Function	Standardized Function Coefficient
1. Tutoring	−.051	0.095
2. Mentoring	−.097	−0.032
3. Advising[a]	.526	1.074
4. College visits[a]	.450	0.738
5. Summer programs[a]	.496	0.436
6. Educational field trips[a]	.454	−0.246

[a] Program elements associated with the function Advising and College Campus Visitation.

lowest scores (scores ranged from 5 = *a great deal* to 1 = *none*, and "not applicable" was a choice). Students who selected "not applicable" were excluded from the analysis. The program elements that were ranked the highest by students and had a mean higher than 3.00 (indicating that the element helped "some" in their decision to go to college) were all related to visiting college campuses or getting college planning information. These elements were visiting college campuses during the school year ($n = 180, M = 4.04, SD = 1.42$), 10th-grade speakers about college ($n = 179, M = 3.59, SD = 1.44$), college information booklets for each grade level ($n = 179, M = 3.59, SD = 1.42$), 6th-grade trip to a 4-year university ($n = 179, M = 3.46, SD = 1.54$), 9th-grade college planning at a 4-year university ($n = 179, M = 3.41, SD = 1.43$), listening to GEAR UP guest speakers ($n = 180, M = 3.31, SD = 1.41$), and 8th-grade career showcase at the community college ($n = 178, M = 3.24, SD = 1.50$). All results are reported in Table 16.3, listed from highest to lowest ranking.

Bivariate correlations were conducted to address the fourth research question regarding which of 14 program elements correlated with students' self-reported

Table 16.3 Pearson Correlations for Student Rankings of Program Activities and Self-Reported Expectations for Going to College

Ranking of Program Activities	n for correlation	M	SD	Expectations for College
1. Visiting college campuses in school year	174	4.04	1.42	.211†
2. Grade-level college information booklets	173	3.59	1.42	.280†
3. 10th-grade speakers about college	173	3.59	1.44	.282†
4. 6th-grade trip to a 4-year university	173	3.46	1.54	.223†
5. 9th-grade college planning at 4-year university	173	3.41	1.43	.074
6. Listening to GEAR UP guest speakers	174	3.31	1.41	.157**
7. 8th-grade career showcase at community college	172	3.24	1.50	.098
8. After-school homework help	172	2.92	1.50	.129
9. 7th-grade event (film festival, Day of the Dead)	172	2.88	1.57	.099
10. Activities with college mentors	172	2.75	1.51	.120
11. Talking with college mentors	173	2.69	1.50	.192**
12. Participating in summer programs at university	171	2.67	1.53	.226†
13. Tutoring	174	2.67	1.47	.101
14. After-school activities (video club, quilting club)	172	2.50	1.44	.020

Note. GEAR UP = Gaining Early Awareness and Readiness for Undergraduate Programs program.

**$p \leq .05$.
†$p \leq .005$.

expectations of going to college. Five activities had significant positive correlations with student expectations about attending college ($p \leq .001$). These activities were 10th-grade speakers about college ($n = 173, r = .282$), college information booklets for each grade level ($n = 173, r = .280$), participating in summer programs at a 4-year university ($n = 171, r = .226$), 6th-grade trip to a 4-year university ($n = 173, r = .223$), and visiting college campuses during the school year ($n = 174, r = .211$). Results are shown in Table 16.3.

Discussion

Results of the regression analysis for the first research question indicate that students who participated in more GEAR UP advising hours also completed more college-track classes. Completing college-track classes is important (Adelman, 1999; Berkner & Chavez, 1997). However, Latina/o students are less likely to be enrolled in them (NCES, 2008) and often attend schools in which opportunities for advanced classes are limited (Gándara, 2005). In addition parents' educational levels and language barriers may mean that students do not receive information about college-track curricula at home. Advising for Latina/o and/or low-income students may be an important element for improving enrollment in and completion of college-track courses. What is interesting is that tutoring hours was negatively correlated with college-track course completion. This may indicate that students receiving more tutoring are not in college-track courses or that those students in college-track courses require less academic support.

The results of the discriminant analysis for the second research question found that the program elements advising hours, summer program hours, educational field trip hours, and college campus visit hours were most associated with the function. The function, Advising and College Campus Visitation, suggests that students who are not involved in advising and college visit activities are less likely to take the PSAT. This finding is consistent with Walpole et al.'s (2005) conclusion that low-SES ethnic minority students need more and better information about standardized tests. Walpole et al. also pointed out the potential impact of the stereotype threat effect. This is the process by which an individual's belief that students like him or her do not do well on a particular task creates a self-fulfilling prophecy. Involvement in advising and visits to college campuses may help counter these perceptions. The elements of the function also represent social and cultural capital. By providing students with information about going to college as well as activities that increase familiarity with college campuses and promote educational attainment, programs increase access to capital that is more readily available in higher income schools.

The results of the third research question suggest that out of 14 program elements, those that students reported were most influential in their decision to go to college were activities designed to welcome them in a college environment and provide them with task-specific information about college and future planning. These activities include visiting college campuses, bringing speakers from colleges to their schools, and being provided with information booklets about college preparation. Again, these elements represent capital in the form of specific information and knowledge as well as socialization to higher education. In addition to impacting objective measures of college readiness, like PSAT participation and college-track course completion, students self-reported that visiting college campuses and receiving direct information about the path to college were most important in their decision to attend college.

The results of the bivariate correlation for the fourth research question reveal that as students' expectations for college attendance increase, so does the influence that they assign to various program elements. Specifically, 10th-grade speakers from college campuses and grade-level college information booklets correlated with expectations for college attendance. Both of these elements represent access to information about navigating the path to college. Participating in summer programs, the 6th-grade trip to a 4-year university, and college campus visits during the school year were also correlated with expectations. Clearly, students who expected to go to college believed that visiting college campuses influenced their decision. What is interesting is that the 6th-grade trip to visit a 4-year university was significant, whereas subsequent grade-level visits were not. This may indicate that an early visit has influence that later trips do not, which may support the importance of beginning college outreach programs prior to eighth grade (Perna, 2002).

Although the results of these research questions are interesting individually, taken together they illustrate the critical role that social and cultural capital plays in the college readiness process for Latina/o and/or low-income students. Perna (2000a) stated that "additional research is required to understand racial/ethnic group differences and the ways in which social and cultural capital influence particular stages of the process" (p. 137). For the Latina/o and/or low-income students in the present study the influence is clear. Students' participation in both the PSAT and college-track classes was related to the number of advising hours. This suggests the critical role that access to information about the college process plays for these students, particularly when one considers the relationship between the students' family backgrounds and social and cultural capital. Similarly, students reported that program activities that put them in contact with the college environment and helped make higher education more tangible were related to their expectations for obtaining a college degree. Furthermore, participation in these same activities was associated with taking the PSAT.

The present study also supports the importance of the critical elements identified by Perna (2002). Overall, the GEAR UP program in this study had a clear goal of college attendance and provided information toward this end through advising, information booklets, and guest speakers. Participation began prior to eighth grade. College tours, fairs, and visits were significant in both PSAT participation and college expectations. Advising was also related to another critical element (Adelman, 1999; Perna, 2002), enrollment in college-track classes.

Several program elements common to many college outreach programs were not found to be significantly related to college readiness as defined in this study, nor were they identified by students as influencing their decision to attend college. Tutoring (e.g., after-school homework help) and mentoring (e.g., after-school activities) were two of these elements. Though these elements may be important to other aspects of college readiness, such as academic performance, the results of this study indicate that it may be important to continue to focus on college campus visits and providing information to at-risk students. This can be challenging because these activities are often logistically difficult and expensive to carry out compared with tutoring or mentoring.

Implications and Limitations

The schools attended by many Latina/o students may offer lower quality educational options than are available to higher income White and Asian students (Gándara, 2005), making it important that traditional academic support activities (e.g., tutoring) be included in GEAR UP and other college readiness programs. However, helping students secure necessary social and cultural capital is also essential. This may become challenging in the present era of accountability and budget pressures. Therefore, continued research into the role of social and cultural capital is necessary.

Several limitations to the present study should be considered when interpreting the findings. The sample represented students for whom complete long-term data were available. There may have been differences between students who participated in the program for shorter periods of time. This study examined only a few elements of college readiness and did not include measures of academic achievement, which may be impacted more by other program elements. Although the participants in this study self-identified as Latina/o, it is known that the communities in which these GEAR UP services were administered were composed primarily of Mexican and Mexican American families. Therefore, the results of this study may not generalize to other Latina/o populations. In addition, the participants in this study were from a rural, agricultural area, and though they faced many of the same challenges as their urban peers, there may also have been important differences in what helps them prepare for college.

In addition to examining the role of social and cultural capital in college preparation for at-risk students, future research should follow students who participated in college readiness programs to learn whether they pursued their stated plans for attending college. In addition, it is important to understand whether students are able to complete their degrees once they do enroll in college and, if they do not, what barriers are preventing them from achieving their goals.

References

Adelman, C. (1999). *Answers in the toolbox: Academic intensity, attendance patterns and bachelor's degree attainment* (Document No. PLLI 1999–8021). Washington, DC: U.S. Department of Education, Office of Education Research and Improvement.

Berkner, L., & Chavez, L. (1997). *Access to postsecondary education for the 1992 high school graduates* (Publication No. 98–105). Washington, DC: National Center for Education Statistics.

Bourdieu, P. (1977). Cultural reproduction and social reproduction. In J. Karabel & A. H. Halsey (Eds.), *Power and ideology in education* (pp. 487–511). New York: Oxford University Press.

Bourdieu, P., & Passeron, J. C. (1977). *Reproduction in education, society, and culture*. Beverly Hills, CA: Sage.

Cabrera, A. F., Burkum, K. R., & La Nasa, S. M. (2003, November). *Pathways to a four-year degree: Determinants of degree completion among socioeconomically disadvantaged students*. Paper presented at the meeting of the Association for the Study of Higher Education, Portland, OR.

Cabrera, A. F., Deil-Amen, R., Prabhu, R., Terenzini, P. T., Lee, C., & Franklin, R. E. (2006). Increasing the college preparedness of at-risk students. *Journal of Latinos & Education, 5*(2), 79–97.

Cabrera, A. F., & La Nasa, S. M. (2000a). Three critical tasks America's disadvantaged face on their path to college. *New Directions for Institutional Research, 2000*(107), 23–29.

Cabrera, A. F., & La Nasa, S. M. (2000b). Understanding the college choice process. *New Directions for Institutional Research, 2000*(107), 5–22.

Cabrera, A. F., & La Nasa, S. M. (2001). On the path to college: Three critical tasks facing America's disadvantaged. *Research in Higher Education, 42*(2), 119–148.

Coleman, J. S. (1988). Social capital in the creation of human capital. *American Journal of Sociology, 94*, 95–120.

College Board. (n.d.). *Student action plans*. Retrieved July 2, 2009, from http://www.collegeboard.com/student/plan/action/index.html

Contreras, F. E. (2005). Access, achievement and social capital: Standardized exams and the Latino college-bound population. *Journal of Hispanic Higher Education, 4*, 197–214.

Gándara, P. (2005). *Fragile futures: Risk and vulnerability among Latino high achievers*. Princeton, NJ: Educational Testing Service.

Gándara, P., & Bial, D. (2001). *Paving the way to postsecondary education: K-12 intervention programs for underrepresented youth*. Washington, DC: U.S. Department of Education, National Center for Education Statistics, Office of Educational Research and Improvement.

Hossler, D., & Gallagher, K. S. (1987). Studying student college choice: A three phrase model and implications for policy makers. *College and University, 62*(3), 207–221.

Hossler, D., Schmit, J., & Vesper, M. (1999). *Going to college: How social, economic and educational factors influence the decisions students make*. Baltimore: The Johns Hopkins University Press.

McDonough, P. M. (1997). *Choosing colleges: How social class and schools structure opportunity*. Albany: State University of New York Press.

National Assessment of Educational Progress. (2005). *Results from the 2005 High School Transcript Study*. Washington, DC: Author.

National Association for College Admissions Counseling. (2004). *Short-term early college awareness: Key strategies for successful intervention and early college awareness programs*. Alexandria, VA: Author.

National Center for Education Statistics. (2008). *The condition of education*. Washington, DC: Author.

Perna, L. W. (2000a). Differences in the decision to attend college among African Americans, Hispanics and Whites. *Journal of Higher Education, 71*(2), 134–141.

Perna, L. W. (2000b). Racial and ethnic group differences in college enrollment decisions. *New Directions for Institutional Research, 2000*(107), 65–83.

Perna, L. W. (2002). Precollege outreach programs: Characteristics of programs serving historically underrepresented groups of students. *Journal of College Student Development, 43*(1), 64–83.

Perna, L. W., & Swail, W. S. (2001). Pre college outreach and early intervention. *Thought and Action, 27*, 99–110.

Stanton-Salazar, R. (1997). A social capital framework for understanding the socialization of racial minority children and youths. *Harvard Educational Review, 67*, 1–40.

Swail, W. S. (2000). Preparing America's disadvantaged for college: Programs that increase college opportunity. *New Directions for Institutional Research, 2000*(107), 85–101.

Swail, W. S., Cabrera, A. F., & Lee, C. (2004). *Latino youth and the pathway to college*. Washington, DC: Pew Hispanic Center.

Tabachnick, B. G., & Fidell, L. S. (1996). *Using multivariate statistics* (3rd ed.). New York: HarperCollins.

Walpole, M., McDonough, P. M., Bauer, C. J., Gibson, C., Kamau, K., & Toliver, R. (2005). This test is unfair: Urban African American and Latino high school students' perceptions of standardized college admissions tests. *Urban Education, 40*, 321–349.

Yampolskaya, S., Massey, O. T., & Greenbaum, P. E. (2006). At risk high school students in the "Gaining Early Awareness and Readiness Program" (GEAR UP): Academic and behavioral outcomes. *Journal of Primary Prevention, 27*, 457–475.

17 Latina/o Parent Organizing for Educational Justice

An Ethnographic Account of Community Building and Radical Healing

Kysa Nygreen

Parent organizing is often promoted as an approach to raising academic achievement in high-poverty, underserved school districts. In contrast to prevailing models of parent involvement that frame parents as subordinate partners or as the recipients of school-centered reforms, parent organizing strives to empower parents as agents of change who struggle for educational justice (e.g., Oakes & Rogers, 2006; Shirley, 1997; Warren & Mapp, 2011). In this article, I offer an ethnographic picture of parent organizing with Latina/o immigrant parents in a large, high-poverty, racially and linguistically diverse urban school district. The effort was led by a grassroots, community-based organization, Alianza, which employed a Freirean popular education approach (see Freire, 1999; Horton & Freire, 1990). This article focuses on weekly parent workshops, sponsored by Alianza, which aimed to strengthen Latina/o immigrant parents' critical consciousness of educational justice and develop advocacy skills to support school improvement. Drawing from ethnographic research at Alianza, I examine the relational processes of community building (Beckett, Glass, & Moreno, 2012) and radical healing (Ginwright, 2010) that occurred in the workshops, and consider their implications for education-based parent organizing in Latina/o communities.

This article contributes to the ethnographic literature on Latina/o parent organizing by examining how one group of Latina/o immigrant parents engaged with and sought to improve the quality of their children's education. Using the theoretical lens of *mujerismo* (Latina womanism) and the methodological tools of ethnography, I highlight Latina women's stories of feeling silenced, invalidated, or excluded in their attempts to engage with their children's schools, and I show how they participated in their own healing and empowerment through processes of community building. Although the practices I document may indeed contribute to school improvement, I contend that they are valuable for their own sake, regardless of their effects on educational outcomes. Consistent with Freire's (1999) emphasis on humanization as the fundamental purpose of liberatory education, I frame the humanizing practices of community building and healing as legitimate ends in themselves, and crucial components of parent organizing for educational justice. Attention to these themes is particularly important in organizing with Latina/o immigrant parents, given the current sociopolitical context of xenophobia, racism, and legal violence (Menjivar & Abrego, 2012). My findings suggest the need for more research that empirically examines the relational, embodied, and pedagogical dimensions of parent organizing work.

Overview: Latina/o Parent Organizing

The goal of parent organizing is to improve the quality of public schools in low-income communities by building a strong constituency of parents who are informed, organized, and mobilized to make political demands. Parent organizing takes as its starting point the assumption that low-income and racially oppressed parents are civic actors and change agents, not powerless or passive recipients of change. Using techniques adapted from Saul Alinsky's model of relational organizing in low-income neighborhoods (Alinsky, 1971), community organizers work directly with parents of children in low-performing schools to cultivate relationships, develop parents' leadership capacities, and build a mobilized political constituency to demand school change and hold educators accountable (e.g., Mediratta, Shah, & McAlister, 2009; Shirley, 1997; Warren, 2011; Warren & Mapp, 2011). The research on parent organizing has drawn attention to the important role of community-based organizations (CBOs) as spaces for mobilizing, educating, and empowering low-income and racially oppressed parents; CBOs may be perceived as safer and more welcoming spaces than schools, and are better positioned to prioritize and represent parents' interests, voices, and concerns (Lawson & Alameda-Lawson, 2012; Warren 2011). In Latina/o immigrant communities specifically, scholars have noted the significance of xenophobia, institutional racism, and fear of deportation as crucial contextual features that may be barriers to parent engagement (e.g., Dyrness, 2011; Lawson & Alameda-Lawson, 2012; Rogers, Saunders, Terriquez, & Velez, 2008). Organizing efforts in Latina/o immigrant communities must be sensitive to these realities; however, as Dyrness (2016) points out, the experience of migration and the "diasporic civic identities" of immigrant parents can also facilitate increased critical consciousness that supports an activist stance. These are some of the themes that research on Latina/o parent organizing has begun to develop and this article extends.

Much of the research on parent organizing provides descriptive accounts of organizing campaigns that demonstrate the rationale, processes, and techniques of parent organizing (e.g., Oakes & Rogers, 2006; Shirley, 1997; Warren & Mapp, 2011), while other works emphasize the potential of organizing for improving schools and raising student achievement (e.g., Mediratta, Shah, & McAlister, 2009; Warren, 2011). A third strand of research focuses more deeply on parents' *subjective* experiences of organizing rather than techniques, products, or outcomes (e.g., Beckett, Glass & Moreno, 2012; Dyrness, 2008, 2011; Lawson and Alameda-Lawson, 2012). For example, Dyrness (2011) used ethnography and participatory action research with Latina immigrant mothers to examine processes of *confianza* (trust) and healing among the women as they participated in organizing for new small schools. Beckett and colleagues (2012) examined Latina/o parent organizing efforts in two CBOs as "spaces of community building" (p. 6), aiming to develop a deeper understanding of "how people come together and build the capacity to change themselves and their environments" (p. 6). Lawson and Alameda-Lawson's study (2012) drew attention to the emotional impacts of trauma, stress, and fear of deportation on Latina/o immigrant parents, and highlighted the key role of the CBO as a safe space. These works all suggest that the relational and emotional dimensions of parent organizing work are important to the process and deserve rigorous theorizing.

In this article, I draw insights from, and seek to contribute to, this third strand of the parent organizing scholarship. Rather than focusing on the outcomes of organizing as measured by policy changes, reforms implemented, or scores raised, I use ethnography to examine the collective practices of teaching, learning, community building, and healing that occurred in one community-based effort. I position these as humanizing practices that are valuable in their own right and integral to educational justice. To advance this argument, I draw from two complementary theoretical lenses: *mujerismo* (e.g., Bryant-Davis & Comas-Diaz, 2016; Dyrness, 2008, 2011, in press) and radical healing (Ginwright, 2010). I describe these in the following section.

Theoretical Framework: *Mujerismo* and Radical Healing

Mujerismo, or Latina womanism, is a theoretical stance that begins from Latina women's concrete daily experiences, struggles, and survival strategies (Nygreen, Saba & Moreno, 2016; Bryant-Davis & Comas-Diaz, 2016; Dyrness, 2008, 2011; Dyrness, in press; Villenas, Godinez, Delgado Bernal, & Elenes, 2006). Like other racially conscious strands of feminism, *mujerismo* emphasizes intersectionality—the idea that Latina women's experiences are shaped by interlocking oppressions of race, class, gender, sexuality, language, nationality, citizenship status, and more. *Mujerismo* assumes that Latina women's positionality at the intersections of multiple oppressions shapes their consciousness in important ways. This framework honors and celebrates Latinas' resilience and survival strategies in the face of oppression; however, it also acknowledges that oppression inflicts pain, harm, and trauma—both physical and psychic—and that the work of political resistance necessarily entails a process of personal and collective healing. Where *mujerismo* differs from other strands of feminism is not so much in content but, rather, in *mujerismo*'s unique emphasis on the embodied, emotional, and spiritual dimensions of healing and wholeness (Nygreen, Saba & Moreno, 2016). As Dyrness (2008) explains, it "acknowledges the need for personal healing and for the emotional, spiritual, and relational resources that Latina women draw on in their struggles against oppression" (p. 27). A *mujerista* theoretical lens invites scholars to pay attention to whether, and how, women's whole selves—their corporal, emotional, intellectual, and spiritual selves—are present and affirmed in particular community spaces (Nygreen, Saba & Moreno, 2016). It further invites us to give central importance in our analysis to the emotional, spiritual, embodied, and relational practices of healing and community building, and to recognize these as acts of resistance (Dyrness, 2008, 2011).

The framework of *mujerismo* resonates with Shawn Ginwright's seminal work on *radical healing* in the Black community (2010). Ginwright's framework recognizes that collective and individual trauma are pervasive in Black urban communities due to high levels of social toxicity (Garbarino, 1995) and the harm inflicted by institutionalized oppression. As such, he argues, the political empowerment of Black youth necessarily requires a process of personal and collective healing, relationship and community building, and reclaiming a sense of wholeness and wellbeing. Radical healing, in this framework, is a crucial dimension of critical consciousness development. It involves recognizing how one's individual struggles are rooted in structures of oppression, reclaiming a sense of wholeness, and reimagining another kind of society where joy, wellbeing, and authentic relationships thrive. This healing process is two-fold because it involves both *individual* liberation from internalized oppression and *collective* liberation from institutionalized oppression. Ginwright's work is exemplary for its careful attention to the emotional, embodied, and spiritual dimensions of liberation work. In this sense, it is consistent with and complementary to the theoretical framework of *mujerismo*.

Research Context and Methods

The context of my study is a small, grassroots, community-based organization, Alianza, located in a large, high-poverty, racially and linguistically diverse city on the West Coast of the US. Within this larger urban context, Alianza is located in a neighborhood that is predominantly Latina/o and home to many newly arrived immigrants from Latin America. The neighborhood contains some of the poorest census tracts and lowest-performing schools in the state. Alianza self-identifies as a Freirean popular education organization (e.g., Freire, 1999; Horton & Freire, 1990), using what its leaders call "popular education methodology" in a variety of locally based projects serving the Latina/o immigrant community. At the time of my research, its array of popular education projects included a day labor center for undocumented workers, a women's empowerment collective, and a family literacy program emphasizing bilingualism and biliteracy in Spanish and English. The family literacy program included free education-based childcare for elementary-aged children during summer, after-school, and intersession periods. When parents enrolled their children in the program, they were recruited into a parent education program consisting of workshops (*talleres*) that usually met on Saturdays. These workshops aimed to deepen parents' critical consciousness of how educational inequality is shaped by larger structures of oppression, while also developing advocacy and navigational skills needed to effect school change.

I learned about Alianza from the director of its children's program, Lidia, a 1.5-generation Mexican-American who, at that time, was a recent college graduate in her early twenties. I am a White, native-born U.S. citizen and university professor with research interests in urban schooling, race, and community-based popular education. Lidia approached me as an ally as she was building and expanding Alianza's family literacy program. She gave a presentation about Alianza in my university classes, and I agreed to sponsor independent study units for undergraduates who volunteered at Alianza during the summer months. As I learned more about Alianza's work, I became interested in the practice and potential of popular education as a framework for parent empowerment and organizing. I approached Lidia with a proposal for community-engaged, ethnographic research to document Alianza's practice of popular education with Latina/o immigrant families and explore its possibilities and challenges. I hoped to contribute to Alianza as an ally and volunteer, creating a reciprocal relationship of trust with its leadership, staff, and volunteers. Through a series of discussions, we negotiated my role, and the aims and parameters of the research.

Over a two-year period, I conducted ethnographic field research on Alianza's family literacy program and parent workshops. This involved extended participant-observation in a range of spaces, including (but not limited to): staff meetings, workshops, and trainings; parent meetings, workshops, and trainings; the children's program; fundraisers; and informal or impromptu gatherings among staff and volunteers. I also conducted semi-structured interviews with eight Alianza educators (paid and volunteer) and analyzed written transcripts made at several different types of meetings. My participation in this larger research study provided important insights about Alianza and the local community that were significant in shaping the analysis in this article. However, this article draws specifically from data collected at weekly parent workshops (*talleres*) during the summer of 2009. These workshops were held on six consecutive Saturdays, for four hours each, and conducted in Spanish. The participants were 14 immigrant mothers from Mexico or Central America. Eleven of the 14 mothers completed all six workshops, receiving certificates of completion in a celebratory graduation ceremony at the end of the summer. All of the women had children in Alianza's summer program, and at one of two neighborhood public elementary schools. Their children's schools served over 700 students each, in grades K–5, with student populations well above 90% Latina/o and 70% ELL-classified at both schools.

All six parent workshops were audio recorded and transcribed verbatim, yielding approximately 20 hours of audio and hundreds of written transcript pages in Spanish. This set of written transcripts, along with ethnographic fieldnotes taken during and immediately after each four-hour workshop, constitute the primary data source used in this article. I analyzed this body of data using inductive thematic coding methods. In the initial coding stage,

I read through the entire dataset looking for recurring patterns or themes. I then grouped these themes into categories and codes, and conducted a secondary round of coding in which I looked for confirming and disconfirming examples, and refined the codes as needed. I repeated this process several times until no new codes were emerging. During the coding process, I also looked for key moments, scenes, or conversations to write up into ethnographic vignettes. Each of these moments poignantly illustrated a significant theme, but was also representative of general patterns observed across the workshop dataset and my fieldwork as a whole. Because I had verbatim transcripts of the workshops, I was able to revisit and recreate much of the activity and dialogue that occurred there. Direct quotes in this article are taken from the transcripts and translated by me; descriptions of the activities are based on my ethnographic fieldnotes.

Findings

The First Workshop

The sounds of children playing, babies fussing, and women working reverberated through the room—a spacious, open, and airy reception hall on the second floor of the United Latinos building (an ally organization from which Alianza rented space). Abundant sunlight poured in through large windows, and high ceilings with exposed pipes lent a loft-like feel to the space. It was the first day of the six-week parent workshop series. After introductions and an overview of the workshop's purpose and expectations, the 14 women were divided into three small groups. They sat around semi-circular tables, discussing with each other and drawing pictures on plain white paper. One woman worked with an infant in her arms. The co-facilitators, Pablo and Sara, circulated among the small groups taking questions and sometimes joining the conversation. The children's program director, Lidia, was in an adjacent playroom attempting to keep a half-dozen children entertained. Their voices were nonetheless audible in the workshop room, and children occasionally entered the space to visit with their mothers or run around.

Pablo called the room back together and asked for a volunteer from each group to share their work. It took several minutes for the women to reconvene in one large circle and decide who would speak. The first person to share was Eugenia, who held the picture she had drawn of the two schools she attended as a child in Mexico City. She said that her mother had moved her from one school to the other—then digressed to share about the closeness of her relationship with her mother, and how deeply she missed her now. Returning to the picture, she explained that it represented a field trip to Teotihuacan she had taken with her class as a girl. Her mother had refused to let her attend because the family could not afford the fee. But, on this occasion, Eugenia shared, a teacher had paid her way, and even purchased *artesanías* for her at the site. Eugenia remembered this as a beautiful moment, and grew emotional as she shared it. Several other women then took turns explaining their drawings. All of them shared stories of school in Mexico, Guatemala, or Honduras, and many grew emotional as they relived warm memories from a home left behind. Pablo explained that the purpose of the drawing was for participants to reflect on their own processes of learning and education, and to remember, in particular, their *positive* experiences of learning.

Pablo explained that much of our childhood learning occurs through the socialization process conveyed through games, songs, and *dichos* (brief sayings that contain a message). In addition to drawing their memories of education, each group had been asked to brainstorm a list of games, songs, or *dichos* from childhood, and they now shared the contents of their lists with the larger group. When one woman began reading her group's list of familiar songs—*El Perrito le Duele la Muela, Tres Cochinitos, La Mochila Azul, Una Rata Vieja, El Chorrito, Marieta, Las Siete ya Van a Dar, Cielito Lindo, y De Colores*—the room quickly filled with sounds of humming and singing. Pablo asked what song they wanted to sing now, and someone started to hum the opening words to *Cielito Lindo*. In no time, most of the group joined in and they sang together in unison.

Pablo kept things moving by asking the third group to share their list of games. One woman read aloud—*los encantados, el bote, las escondidas, arranca cebolla, la víbora del mar, las estatuas*—and again the room filled with laughter and the sounds of joyful recognition. Pablo asked the group to choose a game to play, and after some discussion, they decide to play *la víbora del mar* ("the sea snake"), a children's game in which participants hold hands to become a "snake" that slithers around and passes through an arch formed by two players holding hands. Several women rose from their seats and tried to get themselves into position for the game. Some were reluctant to play, appearing embarrassed as they stayed put in their chairs. Others encouraged them, and most of the group eventually stood and played along. They laughed as they reconstructed the childhood game, singing as they slithered around the room: "*a la víbora, víbora/de la mar, de la mar/por aquí pueden pasar....*" As the song ended and the women made their way back to their seats, Pablo summed up the activity by noting, "*lo que todos tienen que recordar al final es que el proceso de aprendizaje debe ser algo divertido, algo bonito*" ["the thing that you all must remember at the end of this is that learning should be a fun and a good thing"].

These opening activities exemplify Alianza's popular education approach to parent organizing. It is significant that in this, the first of a six-week workshop series on parent engagement, the very first activity was aimed at connecting the mothers to the joy and beauty of learning, and with the popular knowledge they themselves possessed, rooted in their shared experiences as transnational migrants. By starting this way, Alianza set an important tone, placing the joy of learning and the popular knowledge of learners at the center of the work. This process was emotional and several women began to cry, but they were not the embarrassed tears that we shamefully try to fight back as inappropriate displays of emotion. Instead, the space felt safe and affirming—welcoming tears and memories, stories and experiences, the participants' fully humanized selves. The small-group activity was an icebreaker and trust builder that helped the group construct a collective identity while valorizing and making visible their shared popular knowledge. This exercise also represents a practice of community building and collective memory, as the women recalled aspects of their shared histories. In summing up the activity, Pablo explained that everyone is a teacher and a learner; that each of us has important knowledge to share and to bring to the learning process. This is the essence of popular education. It was this vision of learning—as joyful, empowering, embodied, and emotional—that was to guide all of Alianza's work with parents and children that I witnessed during my fieldwork.

After a quick lunch break, the second part of the workshop featured a guest speaker from a prominent national nonprofit/advocacy organization that supports Latino/o parent involvement in schools. It was striking to see the shift in the energy between the first group activity—where the joy and love of learning were celebrated and mothers engaged in practices of collective memory, singing songs and playing a children's game, literally laughing and crying all at once—to the second portion of the workshop, where the mothers' anxieties about their children's educational progress were at the forefront. The speaker, Graciela, was Latina and a native Spanish speaker. She began her presentation by asking the group if they had discussed *No Child Left Behind* (NCLB) Seeing that the answer was no, she asked if anyone had heard of it. Eugenia volunteered that it provided funding for children to get tutoring. Graciela proceeded to explain that NCLB's purpose was to hold schools accountable for the achievement of all students. One of the mothers raised her hand and said that she was upset about a program her son was placed in. She didn't know whom to contact or how to voice her concerns at the school. She had received a form with a phone number but was reluctant to call because she did not know who would answer. Graciela moved on, saying that, because of NCLB, students in every state now had to take tests to demonstrate how well the school was teaching them. She explained the requirement to dis-aggregate test score data by race and language-learner status, and began to review various terminology from the legislation: AYP, API, Title I, and Magnet Programs—writing these up on a white board as she explained each one.

One woman raised her hand to ask how to get tutoring for her children. Another asked if tutoring had to do with AYP. Graciela reiterated that if a school failed to meet AYP for five years, the mothers could move their children to a different school. The first mother persisted in asking how to get tutoring for her children *now*. Eugenia raised her hand and said that her son, a second grader, had low scores. She had asked about moving him to another school already but they said he was not in the correct zone. More questions poured from the mothers—most of them about how to get tutoring for their kids. Graciela kept things moving, taking parents through an institutional diagram of the school system, and the responsibilities of various school committees. But the questions from the mothers didn't stop. They continued to participate: raising their hands and interrupting with questions and concerns, especially on the topic of getting tutoring for their kids. In their persistent requests for support with getting a tutor, the women were not just displaying their engagement in their children's education, but also exercising advocacy— the very sort of advocacy that is routinely practiced by upper middle-class parents on behalf of their children (Demerath, 2009; Lareau, 2003).

Contrary to dominant constructions of Latina immigrant mothers as being less involved in school-based forms of engagement, Graciela's presentation revealed that many of the workshop participants were actively engaged in their children's schooling. One woman told Graciela that she had already served on a school committee; another said that she had organized a parent group to meet in the school cafeteria. All of the participants appeared to be keenly aware of their children's educational progress and anxious to support their achievement. In the following section, I offer additional examples of women's stories about their school engagement and educational advocacy practices, and discuss the significance of these stories in the context of parent organizing. I then return to a discussion of Alianza's popular education approach, highlighting the humanizing practices of community building, collective memory, and healing.

Parent Stories of Engagement and Advocacy

As seen in Graciela's presentation, the women in the workshops often shared stories of their school engagement and educational advocacy practices. They used the space of the workshops to swap stories, teach and learn from each other, and engage in collective problem solving toward working with educational authorities. Their stories reveal a high level of interest and engagement in their children's education, but also the persistence of exclusionary practices that render their engagement invisible, ineffectual, or emotionally draining.

In one workshop, each participant was asked to share a quality that made her proud. One woman shared that she decorated a bulletin board in the entrance of her children's school, changing the display each month according to its major holidays. She was proud of this because she loved art, and felt that it demonstrated her artistic talents as well as her involvement in her kids' education. Another said that she was proud of her involvement in her daughter's education. She told a story about how she discovered that her daughter was not receiving free breakfast at school, even though she was qualified and signed up for it. Had she not been persistent in questioning her daughter about every aspect of her school day, she would not have learned about this failure to receive breakfast. When she did find out, she went to the school and corrected the error, and this gave her great pride. A third woman shared about a time she took her children to the library to read together, and when she didn't know a word in the book, she found a dictionary and looked up the meaning with her children. All three of these examples demonstrate the participants' engagement in the education of their children, and the pride they took in this aspect of their parenting.

In another workshop, a woman asked how decisions were made at the school, who chose the speakers and topics at the events meant to cater to parents, and how she might suggest a topic. Her line of questioning suggests that she had the desire to be more engaged and was actively trying to figure out how to navigate the school as an institution. A woman named Gloria responded by saying that the first step was to ask politely; the second step was to make demands. Gloria gave an example from her own children's school, where she developed a positive relationship with the principal by approaching her with good manners: "*me la hice mi aliada porque le llegué de buenas maneras. Porque si, yo pienso que si la hubiera llegado de mandato, no me habría escuchado*" ["I made her my ally because I approached her with good manners. Because if, I think that if I had approached her with demands, she wouldn't have listened to me"]. She went on to tell about how the principal had refused to make space available for a parent center; however, after making her an ally, Gloria received permission to hold parent meetings in the school cafeteria. As an added bonus, the cafeteria staff even began offering free coffee to the mothers during their meetings. Gloria's advocacy story shows that she had worked hard to forge a positive relationship with her school principal and was able to articulate her strategy for the benefit of other mothers in the room. Although her emphasis on "good manners" rather than "making demands" suggests a deferential and possibly disempowered stance in relation to school authorities, it also shows how the mothers used the space of the workshops to share experiences and strategies with each other, bringing their own knowledge and experience to bear as they supported each other in navigating educational institutions.

In another workshop, a woman named Zoraya shared her own example of educational advocacy. Zoraya's son had recently completed fifth grade, and would be starting middle school in the fall. As a parent, Zoraya could choose which middle school he would attend. However, she said that her son's fifth-grade teacher selected a school for him without communicating about it with her. Most upsetting to Zoraya was that her son had accepted this as normal and internalized the belief that she was incapable of selecting his school because she did not speak English and was not from the United States. In Zoraya's eyes, her son had lost respect for her and the school had displaced her authority as a parent. She recalled: "*mi hijo en ese entonces tenía diez años [. . .] Y ya tenía en su mente que yo no tenía derecho de decidir a que escuela iba a ir. Porque yo no era de acá. Porque yo no hablaba Inglés*" ["My son was ten years old at that time [. . .] and he already had the idea in his head that I didn't have the right to decide what school he would go to. Because I wasn't from here. Because I didn't speak English"]. Yet, rather than accepting this status degradation, Zoraya called a meeting with the teacher and principal to confront them about what happened and assert her right as a parent to make choices about her son's education. In her words:

> *Vine yo y pedí una junta, hablé con la directora y hablé con él [el maestro] y les dije, "agradezco mucho lo que han hecho por mi hijo, pero yo creo que aquí somos dos lo que estamos. . . . Soy yo la que voy a decidir. Soy la madre. Ustedes son el maestro y la escuela y todo, y ustedes tienen su poder aquí. Pero hasta aquí el poder se termina. Al salir de aquí por acá, el poder es mío y yo soy la que voy a decidir adonde va."*
>
> [I came and asked for a meeting, I talked with the principal and the teacher and I told them "thank you for all you have done for my son, but there are two of us here. . . . I am the one who is going to decide. I am the mother. You are the teacher and the school, and you have power here. But your power ends at the school walls. Leaving here, the power is mine and I am the one who is going to decide where he goes to school."]

Zoraya's story demonstrates yet another example of active parent engagement and advocacy. Zoraya confronted school authorities and advocated not only for her son, but also for her own autonomy as a parent to make choices about his education. In her telling of the story, she mentioned twice that she was a single mother (*yo era madre soltera*), suggesting that she perceived this status as further stigmatizing her in the eyes of school authorities. She seemed to feel that the school was attempting to displace her authority as a parent, and this was exacerbated by her multiple-marginalized status as an immigrant, non-English speaker, and single mother. In confronting the school authorities about this and reasserting her authority as a parent, Zoraya demonstrated strength, courage, and a sense of entitlement. But her story also reveals how even the simple act of choosing a middle school for one's child was beset with barriers caused by the "benevolent racism" of well-meaning educators (Villenas, 2001). Zoraya was made to feel that educators questioned and doubted her capacity to make routine choices about the education of her child. Although she was successful in her advocacy story, she also had to contend with feeling disrespected and stigmatized.

As these examples illustrate, the mothers in Alianza's parent workshops engaged in advocacy and often took great pride in these acts. No doubt, confronting school authorities was scary and the mothers offered their anecdotes as points of pride and a demonstration of care. Their stories challenge the deficit view of Latina/o parents as uncaring and uninvolved in their children's education. But their stories also suggest that, even when they did attempt to become more involved in site-based activities at the school, they were sometimes shut out of the process by school authorities attempting to regulate and maintain control of parent involvement. Even Gloria—who was successful in forging a positive relationship with her principal and organizing a parent center in the school cafeteria—emphasized the importance of deference and "good manners" when dealing with school authorities. This is significant because the requirement of deference reproduces the mothers' subordinate status vis-à-vis educators (Cooper, 2009).

My findings in this section are consistent with other critical scholarship on parent engagement, which has consistently documented exclusionary practices through which low-income parents and parents of color feel alienated and stigmatized by school authorities (e.g., Cooper, 2009; Crozier & Davies, 2005; Dyrness, 2011; Lareau & Horvat, 1999). These findings underscore the importance of creating parent organizing spaces that foster healing and community building. I turn to this theme in the following section.

Humanizing Practices: Community Building and Healing

While stories of advocacy and engagement were plentiful in the parent workshops, so too were stories of fear, stigma, and shame. As low-income Latina immigrant women, some of whom were undocumented, the workshop participants lived at the intersections of multiple intersecting oppressions. Alianza's popular education pedagogy created a welcoming space that fostered community building, connectedness, and solidarity, and allowed for practices of healing from the injuries of institutionalized oppression. These humanizing processes of community building and healing should be seen as political processes that constitute acts of resistance—particularly within the context of systemic stigmatization and criminalization of Latina/o immigrants (e.g., Chavez, 2008; De Genova, 2002, 2004; Menjivar & Abrego, 2012)

In one workshop, the group discussed various protests that were happening around the city for immigration reform, an end to racially motivated police violence, and rights for carwash workers. One woman said she would like to attend a protest but was afraid to because of her undocumented status. She feared she might be deported if she came into contact with police or other authorities. Another woman confessed to feeling like she didn't have a legitimate right to protest because she was an immigrant. At the same time, she recognized that these feelings could be based on ideologies perpetuated in the media:

> *La ideología, por ejemplo, donde [usted] dijo la televisión y la radio, también nos venden la idea a los, que venimos dentro país de que, por ejemplo, porque no es nuestro país aquí entonces no tenemos derecho. Y si queremos ejercer nuestro derecho pues tenemos que regresar a nuestro país. Entonces, como que vivimos con eso, o este no es mi país, tenemos entonces, no puedo hacer nada. . . .*

> ["Ideology, for example, when you said the TV and radio sell the idea to people who came to this country that, for example, because it isn't our country here then we don't have rights. And if we want to exercise our right then we have to go back to our own country. So, it's like we live with this idea that this isn't my country so I can't do anything."]

This discussion reveals how their status as immigrants could sometimes lead to feelings of unbelonging or a lack of political entitlement. Even when they recognized the source of these emotions in the media and the processes of ideological hegemony—as the previous speaker did—they did not deny the impact of these emotions on their daily lives and the ways in which fear inhibited them from engaging in more public forms of resistance and advocacy. Emotions of fear, stigma, and shame are not merely ideas that can be overcome through attitude adjustments; they are rooted in a material reality of danger for Latina/o immigrants, perpetuated through the "spectacle of enforcement" (De Genova, 2004) and the ideological processes of immigrant criminalization and stigmatization (Chavez, 2008; Menjivar & Abrego, 2012). Menjivar and Abrego (2012) describe the constant state of fear and vulnerability experienced by Latina/o immigrants as a form of "legal violence," explaining: "Legal violence is at once structural in that it is exerted without identifiable perpetrators, and it is symbolic in that it is so thoroughly imposed by the social order that it becomes normalized as part of the cognitive repertoire of those exposed" (p. 143). This hostile sociopolitical context for Latina/o immigrant parents must be taken seriously in discussions of Latina/o parent organizing and resistance, because it is a reality for many that reaches into all aspects of daily life and routines (Jeffries, 2014; Lawson & Alameda-Lawson, 2012).

In a poignant illustration of this, a mother named Nidya opened up during a discussion of ideological hegemony and anti-immigrant rhetoric to share her own personal experience of pain on this issue. In the preceding week, Nidya said, she had reached out to a neighbor who was active in the parent center at her daughter's school. Nidya wanted to discuss school topics with her and seek ways to increase her own school-based involvement. Nidya said that the woman came to her home and asked a few questions about her daughter. Upon learning that her daughter was undocumented, she told Nidya not to bother with school involvement because her daughter had no educational future. Instead, she should try to help her daughter secure decent under-the-table work because immigration reform was never going to happen. The conversation left Nidya feeling terrible but she reassured herself that, at least, her daughter did not hear it. Then, later that night, she found her daughter crying inconsolably in the bathroom because she had heard the whole thing. Nidya tried to reassure her daughter that these challenges would make her stronger and she had to maintain hope. But she confided to this group, as she broke down in tears, "*me dio mucha tristeza*" ["it made me very sad"].

The women quickly began offering words of encouragement and affirmation to Nidya. Zoraya began with a pep talk about how Nidya could do anything she wanted, and would always be the same person with the same qualities, "*con papeles o sin papeles*" ["with or without papers"]. Others jumped in to agree, talking over each other to offer reassuring words. They told her that some people are negative and not to take it personally; that every negative can be turned into a positive and every challenge into an opportunity. They assured her of her strength, and praised her for succeeding (*sobresaliendo*) and rising up (*estas yendo para arriba y arriba*). They told her that she was right to hold high expectations for her daughter and aspirations of college attendance, and that ultimately her daughter would be better off for it. At this point, Pablo interjected with a brief impromptu teaching on Paulo Freire's educational philosophy. Referring to Freire as "Don Paulo," he said:

> *Don Paulo dice que tenemos que aprender a pensar de la educación de una manera diferente. [. . .] Decía Don Paulo que una de las cosas quizás mas importantes que tenemos que hacer es sacarnos al opresor que nos metieron adentro. Entonces cuando estábamos hablando de la hegemonía y de las ideas y de como nos meten dentro de nosotros un montón de cosas así ¿verdad? Que nos hacen, que tengamos alguien adentro de nosotros que siempre nos está prohibiendo, siempre nos está limitando, y siempre nos está, como que los meten esa cosa por dentro, ¿verdad? Yo no sé si es terapia, pero creo que se necesita una revolución* [laughter from group] *como sacarnos a ese señor que nos impide ser más humanos, más solidarios, más amigos, más todas esas cosas, ¿verdad? Entonces, yo lo que creo, que es importante, es que en este proceso de crecimiento, nosotros tenemos que aprender a romper la barrera individualista de esta sociedad para crear como un proyecto de grupo en el cual nosotros nos fortaleza nosotros como persona, pero nos fortalece como un grupo social. . . .*
>
> ["Don Paulo says we have to learn how to think about education in a different way. He said one of the most important things we have to do is free ourselves from the oppressor inside us. So when we were talking about hegemony and about ideas and how they put so many things into us, right? That they make it like we have someone inside us that is always prohibiting us, always limiting us, always like putting something inside us, right? And I don't know if it's therapy, but I think we need a revolution [*laughter from group*] to free ourselves of this being that keeps us from being more human, more solidary, more friends, more all of these things, right? Then what I think is important in this process of growth, we have to learn how to break society's barrier of individualism in order to create a group project in which we strengthen ourselves as people, but also as a social group.]

Pablo's interjection was significant. First, he listened, validated, and affirmed Nidya's experience of pain and her co-participants' advice to stay strong as an individual. But he also inserted a counternarrative to the mothers' individualistic mobility narrative. Some aspects of the women's supportive pep talk had reproduced the dominant narrative of individual mobility—or "pulling oneself up by their own bootstraps"—as they suggested that Nidya, as an individual, was capable of anything if she put her mind to it and worked very hard. Of course, believing in oneself as an individual, and loving oneself, are important and should not be summarily dismissed. Moreover, nourishing self-love in a context that criminalizes and shames the undocumented is an act of resistance and an essential aspect of healing. But Pablo also made a point to insert a collectivist paradigm as a complement to the individualistic paradigm that was implied in the women's encouragement to Nidya. Referencing Paulo Freire, he suggested that what was needed was a revolution, not therapy. This comment prompted warm laughter from the group. And it conveyed the importance of solidarity, not individualism, for achieving radical social change.

In this, as in many other workshops that I observed, the women engaged in mutual support, encouragement, and affirmation. They shared intimate details of their lives, made themselves vulnerable, and sometimes cried. In other words, they were present as their fully humanized selves and were able to connect authentically with one another. Alianza's popular education approach made this wholeness and human connection possible. Through collective, relational processes of teaching, learning, and healing, the women built community and supported each other in healing the wounds of institutionalized oppression and developing self-love. In the context of hostile criminalization and dehumanization, these processes of humanization constitute acts of resistance.

Discussion

The findings summarized earlier contain two important themes. First, they reveal the variety of ways in which Alianza's workshop participants engaged in their children's education—both through school-based practices of engagement and advocacy, and home-based or community-based practices. They show that many mothers engaged in educational advocacy at their children's schools, even in the face of exclusionary practices that rendered their advocacy challenging or emotionally taxing. These findings lend additional support and a new level of detail to the already robust body of critical scholarship documenting the school engagement practices of Latina/o parents (e.g., Delgado-Gaitan, 1994; Espinoza-Herold, 2007; Moll, Amanti, Neff, & Gonzalez, 1992; Olivos, 2006; Valdes, 2003), and showing that marginalized parents often experience practices of exclusion when they attempt to participate in schools (e.g., Cooper, 2009; Crozier & Davies, 2005; Dyrness, 2011; Lareau & Horvat, 1999). My findings support this previous scholarship while providing a grounded, contextualized, nuanced analysis of Latina immigrant mothers' personal accounts and subjective experiences of exclusion. My findings also reveal the women's resilience and strength in spite of these challenges.

Second, my findings illuminate the relational processes of community building and radical healing that were central to Alianza's popular education approach. As my findings show, community building is a *pedagogical* process because teaching and learning are central and ongoing within it. It is also a *humanizing* process because it invites participants' whole selves to be present and empowers them to challenge dehumanizing social and institutional structures. In my ethnographic vignettes and analysis, I aimed to highlight the extent to which Alianza's parent workshops engaged participants' bodies and emotions—not just their intellect. Similar to the activities that Ginwright (2010) described in his work with urban African American youth, Alianza workshops included a range of "carefully choreographed experiences such as experiential activities or workshops, discussions, or visualizations [that] serve as powerful gateways to self, social, and spiritual awareness" (p. 88). This type of activity allowed for the display of "[r]aw emotion, honest dialogue, and sharing" (p. 88) among participants, thereby cultivating authentic relationships of care and contributing to the healing process. The activity in which Alianza parents recalled songs, games, and *dichos* from their home countries exemplified the use of physical activities that got people on their feet, moving around, drawing, singing, dancing, and playing. It also showcased the act of recalling and sharing collective cultural memories—a crucial practice of community building with a long history of use in liberation movements, as scholars like bell hooks (1999), Shawn Ginwright (2010), and Andrea Dyrness (2011) remind us.

It is crucial for scholars of parent organizing to understand the nature of the work that goes into building the "community" of community organizing. Warren and Mapp (2011) point out that community organizing is not just about bringing individuals together for collective action, but rather, it is about fostering a sense of collective identity by tapping into shared cultural traditions, values, and loyalties. In other words, communities do not simply exist "out there," but rather, they must be consciously constructed and sustained. This active and ongoing process is what Warren and Mapp (2011) call the "deep cultural work of organizing; that is, the effort to engage and reshape values, traditions, cultural practices, and collective identities" (p. 234). This article has provided one account of this "deep cultural work." Community building is central to parent organizing because it cultivates shared commitments and collective identities, but also because it makes space for radical healing and facilitates more public forms of resistance (Beckett et al., 2012; Dyrness, 2008, 2011; Ginwright, 2010). As such, empirical investigations of community building practices make an important contribution to the scholarship on parent organizing.

Conclusions and Implications

In this article, I argued that Alianza's parent organizing workshops were a space of community building and radical healing, and I used ethnographic vignettes to illustrate what these practices looked like. I also drew attention to the hostile sociopolitical context for Latina/o immigrant communities, showing how exclusionary practices in schools as well as legal violence (Menjivar & Abrego, 2012) across social institutions produced trauma and fear for Alianza's participants. Given this adverse and dehumanizing social context, the humanizing practices of community building and radical healing constitute forms of political resistance that warrant scholarly attention and theoretical analysis. As Ginwright notes: "Educational, social movement, and youth development research has not adequately addressed the theoretical significance of suffering or considered the empirical dimensions of healing, hope, and freedom" (p. 9). This article offers one empirical account to help build this field of scholarship. My findings also contribute to emerging scholarship on parent organizing that centers the emotional and relational aspects of organizing rather than its techniques, outcomes, and products.

One implication of my findings is that parent organizers in Latina/o immigrant communities, and scholars of parent organizing, must be conscious of the ways in which xenophobia, racism, and legal violence, as well as poverty and other social toxins (Garbarino, 1995), inflict trauma on Latina/o immigrant parents and youth in ways that profoundly shape everyday life. Parent organizing for educational justice in Latina/o immigrant communities must be cognizant of this hostile sociopolitical context, aim to create safe spaces that are welcoming of participants' fully humanized selves, and incorporate healing as a form of resistance. Community building and radical healing should be framed as legitimate goals of parent organizing and not merely as means to the goal of higher student achievement. Higher test scores in a society that continues to dehumanize, stigmatize, and inflict trauma on immigrant families would surely represent an impoverished notion of educational justice. We must continue to work toward articulating a vision of justice that includes humanization and radical healing for youth, parents, families, and communities. Parent organizing itself may have an important role to play in leading the way.

References

Alinsky, S. (1971). *Rules for radicals: A pragmatic primer for realistic radicals.* New York, NY: Random House.

Beckett, L., Glass, R., & Moreno, A. P. (2012). A pedagogy of community building: Re-imagining parent involvement and community organizing in popular education efforts. *Association of Mexican-American Educators Journal, 6*(1), 5–14.

Bryant-Davis, T., & Comas-Diaz, L. (2016). Introduction: Womanist and mujerista psychologies. In T. Bryant-Davis & L. Comas-Diaz (Eds.), *Womanist and mujerista psychologies: Voices of fire, acts of courage.* Washington, DC: American Psychological Association.

Chavez, L. (2008). *The Latino threat: Constructing immigrants, citizens, and the nation.* Stanford, CA: Stanford University Press.

Cooper, C. W. (2009). Parent involvement, African American mothers, and the politics of educational care. *Equity and Excellence in Education, 42*(4), 379–394. doi:10.1080/10665680903228389

Crozier, G., & Davies, J. (2005). Hard to reach parents or hard to reach schools: A discussion of home-school relations, with particular reference to Bangladeshi and Pakistani parents. *British Journal of Educational Research, 33*(3), 295–313. doi:10.1080/01411920701243578

De Genova, N. (2002). Migrant "illegality" and deportability in everyday life. *Annual Review of Anthropology, 31*, 419–447. doi:10.1146/annurev.anthro.31.040402.085432

De Genova, N. (2004). The legal production of Mexican/migrant illegality. *Latino Studies, 2*(2), 160–18. doi:10.1057/palgrave.lst.8600085

Delgado-Gaitan, C. (1994). Socializing young children in Mexican-American families: An intergenerational perspective. In P. M. Greenfield & R. R. Cocking (Eds.), *Cross-cultural roots of minority child development* (pp. 55–86). Hillsdale, NJ: Erlbaum.

Demerath, P. (2009). *Producing success: The culture of personal advancement in an American high school.* Chicago, IL: University of Chicago Press.

Dyrness, A. (2008). Research for change versus research as change: Lessons from a *mujerista* participatory research team. *Anthropology & Education Quarterly, 39*(1), 23–44. doi:10.1111/j.1548-1492.2008.00003.x

Dyrness, A. (2011). *Mothers united: An immigrant struggle for socially just education.* Minneapolis, MN: University of Minnesota Press.

Dyrness, A. (2016). The making of a feminist: Spaces of self-formation among Latina immigrant activists in Madrid. *Diaspora, Indigenous, and Minority Education, 10*(4), 201–214.

Espinoza-Herold, M. (2007). Stepping beyond "Sí se puede": "Dichos" as a cultural resource in mother-daughter interaction in a Latino family. *Anthropology & Education Quarterly, 38,* 260–277. doi:10.1525/aeq.2007.38.3.260

Freire, P. (1999). *Pedagogy of the oppressed.* New York, NY: Continuum.

Garbarino, J. (1995). *Raising children in a socially toxic environment.* San Francisco, CA: Jossey-Bass.

Ginwright, S. (2010). *Black youth rising: Activism and radical healing in urban America.* New York, NY: Teachers College Press.

hooks, b. (1999). *Yearning: Race, Gender, and Cultural Politics.* Boston, MA: South End Press.

Horton, M., & Freire, P. (1990). *We make the road by walking: Conversations on education and social change.* Philadelphia, PA: Temple University Press.

Jefferies, J. (2014). Fear of deportation in high school: Implications for breaking the circle of silence surrounding migration status. *Journal of Latinos and Education, 13*(4), 278–295.

Lareau, A. (2003). *Unequal childhoods: Class, race, and family life.* Berkeley, CA: University of California Press.

Lareau, A., & Horvat, E. M. (1999). Moments of social inclusion and exclusion race, class, and cultural capital in family-like relationships. *Sociology of Education, 72,* 37–53. doi:10.2307/2673185

Lawson, M. & Alameda-Lawson, T. (2012). A Case Study of School-Linked, Collective Parent Engagement. *American Educational Research Journal 49*(4), 651–684.

Mediratta, K., Shah, S., & McAlister, S. (2009). *Community Organizing for Stronger Schools: Strategies and Successes.* Cambridge, MA: Harvard University Press.

Menjivar, C., & Abrego, L. J. (2012). Legal violence: Immigration law and the lives of Central American immigrants. *American Journal of Sociology, 117*(5), 1380–1421. doi:10.1086/663575

Moll, L., Amanti, C., Neff, D., & Gonzalez, N. (1992). Funds of knowledge for teaching: Using a qualitative approach to connect homes and classrooms. *Theory into Practice, 31*(2), 132–141. doi:10.1080/00405849209543534

Nygreen, K., Saba, M., & Moreno, A. P. (2016). *Mujerista research: Integrating body, emotion, spirit, and community.* In T. Bryant-Davis & L. Comas-Diaz (Eds.), Womanist and mujerista psychologies: Voices of fire, acts of courage (pp. 41–65). Washington, DC: American Psychological Association.

Oakes, J., & Rogers, J. (2006). *Learning power: Organizing for education and justice.* New York, NY: Teachers College Press.

Olivos, E. (2006). *The power of parents: A critical perspective on bicultural parent involvement in public schools.* New York, NY: Routledge.

Rogers, J., Saunders, M., Terriquez, V., & Velez, V. (2008). Civic lessons: Public schools and the civic development of undocumented students and parents. *Northwestern Journal of Law & Social Policy*, *3*(2), 201.

Shirley, D. (1997). *Community organizing for urban school reform.* Austin, TX: University of Texas Press.

Valdes, G. (2003). *Con respeto: Bridging the distance between culturally diverse families and schools: An ethnographic portrait.* New York, NY: Teachers College Press.

Villenas, S. (2001). Latina mothers and small town racisms: Creating narratives of dignity and moral education in North Carolina. *Anthropology and Education Quarterly*, *32*(1), 3–28. doi:10.1525/aeq.2001.32.1.3

Villenas, S., Godinez, F. E., Delgado Bernal, D., & Elenes, C. A. (2006). Chicanas/Latinas building bridges: An introduction. In D. Delgado Bernal, C. A. Elenes, F. E. Godinez, & S. Villenas (Eds.), *Chicana/Latina education in everyday life: Feminist perspectives on pedagogy and epistemology* (pp. 1–10). Albany, NY: State University of New York Press.

Warren, M. (2011). Building a Political Constituency for Urban School Reform. *Urban Education* 6(3): 484–512.

Warren, M., & Mapp, K. (2011). *A match on dry grass: Community organizing as a catalyst for school reform.* New York, NY: Oxford University Press.

18 Dream Big

Exploring Empowering Processes of DREAM Act Advocacy in a Focal State

Brad Forenza and Carolina Mendonca

Literature Review

Background

There are approximately 11 million undocumented immigrants living in the United States (Diaz-Strong, Gomez, Luna-Duarte, & Meiners, 2011). Roughly 5.5 million children reside in households with an undocumented individual (Kim, 2013) and 1.7 million children are undocumented themselves (Diaz-Strong et al., 2011; Ellis & Chen, 2013). An undocumented immigrant is defined as having been born outside of the United States and having not been granted permanent residency, long-term residency, or a work permit (Nienhusser, 2013). Divisive, political rhetoric often frames these individuals as prone to violence and the exploitation of community resources, such as public benefits and job opportunities (Gonzalez, Stein, Prandoni, Eades, & Magalhaes, 2015; Levin, 2013). Undocumented individuals from myriad countries live in the United States, though the pervasive stereotype of an "illegal immigrant" is largely conceptualized as Latino (Saldivar, 2015).

Latinos are the fastest growing immigrant group in the United States (Levin, 2013). In fact, the United States ranks third—behind Mexico and Colombia—as the country with the largest Latino population (Valdez, 2011). According to Gonzalez et al. (2015), one-third of U.S. Latinos are undocumented. Lack of citizenship or residency status poses unique acculturation challenges to both undocumented parents and children alike (see Ishizawa, 2015). Discrimination is common. While parents must concern themselves with finding food, shelter, and work, the undocumented child's mental health needs may be at risk (Perez, Cortes, Ramos, & Coronado, 2010). If appropriate coping skills are not developed, adjustment issues will arise (Ellis & Chen, 2013).

Because of its implication that undocumented individuals are de-facto criminals, the term "illegal immigrant" is assumed to stigmatize undocumented Latinos (Perez et al., 2010; Storlie & Jach, 2012). Stigma happens when an individual feels—or is made to feel—like his or her identity is somehow discredited or sub-par (Goffman, 1963). The stigmatized immigrant is prone to psychological stress and shame (Ellis & Chen, 2013). For example, Jefferies (2014) detailed the inescapable stress that many undocumented students feel (fear of deportation) in their formative, high school years. In the Perception of Undocumented Status and Possible Selves Among Latino/a Youth study, participants used words such as "crushed, disappointing, hard, struggle, and discouraged" to describe perceptions of what lie ahead for other undocumented youth (Gonzalez et al., 2015, p. 1205). These perceptions may be exacerbated when the stigmatized identities of otherwise diligent and applied undocumented students interface with potentially racist educational systems (see Taylor & Fernandez-Bergersen, 2015).

In the 1982 Supreme Court case of *Plyler v. Doe*, the Court ruled that all children—regardless of immigration status—had a right to free, public education from kindergarten through twelfth grade (*Plyler v. Doe*, 1982). Approximately 65,000 undocumented students earn high school diplomas annually (Diaz-Strong et al., 2011; Kim, 2013); thereafter, approximately 7,000–13,000 (or 11–20%) pursue post-secondary education (Diaz-Strong et al., 2011). Post-secondary education is abundantly necessary in the competitive U.S. workforce, as it proves to be a springboard to desirable employment, higher lifetime income, and a host of positive outcomes (Liu, 2011). Yet many U.S. Latinos perceive post-secondary education as unaffordable (Berg & Tollefson, 2014; Sanchez, Usinger, & Thornton, 2015). For undocumented Latinos, college affordability—compounded by residency status—is a paramount concern. In a study of Mexican-Americans and undocumented Mexicans, Covarrubias and Lara (2014) found that Mexican-Americans pursued post-secondary education at noticeably higher rates when compared to their undocumented contemporaries. According to Nienhusser (2013), the disempowering realization that an undocumented young person may not be able to pursue post-secondary education can happen as early as seventh grade, when young people start contemplating what they might do after high school. As middle school and high school commence—and undocumented students interface with school administrators who historically lack capacity to extend targeted information to them (see Erisman & Looney, 2007; Gonzalez, 2015)—these disempowering realizations become impenetrable.

Because post-secondary affordability is a perennial concern for undocumented students—and because out-of-state tuition costs can exceed in-state costs by 140%—In-state Resident Tuition (IRT) policies have proven useful for making in-state college tuition affordable and accessible to undocumented students (Potochnik, 2014). Potochnik (2014) reports that IRT policies have increased the enrollment rates of undocumented students in college, while also reducing the high school dropout rate among the same population. In spite of this welcome, inclusive IRT trend, the National Council of State Legislatures (2014) reports that some states (Arizona, Georgia, and Indiana) have expressly barred undocumented students from receiving in-state tuition, while other states (Alabama and South Carolina) have unilaterally prohibited undocumented students from attending public institutions of higher education. At the federal level, Congress has failed to pass the Development, Relief, and Education for Alien Minors (DREAM) Act. If passed, the federal DREAM Act would extend conditional residency to undocumented young people as they serve in the U.S. military or obtain *at least* an associate's degree (Batalova & McHugh, 2010; Ortega, 2011).

Educational assistance and residency status is a controversial intersection for federal lawmakers (Covarrubias & Lara, 2014; Nienhusser, 2013). In the absence of a federal DREAM Act, token states have enacted permissive local policies. California and Texas were the first to enact IRT laws in 2001; since then, at least 16 states—including the focal state for this research—have followed suit (NCSL, 2014). Local IRT policies/local DREAM Acts are assumed positive for the culture and economy of the enabling state, but also empowering for the undocumented youth that benefit from them. While some outcomes-oriented research has examined local IRT/DREAM Act performance (see Potochnick, 2014), less research has examined the empowering processes that undocumented young people may experience when advocating for such a change on their own behalf, and on behalf of other undocumented students.

Theoretical Framework

Empowerment—gaining control of, or affecting change in, the socio-political environment—refers to one's behavioral, relational, cognitive (interactional), and emotional (intrapersonal) interactions with macro forces (Christens, 2012; Speer, 2000; Zimmerman, Israel, Schultz, & Checkoway, 1992). Scholastically, this type of empowerment—empowerment as an individual outcome—is referred to as "psychological empowerment." Yet the empowerment literature assumes that there are individual processes that one encounters en route to psychological empowerment. Specifically, organizational empowerment refers to "organizational efforts that generate psychological empowerment among members and organizational effectiveness needed for goal achievement" (Peterson & Zimmerman, 2004, p. 130). Intra-organizational empowerment, which happens in a focal organization, associational membership, organized movement, political campaign, etc., is comprised of four dimensions: shared beliefs, opportunity role structure, social support, and leadership. In their seminal article, Maton and Salem (1995) operationalize these dimensions as follows: shared beliefs refers to group based belief systems that support members in achieving individual goals; opportunity role structure refers to the ability of individual members to fill organizational niches; social support refers to the social bonds within an organization; and leadership refers to the direct action of an organizational leader, or that leader's indirect effect on the organization.

Numerous dimensions of oppression (see Windsor, Benoit, & Dunlap, 2010) impose themselves on undocumented youth. As these youth contemplate their post-secondary education and other life prospects, they will inevitably place themselves in a broader societal context (see Erikson, 1968).

Research (see Freire, 1973) assumes that undocumented youth will inevitably question systemic injustices like post-secondary accessibility and affordability, a developmental turning point known as critical consciousness. Critical consciousness encourages individuals to understand, analyze, and take action against oppressive, disempowering forces. Confronting a problem in the socio-political environment is assumed to yield a host of positive outcomes, including civic literacy and social capital (Putnam, 2000); though, in the highest order, activism can yield psychological empowerment (see Forenza & Germak, 2015). Less is known, however, about the processes that an individual—specifically an undocumented young person—will experience en route to psychological empowerment. This research utilized an organizational empowerment framework to answer the question: What are the empowering processes of DREAM Act advocacy among undocumented students in a focal state?

Methods

Research Setting and Sample

"DREAM Big" (a pseudonym) was an activist organization advocating for in-state college tuition and financial aid benefits for undocumented students in a single Northeastern state. Throughout the focal state's 2012–2013 legislative session, DREAM Big was successful at navigating a local version of the DREAM Act through the state's Democratically controlled legislature and onto the desk of its Republican governor. The statewide act was signed into law in December 2013 and was implemented almost immediately (in January 2014), allowing in-state tuition rates for undocumented students. Soon thereafter, DREAM Big disbanded and a new movement-based organization ("Immigration Liberation," also a pseudonym) was formed.

In an effort to explore the potentially empowering processes of DREAM Big membership among college-age youth, the co-investigator of this project attended a conference in the summer of 2015 hosted by Immigration Liberation. There, the co-investigator distributed recruitment flyers inviting college-age DREAM Act advocates into the study (a convenience sample). Per the recruitment flyer, research participants had to be at least 18 years old and able to participate in an English-only interview. Most importantly, research participants had to have been undocumented, DREAM Big volunteer advocates (as opposed to paid staff members). Those willing to participate responded to the co-investigator via contact information provided on the recruitment flyer. Six participants responded in the affirmative, though one ultimately did not meet sampling criteria. Saturation was reached. Demographic characteristics of the final sample ($N = 5$) are described in Table 18.1.

Per Table 18.1, the five research participants were from two countries: Peru and Mexico. At the time of the interview, one participant had received

Table 18.1 Characteristics of Sample (*N* = 5).

		Frequency	Percent
Gender	Male	4	80.0
	Female	1	20.0
Country of Origin	Peru	3	60.0
	Mexico	2	40.0
Age Bracket	20–26	5	100.0

citizenship; the rest were still undocumented. Also, at the time of interview, participants were between the ages of 20 and 26 (mean: 23.2; median: 23.0). Since interviews were conducted almost two years after the statewide DREAM Act was signed into law, we assume these participants were roughly two years younger at the time of their volunteer advocacy (mean: 21.2; median: 21.0). Finally, participants were mostly male (*n* = 4); they all still lived in the focal state.

Data Collection and Analysis

The research team was not affiliated with either the DREAM Big or the Immigration Liberation organizations. Instead, the research team is affiliated with a university in the focal state. After a full IRB review, approval was obtained. Data were collected throughout the summer and fall of 2015. In an effort to illicit rich, narrative data among a small sample—and in an effort to explore the depth of empowering processes encountered through DREAM Act volunteerism and DREAM Big membership—qualitative methods were employed. Specifically, open-ended, qualitative interviewing techniques were utilized. This approach to data collection is useful for exploring perceptions of process among smaller samples (Patton, 2001).

The research questionnaire was organized according to the four dimensions of intra-organizational empowerment (shared beliefs, opportunity role structure, social support, and leadership). It was created in concert with an empowerment expert unaffiliated with the research project, and included questions like: "What connects you to other DREAM-ers?" (shared beliefs); "What, specifically, did you do to advance the DREAM Act in your state?" (opportunity role structure); "Tell me about your relationships with other DREAM-ers" (social support); and "How would someone else describe your contributions to the passage of your state's DREAM Act?" (leadership). All five participants were interviewed at a single point in time (cross-sectional research) at the location of their choice. All five participants received $20 remuneration for their 60-minute interview.

Per full IRB review—and because of the sensitive nature of undocumented statuses—in-depth interviews were not audio or video recorded. Instead, the co-investigator conducted interviews and transcribed responses on her laptop computer in real time. Then, she repeated the transcription back to participants, which functioned as a form of member check (see Koelsch, 2013). Responses were subsequently organized by question in an Excel spreadsheet. There, the PI and co-investigator independently conducted the first round of thematic analysis and a-priori coding. Repeated concepts were noted when they were expressed by a majority ($n = 4$) of the sample. The PI and co-investigator then met to discuss preliminary findings and to conduct deeper analysis, whereby preliminary concepts (for example, challenges associated with DREAM Act advocacy) were parceled into categorical "themes" (i.e., overcoming internalized stigma). These themes, which emerged from the data inductively, comprise the findings of this research.

Reflexivity

In qualitative research, the investigators must interpret participant experiences through their own subjective realities. As such, reflexivity calls on the investigators to be "attentive to and conscious of the cultural, political, social, linguistic, and ideological origins of one's own perspective" (Patton, 2001, p. 65). Since the qualitative investigator is part of the research instrument, reflexivity calls on him or her to disclose personal biases. As such, it is important to note that the PI is a former political aide, having worked for the chair of the focal state's legislative Latino caucus. In that capacity, he interfaced regularly with DREAM Big organization, as DREAM Big and its membership worked to facilitate passage of the statewide DREAM Act. The PI is currently a qualitative methodologist with an expertise in civil society, youth development, and empowerment theory. The co-investigator is an undergraduate student with a personal and scholastic interest in immigration policy, youth organizing, and liberation psychology. As such, this research may classify as heuristic inquiry, which "brings to the fore the personal experience and insights of the researcher" (Patton, 2001, p. 107).

Results

Results are organized according to the explicated dimensions of intra-organizational empowerment: shared beliefs, opportunity role structure, social support, and leadership. Findings—vis-à-vis four emergent themes, which transcended the data inductively (without prompt)—support and extend our current understanding of intra-organizational empowerment as it relates to this population (undocumented, college-age DREAM Act advocates—all of whom happen to be from Latin American countries—in a Northeastern state). The emergent themes are: (1) *Challenging Social Injustice;* (2) *Inherent Connection with other Advocates*; (3) *Combatting Internalized Stigma;* (4) *Civic Literacy*. The themes are described more in the following.

Shared Beliefs

Participants in this sample independently discussed a number of ways in which they saw the world similarly to other DREAM Act advocates. For example, the general belief that immigration was a "broken" system in the United States was a universal ($N = 5$) sentiment. As one participant stated, "Immigration is a huge issue in America and it is breaking many families apart." To quote another: "I am not so worried about myself as I am about my mother, because she can't drive and can be exploited in her job." Tandem to these beliefs was the sentiment among all participants ($N = 5$) that American politicians were not willing or capable to address immigration on a systemic level. As two participants offered:

> The immigrant community is not a priority for any political party, and the immigrant community as a whole is being used as a political soccer ball . . . the Republican Party is not appealing to our community and the Democratic Party takes us for granted.
>
> When it comes to politicians, I do not feel connected to them. All they want is a vote from people. . . . They always worry about other topics and they ignore all the undocumented people. . . . (Politicians) are people you can't depend on, because they change their minds after they're in office.

One particularly colorful quote illustrates the dichotomous views that politicians tend to hold about immigrants:

> We have seen politicians try to divide the people with the narrative of bad versus good immigrant. If you have a D-U-I, you are bad and need to be deported. If you have been here for 10 years with no record, than you're a good immigrant. You are pitting the community against each other. . . . In the youth, if the person has straight A's and not able to go to school because of legal reasons, we are "wasting a great mind." When the student is average, they don't deserve to go to school. . . . Our biggest challenge is that we buy into what politicians say about us.

Universally, these beliefs about politicians and the American immigration system were informed by personal experiences encountered by the youthful sample itself. Because they were undocumented, all participants ($N = 5$) discussed instances of being oppressed or discriminated against in their respective educational settings. "In high school, my guidance counsellor wasn't able to help answer my questions because she wasn't prepared for the issues I was facing," said one participant. "My best friends were really smart, but couldn't study where they wanted to, because they came from poor immigrant families. Their potential was limited, and that was frustrating," said another. Other common experiences among participants included participants not being able to attend certain colleges, even though they felt qualified to attend ($n = 3$), and having to leave college altogether or drop to part-time status due to (lack of) financial aid ($n = 3$). One participant illustrated the latter issue when he explained:

> In my sophomore year (of college), I became the president of the Association for Latin American students. I was re-elected my junior year, but my parents and I were out of money. I had to either take a year off or become a part-time student. Because I would not be able to continue with my schooling, I would not be able to stay president of my organization.

Interestingly, the young man quoted above wound up "going public" with his story of being an undocumented student without financial aid. This led to his eventual involvement in DREAM Big, in pursuit of a statewide tuition equity policy. Shared beliefs refer to group-based belief systems that should support individual members in achieving personal goals (Maton & Salem, 1995). Tuition equity was a personal goal for all research participants ($N = 5$). As an emergent theme, however, what led all participants ($N = 5$) to become DREAM Big members was the desire to challenge what they perceived to be a social injustice. This first emergent theme—*Challenging Social Injustice*—is best illustrated by the participants in the following:

> I had received a scholarship (to college) and I had to give it back (because of my undocumented status). I had to drop out of school and had nothing to do or anywhere to go. . . . I wanted to become politically active because I was undocumented and . . . that [political activity] gave me hope that one day I would go back to school.
>
> I have a brother and a sister who are undocumented. . . . They are the people who influenced me to be who I am today [a volunteer immigration reform advocate]. In the country's eyes, they shouldn't be here. But in my eyes, they should have the same opportunities as everyone else.

These quotes illustrate a desire to change the status quo on behalf of a disenfranchised population (undocumented youth in educational settings). Maton and Salem (1995) state that group-based belief systems must be inspiring of growth, strengths-based, and located beyond the self. To this end, while DREAM Big members may have initially joined the DREAM Act movement due to their own, personal circumstances (e.g., regaining a scholarship), their efforts—in time—became rooted in a desire to help the entire community of undocumented youth (e.g., pursuing equality of opportunity). As one participant stated, "It stopped being about me going back to school and became about others." This shared belief—this commitment to advocating for all undocumented youth—was illustrated by all participants ($N = 5$).

Opportunity Role Structure

Opportunity role structures provide niches in an organization, which members are intended to fill. These niches allow members to develop, grow, and participate. Civil society initiatives (such as DREAM Big) are characterized by a voluntary division of labor, whereby voluntary members have specific functions to perform (see Putnam, 2000). Participants were asked how they personally helped DREAM Big advance the statewide DREAM Act. All participants ($N = 5$) identified specific ways in which they helped the organization achieve its goals. Two individuals explicated macro-level advocacy on behalf of the DREAM Act movement, as illustrated by this quote:

> I was a campaign manager, so most things were filtered to me. I was able to facilitate conversations about direct actions and social media. My role was to keep everything connected and to make sure everyone knew what everyone else was doing. . . . I was involved in 100% of the legislative meetings, phone calls, and media events.

While the aforementioned quote pertains to campaign management and the lobbying of state officials, most participants ($n = 3$) filled DREAM Big niches on the micro-level. One participant discussed facilitating the continuous translation of information about the DREAM Act movement from English into another language. Two participants discussed performing outreach functions with undocumented high school students and their parents.

Social Support

In terms of macro-or micro-advocacy, all participants ($N = 5$) discussed the importance of coalition building with non-members and allied organizations. "We had allies that weren't part of [DREAM Big], but we could work on projects with them," said one participant. To quote another:

> There were lots of faith-based groups, legislators, people, and other groups that helped in their own communities. Some churches had their bishops talk to legislators. . . . The labor unions were great, and at one point I was able to work for one. They gave [DREAM Big] meeting spaces, access to lawmakers, and meetings with decision makers.

This type of social support, while distinct from intra-organizational empowerment, is reflective of bridging social capital. According to Putnam (2000), bridging social capital is a framework that describes the inherent value of extra-organizational social networks. Participants in this study unanimously recognized the utility of coalition building as central to DREAM

Big's success. Nevertheless, from an organizational empowerment perspective, social support should contribute to a DREAM Big member's overall quality of life; it refers more to intra-network bonds. To this end, participants were unanimous ($N = 5$) in recognizing an *Inherent Connection with other Advocates*. Herein lies a second emergent theme from the study.

Participants discussed their DREAM Big relationships using phrases like "We're a family," and "We love each other." The most palpable quotes, however, identify the unspoken experiences of living as an undocumented youth in the United States:

> The relationships were at a personal level. When speaking with (other DREAM-ers) you can talk about your status, parents' status, and parents under-the-table jobs. Many of your friends don't know who you are. They only know the "you" that they see on social media. You assume that all your friends are here legally. . . . With any Dreamer that I met, I opened up really easily. Having the status issue in common, it is easier to become friends. This makes you more connected to them and their families. . . . Dreamers have parents who work long hours and we can connect on a deeper level.
>
> A lot of my closest friends were and are undocumented or have DACA [Deferred Action for Childhood Arrivals]. Many, I worked with on the federal and state DREAM Act and deportation fights. We connected on our cultural identity. Being undocumented is a culture of its own, because you are affected by what your parents and politicians say about you and to you.

The "unspoken experiences" mentioned previously may be reflective of an internalized stigma that, if not for organizations like DREAM Big, participants would still experience. Almost all participants ($n = 4$) discussed this stigma, either in overt or implied terms, as illustrated in the following:

> [Before DREAM Big], I was not used to speaking about my legal status. I once met this girl who was shouting "I am undocumented, unafraid, and unapologetic" and I was like, "Whoa, chill." It was a bit much for me. . . . [But now], my main role is being the emcee and chant leader for civil actions. I am the girl chanting "Undocumented and unafraid."
>
> When you are out advocating for Dreamers, you see, you are fearless. Just holding a poster or signing a petition, you are putting yourself out there. When people see you getting involved they assume you are undocumented. I graduated in the top 10 of my class . . . (but) I would lie to my peers and counsellors about my status because I was fearful.

Through their DREAM Act advocacy and the social support afforded by the DREAM Big organization, participants in this study are assumed to have *Combatted Internalized Stigma* (a third emergent theme).

The social support afforded to participants by DREAM Big membership is also tandem to bonding social capital (AKA the inherent value of intra-network ties). Several participants ($n = 3$) implicitly illustrated ways in which their membership in DREAM Big benefited fellow DREAM-ers. As one young woman offered:

> When I meet other Dreamers, I try to engage them and talk about county colleges and scholarships available to us. I try to help them and connect them with the right people so they can get those supports. I try to [educate them] because the laws are not doing that, and it's up to us to bring each other up to speed.

This ability to make a difference is also reflective of organizational empowerment's leadership dimension (discussed more in the following).

Leadership

Maton and Salem (1995) note that the leadership dimension of organizational empowerment may facilitate individual empowerment through (1) the direct action of a leader; or (2) a leader's indirect effect on organizational members. Leaving a legacy is central to this dimension. The most tangible and overt legacy of one's DREAM Big advocacy is undoubtedly the passage of the focal state's DREAM Act. All participants ($N = 5$) similarly described DREAM Big's ability to force a dialog on immigration and its ability to force residents of the focal state to challenge their assumptions of what undocumented individuals are capable of, instead of what their deficits might be.

A final emergent theme pertains to *Civic Literacy*, whereby all participants ($N = 5$) gained a more thorough understanding of political processes, and how undocumented and/or immigrant populations are treated in policy arenas. Demonstration of civic literacy was evident in quotes like these: "We have to start looking at our community as being powerful. Our contributions through labor and economics make this country run. Collectively, we can stop this country form running"; "What I learned about the political process is that it takes so much (time) to make change . . . politicians are slow"; "I learned that I would never want to run for elected office. No one wants to see how the sausage is made. I saw it and it's not pretty. There are a lot of factors, special interests, and money in politics."

In spite of their mixed feelings about politics and political processes, all participants ($N = 5$) indicated a desire to continue their advocacy on behalf of undocumented youth. As one participant stated:

> I think (advocacy) is something that is part of me, and I do it day-by-day. It might not be at the federal level, but I am involved on my campus and around my state advocating for undocumented students. The only reason I wouldn't continue to advocate so rigorously is that I don't want to think

about it every day. That is a form of self-care, because [the oppression of undocumented individuals] is happening with your family and your parents every day. I don't think it is possible to ever truly stop advocating.

This desire to continue advocating is, in part, responsible for the creation of Immigration Liberation, the organization from which this sample was recruited. The desire to continue advocating is also illustrative of Kieffer's (1984) assertion that empowerment is a developmental process that unfolds over time. To this end, the true legacy of this sample may reveal itself with time. In the interim, however—and perhaps the greatest indicator of civic literacy—is the revelation among all participants ($N = 5$) of a generalized political awakening. As one said:

> The way I grew up, I was made to believe that I should not question authority and I should just follow the system. That event [passage of the statewide DREAM Act] made me realize that everything isn't linear and I *can* question the system.

Psychological empowerment—as mentioned earlier—is an individual outcome and a multidimensional construct, but at its core is one's desire to effect systemic change through advocacy in the sociopolitical environment (Zimmerman, 1995). To the extent that these five participants were part of an organizational initiative (DREAM Big) that effected systemic change (in state resident tuition), we assume that they encountered several empowering processes, vis-à-vis intra-organizational empowerment. As illustrated by the quote earlier, there is perhaps no greater legacy than the imparted belief that an undocumented young person can, in fact, make change in the systems that impact them.

Discussion

This research applied an organizational empowerment framework to explore processes of DREAM Act advocacy in a focal state. Four emergent themes transcended the data inductively (without prompt): (1) Challenging Social Injustice, which pertains to participant motivations for their DREAM Act involvement; (2) Inherent Connection with other Advocates, which pertains to the unique personal experiences among DREAM-ers; (3) Combatting Internalized Stigma, which pertains to overcoming the shame or embarrassment of an undocumented identity; and (4) Civic Literacy, which pertains to political proficiencies that participants acquired throughout their DREAM Act advocacy.

Implications for Policy, Practice, and Future Research

Implications for Policy

Policymakers will benefit from this in-depth exploration of DREAM Act advocacy in myriad ways. First—through participant voice—policymakers can discern what obstacles (e.g., lack of scholarship availability, inability to maintain full-time status, etc.) undocumented Latinos face in pursuit of postsecondary education. Policymakers—especially those in states that have not yet adopted a local DREAM Act—can also benefit from understanding the extent to which undocumented Latinos desire to pursue post-secondary education to better themselves, and—by proxy—their local workplaces and economies. Lastly, policymakers will appreciate the fourth emergent theme of this research, civic literacy. In this study, civic literacy was brought about through DREAM Act advocacy. The cultivation of civic literacy among study participants may, in time, correlate itself with other hallmarks of active citizenry (e.g., voting, recycling, being a leader in one's community, etc.), even though the population at hand lacks citizenship.

Implications for Practice

Secondary educational practitioners must actively educate themselves about what resources and supports may be available to undocumented youth who desire post-secondary attendance. Similarly, post-secondary educators and administrators must institute programs to attract and retain the population; this may include advertising targeted supports and services to incoming students and high school guidance counsellors. Per the "inherent connection" finding of this research, secondary and post-secondary educators must work to bond and connect undocumented populations through the facilitation of informal, social support groups, which may function as a protective factor. Most importantly, all educational practitioners must work to create and maintain stigma-free educational communities, as they relate to issues of residency.

Implications for Future Research

This research contributes generally to a large body of literature on processes allied with positive youth development. This research contributes specifically to a growing body of strengths-based literature on undocumented youth and what they capable of, as opposed to what they are lacking. Future research must examine the empowering processes of DREAM Act advocacy with larger, heterogeneous samples. Additionally, scholars will benefit from quantitative approaches that test theory (e.g., empowerment) as it relates to this type of civic engagement. Per the "inherent connection" findings of this research, future scholarship may wish to further explain the bonding (intra-group) social capital of undocumented youth with the bridging social capital of inter-group dynamics, as protective factors for the population. Future research should also examine the myriad dimensions of stigma, shame, and oppression that are experienced by this otherwise strengths-based population.

Limitations

Like all qualitative research, this study is context-bound and its findings should not be generalized beyond the small sample ($N = 5$) specified earlier.

Similarly, the investigators concede that the sample is homogenous: it is mostly male ($n = 4$) and exclusively Latino, even though undocumented college students in the United States are both male and female, and come from myriad regions across the globe (not just Latin America). Per full IRB review—and out of respect for the privacy of undocumented individuals—the investigators were prohibited from audio or video recording participant interviews. Consequently, they had to rely on real-time transcription using a laptop computer, which was less preferred. Finally, the organization from which this sample was recruited (Immigration Liberation, a pseudonym), is an offshoot of DREAM Big (also a pseudonym), which is—in fact—the disbanded organization responsible for facilitating the passage of the focal state's DREAM Act. As such, it is unlikely that the recruitment flyer reached all members of the disbanded group. In spite of these limitations, the investigators believe that this formative, strengths-based research makes an important contribution to our understanding of undocumented (specifically Latino) youth, and the empowering processes they encounter in their pursuit of sociopolitical change.

References

Batalova, J., & McHugh, M. (2010, July). *DREAM vs. reality: An analysis of potential DREAM Act beneficiaries*. Washington, DC: Migration Policy Institute.

Berg, G. A., & Tollefson, K. (2014). Latino/a student perceptions of post-baccalaureate education: Identifying challenges to increased participation. *Journal of Latinos and Education, 13*(4), 296–308. doi:10.1080/15348431.2014.887470

Christens, B. D. (2012). Toward relational empowerment. *American Journal of Community Psychology, 50*(1–2), 114–128. doi:10.1007/s10464-011-9483-5

Covarrubias, A., & Lara, A. (2014). The undocumented (Im)migrant educational pipeline: The influence of citizenship status on educational attainment for people of Mexican origin. *Urban Education, 49*(1), 75–110. doi:10.1177/0042085912470468

Diaz-Strong, D., Gomez, C., Luna-Duarte, M. E., & Meiners, E. R. (2011). Purged: Undocumented students, financial aid policies, and access to higher education. *Journal of Hispanic Higher Education, 10*(2), 107–119. doi:10.1177/1538192711401917

Ellis, L. M., & Chen, E. C. (2013). Negotiating identity development among undocumented immigrant college students: A grounded theory study. *Journal of Counseling Psychology, 60*(2), 251–264. doi:10.1037/a0031350

Erikson, E. H. (1968). *Identity: Youth in crisis*. New York, NY: Norton.

Erisman, W., & Looney, S. (2007, April) *Open the door to the American dream: Increasing higher education access and success for immigrants*. Washington, DC: The Institute of Higher Education Policy.

Forenza, B., & Germak, A. J. (2015). What ignites and sustains activism: An exploration of processes and competencies. *Journal of Progressive Human Services, 26*(3), 229–245. doi:10.1080/10428232.2015.1063349

Freire, P. (1973). *Education for critical consciousness*. New York, NY: Seabury.

Goffman, E. (1963). *Stigma: Notes on the management of spoiled identity*. New York, NY: Simon & Schuster.

Gonzalez, L. M. (2015). Barriers to college access for Latino/a adolescents: A comparison of theoretical frameworks. *Journal of Latinos and Education, 14*(4), 320–335. doi:10.1080/15348431.2015.1091315

Gonzalez, L. M., Stein, G. L., Prandoni, J. I., Eades, M. P., & Magalhaes, R. (2015). Perceptions of undocumented status and possible selves among Latino/a youth. *The Counseling Psychologist, 43*(8), 1190–1210. doi:10.1177/0011000015608951

Ishizawa, H. (2015). Civic participation through volunteerism among youth across immigrant generations. *Sociological Perspectives, 58*(2), 264–285. doi:10.1177/0731121414556843

Jefferies, J. (2014). Fear of deportation in high school: Implications for breaking the cycle of silence surrounding migration status. *Journal of Latinos and Education, 13*(4), 278–295. doi:10.1080/15348431.2014.887469

Kieffer, C. H. (1984). Citizen empowerment: A developmental perspective. *Prevention in Human Services, 3*, 9–36. doi:10.1300/J293v03n02_03

Kim, C. (2013). Lost American DREAM of undocumented students: Understanding the DREAM (Development, Relief, and Education for Alien Minors) Act. *Children and Schools, 35*(1), 55–58. doi:10.1093/cs/cds041

Koelsch, L. E. (2013). Reconceptualizing the member check interview. *International Journal of Qualitative Methods, 12*, 168–179.

Levin, I. (2013). Political inclusion of Latino immigrants: Becoming a citizen and political participation. *American Politics Research, 41*(4), 535–568. doi:10.1177/1532673X12461438

Liu, O. L. (2011, May). *Examining American post-secondary education* (ETS Research Report #11–22). Princeton, NJ: Educational Testing Service.

Maton, K. I., & Salem, D. A. (1995). Organizational characteristics of empowering community settings: A multiple case study approach. *American Journal of Community Psychology, 23*(5), 631–656. doi:10.1007/BF02506985

National Council of State Legislatures. (2014, June 12). *Undocumented student tuition: State action*. Retrieved from www.ncsl.org/research/education/undocumented-student-tuition-state-action.aspx

Nienhusser, H. K. (2013). Role of high schools in undocumented students' college choice. *Education Policy Analysis Archives, 21*(85), 1–29. doi:10.14507/epaa.v21n85.2013

Ortega, N. (2011). The role of higher education associations in shaping policy that connects immigration to educational opportunity: A social capital framework. *Journal of Hispanic Higher Education, 10*(1), 41–65. doi:10.1177/1538192710391803

Patton, M. Q. (2001). *Qualitative research and evaluation methods* (3rd ed.). Thousand Oaks, CA: Sage.

Perez, W., Cortes, R. D., Ramos, K., & Coronado, H. (2010). "Cursed and blessed": Examining the socioemotional and academic experiences of undocumented Latina and Latino college students. *New Directions for Student Services, 2010*(131), 35–51. doi:10.1002/ss.v2010:131

Peterson, N. A., & Zimmerman, M. A. (2004). Beyond the individual: Toward a nomological network of organizational empowerment. *American Journal of Community Psychology, 34*(1–2), 129–145. doi:10.1023/B: AJCP.0000040151.77047.58

Plyler v. Doe, 457 U.S. 202. (1982).

Potochnick, S. (2014). How states can reduce the dropout rate for undocumented immigrant youth: The effects of in-state resident tuition policies. *Social Science Research, 45*, 18–32. doi:10.1016/j.ssresearch.2013.12.009

Putnam, R. (2000). *Bowling alone: The collapse and revival of American community*. New York, NY: Simon and Schuster.

Saldivar, K. M. (2015). A mute voice? Red tape and Latino political participation. *PAQ Spring, 39*(1), 51–84.

Sanchez, J. E., Usinger, J., & Thornton, B. W. (2015). Predictive variables of success for Latino enrollment in higher education. *Journal of Latinos and Education, 14*(3), 188–201. doi:10.1080/15348431.2014.973565

Speer, P. W. (2000). Intrapersonal and interactional empowerment: Implications for theory. *Journal of Community Psychology, 28*(1), 51–61. doi:10.1002/(ISSN)1520-6629

Storlie, C. A., & Jach, E. A. (2012). Social justice collaboration in schools: A model for working with undocumented Latino students. *Journal of Social Action in Counseling and Psychology, 4*(2), 99–116.

Taylor, K. A., & Fernandez-Bergersen, S. L. (2015). Mexican American women's reflections from public high school. *Journal of Latinos and Education, 14*(1), 6–24. doi:10.1080/15348431.2014.944701

Valdez, Z. (2011). Political participation among Latino in the United States: The effect of group identity and consciousness. *Social Science Quarterly, 92*(2), 466–482. doi:10.1111/ssqu.2011.92.issue-2

Windsor, L., Benoit, E., & Dunlap, E. (2010). Dimensions of oppression in the lives of impoverished Black women who use drugs. *Journal of Black Studies, 41*(1), 21–39. doi:10.1177/0021934708326875

Zimmerman, M. (1995). Psychological empowerment: Issues and illustrations. *American Journal of Community Psychology, 23*(5), 581–599. doi:10.1007/BF02506983

Zimmerman, M. A., Israel, B. A., Schultz, A., & Checkoway, B. (1992). Further explorations in empowerment theory: An empirical analysis of psychological empowerment. *American Journal of Community Psychology, 20*(6), 707–727. doi:10.1007/BF01312604

19 Multiple Ethnic, Racial, and Cultural Identities in Action

From Marginality to a New Cultural Capital in Modern Society

Henry T. Trueba

What does it imply to have more than one identity? Is there a cultural conflict, a conflict of values? Our identity as members of the human species should bring together diverse racial, ethnic, and cultural groups that may see each other as enemies, or even as subhuman, genetically inferior, and undesirable. Yet, our capacity to conceive and create new knowledge; to reflect, accumulate, and transfer information and experiences from one generation to the next (the quintessence of *homo sapiens sapiens*) separates human beings not only from each other, into opposite sociocultural groups, but also from other primates. Chimps, gorillas, and other primates and mammals can feel, recognize, and mimic symbolic codes taught by others, and even generate certain symbols. Yet, humans can create or overcome social barriers. The acquisition of human communicative competence with mastery of codes and concepts requires a clear understanding of one's own position in a given cultural setting (i.e., a clear definition of the self). A person's ability to define their identity in different ways in order to function effectively in different settings and cultural contexts is clearly related to their quest for survival and success. I want to argue here is that there is an intimate relation between people's capacity to endure hardships, challenges, and difficult situations in life (that is what we call *resilience*), and their ability to redefine themselves in order to function effectively in new social, cultural, linguistic, and economic contexts. That is, resilience is a function of psychological and cultural flexibility to define oneself in multiple ways and fashions.

When I speak of multiple identities I do not imply maladjustment, abnormality, lack of loyalty to a given ethnic group, or any other negative characteristic of a person's personality (that was the case in previous decades). I am hypothesizing that simultaneous multiple identities (not serial or sequential identities) require a unique skill and flexibility on the part of immigrant youths from all ethnic groups. The "new" and rapidly evolving postmodern society is more than ever lead by a new youth that does not accept ethnic boundaries as a red light in the development of their potentialities. The rapid immigration and migration waves from many countries to Western industrial societies, and population movements within industrial societies, is not a new phenomenon. What is new is its magnitude and the adaptive strategies of immigrants and migrants. There are unexpected forces leading to these adaptive strategies. Unlike the immigration of the last century from the European countries to the United States, the last 30 years reveal a drastic change:

> Immigration is the driving force behind a significant transformation of American society taking place at the end of the millennium. Few other social phenomena are likely to affect the future character of American culture and society as much as the ongoing wave of "new immigration."... In 1945, just fifty years ago, the U.S. population was 87 percent white, 10 percent black, 2.5 percent Hispanic, and 0.5 percent Asian. Fifty years from now, in the year of 2050, demographic projections suggest a strikingly different population profile: 52.8 percent of the population will be white, 13.6 percent of the population will be black, 24.5 percent of the population will be Hispanic, and 8.2 percent of the population will be of Asian ancestry.... Given ethnic socioeconomic mobility and the high rates of interethnic marriage in the United States along with changing cultural models and practices around ethnicity, there is reason to suspect that these categories, fluid and in constant formation and transformation, may be quite irrelevant in three generations.
>
> (Suárez-Orozco, 1998, p. 5)

Suárez-Orozco (1998) suggested that one in six children in the United States today lives in a household headed by immigrants. Immigrants are concentrated in California, New York, Florida, Texas, and Illinois. In California, for example, about 20% of all school age children are immigrants. In New York City public schools today, 48% of all children come from immigrant households speaking over 100 different languages. In contrast with previous decades, powerful new forms of transnationalism are shaping the immigration flood of the 21st century. Immigrants are culturally and racially heterogeneous and economically stratified. Some are rapidly achieving upward mobility, whereas many others, especially immigrants of color, find themselves isolated in semi-skilled, low-paying service jobs. Finally, other immigrants inconspicuously disappear in mainstream middle class institutions (Suárez-Orozco, 2000).

> New technologies of communication—including computers, discount telephone cards, and faxes; easier and more affordable systems of mass transportation; along with new social practices and cultural models celebrating ethnic and cultural difference seem to subvert the sharp break with the country of origin that was said to characterize earlier waves of European immigration to the United States.... Many immigrants today are apt to remain players both "here" and "there" circuiting back and forth between the country of their birth and the country of their choice.
>
> (Suárez-Orozco, 2000, p. 24)

Previously, psychologists viewed self-identity as a rigid and permanent state incompatible with alternative identities. Suárez-Orozco felt that recent work by anthropologists and sociologists highlights the multiple identities, which is much different from the dysfunctional models alluded to "in the old Freudian/Eriksonian master narrative depicting a unilinear developmental epic journey of separation and individuation into maturity, autonomy, and coherence" (Suárez-Orozco, 2000, p. 29). To assume that each person has only one fixed identity relatively unchanged across the cultural and social experiences that differentiate individuals is simplistic and reductionistic. G. Spindler (1974, 1978, 2000) and G. and L. Spindler (1987, 1994) discussed the nature of the "enduring self," the "situated self," and the "endangered self" to explain changes in self-identity. These identities, however, are conceived of as sequential and for the most part coherent and compatible with the diverse living environments of individuals throughout life. My position (see *Latinos Unidos*; Trueba, 1999; Trueba & Bartolomé, 2000) is that immigrants manage to acquire and maintain different identities that co-exist and function without conflict in different contexts simultaneously. A simple unilinear acculturation or assimilation process from one culture to another would not be functional or even possible for most immigrants. In fact, their resiliency and "success" (defined in terms of psychological adaptation and social mobility), and their powerful influence in mainstream society are the result of their creative ability to become an "other" and participate in different worlds. They must fit the expectations of employers and their own economic needs, and they must acquire communicative skills in other languages and cultures, without depriving themselves from their quintessential selves and from the security of their home culture. Practicing "other identities" is part of the adaptive process. See, for example, the work of Ainslie (1998), who described Mexicanos of Texas who go to the "Flea Market" (or *La Pulga* as they call it) and try to pass for Anglos or at least to adopt the communicative style and dressing codes of the mainstream population. They become more comfortable by "code switching" and entering the Anglo world for a few minutes.

The acculturation and/or assimilation models are too simplistic, and are clearly contradicted by the presence of cultural and economic enclaves of immigrants in Europe and the United States. It seems as if recent generations of immigrants see no conflict in retaining their ethnic identities while they learn the culture of their host country and become proficient in their new home languages. The ability of immigrants to function effectively among members of mainstream society and to compete well with them in school and business does not necessarily mean that ethnic communities become invisible or disappear. On the contrary, young generations of Asian Americans, Latinos, and other immigrants are proud to become both mainstream citizens (aware of their new culture and proud to be fully participating in American institutions) as well as active members of an ethnic group with fluency in Mandarin, Spanish, Cantonese, Korean, or other home languages.

Immigrants who belong to a specific racial group (Black Africans, Black Latinos, Black Cubans, Indians from Mexico or Latin American, Asians from the Pacific Islands, and other people of color) are increasingly aware of belonging to more than one ethnic group, and to use different communicative patterns in each group. Biracial persons, for example, do associate with opposite groups (mainstream Whites and African Americans); they see multiple memberships and the use of multiple linguistic codes as an asset. In fact, they often view their generation as gifted. As they learn the different communication styles and interactive patterns, they manage to mimic codes and patterns and fit well in different groups without any penalties. There is no psychological dysfunctionality or cultural conflict in their daily interaction with opposite groups. Code switching and the assumption of different identities comes natural to them and permits them to function in multiethnic and multicultural environments.

Would increasing miscegenation and intermarriage among ethnic and racial groups in modern America render former ethnic identities as irrelevant? Would multiple identities become commonplace? Would the general population in this country become multiracial, multicultural, and desegregated? If traditional groupings with oppositional political and cultural identities disappear, then racial, ethnic, and other groupings categories should become useless and obsolete. What, if any, stratification will exist to clearly mark the predominance of political and economic power groups across the multiracial and multicultural shades of citizens? One could speculate that the markers of new power hierarchies and distinctive identities will follow educational, socioeconomic, and technological lines.

In fact, the future is here. In some cities in the United States, the diversity of student populations in the public schools has not only ended the predominance of "White" populations, but the associations across ethnic and racial lines have become the dominant pattern in voluntary associations, businesses, and industry.

Self-Identity Among Immigrants and Ethnic/Racial Minorities

In a recent volume edited by Jacobs, Cintrón, and Canton (in press) entitled *The Politics of Survival in Academia: Narratives of Inequity, Resilience, and Success*, we find a number of testimonies that force us to reflect on the nature of academia today. Canton, for example, had to face racism and discrimination year after year, but managed to retain his optimism and integrity, as well as his extraordinary scholarly production. He states,

> Unless you have come face to face with blatant individual prejudice, it is often difficult to recognize it when it presents itself in hidden, sometimes unintentional ways. . . . Given the law enforcement backgrounds of many of my colleagues on the faculty, I was amazed that I wasn't

exposed to it more often. Whatever the reason, what I found was much more organizational discrimination, and institutional racism than the individual variety.

(Canton, in press)

Canton's subtle, elegant, at times painful, but always peaceful account is truly inspiring; a victimized faculty can retain a high degree of self-respect and dignity in the face of unjust treatment by peers. His endurance and sharp analytical skills match the profound respect earned at the university among students and some colleagues. Resilience, courage, and wisdom are not in conflict with intelligent resistance in the face of academic racism. Prejudice is the most challenging and draining conflict in academia.

Another example is that of a woman who is gay, Native American, and Black. Disagreements among faculty of color who had conflicting expectations resulted in bitter disappointment and isolation for her. Unwilling to pass for someone else, or to hide her ancestry, she searches for a new personal identity as a member of the academy:

> Since I didn't know of my Indian heritage in childhood, I only learned how awful it was to be me. Where I've come to now, is the knowledge that being both Black and Indian is rich and full, life-affirming. To deny either is to engage, maybe even affirm, the comfort preferences of the dominant cultures; to support the unspoken contention that Black is bad, except in politics." . . . The politics of the academy boil down to who you know and who you "hang with," from what I can tell. I often find myself in a quandary about when to speak to whom about what, and when to stay silent. On the surface, I feel the most secure when I keep silent. In my waking nightmares, I am the "good little Black girl," one who "doesn't make trouble." In my center, I am ashamed that I do not speak up, ashamed of my fear and sense of insecurity. That has meant checking myself to see that I don't say the "wrong" thing, regardless of its veracity. It has meant that I keep quiet when I feel the need to speak out. It has meant that I've done as instructed, whether I've wanted to or not.

(Cowan, in press)

Cowan feels that her ancestors faced the same challenges and offers the following information. Slaves often told "lies" to White oppressors to keep from being brutally punished or murdered. They had to hide and found that "a false appearance could be useful when dealing with the White master and mistress." Slave narratives are a testimony to their skill in dressing the truth to survive. Cowan confesses,

> I feel pressure to keep quiet or "water down" my opinions, from not only the White folks in charge, but from my colleagues of color, as well.

> More than once, I have compromised my sense of truth and integrity to ensure my survival in this climate.

Then, reflecting on the lessons learned in academia, she states,

> First, I discovered a more hostile environment than I was expecting. Most of my White colleagues prefer to believe that we are somehow above the "isms;" that no one we know is in the least uncomfortable regarding issues of difference. They would rather think that they are sensitive and respectful, and that they have healed all manner of racism, sexism, and homophobia that they spent most of their lives unconsciously learning. My presence seems to be initially for the purpose of proving that. That I'm invited to participate, or that I'm included, comes off like a gesture to demonstrate how together they are. But the second edge of the sword is that I serve as a somewhat thorny reminder, if I speak up, of all that has not been dealt with properly, of the racism, sexism and homophobia that still exist in their world views. . . . I am constantly struggling to maintain a sense of pride and confidence in my abilities. For the first time in a very long time, I doubt my abilities. I doubt myself. I work hard, convinced that I must prove myself, even though my experience is that no amount of proving will make a difference.
>
> (Cowan, in press)

Racism, sexism, and homophobia are suffered not only personally, but vicariously when we observe our colleagues under attack. The silence imposed on many of us should not be taken to mean that everything is smooth and equity is the rule. It only means that we do not have the freedom to express our solidarity, and we feel constrained to protect our own position at any cost. A similar response is observed among colleagues who witness unfair treatment of faculty who are sick and cannot defend themselves. The next example illustrates this point.

A third example shows how indifferent the academy can become when a faculty member faces health problems. Delgado-Gaitan discusses her encounters with academia as a scholar facing health challenges due to an advanced case of lupus. As an immigrant child first, and later as an educational ethnographer doing anthropological literacy fieldwork in poor communities, she acquired first-hand knowledge and experience in having resilience in the face of adversity. She expected that a senior professor at the University of California would receive compassionate treatment following the spirit of the Americans with Disability Act. It was her family and friends that she leaned on while tapping her inner cultural knowledge and strength when her health crisis called for extraordinary measures. She says

> Fundamentally, I learned that while I relied on the support of my family, friends and cultural values to strengthen me, the University of

California did not consider my needs. Instead it dealt with my situation only according to their interpretation of the *Americans with Disability Act*—the bureaucratic law.

(Delgado-Gaitan, in press)

She describes in detail her extraordinary struggle to retain a measure of health. Her problems with the insensitivity of university bureaucrats continued. Her inability to walk long distances at the university to teach her classes made her appear even more impaired. Walking with a cane became impossible. She states,

When I first became ill, I was always assigned to teach in classrooms that were located long distances from my office and designated class hours impossible to meet because I felt too debilitated to get up very early in the mornings or stay late enough in the day on campus to teach. Most quarters I fought with the administration about appropriate scheduling of my classes up to the last minute before class began. This impeded students from taking my course since time and place were often undetermined until the first week of class.

(Delgado-Gaitan, in press)

Her personal accounts of the trials that ensued when she faced physical disabilities illustrate the vulnerability of the individual against a bureaucracy and the power of existing cultural values.

Kiang (in press) contended that transnational themes ("home," "identity," "family ties") represent an important way to use "the curriculum in order to explore the connections of culture, history, economics, and politics across time and distance for specific nationalities." Loo and Chun (in press) presented several case studies of "Asian American Warriors" to expose the myth that "the Asian American experience in academia is exemplary and devoid of any racial/ethnic bias" in American institutions of higher education. Indeed, these Asian Americans were faced with the traumatic experience of being denied tenure and/or promotion. They chose to "fight" rather than "flight." They felt that their careers were placed in jeopardy. One of the "warriors" comments, "Finally, the promotion due me was recommended, seven years later, but even this victory was bittersweet. The summary contained inaccurate statements, prejudicial omissions, discriminatory criteria, and a biased tone, terminology, and biased weighting of evidence" (Loo & Chun, in press). Another warrior describes his reaction to the traumatic battle on tenure and promotion:

An inability to recall the incident, an unwillingness to talk about it, . . . paranoia, . . . loss of self-esteem, self-deprecation, a paralysis in one's capacity to handle professional responsibilities, anger and permanent bitterness toward individuals regarding the incident, desire for revenge, feelings of racial persecution, and the development of a stoic and impenetrable persona. I became a person who would not engage with others. . . . I developed a kind of scar tissue, the development of cynicism. [The denial represented] a total invalidation of my life, of what I pursued, my activities. They made me feel like an inferior person. They weren't judging my competence, only what *they* thought was relevant. . . . These were totally ignorant people judging me.

(Loo & Chun, in press)

This is an extraordinary account of facts we never suspected could exist in academia among Asian Americans. It has an intensity that contrasts with the stereotype of Asian Americans who are presumed to accept inequities stoically. Not all individuals who develop multiple identities are successful in academia. The mechanisms that marginalize certain persons of color may turn into a cultural capital in other settings.

Multiple Identities and Action Research

Cultural anthropology has gone through a number of significant changes during the last century. One of these changes has been the emergence of ethnic anthropologists and their dissenting voices in the interpretation of ethnographic data. Foley, a renowned American anthropologist trained at Stanford who has written extensively on immigrants and ethnic researchers, comments,

> One of the most exciting new developments in educational research is the emergence of the "ethnic educational ethnographer." When I entered the field in the late 1960s educational anthropologists/sociologists were mostly White middle class men. Noted anthropological historian Marcus (1998) cited this rise of "native anthropologists" as the single most important development in anthropology. It signals the end of anthropology as a colonial/neo-colonial enterprise and acknowledges that "insiders" studying their own culture elevates the quality of ethnographic fieldwork. Insiders have obvious political, linguistic, and cultural advantages. On the other hand, neither Marcus nor I would argue that "insider ethnography" is without problems. Nor would we argue that insiders can and should replace outsiders completely. I will not explore the pros and cons of insider vs. outsider ethnographers today.

(Foley, in press)

However, the ride Foley speaks of has not been smooth and without bumps and surprises. The highly respected work of Ogbu (an immigrant from Africa) and his associates developed as an alternative theoretical approach to deficit theories and postulated that "caste-like" (or involuntary) minorities did not achieve academically because they became quintessentially handicapped.

These involuntary (caste-like) minorities had undergone such primary cultural discontinuities (contracted prior to exposure to mainstream culture) and secondary discontinuities (as a result of their oppression from mainstream societies) that they formed an oppositional self-identity that led them to reject school achievement as a desirable goal (Gibson 1987a, 1987b, 1987c, 1988; Gibson & Ogbu, 1991; Ogbu, 1974, 1978, 1981a, 1981b, 1982, 1987a, 1987b, 1989, 1991a, 1991b, 1992; Ogbu & Matute-Bianchi, 1986). It is important to note that although the macro-sociological models of the 1960s and 1970s were seen as a theoretical progress, other "ethnic" social scientists were concerned that such approaches would contribute to stereotype minorities and would not explain their ability to succeed; in other words, an attempt to reject one type of determinism (genetic, biological, etc.) would end up taking us to another type of determinism (cultural). Trueba (1988) and Foley (1991) were clear in pointing out the potential risks of Ogbu's typology and theoretical premises. Valencia (a Mexican American) suggests that

> A close examination of research by deficit thinkers uniformly shows that the scientific method is frequently violated. . . . Typically, the study's assumptions are unsound, instruments used are psychometrically weak and/or data are collected in flawed manners and rival hypotheses for the observed findings are not considered. Of course, the preceding scenario can, and does, characterize just plain sloppy research. How does one draw the line between (a) legitimate scientific research that contains lethal flaws that prevent its publication from (b) pseudoscience? One can argue that the difference lays in the *degree of researcher bias* (which is ubiquitous), as well as the *degree of vigor* [with which] the researcher pursues hypothesis verification.
>
> (Valencia, 1997a, p. 6)

Valencia describes some of the historical currents that affected immigration policies in this country. The passing of the Immigration Act of 1924 followed years of debate and struggles to control European immigration currents from Italy, Russia, Poland, and Greece. The racial and ethnic biases of the act are generally accepted:

> The question remains, however, as the roles of mental testing, hereditarian psychologists and the eugenics movement influencing the passage of the statute. Several scholars have contended that hereditarianists and eugenicists—via intelligence test data—had profound influence in congressional debate and eventual passage of the Immigration Act of 1924. . . . These scholars, for the most part, point to Carl Brigham's 1923 book, *A Study of American Intelligence*, where he reanalyzed the Army intelligence data (WWI) by immigrant background and concluded the innate intellectual superiority of the Nordic-origin men over Army examinees whose ancestry could be traced to southern and eastern Europe. . . .

> Brigham's conclusions were far-reaching: In the sense of restrictive and selected immigration policy, the possibility of racial admixture looms large—that in turn will "allegedly" lead to the overall decline of American intelligence.
>
> (Valencia, 1997b, p. 46)

Foley suggested that in the 1940s and 1950s scholars tried to avoid genetic determinism and deficit models based on pathological notions of biological constitution or biological inferiority. Intelligence testing and notions of racial superiority underwent serious scrutiny. Deficit theorists turned to culture and often used Lewis' work in Mexico, Puerto Rico, and Cuba to identify "inferior" cultural traits and the negative image of peoples of color:

> Lewis' list of "cultural traits" of the poor evokes a powerful negative image of poor people as a lazy, fatalistic, hedonistic, violent distrustful people living in common law unions, as well as in dysfunctional, female-centered authoritarian families who are chronically unemployed and rarely participate in local civil activities, vote, or trust the police and political leaders. Lewis argues that the poor create an autonomous, distinct subculture or way of life that becomes encapsulated and allegedly inferior to the mainstream way of life, [and] keeps them impoverished. For anyone wanting to indict the poor, the culture of poverty theory is a powerful metaphor that spawns a sweeping, holistic image.
>
> (Foley, 1997, p. 115)

Foley felt that the contributions of major nonethnic scholars emanated from various Marxist and cultural reproduction theorists. He stated that schools emphasized the reproduction of class inequalities through institutional mechanisms or through instructional strategies (Anyon, 1981, 1997), or perhaps also in response to teacher and peer interaction; however, early Marxist critique focused mainly on class inequality and ignored racial and gender biases (Foley, in press).

New Cultural Capital of Marginal People

If the most typical human characteristic is to be able to think, talk, and articulate reflectively, both orally and in writing experiences, then Bourdieu's tenets (1977, 1984, 1990, 1992, 1993) in the field of cultural production play a very important role in the role of ethics in academia. Given the theoretical problems faced by theoreticians attempting to explain human behavior by simple notions of biological, genetic, or cultural determinism, Pierre Bourdieu developed the concepts of *habitus* and field. He wanted to generate a concept of an agent free from both deterministic and mechanistic causality. *Habitus* was an alternative to "subjectivism" with its load of consciousness; it was a reaction against structuralism (understood as an unconscious adherence to prescribed behavior) and a way to deal with the concepts of agency and consciousness. Therefore, *habitus* is seen as a system of "durable, transposable dispositions or principles to generate or organize behavior" (regulated and regular). *Habitus* is the result of early socialization and inculcation of values and beliefs. Thus, "Bourdieu shows statistically how the working-class *habitus* generates analogous preferences across a broad range of cultural practices" (Johnson, 1993, p. 5). This concept compares with Spindler's "enduring self."

Because agents do not act in a vacuum but in specific contexts, Bourdieu conceived the notion of "field" (*champ*) as a concrete social situation and a set of objective relations (to avoid deterministic analysis of behavior). Social formations are structured by hierarchically organized series of fields (economic, political, educational, cultural, etc.), each with its own space and laws. Agents determine field structures, and a change in agents brings new field organization. Agents in any given field are in competition for control of resources and interests (not always material). In the cultural field, for example, competition over recognition and prestige is central. Cultural capital is in the crossing roads of a dialectic of "*connaissance*" and "*reconnaissance*" (knowledge and recognition).

In academia the cultural capital required to succeed and compete well consists of intangibles (or "symbolic power" to use Bourdieu's term) such as knowledge and recognition, but beyond those are a set of symbolic systems acquired through family education since early childhood. Cultural field is equivalent to "radical contextualization" because it takes into consideration not only the works or creation of intellectual products but the specific agents in their complex relationships in a given field within a historical context. Bourdieu opposed simple internal analysis of texts in the absence of a historical context. Internal analysis pursues explanations of discourse in the field of discourse itself; that is, this approach would be reductionistic because it would seek as the source of explanations and meaning of a cultural product the product itself, isolated from the conditions of production and utilization without relating the space of the cultural product or discourse and the space of the positions used by those who create such product. Cultural production needs to take into consideration social class difference. Yet Bourdieu granted that the cultural field is relatively autonomous with respect to economic and political fields. The cultural field is structured by the rigid strata formed by a hierarchy of institutions who have differential recognition and power to "consecrate" its affiliates. One can think of Harvard or Stanford as having such power in contrast with a relatively unknown small institution. The actual production of text by a person in top institutions has a higher value in the intellectual field because of the position of the scholar who produces it (see *Homo Academicus*). Bourdieu's theory of the field of cultural production emphasizes symbolic production of cultural works, including the multiple mediators contributing to the meaning and structure of a cultural field. According to Bourdieu (1993), "The literary field . . . is an independent social universe with its own laws of functioning, its specific relations of force, its dominants and its dominated, and so forth" (pp. 163–164). In other words, academia becomes a unique universe of its own with its own rules and its own form of capital.

Bourdieu (1993) described intellectuals (academicians) as entering an autonomous field, a "corner of madness within the field of power" and a "new social game" where academicians are neither dominant nor dominated. They "occupy a dominated position in the dominant class." Bourdieu observed that this "structurally contradictory position is absolutely crucial" (p. 164) to understand university people.

Bourdieu (1992) viewed field as a network or unique configuration of objective relationships among people in various positions. Positions are in turn defined as factors determining the relationships between agents and institutions in structures with their peculiar distribution of power, modes of domination or subordination, and lifestyles (1992).

Cultural Capital in Different Social Settings

Although Bourdieu made us aware of the nature of academia and the ambiguity and complexity of conducting research across social classes and cultures, Wertsch dealt with the nature of human consciousness and the acquisition of knowledge in his discussion of Vygotsky and other developmental psychologists and linguists. Wertsch made us aware of the enormously important role of the social and cultural contexts of behavior. According to Wertsch (1998), we have to ask the question, Are we mindless machines, complexly programmed computers, or robots acting under the influence of unconscious forces? What are the fundamental explanations for the origins of human consciousness? Do we have to consider recent research on brain damage, substitution of functions, and interruption of certain levels of consciousness? Reflective thinking about the past, present, and future, along with a clear connection to action, brings us closer to the crucial differences between the human species and other species. Wertsch reminds us of the narrow intradisciplinary approach to these issues and of the need to consider the so-called "terministic screens" to describe the lack of broad vision and perspectives, or the "learned incapacities" associated with the use of specialized discourse in a given discipline (Wertsch, 1998). Those learned incapacities may explain our myopia in dealing with world crises, such as the projections on China or the Soviet Union as a result of their political systems, and the recomposition of American society and its ability to cope with world problems vis-à-vis immigration and the change in racial and ethnic representation among the general population. The tendency toward reductionist assumptions reflects the provincialism within disciplines.

When Ogbu began to write on the differential achievement levels of ethnolinguistic minorities he combined a number of elements existing in anthropology, sociology, and psychology. His original typology (autonomous, immigrant, and caste-like groups) was already an effort to capitalize on the work of previous scholars. DeVos had used the "caste-like" concept extensively; G. Spindler had studies on "cultural continuities and discontinuities" among native Americans and other groups and had discussed their various adaptive strategies (nativistic, transitional, assimilated, bicultural, etc.). Ogbu capitalized on the sociological literature to recognize the social structural forces impacting behavior in ethnic groups, but also went on to capitalize on the psychological factors related to cultural continuities and discontinuities that affect the formation of self-identity. Thus, for example, among the caste-like minorities (in contrast with immigrant and autonomous minorities that, in the end, he labeled "voluntary" as opposed to the caste-like "involuntary"), Ogbu theorizes that the explanation for their low achievement is not only social constraints (segregation, job ceiling, etc.), but their "oppositional self-identity." This makes them view school achievement as a "White" characteristic and, consequently, one that persons of color ought to avoid if they want to remain consistent with their identity. The very subtle relation of self-identity to adaptive responses in the face of conflict is chosen as central to our understanding of the real or assumed failure of certain groups (Mexican American, Black, Native Americans, and other people of color). But what this theory does not explain is the differential success of some members of these groups who are exposed to the same oppressive societal factors (segregation, poverty, job ceiling, etc.). It is in this context that we see the need to search for a more flexible and sophisticated model (such as that of Bourdieu) in search of special agencies and unique "fields" (economic, cultural, political, etc.) that affect an individual's early socialization and self-identity formation (their "habitus," to use Bourdieu's terms) as a result of the continuous and dynamic interaction with special agents in each field. Furthermore, the complex relationship between fields and the relative autonomy of such fields leaves enough room to explain differential performance of individuals in certain circumstances.

Bourdieu was well aware of the dangers involved in large macro-sociological or macro-psychological models (such as the cultural ecological theories postulated by Ogbu and associates). These macro models can take us directly to the kind of deterministic positions that Ogbu was originally battling against. We all reject biological or genetic determinism on the basis of empirical data showing that socialization patterns, cultural influences, and other learned behavior can render genetic determinism as false, especially if we compound concepts of determinism with racial typologies. The enormous miscegenation among all ethnic groups, on the one hand, and the fundamental comparability of DNA structures across diverse ethnic groups around the world (e.g., the study of disease predominant in certain groups, like high blood pressure among Blacks in the use), on the other hand, shows that environmental influences, adaptive mechanisms, lifestyle, education, and other factors better explain the distribution of health conditions and risks than any fixed racially structured model. South African Blacks have one of the lowest incidences of high blood pressure. Chinese Americans, if compared with their siblings living in Mainland China, develop high cholesterol and high blood pressure, despite sharing the same genetic pool with their relatives. Cancer patients in this country are in clear contrast with their relatives in Mexico who are not exposed to pesticides and the stress associated with migrant life in this country. The same Native American group (e.g., the Yaqui), living on both sides of the border (some in Northern Mexico and others in Arizona), shows an enormous difference in health conditions. The diet and more sedentary life of the Northern Yaqui living in the United States leads to a great deal more fat tissue and higher incidence of high blood pressure, diabetes, and other problems often associated with fattier diets and lack of physical exercise.

Some theorists have assumed that certain peoples of color do not have the cultural capital to achieve academically at the same level as that of mainstream populations. In other words, people of color are handicapped and deprived of the cultural capital necessary to succeed. The source of this lack of capital is viewed as an abnormal self-identity or personality type ("oppositional identity" according to Ogbu, see earlier references), which are related to the rigidity of personality caused by an extended experience of oppression or exploitation, or by other abuses. My hypothesis is that oppression and abuse can also generate precisely the opposite—resilience and cultural capital to succeed—which often creates the psychological flexibility necessary to pass for or assume different identities for the sake of survival. In other words, academic achievement may be viewed as less functional for economic survival than other occupations and, consequently, the person of color pursues other avenues of success in life. Our debate about differential explanations for achievement and the role of language and culture somehow neglected the complexity of specific settings in which populations live. The very notion that human and cognitive development are determined by macrosociological or macropsychological factors is as disturbing as the "black box" of differential intelligence as defended by some psychologists who have no tolerance for deviation from tests (not even the translation of some tests for speakers of other languages). The epitome of arrogance is not only that these psychologists demand all children be tested with the same English instruments, but that the outcomes of their tests measure "intelligence" and predict future achievement. This is the extreme position that learned disabilities or incapacities and Bakhtin's "inherent dialogicality of human life" take us to. For this reason, it is important to reflect on the consequences of reductionism alluded to by Wertsch, and on the intimate relations between politics, social environments, and psychological processes, as suggested in the work of Bourdieu, Vygotsky, Bakhtin, and their associates. These authors are attempting to guard us against the fragmentation that results from myopic intradisciplinary views of complex human phenomena, and how such fragmentation "can be traced to the bureaucratic forces that shape our lives" and is often "reinforced by differing theoretical assumptions about the essence of human nature" (Wertsch, 1998, p. 7).

In the interpretation of Wertsch, if we followed Vygotsky and his followers to understand human consciousness, we must go into the social activities of humans (not inside their minds) and their culture, values, practices, and actions:

> I would argue that most scholars in the social sciences hold some position on this issue of analytic primacy. In some cases, this may simply be a matter of disciplinary orientation. Thus psychologists may assume that we can explain psychological phenomena by appealing to institutional processes, connectionists might try to account for both reducing them to physical processes, and so forth.
>
> (Wertsch, 1998, p. 9)

How much influence does the social environment have to determine a person's behavior. Is the "social conditioning" a blind force that does away with individual freedom? This antinomy between the individual and society can also be oversimplified. Bourdieu (1993) warns us about it.

Research on new cultural capital must be focused on human action. Following Vygotsky, Bakhtin, and others, Wertsch states that the basic unit of analysis is human action. In other words, the effort must be focused on describing, interpreting action, and explaining human action "as opposed to some other phenomenon such as behavior, mental or linguistic structure, or attitudes" (Wertsch, 1998, p. 12). We must reject the idea of breaking human actions in to more basic components, and examine larger action units in their entirety, rather than analyzing specialized dimensions of a single action within given disciplinary perspectives.

In his book, *Mind as Action*, Wertsch (1998) stated,

> A fundamental claim of the sociocultural analysis outlined in this book is that its proper focus is human action. As understood here, action may be external as well as internal, and it may be carried out by groups, both small and large, or by individuals. In the view of many investigators, there are important parallels between action carried out on the social and individual planes and on the external and internal planes. . . . The task of a sociocultural approach is to explicate the relations between human *action*, on the one hand, and the cultural, institutional, and historical contexts in which this action occurs, on the other.
>
> (pp. 23–24)

Human action beyond the academic field requires broader research agendas. Foley (1997) attempted to clarify the grounds for rejection of deterministic notions of success or failure based on either genetic or cultural deficit models. The narratives I presented earlier to illustrate the difficulties faced by faculty of color in academia have the virtue of giving a voice to the very people whose intellectual and academic demise was prematurely predicted by deficit models and who, by a rather unique paradoxical turn of events, are now excelling above any expectations. The challenge of explaining success among the poor, disenfranchised, and oppressed has forced reflection and redirection of theoretical explanations. Foley (1997) presented a critical cultural studies perspective to reinterpret the culture of poverty/cultural deficit debate:

> I have abandoned Lewis' conceit that culture is a "neutral," apolitical transmission or socialization, objective enterprise. Consequently, many cultural anthropologists have redefined the traditional descriptive study of a cultural group as the study of how competing cultural groups—divided along class, racial and gender lines—socially construct images of each other.
>
> (p. 125)

Foley adopted cultural constructs of Foucault, Gramsci, and Habermas to rethink cultural processes and provide a realistic description of the roles of leaders of postindustrial societies in specific political contexts, as well as their use of the media to manipulate public opinion and control social phenomena. Although ethnic researchers and scholars provide counter narratives and alternative explanations of success and failure, a new wave of radical right thinkers pushes old deficit ideologies such as The Bell Curve and the importation of poverty by immigrants of color as a backdoor strategy to revive Eurocentric notions of cultural purity and racial superiority of certain groups. In the end, the outcome of such notions is the belief that investing in the education of children of color is a waste of time and money, that they should be abandoned, and that the investment should be redirected to the White population alone. Education is undoubtedly a must for the poor and racially isolated to move up. Can education change the political structure and power hierarchy? Probably not, but education can create a new set of expectations and in the end open up occupational and status opportunities for excluded persons (persons of color and low-income). Bourdieu (1984) suggested that higher education has maintained inequality by bringing social inequalities into academic circles via a new stratification. In an effort to explain Bourdieu's view of academia, Pearl (1997) stated,

> Bourdieu recognizes the link between education and occupation and that credentials earned in school provide access to desirable work. He also makes clear that there is little to be gained by increasing the number of persons with credential. When qualifications exceed occupational openings the dominant classes redefine the criteria for admission and thus maintain a privileged status for their children (and others with whom they share class membership). Thus Bourdieu is able to show that merely increasing educational achievement in the dominated classes will not necessarily lead to economic success.
>
> (pp. 139–140)

Multiple Identities of Latinos as a New Cultural Capital

In the context of massive immigration waves and of our debates over nationalism, binationalism, and transnationalism, the role of immigrants and their life as immigrants in the United States shows only a part of their reality. Because they move back and forth from their country of origin to the United States, and because they retain a strong network of communication and exchanges with their family, friends, and acquaintances on both side of the border, new Latino immigrants learn to instantly code-switch, adapt, and change their own self-definitions to maximize their survival and obtain economic security. Immigrants play a key role in their home village politics, religious organizations, and economic development. The substantial amount of money sent to Mexico, for example, by persons working in the United States (it is believed that over $6 billion is sent annually to Mexico) restructures the economic and social order in many small towns of central Mexico. The resulting lifestyle of many transnational families often is accompanied by interethnic and interracial marriages, multiple languages used in the homes, and a greater physical mobility across borders. This century will undoubtedly be marked by a blurring of racial boundaries and the sharing of richer multicultural family heritages. The implications of social changes among immigrant families is bound to affect our entire society and in particular some of its most important institutions, such as schools, universities, economic infrastructure, and channels for upward mobility.

We used to conceive of immigrants of color, especially Latinos, as "handicapped" because of their experience of oppression and their low economic status. They were seen as lacking the necessary cultural capital to succeed at the level of mainstream populations. However, as the demographics change drastically from "minority groups" (people of color being marked and indeed fewer than mainstream) to the predominant population in the country (by mid-21st century), those individuals who can best function in a diverse society will be have a large cultural capital and greater ability to function effectively. The mastery of different languages, the ability to cross racial and ethnic boundaries, and a general resilience associated with the ability to endure hardships and overcome obstacles will clearly be recognized as a new cultural capital, not a handicap.

The importance of multiple identities as the new asset, the cultural capital that will be crucial for success in a modern diversified society, must be analyzed from its very foundations. The work by G. Spindler (1955, 1974, 1978, 2000) and by G. and L. Spindler (1987, 1994) offered the theoretical foundations to our understanding of cultural adaptation. G. Spindler is appropriately recognized as the "Father of Educational Anthropology." G. Spindler played a key role in developing a number of subfields in anthropological linguistics, ethnoscience, the ethnography of law, and in educational anthropology. His major theoretical contributions (through his teaching of over 14,000 students during the last 50 years and his numerous publications) were focused on the nature of cultural transmission and cultural adaptation. His basic assumption has been that school plays a key role in the enculturation and socialization of children, and that often schools have ignored or failed certain children, especially children of color. As a psychological anthropologist, G. Spindler described complex processes of self-identity formation and adaptation. His classic study of Menomini acculturation has been applied to other groups (Latinos, Blacks, Native Americans, and others). His discussion of cultural therapy reflects his concern for children whose teachers miscommunicate and have gross misperceptions about their ability and their adjustment to school. The contributions by Louise Spindler, who was the inseparable companion of George, focused on the differential adaptive strategies of women and men within the same society (L. Spindler, 1958, 1962, 1976). With G. Spindler she wrote insightful articles and books (L. Spindler & G. Spindler, 1970, 1971, 1990). The team of George and Louise produced classic pieces such as *Roger Harker* and *Beth Ann* to help us understand equity in its quintessential elements of child–adult interaction.

What we have learned from psychological anthropology is that successful adjustment to different cultural settings requires an enormous mental flexibility; in contrast, rigidity is associated with maladjustment and inability to functions in diverse settings. The theory was that repeated psychological abuse or oppressive situations would lead to mental or cultural rigidity and, consequently, inability to accommodate and achieve in schools (Ogbu 1974, 1978, 1982, 1987a, 1987b, 1989, etc.). Thus, the failure in school of certain ethnic groups (Blacks, Chicanos, Native Americans, etc.) may not necessarily result from a permanent handicap or psychological damage. Such damage does not seem to hinder other successes of persons of color, or at times, later academic success. As we attempt to explain the success of people of color in school and society we begin to redefine cultural capital and interpret social settings and research findings in a different light, in the light of the new experiences, interventions, and studies by other ethnic researchers. The new cultural, social, and linguistic demands require a greater ability to endure hardships and to work with highly diversified groups. Thus, what was originally viewed as a handicap and marginalizing force may indeed provide strength and skills to succeed in settings foreign to mainstream folks.

Ethnographic research (especially critical ethnography) attempts to explore the nature of social and academic settings that lead to or illustrate inequity at work. But critical theory has focused on relatively petty theoretical differences among an elite of intellectuals who claim to follow Freire, while neglecting the pervasive global movements of transnational families, or within countries migrations of culturally and linguistically different groups (as in the case of China). There is no question in my mind that in this century the Southwest will be the theater of rapid population movements in both binational and transnational settings, and that the speed of migration will increase. Edinburg and McAllen in S. Texas, for example, are increasing at a rate of over 60%

every 10 years, and the economic movement resulting from the Free Trade Treaty has opened new economic avenues for both countries and a renewed transnational existence. The implications for school and society are obvious.

Anthropology, sociology, and psychology over the last three decades have remained relatively static and rigid in conceptualizing self-identity, community, and acculturation and adaptation processes. What was once considered contradictory and impossible is viewed as part of everyday life among immigrant youth from different ethnicities. Young immigrants cross linguistic and cultural borders without any conflict. In previous decades, the social sciences had adopted rather static conceptions of community and adaptation. Now they are having serious problems explaining transnational phenomena and multiple identities for people who live in two or more worlds. The politics of Comala, for example (a small town in Colima, central Mexico), are not decided in Comala, but in Southern California, where the most influential members of Comala live and work. They finance all the important religious festivities and they determine the most critical political changes in the village and region. In the meantime, universities and colleges, absorbed in their petty politics, are trying to figure out how to prepare future generations of teachers who will have to work with the new school populations representing many languages and cultures, and get ready to explore new worlds with their more elastic and fluid concept of self-identities. These students of the future belong to new generations of transnational families with ties to many virtual communities on both sides of the border.

The new generations of American youth are more flexible, less ethnically and linguistically polarized, and more willing to adopt lifestyles previously unimaginable to their parents and grandparents. They are also highly literate in modern technologies, beyond the comprehension of our adult generations, and they possess a capacity to imagine worlds we, the senior generations, cannot even imagine. These future generations of postmodern youth will function in a new world with a capacity to communicate and think beyond the expectations of their parents, grandparents, teachers, and mentors. All we can hope for is that we have enough understanding of their goals and ideas to provide them with support and love to grow to their full potential.

Acknowledgments

Henry T. Trueba is Ruben E. Hinojosa Regents Professor Emeritus in the College of Education at the University of Texas, Austin.

References

Ainslie, R. C. (Ed.). (1998). *Cultural mourning, immigration, and engagement: Vignettes from the Mexican experience.* Cambridge, MA: Harvard University Press & D. Rockefeller Center for Latin American Studies.

Anyon, J. (1981). Social class and school knowledge. *Curriculum Inquiry, 11*(1), 3–42.

Anyon, J. (1997). *Ghetto schooling: A political economy of urban educational reform*. New York: Columbia University Teacher's College Press.

Bourdieu, P. (1984). *Distinction: A social critique of the judgement of taste*. Cambridge, MA: Harvard University Press.

Bourdieu, P. (1984). *Homo academicus*. Paris: Minuit.

Bourdieu, P. (1990). *The logic of practice* (R. Nice, Trans.). Stanford, CA: Stanford University Press.

Bourdieu, P. (1993). *The field of cultural production: Essays on art and literature*. New York: Columbia University Press.

Bourdieu, P. P. (1977). *Reproduction: In education, society and culture*. Beverly Hills, CA: Sage.

Bourdieu, P. (1992). *An invitation to reflexive sociology*. Cambridge, MA: Polity.

Canton, C. (in press). From slaveship to scholarship: A narrative of the political and social transformation of an African-American educator. In L. Jacobs, J. Cintrón, & C. Canton (Eds.), *The politics of survival in academia: Narratives of inequity, resilience and success*. Volume in H. T. Trueba (Ed.), *The immigrant and transnational experience series*. New York: Rowman & Littlefield.

Cowan, G. (in press). Hanging in: The journey to good enough. In L. Jacobs, J. Cintrón, & C. Canton (Eds.), *The politics of survival in academia: Narratives of inequity, resilience and success*. Volume in H. T. Trueba (Ed.), *The immigrant and transnational experience series*. New York: Rowman & Littlefield.

Delgado-Gaitan, C. (in press). Disabling institutions. In L. Jacobs, J. Cintrón, & C. Canton (Eds.), *The politics of survival in academia: Narratives of inequity, resilience and success*. Volume in H. T. Trueba (Ed.), *The immigrant and transnational experience series*. New York: Rowman & Littlefield.

Foley, D. (1991). Reconsidering anthropological explanations of ethnic school failure. *Anthropology and Education Quarterly, 22*, 60–86.

Foley, D. (1997). Deficit thinking models based on culture: The anthropological protest. In R. R. Valencia (Ed.), *The evolution of deficit thinking: Educational thought and practice* (pp. 113–131). Washington, DC & London: Falmer.

Foley, D. (in press). *Reconceptualizing ethnicity and school achievement: The rise of ethnic ethnographers*. University of Texas: Austin.

Gibson, M. (1987a). Playing by the rules. In G. Spindler (Ed.), *Education and cultural process: Anthropological approaches* (2nd ed., pp. 274–283). Prospect Heights, IL: Waveland.

Gibson, M. (1987b). Punjabi immigrants in an American high school. In G. S. L. Spindler (Ed.), *Interpretive ethnography of education: At home and abroad* (pp. 281–310). Hillsdale, NJ: Lawrence Erlbaum Associates, Inc.

Gibson, M. (1987c). The school performance of immigrant minorities: A comparative view. *Anthropology and Education Quarterly, 18*, 262–275.

Gibson, M. (1988). *Accommodation without assimilation: Sikh immigrants in an American high school*. Ithaca, NY: Cornell University Press.

Gibson, M., & Ogbu, J. (1991). *Minority status and schooling: A comparative study of immigrant and involuntary minorities*. New York & London: Garland.

Jacobs, L., Cintrón, J., & Canton C. (Eds.). (in press). *The politics of survival in academia: Narratives of inequity, resilience and success*. Volume in H. T. Trueba (Ed.), *The immigrant and transnational experience series*. New York: Rowman & Littlefield.

Johnson, R. (1993). Editor's introduction: Pierre Bourdieu on art, literature, and culture. In R. Johnson (Ed.), *Pierre Bourdieu, The Field of cultural production*. New York: Columbia University Press.

Kiang, P. (in press). Transnational linkages in Asian American studies as sources and strategies for teaching and curricular change. In L. Jacobs, J. Cintrón, & C. Canton (Eds.), *The politics of survival in academia: Narratives of inequity, resilience and success*. Volume in H. T. Trueba (Ed.), *The immigrant and transnational experience series*. New York: Rowman & Littlefield.

Loo, C., & Chun, M. (in press). Eight faculty warriors: Asian Americans who prevailed over academic adversity. In L. Jacobs, J. Cintrón, & C. Canton (Eds.), *The politics of survival in academia: Narratives of inequity, resilience and success*. Volume in H. T. Trueba (Ed.), *The immigrant and transnational experience series*. New York: Rowman & Littlefield.

Marcus, G. (1998). *Ethnography through thick and thin*. Princeton, NJ: Princeton University Press.

Ogbu, J. (1974). *The next generation: An ethnography of education in an urban neighborhood*. New York: Academic.

Ogbu, J. (1978). *Minority education and caste: The American system in cross-cultural perspective*. New York: Academic.

Ogbu, J. (1981a). Education, clientage and social mobility: Caste and social change in the United States and Nigeria. In G. D. Berreman (Ed.), *Social inequality: Comparative developmental approaches* (pp. 277–306). New York: Academic.

Ogbu, J. (1981b). Origins of human competence: A cultural-ecological perspective. *Child Development, 52*, 413–429.

Ogbu, J. (1982). Cultural discontinuities and schooling. *Anthropology and Education Quarterly, 13*, 290–307.

Ogbu, J. (1987a). Variability in minority responses to schooling: Nonimmigrants vs. immigrants. In G. S. L. Spindler (Ed.), *Interpretive ethnography of education: At home and abroad* (pp. 255–278). Hillsdale, NJ: Lawrence Erlbaum Associates, Inc.

Ogbu, J. (1987b). Variability in minority school performance: A problem in search of an explanation. *Anthropology and Education Quarterly, 18*, 312–334.

Ogbu, J. (Ed.). (1989). *The individual in collective adaptation: A framework for focusing on academic underperformance and dropping out among involuntary minorities*. Albany, NY: State University of New York Press.

Ogbu, J. (Ed.). (1991a). *Immigrant and involuntary minorities in comparative perspective*. New York, NY: Garland.

Ogbu, J. (Ed.). (1991b). *Low school performance as an adaptation: The case of blacks in Stockton, California*. New York, NY: Garland.

Ogbu, J. (1992). Understanding cultural diversity. *Educational Researcher, 21*(8), 5–24.

Ogbu, J., & Matute-Bianchi, M. E. (1986). Understanding sociocultural factors: Knowledge, identity and school adjustment. In *Beyond language: Social and cultural factors in schooling language minority students* (pp. 73–142). Sacramento, CA: Bilingual Education Office, California State Department of Education.

Pearl, A. (1997). Cultural and accumulated environmental deficit models. In R. R. Valencia (Ed.), *The evolution of deficit thinking: Educational thought and practice* (pp. 132–159). Washington, DC & London: Falmer.

Spindler, G. (1955). Sociocultural and psychological processes in Menomini acculturation. *Publications in Culture and Society, 5*.

Spindler, G. (Ed.). (1974). *Education and cultural process: Towards an anthropology of education*. New York: Holt, Rinehart & Winston.

Spindler, G. (Ed.). (1978). *The making of psychological anthropology*. Berkeley, CA: University of California Press.

Spindler, G. (Ed.). (2000). *Fifty years of anthropology and education 1950–2000: A Spindler Anthology*. Mahwah, NJ: Lawrence Erlbaum Associates, Inc.

Spindler, G., & Spindler, L. (Eds.). (1987). *Interpretive ethnography of education at home and abroad.* Hillsdale, NJ: Lawrence Erlbaum Associates, Inc.

Spindler, G., & Spindler, L. (Eds.). (1994). *Pathways to cultural anthropology: Cultural therapy with teachers and students.* Thousand Oaks, CA: Corwin.

Spindler, L. (1958). Male and female adaptation in culture change. *American Anthropologist, 60,* 217–233.

Spindler, L. (1962). Menomini women and culture change. *American Anthropologist, 64*(Part 2).

Spindler, L. (1976). The Menonimi Indians. In B. Trigger (Ed.), *Handbook of North American Indians* (Vol. 15, pp. 707–724). Washington, DC: Smithsonian Institution.

Spindler, L., & Spindler, G. (1970). Menomini witchcraft. In D. Walker (Ed.), *Systems of North American witchcraft and sorcery* (Anthropological Monographs, No. 1). Boise, ID: University of Idaho.

Spindler, L., & Spindler, G. (1971). *Dreamers without power: The Menomini Indians.* New York: Holt, Rinehart & Winston.

Spindler, L., & Spindler, G. (1990). Male and female in four changing cultures. In D. Jordan & M. Swartz (Eds.), *Personality and the cultural construction of society* (pp. 182–200). Tuscaloosa, AL: University of Alabama Press.

Suárez-Orozco, M. M. (Ed.). (1998). *Crossings: Mexican immigration in interdisciplinary perspectives.* Cambridge, MA: Harvard University Press and D. Rockefeller Center for Latin American Studies.

Suárez-Orozco, M. M. (in press). Some conceptual consideration in the interdisciplinary study of immigrant children. In H. T. Trueba & L. Bartolomé (Eds.), *Immigrant voices in search of pedagogical reform* (pp. 17–35). New York: Rowman & Littlefield.

Trueba, H. T. (1988). Culturally-based explanations of minority students' academic achievement. *Anthropology and Education Quarterly, 19,* 270–287.

Trueba, H. T. (1999). *Latinos Unidos: From cultural diversity to the politics of solidarity.* New York: Rowman & Littlefield.

Trueba, H. T., & Bartolomé, L. (Eds.). (2000). *Immigrant voices: In search of educational equity.* New York: Rowman & Littlefield.

Valencia, R. R. (1997a). Conceptualizing the notion of deficit thinking. In R. R. Valencia (Ed.), *The evolution of deficit thinking: Educational thought and practice* (pp. 1–12). Washington & London: Falmer.

Valencia, R. R. (1997b). Genetic pathology model of deficit thinking. In R. R. Valencia (Ed.), *The evolution of deficit thinking: Educational thought and practice* (pp. 41–112). Washington & London: Falmer.

Vygotsky, L. S. (1962). Thought and language. Cambridge, MA: MIT Press.

Vygotsky, L. S. (1978). *Mind in society: The development of higher psychological processes.* Cambridge, MA: Harvard University Press.

Wertsch, J. V. (1998). *Mind as action.* New York & Oxford, England: Oxford University Press.

Index

Note: Numbers in *italic* indicate a figure and numbers in **bold** indicate a table on the corresponding page.

abuelitas/grandmothers as educators: in Indigenous communities 242–246; introduction to 239–240; memories of 240–242; subtracting *abuela* as educator 250–253; subtracting *abuela* epistemologies 248–250; subtractive schooling 246–248; summary of 253–254
Academy for Teacher Excellence (ATE) 104
ACPA-College Student Educators International (ACPA) 224
Adams, John T. 125, 131
adolescent econometricians 30
adult education programs 47, 50
advocacy and education 13, 310–313, 329; *see also* DREAM Act advocacy
affordability issues in Hispanic-serving institutions 89
African American education 70–72
Alamosa Courier 130
Alamosa Independent Journal 124–125, 127
Alamosa Journal 122
Alamosa Leader 132
Alamosa School Board of Education 120, 121, 124
Alarcón, Wanda 179–180
Allen, Paula Gunn 239–240
alternative certification paths 109–110
alternative education programs *see* Project Avanzando
Alvarez v. Lemon Grove (1931) 119
American Association of Hispanics in Higher Education 179
American Colonial period 4
American Indian Grandmothers (Schweitzer) 243

Americans with Disability Act 342–343
America's Perfect Storm: Three Forces Changing Our Nation's Future report 79–80
Annie E. Casey Foundation 165
anti-immigrant rhetoric 314
Anzaldúa, Gloria 240, 241, 245
Art, Research and Curriculum Associates (ARC) Proposal 49
Asian American education 70–72
assimilationist curriculum 163
Association for the Study of Higher Education (ASHE) 224
Association for the Study of Hispanics in Higher Education (AAHHE) 224
Astin, Alexander 62
at-risk child literature 7–8

Barrientos, Gonzalo 14
barriers to education 100–101, *147*
barrio-based education 271–273, 283–285
barrio-classroom connections 281–282
Batalla, Bonfil 244, 250
Bean, Luther 122
Bernal, Joe 14
Beverley, John 178
biculturalism 205
bien educado 247, 249
bien preparado 247, 249
bilingual/bicultural education 13, 59, 87, 150–151, 161, 253
Bilingual Hispanic Children on the U.S. Mainland: A Review of Research on Their Cognitive, Linguistic, and Scholastic Development (Dunn) 9–10

bilingualism 13, 152, 205, 253, 257, 265, 305
biliteracy 257, 267, 305
binationalism 353
Black, Edward 277, 279, 281
Black-serving institutions 83
"blowout" (school walkout) 14
Body, Carrie 128
Bourdieu, Pierre 346–348, 352
Bradford, Mary C.C. 121
Brigham, Carl 345–346
Bush, George H. 10

California State University system 86
Canales, Ramiro 11
cantadista 244
Cárdenas, José A. 10
career pathway programs 107–108
caste-like groups 344–345, 348–349
Castro, Crystal 277, 281–282
categorical aggregation analysis 146
Catholic school 206–207
Cavazos, Lauro 10, 12
Census Current Population Survey 75
Chicana(o) educational pipeline: findings 64–75, *65*, *66*, *67–68*, *70*, *71*, *72–73*; intersectionality 61, 62–63; introduction to 59–61; methodology 63–64; overview of 61–62; summary of 75–76; *see also* Mexican American education
Chicana/o identity 239
Chicano movement 180
Chicanx Caucus 223
childcare for students 144
Christensen, Rosemary 241
civic literacy 331
Civil Rights Act of Colorado 134
civil society initiatives 329
Clark County School District's (CCSD) 2007 Dropout Survey Report 160–161, 175–176
collective adaptation 143
collective liberation 305
collective problem solving 310
college enrollment gap study: college plans and expectations 290–291; college-track course enrollment 289–290; discussion 297–299; elements of preparation programs 291; implications and limitations 299; introduction to 288; methodology 292–294; overview of 288–289; purpose of 291–292; results **294**, 294–297, **295**, **296**; standardized testing programs 290

colonial system of knowledge 250–253
Colorado Constitution 124
Colorado State Board of Education 121
Colorado State Supreme Court 132
Combatted Internalized Stigma 330
communication gaps 147–149
community-based education 251
community-based organizations (CBOs) 303
community building and healing 313–316
community cultural wealth 195–196
community of learners 53, 55
confianza (trust) 304
conformist resistance of students 165
connaissance 347
conscientización 164
consejos (advice-giving narratives) 14, 199, 203
constructivism 143
constructivist approach to education 47, 50
corridos musical tradition 244
Crenshaw, Kimberly 61
critical race theory (CRT) 143, 194–195
cross-classified random effects model 35
Cruz, Cindy 180–183
cultural capital 29, 289; in different social settings 348–352; of Latinos 353–355; marginal people 346–348
cultural deficit models 161
cultural deprivation literature 6–7
cultural-ecological theory 143
cultural identity 162, 184; *see also* multiple cultural immigrant identities
culture clashes 149, 155
culture loss 155
Cummings, Mario 277
Cunningham, William 11
Current Population Survey 63–64

Darling, J.H. 127–128
Data Ferret software 63
decision-making authority 50
Decolonizing Methodologies: Research and Indigenous Peoples (Smith) 240
deculturalization 249
deficit thinking 4
degree attainment rates 82
de-indianization 240, 244–245, 250
Deloria, Vine 245
Del Rio ISD v. Salvatierra (1930) 119
democratic success 91
Denious, Nancy 122
Denver Catholic Register 120, 121, 127, 130, 133–134
Denver Times 121

Development, Relief, and Education for Alien Minors (DREAM) Act *see* DREAM Act advocacy
differential intelligence 350
discrimination 59–60, 166–168, 321
diversification of teacher workforce 96
doctoral degree recipients 70
dominant culture normativity 209
DREAM Act advocacy: discussion 332–334; future research 333; leadership 331–332; limitations of 333–334; literature review 321–323; methodology 324–326, **325**; opportunity role structure 329; policy implications 332–333; practice implications 333; reflexivity 326; results of 326–332; shared beliefs 327–328; social support 329–331; theoretical framework 323–324
DREAM Big organization 324
dual language immersion program: background of study 259–260; discussion 263–267; educational implications 267; effective bilingual teachers 264–265; findings 260–262, *261–262*; introduction to 257; leadership and continuity 266–267; literature review 257–258; modes of inquiry 258–259; parent involvement 265–266; pedagogical equity 263–264; summary of 267–268
Dunn, Lloyd M. 9–10

educación, defined 162
educational advocacy *see* advocacy and education
educational pipeline *see* Chicana(o) educational pipeline; Latina(o) teacher pipeline
Education Research Complete database 216
elder epistemology 241
empowerment programs 48, 49–50
endogenous theory of school failure 4
enduring self 339
English as a Second Language (ESL) 87
English language learners (ELLs) *see* Latina(o) English language learners
English learners (ELs) 257–258, 261
enrollment projections/rates 82–84
enrollment rates 82
environmentally induced deficiency 7
environmental scanning 231
environmental scanning data collection 218–219

equal educational opportunity struggles 12–14
ERIC database 216
Escamilla, Kathy 183
ethnic educational ethnographer 344
ethnic minority teachers 96
ethnocentric nearsightedness of education 190–191, 209
exemplary teachers study: *barrio*-based education 271–273, 283–285; *barrio*-classroom connections 281–282; in *el barrio* 271–273; findings 278–282; Hoop City Public Schools 275; immersion experiences 278–280; implications and limitations of 283–286; introduction to 271; language and other assets 282; methodology and participants 275–277; nominated teachers 276–277; teacher preparation programs 273–274

faculty issues in Hispanic-serving institutions 88–89
Fallo, Thomas M. 91–92, 93
familial capital 196, 201
family enterprise approach 53–54
family-school engagement practices 193
feminine gender binary 228–229
feminine in Native cosmology 251–252
financial incentives for teaching 98
Flawn, Peter 11
foreign-born students 69, 73–74, 81, 89
Francisco Maestas et al. v. George H. Shone et al. (1914): arguments against 125–127; discussion 131–134; emergence of 120–121; filing of 123–125; grassroots activism 121–123; introduction to 119–120; legal loose ends 131; media reports 130–131; ruling 129–130; trial records 127–129
Freire, Paulo 315
funding issues in Hispanic-serving institutions 85–86
funds of knowledge 15
funds of knowledge for Latina(o) students' transition to college: college access and 37–38; development of career aspirations 38–39; households' funds of knowledge 33–37, **34**, **36**, 40; limitations of 39; refining units of analysis 40

gay identity 341–342
GEAR UP program 291–294, 297–298

gender binaries 228–230
gender inclusivity 219–221
general education diploma (GED) instruction 44, 49, 52–55
genetic-cultural-familial thinking 4
genetic determinism 349
globalism 79
Gonzales, Patricia 245
González, Deena J. 239
Graglia, Lino 10–12
Great Expectations survey 15–16
group-based belief systems 328
Grow Your Own (GYO) initiative 108

habitus concept 346–347
Hamilton, June 277, 282
Helmsley, Jessica 276–277, 278–279, 282
help-seeking orientation 31
heritage language loss 155
high-stakes testing 13
Hispanic Association of Colleges and Universities (HACU) 83, 84
Hispanic-serving institutions (HSIs): affordability issues 89; challenges facing **85**, 85–91; enrollment projections 82–84; faculty issues 88–89; funding issues 85–86; future research recommendations 91–92; future trends 92–93; higher education and 82; introduction to 78; limitations of study 84–85; literature review 78–82; methodology 84; new economy and 78–80; purpose of study 84; student preparedness issues 87; student retention/success issues 87–88; summary of findings 91; U.S. demographics 80–81, *81*; use of *Latinx* 226–227
Holbrook, Charles 125, 129–130, 131
homophobia 342
Hoop City Public Schools 275
Hooper-Mosca Tribune 132
households' funds of knowledge 33–37, **34, 36**, 40
human capital investment 28
humanizing process of community building 316–317

identity: Chicana/o identity 239; cultural identity 162, 184; gay identity 341–342; Native American identity 341–342; self-identity among minorities 339, 340–344, 345; social identity 62, 231; *see also* multiple cultural immigrant identities

immersion teaching experiences 278–280
Immigration Act (1924) 345
immigration impact on society 338
Immigration Liberation 324
inclusiveness programs 48
individual advocacy for educational opportunities 13
individualism 30, 141, 153, 178, 205–206, 315–316
individual liberation 305
Iniguez, Martha 52
In Lak Ech 247
In-state Resident Tuition (IRT) 322–323
institutional barriers to college 28
institutional racism 161
intellectual deprivation literature 6
intergenerational participation in education 54–55
internalized oppression 249
intersectionality 61, 62–63, 222, 231
involuntary (caste-like) minorities 344–345

Jackson, Linda Guardia 183–184

K-16 pipeline *see* Latina(o) teacher pipeline
Kingery, Elinor 122

Lahrmann, C.L. 128
language of power 59
La Revista de Taos 131
Latina(o) English language learners: communication gaps 147–149; cultural identity concerns 184; culture clashes 149, 155; data collection and analysis 145–146; design and procedures 144–145; findings 146–153, *147*; introduction to 141–143; lack of support systems 151–153; lack of systemic, articulated plan 150; lack of teacher preparation 150–151; methodology 143–146; participants and settings 144; qualitative tradition 143; researcher personal stance 144; summary of 153–156, **154**; theoretical framework 143–144; trustworthiness 146
Latina(o) parent organizing for educational justice: community building and healing 313–316; discussion 316–317; engagement and advocacy 310–313; findings 307–316; first workshop 307–310; introduction

Index 363

to 302–303; *mujerismo* 302, 304–305; overview of 303–304; research context and methodology 305–307; summary of 317–318
Latina(o) school pushout study: apathetic/bad teachers 168; bad/negative school climate 169; behavioral mistakes 170; CCSD Dropout Survey Report 160–161, 175–176; cultural issues 170–171; data analysis 166; discrimination and microaggressions 166–168, 173; discussion 173–175; ESL issues 171–172; grade/coursework problems 170; introduction to 159–160; irrelevant/boring homework 169; literature review 161–163; mental health issues 173; methodology 165–166; personal issues 170–173; pregnancy concerns 172; purpose of 160; results 166–173; school issues 166–170; summary of 175; theoretical framework 163–165; work concerns 172–173
Latina(o) students' transition to college: access and opportunity 27–28; college access 100–103; economic perspective on 28–32; enrollment gap 288–289; funds of knowledge 32–39, **34**, **36**; further research implications 40; introduction to 26–27; sociological perspective on 29–32; summary of 40
Latina(o) teacher pipeline: alternative certification paths 109–110; career pathway programs 107–108; college access to students 100–103; discussion 97–111; in the field 110–111; high school completion by students 99–100; introduction to 95–97; obtaining teaching degree 103–110; paraprofessionals 106–107; summary of 111–112; teacher education 103–104; terminology for 97; two-year college route 104–106
Latinx: in academic journals 219–222; emergence of 218; hashtags categorized 235; in higher education institutional websites 226–227; introduction to 216–217; Latino *vs.* Hispanic 217–218; methodology 218–219; in online media 222–224; in professional conferences 224; recontextualizing 227–230; review of findings 219–230; in social media sites 224–225; summary of 230–231
Lauer, Matt 11

League of United Latin American Citizens (LULAC) 13
learner-centered instruction 56
Lee, Jin Sook 248
legislation for educational opportunities 14
Levinas, Emmanuel 178
liberatory education 302
linguistic capital 196
Lister, Mary 128–129
literacy testing for adults 79
litigation for educational opportunities 13
lxs estudiantes 223

macro-advocacy 329
Maestas, Francisco *see Francisco Maestas et al. v. George H. Shone et al.*
Maestas, Juan 131
Maestas, Miquel 125–126, 128
Mahalanobis Distance values 294
majoritarian narrative 175
marginalization of students 144, 164
masculine gender binary 228–229
McGraw, Loretta 129
media expressions 10–12
mental health issues 173
Mexican American education: cultural identity concerns 162; *educación*, defined 162; state of education 64–75, *65*, *66*, *67–68*, *70*, *71*, *72–73*; university outreach programs 37; *see also* Chicana/o educational pipeline
Mexican American Legal Defense and Educational Fund (MALDEF) 13
Mexican American PhD *educación* aspirations: community cultural wealth 195–196; conceptual framework 194–196; critical race theory 194–195; data analysis 197–198; discussion 209–212; findings 199–209; introduction to 190–191; limitations 199; literature review 191–194; methodological approach to 196–199; parental/familial aspirations 193–194, 200; parental involvement 191–193, 204; participants 196–197; positionality 198–199; trustworthiness 198
Mexican American resistance to segregation *see Francisco Maestas et al. v. George H. Shone et al.*
Mexican Americans don't value education myth: at-risk child literature 7–8; cultural deprivation literature 6–7; debunking of 12–18; fundamental basis of 3–4; introduction to 3; media

expressions 10–12; mythmaking 4–12; parental involvement literature 14–18; scholarly literature 6–10; summary of 19
Mexican-ness 248
Mexquitic Indians 239
micro-advocacy 329
microaggressions 59–60, 166–168
migrant agricultural families 44–47, **45**
Migrant Education Program 45
Mind as Action (Wertsch) 351
missionary schools 251
Mooney, W.B. 127
Morales, Adelaide 277, 282
Morrison Institute for Public Policy 79
Movimiento Estudiantil Chicano de Aztlán (MEChA) 13
mujerismo (Latina womanism) 302, 304–305
multiculturalism 146, 150–151, 153–155
multiple cultural immigrant identities: action research 344–346; cultural capital in different social settings 348–352; cultural capital of Latinos 353–355; cultural capital of marginal people 346–348; introduction to 337–340; self-identity among minorities 339, 340–344, 345
Muxes gender binary 228–229

NASPA-Student Affairs Professionals in Higher Education (NASPA) 224
National Agricultural Worker Survey (NAWS) 45
National Assessment of Educational Progress 289
National Association for College Admissions Counseling (NACAC) 288
National Center for Education Statistics (NCES) 83, 96, 159, 257
National Conference on Race and Ethnicity (NCORE) 224
National Council of State Legislatures 322
National Educational Longitudinal Study (NELS) 15, 99–100
nationalism 353
National Latina/o Psychological Association 197
National Research Council 197
Native American education 71–72, 242–246
Native American identity 341–342
native-born Hispanics 81
nativist racist ideologies 67–68
navigational capital 196
NBC *Today* 11
new economy and Hispanic-serving institutions 78–80
No Child Left Behind (NCLB) Act 141–143, 309
Noddings, Nel 247
non-deficit thinking perspective 5–6
non-English-speaking children 126
non-resident students *see* foreign-born students

opportunity role structure 329
oppositional behavior of students 164
oppressive conditions 60–61, 173, 323–324

paraprofessionals 106–107
Paredez, Domingo Martínez 245
parental involvement: dual language immersion program 265–266; in education 14–18; lack in migrant agricultural families 44–47; Latina(o) English language learners 142; Mexican American PhD *educación* aspirations 191–193, 204; Mexican Americans don't value education myth 14–18
Parents and Teacher Organization (PTO) 46–47
Parent-Teacher Association (PTA) 44, 46
parent-teacher communication gaps 148
parent workshops *(talleres)* 305–306
part-time status of students 328
patriarchy 252
pedagogical equity 263–264
pedagogical process of community building 316
pedagogical retardation 5
Peña, Geraldo 277, 279, 281
Pierda, Jesús 200–201
Plessy v. Ferguson (1896) 132
Plyler v. Doe 322
political demonstrations for educational opportunities 14
politics of representation 27
Politics of Survival in Academia: Narratives of Inequity, Resilience, and Success, The (Jacobs, Cintrón, Canton) 340–341
positionality 198–199, 220–222, 231, 304
pregnancy concerns 172
Preliminary SAT (PSAT) test 290, 292, 293, 295, **295**, 297–299
Pricto, Linda 184–186
privileging conditions 60–61

Project Avanzando (alternative education program): community of learners 53, 55; discussion and reflection 54; empowerment and 49–50, 55; family enterprise approach 53–54; intergenerational participation 54–55; introduction to 44; methodology 48–49; migrant agricultural families 44–47, **45**; role modeling 55; role of 47–48; schooling of migrant's children 50–55; service and 49–50; summary of 55–56; supplemental reading material 54
ProQuest Theses & Dissertations Global database 220

Quintana, Efren 128

racial microaggressions 166–168, 173
racial segregation in public facilities 132
racism 67–68, 149, 155, 161, 183, 342
radical healing 305
ranchera musical tradition 244
Randall, Margaret 178
rational choice theory 30
reconnaissance 347
Red Earth, White Lies (Deloria) 245
reflexivity 326
resistant capital 196
Rising Above the Gathering Storm: Energizing and Employing America for a Brighter Economic Future report 80
Rocky Mountain News, The 121, 130
Rodriguez-Arroyo, Sandra 186–189
Rodriquez, Roberto 244–245
role modeling 55
Ruybal, J.R.C. 122–123

Sacred Hoop, The (Allen) 239–240
SAT test 290
school district communication gaps 148–149
school failure theory 4, 7–8, 12, 161
school financing 13
schooling of migrant's children 50–55
school-to-prison pipeline 97
self-conscious traditionalism 254
self-defeating resistance of students 164–165, 173, 174
self-efficacy 32, 52, 56, 211, 242
self-identity among minorities 339, 340–344, 345
sense-making 48
service programs 49–50
sexism 342

Sharlot, Michael 11
Sheets, Rosa 248
Shone, George 128
Silver, Sara 277, 282
situated self 339
skill distribution 79
Smith, Linda Tuhiwai 240
social capital 31, 196, 289
social deprivation literature 6
social identity 62, 231
social support 31, 329–331
Society for the Advancement of Chicanas/os and Native Americans in the Sciences 197
socioeconomic status (SES): in *barrio* schools 272; college enrollment and 288–290; education impact on 203; Hispanic Americans 88; immigrant parents 151–152; Latina(o) students 26, 46, 102; Mexican Americans 3, 6; migrant agricultural families **45**, 45–46
Soto, William 277, 278, 281
Sowell, Thomas 3, 8–9
Spindler, George 353–354
Spindler, Louise 354
Spirit God 251
standardized testing programs 290
student preparedness issues 87
student retention/success issues 87–88
Students for Equal Opportunity 10–11
student skills 80
student-teacher communication gaps 148
Study of American Intelligence, A (Brigham) 345–346
subtractive schooling 162, 246–248
Subtractive Schooling: U.S.-Mexican Youth and the Politics of Caring (Valenzuela) 246
success, defined 339
Sullivan, Raymond 123–124, 125, 134

Talbert, James 277, 278, 279
Talkwalker tool 225
teacher-parent communication gaps 148
teacher preparation 150–151, 273–274
teacher skills 80
teacher-student communication gaps 148
teacher training magnet schools 108
teacher workforce development 107
Teach for America (TFA) 103, 109–110
teaching certification 105
testimonios/testimonial narratives: Alarcón, Wanda 179–180; Cruz, Cindy 180–183; introduction to 48–49, 178–179; Jackson, Linda Guardia 183–184; Prieto,

Linda 184–186; Rodriguez-Arroyo, Sandra 186–189
Texas Assessment of Knowledge and Skills (TAKS) 259, 261–263
Thompson, George O. 122, 127
three-interview model 35
Tijerina, Pete 13
tradition keeper 243
transformational resistance 165
transnationalism 353
trend spotting 219

undocumented individuals 13, 28, 321
University of Nevada Cooperative Extension 165
University of Texas at Austin 13
University of Texas School of Law 11
U.S. Census 63–64, 273
U.S. Department of Education 49

Valenzuela, Angela 184, 246
Vásquez, James A. 10
Villenas, Sofia 249
voluntary immigrants 143–144

Western modernism 228
White supremacy 195
work concerns 172–173
working-class people 62, 207–209

xenophobia 303

Made in the USA
Coppell, TX
02 June 2020